Salvaging American Defense

Salvaging American Defense
THE CHALLENGE OF STRATEGIC OVERSTRETCH

Anthony H. Cordesman

With the Assistance of
Paul S. Frederiksen and William D. Sullivan

THE CSIS PRESS
**Center for Strategic
and International Studies**
Washington, D.C.

© 2007 by Center for Strategic and International Studies
Washington, D.C.

11 10 09 08 07   5 4 3 2 1

ISBN 978-0-89206-495-3

Library of Congress Cataloging-in-publication Data
Cordesman, Anthony H.
    Salvaging American defense : the challenge of strategic overstretch / Anthony
H. Cordesman ; With Paul S. Frederiksen and William D. Sullivan.
        p. cm.
    Includes bibliographical references.
    ISBN 978-0-89206-495-3 (pbk. : alk. paper) 1. National security—United
States. 2. United States—Military policy. 3. United States—Defenses. 4. World
politics—21st century. I. Frederiksen, Paul S. II. Sullivan, William D. III. Title.
    UA23.C673753 2007
    355'.033573—dc22   2007006774

Contents

Figures

1 ——————————————————————————

Introduction

The Iraq War, the Afghan War, and the war on terrorism are all powerful warnings that the United States faces major new challenges to its national security. Any analysis of these challenges, and of the current pressures on U.S. military capabilities, however, must approach these subjects in a far broader context. It must attempt to deal with all of the complexity involved in assessing what America's overall approach to strategy, force planning, programming, and budgeting should be.

There are important and immediate issues to be dealt with. The war on terrorism, the Afghan conflict, and the Iraq War have revealed that U.S. forces have serious limitations, even in fighting a single major regional contingency. Some of these limitations are the result of past mistakes and strategic failures; some are a matter of resources; some are matters of force structure; and some are the result of the fact that the United States must now adapt its tactics, training, and technology to deal with new kinds of threats.

It is clear that the United States must prepare to fight very different kinds of war with a far higher level of political content and vastly improve its capabilities for tasks like stability operations and nation building. Iraq, Afghanistan, and the broader war on terrorism have also shown that terrorists, insurgents, and other enemies can fight the United States using asymmetric methods that severely limit its advantages in conventional warfighting capability, technology, professionalism, and intelligence. The United States is being forced to make changes to its national strategy to fight a new kind of "long war" against transnational terrorism that is as much an ideological and a cultural struggle as a military one. These developments are forcing the United States to modify many aspects of its strategy, force posture, and military spending, and the way the rest of the federal government organizes for war.

None of the challenges the United States faces mean it cannot remain the world's preeminent military power, although they do mean that the risks the United States faces in military action have increased, and it is becoming steadily more dependent on its allies as well as regional friends and collective diplomatic and military action. The United States has demonstrated that it has an unparalleled capability to fight conventional wars and retains the world's largest and most capable nuclear forces. It deploys its military forces on a global level, and it is supported by a mixture of formal and informal alliances that span the world.

The United States faces far fewer limits to its military capabilities than any potential enemy or rival nation-state. China is an emerging power, but will take a decade or more to seriously modernize its forces. Russia may be slowly recovering economically, but is making only faltering progress toward military reform. Europe has turned inward and is focused on its economic and social future. It acts, if at all, as either individual nations supporting the United States or NATO, or in peacemaking and humanitarian roles. The rest of the world is either allied to the United States or consists of third-rate military powers.

Yet, U.S. strategy and military planning must still recognize that wars like Iraq and Afghanistan are only one example of the kind of war the United States will have to fight in the future. The United States may have to fight major conventional wars in Korea or the Taiwan Strait, which might escalate to the use of nuclear weapons. It must deal with very different kinds of asymmetric threats like an Iran with massive revolutionary forces, long-range missiles, and possible future nuclear weapons. The United States cannot afford to shape or size its strategy, forces, and defense budgets around any one type of war or scenario; it has to find an affordable mix of capabilities that both deals with probable threats and sudden uncertainties.

More broadly, the United States needs to create new civil-military capabilities. It cannot perform key missions like conflict termination, stability operations, and nation-building without the ability to provide far more civilians who can support such military operations and the transition to creating stable postwar outcomes and states. The failures within the Department of Defense are matched by failures in the overall structure of the U.S. national security community and civilian departments and agencies. Effective transformation must go far beyond military forces; it must affect the entire U.S. government.

The United States also must reevaluate its recent approach to alliances and to the world. Military power is only one dimension of power, and the United States must learn that allies and friends must be treated as true partners and not as nations the United States can always lead. The United States needs to relearn a key lesson of the Cold War. This is not a unipolar world, and there are many times the United States should listen and follow. U.S. security depends on working out relations with competing powers, not on dominating them. U.S. strategy can succeed only by minimizing military intervention and relying primarily on patience, diplomacy, and collective action in concert with its allies and other states. A reliance on unilateralism and hard power can succeed only in alienating the world. No matter how well the United States shapes its military strength, multilateralism and soft power must still be the rule and not the exception.

THE RICH STATES HAVE MORE MONEY

Fortunately, the resource limits on U.S. defense efforts are far smaller than those faced by any potential threat or rival. Statistics on world military expenditures are notoriously uncertain, as are efforts to make direct comparisons of national military and security spending. In fact, the United States no longer attempts to make public estimates of global military spending in the *CIA World Factbook* and no longer publishes an annual report on *World Military Expenditures and Arms Transfers*.

Nongovernmental and UN reports generally have limited credibility. The International Institute of Strategic Studies (IISS), however, does draw on a variety of national inputs. The most recent data published by the IISS are compared in Figure 1.1. The IISS reports that the United States has spent well over $400 billion a year by its definition. This compares with a maximum of around $220 billion a year for NATO Europe, $65 billion for Russia, and less than $60 billion for China.[1]

If one looks at total regional expenditures, the IISS estimates that the entire Middle East spends under $60 billion, all of East Asia (including China) spends some $165 billion, all of Central and Latin America spend around $25 billion, and all of Sub-Saharan Africa spend less than $8 billion. Even if one adds in the

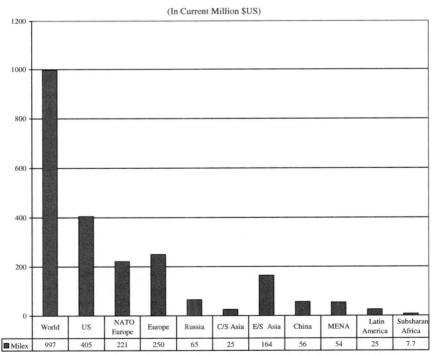

(In Current Million $US)

	World	US	NATO Europe	Europe	Russia	C/S Asia	E/S Asia	China	MENA	Latin America	Subsharan Africa
■ Milex	997	405	221	250	65	25	164	56	54	25	7.7

Source: International Institute of Strategic Studies (IISS), *Military Balance 2004-2005*, Oxford, IISS, 2004, Table 38.

Figure 1.1 Comparative Military Spending in 2003

supplemental costs of the Iraq War and the Afghan War—which are not counted in the IISS estimates—the United States has spent more than 50 percent of all the national security expenditures in the world in recent years.

Nevertheless, as the following chapters show, current U.S. military efforts put only limited pressure on the U.S. gross domestic product and the federal budget. In spite of the Iraq War, the Afghan War, and the war on terrorism, current U.S. military expenditures are close to a historic low as a percentage of both its post–World War II gross national product and total federal spending. U.S. defense manpower is lower than at any time since the beginning of World War II. There are many competing demands for U.S. defense expenditures, but by any practical standard, the current level of U.S. military efforts does not begin to "stretch" U.S. capacity to create much larger forces.

MORE EFFICIENT AND MORE EFFECTIVE FORCES

Money is only one measure of U.S. military power and effectiveness. The United States may face new challenges, but it has already made extraordinary qualitative advances in its forces. The United States has no monopoly on modern tactics, technology, and training or in creating modern professional forces. It is, however, the only nation that has as yet combined high spending levels with a systematic and effective effort to exploit what some have called the "revolution in military affairs."

For all of the challenges the United States now faces in dealing with new kinds of warfare, the Gulf and Iraq wars have shown that the United States leads the world in many areas of military innovation. Moreover, recent wars have given the United States far more practical experience in actually making use of such changes than any other major power. Russia has learned little from its recent struggles in Chechnya and has only begun to modernize an obsolete force structure that used to emphasize mass over quality and relied on low-grade conscripts. China is more active in such modernization, but begins with far less modern forces and a far less developed military-industrial base.

Britain is the only European power with recent meaningful warfighting experience. Efforts to create collective "European" forces are largely rhetorical accounting exercises, and France is the only other European nation seeking modern power projection capability. Europe may be slow to emerge as any kind of independent military force, although the European Union is gradually creating a separate military identity from NATO. Europe does, however, have considerable influence over U.S. security actions that go beyond sheer military force—as French and German actions over the Iraq War made clear. Europe has also shown that it can play a major role in deploying both peacemaking forces and "soft power."

The other regions of the world have some modern military powers like Israel and Japan, but they are comparatively small. The two Koreas represent a highly localized concentration of force, but one where U.S. long-range precision-strike capabilities make a decisive difference in the balance. Aside from a few emerging military powers such as India, most of the world's other military forces consist of small, uncoordinated powers that either have low rates of modernization or buy showpiece equipment they cannot properly man or sustain.

U.S. Advantages in Conventional Warfare

It may be decades before it is clear just how far current changes in technology and tactics will have a lasting impact in changing the nature of warfare and whether such changes can cope with the ability of resourceful enemies to adapt to them, but the United States has had lesson after lesson in how it should use its resources in improving and modernizing its capability to wage conventional war. For all of the problems the United States now faces in dealing with new kinds of warfare, the Gulf and Iraq wars have shown that the United States leads the world in several areas of military innovation:

- *Unity of command:* The level of unity of command, and "fusion," achieved during the Gulf War was scarcely perfect, but it was far more effective than that possible in most states. Advanced powers have improved its unity of command and ability to conduct joint operations.

- *Jointness, combined operations, combined arms, and the "AirLand Battle":* Advanced powers can use technology to train and integrate in ways that allow far more effective approaches to jointness, combined arms, and combined operations. They have developed tactics that closely integrate air and land operations.

- *Emphasis on maneuver:* The United States had firepower and attrition warfare until the end of the Vietnam War. In the years that followed, it converted its force structure to place an equal emphasis on maneuver and deception. This emphasis has been adopted by Britain and France and other advanced states.

- *Emphasis on deception and strategic/tactical innovation:* No country has a monopoly on the use of deception and strategic/tactical innovation. High-technology powers with advanced battle management and information systems will, however, be able to penetrate the enemy's decision-making system and react so quickly that the opponent cannot compete.

- *"24-hour war"—Superior night, all-weather, and beyond-visual-range warfare:* "Visibility" is always relative in combat. There is no such thing as a perfect night vision or all-weather combat system, or way of acquiring perfect information at long ranges. Advanced technology air and land forces, however, have far better training and technology for such combat than they ever had in the past and are designed to wage warfare continuously at night and in poor weather. Equally important, they are far more capable of taking advantage of the margin of extra range and tactical information provided by superior technology.

- *Near real-time integration of $C^4I/BM/T/BDA$:* New $C^4I/BM/T/BDA$ organization, technology, and software systems make it possible to integrate various aspects of command, control, communications, computers, and intelligence (C^4I); battle management (BM); targeting (T); and battle-damage assessment (BDA) to achieve a near real-time integration and decision-making–execution cycle.

- *A new tempo of operations:* Superiority in virtually every aspect of targeting, intelligence gathering and dissemination, integration of combined arms, multiservice forces, and night and all-weather warfare make it possible to achieve both a new tempo of operations and one far superior to that of the enemy.

- *A new tempo of sustainability:* Advanced forces will have maintainability, reliability, reparability, and the speed and overall mobility of logistic, service support, and combat support force activity that broadly match their maneuver and firepower capabilities. The benefits of these new capabilities are already reflected in such critical areas as the extraordinarily high operational availability and sortie rates of Western combat aircraft and the ability to support the movement of heliborne and armored forces.

- *Rapidly moving, armed, computerized supply and logistics:* Rather than steadily occupy and secure rear areas and create large logistic and rear-area supply forces, focus on creating computerized logistic systems capable of tracing the location of supplies and the needs of forward combat units. Send supplies and service support units forward to meet demand on a near real-time basis. Send supply, logistics, maintenance, and recovery units forward to meet demand using airpower and long-range firepower to secure the lines of communication and flanks of land forces. Arm and train logistic and service support units to defend themselves against insurgents and light attacking forces. Ensure that armor, rotary-wing, and fixed-wing combat units can move forward as quickly as possible.

- *Beyond-visual-range air combat, air defense suppression, air base attacks, and airborne C^4I/BM:* The Coalition in the Gulf had a decisive advantage in air combat training, beyond-visual-range air combat capability, antiradiation missiles, electronic warfare, air base and shelter and kill capability, stealth and unmanned long-range strike systems, identification friend or foe and air control capability, and airborne C^4I/BM systems like the E-3 and the ABCCC (Airborne Command and Control Center). These advantages allowed the Coalition to win early and decisive air supremacy in the Gulf and Kosovo conflicts and paralyze the Iraqi Air Force in the Iraq War. Advanced forces will steadily improve the individual capability of these systems and their integration into "netcentric" warfare.

- *Focused and effective interdiction bombing:* Advanced forces organize effectively to use deep strike capabilities to carry out a rapid and effective pattern of focused strategic bombing where planning is sufficiently well coupled to intelligence and meaningful strategic objectives so that such strikes achieve the major military objectives that the planner sets. At the same time, targeting, force allocation, and precision kill capabilities have advanced to the point where interdiction bombing and strikes are far more lethal and strategically useful than in previous conflicts.

- *Expansion of the battlefield: "Deep Strike":* As part of its effort to offset the Warsaw Pact's numerical superiority, U.S. tactics and technology emphasized using AirLand battle capabilities to extend the battlefield far beyond the immediate forward "edge" of the battle area (FEBA) using advanced near real-time targeting systems, precision weapons, and area munitions. The UN Coalition exploited the resulting mix of targeting capability, improved air strike capabilities, and land force capabilities in ways during the Gulf War that played an important role in degrading Iraqi ground forces during the air phase of the war, and which helped the Coalition break through Iraqi defenses and exploit the breakthrough. In Kosovo, the United States and NATO began to employ more advanced deep strike targeting technologies and precision strike systems. These capabilities made striking further advances in the Iraq War, and far more advanced systems are in development.

- *Technological superiority in many critical areas of weaponry:* The West and some moderate regional states have a critical edge in key weapons like tanks, other armored fighting vehicles, artillery systems, long-range strike systems, attack aircraft, air defense aircraft, surface-to-air missiles, space, attack helicopters, naval systems, sensors, battle management, and a host of other areas. This superiority goes far beyond the technical edge revealed by "weapon-on-weapon" comparisons. Coalition forces exploited technology in "systems" that integrated mixes of different weapons into other aspects of force capability and into the overall force structure.

- *Integration of precision-guided weapons into tactics and force structures:* Advanced forces exploit a technical edge in the ability to use precision-guided weapons coupled to far more realistic training in using such weapons and in the ability to link their employment to far superior reconnaissance and targeting capability.

- *Realistic combat training and use of technology and simulation:* During the Gulf and Iraq wars, the United States and Britain took advantage of training methods based on realistic combined arms and AirLand training, large-scale training, and adversary training. These efforts proved far superior to previous methods and were coupled to a far more realistic and demanding system for ensuring the readiness of the forces involved. They show the value of kinds of training that allow forces to rapidly adapt to the special and changing conditions of war.

- *Emphasis on forward leadership and delegation:* Technology, tactics, and training all support aggressive and innovative leadership.

- *Heavy reliance on NCOs and highly skilled enlisted personnel:* Advanced forces place heavy reliance on the technical skills, leadership quality, and initiative of noncommissioned officers (NCOs) and experienced enlisted personnel.

- *High degree of overall readiness:* Military readiness is a difficult term to define since it involves so many aspects of force capability. All professional, combat-experienced forces that rely on high-technology training aids and netcentric systems do, however, have the ability to set more realistic standards for measuring readiness and ensuring proper reporting, and adequate funding over a sustained period of time.

These qualitative advantages more than offset the fact that the United States is not a "superpower" in quantitative terms. Figure 1.2 shows that other powers have substantially larger forces and that the number of forces the United States can credibly project in any one contingency is a small fraction of total U.S. forces. Numbers, however, cannot measure the impact of precision-guided weapons, advances in areas like stealth, "netting" forces for joint operations, and the other advances listed above.

The Vulnerabilities of Less Advanced Powers

Put differently, the United States has shown the world it is able to exploit a range of serious weaknesses in the conventional warfighting capabilities of less advanced powers. These weakness are largely the mirror image of the strengths inherent in

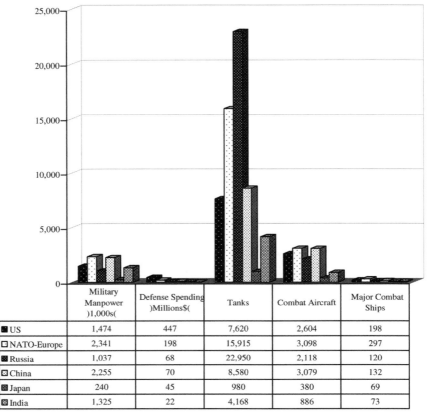

	Military Manpower)1,000s(	Defense Spending)Millions$(	Tanks	Combat Aircraft	Major Combat Ships
US	1,474	447	7,620	2,604	198
NATO-Europe	2,341	198	15,915	3,098	297
Russia	1,037	68	22,950	2,118	120
China	2,255	70	8,580	3,079	132
Japan	240	45	980	380	69
India	1,325	22	4,168	886	73

Source: Adapted from International Institute of Strategic Studies (IISS), *Military Balance 2005-2006*, London, Routledge, 2005

Figure 1.2   Comparative Military Strength of Major Powers and Power Blocs in 2006

U.S. force transformation, and they are weaknesses few potential threat nations have any near-term hope of countering:

- *Authoritarianism and overcentralization of the effective command structure:* The high command of many countries is dependent on compartmentalized, overcentralized $C^4I/$ BM systems that do not support high tempo warfare, combined arms, or combined operations and lack tactical and technical sophistication. Many forces or force elements report through a separate chain of command. C^4I/BM systems often are structured to separate the activity of regular forces from elite, regime security, and ideological forces. Systems often ensure major sectors and corps commanders report to the political leadership, and separations occur within the branches of a given service. Intelligence is compartmentalized and poorly disseminated. Air force command systems are small, unit oriented, and unsuited for large-scale force management. Coordination of land-based air defense and strike systems is poorly integrated, vulnerable, and/or limited in volume-handling capability. Combined operations and combined arms coordination are poor, and command interference at the political level is common.

- *Lack of strategic assessment capability:* Many nations lack sufficient understanding of Western warfighting capabilities to understand the impact of the revolution in military affairs, the role of high-technology systems, and the impact of the new tempo of war. Other countries have important gaps in their assessment capabilities reflecting national traditions or prejudices.

- *Major weaknesses in battle management, command, control, communications, intelligence, targeting, and battle-damage assessment:* No Middle Eastern country except Israel has meaningful access to space-based systems, or advanced theater reconnaissance and intelligence systems, unless data are provided by states outside the region. Most lack sophisticated reconnaissance, intelligence, and targeting assets at the national level or in their individual military services. Beyond-visual-range imagery and targeting is restricted to largely vulnerable and easily detectable reconnaissance aircraft or low performance unmanned aerial vehicles (UAVs). Many rely on photo data for imagery and have cumbersome download and analysis cycles in interpreting intelligence. Many have exploitable vulnerabilities to information warfare. Most are limited in the sophistication of their electronic warfare, signals intelligence (SIGINT), and communications intelligence (COMINT) systems. Their communications security is little better, or worse, than commercial communications security. They have severe communications interconnectivity, volume handling, and dissemination problems. Additionally, they cannot provide the software and connectivity necessary to fully exploit even commercial or ordinary military systems. They lack the C^{4}I/BM capability to manage complex deep strikes, complex large-scale armor and artillery operations, effective electronic intelligence, and rapid cycles of reaction in decision making.

- *Lack of cohesive force quality:* Most countries' forces have major land combat units and squadrons with very different levels of proficiency. Political, historical, and equipment supply factors often mean that most units have much lower levels of real-world combat effectiveness than the best units. Further, imbalances in combat support, service support, and logistic support create significant additional imbalances in sustainability and operational effectiveness. Many states add to these problems, as well as lack of force cohesion, by creating politicized or ideological divisions within their forces.

- *Shallow offensive battlefields:* Most states face severe limits in extending the depth of the battlefield because they lack the survivable platforms and sensors, communications, and data processing to do so. These problems are particularly severe in wars of maneuver, in wars involving the extensive use of strike aircraft, and in battles where a growing strain is placed on force cohesion.

- *Manpower quality:* Many states rely on the mass use of poorly trained conscripts. They fail to provide adequate status, pay, training, and career management for NCOs and technicians. Many forces fail to provide professional career development for officers and joint and combined arms training. Promotion often occurs for political reasons or out of nepotism and favoritism.

- *Slow tempo of operations:* Most military forces have not fought a high-intensity air or armored battle. They are at best capable of medium-tempo operations, and their pace of operations is often dependent on the survival of some critical mix of facilities or capabilities.

- *Lack of sustainability, recovery, and repair:* These initial problems in the tempo of operations are often exacerbated by a failure to provide for sustained air operations and high sortie rates, long-range sustained maneuver, and battlefield/combat unit recovery and repair. Most forces are heavily dependent on resupply to deal with combat attrition, whereas Western forces can use field recovery, maintenance, and repair.

- *Inability to prevent air superiority:* Many states have far greater air defense capability on paper than they do in practice. Most have not fought in any kind of meaningful air action in the last decade, and many have never fought any significant air action in their history. C^{4}I/BM problems are critical in this near real-time environment. Most countries lack sophisticated air combat and land-based air defense simulation and training systems and do not conduct effective aggressor and large-scale operations training. Efforts to transfer technology, organization, and training methods from other nations on a patchwork basis often leave critical gaps in national capability, even where other capabilities are effective.

- *Problems in air-to-air combat:* Air combat training levels are often low and the training unrealistic. Pilot and other crew training standards are insufficient, or initial training is not followed up with sustained training. There is little effective aggressor training. Airborne warning and control system and ABCCC capabilities are lacking. Electronic warfare (EW) capabilities are modified commercial-grade capabilities. Most aircraft lack effective air battle management systems and have limited beyond-visual-range and lookdown/shoot-down capability. Most air forces supplied primarily by Russia or Eastern European states depend heavily on obsolete ground-controlled vectoring for intercepts. Key radar and control centers are static and vulnerable to corridor blasting.

- *Problems in land-based air defense:* Many states lack anything approaching an integrated land-based air defense system and rely on outdated or obsolete radars, missile units, and other equipment. Other states must borrow or adapt air defense battle management capabilities from supplier states and have limited independent capability for systems integration—particularly at the software level. They lack the mix of heavy surface-to-air missile systems to cover broad areas or must rely on obsolete systems that can be killed, countered by EW, and/or bypassed. Most Middle Eastern short-range air defense systems do not protect against attacks with standoff precision weapons or using stealth.

- *Lack of effective survivable long-range strike systems:* Many nations have the capability to launch long-range effective air and missile strikes, but have severe operational problems in using them. Refueling capabilities do not exist or are in such small numbers as to be highly vulnerable. Long-range targeting and battle-damage assessment capabilities are lacking. Training is limited and unrealistic in terms of penetrating effective air defenses. Platforms are export systems without the full range of supplier avionics or missile warheads. Assets are not survivable or lose much of their effective strike capability once dispersed.

- *Combined (joint) operations, combined arms, and interoperability:* Many states fail to emphasize the key advances in the integration of warfighting capabilities from the last decade. They have not developed combined arms capabilities within each service, much less interservice joint warfare capabilities. When they do emphasize combined arms and joint operations, they usually leave serious gaps in some aspects of national warfighting capability. There is little or no emphasis on interoperability with neighboring powers.

- *Rough/special terrain warfare:* Although many forces have armed helicopters, large numbers of tracked vehicles, and can create effective rough terrain defenses if given time; they have problems in conducting high-tempo operations. Many tend to be road-bound for critical support and combined arms functions, and lack training for long-range, high-intensity engagements in rough terrain. Many are not properly trained to exploit the potential advantages of their own region. They are either garrison forces or forces that rely on relatively static operations in predetermined field positions. These problems are often compounded by a lack of combat engineering and barrier crossing equipment.

- *Night and all-weather warfare:* Most forces lack adequate equipment for night and poor-weather warfare and particularly for long-range direct and indirect fire engagement and cohesive, sustainable, and large-scale maneuver.

- *Armored operations:* Most countries have sharply different levels of armored warfare proficiency within their armored and mechanized forces. Few units have advanced training and simulation facilities. Most land forces have interoperability and standardization problems within their force structure—particularly in the case of other armored fighting vehicles where they often deploy a very wide range of types. Many are very tank heavy, without the mix of other land force capabilities necessary to deploy infantry, supporting artillery, and antitank capabilities at the same speed and maneuver proficiency as tank units. Most forces have poor training in conducting rapid, large-scale armored and combined operations at night and in poor weather. Effective battle management declines sharply at the force-wide level—as distinguished from the major combat unit level—and sometimes even in coordinating brigade or division-sized operations.

- *Artillery operations:* Many states have large numbers of artillery weapons, but serious problems in training and tactics. They lack long-range targeting capability and the ability to rapidly shift and effectively allocate fire. Many rely on towed weapons with limited mobility or lack off-road support vehicles. Combined arms capabilities are limited. Many units are effective in using mass fire only against enemies that maneuver more slowly than they do.

- *Attack and combat helicopter units:* Some countries do have elite elements, but many do not properly train their helicopter units or integrate them into combined or joint operations.

- *Commando, paratroop, and Special Forces:* Many countries have elite combat units that are high-quality forces at the individual combat unit level. In many cases, however, they are not trained or organized for effective combined and joint warfare or for sustained combat. This seriously weakens their effectiveness in anything but limited combat missions.

- *Combat training:* Training generally has serious problems and gaps, which vary by country. Units or force elements differ sharply in training quality. Training problems are complicated by conversion and expansion, conscript turnover, and a lack of advanced technical support for realistic armored, artillery, air-to-air, surface-to-air, and offensive air training. Mass sometimes compensates, but major weaknesses remain.

- *Inability to use weapons of mass destruction effectively:* Any state can use weapons of mass destruction to threaten or intimidate another or to attack population centers and fixed area targets. At the same time, this is not the same as having an effective capability and doctrine to obtain maximum use of such weapons, or to manage attacks in ways that result in effective tactical outcomes and conflict termination. Many states are acquiring long-range missiles and weapons of mass destruction with very limited exercise and test and evaluation capabilities. This does not deny them the ability to target large populated areas, economic centers, and fixed military targets, potentially inflicting massive damage. At the same time, it does present problems in more sophisticated military operations. Many will have to improvise deployments, doctrine, and warfighting capabilities. In many cases, weaknesses and vulnerabilities will persist, and they will be able to exploit only a limited amount of the potential lethality of such systems.

THE LIMITS TO U.S. CAPABILITIES AND THE CHALLENGE OF ASYMMETRIC WARFARE

In spite of all these U.S. advantages in fighting conventional wars, however, the recent fighting in Iraq, Afghanistan, and against transnational threats like Al Qa'ida has shown that there are major gaps in U.S. capabilities that current and potential enemies can exploit. Some of these gaps are dictated by the size of U.S. forces and the problems it faces in power projection. China, North Korea, and Russia maintain massive conventional forces, and mass still tells. The threat of a major war between the Koreas and the escalation of a clash over the Taiwan Strait remain major threats. Even a nation like Iran has sufficient conventional capability to be a major deterrent to U.S. ability to actually invade and occupy its territory.

The technological advantages the United States now enjoys are also often going to be temporary and subject to the laws of diminishing returns as other nations approach U.S. levels of capability. Other powers and key potential enemies have realized that they can benefit from adapting the tactics, technologies, and training methods that have given the United States such outstanding conventional warfighting capabilities. The United States cannot ignore the fact that some potential threat nations can and will go further and eventually develop conventional warfighting capabilities that can compete directly with those of the United States.

Russia continues to develop highly advanced military technology and weapons systems. China is actively modernizing its forces in ways that improve its conventional capabilities, but also strengthen its nuclear forces and ability to wage asymmetric warfare. More than any other potential rival, it has sought to develop a new force structure that could both match the United States in some of the areas where it is strongest and exploit the areas where U.S. forces currently seem less capable. Chinese force transformation is only beginning to gather serious momentum, but it represents the one serious effort to bring new and different mixes of tactics, training, and technology together in a form that is truly innovative and modern.

The United States may not want peer competitors or the rebirth of a multipolar world, but it will happen. Much of America's present qualitative edge will inevitably diminish or vanish as nations like China modernize their forces. The United States has recognized this reality in its new national strategy and in the Quadrennial Defense Review it issued in February 2006.[2]

The choices of major and emerging powers, including India, Russia and China, will be key factors in determining the international security environment of the 21st century.

India is emerging as a great power and a key strategic partner. On July 18, 2005 the President and Indian Prime Minister declared their resolve to transform the U.S.–India relationship into a global partnership that will provide leadership in areas of mutual concern and interest. Shared values as long-standing, multi-ethnic democracies provide the foundation for continued and increased strategic cooperation and represent an important opportunity for our two countries.

Russia remains a country in transition. It is unlikely to pose a military threat to the United States or its allies on the same scale or intensity as the Soviet Union during the Cold War. Where possible, the United States will cooperate with Russia on shared interests such as countering the proliferation of weapons of mass destruction, combating terrorism, and countering the trafficking of narcotics. The United States remains concerned about the erosion of democracy in Russia, the curtailment of non-governmental organizations (NGOs) and freedom of the press, the centralization of political power and limits on economic freedom. Internationally, the United States welcomes Russia as a constructive partner but views with increasing concern its sales of disruptive weapons technologies abroad and actions that compromise the political and economic independence and territorial integrity of other states.

Of the major and emerging powers, China has the greatest potential to compete militarily with the United States and field disruptive military technologies that could over time off set traditional U.S. military advantages absent U.S. counter strategies. U.S. policy remains focused on encouraging China to play a constructive, peaceful role in the Asia-Pacific region and to serve as a partner in addressing common security challenges, including terrorism, proliferation, narcotics and piracy. U.S. policy seeks to encourage China to choose a path of peaceful economic growth and political liberalization, rather than military threat and intimidation. The United States' goal is for China to continue as an economic partner and emerge as a responsible stakeholder and force for good in the world.

China continues to invest heavily in its military, particularly in its strategic arsenal and capabilities designed to improve its ability to project power beyond its borders. Since 1996, China has increased its defense spending by more than 10% in real terms in every year except 2003. Secrecy, moreover, envelops most aspects of Chinese security affairs. The outside world has little knowledge of Chinese motivations and decision-making or of key capabilities supporting its military modernization. The United States encourages China to take actions to make its intentions clear and clarify its military plans. Chinese military modernization has accelerated since the mid-to-late 1990s in response to central leadership demands to develop military options against Taiwan scenarios.

The pace and scope of China's military build-up already puts regional military balances at risk. China is likely to continue making large investments in high-end, asymmetric military capabilities, emphasizing electronic and cyber-warfare; counter-space operations; ballistic and cruise missiles; advanced integrated air defense systems; next generation torpedoes; advanced submarines; strategic nuclear strike from modern, sophisticated land and sea-based systems; and theater unmanned aerial vehicles for employment by the Chinese military and for global export. These capabilities, the vast distances of the Asian theater, China's continental depth, and the challenge of en route and in-theater U.S. basing place a premium on forces capable of sustained operations at great distances into denied areas.

The United States will work to ensure that all major and emerging powers are integrated as constructive actors and stakeholders into the international system. It will also seek to ensure that no foreign power can dictate the terms of regional or global security. It will attempt to dissuade any military competitor from developing disruptive or other capabilities that could enable regional hegemony or hostile action against the United States or other friendly countries, and it will seek to deter aggression or coercion. Should deterrence fail, the United States would deny a hostile power its strategic and operational objectives.

Shaping the choices of major and emerging powers requires a balanced approach, one that seeks cooperation but also creates prudent hedges against the possibility that cooperative approaches by themselves may fail to preclude future conflict. A successful hedging strategy requires improving the capacity of partner states and reducing their vulnerabilities. In this regard, the United States will work to achieve greater integration of defensive systems among its international partners in ways that would complicate any adversary's efforts to decouple them. The United States will work with allies and partners to integrate intelligence sensors, communication networks, information systems, missile defenses, undersea warfare and counter-mine warfare capabilities. It will seek to strengthen partner nations' capabilities to defend themselves and withstand attack, including against ambiguous coercive threats.

The United States needs to shape its strategy and force plans around the fact that it has never been a military "superpower" in the sense that it has had enough military strength to dominate every military encounter anywhere in the world. It has always faced severe limits and risks in using military force, particularly where it has faced major powers like Russia and China or in conflicts involving nations with different cultures and religions. Its ability to project air and missile power, or control sea-lanes, has never been matched by a similar ability to project land power, and much of its strength has always been dependent on its structure of formal and informal alliances.

The breakup of the Soviet Union and the dissolution of the Warsaw Pact may have deprived the United States of a direct military rival, but "globalism" and massive changes in the world economy are creating rivals of a very different kind. The United States may not want national or regional rivals, but the reemergence of a more multi-polar world is almost inevitable. This, in turn, will increase the challenge to U.S. capabilities imposed by time, distance, and geography. The United States must act regionally, regardless of its global capabilities, and fighting half way across the world is still a daunting challenge. The United States also cannot always choose its enemies according to its own priorities or concentrate its forces accordingly. History has shown that U.S. power projection must be equally capable to dealing with conventional threats all over the world, and often in unexpected areas and with little warning.

Most important, the United States faces an increasing range of threats that do not rely on conventional forces. The United States faces new threats from nonstate actors and from combinations of hostile states and nonstate actors. These include threats like neo-Salafi Islamist extremist groups such as Al Qa'ida that oppose the United States on ideological and religious grounds and fight through combinations of asymmetric warfare and terrorism. Such nonstate actors cannot be defeated simply by defeating their "fighters" or destroying their leadership. New movements will emerge and old movements will mutate as long as the ideological, cultural, political, and economic forces that create such movements continue to exist. Many such nonstate actors already consist of clusters of affiliated groups that do not have formal ties or clear hierarchies. Defeating any given groups or element is at best a tactical victory. New or existing movements will adapt and expand to take their place.

U.S. Military Vulnerabilities

Both states and nonstate actors can fight the United States at political and ideological levels where U.S. military strength cannot determine the outcome. They can also attack the United States using insurgency, terrorism, and other asymmetric means where the United States has less or no advantage because of its conventional and nuclear strength. The most important near- and midterm challenge the United States faces is that the world does not have to fight the United States on its own terms. Conventional combat is only one way of waging war or exerting military power. The fighting in Iraq and Afghanistan has made it clear that U.S. preeminence in conventional warfighting does not mean the United States has any lead in counterterrorism or counterinsurgency, that it has mastered conflict termination, or that it is effective in stability operations and nation building.

The United States has entered the war on terrorism, the Afghan conflict, and the Iraq conflict with a force posture and national security system designed to fight states and the conventional forces of the Cold War and has shown it has many gaps and shortcomings in dealing with the new kind of wars that the United States now has to fight. These struggles have all exposed many of the long-standing vulnerabilities that the United States had previously exposed in Vietnam, Lebanon, Haiti, and Somalia, as well as new ones:

- *Sudden or surprise attack:* Power projection is dependent on strategic warning, timely decision making, and effective mobilization and redeployment for much of its military effectiveness.

- *Saturation and the use of mass to create a defensive or deterrent morass:* There is no precise way to determine the point at which mass, or force quantity, overcomes superior effectiveness, or force quality—historically, efforts to emphasize mass have been far less successful than military experts predicted at the time. Even the best force, however, reaches the point where it cannot maintain its edge in C^4I/battle management, air combat, or maneuver warfare in the face of superior numbers or multiple threats. Further, saturation may produce a sudden catalytic collapse of effectiveness, rather than a gradual degeneration from which a high-technology force dependent upon such systems recover. This affects forward deployment, reliance on mobilization, and reliance on defensive land tactics versus preemption and "offensive defense."

- *Limited capability to take casualties:* Warfighting is not measured simply in terms of whether a given side can win a battle or conflict, but how well it can absorb the damage inflicted upon it. Many powers are highly sensitive to casualties and losses. This sensitivity may limit its operational flexibility in taking risks and in sustaining some kinds of combat if casualties become serious relative to the apparent value of the immediate objective.

- *Limited ability to inflict casualties and collateral damage:* Dependence on world opinion and outside support means some nations increasingly must plan to fight at least low- and mid-intensity conflicts in ways that limit enemy casualties and collateral damage to its opponents.

- *Low-intensity and infantry/insurgent dominated combat:* Low-intensity conflict makes it much harder to utilize most technical advantages in combat—because low-intensity wars are largely fought against people, not things. Low-intensity wars are also highly political. The battle for public opinion is as much a condition of victory as killing the enemy. The outcome of such a battle will be highly dependent on the specific political conditions under which it is fought, rather than RMA-like capabilities.

- *Hostage-taking, kidnapping, executions, and terrorism:* Like low-intensity warfare, hostage taking, kidnapping, executions, and terrorism present the problem that advanced technology powers cannot exploit their conventional strengths and must fight a low-level battle primarily on the basis of infantry combat. Human intelligence (HUMINT) is more important than conventional military intelligence, and much of the fight against terrorism may take place in urban or heavily populated areas.

- *Urban and built-up area warfare:* Advanced military powers are still challenged by the problems of urban warfare. In spite of the performance of U.S. forces in the Iraq War, cases like Fallujah's and Sadr's urban operations have shown that truly pacifying a hostile city or built-up area can be extremely difficult. It also is not clear what would happen if a more popular regime—such as the government of Iran—tried to create an urban redoubt. Moreover, most Western forces are not trained or equipped to deal with sustained urban warfare in populated areas during regional combat—particularly when the fighting may affect large civilian populations on friendly soil.

- *Extended conflict and occupation warfare:* Not all wars can be quickly terminated, and many forms of warfare—particularly those involving peacekeeping and peace enforcement—require prolonged military occupations. The result imposes major strains on the United States politically, economically, and militarily.

- *Weapons of mass destruction:* The threat or actual use of such weapons can compensate for conventional weakness in some cases and deter military action in others.

- *Proxy warfare and false flags:* As the Lockerbie case demonstrated, states can successfully carry out major acts of terrorism through proxies without having their identity quickly established or suffering major military retaliation. Al Khobar is a more recent case where Iran's full role still remains uncertain and no retaliation has occurred. Similarly, the various charges that Iraq was the source of the first World Trade Center attack, and the conspiracy theories that follow, indicate that false flag operations are feasible. So do the number of terrorist incidents where unknown groups or multiple groups have claimed responsibility, but the true cause has never been firmly established.

- *HUMINT, area expertise, and language skills:* U.S. and Western capabilities to conduct operations requiring extensive area knowledge and language skills are inherently limited. Similarly, high-technology intelligence, surveillance, and reconnaissance (IS&R) assets have not proved to be a substitute for HUMINT sources and analytical skills, although they can often aid HUMINT at both the operational and analytical levels.

- *Attack rear areas and lines of communication:* The United States talks about "swarm theory" and discontinuous battlefields, but Iraqi regular and irregular forces quickly learned—as Iraqi insurgents did later—that U.S. rear area, support, and logistic forces are far more vulnerable than U.S. combat elements. Such "swarming" may be slow, if irregular forces are not in place, but potential opponents understand this and can fight discontinuous battles of their own.

- *Political, ideological, and psychological warfare:* As has been discussed earlier, the United States is vulnerable to such attacks on the grounds of ethnicity, religion, its status as a superpower active in the region, and its ties to Israel. Ironically, some can exploit its ties to moderate and conservative regimes on the grounds it fails to support reform, while others can exploit its efforts to advance secular political and economic reforms on the grounds they are anti-Islamic.

Threat of Asymmetric Innovation

Experts may indulge in petty semantic arguments over whether the United States must now call such forms of warfighting "asymmetric," "irregular," or "fourth-generation war." The fact remains that guerrilla, terrorist, and insurgent movements have repeatedly shown that they can exploit such vulnerabilities. It has also been shown that they now are able to draw on the history of past successes, adopt new tactics proven by other movements and actors on a near real-time basis, and innovate on their own.

For all the talk of such conflicts involving new forms of warfare, there is a vast pool of historical experience that such attackers can draw upon. The United States sometimes confuses an enemy's knowledge of history with innovation, largely because Americans do not have the same collective memory as states and movements in the region. Hostile actors can draw on a long historical menu of past tactics and their results and adapt them to specific tactical circumstances. One has only to read Sun Tzu to find that many of the tactics that today's nonstate actors exploit in Afghanistan and Iraq are the same as those that other practitioners of asymmetric and irregular warfare have practiced for centuries.

In fact, America's very strengths have forced many of its enemies to find new ways to exploit its weaknesses. As a result, Iraq and Afghanistan have provided so many case examples of "lessons" that mix innovation with historical experience that it is possible only to touch upon some of the more specific "innovations" that insurgents have used in Iraq and Afghanistan, but even a short list is impressive:

- *Attack the structures of governance and security by ideological, political, and violent means:* Use ideological and political means to attack the legitimacy of the government and the nation-building process. Intimidate and subvert the military and security forces. Intimidate and attack government officials and institutions at the national, regional, and local levels. Strike at infrastructure, utilities, and services in ways that appear to show the government cannot provide essential economic services or personal security.

- *Create alliances of convenience and informal networks with other groups to attack the United States, moderate regional governments, or efforts at nation building:* The informal common fronts operate on the principle that the "enemy of my enemy" is my temporary friend. At the same time, movements "franchise" to create individual cells and independent units, creating diverse mixes of enemies that are difficult to attack.

- *Link asymmetric warfare to crime and looting; exploit poverty and economic desperation:* Use criminals to support attacks on infrastructure and nation-building activity, raise funds, and undermine security. Exploit unemployment to strengthen dedicated insurgent and terrorist cells. Blur the lines between threat forces, criminal elements, and part-time forces.

    At the same time, insurgents and Islamists have shown a steadily more sophisticated capability to exploit holidays, elections and other political events, and sensitive targets both inside the countries that are the scene of their primary operations and in the United States and the West. Attacks on Kurdish and Shi'ite religious festivals and the Madrid bombings are cases in point.

    Terrorists and insurgents know that such targeted and well-timed attacks can successfully undermine the Israeli-Palestinian peace process and can help drive the Israeli-Palestinian conflict. A handful of terrorists in Hamas and the Palestinian Islamic Jihad (PIJ), and the Israeli who killed Rabin, effectively defeated both Israel and the Palestinian Authority. Dramatic incidents of violence in Beirut and Somalia have also created political and psychological conditions that have helped catalyze U.S. withdrawal.

- *Push "hot buttons." Try to find forms of attack that provoke disproportionate fear and "terror" and force the United States and its allies into costly, drastic, and sometimes provocative responses:* Terrorists and insurgents have found that attacks planned for maximum political and psychological effects often have the additional benefit of provoking overreaction. Hamas and the PIJ exploited such tactics throughout the peace process.

    The U.S. response to the attacks on the World Trade Center and the Pentagon led to U.S. overreactions—particularly at the media and Congressional levels—that helped alienate the Arab and Islamic worlds from the United States. At a different level, a limited anthrax attack had a massive psychological impact in the United States, inflicted direct and indirect costs exceeding a billion dollars, drew immense publicity, and affected the operations of a key element of the U.S. government for several weeks.

- *Use media as an intelligence and communication system and for information warfare:* Islamist movements, Palestinian groups, and many others have learned how to capture maximum exposure in regional media, use the Internet, and above all exploit the new Arab satellite news channels. In contrast, U.S. officials often confuse their occasional presence with successful impact.

- *"Game" and manipulate regional, Western, and other outside media:* Use interview access, tapes, journalist hostage takings and killings, politically led and motivated crowds, drivers, and assistants to journalists, and timed and targeted attacks to attempt to manipulate Western and outside media. Manipulate U.S. official briefings with planted questions.

- *Externalize the struggle:* Bring the struggle home to the United States and its allies as in the cases of the World Trade Center, the Pentagon, and Madrid. Get maximum media and political impact. Encourage a "clash between civilizations." Avoid killing fellow Muslims and collateral damage. Appear to be attacking Israel indirectly. Undermine U.S. ties to friendly Arab states.

- *Use Americans and other foreigners as proxies:* There is nothing new about using Americans and other foreigners as proxies for local regimes or attacking them to win support for ideological positions and causes. There has, however, been steadily growing sophistication in the timing and nature of such attacks and in exploiting softer targets such as American businessmen in the country of operations, on striking at U.S. and allied targets in other countries, or in striking at targets in the United States. It is also clear that such attacks receive maximum political and media attention in the United States.

- *Attack UN, NGO, embassies, aid personnel, and foreign contractor business operations:* Attacking such targets greatly reduces the ability to carry out nation building and stability operations to win hearts and minds. Attacking the "innocent," and curtailing their operations or driving organizations out of the country, has become an important focus of insurgents and Islamist extremist attacks.

- *"Horror" attacks, atrocities, and alienation:* Whether or not the tactics were initially deliberate, insurgents in Iraq have found that atrocities like desecrating corpses and beheadings are effective political and psychological weapons for those Islamist extremists whose goal is to divide the West from the Islamic world and create an unbridgeable "clash of civilizations."

  Experts have long pointed out that one of the key differences between Islamist extremist terrorists and previous forms of terrorists is that they are not seeking to negotiate with those they terrorize, but rather to create conditions that can drive the West away, undermine secular and moderate regimes in the Arab and Islamic worlds, and create the conditions under which they can create "Islamic" states according to their own ideas of "Puritanism."

  This is why it serves the purposes of Islamist extremists, as well as some of the more focused opponents of the United States and the West, to create massive casualties and carry out major strikes, or carry out executions and beheadings, even if the result is to provoke hostility and anger. The goal of Osama bin Laden and those like him is not to persuade the United States or the West; it is rather to so alienate them from the Islamic and Arab worlds that the forces of secularism in the region will be sharply undermined and Western secular influence can be controlled or eliminated. The goal of most Iraqi insurgents is narrower—drive the United States and its allies out of Iraq—but involves many of the same methods.

  Seen in this context, the more horrifying the attack, or incident, the better. Simple casualties do not receive the same media attention. They are a reality of war. Killing (or sometimes releasing) innocent hostages does grab the attention of the world media. Large bombs in crowds do the same, as does picking targets whose innocence or media impact grabs headlines. Desecrating corpses, beheadings, and similar acts of violence get even more media attention—at least for a while.

Such actions also breed anger and alienation in the United States and the West and provoke excessive political and media reactions, more stringent security measures, violent responses, and all of the other actions that help provoke a clash of civilizations. The United States and the West are often provoked into playing into the hands of such attackers.

At the same time, any attack or incident that provokes massive media coverage and political reactions appears to be a "victory" to those who support Islamist extremism or those who are truly angry at the United States—even though the actual body count is often low, and victory does not mean creating stronger forces or winning political control. Each such incident can be used to damage the U.S. and Western view of the Arab and Islamic worlds.

- *Keep "failed states" failed and/or deprive local governments and nation-building efforts of legitimacy. Attack nation building and stability targets:* There is nothing new about attacking key economic targets, infrastructure, and aspects of governance critical to the functioning of the state in an effort to disrupt its economy, undermine law enforcement and security, and encourage instability. The Al Qa'ida and Taliban attacks on road works and aid workers; Iraqi insurgent and Islamist attacks on aid workers and projects; and their role in encouraging looting, sabotage, and theft does, however, demonstrate a growing sophistication in attacking stability efforts and tangible progress in aid and governance. These tactics also interact synergistically with the above tactics.

- *Confuse the identity of the attacker; exploit conspiracy theories:* Insurgents and Islamists have learned that a mix of silence, multiple claims to be the attacker, new names for attacking organizations, and uncertain levels of affiliation all make it harder for the United States to respond. They also produce more media coverage and speculation.

  As of yet, the number of true false-flag operations has been limited. However, in Iraq and elsewhere, attacks have often been accompanied by what seems to be deliberate efforts to advance conspiracy theories to confuse the identity of the attacker or to find ways to blame defenders of the United States for being attacked. In addition, conspiracy theories charging the United States with deliberately or carelessly failing to provide an adequate defense have been particularly effective.

- *Shelter in mosques, shrines, high-value targets, and targets with high cultural impact:* Again, exploiting facilities of religious, cultural, and political sensitivity is not a new tactic. However, as operations against Sadr and in Fallujah have shown, the tactics raise the media profile, create a defensive deterrent, and can be exploited to make the United States seem anti-Islamic or to be attacking a culture and not a movement.

- *Exploit, exaggerate, and falsify U.S. attacks that cause civilian casualties and collateral damage, friendly fire against local allies, and incidents where the United States can be blamed for being anti-Arab and anti-Islam:* Terrorists and insurgents have found they can use the media, rumor, and conspiracy theories to exploit the fact the United States often fights a military battle without proper regard to the fact it is also fighting a political, ideological, and psychological war.

  Real incidents of U.S. misconduct, such as the careless treatment of detainees and prisoners and the careless and excessive security measures are cases in point. So too are careless political and media rhetoric by U.S. officials and military officers.

Bin Laden, the Iraqi insurgents, etc., all benefit from every Western action that unnecessarily angers or frustrates the Arab and Islamic worlds. They are not fighting to influence Western or world opinion; they are fighting a political and psychological war to dominate Iraq and the Arab and Islamic worlds.

- *Mix crude and sophisticated IEDS:* Hezbollah should be given credit for having first perfected the use of explosives in well-structured ambushes, although there is nothing new about such tactics—the Afghans used them extensively against the Soviets. Iraq has, however, provided a unique opportunity for insurgents and Islamist extremists to make extensive use of improvised explosive devices (IEDs) by exploiting its mass stocks of arms. The Iraqi attackers have also learned to combine the extensive use of low-grade IEDs, more carefully targeted sophisticated IEDs, and very large car bombs and other devices to create a mix of threats and methods that is much more difficult to counter than reliance on more consistent types of bombs and target sets.

- *Suicide bombs, car bombs, and mass bombings:* The use of such tactics has increased steadily since 1999, in part due to the high success rate relative to alternative methods of attack. It is not always clear that suicide bombing techniques are tactically necessary outside struggles like the Israel-Palestinian conflict, where one side can enforce a very tight area and perimeter, and point target security. In many cases, timed devices might produce the same damage.

  Events in Iraq have shown, however, that suicide bombers still have a major psychological impact and gain exceptional media attention. They also serve as symbols of dedication and commitment, can be portrayed as a form of Islamic martyrdom, and attract more political support and attention among those sympathetic to the cause involved.

  At the same time, regional experts must be very careful about perceiving such methods of attack as either a recent development or as Islamic in character. For instance, Hezbollah used suicide bombings in the 1980s, with an attack on the U.S. Embassy in Beirut in 1981 and in six attacks in 1983 killing 384 people—including 241 U.S. Marines. Moreover, Hindu terrorists and the Tamil Tigers made extensive use of suicide bombings long before the Palestinians. In fact, Hindu terrorists still lead in the amount of suicide bombings committed by a particular group. The Tamil Tigers have carried out 168 such attacks since 1987 versus 16 for Hezbollah versus Israel (1983–1985), 44 for the Palestinians (1999–2004), and 28 for Al Qa'ida (1999–2004). A profiling of the attackers in some 168 attacks also found that only a comparative few could in any sense be called religious fanatics rather than believers in a cause.[3]

- *Attack lines of communication (LOCs), convoys and logistic movements, rear areas, and support activity:* Iran and Afghanistan have shown that dispersed attacks on logistics and support forces often offer a higher chance of success than attacks on combat forces and defended sites and make the fight based on "deep support" rather than on "deep strikes" beyond the FEBA.

- *Better use of light weapons and more advanced types; attack from remote locations or use timed devices:* While much will depend on the level of insurgent and Islamist extremist access to arms, Iraq and Afghanistan have seen a steady improvement in the use of systems like mortars and antitank weapons and efforts to acquire Manpads, antitank guided missiles (ATGMs), mortars, rockets, and timed explosives. The quality of urban and road ambushes has improved strikingly in Iraq, as has the ability to set up rapid attacks and exploit the vulnerability of soft-skinned vehicles. Hezbollah successfully exploited such weapons in its war with Israel in 2006 and showed that nonstate actors are capable of making effective use of advanced ATGMs, antiship missiles, and the threat of using advanced short-range air defense systems.

- *Create informal distributed networks for C^4IBM and IS&R—deliberately or accidentally:* Like drug dealers before them, Islamist extremists and insurgents have learned enough about COMINT and SIGINT to stop using most vulnerable communications assets and to bypass many—if not most—of the efforts to control cash flow and money transfers.

The use of messengers, direct human contact, and more random methods of electronic communication are all cases in point. At the broader level, however, insurgents in Iraq seem to have adapted to having cells and elements operate with considerable autonomy and by loosely linking their operations by using the media and reporting on the overall pattern of attacks to help determine the best methods and targets.

Smuggling, drug sales, theft and looting, and direct fund transfers also largely bypass efforts to limit operations through controls on banking systems, charities, etc. Under these conditions, a lack of central control and cohesive structure may actually be an asset, allowing highly flexible operations with minimal vulnerability to roll-up and attack.

The existence of parallel, and not conflicting, groups of hostile nonstate actors provides similar advantages and has the same impact. The fact that insurgent and Islamist extremist groups operate largely independently, and use different tactics and target sets, greatly complicates U.S. operations and probably actually increases overall effectiveness.

The war on terrorism, the Afghan conflict, and the Iraq War are only the most recent catalysts teaching state and nonstate actors to exploit these vulnerabilities. Other post–Cold War struggles like the Western intervention in Bosnia and Kosovo, peacemaking efforts in Lebanon, nation building in Somalia, and civil struggles in places like Chechnya and Sri Lanka have all shown that such tactics are often the only options that offer a credible hope of deterrence or victory against the United States.

THE CHANGING STRATEGIC ENVIRONMENT: THE "LONG WAR"

As a result, the United States is forced to look far beyond the challenges of any "overstretch" emerging from the Iraq War and focus on the emerging strategic environment that it now calls the "long war." The United States not only faces a strategic environment that is very different from the strategic environment it faced in structuring its forces to fight during the Cold War, it faces far more challenges than it did immediately after "9/11," when it first defined its response to what it then called the "global war on terrorism" or "GWOT."

The real message of the Iraq War is not that there is a major strain on U.S. forces because of the overall size of its forces, because of the limits imposed by current levels of U.S. defense spending, or because of any strain military spending puts on the U.S. economy. It is rather that the United States has driven other powers to try to emulate some aspects of U.S. advances in conventional warfare. Warfare is scarcely an exercise in Newtonian physics, but every reaction does tend to create an equal and opposite reaction.

Recent wars have driven both hostile states and nonstate actors to find asymmetric or "irregular" ways of fighting the United States in precisely those areas where its gaps and shortcomings are greatest. Nations and nonstate actors have already shown that they can use tactics like terrorism, covert attack, insurgency, wars of attrition, and a host of other means to fight the United States below the threshold of operations where it can take advantage of its superior conventional capabilities.

The United States must redefine force transformation to fight on the ideological, political, and asymmetric levels, as well as the conventional and nuclear levels. It must also be prepared for long wars of attrition where opponents seek to create sanctuaries and centers of operation, and to dominate countries and regions in terms of a hostile or insurgent presence, rather than defeat U.S. forces in battle. The center of gravity in such wars is not military in the classic sense; it is political, ideological, and perceptual. Civil-military and stability operations, nation building, and conflict termination may all be as important, or more important, than tactical success. In fact, military success without political and ideological success may often prove as irrelevant as it did in Vietnam.

The Threat of Nonstate Actors

U.S. ideological, political, and military vulnerabilities do not provide most hostile or potentially hostile states with a clear way of defeating the United States *if* the United States determines that stakes are worth escalating to the point where it is willing to use decisive military action. Few regimes are strong and capable enough to risk trying to exploit such vulnerabilities if the United States is determined to pursue a truly critical national interest. Moreover, such tactics often sharply increase the cost of combat to the nations that use them, as well as to the United States, and greatly increase the risk the United States will escalate to remove the regime involved—if this is not part of the original war plan.

This scarcely means that hostile states will not try to exploit U.S. weaknesses if they perceive their own critical interests to be at stake. Nations will pursue the best option they have under duress. They have the option of trying to use violent extremist groups and other nonstate actors as proxies to carry out covert attacks and/or to attempt false-flag operations. Moreover, the distinction between state and nonstate actors is often blurred for other reasons. Failed states with weak or ineffective governments, states involved in civil war, and states that are on the edge of dividing along sectarian, ethnic, or other lines do not have regimes that can be deterred, held responsible, or attacked along conventional military lines. For all intents and purposes, they are nations of nonstate actors.

Many of the vulnerabilities in U.S. warfighting capabilities do, however, tend to favor attacks by nonstate actors. Like many similar wars before them, the Iraq and Afghan conflicts have shown nonstate actors face fewer problems than hostile states in exploiting asymmetric warfare and U.S. and allied vulnerabilities. Such conflicts, and the outcome of a host of major terrorist incidents, have all shown how difficult it is to deter and defeat true ideologues, those who are willing to be "martyrs," and those who believe their cause is predetermined to win and will survive even if they and their movement are destroyed. They have shown that insurgents and terrorist groups can hide and disperse in ways that national forces cannot and that some are willing to take serious losses to achieve an ideological or political goal.

Moreover, these wars have shown that nonstate actors now operate in informal and loosely affiliated global networks that draw on the Internet, DVDs and videotapes, cell phones, and satellites to carry out their own "revolution in military affairs." They also have shown that extremist and insurgent movements carefully study the history of past terrorist/asymmetric warfare/unconventional warfare attacks and work from a long menu of options. They use both history to try to repeat past successes and modern communications to avoid repeating tactics after they fail.

Several key nonstate actors have shown they can do a better job than states at fighting at the political and ideological levels. Movements like Al Qa'ida have shown that even the most successful U.S. tactical victories can sometimes be turned into reasons for calling the United States an enemy of Islam, getting media coverage hostile to the United States, and recruiting new cadres. At the risk of using a terrible pun, post–Cold War conflicts and terrorism have shown that the United States is culturally vulnerable to eschatological warfare and has serious trouble in countering the extremist ability to climb the "eschatological ladder."

The United States again has recognized these shifts as a key aspect of its most recent Quadrennial Defense Review:[4]

> "globalization" enables many positive developments such as the free movement of capital, goods and services, information, people and technology, but it is also accelerating the transmission of disease, the transfer of advanced weapons, the spread of extremist ideologies, the movement of terrorists and the vulnerability of major economic segments. The U.S. populace, territory and infrastructure, as well as its assets in space, may be increasingly vulnerable to these and a variety of other threats, including weapons of mass destruction, missile and other air threats, and electronic or cyber-attacks.
>
> "globalization" also empowers small groups and individuals. Nation-states no longer have a monopoly over the catastrophic use of violence. Today, small teams or even single individuals can weaponize chemical, biological and even crude radiological or nuclear devices and use them to murder hundreds of thousands of people. Loosely organized and with few assets of their own to protect, non-state enemies are considerably more difficult than nation-states to deter through traditional military means. Non-state enemies could attempt to attack a wide range of targets including government facilities; commercial and financial systems; cultural and historical landmarks; food, water, and power supplies; and information, transport, and energy networks. They will employ unconventional means to penetrate homeland defenses and exploit the very nature of western societies—their openness—to attack their citizens, economic institutions, physical infrastructure and social fabric.

The threat to the U.S. homeland, however, is broader than that posed by terrorists. Hostile states could also attack the United States using WMD delivered by missiles or by less familiar means such as commercial shipping or general aviation. They could attack surreptitiously through surrogates. Some hostile states are pursuing advanced weapons of mass destruction, including genetically engineered biological warfare agents that can overcome today's defenses. There is also a danger that the WMD capabilities of some states could fall into the hands of, or be given to, terrorists who could use them to attack the United States.

The Threat of Ideology and Alliance

Afghanistan and Iraq have shown just how well enemies can successfully challenge the United States on political, ideological, and cultural terms. The world perceives the United States as a largely Christian nation, allied to a Jewish state, fighting Islamist extremist enemies that consist of loose and ever-changing "networks" of affiliated groups and cells. So far, the United States has not been able to demonstrate that it can convince the world, particularly the Islamic world, that its commitment to democracy, "globalism," and secular culture is the path that other states and cultures should follow.

The United States faces an ideological challenge from a range of Islamist extremist movements that have developed methods of complex insurgency that allow them to attack the United States both below and above its threshold of conventional operations. At the tactical level, the United States faces a mix of informal networks of extremist and terrorist groups that have a host of low-cost ways of challenging or attacking the United States and its allies. At the grand strategic level, the United States faces an ideological struggle that is religious and focused on Islam, not Western political values or economic systems.

This struggle has several new elements to which the United States must now respond:

- *The ideological threat is not driven by Western values or the norms of Western culture:* The United States and its allies know how to carry out ideological struggles based on secular political and economic values. Islamic extremism, however, is based on a rejection of such values. It is not concerned with democracy, communism, or fascism; it is concerned with religion and specifically with Islamic norms and values. Issues like human rights and the rule of law are seen from the perspective of a different culture and often the perspective and priority of religious law. The United States is not seen in terms of its own self-image, but as an alien "crusader," "imperialist," and "occupier" that rejects Islam and does not respect Muslims or Arabs. Moreover, Islamic extremism rejects most Middle Eastern regimes, and local reformers, for many of the same reasons. Its goal is religious Puritanism and a unified Islam defined by its own rules and terms.

  For those who support such movements, this struggle is one about religious ideology and ideas, not about who wins battles or Western concepts of democracy. It also is a belief structure that lends itself to wars of attrition and which does not see victory or defeat in national terms. They are well aware that the United States was pushed out of

Lebanon and Somalia and that it won every important battle in Vietnam and still lost the war at the political, psychological, and ideological levels. For many Islamist extremists, defeat at the tactical or even organizational level is far less important than winning what they perceive as political, psychological, and symbolic victories. This not only helps explain their actions in Afghanistan and Iraq, but throughout the Islamic world and in the West.

- *It is a transnational struggle fought by many different movements with no clear hierarchy and relying on informal and constantly changing networks and patterns of affiliation:* The United States, most Arab and Islamic states, and many other nations are now fighting various forms of asymmetric struggle against Islamist extremists. The Afghan and Iraq conflicts are just one set of lessons in such warfare.

  It is far from clear that the United States yet knows how to win this broader war on terrorism. While Al Qa'ida's initial leadership cadre has taken serious losses since September 11, 2001, a recent IISS estimate indicates that its strength has probably grown if one counts the full range of affiliates throughout the world. Some estimates indicate that as many as 70,000–100,000 men have been trained in various camps in Afghanistan, the Philippines, and elsewhere in the Muslim world in recent decades, and religious schools throughout the Middle East still train young men in Islamist extremist beliefs. The growing anger over the Israeli-Palestinian conflict and the U.S. and British roles in Iraq have served as another cause of new cadres of terrorists, Islamist extremists, and insurgents.

  The situation in Afghanistan and Iraq is still fluid, whereas Pakistan remains a question mark. Regional governments have done far better and have generally brought Islamic extremists under control or have defeated them, but there still is fighting at some level in Algeria, Egypt, Libya, Morocco, and Saudi Arabia. Moreover, extremist cells or movements still exist—many growing in strength—in virtually every Arab or Islamist country.

- *Many of the underlying forces that cause such threats are coupled to much broader political, social, economic, and ideological struggles within the developing world—and particularly the Arab and Islamic worlds:* Figure 1.3 shows that much of the world is still being driven by a lack of global economic competitiveness, slow rates of growth in per capita income, rapid population growth, and a virtual "youth explosion" in a region where unemployment is already critically high.

  Failed secularism is a problem at the ideological and political levels. Secular regimes are often repressive and ineffective and do not meet social and economic challenges. Traditional political parties and ideologies like Pan-Arabism, Arab socialism, Marxism, and free market capitalism have failed at the popular level and many turn back to Islam and social custom.

  The resulting "clash within a civilization" can lead to either evolution or revolution, and it inevitably interacts with Islamist extremism. These forces create an ongoing and much broader-based political, psychological, and ideological struggle for influence throughout the Middle East.

  So far, the United States has shown limited skill in dealing with this ideological struggle. American public diplomacy is weak, underfunded, and undermanned, and often highly ethnocentric U.S. policy is faltering and there often is far too little useful substance to "sell." U.S. attempts at political, psychological, and information warfare

Figure 1.3   Regional Breakdown of Poverty in Developing Countries (Less Than $2 Daily Income)

	1990	2002	2015
Millions of People Living on Less Than $2/day			
East Asia and Pacific	1116.0	748.0	260.0
China	825.0	533.0	181.0
Rest of East Asia and Pacific	292.0	215.0	78.0
Europe and Central Asia	23.0	76.0	39.0
Latin America and Caribbean	125.0	119.0	106.0
Middle East and North Africa	51.0	61.0	40.0
South Asia	958.0	1091.0	955.0
Sub-Saharan Africa	382.0	516.0	592.0
Total	**2654.0**	**2611.0**	**1993.0**
Percent of Population Living on Less Than $2/day			
East Asia and Pacific	69.9	40.7	12.7
China	72.6	41.6	13.1
Rest of East Asia and Pacific	63.2	38.6	11.9
Europe and Central Asia	4.9	16.1	8.2
Latin America and Caribbean	28.4	22.6	17.2
Middle East and North Africa	21.4	19.8	10.4
South Asia	85.5	77.8	56.7
Sub-Saharan Africa	75.0	74.9	67.1
Total	**60.8**	**49.9**	**32.8**

Source: World Bank, *Global Economic Prospects 2006,* November 16, 2005.

often do far more to build false confidence than defeat Islamist extremists or influence perceptions in the region.

- *The means of attack are escalating to include proliferation by both states and nonstate actors:* Both hostile state and nonstate actors see weapons of mass destruction as a potential a way of compensating for conventional weakness. Nations are still comparatively slow to develop chemical, biological, radiological, and nuclear (CBRN) weapons, but slow does not mean that the threat is not growing. Iraq has failed to retain its weapons of mass destruction, but India and Pakistan have not. Iran and North Korea seem determined to develop nuclear forces. A range of Islamist extremist movements have examined the option of acquiring various CBRN weapons, and Al Qa'ida has made crude attempts to acquire them. Proliferation by nonstate actors is particularly dangerous because extremist movements seek such weapons to magnify the nature of the attack, not to deter or defend.

The United States has recognized these threats in the National Strategy it issued in 2006 and in the Quadrennial Defense Review Report it issued in February 2006. It recognized the need to focus on stability and operations in Department of Defense Directive 3000.05, "Military Support for Stability, Security, Transition, and Reconstruction (SSTR) Operations, which it issued on November 28, 2005[5] They are key centers of attention in the new U.S. Army and U.S. Marine Corps field manuals on counterinsurgency issued in December 2006, and the focus of major new training programs in each military service.[6]

But this does not mean that the United States is ready to meet such threats or has effective plans to do so. The United States has shown that it is still inept in dealing with many aspects of political, psychological, and information warfare, and it can be self-deluding and ethnocentric in dealing with different religions, ideologies, and cultures. It has shown that its advantages in defeating conventional forces do not extend to dispersed asymmetric warfare and that its current forces have been vulnerable to strategic overstretch in trying to carry out counterinsurgency and stability operations in even one major contingency. Unless the United States adapts to fight new kinds of war on a continuing and more realistic basis, it risks winning military engagements and losing the real war.

The United States has also shown that it cannot win such wars unless it learns how to succeed in conflict termination and win the peace. Iraq and Afghanistan have made it clear that unless the United States makes stability and nation building a goal and course of action from the first day of planning, then throughout the course of combat, and from the "stabilization" phase to a true peace, its so-called revolution in military affairs will be a tactical triumph and a grand strategic failure.

Uncertain Coalitions of the Willing

Finally, there has been another important, if less threatening, change in the security environment. The Iraq War has made it clear that the United States no longer benefits from the polarization of the Cold War and its focus on the secular differences between alliances based on democracy and a Soviet empire based on "communism." More than at any time since the beginning of World War II, the United States needs to firmly understand that it cannot lead its allies unless it treats them as partners, listens to their concerns and advice, and defers to them when necessary.

This is even truer in the many parts of the world where the United States does not share a common culture, political system, or set of values. The Iraq and Afghan conflicts are just two of the wars that have shown the United States must now deal with nations and cultures with different religions and values. It also faces a world in which many and where many such states and the people feel that the United States is an outside power that is a crusader and a "neoimperialist."

The idea that the United States can lead and other nations must follow has already been proven decisively wrong, and at a high cost to some key allies like Britain. Elsewhere, U.S. political and military power is also limited by the fact that it is becoming steadily more dependent on local allies and coalitions of the willing. The twenty-first century West is no more united than ancient Greece, and the United States cannot compel loyalty or support from any regional power, no matter how small. Formal alliances do not bind a single ally to follow the U.S. lead or to provide political, military, and economic support. If anything, the Iraq War has been a warning that no power can lead where others do not follow.

A CLIMATE OF ONGOING CHALLENGES

Any discussion of the strains or overstretch in U.S. forces must consider all these realities in the context of both current U.S. military capabilities and what the United States can and should do to improve them. It is always easy to postulate some crisis in U.S. defense, exaggerate trends, and postulate some simple solution. As the following chapters show, however, the United States scarcely has "hollow forces." Iraq, Afghanistan, and the war on terrorism have not strained its forces to the breaking point or even engaged most of its high-technology strike forces. It does not face crippling resource problems, and it continues to innovate. There is no evidence that its current military efforts place a serious strain on its economy or that it cannot sustain a similar level of military effort indefinitely.

Yet, the United States not only needs to adapt to the long war, it needs to broadly reshape many other aspects of its strategy and defense plans, decide what national and federal resources to allocate to defense, deal with the problems in force transformation, and restructure its approach to alliances and coalitions.

Recent conflicts have shown that there are ten major types of challenges that require attention over the next few years or during the coming decade:

- *Challenge One is the extent to which strategic and planning problems in Iraq and in meeting other U.S. strategic commitments have created the present strains on our forces.* It is time to remember that major failures in planning and policy can put serious strains on virtually any force the United States can afford.

- *Challenge Two is determining the level of burden that defense should place on the national economy and federal spending.* The United States must decide on the future priority defense should have in American society and determine what level of national effort is affordable and justified.

- *Challenge Three is meeting the needs of the U.S. active and reserve military.* The United States not only faces serious recruiting and retention problems, it has violated the unwritten "social contract" that has made an all-volunteer military possible.

- *Challenge Four is the challenge of measuring the extent to which the United States has too few forces or the wrong forces.* "More" can be the answer to virtually every problem, but resources are always limited in the real world, and trade-offs and prioritization are necessary.

- *Challenge Five is determining what kind of force transformation is affordable and needed and the extent to which it can or cannot deal with the other aspects of overstretch.* Transformation is far easier to postulate than to execute, and transformational strategy and doctrine are meaningless and wasteful unless they take the form of a successful Future Year Defense Program (FYDP) and National Budget. At the same time, the United States must make the transition from a "legacy force" shaped for conventional warfare to one that can also support counterinsurgency, counterterrorism, stability and peacemaking operations, and homeland defense.

- *Challenge Six is dealing with the legacy of Cold War transformation programs and past efforts at force transformation that are fundamentally unaffordable.* It is dealing with the reality that "cost containment" is now a leading priority for virtually every aspect of procurement and dealing with technology in force transformation. Yet, it is equally important to find the right balance among modernization, continued technological change, and tactical and strategic innovation.

- *Challenge Seven is the challenge of creating an effective interagency capability to perform national security missions.* The current U.S. approach is to layer committee on committee and leave "jointness" largely to the military. New intelligence structures have been created that partly act in parallel with the interagency bodies operating under the nominal direction of the National Security Council. The Office of the Vice President has become another parallel policy structure, as have some functions of the Office of Homeland Defense. The United States needs both a new form of civil-military partnership and a new interagency process capable of planning and managing military, stability, and peacemaking operations on an integrated basis. This process must also (1) tie the use of military force to strategic and grand strategic assessment of risk; (2) integrate the military with political, diplomatic, and economic operations; and (3) emphasize successful conflict termination, stability operations, and nation building.

- *Challenge Eight is creating effective local forces and capabilities for government.* This means creating new approaches to interoperability and alliances on the national level, such as creating effective Iraqi forces and effective Iraqi capabilities for governance that are necessary to allow the United States to reduce its presence and expenditures in Iraq. It is also the broader need to determine the extent to which we can and cannot create effective allied capabilities for asymmetric warfare, counterinsurgency, and counterterrorism.

- *Challenge Nine is the challenge of dealing with the problem of alliances, international cooperation, and interoperability at the regional and global levels.* The United States cannot create an effective force structure on its own. It can solve the problem of overstretch only by creating a more effective structure of regional security partnerships and alliances.

- *Challenge Ten is the challenge of responsibility.* It is one of finding ways that actually hold senior civilian and military policy makers responsible for achieving success, for realism and transparency in their actions, and for solving key long-standing problems in areas like procurement and cost containment.

No single analysis can fully cover every aspect of these challenges. There are too many uncertainties involved and too many complex variables. At the same time, there is a serious danger in not providing an overview of how each challenge affects U.S. security and attempting some integrated approach to suggesting solutions. Whatever the United States does, it must make hard trade-offs throughout its entire national security community. To do so with success, it must find some integrative course of action that ties together the efforts of the U.S. government into a far more effective interagency process and links U.S. efforts to those of its friends and allies.

This analysis attempts this task in ways that focus on options for improving the existing structure of the U.S national security apparatus and particularly on the efforts of the Department of Defense. It does not attempt to examine the full range of options for radical defense reform, nor does it attempt to deal with broader grand strategic issues like globalism, whether the United States is becoming an imperial power, the role of soft power and civil society, the future of arms control, or ways to make the "international community" more effective.

These are all important issues, and the United States will have to deal with them on an ongoing basis. There is a limit, however, to what any given analysis can cover, and this study focuses on the challenges the United States must deal with over the next few years, and certainly no later than the early years of the next Administration. The most pressing task, however, is to adapt to the immediate challenges Iraq, Afghanistan, and the long war pose to transforming both U.S. strategy and the U.S. force posture and to do so in ways the United States can actually implement and afford.

2

Challenge One: The Extent to Which Strategic and Planning Problems in Iraq and in Meeting Other U.S. Strategic Commitments Have Created the Present Strains on Our Forces

Ideology and the arrogance of power are no substitute for reality and a strategy based upon it. Even the best strategy cannot be imposed on a constantly changing reality, and nothing about the U.S. strategy in the Iraq War indicates the United States has pursued the best available options. If anything, Iraq is a grim warning for the United States. For all of America's strengths, the claim that the United States is the "world's only superpower" ignores the fact that it has many critical limitations. The United States may have immense power and influence, but it cannot shape the world. In fact, there are many areas in the world where the best U.S. strategy is to avoid or minimize involvement, and especially to avoid the use of force.

Whatever else the Iraq War may reveal about the nature and adequacy of U.S. strategy and forces, it has been a practical demonstration of the limitations to U.S. power. It has shown that the United States must find the best match it can among strategy, force plans, programs, and actual resources. It has also shown that rethinking U.S. strategy, force plans, and defense expenditures is a constant necessity. Military history provides a long series of warnings that planning for the last war can be a recipe for losing the next and that a contingency plan rarely predicts the forces needed for the future; Iraq is yet another example.

"OVERSTRETCH" IN IRAQ AS A PRODUCT OF STRATEGIC MISTAKES

Many of the following chapters focus on problems in resources, manpower, force plans, procurement and technology, and other more tangible forms of defense challenge. Yet, strategy consistently emerges as being as equally important, if not more so. The strategic choices a nation makes before, during, and after a conflict often do far more to determine its success than the quality and strength of its military forces, and the current debate over how the United States should approach the Iraq War is a case in point. There is less and less debate over the facts that the United States went to war with a series of deeply mistaken assumptions, was not ready to bring stability to Iraq after the fall of Saddam Hussein, and was not ready to deal with the insurgency that developed as a result.

It is one of the ironies of the Quadrennial Defense Review (QDR) the Bush Administration issued in February 2006 that many of its recommendations mark a *de facto* rejection of many of the major strategic assumptions the Administration made in coming to power and in shaping the invasion of Iraq. The Administration came to office focused on strengthening U.S. conventional warfighting capability and on the emergence of China as a potential future rival in terms of its conventional and nuclear forces. Its concept of force transformation was based largely on a high-technology revolution in military affairs that emphasized net-centric warfare; advanced intelligence, surveillance, and reconnaissance (IS&R) systems; precision-strike, long-range attack; and stealth. It believed that technology could produce not only decisive advantages in warfighting, but major savings in military manpower and the cost of U.S. forces.

The attack on the World Trade Center and the Pentagon on September 11, 2001, showed the Administration and the world that the United States faced very different kinds of war in which ideology, asymmetric methods of fighting, and wars of attrition were dominant factors. What appeared to be a quick victory in Afghanistan became a lasting conflict, as did a similar apparent victory in driving Saddam Hussein from power. The United States found itself locked in counterinsurgency campaigns, not conventional wars, and what it came to call a "long war with Islamist extremists and nonstate actors."

As a result, the 2006 QDR and the other transformations the United States has had to make in its strategy, tactics, and military forces have become a transformation of the transformation the Administration originally intended. Military technology has continued to advance, but the United States has had to recognize that no war is meaningful if it simply defeats the enemy. It is the quality of conflict termination and the lasting grand strategic impact of the war that matters. Stability operations and nation building are now accepted as critical tools and priorities for both the military and joint civil and military action. A naive unilateralism, and the idea the world would inevitably follow a "just" United States, has been replaced with a new emphasis on allies and international cooperation. American performance in public diplomacy may still be grossly inept, but its importance has been recognized.

Where the changes in U.S. strategy have been less frank is in admitting the cost of stability operations, how long they can take, just how difficult they can be, and the fact that the quantity and quality of military personnel are often far more critical than advanced military technology. In the case of both Afghanistan and Iraq, the United States has already been involved in wars and operations far longer than it originally planned. In the case of Iraq, it is claiming a degree of success it has not really achieved, understating the time required to bring lasting stability, and understating the cost, risk, and sacrifice involved. The fact the United States can win virtually any conventional war does not mean it can win every peace.

There is an understanding that the United States needs major reforms and improvements in the quality of its intelligence and in the way that the policy community uses intelligence, although the Administration and the Congress have done far more to blame the Intelligence Community for its failures than admit their own gross failures at the policy level. There is an explicit understanding in the Quadrennial Defense Review that war is not simply the task of the Department of Defense (DoD) and that "jointness" goes far beyond the U.S. military.

It is still unclear whether this understanding will lead to an effective new interagency structure to plan, fight, and terminate conflicts or carry out crisis, peacekeeping, and homeland defense activities. In August 2004, the Department of State created a new Office of the Coordinator for Reconstruction and Stabilization, designed to coordinate an interagency approach to the same issue. In November 2005, the Department of Defense issued DoD Directive 3000.05, titled "Military Support for Stability, Security, Transition, and Reconstruction (SSTR) Operations," which calls for the U.S. military to fully accept the need for stability operations, nation building, and the politico-military nature. In December 2006, it issued a new field manual on counterinsurgency that stressed the need to combine military, political, and economic action, the role of civilians in warfighting, and the need to develop effective in-country allied forces. So far, however, these advances in strategy have outstripped the U.S. ability to put them into practice.

There are other problems that extend from the Department of Defense to the interagency community. The ultimate result of the new intelligence organization the United States has progressively adopted since September 11, 2001, is less clear, but it has certainly called for greater capabilities for counterterrorism, counterinsurgency, and the political and the economic analysis of stability and nation-building efforts in cases like Iraq and Afghanistan. What is less clear is whether the United States can match the technical advances it is making in intelligence, surveillance, and reconnaissance with similar advances in human intelligence collection (HUMINT) and in analyzing a fusion of open source material, HUMINT, and technical intelligence. So far, there often has been more turmoil within the intelligence community than change, and the necessary area skills, experience in dealing with counterinsurgency and asymmetric warfare, and basic skills like translation capability are all a work in progress.

The level of change required in all of these areas is probably too great for the United States to deal with effectively in the near term. The United States will certainly make progress, but make it slowly and in ways that leave many gaps. It is likely that full success in creating effective new institutions will take another catalytic war or major national security failure and lie at least a decade in the future. There has, however, at least been the recognition of the need to bring together every major element of the Executive Branch and the Intelligence Community, provide clear and effective central direction, and deploy the proper mix of civil-military capabilities in the field.

More generally, the Afghan conflict and the Iraq War have shown that the U.S. military must vastly broaden its strategic focus. It still needs to be able to fight decisive conventional wars and nuclear conflicts. However, it must be shaped to fight terrorist and extremist movements, deal with complex insurgencies, and fight ideological battles with both state and nonstate actors. It needs the force posture, deployability, and special skills for long, low-level wars in areas where the ability to understand different beliefs, social customs, and languages is as critical as military technology. It needs all the essential military tools for stability operations, nation building, peacemaking, and crisis operations.

The United States also needs to learn how to fight at the grand strategic and political levels, not simply at the strategic and military ones. The United States has been too wrapped up in a narrow focus on winning the long war through the moral and political superiority of democracy and Western values, rather than accepting the understanding that other nations and other cultures will evolve at their own pace and in their own ways. The United States operates in a world with many failed and dangerous regimes, but in many cases it must deal with the immediate threat of terrorism before it can hope for political reform. Its primary ideological challenge is religious in nations where religion is more important than politics and which, at best, see the United States as an outsider, and sometimes as a "crusader," invader, or imperial power. Only Islam, and regional governments and clergy, can defeat Islamic extremism in many such cases.

Democracy is a political system, not an end goal. Many societies have a higher priority for economic reform, dealing with demographic issues, and providing basic security for their ordinary citizens. More representative governments are needed, but productive democratic change requires social and economic stability, effective political parties, human rights, and the rule of law. The United States should have learned more from its experience in Iraq. The idea that a deeply divided and political primitive Iraq would become an instant shining example that transformed the Middle East always bordered on the theater of the absurd. The United States still, however, tends to act as if elections alone could resolve hard-fought political battles over national building, trigger economic reform, and bring a modern social order. This simply cannot happen. At best, Iraq will transform slowly and uncertainly over time.

OVERSTRETCH AS A PRODUCT OF FAILURES IN PLANNING, PROGRAMMING, AND BUDGETING

The U.S. national security community will also have to learn how to properly transform strategy into actual military capabilities. The strains imposed by the Iraq War—as well as by the Afghan conflict and the broader war on terrorism—have shown that the United States had never adapted its forces to the kind of strategic concepts necessary for modern counterterrorism, counterinsurgency, stability operations, and nation building. As a result, the United States found it difficult to use the force posture it had in 2003 to provide the forces needed for even one major regional contingency in Iraq plus a minor contingency in Afghanistan.

These strains should not have come as a surprise. The United States has had a serious mismatch between its strategy, its force plans, what it actually needs, and what it can afford. The current mix of such mismatches is the product of decisions that date back to the Cold War and planning, programming, and budgeting systems developed in the late 1950s and the early 1960s. Long before the Bush Administration came to office, and "9/11" and the Iraq War, the United States committed itself to a series of major procurement programs designed to "transform" its forces and support a "revolution in military affairs."

Some of these programs had their genesis at the time of the Cold War; others grew out of the perceived lessons of the Gulf War and more recent conflicts. What all virtually had in common was a massive failure to predict their real-world cost, the time they could be available, and their actual effectiveness. The United States committed itself to a fundamentally unaffordable mix of research, development, and procurement programs that date back at least 15 years.

At the same time, the United States developed force plans and manpower plans that were just as unrealistic. While many U.S. force and manpower plans may have set desirable goals, they were never properly costed or were affordable, and this meant they could not be shaped into realistic program budgets and annual defense budgets. U.S. planners also often failed to try. Rather than honestly address the trade-offs among increases in total U.S. defense budgets, manpower, and forces, assumptions were made that gave plans the appearance of affordability, and "force transformation" became a *deus ex machina* that claimed the United States could do more and more with less and less. The result was an overarching failure to contain costs, and to create truly unaffordable defense plans that began in the 1980s, and has since done much to create unrealistic force plans and projections of future U.S. warfighting capabilities.

This ongoing series of failures was the product of failures of the "system" and not of any given Administration. They were driven by a long series of Secretaries of Defense, the Joint Staff, and each of the four military services. They occurred under both Democratic and Republican presidents and were tolerated and often encouraged by both houses of Congress. In many cases, outside defense analysts and reformers played a major role and did far more harm than good.

This is not to say that the United States did not have many successes, and ones that produced many of the advances in conventional warfighting capability discussed earlier. These successes included creating an efficient all-professional force, major improvements in jointness and the realism of training, and new standards of readiness and sustainability. They included major advances in precision warfare, IS&R, near real-time integration of information and "net-centric" warfare, battle management, power projection, and many other capabilities. They enabled the United States to achieve a dominant edge in conventional warfighting capability—at least in limited to medium-sized conflicts.

Nevertheless, the cumulative fiscal impact of the failure to effectively integrate strategy, force plans, and defense budgets forced each service to progressively downsize its active forces, or the amount of major combat equipment in each service, to levels far lower than the service originally planned. This was not as apparent from the gross number of major combat units as in the number of active personnel and major weapons, but the reductions in planned force strength were all too real. Almost regardless of U.S. strategy and force plans, the reality often became what the United States could afford to maintain.

The rising cost and size of military and civilian manpower was another factor that contributed to these pressures. The United States was forced to compromise and downsize its plans in many areas other than procurement: operations, maintenance, and construction to name a few. Almost inevitably, however, it steadily reduced military personnel just as it reduced its forces and the amount of combat equipment they deployed.

These manpower problems were compounded by the need to fund an all-volunteer force structure with higher and higher skill levels and experience. The cost of "quality" rose steadily, often faster than the United States could make feasible cuts in "quantity." Maintaining a suitable flow of recruits and retaining experienced personnel became more demanding, while cost pushed numbers down toward a critical minimum.

There were cases where improvements in tactics, technology, and training did allow significant reductions in the numbers of personnel and weapons required. In most cases, however, the benefits of such reductions had been included in U.S. force plans and procurement plans from the start. In other cases, the steady growth of technological sophistication raised other aspects of force costs or required more skills and experience and put new stresses on the manpower that remained.

The long series of ongoing cuts in personnel that were driven by cost escalation also were almost never made on the basis of finding the most desirable trade-offs for force effectiveness. They were made under pressure because of immediate fiscal necessity, in spite of the original strategy and plan. Necessity can always be explained as a virtue after the fact, but the reality was forced and unplanned reductions in capability.

THE IMPACT OF THE IRAQ WAR

The seriousness of these problems was not apparent as long as the United States could fight short, selected, conventional wars on its own terms like the Gulf War. It could back away from asymmetric conflicts in areas with little strategic value like Lebanon, Somalia, and Haiti. It also could limit the level of its stability, peacemaking, and nation building in crises like the Balkan and humanitarian interventions and rely on other powers in cases like Cambodia and East Timor. The mismatch between its strategy and its forces also was not apparent during the initial conventional phases of the Afghan and Iraq wars. The problems became far more serious, however, the moment the United States needed to fight a long, sustained, manpower-intensive conflict where it could not exploit its technological advantages in conventional warfare.

The Iraq and Afghan wars may have been optional at the start, but once the United States became deeply involved (it became involved in wars that it *had* to fight versus wars that it wanted or had planned to fight) the limits to U.S. strategy and force planning became all too clear. It also quickly became clear that the United States lacked the suitable ability to fight counterinsurgency warfare, had a force posture that lacked sufficient capability to sustain long deployments, and had put too much emphasis on technology over personnel and sustainability.

Failures Before and During the War

The situation was made worse by the fact that the United States made major mistakes in planning the Iraq War and in failing to plan for stability operations, conflict termination, and nation building. America chose a strategy whose goals were unrealistic and impossible to achieve and planned only for the war it wanted to fight and not for uncertainty and the problems in stability operations and nation building that were almost certain to follow.

The full chronology of what happened in U.S. planning and operations before, during, and after the fight to drive Saddam Hussein from power is still far from clear. It is now much easier to make accusations than it is to understand what really happened or assign responsibility with credibility. It is clear, however, that many of the key decisions involved were made in ways that bypassed the interagency process within the U.S. government, ignored the warnings of U.S. area and intelligence experts, ignored prior military war and stability planning by the U.S. Central Command, and ignored the warnings of policy makers and experts in other key coalition states like the United Kingdom.

During the invasion and the battles that drove Saddam Hussein from power, the United States demonstrated that it could fight the war it planned to fight—a conventional regional war—with remarkable efficiency, at low cost, and very quickly. At the same time, too much credence was given to ideologues and true believers, and little attention was paid to the problems that would arise once Saddam fell from power.

Leading neoconservatives in the Office of the Secretary of Defense, the Office of the Vice President, and some officials in the National Security Council, as well as in several highly politicized "think tanks," assumed that Iraq would preserve virtually all of its existing government, require little more than the toppling of a dictator, be wealthy enough to carry out its own development, and would not present major internal security problems like ethnic and sectarian conflicts. This lack of realism was compounded by various Iraqi exile groups that grossly exaggerated the level of Iraqi popular support for a "liberating" invasion and the ease with which Saddam Hussein's regime could be replaced and underestimated both the scale of Iraq's ethnic and sectarian divisions and economic problems.

The Office of the Secretary of Defense put intense pressure on the U.S. military to plan for the lowest possible level of U.S. military deployment. It assumed it would get access to Turkey for an American invasion from the north, which Turkey did not approve, and delayed some deployments because of the political need to avoid appearing precipitous to the UN. At the same time, the leadership of the U.S. military actively resisted planning for, and involvement in, large-scale and enduring stability and nation-building activity and failed to plan and deploy for the risk of a significant insurgency. Factors that contributed to U.S. planning failures follow:

- *Inaccurate threat estimates that created a false rationale for the war:* U.S. and British intelligence made major errors in estimating the level of Iraq's programs to develop weapons of mass destruction and delivery systems. Such errors were in many ways the outgrowth of Iraq's history of lies and concealment efforts, but still produced estimates far less accurate than those of UN inspection teams. These errors were compounded by efforts to spin intelligence indicators and analyses to support the private and the public case for war. Lesser errors were made in exaggerating the importance of peripheral Iraqi intelligence contacts with terrorist groups, and the role of Ansar al-Islam. The resulting focus on weapons of mass destruction and terrorism seems to have helped lead the United States to underestimate the importance of Phase IV or stability operations.

- *Diplomatic estimates that exaggerated probable international support and the ability to win an allied and UN consensus:* The United States and Britain initially planned for far more support from their allies and the UN than they received. It was assumed that allies like France and Germany could be persuaded to go along with the U.S. and British position, that UN inspectors would validate U.S. and British concerns regarding Iraqi concealment of weapons of mass destruction, and that they could win the support of the Security Council. In practice, none of these estimates proved to be correct, and the United States and Britain found themselves moving toward war in an unexpectedly adversarial diplomatic position.

- *Overreliance on exile groups with limited credibility and influence in Iraq:* U.S. and British plans to preserve cadres of friendly Ba'ath officials and Iraqi forces proved to be illusory. The exile groups the United States dealt with grossly exaggerated their influence and understanding of Iraq, while the exile groups that did have significant influence were largely Shi'ite religious groups with ties to Iran and independent militias. This resulted in strong pressure to push secular officials and the military out of the political system even if they had no serious ties to Saddam Hussein and helped to polarize Iraq's sectarian and ethnic divisions.

- *Broader failures in intelligence and analysis of the internal political and economic structures of Iraq:* There were failures that a leading intelligence expert involved in planning the operations in Iraq said were the result of "quiescent US military and Intelligence community leaders who observed the distortion/cherry picking of data that led to erroneous conclusions and poor planning," but failed to press their case or force the issue.

- *Inability to accurately assess the nature of Iraqi nationalism, the true level of culture differences, and the scale of Iraq's problems:* This failure in strategic assessment included the failure to see the scale of Iraq's ethnic and sectarian differences, its economic weaknesses and problems, the difficulty of modernizing an infrastructure sized more to 16–17 million people rather than the current population of 27–28 million, unrealistic estimates of "oil wealth," the probable hard-core support for the former regime in Sunni areas, secular versus theocratic tensions, the impact of tribalism, the impact of demographics in a society so young and with so many employment problems, and a host of other real-world problems that became U.S. and Coalition problems the moment Coalition forces crossed the border.

- *Overoptimistic plans for internal Iraqi political and military support:* The full details are not yet public, but the United States expected more Iraqi military units to be passive or even welcome the Coalition and at least one leading Iraqi official to openly turn against Saddam Hussein.

- *Failure to foresee sectarian and ethnic conflict:* Somewhat amazingly—given its problems in Lebanon, Somalia, and the Balkans—the United States did not plan for major tensions and divisions among Arabs, Kurds, and other minorities. It did not plan for the contingency of tension and fighting among religious Sunnis, religious Shi'ites, and more secular Iraqis. For all of its talk about Saddam's links to terrorism, it did not plan for attacks and infiltration by Islamist extremists into a post-Saddam Iraq.

- *Failure to anticipate the threat of insurgency and outside extremist infiltration, in spite of significant intelligence warning, and to deploy elements of U.S. forces capable of dealing with counterinsurgency, civil-military operations, and nation building as U.S. forces advanced and in the immediate aftermath of the collapse of the regime:* Regional commands were created based on administrative convenience, rather than need, and most of the initial tasks of stability operations and nation building were left up to improvisation by individual local commanders who had minimal or no expert civilian support. This compounded the broader problem that the U.S. military was not organized, trained, or equipped for counterterrorism and counterinsurgency missions at the start of the war, and it had only a minimal number of experienced fighters to draw upon. Force transformation and the revolution in military affairs had greatly weakened U.S. core competence in the area it needed most.

- *Failure to anticipate asymmetric threats in rear areas and occupied territory:* U.S. forces assumed that the defeat of conventional enemy forces would leave rear areas and occupied territory largely secure. They did not anticipate threats to convoys, towns, and rear areas like Saddam's Fedayeen during the fight to drive Saddam from power, or the much larger threat that would develop to U.S. lines of communication and forward deployed forces over time.

- *Rejection of the importance of stability operations and nation building before, during, and immediately after the war:* Policy makers and many military commanders sought a quick war without the complications and problems of a prolonged stability or Phase IV effort and without the commitment and expense of nation building. Many policy makers saw such efforts as both undesirable and unnecessary. U.S. commanders saw them as a "trap" forcing the long-term commitment of U.S. troops that should be avoided if possible.

- *Shortfalls in U.S. military strength and capability to provide the personnel and skills necessary to secure Iraqi rear areas and urban areas as the Coalition advanced and to prevent the massive looting of government offices and facilities, military bases, and arms depots during and after the fighting:* The inability to secure key centers of gravity and rear areas helped create a process of looting that effectively destroyed the existing structure of governance and security.

- *Planning for premature U.S. military withdrawals from Iraq before the situation was clear or secure:* Major reductions were initially planned to begin some three months after the fall of Saddam's regime, rather than planning, training, and equipping for a sustained period of stability operations.

- *Inability to execute a key feature of the war plan by miscalculating Turkey's willingness to allow the deployment and transit of U.S. forces through Turkey:* A lean U.S. troop deployment in the original war plan could not be executed because Turkey did not allow the basing and transit of either U.S. ground troops or aircraft. A reinforced division had to be omitted from the war plan, and the United States lacked the kind of presence that might have occupied and stabilized northern Iraq and the Sunni triangle.

- *Failure to anticipate and prepare for Iraqi expectations after the collapse of Saddam's regime:* Indeed, many policy makers failed to realize that many Iraqis would oppose the invasion and see any sustained U.S. and Coalition presence as a hostile occupation.

- *Failure to plan and execute effective and broadly based information operations before, during, and after the invasion to win the "hearts and minds of Iraqis":* The United States did not persuade the Iraqis that the Coalition came as liberators who would leave, rather than as occupiers who would stay and exploit Iraq, and that the Coalition would provide aid and support to a truly independent government and state. A secondary failure was to anticipate and defuse the flood of conspiracy theories certain to follow Coalition military action.

- *Failure to react to the wartime collapse of Iraqi military, security, and police forces and focus immediately on creating effective Iraqi forces:* This placed a major and avoidable burden on U.S. and other Coalition forces and compounded the Iraqi feeling that Iraq had been occupied by hostile forces.

- *Lack of effective planning for economic aid and reconstruction:* While some efforts were made to understand the scale of the economic problems that had developed in Iraq since the early years of the Iran-Iraq War, the United States initially operated on the assumption that Iraq was an oil-rich country that could quickly recover just by a change in leadership. There was little understanding of just how far short every aspect of Iraq's infrastructure fell short of its current needs and of the problems that would arise in trying to construct adequate facilities and services. The problems in Iraq's state industries received only limited attention, particularly the importance of its military industries. Weaknesses in its agricultural sector were also misunderstood. The United States did correctly understand many of the limits in its financial sector, but was unprepared to deal with virtually all of the realities of an economy that had effectively become a "command kleptocracy."

- *Initial lack of a major aid program for stability operations:* Before and during the war, the United States planned for two sets of economic problems, neither of which occurred. One was a major attempt to burn Iraq's oil fields, and the second was the risk of a major collapse in the oil for food program. There was no serious plan to provide Iraq with large-scale economic aid once Saddam Hussein was driven from power. The Coalition Provisional Authority (CPA) was forced to rush a proposal forward calling for more than $18 billion worth of aid, plus Iraqi oil-for-food money and international aid, with no real basis for planning.

- *Lack of giving the Office of Reconstruction and Assistance (ORHA) a meaningful mandate for conflict termination, stability operations, and nation-building efforts:* A small cadre of civilians and military personnel were selected to create ORHA; many of the group were initially recruited for only three-month tours. ORHA planned to operate in an Iraq where all ministries and functions of government remained intact. It was charged with a largely perfunctory nation-building task, given negligible human and financial resources, not allowed a meaningful liaison with regional powers, and not integrated with the military command. Effective civil-military coordination never took place between ORHA and the U.S. command during or after the war, and its mission was given so little initial priority that it did not even come to Baghdad until April 21, 2003—12 days after U.S. forces—on the grounds that it did not have suitable security.

It is a grim lesson of military history that the initial war plan virtually always competes with truth to become the first casualty of any conflict. It is equally true that accurate foresight is difficult where "20-20 hindsight" is easy. Many, if not most, of the factors that led to these failures were, however, brought to the attention of the President, the National Security Council, the Department of State, the Department of Defense, and the Intelligence Community in the summer and fall of 2002. No one accurately prophesied all of the future, but many inside and outside the government warned what it might be.

The key problem was not that the interagency system did not work in providing many key elements of an accurate assessment, serious as this problem sometimes was. The problem was the most senior political and military decision makers ignored what they felt was negative advice. They did so out of a combination of sincere belief, ideological conviction, and political and bureaucratic convenience. However, the cost to the United States, its allies, and Iraq has been unacceptably high. Furthermore, these decision makers laid the groundwork for many of the problems in creating effective Iraqi forces and an inclusive political structure that could unite the country.

The end result was that the United States made major strategic mistakes in planning and executing the first phase of the Iraq War that greatly exacerbated the impact of its previous failures in adopting a workable post–Cold War strategy, focusing on the right capabilities, shaping the right forces, and providing the right resources. It failed both in its overall grand strategy and in the strategy it selected in going to war.

Its first mistake was its basic rationale for going to war: a threat based on intelligence estimates of Iraqi efforts to create weapons of mass destruction that the United States later found out did not exist. It seems doubtful that the Intelligence Community was asked to lie, but it was certainly pressured to provide intelligence to please. The policy community selected the information it wanted to coax and filtered out the information it did not want. The system did not so much consciously lie to the world as unconsciously lie to itself.

At a grand strategic level, the Bush Administration and the senior leadership of the U.S. military made far more serious mistakes. They underestimated the importance of the UN, of winning a broader allied consensus, and of shaping information operations to win the support of the people in the region. They assumed that conflict termination would be easy, wished away virtually all of the real-world problems in stability operations and nation building, and made massive policy and military errors that created much of the climate of insurgency in Iraq. This U.S. failure to plan for meaningful stability operations and nation building was the mistake that ultimately did the most to help lead to the insurgency in Iraq, but it was only one mistake among many. All serve as a warning that no force can ultimately be more effective than the strategy and grand strategy behind it.

Failures After the Fall of Saddam Hussein

The U.S. failures in preparing for and executing the war to drive Saddam Hussein from power almost inevitably laid the groundwork for failure during the year that followed. During April 2003 to June 2004, the United States made many additional errors:

- *Failure to create and provide the same kind and number of civilian elements in the Iraqi government as in the U.S. government necessary for nation building and stability operations:* A lack of core competence in the U.S. government meant the United States did not know how to directly plan and administer the aid once the Administration and Congress approved it and so had to turn to contractors who also had no practical experience working in Iraq or with a command economy. They, in turn, were forced to deal with local contractors, many of whom were corrupt or inept. These problems were particularly serious in USAID, but affected other parts of the State Department and other civilian agencies, and much of the civilian capability the United States did have was not recruited or was not willing to take risks in the field.

- *Lack of understanding of the level of sectarian and ethnic tension and the risk of civil conflict:* Experts disagreed over the level of sectarian and ethnic tension and violence that the fall of Saddam Hussein would unleash, and many Iraqis felt such problems would be minimal. The fact was, however, that the differences between Arab Shi'ites, Arab Sunnis, Kurds, and other Iraqi minorities were severe. The Arab Shi'ites wanted control and revenge. The Arab Sunnis sought to preserve power and feared the dominance of a large Arab Shi'ite faction. The Kurds wanted autonomy or independence, and the smaller minorities wanted security and to survive. The United States did not see the ethnic and sectarian fault lines that could divide the country, that insurgents could exploit them, and that such tactics could lead to civil war.

- *Inability to see that excessive de-Ba'athification could deprive the country of its secular core:* The United States saw Iraqi exiles—many who had strong sectarian and ethnic ties—as the force for change and the Iraqis who stayed in Iraq and supported the Ba'ath to survive as potential threats. The bulk of Iraq's secular leaders and professionals, however, had at least some ties to the Ba'ath and many had senior positions. So many of these Iraqis were disqualified from office, government, and the military that Iraq lost much of its secular leadership core, and many Sunnis were needlessly alienated. At the same time, Shi'ites with strong ties to Iran, who were sectarian and sometimes Islamist, and with links to various militias, were elevated to power.

- *Fundamental misunderstanding of the Islamist extremist threat:* At one level, the United States simply could not understand how deeply religious many Iraqis were and that

Islam was their primary value system, not democracy, human rights, or Western secular values. At a more serious level, the United States was engaging in a war on terrorism without understanding it had opened up a major new window of vulnerability for neo-Salafi Islamist extremists to exploit—they could take control of most of the insurgency by exploiting the isolation of Arab Sunnis and push the country to the edge of civil war by attacking sensitive Shi'ite and Kurdish targets. It focused on the Ba'ath, not the entire mix of threats.

- *Failure to plan and execute efforts to maintain the process of governance at the local, provincial, and central levels; failure to anticipate the risk if the structure of government would collapse and the risk of looting; and failure to create a plan for restructuring the military, police, and security forces:* All such plans needed to be proclaimed and publicized before, during, and immediately after the initial invasion to win the support of Iraqi officials and officers who were not linked to active support of Saddam Hussein and past abuses and to preserve the core of governance that could lead to the rapid creation of both a legitimate government and security.

- *Lack of early reaction to the wartime collapse of Iraqi military, security, and police forces and failure to focus immediately on creating effective Iraqi forces:* This failure placed a major and avoidable burden on U.S. and other Coalition forces and compounded the Iraqi feeling that Iraq was being occupied by hostile forces. This failure was compounded by the failure to see the need to rush a working criminal justice system into place and the failure to ensure that the central government established a presence and services at the local level.

- *Formal dissolution of the Iraqi military without making an adequate effort to replace it:* It was not until May 2003, roughly two months after the fall of Baghdad, that a 4,000-man U.S. military police effort was authorized for deployment to Baghdad, and it then took time to arrive. No serious effort to rebuild Iraqi police forces took place until June 2004, in spite of mass desertions right after the fighting and the turmoil caused by disbanding the Ba'ath Party and military and security forces.[1]

- *Failing to honestly assess the nature and size of the Iraqi insurgency as it grew and became steadily more dangerous:* While the United States, the CPA, and the U.S. command in Iraq did gradually recognize that a military threat was developing, it was initially seen as a small group of Ba'athist former regime loyalists or "bitter enders." It was not until late 2003 that the United States began to realize just how serious the insurgency really was and then react to it. It was not until winter that a major planning effort was made to determine how the United States should seek to rebuild Iraqi military, security, and police forces capable of dealing with the rising threat; it was not until late in 2004 that a critical mass of funds, advisors, equipment, and facilities were really in place.

- *Leaving many elements of the various militias intact, and leaving Iraq an armed society:* The CPA did make plans to disband the militias but never gave the effort serious high-level support, and these plans were largely aborted when the CPA was dissolved in June 2004.

- *Replacing ORHA after the fall of Saddam Hussein with the CPA and suddenly improvising a vast nation-building and stability effort, recruiting and funding such an operation with little time for planning:* Then the United States tried to carry out the resulting mission along heavily ideological lines that attempted to impose American methods and values on Iraqis.

- *Inability to assess and react to the overall scale of Iraq's economic problems:* The United States proved unwilling or unable to see just how serious the impact of the command kleptocracy the Ba'ath had established was, and the impact of war, favoritism, corruption, and sanctions over a 30-year period. It grossly underestimated the level of effort needed to reconstruct and modernize the Iraq economy, the shortcomings and the vulnerability of the oil sector, the problems in infrastructure and services, the problems in a state-dominated industrial sector, and the problems in the agriculture sector. The United States at best saw only the "tip of the iceberg" and was unprepared for the level of economic problems, unemployment, waste, corruption, and overall economic vulnerability that followed.

- *Allowing, if not encouraging, the CPA to adopt a "revolutionary" approach to transform Iraq's economy and society:* It initially planned for a situation where the U.S.–led Coalition could improve its own values and judgments about the Iraqi people, politics, economy, and social structure for a period of some three years—rather than to expedite the transfer of sovereignty back to Iraq as quickly as possible. The record is mixed, but the CPA only seems to have decided to expedite the transfer of sovereignty in October 2003, after the insurgency had already become serious, and its choice of June 2004 for doing so was largely arbitrary.

- *When a decision was taken to create a major aid program, the overall plan for reconstruction and aid was rushed into place and never was validated with proper plans and surveys:* By late 2003, the pressure to find funds for short-term projects designed to bring (or buy) local security had already become acute. Over time, more and more aid money had to be reprogrammed to meet such short-term needs. This often did more to give Iraqis funds and security than the longer-term aid programs, but it further disrupted an already poorly planned and executed formal aid plan.

- *Placing the CPA and U.S. commands in separate areas, creating large, secure zones that isolated the U.S. effort from Iraqis, and carrying out only limited coordination with other Coalition allies:* The United States did not develop a fully coordinated civil-military effort and initially let a system develop with major differences by region and command. This situation was made far worse by forcing most civilians, including State Department personnel, to rely on contract security personnel, and by not creating an integrated system of secure in-theater transportation that allowed State Department and other civilian personnel to move with security throughout the country. The net result was often to virtually imprison civilians in the "Green Zone" and secure U.S. compounds, and make movement for the rest far more difficult. It also created civilian mercenary forces that showed little concern for local political and culture sensitivities and often became serious problems in causing friction with Iraqis and even Americans in other agencies.

- *Inability to deploy the necessary core competence for stability operations and nation building within the U.S. military and government:* This failure was compounded by a lack of language and area skills and training on the part of most U.S. military forces and intelligence capabilities designed to provide the HUMINT, technical collection, analytic capabilities, and "fusion" centers necessary for stability, counterterrorist, and counterinsurgency operations.

- *Staffing the CPA largely with people recruited for short tours, often chosen on the basis of political and ideological vetting rather than on experience and competence:* Civilians were often chosen more on the basis of political vetting than experience and competence. Many were on three- to six-month tours, and permissive rotation policies allowed most who wanted to take an early departure to do so. Most military personnel were deployed on short rotations. There was little effort to establish a stable cadre of experienced personnel who remained in their positions and developed stable relations with the Iraqis.

- *Grossly over-relying on contractors in critical mission areas:* The United States relied on contractors to perform duties for which contractors often had little or no core competence. U.S. prime contractors had little or no practical experience in dealing with command economies, particularly one that was corrupt to the point of being a kleptocracy. They were not able to draw on a pool of experienced and reliable subcontractors and were unprepared to provide their own security. These problems were compounded by the lack of effective Department of Defense and Department of State systems for managing such efforts, auditing them, and monitoring their effectiveness.

Failures from June 2004 to the Present

The United States slowly improved its efforts in Iraq after the transfer of power back from the Coalition to the interim Iraqi government in June 2004. At the same time, it made a series of new and often equally serious mistakes:

- *The Coalition and the CPA had deprived Iraq of much of its secular leadership when it removed most Ba'athist officials from office:* The end result was to restructure the nature of political power in Iraq along secular and ethnic lines—divided between an emerging Shi'ite majority, with strong religious ties and links to Iran, separatist Kurdish elements, and Sunnis who now were being pushed toward taking religious rather than secular nationalist positions. While some "national" political leaders did emerge, the end result was to attempt democracy in a nation with few experienced political leaders, emerging political parties divided largely on sectarian and ethnic lines, and no underpinning experience in enforcing human rights and a rule of law. Elections and formal documents like constitutions were confused with a functioning political base that could make democracy work. One key impact was that such efforts helped push the Iraqis into polarizing and voting on sectarian and ethnic lines. When the first true national election took place on December 15, 2005, Iraqis voted in very large numbers, but they voted to divide and not to unite.

- *The political process the United States imposed was too demanding in terms of time and complexity:* The sudden end to the Coalition in June 2004 left a partial political vacuum. Then, a focus on elections and the constitution created a schedule where Iraqis had to vote for an interim government, then for a constitution, and hold another election for a permanent government in a little over a year during 2005. Iraqis were then left with the need to form a new government, create new methods of governance, resolve over 50 issues in the constitution within a nominal period of four months after a government was in place, campaign for 60 days for a new constitutional referendum, and then implement whatever new political system emerged during the course of 2006. This process inevitably further polarized Iraqi politics along sectarian and ethnic lines.

- *The United States emphasized elections and politics over governance at every level from the national to the local:* It did not provide strong advisory teams for key ministries, including the Ministry of Defense and the Ministry of Interior. It had very small and weakly organized interagency teams at the governorate or provincial level, with tenuous coordination and often with only a token civil presence in the field. It did not organize and man provincial reconstruction teams for Iraq's 18 governorates until 2006, and none were in place as of April 2006—more than three years after the war. Little effort was made to deal with local government, leaving the government of key cities up to the political leadership that could take control and that had the militia or police forces to enforce it. This created major problems in Baghdad and helped allow Shi'ite Islamist extremists to take *de facto* control of Basra.

- *The United States and its allies became involved in serious military operations and urban warfare against Sunni insurgents in western Iraq, but they still continued to underestimate the seriousness of the emerging Sunni insurgency and the extent to which it might push Iraq toward division and civil war:* They continued to treat the insurgents as a relatively small group of activists with a limited base. At the same time, the United States was slow to see how serious the rise of neo-Salafi extremist groups was or that their strategy included a deliberate effort to divide Iraq and provoke a civil war, rather than simply attack Coalition and allied forces. As a result, it underestimated the seriousness of the Shi'ite reaction and the creation of Shi'ite militia forces and covert forces designed to attack Sunni targets.

- *U.S. military operations often occurred at a level that resulted in short-term tactical success —sometimes seriously damaging urban areas in the process—but which did not bring lasting security or stability:* It took considerable time for the United States to understand that either U.S. or Iraqi forces had to occupy the areas where the insurgents were defeated and that providing aid and security after military action was critical. It took equally long to realize that stability operations required immediate and effective aid, police activity, and an Iraqi government presence.

- *By mid-2004, the United States came to recognize that the creation of effective Iraqi forces was critical to creating a secure and stable Iraq, but was slow to staff such an effort, provide the funds required, and see the scale of effort required:* It was not until late 2004 that it provided the resources needed to train the regular military forces, and it was not until 2005 that it recognized that new Iraqi units would need embedded training teams and partner units to become effective. As late as the end of 2005, it still provided only limited equipment to the Iraqi regular forces. It still did not have credible plans for making them fully independent of a need for support from U.S. air, artillery, and armor, and it was slow to see the need to give them independent command, control, communications, computers, and intelligence/battle management (C4I/BM) and IS&R capabilities and a proper mix of sustainment and combat and service support units.

- *The United States was slow to see that the emergence of civil violence, and sectarian and ethnic conflict, was becoming at least as serious a threat as the Sunni insurgency:* Sectarian and ethnic violence had been an issue from the start, but it grew steadily more serious during 2004 as the Sunni insurgents shifted the focus of their attacks from Coalition targets to include Shi'ite, Kurdish, and pro-government Sunnis. This provoked a Shi'ite and Kurdish response in terms of ethnic cleansing, killings and kidnappings, death squads, and other forces of divisive civil violence. Shi'ite militias and local Sunni security forces became a major new source of violence, compounded by escalating violent crime.

- *The United States did not pay proper attention to the emergence of the Ministry of Interior, and some of its key special security units, as Shi'ite, rather than national forces:* The end result was a series of prison abuses, the division of part of Iraq's forces along sectarian lines, and the involvement of at least some Ministry of Interior forces in "death squads" attacking Sunni targets and increasing the risk of civil war. It was not until October 2005 that the United States resolved jurisdictional squabbles between the Department of State and the Department of Defense over who should control the advisory effort for the Ministry of Interior and its forces.

- *These problems were compounded by the relatively low priority that continued to be given to the development of effective police forces, courts, and a government presence tied to the national government:* The police the Coalition trained and equipped were sometimes corrupt and lacking in leadership, and often they were too poorly equipped but yet deployed to operate in areas where insurgents, militias, or hostile political groups were present. A functioning court system was often lacking, and the central government often did little more than make token appearances and give promises it did not keep. While the insurgency was contained to the point where some 85 percent of attacks occurred in only four provinces (albeit with 42 percent of the population), violence was endemic in many other areas. Crime was a major factor, and so was the threat to minorities in areas dominated by a given ethnic group. While insurgent violence was a key factor in Baghdad and Mosul, few areas were really secure, and in many Shi'ite areas ordinary Shi'ites faced pressure or threats from Shi'ite militias or extremists.

- *By the spring of 2003, the tensions between sects and ethnic groups had already begun to produce a process of ethnic separation and ethnic cleansing that became truly serious in 2004 and 2005, to which the United States was slow to respond:* In mixed cities, the separation was often by neighborhood, with minorities being forced to relocate to areas where they were in the majority. In cities like Kirkuk and Basra, the lines were far clearer. In Kirkuk, the Kurds pushed for ethnic separation. In Basra, Shi'ite puritans attempted to push out other sects and Shi'ites who would not practice their beliefs. The United States had no clear policy or instruments for dealing with these problems.

- *The Department of State and other civil branches of the U.S. government (USG) continued to have serious problems in recruiting and retaining suitable personnel:* Many career foreign service officers would not volunteer and inexperienced contract personnel had to be deployed. While some professionals did serve at considerable personal sacrifice, the USG could not find enough qualified civilians willing to go into the field and partner with U.S. military forces. This put additional strains on the U.S. military, which simply did not have the necessary cadres of civil-military experts, military police, area experts and linguists, etc. Moreover, the combination of security and recruiting problems tended to keep personnel in Baghdad's Green Zone around the Embassy, overmanning that area and further undermanning operations in the field.

- *USAID and the contracting officers in the Department of Defense lacked the experience and expertise to plan and manage aid on anything like the scale required:* They also lacked basic competence in managing and planning such an effort. Vast waste and corruption occurred in the aid effort, most of which was spent outside Iraq. Spending was used as a measure of effectiveness, not impact on the Iraqi economy or meeting Iraqi needs. Many long-term projects did not meet a valid requirement or were executed in ways where it was impossible to sustain them and/or provide security. Serious problems occurred because the United States imposed its own methods and standards on an aging, war-worn infrastructure that Iraqis could maintain but not effectively integrate with U.S. equipment and standards.

- *Interagency rivalry and recruiting problems prevented the timely staffing and deployment of provincial reconstruction teams:* The Department of State and the Department of Defense could not agree on some aspects of how to staff and organize its provincial reconstruction teams (PRTs) until April 2006. Major recruiting problems meant that the pool of civilians recruited for the teams often lacked real professional experience, and most teams remained largely unmanned as of the end of March 2006.

- *The Special Inspector General for Iraqi Reconstruction (SIGIR) has found massive accounting abuses and fraud in the most expensive aid effort since the Marshall Plan:* The Congressional Research Service estimates the total cost of U.S. aid allocations (all grant assistance) for Iraq appropriated from 2003 to 2006 totals $28.9 billion. It estimates that $17.6 billion (62 percent) went for economic and political reconstruction assistance, while $10.9 billion (38 percent) was used to aid Iraqi security.[2] The SIGIR includes the Iraqi government funds the United States took control of in 2003 in its audits, which produces a total cost of over $34 billion. It found massive waste and corruption in its audit of various uses of this money, as well as many projects that failed or served little progress. It also found, however, that the United States had never established proper auditing procedures or ways of measuring project completions and effectiveness, which makes accurate estimates impossible.[3]

- *The aid process made some progress, but was seriously crippled by the fact that the U.S. military did not provide security for most projects, and contract security personnel were extremely expensive and often would operate only in limited areas:* Some 25 percent or more of aid spending went to security, and aid projects tended to be concentrated in safe areas. Efforts to push the security problem down onto the contractors compounded the problem.

- *Rather than honestly admit and assess these political, military, economic, and aid problems, the U.S. government tended to systematically exaggerate what were sometimes very real successes, downplay risks and problems, and provide public and media reporting that "spun" the facts to the point where such reporting lost credibility with Iraqis and the U.S. public:* The United States seemed unable to develop an effective approach to public diplomacy in Iraq and the region and slowly lost credibility in the United States and the rest of the world.

- *These problems were compounded by the misuse of public opinion polls to try to find propaganda arguments rather than honestly understand the perceptions and needs of the Iraqi people:* From the summer of 2003 on, polls of Iraqis provided serious warnings about anger against the Coalition and distrust of its motives and actions, willingness to support attacks on Coalition forces, divisions within Iraq, and the perceived failure of U.S. efforts to support reconstruction. U.S. officials largely ignored the negative results and cherry-picked any favorable results for propaganda and political purposes.

It is important to note that by the spring of 2006, the United States finally did have many elements of a potentially successful strategy to win the Iraq War in place. By that time, however, it was questionable whether the United States still had the time, resources, and opportunities to implement its strategy. It faced a very real risk that Iraq would collapse into civil war, and it was now far harder to even help Iraqis create a government, much less make it operate effectively. The bulk of aid funds had been obligated with few lasting real-world achievements. The drift toward a higher level of civil conflict threatened progress in developing the regular military, and progress in reforming the Ministry of Interior, security forces, and the police was delayed by months without an effective government. America had made a long series of strategic, tactical, and operational mistakes from the initial war-planning phase in 2002 through early 2006, and the United States, its allies, and the Iraqis were paying the price.

THE COST IN BLOOD AND DOLLARS OF AMERICA'S STRATEGIC MISTAKES AND "MISMATCH"

The mismatch among America's strategy, force plans, programs, and actual resources during the period from the end of the Cold War to the beginning of the Iraq War and its strategic mistakes in Iraq and Afghanistan have so far had a limited impact in terms of money. The cost has been high in dollar terms, but too small relative to the U.S. national budget to put intense pressure on the U.S. economy or drain the pool of American military capabilities.

Iraq, Afghanistan, and the war on terrorism have, however, gradually pushed the United States to the limit of the ground forces it could easily deploy in such conflicts with its existing force structure. These conflicts showed that the United States had lost most of its counterinsurgency capability and had never funded the mix of area expertise and warfighting capabilities it needed for asymmetric wars. They showed that a serious imbalance existed between its active and reserve forces and how easily a conventional victory could be turned into the risk of an asymmetric defeat. Finally, they showed how costly peacetime failures in matching strategy, planning, and resources could be in more serious conflicts.

The Cost in Blood: American, Allied, Friendly, and Civilian

Whatever the final outcome may be, the cost in blood has already been far more serious than any U.S. planners estimated in going to war, and it has had tragic consequences for the United States, its allies, and the Iraqi people. The casualties during the conventional fighting that defeated Iraq's regular forces and drove Saddam Hussein from power were negligible. Yet, the human cost to Iraq after Saddam was driven from power steadily escalated to very serious proportions—every number in Figure 2.1 represents a human life, and every current casualty is only a symbol of the broader level of suffering caused by war. There also is no way to estimate how high the cost of such a war will be if Iraq drifts into full-scale civil war or sectarian and ethnic "cleansing."

As a comparison of Figures 2.1 and 2.2 shows, the cost in U.S. casualties in Iraq and Afghanistan was limited by the standards of past wars, at least as of November 2006. As shown in Figure 2.1, as of September 1, 2006, the United States had

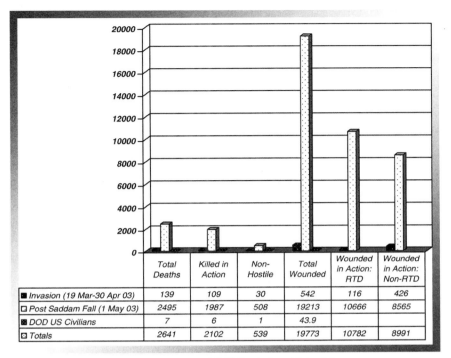

	Total Deaths	Killed in Action	Non-Hostile	Total Wounded	Wounded in Action: RTD	Wounded in Action: Non-RTD
■ Invasion (19 Mar-30 Apr 03)	139	109	30	542	116	426
□ Post Saddam Fall (1 May 03)	2495	1987	508	19213	10666	8565
▨ DOD US Civilians	7	6	1	43.9		
◨ Totals	2641	2102	539	19773	10782	8991

Source: Department of Defense, Operation Iraqi Freedom (OIF) US Casualty Status." Defenselink: http://www.defenselink.mil/news/, September 1, 2006.

Note: Does not include casualties in enforcing no fly zones before March 19, 2003. Wounded-RTD indicates lighter wounded where personnel were returned to duty within 72 hours. Wounded-Non-RTD indicates more serious wounds where personnel could not be returned to duty within 72 hours.

Figure 2.1   U.S. Casualties in the Iraq War: Total Killed versus Wounded, March 2003–September 1, 2006

suffered 2,641 deaths, of which 2,102 were killed in hostile action, and well over 19,000 Americans had been wounded. U.S. losses intensified, however, as the fighting became more serious. As of November 18, 2006, the Department of Defense reported a total of 24,636 U.S. casualties in the fighting in Iraq. These included 2,295 killed in hostile action, 563 other deaths, and 21,778 wounded. There had been a total of 1,399 casualties in Afghanistan. These included 189 killed in hostile action, 156 other deaths, and 1,054 wounded.[4] These figures rose to nearly 3,000 U.S. killed and 22,000 wounded by the end of 2006, plus over 6,000 injured and 18,000 suffering from disease where the case was serious enough to require air transportation. Britain had lost 126 soldiers by the end of 2006, and other Coalition partners had lost 121.[5]

U.S. and Coalition losses, however, have been only part of the story and Iraqi casualties have risen steadily. In September 2005, Coalition forces absorbed 82 percent of all attacks and Iraqis 18 percent. By February 2006, 65 percent were

Figure 2.2 U.S. Casualties in War: A Historical Summary

War	Duration	Number Serving	Total Deaths	Battle Deaths	Other Deaths	Serious Wounds
Revolutionary	1775–1783	184,000–250,000	4,435	4,435	–	6,188
War of 1812	1812–1815	286,730	2,260	2,260	–	4,505
Mexican War	1846–1849	78,718	13,283	1,733	11,550	4,152
Civil War (Union)*	1861–1865	2,213,363	364,511	140,414	224,097	281,811
Spanish-American	1898	306,760	2,446	385	2,061	1,662
World War I	1917–1918	473,499	116,516	53,402	63,114	204,002
World War II	1941–1946	16,112,566	405,399	291,557	113,842	671,846
Korean War	1950–1953	5,720,000	36,574	33,741	2,833	103,284
Vietnam	1964–1973	874,400	58,209	47,424	10,785	153,303
Iranian Hostage	8-25-1989	–	8	–	8	–
Lebanon	1982–1984	–	265	256	9	–
Grenada	1983	–	19	18	1	–
Panama	1989	–	23	23	–	–
Gulf War	1990–1991	2,225,000	382	147	235	467
Somalia	1992–1994	–	43	29	14	–
Haiti	1994–1996	–	4	–	4	–

* Confederate data are uncertain. Some 600,000–1,500,000 served. Reports indicate 133,821 Confederate deaths (74,524 battle and 59,297 other). Some 26,000–31,000 Confederates died in Union prisons.

Source: U.S. Department of Defense.

aimed at the Coalition and 35 percent at Iraqis.[6] Iraqi police, soldiers, and civilians were being killed at about a rate of 75 per day by April 2006.[7] By some estimates, 2,500 to 5,000 Iraqi troops and police had died by July 2006, following Saddam's fall some three years earlier. These figures rose to over 12,000 by the end of 2006.

Iraqi civilian casualties were far more substantial than Coalition casualties. Estimates ranged from 39,702 to 44,191 dead as of August 4, 2006, and rose quickly as both the insurgency and civil violence intensified.[8] In November 2006, the UN reported that "according to information provided by the Ministry of Health, the number of civilians violently killed in the country was 3,345 in September (including 195 women and 54 children) and 3,709 in October (including 156 women and 56 children).[9] The number of wounded reached 3,481 in September (including 251 women and 125 children), and 3,944 in October (including 276 women and 112 children). As a way of comparison, the total figure of civilians killed in Iraq was 3,590 in July and 3,009 in August 2006. In Baghdad the total number of civilians violently killed in September and October was 4,984 (2,262 in September and 2,722 in October).

Iraq Body Count estimated that a total of some 52,000 to 54,5000 Iraqi civilians had died by the end of 2006.[10] Other efforts to calculate total casualties, such as one line published in *The Lancet* magazine, put the total number of Iraqis killed since the invasion in 2003 at slightly over 650,000 (give or take a quarter of a million) deaths. While such high-end estimates were extremely suspect, they achieved considerable credibility and illustrated the dangers of failing to provide detailed and credible figures.[11]

The UN also provided estimates that illustrate the indirect human costs of war:

> The numbers of displaced persons continued to grow steadily, primarily as a result of sectarian and criminal violence. Some 418,392 people have been displaced due to sectarian violence and 15,240 due to military operations since the attack on the Samarra Al Asker Shrine on 22 February 2006. UNHCR [Office of the UN High Commissioner for Refugees] estimates that [an] additional 1.6 million people have left the country since 2003, of whom between 500,000 and 700,000 people are currently in Jordan; approximately 800,000 in Syria, and about 100,000 in Saudi Arabia and Kuwait. A total 436,000 of Iraqis moved to Europe, Americas, Africa and Asia. Of these, UNHCR has characterized 240,300 as migrants, 180,700 as recognized refugees, mainly from before 2003, and 15,000 as asylum-seekers. According to UNHCR officials, nearly 100,000 Iraqis are fleeing each month to Syria and Jordan. UNHCR is in the process of compiling statistics about the recent increase in asylum applications by Iraqis. It appears that there has been:

> - —50% increase in asylum claims by Iraqis in industrialized states over the year from January to June 2006;

> - —a 94% increase in asylum claims by Iraqis in industrialized states in the period from June 2004 to June 2006.

No one can predict what the ultimate human cost of this war will be after the war. Hopefully, Iraq will not become a case study of failures in nation building and stability operations that lead to mass casualties. The fact remains, however, that such failures have already become a serious possibility, and Iraq is only one theater where terrorism and insurgency have created such a risk. Afghanistan also tilted toward rising civil violence in 2006, and there is a wide range of civil wars throughout the world where any new failures in U.S. intervention could escalate into extreme violence.

The wars in Iraq and Afghanistan also illustrate the need to tie U.S. military planning and operations in real time to estimates of civilian casualties and collateral damage. It is one thing to fight existential wars for survival with blunt instruments that cannot avoid large-scale civilian casualties and collateral damage. It is another thing to fight limited wars where modern intelligence, surveillance, and reconnaissance; time sensitive targeting and battle management; and precision weapons allow the United States to minimize both casualties and collateral damage and estimate their cost in near real time if it chooses to do so.

Modern warfare has evolved to the point where the ethical and moral nature of Western values requires a different approach to warfighting. The U.S. military has already recognized this fact in many respects, and the recent employment of precision 250-pound guided weapons in place of the 2,000-pound precision weapons used a decade earlier is only one such example. Where the United States has so far failed to adapt is in failing to provide (1) credible unclassified estimates, (2) transparency in its efforts to count allied, friendly, and civilian casualties, and (3) collateral damage estimates. This is partly a result of the legacy of the political backlash and emphasis on casualties rather than on meaningful tactical success exemplified by the "body counts" of Vietnam. It is partly a tragically misguided effort to deal with the reality that war is steadily more political, and shaped by local and global perceptions, than by trying to avoid reporting on its tragic realities.

The end result, however, is to create a vacuum in which exaggerated and false estimates can be used against the United States, U.S. reporting and denials lose credibility, and there are no coherent campaign plans, set of metrics, and validated rules of engagement for dealing with a critical new element of war. Honesty, transparency, credibility, and political and perceptual victory can be established only by a different approach to public affairs and by an explicit and open effort to communicate what the United States is doing and the level of unavoidable friendly and civilian casualties and collateral damage that actually does occur. Equally important, the United States needs to strengthen the trust of allied forces—both international and local—by reporting on these casualties and showing its deep ongoing concern for friendly dead and wounded.

The costs of terrorism, insurgency, and asymmetric war to the United States also go well beyond direct casualties. Figure 2.1, for example, shows that intense combat produces much sharper swings in the number of U.S. wounded than it does in U.S. killed. As a result, the number of both killed and wounded is both a much better measure of combat activity and of the sacrifice that military forces make in combat. The failure to report on wounded is incompetent analysis and incompetent reporting.

On the one hand, the lower totals of U.S. killed reflect major improvements in military professionalism, military technology, and military medical care. On the other hand, they represent sacrifice on the part of the small portion of Americans who now bear the burden of military service, and many of these casualties could have been avoided had the United States made fewer strategic mistakes.

As Figure 2.3 shows, the human cost to the United States is measured in mental as well as physical terms. The psychological impact of war, and lingering medical effects, has always been a serious problem. Declines in physical casualties do, however, seem to be accompanied by a rise in combat-related stress and psychological effects, a factor no effort to assess the cost of strategic mistakes can afford to ignore.

In December 2006, for example, the Army released its third Mental Health Assessment in Iraq, which showed some disturbing mental health realities associated with redeployments. Repeat deployers reported notably higher acute stress than initial deployers. The 1,500 soldiers surveyed told the mental health experts they were unhappy with the length of tour deployments and said their families were experiencing more stress. Some of the results of the report were as follows:[12]

- Stress levels jumped back to 2003 levels as did the suicide rate for troops in Iraq which doubled and returned to where it was in 2003.

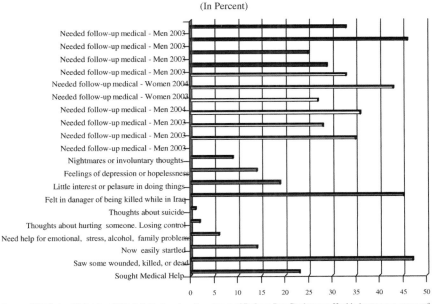

(In Percent)

Source: *USA Today*, 19 October 2005: 1 & 11. Based on Department of Defense Post-Deployment Health Assessment survey of 193,131 personnel.

Note: "Medical" includes both physical and psychological problems.

Figure 2.3   Medical and Psychological Impact on Returning U.S. Forces

- The Iraq suicide rate in 2003 was 18.8 per 100,000, then dropped to 10.5 per 100,000 in 2004. In 2005, the suicide rate for troops deployed to Iraq rose again to 19.9 per 100,000 soldiers, an increase over the previous year and higher than the Army's overall rate of 13.1 per 100,000 that same year.

- Overall in 2005, there were 88 suicides worldwide in the U.S. Army in 2005; 22 soldiers committed suicide in Iraq, 5 of them were soldiers on their second deployment to Iraq.

- There was a significant decline from the soldiers surveyed in 2004 who said their predeployment training for suicide prevention was adequate.

- Fourteen percent of the nearly 1,500 soldiers surveyed said they experienced acute stress and 17 percent said they experienced a combination of depression, anxiety, and acute stress. These numbers were similar to the rates found in 2003 and higher than in 2004.

- The top noncombat stressors were deployment length and family separation.

- Soldiers were more likely than in the previous two studies to report more intense and predictable combat experiences resulting from the use of improvised explosive devices.

- Between 20 and 40 soldiers were taken out of theater per month and sent back to the states for follow-on care. These troops do not return to duty in Iraq. There is no data on how many seek short-term care in Iraq and are returned to duty. This can mean access to a primary physician, a chaplain, or a mental health professional.

- Difficulty in access to care was reduced from 13 percent in 2003 to 5 percent. Figures 2.1 and 2.3 do, however, examine only such costs of war to the United States. Iraq has shown that enemies may concentrate on attacking the local allies of the United States, local civilians in an effort to block nation building and trigger civil war, and nongovernmental organizations (NGOs) and international organizations in efforts to end civil and foreign support for the U.S. effort. Violence can expand to include death squads, massive suicide bombings of civilians, kidnappings, disappearances, forced relocations, attacks on cultural and religious centers, and attacks on every element of civilian life. It is easier and often more effective to attack America's allies, and local peoples, than to attack U.S. forces. American grand strategy, strategy, and tactics must deal with the total human cost of war, not simply the cost to U.S. forces.

The Cost in Dollars

The economic cost of war is less important than the human cost, but scarcely something that U.S. strategy and military planning can ignore. There is no agreement as to how the dollar cost of the Iraq War and other recent U.S. conflicts should be costed, and there is no way to predict their ultimate cost. The same is true of the conflict in Afghanistan and the overall war on terrorism. What is clear is that the cost of the Iraq War in dollars has been much greater than the Bush Administration planned in going to war. Figure 2.4 shows that the United States incurred incremental costs that have gone far beyond the level of the global war on terrorism before the invasion of Iraq and beyond the estimate of a total near $70 billion that U.S. officials used in planning what they initially thought would be a short and decisive war against Saddam Hussein.

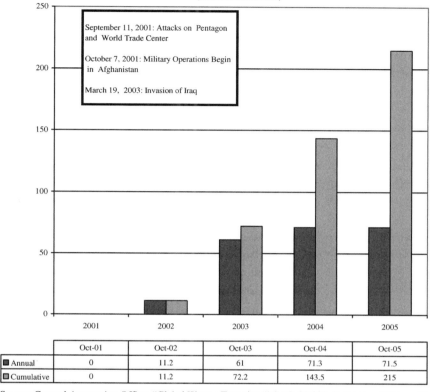

($US Current Billions)

Source: General Accounting Office, "Global War on Terrorism," GAO-05-882, September 2005, p. 34

Figure 2.4   GAO Estimate of Incremental and Unanticipated Spending on Iraq and the Global War on Terrorism: 2001–2005

In fact, the rising costs of the Iraq War provide a grim warning about the inability to anticipate how U.S. forces should be shaped on the basis of even the best strategic thinking and plans. As has been touched upon earlier, the Bush Administration came to office focused on China and Korea. The attacks on the World Trade Center and the Pentagon on September 11, 2001, however, suddenly thrust it into a totally different direction with the war in Afghanistan that began on October 7, 2001.

By the end of fiscal year 2002 (FY2002), this "global war on terrorism" had led to major redeployments of U.S. forces, significant changes in tactics and force employment concepts, and an unforeseen expenditure of $11.6 billion.[13] The decision to invade Iraq on March 19, 2003, then shifted the United States from the Afghan War, focused on precision air strikes and light forces, to a conflict in the Gulf that required a major deployment of heavy land forces, including Marine units that had previously planned for littoral warfare.

Costing the War to Date

There are many different ways to estimate the cumulative cost of the war that followed. According to the Government Accountability Office, the expansion of the war on terrorism to include the Iraq War raised the direct annual cost in *outlays*—approved expenditures only for the current fiscal year—for the global war on terrorism in both Afghanistan and Iraq to $61 billion in FY2003 and led to unplanned expenditures for a counterinsurgency campaign in Iraq that cost $71.3 billion in FY2004 and an estimated $71.5 billion in FY2005. This was a total of $215.1 billion in direct, current spending for the period from FY2002 to FY2005.[14]

Since that time, the monetary cost of the wars in both Iraq and Afghanistan has risen steadily in ways that the United States has not been able to control and predict. A June 2006 report by Amy Belasco of the Congressional Research Service (CRS) found that the overall cost of the wars in Iraq and Afghanistan and other global war on terror operations since September 11, 2001, totaled $437 billion through the fiscal year ending September 30, 2006.

This amount included appropriations for military operations, base security, reconstruction, foreign aid, embassy costs, and veterans' health care for Operation Enduring Freedom (OEF), Operation Noble Eagle (ONE), and Operation Iraqi Freedom (OIF).

The total dollar amount combined the $50 billion for war costs included in the DoD's regular FY2006 appropriations and the $69 billion in the FY2006 Supplemental.[15] If one adds to the $437 billion the roughly $1.5 billion in FY2007 Foreign Operations funds for Iraq and Afghanistan, the $70 billion in Pentagon "bridge funds" for FY2007, plus the undetermined supplemental funds for the remainder of FY2007, the total war-related costs easily exceed $507 billion by the end of FY2007.[16] A CRS update of its study of the cost of the war, issued in September 2006, projected the total cost at $549 billion for both Iraq and Afghanistan through all of FY2007.[17]

There is no end in sight to either the conflict in Iraq or Afghanistan, and there is no way to predict the final cost in either blood or dollars. The United States does, however, now have enough experience to show how difficult it is to control such costs and even calculate them accurately. If one looks at past estimates based on *budget authority*—approved expenditures for the current and future fiscal years—Belasco estimated that of the $437 billion likely to be appropriated for FY2006, Iraq would receive about $319 billion (73 percent), OEF $88 billion (20 percent), and enhanced base security about $26 billion (6 percent), leaving about $4 billion that could not be allocated based on available information.

The CRS report also estimated that budget authority for operations and maintenance (O&M) costs would rise from $42.7 billion in FY2004 to $60.9 billion in FY2006. During the same period, procurement budget authority would grow from $7.2 billion to $22.9 illion. Some of the reasons for these cost increases are known and reflect the purchase of more body armor, the rise in oil prices, required maintenance on worn equipment, and funds to train and equip Afghan and Iraqi forces, previously carried in foreign operations accounts. However, these factors do not adequately explain a 50-percent increase of over $20 billion in operating costs.

The rise in investment costs since FY2004 has also been dramatic with budget authority costs rising from $7.2 billion in FY2003 to $24.4 billion in FY2006. The known reasons for this upsurge in war-related investment reflects the following:[18]

- A push by both DoD and Congress to provide more force protection equipment and increase situational awareness;
- A decision to temporarily fund equipment for new Army and Marine Corps units, known as modularity and restructuring;
- The growing bill to rebuild or replace damaged equipment, a process known as reset; and
- The building of more extensive infrastructure to support troops and equipment in and around Iraq and Afghanistan.

But as with O&M costs, these reasons are insufficient to explain the level of increases or predict whether these procurement levels are temporary or likely to continue to rise.

While the CRS study seems to be the best estimate of the costs of the ongoing U.S. military engagements to date, it clearly states that there are costs it cannot properly estimate and that the DoD declined to provide a detailed breakdown of the costs by war. The big questions for which the CRS lacked accurate data to make precise cost estimates included the following:[19]

- What is the estimated cost to reset—repair and replace—war-worn equipment, and how might that affect the DoD's regular or baseline budget?
- How are some types of war costs affected by policy and contracting decisions, as well as by operational needs and troop levels?
- How have deployed troop levels changed after the 9/11 attacks, and how could Congress get accurate information on past and future troop levels?
- What is the average cost per deployed troop of OIF and OEF, and how might that cost affect future war costs?
- What are estimates of future war costs?
- How might Congress improve reporting of war costs to get accurate and complete information to be used to assess current and future requests?

Answers to all of these questions would help Congress and independent analysts compare war spending to other spending, assess current requests, and project future costs.

Estimates of Monthly Costs

Another way of illustrating both how high the costs of asymmetric war can be and how difficult it is to manage and predict them is to examine costs and burdens in terms of expenditures per month, or what DoD personnel commonly refer to as the "burn rate." This figure covers what might be characterized as the immediate costs of ongoing military operations—i.e., the war-related costs of military personnel and O&M—but it excludes funds for military equipment; research, development, test, and evaluation; and military construction intended to upgrade or replace equipment or facilities deemed necessary to conduct war operations. In FY2006, the immediate operations costs associated with military personnel, O&M, and working capital funds accounted for only about $73.5 billion, or 70 percent of the $105 billion for DoD in FY2005.[20]

According to the CRS, the only figures that show average monthly spending rates are based on obligations, which reflect contracts signed to provide goods or services and pay to military and civilian personnel as reported by the Defense Finance Accounting Service (DFAS). These average monthly obligation costs tend to vary sharply according to the intensity of operations and the size of the contracts signed in a given month. In June 2005, for example, the DoD's obligations costs leapt from $3.0 billion the previous month to $12.8 billion because a large number of high-value contracts were signed in June. For the same reason, the cumulative average monthly obligation costs for FY2005 spiked to $7.1 billion as of June from $6.4 billion as of May simply because a new, war-related supplemental allowed for the signing of so many contracts. This one month peak in expenditures changed the estimated total obligation costs for OEF, ONE, and OIF for all of FY2005 from $76.8 billion to $85.2 billion.[21]

Ongoing expenditures continued to change these estimates. In a later costing of the monthly totals for FY2005, which included funds that the DFAS did not capture, the CRS estimated that the DoD's obligations averaged $6.4 billion per month for Iraq, $1.3 illion for Afghanistan, and $200 million for enhanced security. This totaled $7.9 billion per month. From FY2004, these costs were 28 percent higher for Iraq, 18 percent higher for Afghanistan, and 33 percent lower for base security.[22]

The total CRS estimate of DoD obligations in FY2006 rose to a monthly average of $9.7 billion by June 2006, as the average cost for the DoD's obligations in Iraq alone reached $8.0 billion. These estimates compare with an average of some $5.1 billion per month in FY2006 dollars for the war in Vietnam.[23]

Authority versus Obligations

The CRS breakdown of expenditures is shown in detail in Figures 2.5 through 2.7. It is clear from these totals that if one considers only the cost of the Iraq War, and not the Afghan conflict and other costs for the war on terrorism, the totals are much lower than for the overall cost of the "long war" plus Iraq since 9/11:[24]

- The cumulative estimated costs in *budget authority* for all spending for the Iraq War alone for FY2001–FY2006 were $318.5 billion versus $432.8 billion for Iraq, Afghanistan, and the supplementals for the war on terrorism.

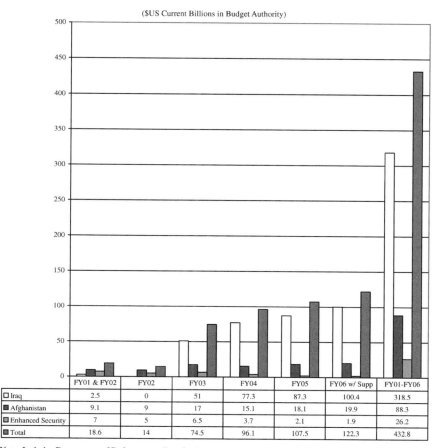

($US Current Billions in Budget Authority)

	FY01 & FY02	FY02	FY03	FY04	FY05	FY06 w/ Supp	FY01-FY06
☐ Iraq	2.5	0	51	77.3	87.3	100.4	318.5
▣ Afghanistan	9.1	9	17	15.1	18.1	19.9	88.3
▣ Enhanced Security	7	5	6.5	3.7	2.1	1.9	26.2
▣ Total	18.6	14	74.5	96.1	107.5	122.3	432.8

Note: Includes Department of Defense spending, foreign aid and diplomatic operations, and foreign operations.

Source: Amy Belasco, "The Cost of Iraq, Afghanistan, and Other Global War on Terror Operations Since 9/11." Congressional Research Service, 14 June 2006: 10.

Figure 2.5 CRS Estimates of Incremental and Unanticipated Spending on Iraq, Afghanistan, and the Global War on Terrorism: FY2001–FY2006 Supplemental Request

- The annual totals in *budget authority* estimated for the Iraq War alone were $51 billion in FY2003, $77.3 billion FY2004, $87.3 billion for FY2005, and $100.4 billion for FY2006. The annual totals in *budget authority* estimated for all the wars were $74.5 billion in FY2003, $96.1 billion FY2004, $107.5 billion for FY2005, and $122.3 billion for FY2006.

- The cumulative reported *obligations* for DoD spending for the Iraq War alone from the start through March 2006 were lower still: $219.4 billion, including both operations and investment costs. This compared with $58.3 billion for Afghanistan and

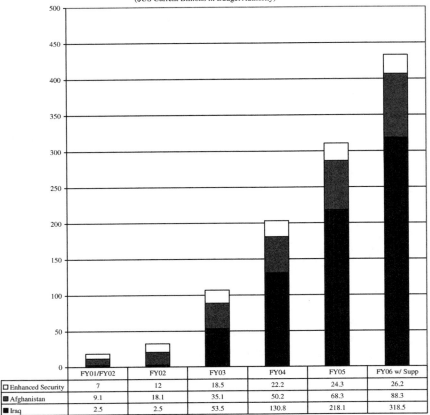

($US Current Billions in Budget Authority)					
	FY01/FY02	FY02	FY03	FY04	FY05	FY06 w/ Supp
☐ Enhanced Security	7	12	18.5	22.2	24.3	26.2
■ Afghanistan	9.1	18.1	35.1	50.2	68.3	88.3
■ Iraq	2.5	2.5	53.5	130.8	218.1	318.5

Note: Includes Department of Defense spending, foreign aid and diplomatic operations, and foreign operations.

Source: Adapted from Amy Belasco, "The Cost of Iraq, Afghanistan, and Other Global War on Terror Operations Since 9/11." Congressional Research Service, 14 June 2006: 10.

Figure 2.6   CRS Estimates of Cumulative Costs of Incremental and Unanticipated Spending on Iraq, Afghanistan, and the Global War on Terrorism: FY2001–FY2006 Supplemental Request

$24.5 billion for enhanced security. The total cost in obligations through March 2006 was $302.2 billion versus $310.7 billion in budget authority. Since only obligations are counted in estimating the extent to which the budget is balanced, and given the strain placed on the U.S. economy, the spend-out rate created a significantly lower burden figure.

- The CRS estimates of the monthly averages in *obligations* for the Iraq War alone were also significantly lower: $4.4 billion in FY2003, $5.0 billion in FY2004, $6.4 billion in FY2005, and an estimated $8 billion in FY2006. The same is true for the CRS

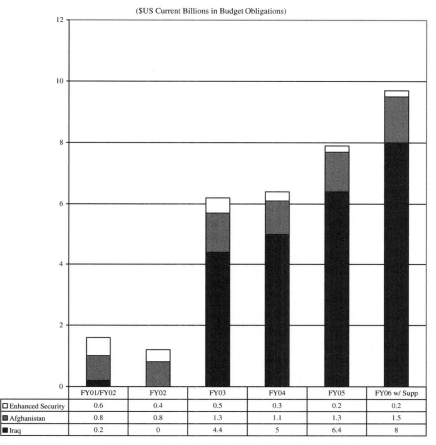

($US Current Billions in Budget Obligations)

	FY01/FY02	FY02	FY03	FY04	FY05	FY06 w/ Supp
☐ Enhanced Security	0.6	0.4	0.5	0.3	0.2	0.2
▦ Afghanistan	0.8	0.8	1.3	1.1	1.3	1.5
■ Iraq	0.2	0	4.4	5	6.4	8

Note: Includes Department of Defense spending, foreign aid and diplomatic operations, and foreign operations.

Source: Adapted from work by Amy Belasco. "The Cost of Iraq, Afghanistan, and Other Global War on Terror Operations Since 9/11." Congressional Research Service, 14 June 2006: 10 & 14.

Figure 2.7 CRS Estimates of Average Monthly Costs of Incremental and Unanticipated Spending on Iraq, Afghanistan, and the Global War on Terrorism: FY2001–FY2006 Supplemental Request

estimates of the monthly cost of all the wars: $6.3 billion in FY2003, $6.4 billion in FY2004, $7.9 billion in FY2005, and an estimated $9.7 billion in FY2006.

The CRS did find that the estimates of expenditures being issued by the U.S. government understated the real cost of operations because they included only current obligations, not the cost in terms of worn equipment, future replacements, paying the long-term costs of increased pensions and payments for killed and wounded, and paying for a long list of additional costs such as support by the national intelligence agencies.

Outside Estimates and Future Costs

As might be expected, experts can only guess at the total cost of the war, including the cost of the expenditures not reported by DoD and the State Department and which will be incurred in future years. Such estimates generally put the direct cost of the war from 2002 to March 2006 in the range of $350 billion to $700 billion.[25] The Center for Strategic and Budgetary Analysis, for example, made an estimate very close to the CRS estimate: $48 billion in 2003, $59 billion in 2004, $81 billion in 2005, and $91 billion in 2006.[26]

Calculations of different types of estimates, ranging from opportunity cost to total economic direct and indirect impacts on the U.S. economy, can be lower or much higher. There also are no reliable estimates as yet of just how much it will cost in future years to deal with accelerated equipment wear, replace equipment earlier than planned, or deal with deferred expenditures.[27]

There is no way to do more than guess at the ultimate cost of the Iraq War, the Afghan War, and the war on terrorism. One outside study put the cost at $2.2 trillion by assuming the United States would still be active in Iraq through 2015, and one of the Congressional staff experts working on such figures put the figure at "well over a trillion dollars."[28]

A CRS study by Amy Belasco estimated that the total cost of the global war on terror could easily reach $808 billion by FY2016.[29] This estimate was based on a Congressional Budget Office (CBO) estimate based on a projected drawdown from some 258,000 troops deployed for all the wars in FY2006 to 74,000 in FY2010. In this study, the CBO estimated that the war could cost another $371 billion between FY2007 and FY2016. If that was added to the $435 billion total estimated spending during FY2001–FY2006, the total would be $806 billion—an average of around $80 billion a year or $6.7 billion a month. The CBO has, however, examined other cases involving more and less intense levels of combat during the period from FY2007 to FY2016. The baseline cost for military operations during this period ranged from $472 billion in outlays ($483 billion in authority) to $1,188 billion in outlays ($1,297 billion in authority). These expenditures would be incremental to around $400–440 billion in previous expenditures on Iraq, Afghanistan, and other aspects of the war on terrorism, between FY2001 and FY2006. The truth is that no one can predict the total cost of the Iraq War, the Afghanistan conflict, and the war on terrorism, but it seems almost certain that they will eventually exceed $1 trillion —even if one ignores issues like opportunity cost, trade impacts, and the host of indirect costs that some outside governments add to such figures.[30] These figures also do not include the expenditures of allies in such wars or their aid programs.[31]

The Costs to the Total Force

The high tempo of ongoing operations in Iraq and Afghanistan has also taken its toll on warfighting equipment and sharply affected the force posture on which the United States bases both its current contingency plans and efforts to plan force readiness and transformation. As part of the $70-billion "bridge fund" for the DoD's war costs attached to the 2007 Defense Authorization Act, and its companion Defense Appropriations Act, Congress gave the Army around $17 billion and the Marine Corps $5.8 billion to reset—repair, upgrade, and replace—equipment, including helicopters, tanks, and other vehicles destroyed in Iraq and Afghanistan. This came two months after the Army's Chief of Staff, General Peter Schoomaker, told Congress that the Army needed $17.1 billion in 2007—more than double the amount appropriated for repairs in FY2006—and $13 billion a year for at least two to three years after 2007 just to cover reset costs. The Congressional appropriators' conference report identified $2.9 billion for specific Army combat losses, including the following:[32]

- $621 million to replace 18 AH-64 Apache helicopters,
- $511 million to replace 17 CH-47 Chinook helicopters,
- $225 million to replace 15 UH-60 Black Hawk helicopters,
- $700 million for M1 tank losses, and
- $82 million for Stryker vehicle losses.

Beyond combat losses, the funding would also cover the following:

- $3.7 billion for maintenance costs,
- $1.1 billion for new up-armored Humvees,
- $1.4 billion to buy new medium and heavy trucks,
- $1 billion for body armor and other force protection items,
- $160 million for night vision gear, and
- $61 million for foreign language proficiency pay.

The Army's demand for additional funds should come as no surprise. Equipment wears out much faster in wartime, and Congress does not fund replacement costs in peacetime unless the Department of Defense provides honest projections of their cost and the funds necessary to replace them.

The failure to make honest and timely requests to preserve readiness and the force structure can, however, seriously compromise the warfighting capabilities of the United States. As James Jay Carafano, Assistant Director and Senior Research Fellow at the Heritage Foundation, pointed out, "Operations in Iraq are wearing out trucks three to five times faster than normal. Helicopters are being used at five times their normal rate. Stockpiles of ammunition that sat around during the Cold War have been used up."[33]

As is discussed in the following chapters, the Army's problems go well beyond resetting equipment. The service's active duty force numbers around 504,000. Around 400,000 soldiers have done at least one tour of combat duty in Iraq or Afghanistan, and more than one-third of these soldiers have been deployed twice.

Commanding officers have increasingly complained of the strain on the force and have pointed out that sustaining current troop levels will likely require more help from the National Guard and Reserve or an increase in the active-duty force.[34]

The Army also is only one of the services involved. The burden on the Marine Corps has been just as great. The Air Force has worked its bomber, fighter, tanker, and transport aircraft far beyond the rates it planned. It, too, is badly in need of funds to maintain and rehabilitate its forces and equipment that the Department of Defense failed to fund for political reasons, and it has "aged" its fleet far more quickly than its force plans call for. A similar burden has been placed on some elements of the United States Navy. Deferring such spending may be a politically expedient way of deferring and disguising the cost of war, but it is a terrible way of preserving readiness and of planning, programming, and budgeting.

Reconstruction of Iraq versus Japan and Germany

It is also interesting to look at the cost of the Iraq War in terms of U.S. reconstruction efforts and political, economic, and security aid. The CRS estimated the cost of U.S. aid allocations (all grant assistance) for Iraq appropriated from 2003 to 2006 to total $28.9 billion. The CRS estimated that $17.6 billion (62 percent) went for economic and political reconstruction assistance, while $10.9 billion (38 percent) was used to aid Iraqi security.[35]

A higher proportion of Iraqi aid was spent on economic reconstruction of critical infrastructure than in the case of Germany and Japan. Total U.S. assistance to Iraq through March 2006 was already equivalent to total assistance provided to Germany—and almost double that provided to Japan—from 1946 to 1952. The United States provided Germany with a total of $29.3 billion in assistance in constant 2005 dollars from 1946 to 1952 with 60 percent in economic grants, nearly 30 percent in economic loans, and the remainder in military aid. Total U.S. assistance to Japan for 1946 to 1952 was roughly $15.2 billion in 2005 dollars, of which 77 percent was in grants and 23 percent was in loans.[36]

The one clear message from all these conflicting figures is that "long wars" are very unlikely to be cheap simply because they do not involve extensive periods of combat between modern conventional and high-technology forces. The costs in both the Afghan and Iraq wars rose sharply after the conventional phase and have been far higher in the counterterrorism/counterinsurgency phases of each war that have followed.

Looking beyond Iraq

All of these mistakes, problems, and issues show that the Iraq War and other recent conflicts provide important lessons and warnings about the need for changes in U.S. strategy and military planning. At the same time, Americans must not use the Iraq War to judge what is and is not overstretch or to seek the right match between strategy and resources. U.S. strategy and commitments, U.S. defense resources, and the future U.S. force posture cannot be shaped on the basis of the strains that operations in Iraq have placed on U.S. forces. Iraq is at most a symptom, not the disease.

Iraq has pushed some elements of U.S. land forces to the limit of what its currently deployable forces can sustain—and probably well beyond that point in terms of the burden placed on some elements of its active forces, Reserves, and National Guard. *But,* as the following chapters explain in detail, many of today's problems in Iraq are the result of mistakes the United States made in the way it deals with strategy, planning, programming, and budgeting that began decades before the Iraq War. Many of America's problems are at least as much a result of the fact that much of the U.S. force structure is a legacy of the Cold War era.

The last thing on earth the United States needs to do is to plan its overall strategy, force plans, programs, and budgets around the fighting in Iraq. There is a reason that military strategists have warned for generations against planning for the last war. This may well be truer of the Iraq War than most conflicts. In many ways, it is the kind of war that the United States should do everything possible to avoid in the future. It has forced the United States to fight a major asymmetric war on a largely hostile or indifferent territory halfway around the world. It has involved it in an ideological and religious struggle in a nation with a different faith and culture. It has involved the United States in Iraq's sectarian, ethnic, and tribal tensions and conflicts. It has forced the United States to simultaneously try to defeat an enemy, rebuild a relatively modern state with some 27 million people, and reshape that state's politics and economy.

Nations cannot always choose the wars they want to fight, but Iraq has presented the kind of grand strategic challenge the United States has every reason to avoid repeating in the future. The United States also faces major challenges of a different kind that could easily put very different strains on its ability to match its global strategy to its force plans, programs, and budgets, and the United States must always plan for the historical reality that surprise and uncertainty shape the strategic future of even the most powerful nations.

OTHER STRATEGIC CHALLENGES: WHY IRAQ AND CURRENT WARS CANNOT BE USED TO DEFINE OVERSTRETCH

More broadly, the United States must consider the full range of global trends and problems that should shape its strategy over the coming decades. One key trend that the United States must consider is that military power is only one element of global power, and the United States has far less strength in economic terms than it does in military terms. There is no consensus among experts as to the future trends in economic power or even how to make estimates of even summary measures of economic strength like gross domestic product (GDP) or gross national product (GNP). Past estimates have often sharply exaggerated how long current trends will last and sharply under- or overestimated changes in global economic strength.

The fact remains, however, that many experts feel that fundamental changes are coming in the relative economic power that has determined both the civil and

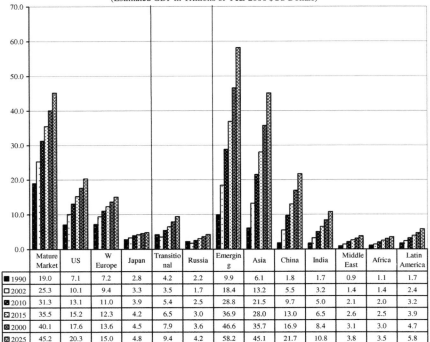

(Estimated GDP in Trillions of Year 2000 $US Dollars)

	Mature Market	US	W Europe	Japan	Transitional	Russia	Emerging	Asia	China	India	Middle East	Africa	Latin America
■ 1990	19.0	7.1	7.2	2.8	4.2	2.2	9.9	6.1	1.8	1.7	0.9	1.1	1.7
☐ 2002	25.3	10.1	9.4	3.3	3.5	1.7	18.4	13.2	5.5	3.2	1.4	1.4	2.4
▨ 2010	31.3	13.1	11.0	3.9	5.4	2.5	28.8	21.5	9.7	5.0	2.1	2.0	3.2
▨ 2015	35.5	15.2	12.3	4.2	6.5	3.0	36.9	28.0	13.0	6.5	2.6	2.5	3.9
▨ 2000	40.1	17.6	13.6	4.5	7.9	3.6	46.6	35.7	16.9	8.4	3.1	3.0	4.7
▨ 2025	45.2	20.3	15.0	4.8	9.4	4.2	58.2	45.1	21.7	10.8	3.8	3.5	5.8

Source: Energy Information Administration, International Energy Outlook, 2005, Washington, DC, Department of Energy, pp. 92.

Figure 2.8   The Changing Nature of Global Economic Power

military preeminence of the United States. The projections shown in Figure 2.8 are typical of projections that show that U.S. economic power will steadily decline in relative terms and may lead to a far more multipolar world than the one that emerged out of the Cold War.

Such estimates do show that "globalization" will produce a continued growth in the economies of mature or industrialized states, with the United States taking the lead followed by Western Europe and Japan. Most experts also agree that the economies of the transitional states—Russia, other former Soviet Union (FSU) states, and Eastern Europe—will also grow, but more slowly, and that Russia will not come close to economic superpower status. If anything, Russia is increasingly seen in terms of its importance to the export of oil and gas to Europe and Asia, both from its own resources and because of its control of pipelines from Central Asia.

At the same time, a major shift in economic power is projected as a result of the growth of emerging economies, although this growth reflects the sharp difference between the "winners" and the "losers" in globalization. The emergence of new economic powers is dominated by Asia, and particularly by China. Latin America comes in a distant second, and the Middle East and Africa are projected to lag in competitiveness and success (as they have ever since the end of World War II). Put simply, economic globalization is projected to change the balance of economic power—and the ability to buy military power—in ways that will lead to a striking increase in the relative strength of emerging Asia and particularly China and India.

There is no way to predict precisely what this will mean in strategic terms, or whether given winners and losers will change in the ways that experts currently project. Asian countries have become economic powers through their export-oriented economic, industrial, and trade policies, but can still falter. Other regions also may find ways to develop and exploit their own comparative advantage. Countries and regions that were considered losers in the past may become the winners of the future, which would further "multipolarize" the world. Emerging countries in Asia, the Middle East, and Africa can emerge as economic centers, increase their purchasing power of military hardware, and improve their power status.

Nations may also chose to compete primarily in economic terms and not in military ones. Traditional warfighting capability is only a measure of power if nations compete in terms of conventional wars. Nations like China, and regions like the EU, may see economic strength as providing a far more useful investment than military strength if they do not see a military challenge or threat.

The "Reglobalization" of Military Power

The United States may well, however, face a world in economic globalization that gradually changes the balance of military power as well as the balance of economic power. Over time, the United States may go from being the world's only superpower to being one of several major powers in a world where other nations, particularly China, emerge as peer competitors.

If so, this shift to a more multipolar world will take at least a decade. At least for the present, the United States is able to exploit its economic strength in ways that steadily enhance its military power. This relative advantage is not as apparent if one looks only at force quantity and not at force quality.

The data in Figure 2.9 do show that if military power is measured in quantitative terms, the vestiges of the Cold War have still left Russia as a military superpower in spite of the economic strains and collapse that caused the breakup of the FSU and the dissolution of the Warsaw Pact. Similarly, China appears to be a major military power, and NATO Europe appears to be more powerful than the United States.

The qualitative reality, however, is very different. Numerical strength, or military "mass," has lost much of its value. Figure 2.9 shows the United States has the ability to vastly outspend other nations in pursuing force quality. As a result, it can now project power on a basis that is impossible for any other nation or regional bloc, including the European Union. The United States deploys all-professional forces with a decisive lead in most critical areas of military technology. Regardless of the size of total Chinese and Russian forces, they lack the mix of experience, precision-strike assets, stealth, IS&R capabilities, and other qualitative advances to compete with the United States in conventional warfare.

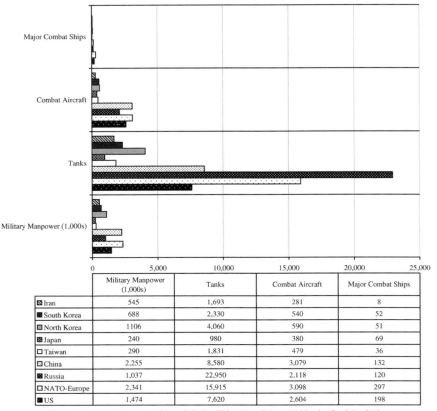

	Military Manpower (1,000s)	Tanks	Combat Aircraft	Major Combat Ships
Iran	545	1,693	281	8
South Korea	688	2,330	540	52
North Korea	1106	4,060	590	51
Japan	240	980	380	69
Taiwan	290	1,831	479	36
China	2,255	8,580	3,079	132
Russia	1,037	22,950	2,118	120
NATO-Europe	2,341	15,915	3,098	297
US	1,474	7,620	2,604	198

Source: Adapted from data in International Institute of Strategic Studies (IISS), *Military Balance 2006*, London, Routledge, 2006

Figure 2.9 Comparative Military Strength of U.S. Forces, Allied Power Blocs, and Key Contingency Forces in 2006

As Chapter 3 documents in detail, the United States has also shown that it is able to support such levels of spending—even for a combined mix of wars in Afghanistan, Iraq, and against terrorism—at a lower cost in terms of a percentage of its GDP and national budget than it spent during the 1990s and the Cold War. Even if one includes the cost of budget supplements for three wars, it spent around 5–6 percent of its GDP on national security during FY2003–FY2006 versus an average of around 6–7 percent during the last decade of the Cold War.[37]

This situation is almost certain to change over time, but it will change slowly. Russian weakness, China's slow rate of modernization, and Europe's focus on Europe mean that any reglobalization of military power will be slow and will begin at the regional rather than the global level. It is difficult to believe, however, that China will not emerge as a major military as well as economic power center or that Japan and South Korea will not respond by taking a more national and independent stand.

Europe may be slow to emerge as any kind of independent military force, although the EU is gradually creating a separate military identity from NATO. Europe does, however, have considerable influence over U.S. security actions that go beyond sheer military force—as French and German actions over the Iraq War made clear. Europe has also shown that it can play a major role in deploying both peacemaking forces and "soft power."

The question of whether nations like India will also become major regional military powers is equally important. Moreover, for all of their current failures to create any meaningful military unit, regional organizations like the Association of Southeast Asian Nations and the Gulf Cooperation Council at least have the potential to become more significant blocs.

U.S. strategy, however, cannot be based on the assumption that this will be an American century or one of U.S. military preeminence. Other nations will almost certainly eventually become wealthy enough to create truly modern conventional and nuclear forces that can rival America's qualitative "edge." The United States may not want such national or regional rivals, but there is little it can do about them as long as they are hostile to the point where war resolves the issue.

The United States must prepare for a world in which it establishes stable strategic relations with the major winners in the economic side of globalization. It must begin to reinforce existing alliances, create new ones, and find ways of dealing with emerging major powers that minimize the risk of future conflicts.

This should be relatively easy if the United States places the proper emphasis on diplomacy and negotiation, rather than on pressure and military intervention. The United States faces serious conflicts of interest with ideological threats, but has no vital strategic interests that require it to come into conflict with such nations or other power blocs. Europe's growing unity and economic power does not mean that NATO will split or Europe will reorient is military capabilities toward independent action. Europe may, in fact, continue to cooperate with the United States in most cases, strengthening the West even as it faces emerging power blocks in Asia. India and China have local interests that may lead to local friction and conflict, but it is not clear why their emergence should create vital national security interests that put them at odds with the United States.

The Reglobalization of Military Power, the Koreas, and Taiwan

There are, however, important potential regional states that can test the limits of U.S. military capabilities. One is the risk of another Korean conflict, and here the United States not only faces the prospect of a nuclear armed North Korea, equipped with long-range ballistic missiles, but the United States is forging a new and more stable military partnership with South Korea.

Figure 2.10 (Part 1) and Figure 2.10 (Part 2) show the balance of forces in Northeast Asia, and it is important to note that U.S. forces in South Korea are almost too small to play a significant role. By early 2006, the U.S. Army still had over 21,000 men in country, but the U.S. 8th Army was little more than a brigade equivalent,

Figure 2.10 Northeast Asian Military Forces in 2006: Part 1

	China	Japan	Taiwan	N. Korea	S. Korea
Manpower (1,000s)					
Total Active	2,255	239.9	290	1,106	687.7
Regular	2,255	239.9	290	1,106	687.7
National Guard & Other	–	–	–	–	–
Reserve	800	44.34	1,653.5	4,700	4,500
Paramilitary	3,969	12.25	22	189	4.5
Strategic Missile Forces (1,000s)	100	–	–	–	–
ICBM	46	–	–	–	–
IRBM	35	–	–	–	–
SRBM	725	–	–	–	–
Army and Guard Manpower (1,000s)	1,600	148.2	200	950	560
Regular Army Manpower	1,600	148.2	200	950	560
Reserve (1,000s)	–	–	1,500	600	–
Total Main Battle Tanks	7,580	980	926	3,500	2,330
Active OAFV/Lt. Tanks	2,000	70	1,130	560	40
Total APCs	5,500*	730	950	2,500	2,480
Self-Propelled Artillery	1,200	250	405	4,400	1,089
Towed Artillery	17,700	480	1,060	3,500	3,500
MRLs	2,400	110	300	2,500	185
Mortars	some	1,140	–	7,500	6,000
SSM Launchers	7,200	910	1,000	some	some
Light SAM Launchers	284	550	581	10,000	1,090
AA Guns	7,700	60	400	11,000	600
Air Force Manpower (1,000s)	**400**	**45.6**	**45**	**110**	**64**
Air Defense Manpower	210	–	–	–	–
Total Combat Aircraft	2,643	300	479	590	540
Bombers	222	–	–	80	–
Fighter/Ground Attack	1,169	130	128	211	283
Fighter	1,252	150	293	150	210
RECCE/FGA RECCE	53	20	8	–	57
COIN/OCU	–	–	–	–	–
AEW C41/BM/EW	4	10	6	–	4

MR/MPA	–	–	–	–	–
Transport Aircraft	296	30	39	318	34
Tanker Aircraft	10	–	–	–	–
Total Helicopters	80	40	35	308	28
Armed Helicopters	–	–	–	24	–
Major SAM Launchers	1,078	720	–	38	–
Light SAM Launchers	500	–	–	760	–
AA Guns	16,000	some	–	–	–

* Includes Lt. Tanks, AIFVs, and APCs. Note: ICBM = intercontinental ballistic missiles, IRBM = intermediate-range ballistic missiles, SRBM = short-range ballistic missiles; OAFVs = other armored fighting vehicles, APC = armored personnel carrier, MRL = multiple rocket launcher, SSM = surface-to-surface missile, SAM = surface-to-air missile, AA = antiaircraft, RECCE = reconnaissance, COIN = counterinsurgency, OCU = other combat unit, AEW = airborne early warning, BM = battle management, EW = electronic warfare, MR = maritime reconnaissance, and MPA = maritime patrol aircraft.

with only 116 M-1 tanks, 126 armored fighting vehicles, 111 armored personnel carriers, and 45 artillery weapons and mortars. The U.S. 7th Air Force had over 9,000 men, but its air strength consisted of only 40 F-16C and 24 A-10 II combat aircraft, plus some Special Forces and support aircraft.

The United States can deploy immense precision strike power by sea, from bases in Japan, and from locations like Guam. It can use stealth and stand-off weapons to do massive damage to North Korea without using nuclear weapons. It cannot, however, rush large conventional forces to South Korea, and it is steadily reducing its forces in country.

The United States already has begun force changes that make South Korea the *de facto* senior partner in any future conventional conflict. The Pentagon announced in the summer of 2006 that it planned to give South Korea wartime operational control over U.S. troops within three years, or by 2009. Stated plans were to cut troop levels in South Korea to 25,000 by 2008 and to maintain 20,000 to 25,000 troops on the peninsula "for the foreseeable future."[38]

By the late summer of 2006, however, the notion of a total withdrawal of troops in South Korea—or a reduction to a much more token force—had begun to gather additional momentum. Such a move would have brought to final conclusion a slow process of disengagement from Korea that had seen total U.S. troop levels fall from 326,800 at the end of the Korean War, to 55,800 by 1960, and finally to 29,500 by the summer of 2006.[39]

The other war where there is a near- or midterm danger that the United States might face a peer challenge in terms of the forces it can rapidly deploy is the risk of a conflict in the Taiwan Strait. More broadly, China also seems to be the only potential threat that has a mid- to long-term capability to create a modern conventional and nuclear warfighting capability that can rival the United States. The United States

Figure 2.10   Northeast Asian Military Forces in 2006: Part 2

	China	Japan	Taiwan	N. Korea	S. Korea
Total Naval Manpower (1,000s)	255	44.4	45	46	63
Major Surface Combatants					
Carriers	–	–	–	–	–
Destroyer-Guided Missile	21	39	11	–	–
Other Destroyer	–	5	–	–	–
Frigate-Guided Missile	42	9	21	–	9
Other Frigate	–	–	–	3	–
Corvettes	–	–	–	6	28
Patrol Craft					
Missile	96	9	59	43	5
Torpedo and Coastal	130	–	–	125	–
Inshore, Riverine	117	–	–	133	75
Submarines					
SLBN*	1	–	–	–	–
SSN	5	–	–	–	–
SSG	1	–	–	–	–
SS/SSK	61	16	4	88	20
Mine Vessels	130	31	12	23	15
Amphibious Ships	50	4	18	10	12
Landing Craft	285	23	325	260	36
Support Ships	163	28	20	7	14
Marines (1,000s)	10	–	15	–	28
Naval Air	26,000	9,800	–	–	–
Naval Aircraft	436	80	32	–	16
Bomber	68	–	–	–	–
FGA	274	–	–	–	–
Fighter	74	–	–	–	–
MR/MPA	4	80	–	–	8
Armed Helicopters	16	98	20	–	11
ASW Helicopters	8	88	20	–	11

SAR Helicopters	27	18	–	–	–
Mine Warfare Helicopters	–	10	–	–	–
Other Helicopters	8	27	–	–	34

* Note: SLBN = nuclear powered ballistic missile submarine; SSN = nuclear powered submarine, SSG = cruise missile submarine, SS = diesel-battery powered submarine, SSK = hunter killer submarine, ASW = antisubmarine warfare, and SAR = search and rescue.

recognized this reality in the national strategy it issued in February 2006 and in the Quadrennial Defense Review it issued that same month, stated as follows:[40]

> The choices of major and emerging powers, including India, Russia and China, will be key factors in determining the international security environment of the 21st century.
>
> India is emerging as a great power and a key strategic partner. On July 18, 2005 the President and Indian Prime Minister declared their resolve to transform the U.S.–India relationship into a global partnership that will provide leadership in areas of mutual concern and interest. Shared values as long-standing, multi-ethnic democracies provide the foundation for continued and increased strategic cooperation and represent an important opportunity for our two countries.
>
> Russia remains a country in transition. It is unlikely to pose a military threat to the United States or its allies on the same scale or intensity as the Soviet Union during the Cold War. Where possible, the United States will cooperate with Russia on shared interests such as countering the proliferation of weapons of mass destruction, combating terrorism, and countering the trafficking of narcotics. The United States remains concerned about the erosion of democracy in Russia, the curtailment of non-governmental organizations (NGOs) and freedom of the press, the centralization of political power and limits on economic freedom. Internationally, the United States welcomes Russia as a constructive partner but views with increasing concern its sales of disruptive weapons technologies abroad and actions that compromise the political and economic independence and territorial integrity of other states.
>
> Of the major and emerging powers, China has the greatest potential to compete militarily with the United States and field disruptive military technologies that could over time off set traditional U.S. military advantages absent U.S. counter strategies. U.S. policy remains focused on encouraging China to play a constructive, peaceful role in the Asia-Pacific region and to serve as a partner in addressing common security challenges, including terrorism, proliferation, narcotics and piracy. U.S. policy seeks to encourage China to choose a path of peaceful economic growth and political liberalization, rather than military threat and intimidation. The United States' goal is for China to continue as an economic partner and emerge as a responsible stakeholder and force for good in the world.
>
> China continues to invest heavily in its military, particularly in its strategic arsenal and capabilities designed to improve its ability to project power beyond its borders. Since 1996, China has increased its defense spending by more than 10% in real terms in every year except 2003. Secrecy, moreover, envelops most aspects of Chinese security affairs.

The outside world has little knowledge of Chinese motivations and decision-making or of key capabilities supporting its military modernization. The United States encourages China to take actions to make its intentions clear and clarify its military plans. Chinese military modernization has accelerated since the mid-to-late 1990s in response to central leadership demands to develop military options against Taiwan scenarios.

The pace and scope of China's military build-up already puts regional military balances at risk. China is likely to continue making large investments in high-end, asymmetric military capabilities, emphasizing electronic and cyber-warfare; counter-space operations; ballistic and cruise missiles; advanced integrated air defense systems; next generation torpedoes; advanced submarines; strategic nuclear strike from modern, sophisticated land and sea-based systems; and theater unmanned aerial vehicles for employment by the Chinese military and for global export. These capabilities, the vast distances of the Asian theater, China's continental depth, and the challenge of en route and in-theater U.S. basing place a premium on forces capable of sustained operations at great distances into denied areas.

The United States will work to ensure that all major and emerging powers are integrated as constructive actors and stakeholders into the international system. It will also seek to ensure that no foreign power can dictate the terms of regional or global security. It will attempt to dissuade any military competitor from developing disruptive or other capabilities that could enable regional hegemony or hostile action against the United States or other friendly countries, and it will seek to deter aggression or coercion. Should deterrence fail, the United States would deny a hostile power its strategic and operational objectives.

Shaping the choices of major and emerging powers requires a balanced approach, one that seeks cooperation but also creates prudent hedges against the possibility that cooperative approaches by themselves may fail to preclude future conflict. A successful hedging strategy requires improving the capacity of partner states and reducing their vulnerabilities. In this regard, the United States will work to achieve greater integration of defensive systems among its international partners in ways that would complicate any adversary's efforts to decouple them. The United States will work with allies and partners to integrate intelligence sensors, communication networks, information systems, missile defenses, undersea warfare and counter-mine warfare capabilities. It will seek to strengthen partner nations' capabilities to defend themselves and withstand attack, including against ambiguous coercive threats.

As a result, any analysis of the challenges to U.S. security must recognize the fact that America faces the prospect of two conflicts in Asia that are radically different from the conflicts it is fighting in Iraq and Afghanistan, and which Figure 2.9 shows would involve vastly larger conventional forces as well as weapons of mass destruction. One would be a conflict between North and South Korea that would inevitably involve the United States in a major land and air war that could involve the use of ballistic missiles and nuclear and chemical weapons. While North Korea has a very slow rate of modernization and its inept regime almost ensures that it will be a continuing loser in economic globalization, its sheer military mass and readiness for conflict make it a serious problem.

The Koreas have a close balance of conventional strength. North Korea, however, has long had theater-range ballistic missiles and chemical warheads. It now seems determined to acquire nuclear weapons and possibly biological weapons as well. South Korea relies on the United States for both conventional reinforcement and to deter North Korean use of chemical, biological, radiological, and nuclear weapons. This should produce a secure pattern of mutual deterrence, but North Korea's erratic regime is no guarantee of stability or rational decision making. If North Korea did use nuclear weapons, that would thrust the United States into a totally different kind of asymmetric war from the one it is fighting in Iraq, and one with far higher costs and casualties.

The other tensions in Northeast Asia seem less serious, although the tensions between China on the one hand and the United States and Japan on the other are an issue, as are tensions between Japan and Korea. The United States could, however, find itself dragged into a conflict over the Taiwan Strait.

China has made it repeatedly clear that it will not accept Taiwanese independence and will use military force to prevent this from happening. It has built up a major air and missile presence opposite Taiwan, is modernizing its navy, and is developing more amphibious assault capability. While China and the United States may not have any clear strategic reason to challenge each other, the fact that the United States has made it clear that it will defend Taiwan against any such Chinese attack could thrust it into a major naval and air conflict with the Chinese. Once again, such a conflict would be radically different from the kind of war the United States is now fighting and place a far more serious strain on U.S. military resources.

Any clash between China and another major Asian power or the United States would not only destabilize the global flow of trade in the short run, but could potentially trigger an arms race that would affect all of Asia and the United States for decades to come. It is difficult to see how any side could "win" such a clash. Any defeat or reversal would at best be temporary or tactical: It would push the losing side into a much more competitive position and into seeking to become dominant in the future, essentially making it the probable prelude to future violence. In fact, the United States, China, and the world probably have no greater single strategic priority than avoiding military and strategic competition, a new high-technology arms race, and the risk of region-wide or global strategic conflict. The key strategic goal for both nations must not be to establish some new form of mutual assured destruction or seek dominance relative to the other. It must be to establish a pattern of cooperation and partnership that will avoid this.

The Problem of Proliferation and New Forms of Warfare

Another key uncertainty is how rapidly the transfer of wealth, technology, and advanced arms to other nations and nonstate actors will create a global "revolution" in military affairs that leads to the added proliferation of weapons of mass destruction, the use of precision warfare and near real-time battle management, and new forms of information warfare.

To understand the forces at work, it is necessary to understand that several different trends are interacting on a global basis:

- The technology for both weapons of mass destruction and advanced conventional weapons is becoming steadily more available through information flow, improved national industrial and technological bases, and the sale of arms and dual-use technologies.

- The availability of nuclear fissile material and heavy hydrogen is still an issue. Increases in nuclear power reactors and the steady spread of improved centrifuge and laser isotope separation (LIS) technology are, however, easing this problem. The technology and equipment needed for neutron initiators, reflectors, explosive lens, and simulated test explosions is widely available, and at least one weapons design has been sold on the international market.

- Chemical weapons technology is broadly available, and access to precursors is growing. "Dusty" and "third-generation" weapons are far less secret. Cluster munitions and line source attack technology is spreading. At the same time, the steady spread of chemical technology and manufacturing capability ensures that nations that choose to draw upon dual-use technology to make chemical weapons can do so.

- Advances in biotechnology and genetic engineering and the global spread of advanced biotech manufacturing and equipment are interacting with natural risks like the globalization of immune strains of chronic diseases and pandemics. At the same time, the steady spread of biotechnology, pharmaceutical and food processing technology, and manufacturing capability ensures that nations that choose to draw upon dual-use technology to make biological weapons can do so.

- Long-range ballistic missile and cruise missile technology is steadily spreading. Creating long-range ballistic missile forces is still a major challenge, requiring extensive resources and either an advanced technology base or purchases from other countries. The number of powers with such missiles does, however, continue to increase, and the cost and technical challenges in acquiring missiles continue to drop, particularly in the case of cruise missiles.

- Commercial satellite coverage and the Global Positioning System provide major aids in targeting and strike capability. More nations are able to launch military and intelligence satellites. Long-range unmanned aerial vehicles and unmanned combat air vehicles are likely to enter the world arms market in the next decade. The globalization of intelligence, surveillance, and reconnaissance assets is now unavoidable.

- The world arms and dual-use markets are, however, making precision-guided weapons, advanced sensors, and all of the basic equipment and technology to implement the revolution in military affairs more on a global basis. After a period of decline following the Cold War, the value of new arms agreements signed with developing nations has increased sharply. It reached $21.8 billion in 2004, with a total of some $17 billion for the developed world. A steadily larger amount of these new agreements has been for the sensors, battlement management systems, missiles, and precision-guided or smart weapons that support the revolution in military affairs (RMA), rather than the large weapons platforms that dominated the arms races of the 1960s–1990s.[41]

- Globalization and interdependence are changing the "target base" affecting national, regional, and global security. Nations are far more dependent on the smooth flow of global and regional trade and near real-time delivery. New, high-value targets like desalination plants supplement the ability to use conventional precision weapons to strike at both global shipping and communication routes and at vital facilities like power plants, refineries, communications hubs, etc.

- The globalization of information warfare is occurring at several levels. One is the "CNN effect," the ability to immediately communicate anywhere in the world and use propaganda or information as weapons. Another level is the growing dependence on global information systems such as the Internet, direct financial and other data links, world media, phone systems, TV, etc., which are vulnerable to kinetic, electronic, and cyber attacks.

The United States must deal with these developments at several different levels. Existing arms control arrangements have some value in deterring proliferation and in providing mechanisms that add the kind of transparency that can avoid needless arms races and tensions. At the same time, the United States must face the fact that no foreseeable mix of global arms control agreements can halt the flow of dual-use technology in any of the above areas, develop enough transparency and enforcement capability to halt secret or "black programs," or cover all of the options now open to state and nonstate actors.

The United States can seek to deter proliferation through a mix of arms control, pressure, and deterrence, but cannot really succeed in most cases against a determined power. North Korea is already such a threat, but Iran could become another. This would confront the United States with both a nuclear threat and the kind of asymmetric threat discussed in the previous chapter. The United States might deal with Iran by containment or by focused strikes on its military forces, but any decisive action might confront it with having to launch a major invasion against a much larger nation than Iraq with a far more popular regime—effectively raising the scale of an Iraq-like conflict by a factor of two or more.

As the United States tries to create a balance among its future strategy, forces, and resources, it must also face the fact that other developing powers will see such proliferation as a potential counter to the major powers, as well as a necessary way to adopt at least part of the revolution in military affairs. At the local and regional levels, the ability to use such mixes of proliferation for both a local advantage or to check or counter outside powers will lead some nations to openly or covertly proliferate, and it will certainly increase suspicion and uncertainty.

Over the next few decades, advances in centrifuges and laser isotope separation will make acquiring nuclear weapons easier. Advances in biotechnology and genetic engineering may well create threats that are far cheaper and easier to create than nuclear weapons. Ballistic and cruise missile technology is already largely beyond control. Precision-guided weapons and much of the technology necessary to target them has already reached the world market. Information warfare is an ongoing activity in the form of cybercrime and "cracking" for sport.

Globalization will continue to increase the transfer of dual-use technology and the ability to weaponize it, while it simultaneously increases economic interdependence at the national, regional, and global levels. The sheer density of trade and communications will increase vulnerability, but so will the search for cost-effectiveness and efficiency. Near real-time delivery, minimal inventory, minimal redundancy, and security expenditures are just a few of the market forces that push toward added vulnerability.

The Globalization of Nonstate Actors as a Transnational Threat

As has been discussed in the previous chapter, globalization is giving new power to transnational threats such as Al Qa'ida, and such movements will be a lasting force. U.S. strategy is now based on the thesis that there will be a long war against a loose and changing informal network of such threats, dominated by neo-Salafi Islamist extremists. The United States defined this threat as follows in its 2006 Quadrennial Defense Review:[42]

> "globalization" enables many positive developments such as the free movement of capital, goods and services, information, people and technology, but it is also accelerating the transmission of disease, the transfer of advanced weapons, the spread of extremist ideologies, the movement of terrorists and the vulnerability of major economic segments. The U.S. populace, territory and infrastructure, as well as its assets in space, may be increasingly vulnerable to these and a variety of other threats, including weapons of mass destruction, missile and other air threats, and electronic or cyber-attacks.
>
> "globalization" also empowers small groups and individuals. Nation-states no longer have a monopoly over the catastrophic use of violence. Today, small teams or even single individuals can weaponize chemical, biological and even crude radiological or nuclear devices and use them to murder hundreds of thousands of people. Loosely organized and with few assets of their own to protect, non-state enemies are considerably more difficult than nation-states to deter through traditional military means. Non-state enemies could attempt to attack a wide range of targets including government facilities; commercial and financial systems; cultural and historical landmarks; food, water, and power supplies; and information, transport, and energy networks. They will employ unconventional means to penetrate homeland defenses and exploit the very nature of western societies—their openness—to attack their citizens, economic institutions, physical infrastructure and social fabric.
>
> The threat to the U.S. homeland, however, is broader than that posed by terrorists. Hostile states could also attack the United States using WMD delivered by missiles or by less familiar means such as commercial shipping or general aviation. They could attack surreptitiously through surrogates. Some hostile states are pursuing advanced weapons of mass destruction, including genetically engineered biological warfare agents that can overcome today's defenses. There is also a danger that the WMD capabilities

of some states could fall into the hands of, or be given to, terrorists who could use them to attack the United States.

Ideologies and politics can now cut across national, regional, and global lines. The Internet and satellite television are two obvious tools that radicals and extremists have learned to manipulate on a global basis. The same is true of some aspects of the international financial structure and charities.

The key question is whether extremists can continue to capitalize on these tools and the vulnerabilities of various nations and political systems or whether they will provoke so much reaction that they are defeated by their own extremism.

U.S. strategy now assumes that there will be a continuing global struggle with neo-Salafi Islamist extremism and constantly muting informal networks of nonstate actors. The new U.S. national strategy makes this a central focus of U.S. policy. This assumption is based on the thesis, however, that Islamic states and Islam is fragile and cannot respond effectively on a political and an ideological level and that state actors will provide covert or overt support and sanctuary.

More generally, the question arises as to what extent advances in intelligence collection and analysis, and international cooperation in counterterrorism are necessary to counter such nonstate threats, and how the United States can work with the governments concerned to check the nonstate actors that operate on their soil. Nations may be unwilling to subordinate their military security to international bodies, but many are willing to cooperate against nonstate actors and terrorism. The UN and regional security organizations may be more effective on a global level than some experts estimate.

The dilemma for the United States is that the past success of national and nonstate actors in fighting the United States on asymmetric terms has already forced it to make massive, ongoing shifts in virtually every aspect of its national security structure and to do so at vast expense while fighting three wars. At the same time, it has shown the United States that the exercise of unilateral power is no substitute for global, regional, and national allies. It must deal with opponents that fight *above* the level where its conventional advantages apply by using religion, ideology, and wars of ideas. At the same time, it must fight opponents in asymmetric ways where they can fight *below* the level where its conventional advantages have great effectiveness.

The Possibility of Resource Wars

The United States cannot totally ignore the prospect of global struggles over the control of critical goods like oil, or "resource wars." During the Cold War, many postulated future struggles over scarce minerals and metals. In practice, however, both superpowers had enough control over most such materials on their own soil to limit competition, and the rising price of scarce materials led to new technologies and manufacturing methods that steadily reduced demand. Substitution effects reduced the risk of conflict to low, if not negligible levels.

Some have postulated the idea of "water wars," but water is so heavy and difficult to move that such conflicts are difficult to wage in practical terms except in contiguous areas or those served by the same major rivers. The major winners in globalization have little reason to compete for water, and they have the ability to pay for substitutes.

If there is a reason for such resource wars, it may lie in the growing global demand for energy, and particularly oil and gas imports. Virtually every expert estimates a massive increase in the need emerging economies will have for energy, particularly in Asia.

One such projection is shown in Figure 2.11, and there is a broad consensus among experts that while their individual figures may differ, emerging economies will go from consuming less than half the energy of mature economies in 1990 to consuming more energy at some point around 2020.[43]

This projected growth in global and Asian energy demand does not mean that struggles over energy resources are certain, or even probable. It is important to note

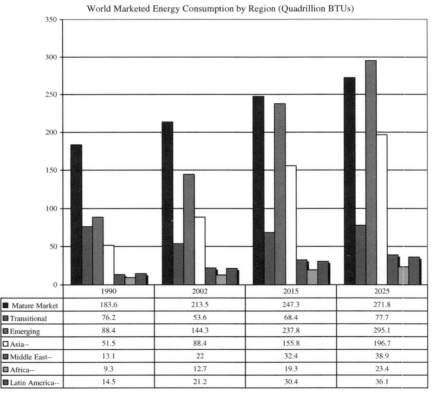

World Marketed Energy Consumption by Region (Quadrillion BTUs)

	1990	2002	2015	2025
■ Mature Market	183.6	213.5	247.3	271.8
▨ Transitional	76.2	53.6	68.4	77.7
▧ Emerging	88.4	144.3	237.8	295.1
☐ Asia--	51.5	88.4	155.8	196.7
■ Middle East--	13.1	22	32.4	38.9
▨ Africa--	9.3	12.7	19.3	23.4
■ Latin America--	14.5	21.2	30.4	36.1

Source: Energy Information Administration, *International Energy Outlook, 2005*, Washington, DC., Department of Energy, pp. 7-8.

Figure 2.11 Comparative Growth in Global Energy Consumption

that rises in oil and gas prices steadily make environmentally safe coal use, nuclear power, alternative fuels, conservation, and investments in increased efficiency more attractive. China, India, and the United States all have large coal reserves, gas and gas liquids can supplement or replace oil imports, oil shale/sands and heavy oil become more competitive as prices rise, and nuclear power is available to all advanced economies.

Oil imports, however, are likely to be an increasingly sensitive issue. There is no near-term substitute for petroleum for transportation use except for gas liquids that generally have to be imported to much the same extent as oil. Once again, experts differ over the details, but most agree that globalization will help expand the demand for imports as shown in Figure 2.12.

Chinese strategic thinkers have already postulated future struggles for oil resources, and China has already sought to secure at least some of its sources of oil

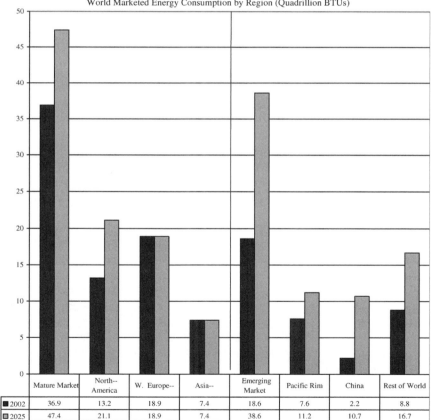

World Marketed Energy Consumption by Region (Quadrillion BTUs)

	Mature Market	North-- America	W. Europe--	Asia--	Emerging Market	Pacific Rim	China	Rest of World
2002	36.9	13.2	18.9	7.4	18.6	7.6	2.2	8.8
2025	47.4	21.1	18.9	7.4	38.6	11.2	10.7	16.7

Source: Energy Information Administration, *International Energy Outlook, 2005*, Washington, DC., Department of Energy, pp. 34-35.

Figure 2.12 Trends in World Petroleum Imports

and gas imports. Other powers are increasingly concerned with the prospect that various powers may seek the kind of contracts and oil investments that would guarantee emergency supply without full sensitivity to market forces, will use oil and gas exports as an economic weapon, or will be subject to pressure from global or regional military powers.

Gas resources and exports could also be an issue. Russian manipulation of gas prices to the Ukraine and pipeline politics have already raised the issue of "gas wars." So has Chinese and Japanese competition over the route and output of Russian pipelines, and efforts by the Caucasus and Central Asian states to find alternative gas pipelines that reduce dependence on Russia. The fact that some Middle Eastern countries still allow outside investment in their gas fields and need massive investments in long-range pipelines and natural gas liquids gas export facilities that can lead to guaranteed supply contracts is another feature.

In theory, such struggles should not take place. All major industrialized states and energy exporters operate in the same global economy. The maximum flow of energy imports and exports at market-driven prices is critical to both global economic growth and the economies of all such states. Developed nations must sustain trade with other developed nations, and developing nations must trade to develop and survive. China needs a U.S. and a global market for its exported goods (which means those economies must function efficiently, and the United States and the global import market need Chinese exports, which can come only if China has energy. Russia may be able to profiteer from trying to manipulate oil and gas exports to Europe for a while, but that would drive its import markets to find substitutes and retaliate in kind.

This makes a clear case for global interdependence at market prices with supplier agreements to ensure the flow of the total pool of supplies at the same world price in spite of sanctions, boycotts, wars and revolutions, and natural catastrophes. In fact, it led to the creation of emergency sharing arrangements within the Organisation for Economic Co-operation and Development (OECD) back in the 1970s. It will increase steadily with every expanding of globalization and the flow of exports. A race to grab secure sources of oil and gas imports, in spite of market needs and the priorities set by the global economy, can have only negative effects. Like similar struggles during the Colonial Era, it can create a wide range of losers, but no long-term winners.

No one looking back over recent human history, however, can base a strategy or force posture on the assumption that the world is filled with "rational actors."

PLANNING FOR STRATEGIC UNCERTAINTY

No amount of improvement in strategic thinking, military planning, or intelligence estimates can protect any nation against uncertainty and the unexpected. Every such effort is, at best, a quest that future events inevitably show at least partially fails. H. L. Mencken once described Americans and their desire for prophecy as "[t]he virulence of the national appetite for bogus revelation."

There is some truth in this canard. The United States is the country that did not predict Pearl Harbor, did not predict Korea, failed to predict the timing of the Russian acquisition of nuclear weapons, and then failed to predict its development of intercontinental ballistic missiles and its ability to increase its number of multiple independent reentry vehicles per missile, or "MIRVing." It mischaracterized the threat in Vietnam and initially disregarded the Sino-Soviet split. It did not predict the risks in Lebanon, Haiti, and Somalia. America is the country that did not predict the threat Iraq would be to Kuwait or its level of proliferation, and then it exaggerated the probable effectiveness of the Iraqi Army before the Gulf War. It failed to accurately predict 9/11 and the threat posed by Islamic extremism. It blundered into the Iraq War with the wrong threat analysis of the reasons for going to war, and it totally failed to understand the importance of stability operations.

Wealth as a Substitute for Strategy

As has been touched upon earlier, the traditional American solution is to fight on the strength of its wealth rather than to fight smart. The United States has faced far greater strains on its budget and economy in the past than it faces in the Iraq War. There is no easy way to compare the cost of American wars in constant dollars, but Figure 2.13 provides a rough comparison of the cost of such wars. It shows that the Iraq War has not been more expensive than other recent wars, although it is moving quickly toward the total cost of the Korean and Vietnam wars, and it could easily cost twice as much in constant dollars. At the same time, the U.S. economy is far larger than in past conflicts, and there is no evidence that the Iraq War alone—or the combination of the Iraq War, Afghan War, and the war on terrorism—have placed a crippling or even a major burden on the U.S. defense budget, the U.S. federal budget, or the national economy.

Figure 2.14 shows that the Iraq War has placed a relatively mild strain in economic terms compared to such conflicts. The total Department of Defense budget has consumed 17–19 percent of the federal budget during the period covered by the Iraq War, the Afghan War, and the war on terrorism and 3.9–4.0 percent of the U.S. GDP. The direct costs of the Iraq War alone represented something approaching 10–20 percent of the U.S. defense budget during the period, 3–5 percent of the federal budget, and less than 1 percent of the GDP.[44]

However, as the previous analysis has just shown, the United States already faces potential challenges that could individually or collectively stretch U.S. forces far beyond the military and economic burdens imposed by the Iraq War. There are three obvious cases in point:

- One is the risk of nuclear proliferation in Iran, the potential impact of a nuclear conflict involving Israel, or the use of nuclear weapons in the Gulf—a region with more than 60 percent of the world's proven conventional oil reserves and nearly 40 percent of its proven gas reserves.

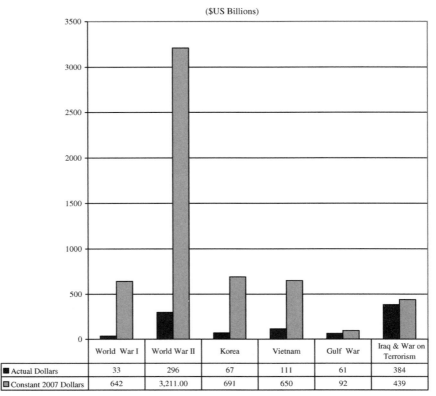

Source: Adapted by the author from data provided by the Congressional Research Service as quoted in Defense News, May 8, 2006, p. 3.

Figure 2.13   The Cost of American Wars

- The second is a conflict in the Taiwan Strait, which would involve very different forces and force development priorities from the war in Iraq, and it would lead to very different kinds of a strategic aftermath. It could push the United States and China into a kind of enduring strategic competition where the real-world impact of the law of untended consequences would make the cost of Iraq seem minor by comparison.

- A war in Korea would be very different from the war on terrorism, the war in Iraq, and a Taiwan Strait conflict. It also would now involve the United States in a major regional conflict in which an allied government and allied forces would have the lead role, and it would require a different kind of alliance warfare and interoperability.

The United States needs to fight smart as well as with its wealth, particularly in a world where major rival economic powers and blocs are emerging that can compete with the United States. The Iraq War is simply one more warning that the United States must structure its strategy and plans to deal with the probability that its strategy and plans will often be wrong as well as right. Military capabilities will always

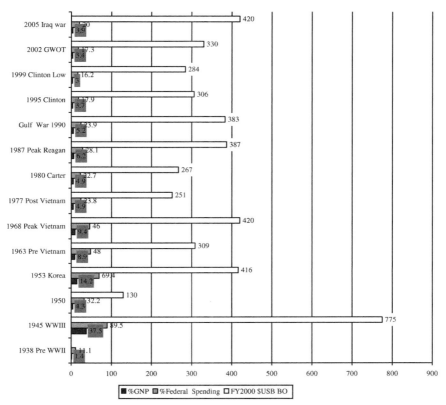

Source: Office of the Under Secretary of Defense (Comptroller), National Defense Budget Estimates for FY2006, Washington, Department of Defense, April 2005, Table 7-2, and National Defense Budget Estimates for FY2007, March 2006, Table 7-2. Budget total is for entire national defense, not just the Department of Defense.

Figure 2.14   National Defense Spending in Constant Dollars and as a Percent of GNP and Total Federal Spending in Previous Conflicts and Crises (Total Federal Outlays)

need to be more flexible than today's thinking and events can justify, and efforts to find some critical minimum level of forces and defense expenditures will inevitably create forces that are inadequate. No matter how well one reads one's cards, the wild card will often be the most important card in the deck.

STRATEGY, GRAND STRATEGY, AND OVERSTRETCH

This need to plan for contingencies very different from Iraq, and for a wide range of uncertainties which include future wars similar to the struggle in Iraq and Afghanistan, forces the United States to make hard choices. The United States needs to decide very clearly what global strategy it intends to pursue in the future before it decides whether it faces overstretch in any given area of its forces. The strategy and force posture the United States chooses must both fit its resources and be one that it has high confidence in to actually be implemented from initial engagement to "victory," as defined by achieving U.S. political and grand strategic goals and not simply as by defeating enemy forces. It is equally clear that such a strategy must involve hard choices about the role of friends and allies:

- If the United States does plan to change nations by force, and do so without massive native or Coalition support, it needs a fundamentally different force posture. The Iran invasion scenario is a case in point.
- If it intends to work with a local ally and have the ally assume the burden, then it needs to plan accordingly. The Korea scenario is an example.
- If it intends to fight a regional war without using force to change the regime, the nation building and stability burden does not exist. The Taiwan Strait is this kind of scenario.
- If it intends only to conduct nation building and stability in small, weak nations, the issues are still different, and Afghanistan and Liberia are cases in point.

It is all too easy for a nation as powerful as the United States to forget that there are many parts of the world where it may have some strategic and economic "interests," but where these do not create any compelling need for military involvement. Americans do not think in terms of deliberate "strategic indifference" or "strategic neglect"—the process of triage where they carefully assess the engagements they should avoid.

The United States also needs to remember that it is often far better to rely on allies and friends than take the lead. In the past, the United States has relied heavily on other states to handle local security missions and has used arms transfers, arms sales, and advisory efforts to create regional stability. The United States has rarely, however, seen such efforts as part of its own force sizing, force planning, and force transformation process. The same has been true of U.S. diplomacy and economic strategy. The United States may be a global superpower, but it does not really shape its military strategy in global terms; it prefers to rely on American military power and military presence.

Since the start of the Bush Administration, the United States has also become increasingly impatient with deterrence, co-option, and compellence, as distinguished from warfighting. This emphasis on confrontation and intervention is one the United States needs to reverse. During the Cold War, the United States understood that it could not size its forces, or create war plans, that could win an actual strategic exchange with the Soviet Union. It understood that it faced similar problems in fighting theater-wide war in Europe with the Warsaw Pact, and that either a conventional or theater nuclear conflict would be a disaster. The same reality has long existed in the Korean Peninsula.

The end of the Cold War, however, left the United States the world's preeminent military power. The United States went from an era of existential threats that united the West to an era of largely optional limited wars in other regions. This, in turn, has led at least some Americans to place a growing emphasis on unilateral or U.S.–dominated strategies that involve direct warfighting and intervention. The United States has already shown it was unwilling to continue a strategy of "containment" in dealing with Iraq. While most U.S. military planners show great caution in talking about the use of military force, some American politicians and analysts now talk of strikes on Iran, or conflicts with states like Syria, rather than about how to use U.S. military power to achieve U.S. strategic goals without actual fighting.

Since the Cold War, U.S. policy makers and the U.S. military have been too ready to make an overt use of force. They sometimes seem to have forgotten the fact that deterring war while achieving U.S. strategic goals is the superior grand strategy and the best "force multiplier." They have been equally slow to make conflict termination and to see stability operations and nation building as a vital part of the mission. If war is the only option, shaping the battle to achieve the right conflict termination and peace will always be as important as defeating the enemy. Managing the aftermath of conflict termination—which may well involve stability operations, nation building, and/or a lingering counterinsurgency or counterterrorism campaign—is often the only way to give war strategic purpose and meaning.

The United States has been slow to see the potential strategic cost of any direct competition with China or a conflict over the Taiwan Strait. It has not coupled its efforts to check North Korea with equal efforts to keep South Korea as an effective partner. It has been so enmeshed in its war on terrorism that it has not understood the risks and complications of becoming involved in Central Asia, and in Russia and China's backyard.

Legitimate European security concerns are treated more as outside interference than as problems in preserving a vital structure of alliances. The need to avoid or minimize long-term strategic competition has been subordinated by military interventionism—even when it is not clear whether such intervention creates nearly as many, or more, problems than it solves. U.S. policy makers confuse military power with the ability to control the course of events and ignore the "law of unintended consequences."

Americans should remember that Iraq is only one example of U.S. failures in planning and executing a war. American strategic and grand strategic blunders had a high cost in the Korean and Vietnamese wars and in terminating the Gulf War in 1991. They have been costly in smaller actions like Haiti, Lebanon, and Somalia. Neither U.S. policy makers nor the U.S. military had a plan for ending the Gulf War in 1991. The United States did not blunder into the Balkans, and Bosnia and Kosovo, but neither did it have clear plans to end the use of military force or deal with the aftermath. Haiti and Somalia provide further examples of the inability to link the use of military strength to both strategy and nation building.

If the problems raised by the Iraq War teach any one overarching lesson, it is this: the requirement is to make U.S. strategy realistic and successful, not that the United States should make greater efforts to disengage from the world. Too much U.S. restraint can just as easily create as many problems as pursuing ill-planned and ideological strategic fantasies. The kind of strategic vacuum that would almost inevitably result would then be filled with instability and violence. America cannot afford a strategy of denial—rejecting the need to develop U.S. military capabilities to deal with any key aspect of a probable mission until it is forced upon it. Planning only for the parts of war the United States wants to fight, rather than for burdens like conflict termination and nation building, means the United States cannot achieve all of its grand strategic objectives and is virtually certain to find American forces unready for reality as it evolves in the field. It also will almost inevitably mean the "overstretch" of a major part of U.S. forces because they will not have been prepared for the entire warfighting mission.

This does not mean the United States will not need to use force in the future. The world is not a kind or gentle place and is not becoming one. As the new Quadrennial Defense Review correctly declares, the United States faces new asymmetric threats, new forms of proliferation, new kinds of insurgents and terrorists, and a growing dependence on a global economy. The United States can never ignore the need for actual warfighting, and fighting in unpredictable conflicts for reasons that no one foresaw before they started. If Iraq provides lessons about strategic overstretch, they are rather that U.S. policy makers must insist that U.S. policies and plans include an assessment of the costs and risks of the entire war—including nation building and stability operations—and provide detailed operational plans from conflict preparation to final termination.

Challenge Two: Determining the Level of Burden That Defense Should Put on the National Economy and Federal Spending

America needs to conduct a much broader examination of what it must really spend to remain the world's preeminent superpower, and it must make wiser and more decisive choices about its national priorities. The United States has no guarantee that it will not fight serious conventional wars, fight more serious forms of asymmetric war, or confront periods like the one it faces today where it has three simultaneous conflicts: Afghanistan, Iraq, and the global "war on terrorism."

The United States must closely examine the resources it spends on defense for several key reasons:

- It badly needs to create more effective tools for linking strategy, force plans, programs, and budgets.
- It needs to understand what the Iraq War, the Afghan War, and the war on terrorism do and do not explain about the overall adequacy of U.S. defense resources.
- It needs to examine the overall stress that defense spending puts on the federal budget and the gross domestic product (GDP) in both wartime and peace.
- It should consider whether defense spending is the main challenge in terms of priorities for federal or social spending or whether on a national level there are actually major greater strains that may argue for major shifts in resources to higher priority areas like defense.

UNDERSTANDING THE CHALLENGE OF RESOURCES

Strategy, force plans, and technology seem to have a level of glamor that makes the details of money, manpower, and other resource issues seem boring by comparison.

Strategy, force plans, and technology almost inevitably receive far more attention than planning and managing resources, and far too often the focus on strategies, force plans, and weapons means little attention is paid to their real-world affordability and cost. Even the best plans have little practical value unless they are affordable and are properly funded. Strategy, tactics, doctrine, and force transformation plans are meaningless unless they are actually executed, and the limiting factor is almost always resources.

These problems are compounded by an archaic method of reporting defense spending and managing the details of defense budgets that make it difficult to impossible to tie most defense spending data to the ability to execute a given strategy or force plan. The United States provides a flood of data on military spending, but most of this apparent transparency has severe limits and many of the data are totally dysfunctional in showing what forces or missions cost—much less whether the resources provided are adequate.

Figure 3.1 shows the two major ways in which the United States categorizes its defense budget. The first is by major type of spending—the so-called input budget. The second is a list of categories used in the so-called program budget—categories that have nothing to do with real-world missions and capabilities and are little more than an intellectual farce.

Input Budgeting: Helping Pork and Earmarks at the Expense of the Nation

The first series of input budget categories would have far more value in planning, programming, and budgeting if they could be tied to major force components, missions, and commands. They would then provide some picture of how the United

Figure 3.1   Major Categories in the U.S. Defense Budget

Input Budget	Program Budget
Military Personnel	Strategic Forces
Retired Pay	General Purpose Forces
Operations and Maintenance	C3, Intelligence, and Space
Procurement	Mobility Forces
Research, Development, Test, and Evaluation	Guard & Reserve Forces
Military Construction	Research and Development
Family Housing	Central Supply and Maintenance
Revolving and Management Funds	Training, Medical, and Other
Special Foreign Currency	Administration and Associated Expenditures
Offsetting Receipts	Support of Other Nations
Trust Funds	Special Operations Forces
Interfund Transfers	Undistributed

Source: Table 6-4 and Table 6-8, *National Defense Budget Estimates for FY2007,* Office of the Under Secretary of Defense (Comptroller), March 2006.

States is allocating resources to create given kinds of military and warfighting capabilities. They would be particularly valuable if they could be tied to the cost of the major unified and specified commands, the cost of major combat units, and major types of forces in ways that allowed the rapid examination of the cost of alternative plans and strategies, future force costs, and all of the other major "what ifs" needed for effective defense planning and management.

In practice, however, no such review takes place within the Department of Defense or the Executive Branch. Spending is reviewed largely by input category with no real linkage to strategy, plans, and programs. The Department of Defense budgets in this way because it has done so in the past, because it has never modernized its budgeting and accounting practices, and because it has separated its comptroller functions from programming and systems analysis. Its budgeting processing is a cumbersome, ill-coordinated, management nightmare focused far more on accounting needs and fiscal control than on making U.S. forces effective. Accounting is not properly automated, standardized, or structured to examine strategy and alternative force plans, and it focuses on tens of thousands of line item categories that cannot be broken down by force element, command, or mission.

Secretary Robert McNamara failed to fix this budgeting and accounting disaster in the early 1960s, and no Secretary since has had the courage or competence to even attempt serious further reform. The failure to effectively link planning and programming to budgeting has left a major gap in planning and management capability, compounded by the failure to force the services and defense agencies to standardize on a single automated accounting system capable of being used for near real-time planning and programming purposes.

The problem is further compounded by the fact the Congress insists on reviewing such costs on a defense-wide basis for the total budget for only one year in the future and concentrates far more on the needs of constituents and special interests than on the overall strategic needs of the United States. The Congressional review of the defense budget has many defects, including a time-consuming process of hearings and far too many committees with overlapping jurisdiction. The main problem, however, is that most Congressional action to change the defense budget focuses on supporting the interests or "hobbies" of major committee leaders, parochial interests and add-ons in the form of special interest "pork," and sometimes what is little more than legalized corruption.

Even the two armed services committees in the Senate and the House do little to review the program budget or links between strategy, programming, and budgeting in any meaningful detail. Hearings on these issues are largely exercises in political visibility with little substantive impact on force plans and major programs. The two major appropriations committees do little more than serve party and personal interests by raising or cutting given items in the next year's budget.

This process culminates in closed markup sessions in each committee that are kept secret largely to disguise the degree to which members seek their own personal goals or "earmarks" of the budget for political, constituent, and purely selfish ends. They are followed by similar meetings between the Senate and House committees. The end result can sometimes serve the national interest, but it is far more likely to be parochial and compound the problems in the original budget submission.

As a case in point, Congressional action on the FY2007 defense budget was no different in this respect than that of any other year in recent memory. The four major Authorizations and Appropriations Committees in the House and the Senate made hundreds of program changes that served the interests of members, but did little or nothing to alter strategy, force plans, or the procession of force transformation. As from some minor adjustments in end strength, the major changes in the line item budget moved money largely to pay for Congressional earmarks affecting procurements and member ties to defense industries.[1]

Program Budgeting: A Vacuous Farce

Even a glance at the program budget categories in Figure 3.1 shows that most are meaningless. Virtually all real-world military capability is buried in a meaningless category called "General Purpose Forces." This is a heading that even one of its key creators came to call "No Purpose Forces" and felt that it had to be divided into major unified and specified commands by the mid-1960s.

"Strategic Forces" has become almost meaningless since the end of the Cold War. "Strategic" to do what? Located where? Consisting of what? Being transformed to do what? For more than a decade, Strategic Forces have largely performed regional or theater tactical missions.

The heading for Special Forces is more the product of the personal "hobby" of past Congressmen and a single Secretary of Defense than something that can be related to a given mission, but it is the only category that now comes close to explaining how one aspect of the defense budget is spent to buy a given type of military category. As for the other categories shown in Figure 3.1, they have no meaningful relation to strategy, planning, or programming. They are simply a warmed-over form of input budgeting.

Abdicating Real-World Responsibility for Managing Resources

The need to restructure this approach to programming and budgeting to provide a real-world capability to link strategy and force planning to both immediate budget costs and future program costs has been obvious for decades. The repeated failure of various Secretaries of Defense to act on this need helps explain why the latest Quadrennial Defense Review (QDR) is one more milestone in a long line of well-intentioned failures to link American strategy to implementable force plans and practical program budgets.

There is nothing new about the challenge of matching strategy and plans to resources. Generations of U.S. defense officials have talked about fixing the U.S. defense planning, programming, and budgeting system (PPBS), but the current system still has all the same flaws it did when it was formed under Secretary Robert McNamara in the early 1960s.

Nearly half a century after the U.S. defense PPBS was created, most of the "programs" in the U.S. program budget are categorized in ways that have little or no practical meaning in terms of key missions. It is far more a crude budgeting tool than a planning or programming tool, and its future-year defense plan (FYDP) is heavily decoupled from both U.S. military force plans, civilian force transformation efforts, and the real-world costs of future procurement plans and programmed force changes.

However, the problems in the way the United States shapes and reports on defense spending go far beyond military taxonomy and the nature of the data presented. Planning, programming, and budgeting have little meaning unless they are executed efficiently within the planned level of funding and costs. The PPBS and the budgeting effort have also become one of the most inefficient bureaucratic nightmares in human history. The ability to formulate the FYDP has become steadily more cumbersome and time-consuming in spite of computers, word processors, and countless efforts to improve and integrate the Department's accounting and budgeting systems.

It is the ability to create plans and management tools that ensure plans are affordable; however, that has proven to be the most serious problem the United States has in managing its defense resources. As the following chapters show, the Department of Defense has an appalling record in costing its forces, particularly major force changes and major new procurement programs. In case after case, the Department has to make drastic cutbacks in some aspects of its force or procurement plans, but such exercises in "cost containment" at best are exercises in living with failure after the fact.

The United States does not effectively program or manage defense spending. It lets costs escalate to the crisis point and then either reduces program costs to fit its budget goals or increases expenditures on a crash basis. It manages by correcting past failures. When major equipment purchases or force transformations finally escalate too much in cost, the level of activity is cut back to fit the budget, or parts of the spending are slipped into future years. The Department has a long history of compensating for undercosted plans by not fully executing the plan or entirely canceling the program. In fact, every major Department of Defense procurement and force transformation plan has been subject to such cuts or deferrals for at least the last quarter century. American defense plans simply do not survive engagement with reality.

There are several other techniques for managing through failure that the Department uses to reduce the burden of defense spending and that compound its future problems in bringing plans into balance with resources. One is to defer spending during wartime or periods of peak spending in areas like maintenance, housing, construction, and every other area where it is possible to put spending off for several years. Another is to play with the annual flow of spending on major programs so they do not appear in the current year's outlays and become visible in terms of their impact on the overall budget deficit. Still another is to slip major spending on new procurement or forces beyond the tenure of the current President or the period of the FYDP. This "slipping expenditure to the right" either forces the next President to make hard decisions about cutting programs or increasing spending or hides the full budget impact of defense plans from the Office of Management and Budget and the Congress.

FIGHTING WEALTHY RATHER THAN FIGHTING SMART: THE COST OF U.S. DEFENSE EFFORTS

Fortunately, the United States has been able to buy its way out of its incompetence in managing defense resources. Fighting on the strength of its wealth, rather than fighting smart, has helped in the past. Some of the cost containment problems put on U.S. forces have been eased by the fact that U.S. defense budgets have risen steadily in recent years, compounded by the ability to use wartime budget supplementals to pay for a host of planning and management mistakes. This rise has been far smaller in constant dollars than in current dollars, and defense costs have continued to escalate more quickly than resources, but throwing more money at the problem does conceal a multitude of evils and mistakes.

Department of Defense Spending: Supplementals

The data in Figure 3.2 show the trends in past and projected national security spending by the Department of Defense. They show the recent trends in U.S. defense spending in current and constant FY2006 dollars and the new authority to spend incurred in a given year (Budget Authority or BA), which may actually be spent over a period of future years, and the actual money that will be obligated from the federal budget in a given fiscal year (Budget Outlays or BO).[2]

Such figures provide a good gross estimate of the cost of U.S. defense burdens, although they do not include such other national security spending as the cost of programs in the Department of Energy, some aspects of intelligence, homeland security efforts by civilian agencies, and some aspects of pensions.

The data that project future spending also conceal the cost of most wartime expenditures, and an increasing number of programs with no direct links to war, which have recently been paid for using the budget supplementals mentioned in the previous chapter. These budget additions authorized by Congress, and included in the actual spending totals through FY2007 in Figure 3.3, amounted to $19.8 billion in FY2001, $17.3 billion in FY2002, $72.6 billion in FY2003, $65.3 billion in FY2004, $75.9 billion in FY2005, $65.8 billion in FY2006, and will total at least $60 billion in FY2007.[3]

They will almost certainly be far higher in the future. Reports surfaced in November and December 2006 that the total cost of FY2007 supplementals could climb to $100 to $128 billion—driven by the need to fund a major backlog of readiness problems and the fact that the Afghan and Iraq wars were lasting far longer than budget planners had funded in the baseline budget request.[4]

Congress and honest defense planners and programmers have every reason to distrust funding wars through emergency supplementals and so-called "bridge funds"

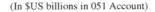

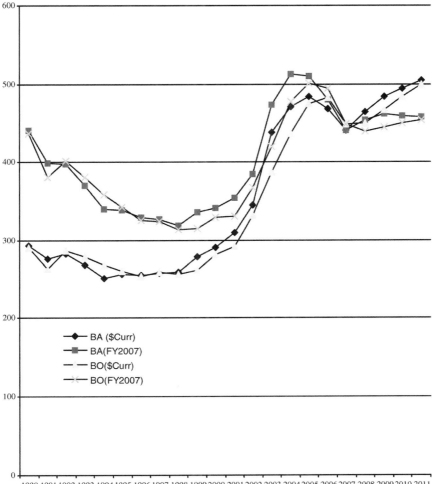

Source: Adapted by Anthony H. Cordesman from data provided by Office of the Under Secretary of Defense (Comptroller), "National Defense Budget Estimates for FY2006", Washington, Department of Defense, March 2006, Table 1.1 and 1.2.

Figure 3.2   Department of Defense Expenditures since the End of the Cold War: FY1990–FY2011

that bridge the gap between appropriations bills or between appropriations bills and supplementals. No one can precisely plan, program, and budget for a war, but this is no excuse not to try. National policy should be made on the basis of clear projections of the overall cost of national security, including ongoing wars.

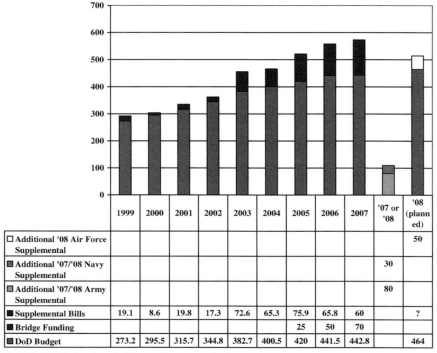

	1999	2000	2001	2002	2003	2004	2005	2006	2007	'07 or '08	'08 (planned)
☐ Additional '08 Air Force Supplemental											50
▣ Additional '07/'08 Navy Supplemental										30	
▣ Additional '07/'08 Army Supplemental										80	
▪ Supplemental Bills	19.1	8.6	19.8	17.3	72.6	65.3	75.9	65.8	60		?
▪ Bridge Funding							25	50	70		
▣ DoD Budget	273.2	295.5	315.7	344.8	382.7	400.5	420	441.5	442.8		464

Note: The DoD budget figure includes nuclear-weapons funds.

Source: Adapted by the author from data provided by the Office of Management and Budget as quoted in *Defense News*, 6 November 2006: 3.

Figure 3.3   When You Truly and Sincerely Cannot or Will Not Plan: The Growing Impact of Budget Supplementals (in $U.S. Billions)

    Instruments like supplementals and bridge funds provide for far less Congressional and public scrutiny over how the money will be spent. For instance, supplementals must be approved by appropriations committees, but not by authorizing committees. Defense budgets must be approved by both.[5] More generally, the Department of Defense finds it easier to hide a failure to fully fund all of the needs of the military, bury potentially unpopular expenditures in unfamiliar areas, and conceal the deferral of key aspects of readiness like major depot repairs. It also becomes difficult to develop effective multiyear programs and budget requests.

    There are political problems as well. Emergency spending bills usually directly fund troops in the field. Lawmakers from both parties are hard-pressed to vote against them and appear weak on defense. Supplemental funding does not count against spending limits set by the Office of Management and Budget or against limits that Congress imposes on itself each year.[6]

    At another level, reliance on supplementals and bridge funds reflects a fundamental failure to lead on the part of the Secretary of Defense and the Joint Chiefs. War planning requires constant efforts to bring budget requests and the FYDP to the proper level to both fund current operations and preserve longer-term readiness, manpower, modernization, and the key elements of force transformation.

Once again, political expediency comes at the cost of effective planning and budgeting. It means that the true costs of war are disguised and key spending efforts are omitted or slipped far too far into the future. The entire defense program slides out of balance, and no serious effort is made to plan and budget for what are "long wars." Emergency supplementals are inevitable in major conflicts. Relying on supplementals and unrealistic budget requests and baseline programs and FDYP proper planning and management disguise the true cost of war and makes the effective planning and funding of America's defense posture impossible.

Congress has been correct in putting increasing pressure on the Executive Branch to include such costs in its formal budget submissions, rather than financing wars with emergency supplemental appropriations and bridge funds. While the 2007 Defense Authorization Act authorized $532.8 billion in defense spending and included a $70-billion bridge fund in partial payment for the wars in Iraq and Afghanistan, Section 1008 of the Act stated that the President's—and hence the DoD's—budget for each fiscal year, after fiscal year 2007, shall include the following:

1. A request for the appropriation of funds for such fiscal year for ongoing military operations in Afghanistan and Iraq,

2. An estimate of all funds expected to be required in that fiscal year for such operations, and

3. A detailed justification of the funds requested.

But no law prevents the President from submitting proposals for supplemental funding, and Congress has often been grossly irresponsible in adding pork and a host of unnecessary spending activities to the original request. In truth, for the political reasons outlined above, as Steven Kosiak of the Center for Strategic and Budgetary Assessments said, "there are lots of incentives to put things in supplementals" and very few not to.[7]

Unfortunately, this situation is more likely to get worse in the near future than to get better. President George W. Bush indicated in a "signing statement" released when he signed the 2007 Defense Authorization Act on October 17, 2006, that he may or may not abide by the provisions in Section 1008. As of November 2006, the DoD had already begun assembling unprecedented supplemental requests for 2007 and 2008.

Moreover, the failure to include predictable costs in the baseline budget request was growing worse and not better. In an October 25, 2006, memo, Gordon England, Deputy Defense Secretary, indicated that the Pentagon would allow the services to use 2007 supplemental funding for any "efforts related to the Global War on Terrorism, and not strictly limited" to wars in Iraq and Afghanistan.[8] Unfortunately, the Executive Branch will be naturally reluctant to check its supplemental spending binge as long as supplementals offer the promise of "easy money" and help reduce political resistance to raising spending.

Department of Defense Spending: 050 and 051 Accounts

The analysis of U.S. defense spending is further complicated by the fact that the United States does not include most homeland defense and other internal security spending in its defense budget, and it uses two different totals for defense spending. The first total, called the 051 account, covers spending only by the Department of Defense. The second, called the 050 account, includes spending by the Department of Energy on defense-related items like nuclear weapons and limited transfers from other agencies. This spending adds from $20 billion to $24 billion a year to Department of Defense budget authority and budget outlays and is planned to average about $20–billion during FY2007–FY2011.

Figure 3.2 has focused on Department of Defense spending and shows the 051 account, because this provides the best picture of how U.S. strategy, force plans, programs, and budgets are being shaped. In spite of the limitations in the data, the spending trends and estimates in Figure 3.2 illustrate several important points:

- The rise in real defense expenditures is much smaller than the trends in current dollars indicate. There is a tendency to focus on current dollars, but such rises are never a particularly meaningful measure of the burden defense spending imposes or of the real resources available. In fact, if one looks at the longer-term pattern in outlays—which is the key measure of the burden on the budget—the levels programmed for 2007–2010 are not higher than the spending in constant dollars during the Vietnam War (FY1968 and FY1969) or during peak peacetime spending before the end of the Cold War (FY1986–FY1988).9

- While U.S. budget outlays and authority differ from year to year, they generally follow a consistent pattern. From the viewpoint of measuring defense resources, or overstretch, the trends in one type of spending are generally valid in shaping the other.

- The spending through FY2004 consists of "actual" spending (figures can be revised in minor ways for several years later). The sudden peak shown for FY2003–FY2007 reflects both a planned increase in spending by the Bush Administration and the impact of unprogrammed and unanticipated spending on the Iraq War. This sudden rise is scarcely a minor amount. At the same time, one needs to be careful about talking about any strain or overstretch coming from such wartime spending. Even the peaks remain close to the levels the United States spent during the Cold War when there was no conflict at all.

- The future-year defense plan for FY2007–FY2011 presents several problems for future-year spending. Out-year costs legitimately do not include what is not yet planned and programmed and undercost current forces and capabilities by definition. The data shown, however, are far less realistic than usual. They do not include any estimate of the future costs of the Iraq and Afghan wars, which have been left to budget supplementals that will cost $120 billion more in FY2007 alone.

- As will be discussed later in more detail, these totals do not reflect anything approaching the real-world cost of the force transformations and new weapons systems and equipment the Department is counting on. This is partly because the Department includes only "known" expenditures in its forecasts. For decades, however, the main problems in such underestimates have been budgeting tricks that slip much of the main wave of such spending for the years beyond the budget projections and by perpetually undercosting procurement and research and development.

At this point in time, the out-year data the Department of Defense is using to estimate future defense costs are so meaningless that it is hard to do more than guess at how much the United States will really spend as long as the wars in Afghanistan and Iraq last. The unfortunate reality is that it is far easier to analyze the adequacy of past defense spending—and the extent to which it places a burden on the federal budget and economy—than the impact of current and probable spending in war time (where a reliance on supplementals means the Department fails to attempt to cost ongoing conflicts) or future spending involving major force shifts or new procurements.

Total Defense Spending

Figure 3.4 supplements Figure 3.2 and provides a more comprehensive estimate of the possible trends in future total defense spending, as calculated by both the Department of Defense and the Congressional Budget Office (CBO). The DoD figures compare both the projections the Department of Defense makes for its own expenditures (051) and the national total of defense-related spending by other agencies like the Department of Energy (050). CBO estimates are similar to the DoD estimates, but the CBO projects through 2016, which provides a more realistic period for forecasting future defense spending, given the long periods necessary to implement force transformation and major procurement programs.

Aside from some major procurement expenditures, however, these spending projections are essentially "business as usual" projections of the peacetime costs of current forces. The DoD and CBO estimates do not attempt to project the future costs of the Iraq War and cannot compensate for the undercosting of major defense procurements and force changes. The CBO estimate of the cost of civilian spending on homeland defense is also shown separately from defense spending since it is not normally counted as part of military spending.

The data also show estimated budget outlays, not authorized funding in years. Neither estimate deals with the probable cost of ongoing wars, the issue of force transformation, or attempts to estimate the cost of the changes recommended in the national strategy, QDR, and service strategies. Neither is linked to a realistic analysis of the cost of present force plans. As such, neither provides a realistic basis for the level of overstretch in spending, and the level of burden on federal spending and gross national product (GNP).

As such, the trends in Figure 3.4 show that current defense spending projections based on Department of Defense forecasts do little more than provide a broad

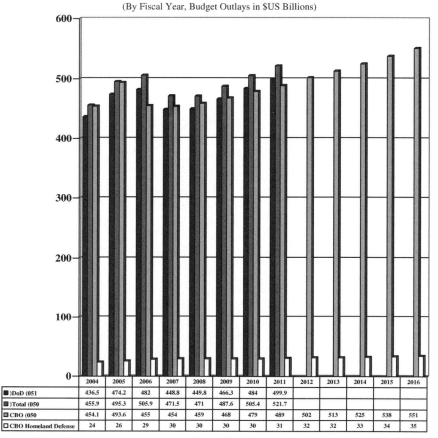

(By Fiscal Year, Budget Outlays in $US Billions)

	2004	2005	2006	2007	2008	2009	2010	2011	2012	2013	2014	2015	2016
■)DoD (051	436.5	474.2	482	448.8	449.8	466.3	484	499.9					
■)Total (050	455.9	495.3	505.9	471.5	471	487.6	505.4	521.7					
▨ CBO (050	454.1	493.6	455	454	459	468	479	489	502	513	525	538	551
□ CBO Homeland Defense	24	26	29	30	30	30	30	31	32	32	33	34	35

Source: Office of the Under Secretary of Defense (Comptroller), National Defense Budget Estimates for FY2006, Washington, Department of Defense, March 2006, Table 1-1 and 1-2; and Congressional Budget Office, "An Analysis of the President's Budgetary Proposals for FY2006, Washington, CBO, March 2005, Table 1-6. For detailed CBO projections by major area of activity, see "The Long-Term Implications of Current Defense Plans and Alternatives: Summary Update for Fiscal Year 2007." Congressional Budget Office, October 2006.

Figure 3.4   Patterns in Future Department of Defense and U.S. National Security Spending: FY2004–FY2016

illustration of current estimates of future trends, and little insight into the future. This is made even clearer in other work done by the CBO. It has made other forecasts of U.S. defense spending through 2024. These forecasts indicate that the Department of Defense's plans, which do not include the war costs now in supplementals, would average about $492 billion in outlays in FY2007 dollars from 2012 to 2024, about 12 percent more than the obligational authority that the Bush Administration requested for FY2007. If, however, the higher-than-average risk of war is added in, the CBO estimates that the average cost could be $560 billion a year, or 27 percent higher that the FY2007 request.[10] This is a clear warning as to just how uncertain the future can really be.

THE CURRENT BURDEN OF U.S. DEFENSE SPENDING

The current trends in U.S. defense spending can be interpreted in several ways. One way is to focus on the fact that U.S. military spending has risen sharply since FY2000 and may well exceed $500 billion a year in constant dollars indefinitely into the future. As the previous chapter has shown, the United States has found that the cost of fighting asymmetric wars in Iraq and Afghanistan has been far higher than the Department of Defense had planned. The United States will either have to increase spending in the future or cut some aspect of U.S. defense programs. As the chapters that follow show, the United States also faces major problems in funding current force transformation and procurement programs that require either significant force cuts or additional spending.

At the same time, it is important to note that Americans need to be careful about talking about overstretch in ways that imply that the current level of total defense spending reflects the limits on U.S. capability to fund America's strategic posture. Any discussion of overstretch must be based on a broad look at the patterns in federal spending and at what America can and cannot afford.

The trends in U.S. defense spending do not show that the United States is sharply increasing the level of spending as a percentage of total federal spending or as a burden on the U.S. economy. The risk in U.S. defense spending has been offset by major ground gaining in the U.S. economy, and the problems in U.S. defense spending are relatively minor in terms of the overall problems in federal spending and when compared to the problems raised by the rising cost of mandatory civil spending.

Currently projected spending puts only a limited burden on the total U.S. economy and federal spending. In 2006, the United States had a GNP of well over $11 trillion. The Bush Administration projected in its official budget submission to Congress for FY2007 that the United States would spend only 3.3 percent of its GDP for the DoD and 3.8 percent for all defense spending. Such estimates for FY2007 ignored wartime supplementals, but if one looks at actual spending that included such supplementals during FY2003–FY2006, the DoD accounted for 3.6–3.9 percent of all federal spending, and total defense spending accounted for 3.9–4.1 percent.[11]

The figures for federal spending reveal an equally limited strain on the total federal budget. The United States is now talking about annual budgets in excess of $2.4 trillion a year, and the Bush Administration budget for defense spending as a percent of total federal spending in FY2007 was projected at 16.2 percent for the DoD and 19.0 percent for all defense spending. If one looks at actual spending during FY2003–FY2006, the DoD accounted for 17.9–19.0 percent of all federal spending, and total defense accounted for 18.7–20.0 percent.[12]

As is true of all of the following comparisons and figures, these data are based on President Bush's FY2007 budget request. This means that they do not project the impact of bridging funds and budget supplementals that the Administration has not yet requested. In broad terms, however, Congress made so few changes to the President's FY2007 budget request in the FY2007 authorization and appropriations bills that they are an accurate representation of the current trends in both the U.S. defense budget and the overall federal budget.[13]

The Burden on the U.S. Economy

These burdens scarcely argue for an unusual burden or major overstretch in U.S. defense spending. Figure 3.5 shows the burden that national security expenditures have placed on the U.S. economy and gross national product during recent wars.

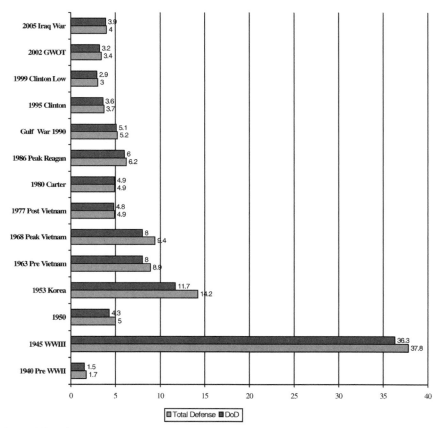

Source: Office of the Under Secretary of Defense (Comptroller), National Defense Budget Estimates for FY2007, Washington, Department of Defense, March 2006, Table 7-7, pp. 216-217. Budget Total is for entire national defense, and not just Department of Defense.

Figure 3.5   National Defense Spending as a Percent of GNP in Previous Conflicts and Crises (Total Federal Outlays)

In general, the development of the U.S. economy has at least kept pace with defense spending, in spite of the war on terrorism, the Afghan conflict, and the Iraq War.

Figures 3.6 and 3.7 expand this analysis and show that this percentage compares with a defense burden of 6–14 percent of the U.S. GNP during the Cold War. Historically, defense spending reached annual peaks of 38 percent of the GNP during World War II, 14 percent during the Korean War, 9.4 percent during Vietnam, and 6.2 percent during the Cold War following Vietnam.[14] The historical low in

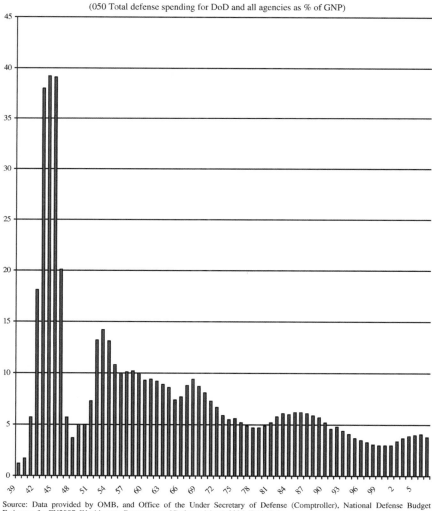

(050 Total defense spending for DoD and all agencies as % of GNP)

Source: Data provided by OMB, and Office of the Under Secretary of Defense (Comptroller), National Defense Budget Estimates for FY2007, Washington, Department of Defense, March 2006, Table 7-7.

Figure 3.6   National Defense Spending as a Percent of GDP: 1939–2007

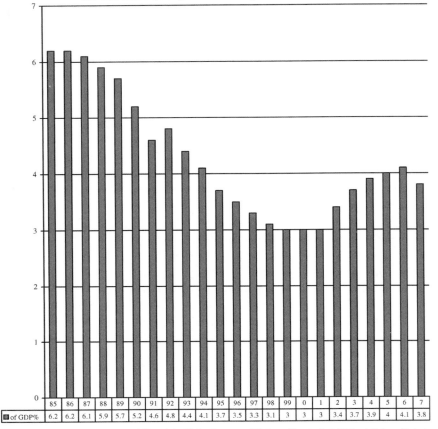

(050 Total defense spending for DoD and all agencies as % of GNP)

	85	86	87	88	89	90	91	92	93	94	95	96	97	98	99	0	1	2	3	4	5	6	7
■ of GDP%	6.2	6.2	6.1	5.9	5.7	5.2	4.6	4.8	4.4	4.1	3.7	3.5	3.3	3.1	3	3	3	3.4	3.7	3.9	4	4.1	3.8

Source: Data provided by OMB, and Office of the Under Secretary of Defense (Comptroller), National Defense Budget Estimates for FY2006, Washington, Department of Defense, April 2005, Table 1-1 and 1-2

Figure 3.7   Shift in National Defense Spending as a Percent of GNP since the End of the Cold War

the post–Cold War era reached 3.0 percent in FY1999–FY2001, but the average since 1992 has been around 3.6 percent. If one looks at the averages by decade, defense spending has so far placed a smaller burden on the U.S. economy than during any decade since 1940.[15]

The creation of professional forces and the end of conscription have also limited the burden on the labor force. The Bush Administration projects that the Department of Defense military and civilian manpower accounted for only 1.4 percent of the American work force in FY2006 and that Defense would account for 3.8 percent of the labor force if all defense-related industry is included.[16] A CBO study that looked at the economic burden imposed by the Department's current plans and baseline defense FYDP concluded that the percentage of the GDP spent on defense had declined from an average of 6 percent in 1980s to 3.8 percent in the 1990s, and would drop to 3 percent by 2011 and 2.3 percent by 2024.[17]

They compare with a Department of Defense total of 2.5–3.8 percent of the U.S. work force during the Cold War and annual peaks of 22 percent during World War II, 7.8 percent during the Korean War, 5.9 percent during Vietnam, and 3.3 percent during the Cold War following Vietnam.[18] If all defense-related labor in the Department and in the defense industry is counted, these percentages compare with 4.8–14 percent of the U.S. work force during the Cold War and annual peaks of 40 percent during World War II, 14 percent during the Korean War, 9.8 percent during Vietnam, and 6.1 percent during the Cold War following Vietnam.[19]

Such estimates are always uncertain, and past wars and crises have shown that they can change radically by the year. They reflect the current strategic and political conditions that would shape U.S. defense spending under current plans. They could become real only *if* U.S. defense plans were accurately costed, *if* defense costs were properly controlled, and *if* no further supplementals were required for Iraq, Afghanistan, an ongoing war on terrorism, and other future conflicts.

The U.S. Congress is increasingly more reluctant to approve supplemental funding and bridge funding for wars that are ongoing and whose costs are somewhat predictable, but this does not mean that the Department will present better or more realistic budgets. As discussed in the following chapters, it also seems virtually certain that the Department of Defense will not improve its consistent history of failing to accurately cost its plans or control escalation in the foreseeable future. The Department has already spent decades talking about such reforms and has made no meaningful progress in implementing them.

Nevertheless, even if U.S. defense expenditures rose to $750 billion a year, it would still be under the average level of economic burden that defense spending imposed during the Cold War when the United States was not fighting a conflict anywhere in the world.

The "worst-case" estimate for the cost of a peacetime U.S. force posture, based on current strategic needs and programs, would probably total no more than 7 percent of its GNP, even after a realistic estimate of force transformation costs. The actual burden could average several percent less. Is this really overstretch in any practical sense in today's world? It is certainly affordable in terms of the size of our economy. We know that the United States spent at similar or far greater levels for half a century. While the cost in wartime could be much higher, the issue then becomes the necessity of the war, and not the economic burden. If the war is necessary, it must be paid for. If the war is not necessary, it should not be fought. In any case, America has accepted sustained burdens well over 20 percent of its GDP in past wars.

The Burden on the Federal Budget

Another way to examine the possibility of overstretch is to look at the burden that maintaining an effective force posture would place on the federal budget. As might be expected, the past and current trends in U.S. defense spending as a percent of the federal budget exhibit much the same pattern as defense spending as a percent of GNP.

Figure 3.8 shows that this percentage has been far higher in past times of war or crisis. Figure 3.9 shows the decline in national security spending as a percentage of total federal spending since the end of the Cold War.

Current CBO projections of the U.S. budget and federal defense spending for FY2006–FY2015 indicate defense spending will make up around 18–20 percent of the federal budget. In practice, actual spending could be over 20 percent, but not drastically so, and this level has generally been higher for virtually all of the period since 1941:

- The projected FY2006 level is about 2 percent less than in 1992, when we were taking the "peace dividend" from the end of the Cold War.

- It is only about 2 percent lower as a share of the federal budget than during the lowest year for defense spending in the Clinton Administration.

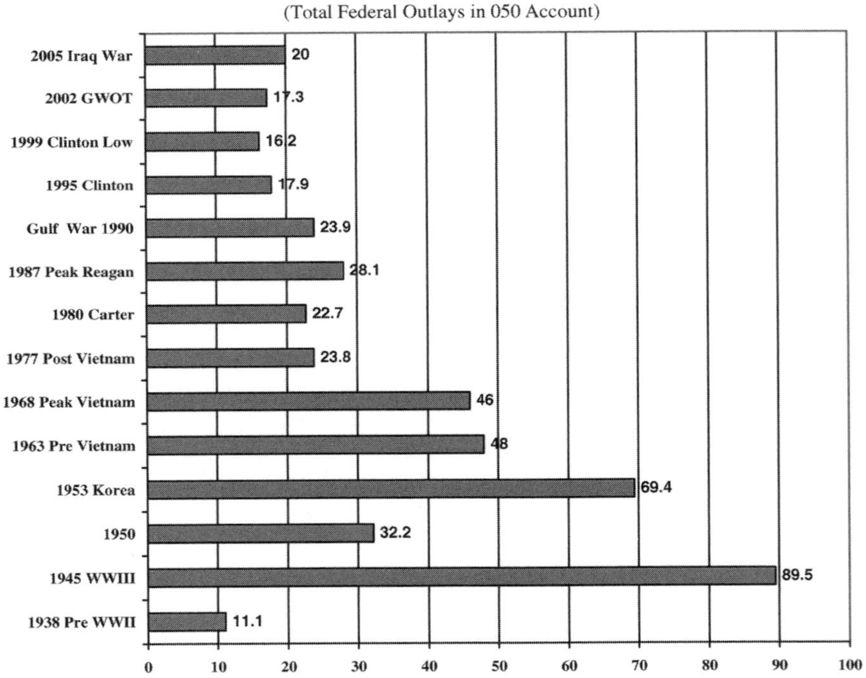

(Total Federal Outlays in 050 Account)

Year	Value
2005 Iraq War	20
2002 GWOT	17.3
1999 Clinton Low	16.2
1995 Clinton	17.9
Gulf War 1990	23.9
1987 Peak Reagan	28.1
1980 Carter	22.7
1977 Post Vietnam	23.8
1968 Peak Vietnam	46
1963 Pre Vietnam	48
1953 Korea	69.4
1950	32.2
1945 WWIII	89.5
1938 Pre WWII	11.1

Source: Office of the Under Secretary of Defense (Comptroller), National Defense Budget Estimates for FY2007, Washington, Department of Defense, March 2006, Table 7-7, pp. 216-217. Budget Total is for entire national defense, and not just Department of Defense.

Figure 3.8   National Defense Spending as a Percent of Total Federal Budget: 1939–2005

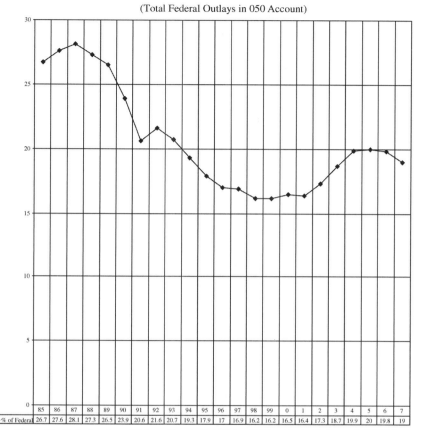

(Total Federal Outlays in 050 Account)

	85	86	87	88	89	90	91	92	93	94	95	96	97	98	99	0	1	2	3	4	5	6	7
◆ % of Federal	26.7	27.6	28.1	27.3	26.5	23.9	20.6	21.6	20.7	19.3	17.9	17	16.9	16.2	16.2	16.5	16.4	17.3	18.7	19.9	20	19.8	19

Source: Office of the Under Secretary of Defense (Comptroller), National Defense Budget Estimates for FY2007, Washington, Department of Defense, March 2007, Table 7-2; and Congressional Budget Office, "An Analysis of the President's Budgetary Proposals for FY2006, Washington, CBO, March 2005, Table 1-6.

Figure 3.9   Cuts in National Defense Spending as a Percent of Federal Budget since the End of the Cold War

- Once again, the Bush Administration's out-year projections for defense spending seem much too low. Some estimates put the spending levels necessary to buy current forces, required additional forces, and all the necessary transformational weapons systems and equipment at closer to $700 billion than some $550 billion. That still, however, is unlikely to push defense spending much above 21 percent of the federal budget.

THE RISING COST OF PROFESSIONALISM

Keeping the burden of defense spending at these levels has had a major impact on force strength, particularly on military and career civilian manpower. As has been touched upon earlier, the size of the U.S. active military has dropped significantly since the end of the Cold War. It has dropped from over 2 million in 1990 to less than 1.5 million in 2006—a drop of roughly 25 percent—in spite of an increase in the number of men and women in this total who have been deployed in actual military and warfighting assignments.

A similar drop has occurred in career Department of Defense civilians, which dropped from nearly 1 million in 1990 to under 700,000 in 2006—a drop of more than 30 percent.[20] The net result has been to reduce the total burden that DoD manpower has put on the national labor force from around 2.5 percent in 1990 to 1.4 percent in 2006.[21]

Trends in Total Defense Manpower Costs

As Figure 3.10 shows, however, more is involved in calculating total defense manpower than simply counting uniformed military and government civilians. The U.S.

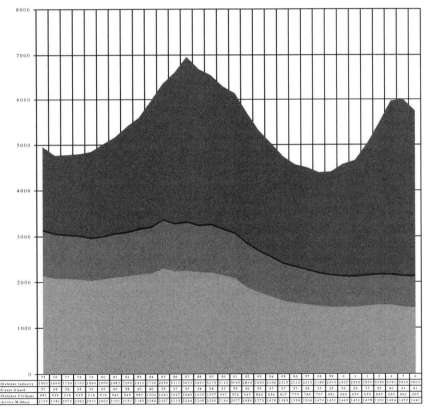

	75	76	77	78	79	80	81	82	83	84	85	86	87	88	89	90	91	92	93	94	95	96	97	98	99	0	1	2	3	4	5	6
■ Defense Industry	1800	1690	1730	1765	1860	1990	2085	2290	2415	2735	2980	3315	3625	3430	3225	3135	3045	2840	2620	2480	2315	2210	2115	2180	2240	2425	2520	2850	3285	3780	3850	3600
■ Coast Guard	37	38	38	38	39	39	40	38	40	40	38	37	39	38	38	37	39	39	37	37	35	35	33	36	36	37	39	40	41	41		
■ Defense Civilians	989	959	938	935	916	916	940	945	980	1009	1045	1027	1049	1010	1037	997	974	945	885	854	807	779	748	707	681	660	650	650	649	650	660	665
■ Active Military	2129	2081	2075	2062	2031	2063	2101	2130	2163	2184	2297	2233	2244	2209	2003	2144	2077	1880	1775	1678	1585	1538	1394	1476	1451	1449	1451	1478	1500	1494	1495	1441

Source: Office of the Under Secretary of Defense (Comptroller), National *Defense Budget Estimates for FY2006*, Washington, Department of Defense, April 2005, Table 7-6.

Figure 3.10   Trends in Defense Manpower (End Strength in Millions)

defense establishment has become steadily more dependent on contract employees. The number of employees in defense-related industries increased from 1.8 million in 1975 to 3.1 million in 1990 and to over 3.6 million by the mid-2000s. As a result, the total number of men and women in the military, civil service, and private sector related to defense remained far more constant than the drop in career military and government personnel would indicate. It dropped from around 6.3 million in 1990 to 5.7 million in 2006—a drop of roughly 10 percent. (These figures do not include the Coast Guard and foreign hires.)

The high level of defense industry employment has been sustained in part because of the high cost of an all-volunteer military and career civil servants. In effect, the United States has reduced the burden of career expenditures by going to what was supposed to be lower cost manpower in the public sector—although the postulated cost savings sometimes did not materialize or were more than offset by inefficiency. Unfortunately, the Department of Defense and the federal government do not report on total manpower costs, including civilians outside government—and there is no way to cost the overall impact of the manpower shift from a part-draft to an all-volunteer force structure, or the gross cost burden imposed on the nation by total defense-related manpower.

Trends in Military Manpower Costs

Figure 3.11 shows the DoD estimate of trends in military compensation per active-duty service member for FY2005–FY2011 *in current dollars* as presented in the President's budget request for FY2006. This figure includes both budget authority direct outlays on military personnel costs in the discretionary and entitlements budget in the 051 account. It does not include substantial indirect costs like family housing, which now total close to $4 billion a year.[22]

What is striking about Figure 3.11 is that it projects significant reductions in near-term defense manpower costs during FY2007–FY2008, which now seem very unlikely to be practical in wartime. These are followed by a steady rise in cost in the out-years after FY2008. This rise in spending, however, does not come from adding end strength, but rather from steadily rising costs per man or woman in service. Actual military end strength is projected to decline.

To put such projections in perspective, the annual cost of pay and training for the average active-duty soldier rose from $75,000 in 2001 to $120,000 in 2006. The cost per reservist rose from $17,000 a year in 2001 to $34,000.[23] This is a roughly 60-percent rise per active and a 100-percent rise per reservist. The problems in getting adequate recruiting and retention for the Army alone required the service to spend $735 million on retention bonuses in 2006 versus $85 million in 2003, and some $300 million more on recruiting in 2006 than it did in 2005.[24]

A related rise in the cost of entitlements and mandatory spending has sharply increased military manpower costs in ways that make it increasingly more difficult to pay for added end strength, and the CBO estimates a much higher estimate for total mandatory expenditures than the Department of Defense. For example,

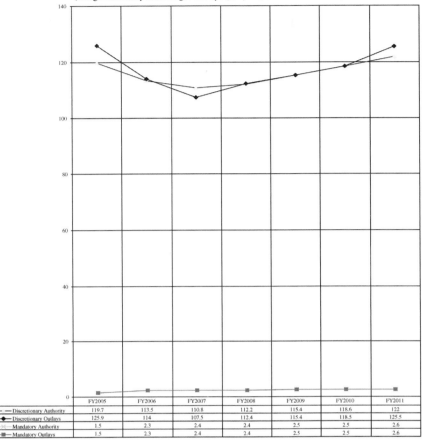

(Budget Authority and Budget Outlays (051) in $US Current Billions)

	FY2005	FY2006	FY2007	FY2008	FY2009	FY2010	FY2011
Discretionary Authority	119.7	113.5	110.8	112.2	115.4	118.6	122
Discretionary Outlays	125.9	114	107.5	112.4	115.4	118.5	125.5
Mandatory Authority	1.5	2.3	2.4	2.4	2.5	2.5	2.6
Mandatory Outlays	1.5	2.3	2.4	2.4	2.5	2.5	2.6

Source: Office of the Under Secretary of Defense (Comptroller), *National Defense Budget Estimates for FY2006*, Washington, Department of Defense, March 2006, Table I-10.

Figure 3.11   Trends in Military Manpower Costs: FY2005–FY2011

military health care and other medical spending has increased significantly. According to the CBO, during the 15-year period between 1988 and 2003 annual military medical spending nearly doubled, from $14.6 billion to $27.2 billion (in constant FY2003 dollars). During this same period, the size of the total active force decreased from 2.2 million personnel to 1.4 million, meaning that medical spending per active-duty service member increased 7.5 percent annually in real terms.[25]

Two key factors accounted for 40 percent of the medical spending increase during this period. First, the number of retirees and other dependents increased sharply relative to active-duty personnel because of the post–Cold War drawdown in troop levels. In 1988, 3.1 non-active-duty individuals for each active-duty service member were eligible for military medical benefits. By 2003 this figure had increased to 4.7. Second, accrual budgeting for the benefits of military retirees eligible for Medicare was introduced in 2003, which forces the future expense of medical care to be financially recognized in current budget documents.[26]

Military retirement and disability costs have also gone up. The CBO projects the cost of military manpower as rising sharply over the next decade. Its estimate of the total cost of mandatory military retirement and disability outlays was $39 billion in FY2005, rising to $55 billion in outlays in FY2016. The cost of mandatory veterans programs rose from $36 billion in FY2005 to $50 billion. This would bring the total cost of mandatory programs from $75 billion in FY2005 to $105 billion in FY2016—a rise of 40 percent. Similar data are not available for career defense civilians.[27]

As CBO studies note, these Department of Defense projections of manpower cost are unrealistic because they project significant cuts in end strength, savings in medical costs, and savings in housing and other costs. As a result, projections based on Department of Defense figures show that military personnel will consume a relatively constant percentage of the defense budget through FY2024. In practice, end strengths will be higher, and the cost of benefits and entitlements per soldier will continue to rise sharply in the future.[28] To put these differences in perspective, the Department of Defense projected that with its planned cuts in end strength, medical spending would rise by only $1.8 billion from FY2007 to FY2011 ($38.4 billion to $40.1 billion. The CBO projects that with the same manpower, the real increase will be $25 billion and the FY2011 cost will be $63.3 billion, accounting for 37 percent of all increases in operations and support spending during this period.[29]

New retirement benefits will add substantially to these totals. Again, even with the Department's manpower assumptions in the FY2006 budget request, shifts in retirement options are projected to add $1.8 billion in FY2007, rising to $2.1 billion annually in FY2024. Providing better health care benefits for life for retirees and their families will raise costs from $9.3 billion in FY2007 to $19.9 billion in FY2024. Changes in social security and concurrent receipts will add hundreds of millions of dollars more.[30]

The CBO also examined a case in which end strengths were not cut because of the pressure of ongoing wars. This could mean an average of some $25 billion more a year almost indefinitely into the future. Such estimates also acquired added credibility in January 2007 when Secretary of Defense Robert Gates announced that he had reversed Secretary Rumsfeld's previous decisions, and that the Army would grow to 547,000 total soldiers from a then current strength of 507,000 soldiers, rising to 512,000 by the end of the year as part of an ongoing 30,000-man increase that had been taking place over the past three years. Gates proposed making this 30,000-man increase permanent and further boosting the size of the Army by an additional 35,000 soldiers over the next five years. The Marines were to grow from 180,000 to 202,000 by adding 22,000 new Marines and making permanent the 5,000-increase of the past three years.[31]

Such changes show how dangerous unrealistic assumptions about defense plans and costs can be in underestimating real-world defense costs. Yet, any analysis of the resulting manpower costs again requires a broader historical perspective. The fact that military manpower is increasingly costly does not make raising today's end strength unaffordable by historical standards. Figure 3.12 shows the trend in constant FY2007 dollars and goes back to the end of the Cold War. Even if one assumes that the Iraq War peak shown in these figures continues through FY2010, the total costs for an all-volunteer force would still be lower than the military manpower costs during much of the Cold War, when the United States had a much smaller economy

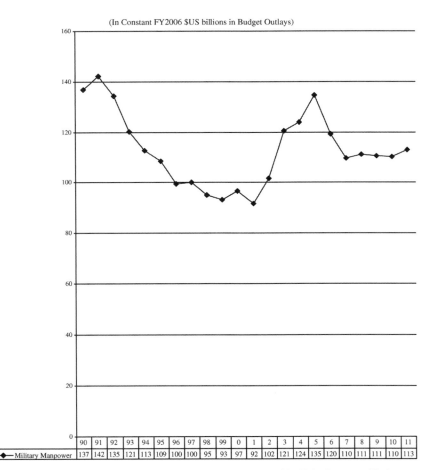

(In Constant FY2006 $US billions in Budget Outlays)

	90	91	92	93	94	95	96	97	98	99	0	1	2	3	4	5	6	7	8	9	10	11
◆ Military Manpower	137	142	135	121	113	109	100	100	95	93	97	92	102	121	124	135	120	110	111	111	110	113

Source: Adapted by Anthony H. Cordesman from data provided by Office of the Under Secretary of Defense (Comptroller), *National Defense Budget Estimates for FY2006*, Washington, Department of Defense, April 2005, Table 6-8 and 6-11.

Figure 3.12   Military Manpower Costs since the End of the Cold War: FY1990–FY2011

and a lower level of overall federal spending. Moreover, during the Korean War and the Vietnam War, the cost of military manpower reached peaks of well over $160 billion in constant FY2007 dollars, an average that was about 33-percent higher in real terms than the spending projected during FY2005 to FY2011.[32]

Force quality is not necessarily more expensive than force quantity and—with the right strategy, tactics, and technology—can often accomplish far more.

FORCE TRANSFORMATION AND EQUIPMENT COSTS

The Department of Defense has never provided a detailed spending plan for force transformation. As the following chapters make clear in detail, it has also never done anything approaching an adequate job of costing and finding future procurement, controlling cost escalation, ensuring effectiveness, or ensuring on-time deliveries. Far too often, the spiraling costs of new systems have also forced premature cuts in existing forces and equipment holdings or led to major cuts in the number of new systems to be procured. It may be ironic to state that force transformation is often the worst enemy of force transformation, but this has often been the case.

Governmental Accountability Office (GAO) study after GAO study has shown that the Department's efforts to estimate the cost of future-year procurements fall short of the true cost of such procurement efforts. Coupled with the fact that the Department also perpetually downsizes its plans to fit the budget, this makes it impossible to know what level of resources the Department needs to actually execute its plans and buy the equipment the services have, in theory, been given permission to procure.

Figure 3.13 shows the Department's actual procurement spending since the Cold War and its plans through FY2011. These data project a major increase in research, development, test, and evaluation (RDT&E) spending in the out-years—presumably driven in part by the cost of the "transformational" systems discussed in later chapters. The projected levels of outlays on RDT&E are higher in constant dollars than the United States spent during much of the Cold War, but they also would be much lower than during some earlier periods, such as the late 1980s, when RDT&E outlays averaged well over $100 billion in constant dollars and reached peaks of over $120 billion—roughly twice the planned level for 2010.

The procurement expenditures shown in Figure 3.13 rise sharply in the period between 2000 and 2010, but will again still be similar in constant dollars to spending at the end of the Cold War. They will be far lower than peak periods during the Cold War, when they reached levels well above $100 billion a year, and outlays reached $132 billion in FY1986.

If one looks closely at Figure 3.13, however, one also sees that the rise in RDT&E and procurement costs is sharply limited in the last years of the Bush Administration and then resumes a major rise once the current President leaves office. This is all too typical of Presidents who are leaving office or are defeated. They try to balance the budget or control defense spending during the last years of their own time in office, but then burden the next President with major expenditures that he or she may or

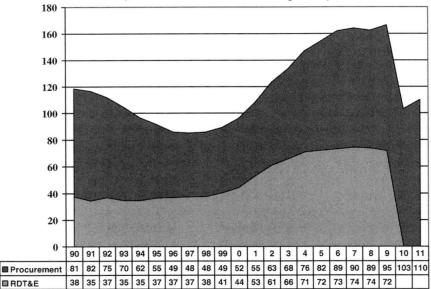

(Constant FY2007 $US billions in Budget Outlays)

	90	91	92	93	94	95	96	97	98	99	0	1	2	3	4	5	6	7	8	9	10	11
■ Procurement	81	82	75	70	62	55	49	48	48	49	52	55	63	68	76	82	89	90	89	95	103	110
▢ RDT&E	38	35	37	35	35	37	37	37	38	41	44	53	61	66	71	72	73	74	74	72		

Source: Adapted by Anthony H. Cordesman from data provided by Office of the Under Secretary of Defense (Comptroller), *National Defense Budget Estimates for FY2007*, Washington, Department of Defense, March 2006, Table 6-8 and 6-11. For more detailed projections by procurement area, see "The Long-Term Implications of Current Defense Plans and Alternatives: Summary Update for Fiscal Year 2007." Congressional Budget Office, October 2006.

Figure 3.13 Procurement and RDT&E Spending since the End of the Cold War: FY1990–FY2011

may not be able to afford. This particular programming trick can be used for both individual procurement and force transformation efforts by putting spending into future years, where it is generally called "slipping to the right." When it is applied to entire sections of the defense budget, it might better be called "dancing to the right." It is simply fiscal dishonest slight of hand.

It is particularly dishonest when many past programming and force transformation decisions proved to be wrong, and the Department of Defense must now pay for the kinds of real-world force transformation it failed to include in its plans. Instead of major high-technology weapons and systems, the Afghan and Iraq wars forced major upgrades in ordinary combat equipment. Improving the protection, weapons, and communications of the average solider raised the cost of the equipment soldiers must carry into combat from $7,000 in 1999 to $25,000 in 2006. The cost of upgrading highly vulnerable Humvees with added armor, weapons, electronic jammers, and GPS raised the cost per vehicle from $32,000 in 2001 to nearly $225,000 in 2006.[33] The Department may well be planning to spend vast amounts of money on systems of marginal value, having failed to plan, budget, and program for the force transformation it has actually needed.

In addition—as future chapters show in brutal detail—any such estimate of the total spending levels needed to buy the planned equipment for transformation and to sustain a proper RDT&E effort is highly speculative. The Department of Defense has consistently undercosted RDT&E and procurement plans for decades. It seems likely that actually paying for the RDT&E and procurement activities called for in current U.S. defense plans could require funding at levels well in excess of $200 billion a year versus the $150 billion shown in the FY2006 FYDP and the peak of $180 billion shown for FY2001. It is possible that the true cost of all current plans could reach levels approaching $250 billion.

This is an ambitious increase, to put it mildly, and even the projected rise after FY2008 may well reflect an effort by the Bush Administration to defer much of the spending and burden on the budget until after he leaves office. While this may not be a deliberate "poisoned chalice" that forces all the truly hard resource decisions on the next administration, it follows a pattern of many administrations that dodge really hard decision making and budget problems by leaving them to their successors.

These games with out-year budgets compound all of the problems in major procurement and transformational programs described in detail in Chapter 6. About all that can be said in their defense is that the United States was spending roughly $250 billion a year for procurement and RDT&E in the late 1980s, and it is difficult to describe such spending levels as overstretch.[34] As a study by the CBO indicates, however, it can create massive cost risks. A CBO analysis of defense spending through FY2024 noted that Department of Defense investment projections for FY2007 to FY2011 called for RDT&E and procurement to rise by an annual rate of 2.8 percent in real terms, and from $158 billion in FY2007 to $176 billion in FY2011. Even with no further rise in weapons costs, this meant the Department's investment costs would rise to $195 billion by FY2013. If more realistic assumptions were made about cost escalation, however, investment spending would be $224 billion in FY2013 (some 15 percent percent higher). Investment costs would average $201 billion a year in constant FY2007 dollars over the period from FY2007 to FY2024.[35]

OTHER COST FACTORS

The Iraq War has driven Operation and Maintenance (O&M) spending to very high levels. O&M spending dropped from annual levels of more than $140 billion in constant FY2007 dollars during the Cold War to levels below $120 billion during the late 1990s. It rose sharply after the beginning of the war on terrorism in 2001. O&M outlays surged from $131 billion in FY2000 to $134 billion in FY2001, $152 billion in FY2002, $173 billion in FY2004, and have been over $190 billion a year ever since. This is a rise of over 40 percent in real terms between FY1990 and FY2005.[36]

At the same time, the data used in creating Figure 3.14 make it all clear that far too few provisions have been made in the budget projections for FY2007–FY2010 to pay for the massive costs of recovering readiness, parts, and other capabilities that come

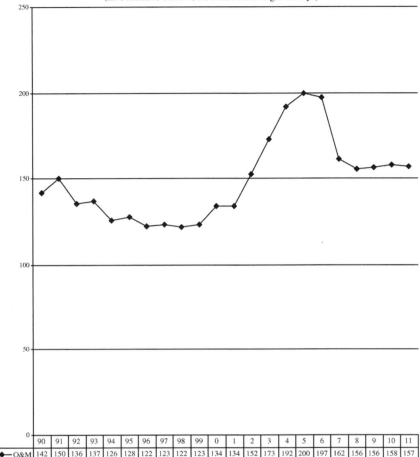

(In Constant FY2007 $US billions in Budget Outlays)

	90	91	92	93	94	95	96	97	98	99	0	1	2	3	4	5	6	7	8	9	10	11
O&M	142	150	136	137	126	128	122	123	122	123	134	134	152	173	192	200	197	162	156	156	158	157

Source: Adapted by Anthony H. Cordesman from data provided by Office of the Under Secretary of Defense (Comptroller), *National Defense Budget Estimates for FY2007*, Washington, Department of Defense, March 2006, Table 6-8 and 6-11.

Figure 3.14   Operations and Maintenance Spending since the End of the Cold War: FY1990–FY2011

after a war. This problem is also greatly further compounded by the underfunding of readiness and modernization before the war. The Chief of Staff of the Army, General Peter J. Schoomaker, summarized these problems as follows in his testimony to Congress in June 2006:

> Historically, the Army has been under resourced—and it is a fact that the decade preceding the attacks of September 11, 2001 was no exception. Army investment accounts were underfunded by approximately $100 billion and 500,000 soldiers were reduced from

total Army end strength. There were about $56 billion in equipment shortages at the opening of the ground campaign in Iraq in the spring of 2003.[37]

This has already become all too apparent in the supplementals prepared for the FY2007 budget request, which included some $23.8 billion to replace worn-out equipment. The U.S. Army alone already has stated that some $17 billion to $19 billion a year's worth of Army equipment is destroyed or worn out each year in the fighting in Afghanistan and Iraq.[38] The Army had a major maintenance backlog in the United States of at least 530 M-1 tanks, 220 M88 wreckers, 700 Bradley M-2 fighting vehicles, 160 M113 armored personnel carriers, 450 medium and heavy trucks, and more than 1,000 Humvees in November 2006. It estimated that some 280,000 items would eventually have to be fixed or replaced and that this level of expenditure will go on for at least several more years; this compares with annual costs of $2.5 billion to $3 billion before the war.

The wear on equipment, and repair backlog, is already so high that Army units now have to exchange equipment sets to train for war in Iraq. Helicopters are flying at two to three times the normal number of annual flying hours. Tanks are being driven at averages of 4,000 miles a year, five times the normal annual rate. The truck fleets in Iraq operate at more than six times the normal annual rate of driving hours. This has already raised the workload on Army maintenance depots from 63,000 items in 2005 to 130,000 in 2006—a predictable workload that did not lead to increases in the O&M areas in the regular budget request.[39] When these problems are added to the underfunding of other Army needs, the Army estimates that it was underfunded by at least $24 billion in FY2007 in areas that should not have been included in supplementals.[40]

The U.S. Air Force has slowed its modernization to pay for new aircraft that will not be delivered until after 2011 and raised the average age of its aircraft to over 25 years. This is forcing the Air Force to place limits on how some types of aircraft can be flown.[41] This has helped to force the Air Force to ask for an additional $33 billion in FY2007 funding, and the problem will require additional funding for at least another half decade.

An analysis by Andrew Feickert of the Congressional Research Service provides a more detailed picture of the cost of bringing the U.S. Army and the U.S. Marine Corps back to its prewar equipment readiness, a process that the services call "reset."[42] There is no agreement on the costs the military services have already incurred, although they clearly exceed some $20 billion in current backlogs, and the Army has estimated its reset costs at $17.1 billion for FY2007 alone.[43] The U.S. Marine Corps requested $11.9 billion for both reset and operations in FY2007 and received $5.8 billion for reset. Moreover, all such cost estimates do not reflect the lessons of the war regarding the fact that a very different equipment mix is needed in the future, with more armored systems, uparmored and upgunned vehicles, much better communications and electronic aids and a host of other expensive upgrades.

The Iraqi War has also shown that the only way the U.S. Army and the U.S. Marine Corps could meet their equipment needs in Iraq was to take equipment from units that were not deployed, from the Reserves, or from other services—again for one regional contingency where the enemy had no heavy military weapons or equipment. The Army National Guard, for example, had to transfer over 100,000 pieces of equipment from nondeploying to deploying units as early as July 2005.[44]

The FYDP presented in the Department of Defense FY2007 budget request simply does not consider or cost the problem. In this case, any impact on overstretch is simply ignored. The failure to program adequate expenditures in the out-years is the opposite form of slight of hand in programming and budgeting from programming expenditures that will never take place, but—like dancing to the right—it is no less dishonest.

Aside from military personnel costs, some analysts have also suggested that certain O&M costs are likely to increase significantly over time:[45]

- **Equipment Maintenance and Repair:** Through most of the 1990s, the age of the services' weapons inventory increased only modestly, despite the fact that relatively few weapons were purchased during the decade. This is because the services bought large quantities of new weapons systems in the 1980s and then in the 1990s cut the size of the force structure by about one-third, with the oldest equipment generally being retired first. However, the buildup of the 1980s is now receding further into the past, and most of the planned force structure cuts were completed by the middle of the decade.

    As a result, the average age of most major weapons systems is projected to increase substantially over the next decade. To date, the aging of the services' weapons inventory does not seem to have resulted in a substantial increase in operations and maintenance costs. This has been dominated by the failure to provide for the timely repair and rehabilitation of the major combat equipment damaged in the Iraq and Afghan conflicts. However, as the aging of the force accelerates over the coming decade, age-related O&M costs could grow significantly, perhaps by as much as $5 billion annually by 2010. According to CBO, by 2022, cost growth associated with operating older equipment could cause O&M funding requirements to increase by as much as $14 billion annually. Moreover, replacing aging weapons systems with newer systems may, at best, only partially offset this cost growth, since the greater complexity of some new weapon systems can also lead to higher O&M costs.

- **Facilities Maintenance and Repair:** It was widely believed that the DoD operated an excessive number of military bases. In an attempt to address this problem, for the first time in a decade, the United States began a new round of military base closures. Under the Base Realignment and Closure (BRAC) process, the President appointed an independent commission that, by September 2006, recommended—based on advice from the services, as well as from its own analysis—the closure of a number of U.S. bases. Currently the U.S. military operates about 425 major U.S. bases. Former Defense Secretary Donald Rumsfeld has suggested that some 20 percent of those bases might be selected for closure. As part of the ongoing 2005 BRAC commission process, a list of more than 500 bases and other facilities—such as terminals, medical, and support centers—was presented with recommendations for closing, realigning, and consolidating these assets.

The Congress did not bloc the Secretary of Defense from acting on the Commission's recommendations, and he has until the end of 2011 to implement them. The Department of Defense has claimed these closures could yield savings of perhaps $2 billion a year on the long term. However, over the next five years, these closures may cost more money than they will save. Moreover, the accounting for these savings often omits major expenditures to correct environmental and safety problems, which were not included in the costs of base closings the Department uses in its accounting on the grounds the Department would eventually have had to pay for them in any case. Such accounting also sometimes assumes that the closed bases will be sold at market value when they are often given away to local causes or sold for far under their market value. The projected budget savings also ignore the Department's need to increase its funding for facility upkeep and construction substantially over the long term. The DoD appeared to have spent too little over the past decade or more on maintaining, repairing, and constructing military bases, housing, and other facilities.

Even so, future O&M expenditures may not cause any serious form of future "overstretch." Even if average future O&M spending levels have to be sustained at levels closer to the $185 billion wartime levels shown for FY2004, they would not —by themselves—pose a major burden on federal defense spending or pose more than a minor burden on the federal budget. It would take a truly massive increase in O&M spending to make that kind of difference.

SHORT-TERM PROSPECTS FOR FY2007–FY2011

It is always dangerous to focus on short-term trends and current projections. Reality often intervenes, and this is particularly true in wartime and when so much U.S. defense spending is not included in supplements and not in the President's formal budget request and forecasts. Even so, if one looks at what the previous analysis means for the Department of Defense budget projections for FY2007–FY2001, issued as part of the FY2007 budget request, the near-term trends highlight the kind of problems that emerge in U.S. defense budgeting and programming, and in tying them to strategy and force planning:[46] While the Congress did not act on these targets as part of its authorization and appropriations bills dealing with the FY2007 budget submission, the Congress made so little change in the FY2007 request and supplemental request, and programs with long-term spending implications, that they seem representative of at least the current level of U.S. planning.[47]

- Total national security costs in outlays rose from $298 billion in FY2001, in constant FY2000 dollars, to $442 billion in FY2007—a rise of 48 percent in real terms since 9/11.[48] They rose from $305 billion in FY2001, in current dollars, to $536 billion in FY2007—a rise of 75 percent.

- Such increases mark a very sharp rise, but defense costs have never been stable in real terms. Total national defense costs in outlays in constant 2000 dollars rose from $267 billion in 1980 to $399 billion in 1989 (49 percent). They dropped from $383 billion in 1990 to $284 billion in 1999 (–26 percent). They then increased by

50 percent from $295 billion in 2000 to $443 billion in 2007. They are projected to drop to $392 billion in FY2008 and then decline to $389 billion in 2011.[49]

- In spite of such rises, the burden national security spending puts on the national economy has dropped sharply over time. Total national security expenditures averaged around 9 percent of the GDP throughout the 1960s, and Department of Defense spending averaged around 8 percent. Both declined to levels around 6 percent in the 1970s and remained at close to these levels in the 1980s. The end of the Cold War allowed them to drop to levels closer to 3.0 percent during the 1990s. Total national security expenditures rose back to around 4 percent of the GDP after "9/11" and Department of Defense to around 3.7 percent.[50]

- The burden national security spending puts on the federal budget has also tended to decline. Total national security expenditures declined from 52 percent at the start of the 1960s to 45 percent at the end. They dropped from 42 percent in 1970 to 23 percent in 1979, then rose to 27 percent in 1989. They dropped from 23 percent to 16 percent in the 1990s and have since risen back to around 19–20 percent. The Department of Defense share has generally been about 1.5–2.7 percent lower.[51]

Once again, this does not mean the United States faces overstretch in terms of defense resources. The pressures defense puts on the economy and federal budget are low by historical standards and minor compared to the pressures put on the budget by mandatory expenditures and entitlements. Moreover, even if defense spending rose by another third, it would still only equal the burden defense placed on the economy during the less expensive periods of the Cold War.

It does mean that the Bush Administration has submitted a FY2007–FY2011 defense plan that is deeply unrealistic. It does not fund ongoing wars after FY2007, and even its 2007 figures are unrealistic given current supplementals. Less such supplementals, the Department of Defense projects spending in outlays as follows:

- In current dollars, projected national security expenditures go from $536 billion in 2006 to $527 billion in 2007, $494 billion in 2008, $494 billion in 2009, and then rise sharply to $507 billion in 2010 and $523 billion in 2011.

- In constant 2000 dollars, projected expenditures go from $443 billion in 2006 to $427 billion in 2007, $392 billion in 2008, $384 billion in 2009, and then rise much more slowly because of assumptions about inflation to $386 billion in 2010 and $389 billion in 2011.

The Bush Administration also manipulates the FYDP for FY2007 to FY2011 by allowing the BA (which does not affect the "balanced budget") to rise much more sharply and quickly in the out-years to fund the defense program and force transformation, while delaying the rise in outlays (which does not affect the politics of budget balancing) until President Bush leaves office. This has become standard practice for outgoing administrations since the Eisenhower Administration and allows a President to understate the true cost of defense by slipping expenditures to the out-years.

The problem is that the United States not only has to pay for its wars, but must be able to implement its strategy and carry out a continuous process of force transformation. If one looks at the levels of defense spending projected in Figure 3.15, it again highlights the fact that future spending by the Department of Defense should almost certainly be budgeted at an average approaching $100 billion more a year during much of FY2008–FY2011.[52]

COSTS OTHER THAN DEFENSE NOW DRIVE THE FEDERAL BUDGET AND THE TAX BURDEN

That said, the United States still sorely needs to look beyond the narrow issue of defense spending and consider what forces are actually putting pressure on the

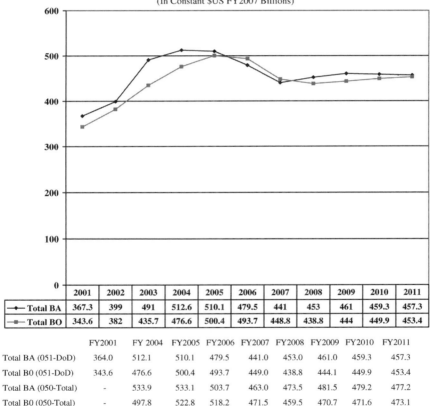

(In Constant $US FY2007 Billions)

	2001	2002	2003	2004	2005	2006	2007	2008	2009	2010	2011
Total BA	367.3	399	491	512.6	510.1	479.5	441	453	461	459.3	457.3
Total BO	343.6	382	435.7	476.6	500.4	493.7	448.8	438.8	444	449.9	453.4

	FY2001	FY 2004	FY2005	FY2006	FY2007	FY2008	FY2009	FY2010	FY2011
Total BA (051-DoD)	364.0	512.1	510.1	479.5	441.0	453.0	461.0	459.3	457.3
Total B0 (051-DoD)	343.6	476.6	500.4	493.7	449.0	438.8	444.1	449.9	453.4
Total BA (050-Total)	-	533.9	533.1	503.7	463.0	473.5	481.5	479.2	477.2
Total B0 (050-Total)	-	497.8	522.8	518.2	471.5	459.5	470.7	471.6	473.1

Source: Adapted from Office of the Under Secretary of Defense (Comptroller), *National Defense Budget Estimates for FY2007*, March 2006, pp. 4 -5.

Figure 3.15   Budgeting for a "Warless World" in an Era of Long Wars after FY2007: Total DoD Budget FY2001–FY2011

federal budget and the U.S. economy. If one examines what is happening within the federal budget, there may well be a need for a very different kind of debate over the budget deficit, the federal debt, and the growth of mandatory federal spending and other sharply rising domestic expenditures—rather than simply focusing on defense.

The Budget Deficit and the Federal Debt

The budget deficit is driven largely by domestic and mandatory programs and not by defense spending. If the United States is to be both secure and globally competitive, it needs basic fiscal responsibility, regardless of the importance of the public policy issue. This means hard trade-offs, not deferring decisions, or letting future (out-year) costs escalate while appearing to control budget obligations (BO) during the current and next fiscal years. It means matching revenues and expenditures and asking the American public to assume equal fiscal responsibility for the individual.

At this point in time, it is difficult, if not impossible, to determine how bad the level of American fiscal irresponsibility is getting. Estimates of the trends in the national debt, budget deficit, or the future costs of mandatory expenditures/entitlement programs are so subject to political views and problems in cost estimates that the only thing really clear is a steadily growing vector of overspending. This situation is made worse by Congressional gimmicks to get through the current year, like the Budget Reconciliation Act, games with supplementals, and undercosting out-year expenditures.

The near-term projections made in the President's budget request are shown in Figure 3.16. They are conservative in estimating the growth of civilian spending and mandatory programs, but they also show that it is these programs, and not defense, that are projected to dominate the overall growth of federal spending and its impact on the U.S. economy.

The baseline data in the CBO budget outlook for FY2007–FY2016, which was issued in February 2006, make very favorable assumptions about Congressional willingness to reimpose a massive tax burden when past cuts begin to expire in 2010. Even so, one sees the following trends:[53]

- A $337-billion baseline deficit costing 2.6 percent of the U.S. GDP for FY2007, with a more realistic total of $360 billion, or 2.8 percent of the GDP, including supplementals for the wars.

- Mandatory expenditures will continue to increase by 5.8 percent per year during FY2007 through FY2016 versus 2 percent for discretionary expenditures (a pace less than half the assumed average growth in GDP).[54]

- Total Social Security, Medicare, and Medicaid costs will rise from 43 percent of all federal spending in 2006 to 56 percent in 2016, and from 8.7 percent of GDP to 18.8 percent.[55]

- A rise in Medicare costs from 7.4 percent in 2008 to 8.3 percent in 2016.[56]

- A rise in Medicaid spending to 8.3 percent of GDP by 2016.[57]

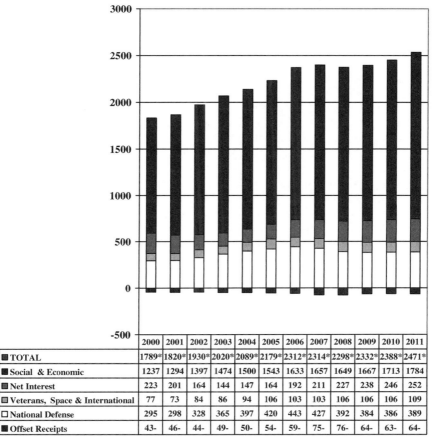

(By Fiscal Year, in Constant $US FY2000 Billions)

	2000	2001	2002	2003	2004	2005	2006	2007	2008	2009	2010	2011
■ TOTAL	1789*	1820*	1930*	2020*	2089*	2179*	2312*	2314*	2298*	2332*	2388*	2471*
■ Social & Economic	1237	1294	1397	1474	1500	1543	1633	1657	1649	1667	1713	1784
■ Net Interest	223	201	164	144	147	164	192	211	227	238	246	252
▣ Veterans, Space & International	77	73	84	86	94	106	103	103	106	106	106	109
□ National Defense	295	298	328	365	397	420	443	427	392	384	386	389
■ Offset Receipts	43-	46-	44-	49-	50-	54-	59-	75-	76-	64-	63-	64-

Source: Office of the Under Secretary of Defense (Comptroller), *National Defense Budget Estimates for FY2006*, Washington, Department of Defense, April 2005, Table 7-2.

VS&I = Veterans, Space, and International; Offset Receipts = Offsetting Receipts.

Figure 3.16 U.S. National Defense Spending Relative to Other Federal Budget Costs: FY2000–FY2011

According to the CBO baseline forecast, the federal budget deficit is estimated to change from $318 billion in 2005 to $337 billion in 2006, $271 billion in 2007, $259 billion in 2008, $241 billion in 2009, $222 billion in 2010, and $114 billion in 2011.[58]

Moreover, the CBO baseline forecast estimates that the federal debt will increase from $3.3 trillion in 2005 to $3.5 trillion in 2006, $3.8 trillion in 2007, $4.1 trillion in 2008, $4.5 trillion in 2009, $4.8 trillion in 2010, and $5.2 trillion in 2011.[59]

More recent CBO projections, made after the Congress acted on the FY2007 budget, are no more optimistic. The Director of the CBO estimates that the cost of social security will rise from 4 percent of the GDP in 2006 to 6 percent in 2030 and increase steadily thereafter. He estimates that the cost of Medicare and Medicaid will rise much faster because demographic factors combine with a sharp real rise in medical costs. As a result, even if such cost escalation slows significantly, the cost of Medicare and Medicaid will rise from 4.6 percent of the GDP in 2006 to 9 percent in 2030. These three programs already account for a total of 9 percent of the GDP and more than 40 percent of all federal spending. Unless they are brought under control, the CBO estimates that they will rise to 15 percent of the GDP, and to over 75 percent of all current federal spending, by 2030.[60] An analysis by the Congressional Research Service is even more pessimistic about the cost of Medicare and Medicaid. It projects a rise to 12 percent of the GDP in 2030 and 22 percent in 2050.[61]

Other projections forecast that if current policy trends continue, they will lead to large sustained deficits. For example, the Concord Coalition baseline projection estimated that the federal budget deficit would reach approximately $380 billion in 2007, $390 billion in 2008, $400 billion in 2009, $410 billion in 2010, and $500 billion in 2011. In addition, this projection estimated that the U.S. federal budget deficit will reach approximately $800+ billion in 2015.[62]

Studies by groups like the GAO have raised the need to reexamine the very base of the U.S. government.[63] It has warned that current spending trends—driven by net interest, Medicare and Medicaid, and Social Security—could easily raise baseline federal spending from some 20 percent of GDP through 2015 to 25 percent by 2030 and close to 30 percent by 2040. If all current tax cuts and relief were sustained, and spending grew at recent rates, these figures would drive federal spending to around 24 percent of GDP by 2015, 34 percent by 2030, and over 45 percent by 2040.[64] The Brookings Institution raised many of the same issues in its study on *Restoring Fiscal Sanity 2005,* by Alice M. Rivlin and Isabel Sawhill.[65]

The United States needs prudent federal fiscal polices. If it wants national security in an era where geoeconomics are at least as important as geopolitics and military forces, it needs a society that is competitive, that allows free markets to work while protecting those who truly need public aid, and where individuals remain productive and pay their own way. Yet, fiscal responsibility does not mean cutting defense first.

The United States may not fight another version of the Iraq War, but the previous chapter has shown that it faces very real external threats, rivals, and foreign enemies. It needs to fight the "long war" against extremism and terrorism, to aid its allies, deter potential enemies, and defeat real ones.

The "Threat" to the United States from Mandatory Programs

If one looks beyond defense per se, and at the best ways to keep federal expenditures from limiting U.S. economic growth, one key priority may be to keep federal spending capped at the current level of roughly 19–20 percent of GDP and do so in ways that do not drive states to increase their share of GDP. In reality, this will be possible only if Americans openly debate the trade-offs between increased reliance on the federal government and/or increased federal debt and by limiting public spending generally.

This cannot be done without bringing mandatory programs like Social Security, Medicaid, Medicare, and other social welfare programs under control. Figure 3.16 has already illustrated this point, but Figures 3.17 through 3.19 illustrate it in more detail. Figure 3.17 shows the growth of mandatory programs by type relative to defense in both percentage and absolute terms as projected in the material prepared for the President's FY2007 budget request. Figure 3.18 shows a conservative Congressional Budget Office projection made through FY2016, based on the budget baseline in outlays. Both serve as a clear warning about the need to bring mandatory programs under control even under the most conservative estimates.

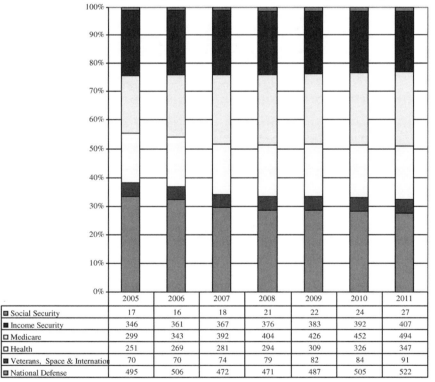

(Percentage of outlays by function in Current $US Billions by Fiscal Year)

	2005	2006	2007	2008	2009	2010	2011
▣ Social Security	17	16	18	21	22	24	27
■ Income Security	346	361	367	376	383	392	407
▢ Medicare	299	343	392	404	426	452	494
▢ Health	251	269	281	294	309	326	347
■ Veterans, Space & International	70	70	74	79	82	84	91
▣ National Defense	495	506	472	471	487	505	522

Source: Office of the Under Secretary of Defense (Comptroller), *National Defense Budget Estimates for FY2006*, Washington, Department of Defense, April 2005, Table 7-2.

VS&I = Veterans, Space, and International; Offset Receipts = Offsetting Receipts.

Figure 3.17 The American Threat to the United States: U.S. National Defense Spending versus Major Health and Mandatory Programs: FY2005–FY2011

(Percentage of outlays by function in CBO projection under baseline assumptions in $US Billions by Fiscal Year)

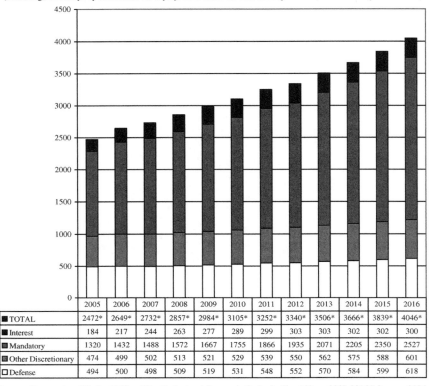

	2005	2006	2007	2008	2009	2010	2011	2012	2013	2014	2015	2016
■ TOTAL	2472*	2649*	2732*	2857*	2984*	3105*	3252*	3340*	3506*	3666*	3839*	4046*
■ Interest	184	217	244	263	277	289	299	303	303	302	302	300
■ Mandatory	1320	1432	1488	1572	1667	1755	1866	1935	2071	2205	2350	2527
■ Other Discretionary	474	499	502	513	521	529	539	550	562	575	588	601
□ Defense	494	500	498	509	519	531	548	552	570	584	599	618

Source: Congressional Budget Office, "The Budget and Economic Outlook: Fiscal Years 2007-2016," January 2006, p. 52.

VS&I = Veterans, space, and International; Offset Receipts = Offsetting Receipts.

Figure 3.18   CBO Projection of U.S. National Defense Outlays versus Other Entitlements and Mandatory Programs: FY2005–FY2016

The Bush Administration and the Congress, however, have so far chosen politics over fiscal responsibility, and spending could be far higher. It has already been mentioned that the GAO has warned that current spending trends—driven by net interest, Medicare and Medicaid, and Social Security—could easily raise baseline federal spending from some 20 percent of GDP through 2015 to 25 percent by 2030 and close to 30 percent by 2040. If all current tax cuts and relief were sustained, and spending grew at recent rates, these figures would drive federal spending to around 24 percent of GDP by 2015, 34 percent by 2030, and over 45 percent by 2040.[66]

The CBO has made a similar estimate, and typical CBO projections of spending based on past trends in economic growth and federal spending are shown in Figure 3.19. Even if Medicare and Medicaid alone are kept under tight control through 2050, cost will still have risen from 0 percent of the GDP in 1966 to some

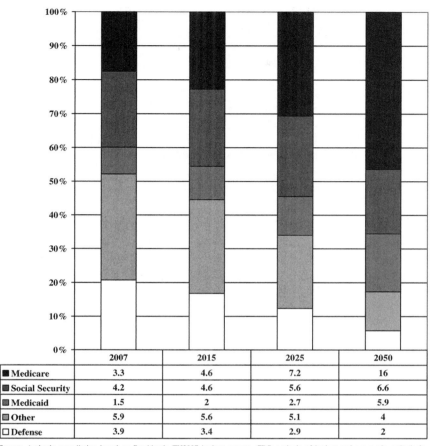

	2007	2015	2025	2050
■ Medicare	3.3	4.6	7.2	16
■ Social Security	4.2	4.6	5.6	6.6
■ Medicaid	1.5	2	2.7	5.9
▣ Other	5.9	5.6	5.1	4
☐ Defense	3.9	3.4	2.9	2

Source: Author's compilation based on President's FY2007 budget request, CBO analysis of budget and economic outlook for FY2007-FY2016, and primarily on the range of extrapolations in Congressional Budget Office, The Long Term Budget Outlook, December 2005, p. 10. For additional analysis, see US Government Accountability Office, "21st Century Challenges: Reexamining the Base of the Federal Government," GAO-05-325SP, February 2005.

Figure 3.19   Entitlements "Hell": CBO FY2006 Estimate of Cost of Programs as a Percent of GDP

4 percent today and will rise to 5.9 percent by 2050. U.S. medical costs for the normal population have exceeded the annual rate of GDP growth by an average of 2.6 percent a year from 1960 to 2003.[67]

If their cost growth in real terms were controlled to only 1 percent annual real growth—a level of Administration and Congressional restraint that would approach a historical miracle—they would rise to over 12 percent of the GDP by 2050. At a historical trend of a 2.5-percent annual rise in real cost, they would rise to about 8 percent of the GDP in 2020 and well over 20 percent of the GDP by 2050.[68] These figures do not include Social Security, which the CBO estimates is on track to rise from 4.2 percent of the GDP in 2006 to 6.0 percent in 2030 and 6.6 percent in 2050—a rise of more than 50 percent.[69]

The United States is a rapidly aging society, and this is having a massive impact on federal spending, as well as on the structure of the American labor force:

- The percent of the U.S. population over 65 will continue to rise from 14 percent in 2016 to more than 19 percent in 2030.[70]
- CBO estimates that the number of U.S. adults under 65 will grow by 12 percent over the next 30 years, but the number over 65 will double. Older adults will rise from one-fifth of the population to one-third between 2005 and 2050.[71]
- Social Security costs must rise, driven by the first baby boomers reaching age 62 in 2003. That means that the burden Social Security puts on the U.S. economy will rise from 4.8 percent of the GDP in 2008 to 6.5 percent in 2016.[72]
- Medicare costs increased by more than 10 times as a percent of GDP between 1970 and 2004, from 0.7 percent to 2.6 percent. Medicaid costs increased by more than 15 times as a percent of GDP between 1970 and 2004, from 0.3 percent to 1.5 percent.[73] Total was 0.1 percent in 1970 and 4.1 percent in 2004.
- The cost of budget outlays for Social Security and Medicare will rise by a trillion dollars from FY2007 to FY2016 ($1.4 to $2.5 trillion).[74]
- The CBO estimates that combined federal spending on Social Security and Medicare will rise by 2 percent of GDP over the next decade, from around 6.5 percent to 8.7 percent. Last year, the CBO projected it would rise to 12.8 percent by 2025 and 22.6 percent by 2050.[75]
- To keep such programs funded, and to keep the federal budget under some sort of control, the CBO estimates discretionary spending must drop from about 8 percent of GDP to 6 percent.

Asking a given Congress or President to act decisively without popular support is almost certainly a triumph of hope over experience. There are, however, measures that might help:

- Focus federal planning and budgeting on controlling both BA and BO. Require every federal department and agency to submit a five-year rolling program budget, and require Congressional approval of the program budget, not just BA and BO in a single year.
- Require the Executive Branch to provide at least a 30-year projection of all mandatory program costs. Require all bills with mandatory provisions and costs to be costed for 30 years, and require Congress to vote on the out-year estimates and not simply BA and BO in a single year.
- Put an end to phony reconciliation acts. Do not ignore the real-world need to bring taxation back to the levels to sustain the budget without more deficits and increases in the national debt, and halt entitlement creep.

THE BROADER PROBLEM OF OVERSTRETCH

There is no simple way to resolve the problems the United States faces in allocating and managing defense resources or in bringing them into balance with other federal and social needs. There is a clear need to improve the planning, programming, budgeting, and management of U.S. defense spending. Part of the solution is to ensure that strategy and planning are formulated as an integrated part of programming and budgeting, part is to improve the quality of the programming and budgeting process, part is to tightly control actual costs rather than let them escalate, and part is to reduce the kind of waste and mismanagement that the following chapters show exist in many defense activities, particularly in force planning and procurement.

It should be clear, however, that the United States needs to look far beyond the Iraq War, and look far beyond simply controlling total defense spending. The United States needs a national strategy for shaping the size and cost of all its federal program, and this strategy must take account of the fact that national security is a key function of government, while many of today's mandatory programs are ones that individual citizens may have to pay for. Defense is only one priority among many, but the early part of the twenty-first century is clearly not going to be more stable or safer than the twentieth century.

The United States does not need radical rises in defense expenditures as a percent of its GDP. But it does need to recognize that it needs to maintain levels much closer to those it spent during the Cold War—particularly as long as it faces challenges like Iraq, Afghanistan, and the war on terrorism—and it must prepare for potential conflict in Korea and over the Taiwan Strait.

When defense is considered in the broader context of Homeland Defense and emergency preparedness, it is also clear why mandatory expenditures should not be allowed to either force further reductions in discretionary expenditures or drive up the total burden on the economy that is imposed by federal spending.

The United States needs to make major trade-offs in the cost of mandatory programs that are estimated to rise in cost from $1.4 trillion in 2007 to $2.5 trillion in 2016.[76] The pressures defense puts on the economy and the federal budget are low by historical standards, and minor compared to the pressures put on the budget by mandatory expenditures and entitlements. Moreover, even if defense spending rose by another third, it would still only equal the burden defense placed on the economy during the less expensive periods of the Cold War. The real issue, therefore, is not to seek ways to reduce defense costs or resources, but rather to determine what levels of spending are actually needed and provide them. The United States can almost certainly afford all of the national security it needs if it can manage other aspects of social programs and defense spending.

Challenge Three: Meeting the Needs of the U.S. Active and Reserve Military

Dollars are only one measure of overstretch and of U.S. ability to develop and sustain an effective strategy and force posture. Military manpower is another critical measure of the strains of the U.S. force posture, one that raises equally serious questions about the viability of U.S. strategy and whether the United States has enough resources to avoid a critical degree of "overstretch."

The ability to provide the skilled military personnel necessary for modern warfighting is the most important single measure of U.S. military capability. Skilled military professionals cannot simply be paid for: they have to be trained, motivated, experienced, and committed. They also have to be retained on a career basis.

The history of modern war has shown that technology is no substitute for such professionalism or for the ability of all ranks to adapt and deal with the unexpected. In case after case in the Gulf War, the Afghan conflict, and the Iraq War—as in previous wars—it was the ability of skilled military professionals to work around the limits of weaponry, technology, and information systems that led to success.

Technology can be a powerful aid for "boots on the ground" and qualified personnel, but it is a miserable substitute for inadequate numbers of trained soldiers. Machines cannot interface with allies, they cannot translate, they cannot develop human contacts and intelligence, and they cannot patrol the streets or discern between insurgents and terrorists and the normal population.

The history of modern military technology is also the history of pushing human skills to new limits, not one of reducing work burdens or training requirements. Each new weapon and system requires more advanced training, more experience to make use of its new capabilities, higher levels of maintenance, and more effort at system integration. The areas where workloads are reduced are offset by new tasks or personnel cuts that end in increasing the need for personnel quality.

HOW MUCH MILITARY MANPOWER IS ENOUGH?

The U.S. experience in Iraq has raised serious questions about the adequacy of the total pool of active and reserve U.S. military personnel. This is not simply a matter of whether the United States has enough military manpower to fight this particular war. It is a matter of whether the United States has enough military manpower to meet its global commitments and implement its global strategy. It is a matter of whether it has the right mix of active and reserve manpower to deal with the kind of wars it may face.

As has been noted earlier, Secretary of Defense Robert Gates announced in January 2007 that the Army would grow from 507,000 to 547,000 total soldiers, and end strength would rise to 512,000 by the end of the year. The Marines would grow from 180,000 to 202,000 by adding 22,000 new Marines and making permanent the 5,000 increase of the past three years.[1]

A growing number of experts feel that further major increases may be required in the end strength of the U.S. Army and the U.S. Marine Corps and that plans to cut Air Force and Navy manning and end strength should be halted. Some experts feel that the end strength of the U.S. Army needs to be close to 600,000 men to avoid excessive deployments and meet America's strategic commitments. No consensus exists about the scale of such increases, however, because the Department of Defense is the only source of clear data on the need, cost, and feasibility of such options, and it has failed to provide such studies, choosing to fund modernization over manpower.

The problem has been increased by the rising military manpower costs described in the previous chapter. The irony is that as military manpower has shrunk, the cost per solider has risen steadily because of the pay and incentives necessary to recruit and retain a force that is excessively deployed and put under steadily greater strain. Military manpower has become subject to the equivalent of "Augustine's Law." The cost per solider is rising steadily and at current rates, the time will eventually come when the United States can afford only a single man or woman in uniform.

Equally serious questions have arisen as to whether the United States can recruit and retain the skilled and experienced manpower it needs, and it is a matter of the moral and ethnical commitment the United States must make to an all-volunteer force structure that fights the battles of all its citizens. The United States has an obligation to both its military personnel and their families not to overdeploy them and not to raise the level of risk of military service to levels that go beyond what men and women in uniform should be asked to accept. The United States has a *de facto* social contract with its military that it must be prepared to honor.

For decades, U.S. strategy has talked about how many wars U.S. forces should be able to fight at or near the same time. In the process, the United States has gone from 2.5 theater wars to 2 major regional contingencies. Now, according to the 2006 Quadrennial Defense Review (QDR), it is supposed to size its forces for two wars of undefined character, size, intensity, and duration that may include irregular long wars and conventional campaigns. There is a new emphasis on asymmetric warfare, but no indication that the United States will need less military capability.

The reality is, however, that for more than half a century, the United States has maintained a pool of military personnel and human skills suitable to fight one serious, enduring major regional or theater conflict. These limits were clear during the Korean and Vietnam conflicts and throughout the Cold War. The United States could not fight one major theater conflict without critically weakening its capability to fight a theater war in Europe. At the time of the Gulf War, in 1990–1991, the United States had to deploy nearly 100 percent of its pool of many key categories of military forces and manpower.

The Iraq War has made this gap between manpower and strategy all too clear. It has become an unexpected war of attrition, one that the United States never designed its force posture to fight. Deploying peaks of far less than 200,000 men and women has put a major strain on the ability of the present U.S. force structure and pool of military manpower to sustain even one major regional contingency. Moreover, the United States has had to deploy and redeploy critical parts of its uniformed manpower to Iraq and Afghanistan in ways that have violated the implied "social contract" that led many men and women to join and stay in the all-volunteer force.

The military repercussions of these strains are all too apparent. An annual risk assessment conducted by General Richard B. Myers, Chairman of the Joint Chiefs of Staff, in 2005 reported that if the United States were to engage in a new war, it would be at a higher risk of not defeating the enemy as quickly as it previously could.[2] Such short-term assessments, however, do not address emerging longer-term requirements. The United States must find ways to restructure its force posture to reduce the strains new types of wars are putting on military manpower.

It must find ways to reduce the overdeployment of part of its forces and find viable incentives to recruit and retain an all-volunteer force structure for what may be an era of long wars. It must find a new balance between its active and reserve components and simultaneously reorganize its manpower to provide new skills. As this chapter notes, some of these changes are under way, but many are still at the conceptual stage or raise serious issues about practicality and affordability.

At some point, the United States must go further and honestly address its real requirements for total active and reserve end strength. The potential need for more active and reserve military manpower is an issue that the Department of Defense has largely dodged by assuming that changes in the U.S. force posture, changes in the mix of military personnel, and advances in technology and organization will allow the United States to meet its needs with its existing military manpower pool. The fact is, however, that such substitutes cannot allow the United States to do more and more with less and less, or even with its existing manpower pool. The Iraq War has shown that the United States may well need a significant increase in military end strength, particularly in its active forces. At a minimum, it needs a zero-based and independent inquiry into the adequacy of its military manpower pool that is not shaped by current budget guidance, the internal bureaucratic momentum of the Department of Defense, or considerations like balanced budgets and domestic politics.

These issues are also being brought to a head by the current QDR and the future-year defense plan (FYDP). The QDR essentially dodged the issues of both end strength and cost; it called for radical improvements in the manpower skills needed for asymmetric warfare without explaining how they could be funded or achieved within the existing manpower pool, and it failed to examine the issue of either over-deployment or total warfighting needs.

The FY2007 budget called for personnel cuts and not increases. While it raised the amount of money programmed for military personnel by 4 percent, it put a much higher emphasis on procurement, which rose by more than 8 percent), and on readiness (operations and maintenance) which rose by 9.4 percent). The planned rise in spending for military personnel did little more than handle pay raises and previous increases in benefits. At the same time, the Iraq War has exposed a host of other problems in the way the United States deals with military personnel, only some of which are as yet being addressed.

As Figure 4.1 shows, the FY2007–FY2011 FYDP made no allowance for added military manpower, and the fact it provides no increases in the out-years meant substantial potential cutbacks in end strength because of the rising direct costs of military personnel in terms of pay and benefits, and of the cost of recruiting and retention. These problems are greatly compounded by the cost escalation in research, development, test, and development (RDT&E) and procurement, and chronic underfunding of operations and maintenance, described in other chapters.

President Bush began to take a more realistic approach to these manpower issues in a speech on January 10, 2007, when he announced plans to surge U.S. forces in Iraq as part of a new strategy for bringing stability to that country. His speech clearly illustrated the importance of adequate military manpower in an era of asymmetric wars. The ability to surge force deployments was seen as critical to gaining control over an increasingly restive and divided Baghdad. While it was far from clear that such a buildup would give the United States any kind of victory, the Bush plan called for the following:

- Five additional Army brigades (about 18,000 troops) to Baghdad,
- Two additional Marine battalions (about 2,000 troops) to Anbar,
- Army brigades currently in Baghdad could see their time extended by three to seven months, and
- Marines in Anbar could see their time extended by up to five months.

The President also had to take the growing strains on the Reserves into account. According to a National Security Council Iraq Strategy highlights briefing, the United States was to "remobilize the National Guard to support rotations." A day after the President's speech, on January 11, the Pentagon announced that steps would be taken to make more Reservists available for duty in Iraq and Afghanistan by changing the policies that governed how often members of the Army National Guard and the Reserve could be mobilized.

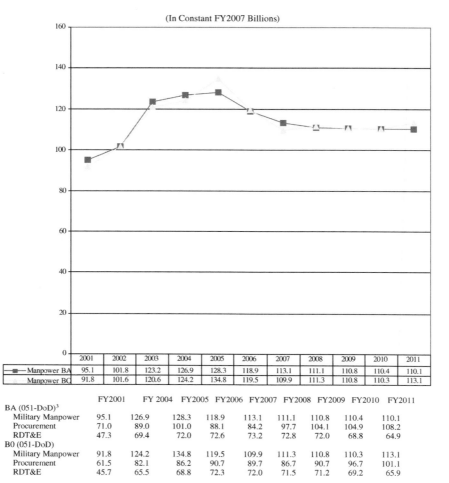

	FY2001	FY 2004	FY2005	FY2006	FY2007	FY2008	FY2009	FY2010	FY2011
BA (051-DoD)[3]									
Military Manpower	95.1	126.9	128.3	118.9	113.1	111.1	110.8	110.4	110.1
Procurement	71.0	89.0	101.0	88.1	84.2	97.7	104.1	104.9	108.2
RDT&E	47.3	69.4	72.0	72.6	73.2	72.8	72.0	68.8	64.9
B0 (051-DoD)									
Military Manpower	91.8	124.2	134.8	119.5	109.9	111.3	110.8	110.3	113.1
Procurement	61.5	82.1	86.2	90.7	89.7	86.7	90.7	96.7	101.1
RDT&E	45.7	65.5	68.8	72.3	72.0	71.5	71.2	69.2	65.9

Source: FY2007 Green Book, p. 115 and 133

Figure 4.1   Less Money for Boots on the Ground and Minds above Them: Total DoD Manpower Expenditures: FY2002–FY2011

The new Secretary of Defense, Robert Gates, followed up a few days later by announcing an increase in the permanent end strength of the Army and Marine Corps over the coming five years. Combined, both services were to grow by 92,000 forces, although that number included the permanent increase of 30,000 in the Army, which had already been taking place over the preceding three years. These increases were to take place as follows:

Army

- The Army is to grow to 547,000 total soldiers.

- The number of 507,000 soldiers as of 2007 is to rise to 512,000 by the end of the year as part of the ongoing 30,000 increase taking place over the preceding three years.

- Gates is to make this 30,000 increase permanent and will further boost the size of the Army by an additional 35,000 soldiers. These 35,000 soldiers are to be recruited over the coming five years.

- The 2007 recruiting goals for the Army stand at 80,000 new recruits per year, meaning the Army has to raise its goals to 87,000 for the coming five years to meet the new needs.

Marines

- The number of 180,000 Marines as of 2007 is to grow to 202,000.

- The goal is to add 22,000 new Marines and make permanent the 5,000 increase of the preceding three years.

- The Marines had annual recruiting goals of 39,000 as of 2007; those numbers are to rise over the coming five years.

- The Marines had wanted this increase because it would add significantly more combat battalions into the mix to make Marine deployments easier: in effect, providing Marines with one year of overseas duty and two years at home.

These new manpower polices allowed Guard members and units that had been called up in the previous five years to be called up again for a tour of up to 24 consecutive months. This departed from a previous policy that sought to keep rotations to once every five year. Secretary Gates announced that this change would enable the Bush Administration to call up tens of thousands of Guard members who were off limits under the previous rules. General Peter Pace, current Chairman of the Joint Chiefs of Staff, told reporters that some of the Guard units "that will be mobilized in the coming period will not have had five years since their last mobilization," that some will have been home for only four years, and others three.[4] As of January 2007, of the 650,000 soldiers who had served in Iraq thus far, about 170,000 had already served more than one tour, according to the Army.[5]

The fact remains, however, that far more serious planning and resource decisions still need to be made. Manpower and procurement need to be brought into balance, major resource trade-offs need to be made, and the top leadership of the Department and the military services has to be made to actually lead and make hard decisions. Better planning and management systems, and procurement reform, will be largely a disruptive waste of time if they are not preceded by such actions. Above all, current useful legacy systems and forces in existence should not be sacrificed for a field of dreams.

THE IMPACT ON MILITARY MANPOWER ON THE HUMAN COST OF WAR

Any discussion of military manpower must be prefaced with the fact that the men and women in uniform face fundamentally different burdens and risks. They face the burden of having to follow the career path set by the service, living with constant moves and relocations, and facing long deployments away from home and family. The risks they face can be measured in several different ways. The most obvious is the number of casualties. At the same time, it is the overall pattern of strain on the men and women in uniform that is the measure of U.S. ability to recruit and retain the personnel it needs. Such strains are hard to measure, but the data available raise serious questions as to whether the United States has a large enough pool of actives and reserves to implement its strategy in an era that mixes the risk of serious regional contingencies with "long wars" of attrition.

The most direct cost of war, and the highest level of sacrifice, is paid in human blood. As Chapter 2 has shown, recent wars have been less costly in terms of this price tag than their predecessors, but this scarcely means they are "affordable" to the men and women concerned. If one looks at how the detailed patterns behind the total casualties discussed in Chapter 2 have developed over time, the human impact of war on America's military manpower resources becomes all too clear.

- Figure 4.2 shows the daily rate of Coalition and Iraqi casualties, by month, from January 2004 through August 11, 2006. It is important to note that U.S. casualties were substantially lower than Iraqi casualties over time, but made up the most Coalition casualties. As of September 1, 2006, U.S. losses accounted for 92 percent of all Coalition troops killed versus 4 percent for the United Kingdom, and 4 percent for all other Coalition partners.[6]

- Figure 4.3 shows overall Coalition casualties and Iraqi troop fatalities from October 2005 through August 2006.

- Figure 4.4 shows trends in U.S. casualties by month, March 2003 through July 2006. While emphasis is often placed on killed-in-action casualties, the data show the significant numbers of wounded in Iraq. Such casualties can also bear significantly on recruiting and retention scenarios.

- Figure 4.5 provides data on some of the follow-on effects of combat for troops returning from action. While not counted among the casualty figures, troops returning home with emotional stress—often leading to problems in personal/familial relationships—can stand as a barrier to recruiting and retention efforts.

If nothing else, Figures 4.2 through 4.5 make it clear that "overstretch" involves far more than force numbers and defense spending. It is clear that wounds dominate the human cost of war in an era of extraordinary military medical services and that even those who do not receive any physical injury pay a price that extends far beyond their time in theater. At the same time, it is important to note that it may be years, and take several future wars, to determine just how much stress direct and indirect psychological and physical problems put on U.S. military manpower and what kind of manpower pool and deployment cycles are sustainable in recruiting and retaining an all-volunteer force structure.

The Gulf War was too short to provide a model of the burdens and risks that would emerge with the mix of long wars, regional conflicts, and crisis-driven

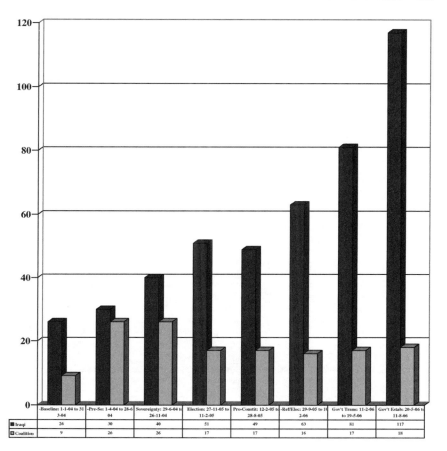

	-Baseline: 1-1-04 to 31 3-04	-Pre-So: 1-4-04 to 28-6 04	Sovereignty: 29-6-04 to 26-11-04	Election: 27-11-05 to 11-2-05	Pro-Constit: 12-2-05 to 28-8-05	-Ref/Elec: 29-9-05 to 16 2-06	Gov't Trans: 11-2-06 to 19-5-06	Gov't Estab: 20-5-06 to 11-8-06
▪ Iraqi	26	30	40	51	49	63	81	117
☐ Coalition	9	26	26	17	17	16	17	18

Note: the Department of Defense states that these "Casualty data reflect updated data for each period from unverified reports submitted by Coalition elements responding to the incident; the inconclusivity of these numbers constrains them to be used only for comparative purposes."

Source: Department of Defense, Measuring Stability and Security in Iraq, Report to Congress in Accordance with the Department of Defense Appropriations Act 2006 (Section 9010), September 1, 2006, p. 32.

Figure 4.2   Overall Casualty Patterns Multinational Security Transition Command-Iraq (MNSTC-I) Estimate of Daily Killed and Wounded, January 2004–August 11, 2006

missions the United States now projects for the future. The Iraq War will provide more useful data once sufficient time is available to measure its overall impact. It may well be the first war in which the United States has reliable data on the longer-term psychological and physical costs—or casualties—of war. It still, however, may be an atypical data point.

The United States faces the prospect of putting an all-volunteer force structure through one to two decades of repeated combat deployments that depend on high

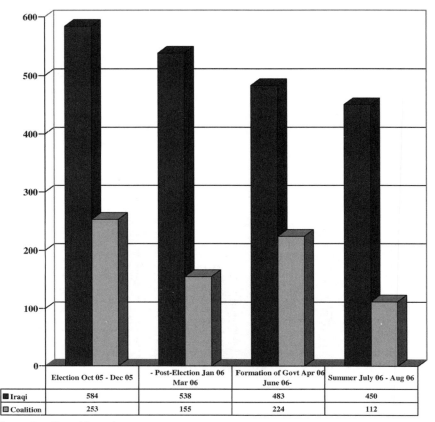

	Election Oct 05 - Dec 05	- Post-Election Jan 06 Mar 06	Formation of Govt Apr 06 June 06-	Summer July 06 - Aug 06
■ Iraqi	584	538	483	450
▣ Coalition	253	155	224	112

Source: http://icasualties.org/

Figure 4.3   Overall Casualty Patterns: Coalition and Iraqi Military Fatalities, October 2005–August 2006

levels of retention in the face of both significant casualties and serious lasting psychological and physical aftereffects. It is easy to speculate about what this means in terms of its impact on the all-volunteer force structure and the men and women who serve in it, but psychobabble and sociological jargon will remain psychobabble and sociological jargon until far more data are available than are available today.

The Issue of Ethics and Morality

There are a number of different ways to reduce the burden and risk faced by the U.S. military, but the following options still leave open the question of the ethics of relying on an all-volunteer force structure that pays a small number of Americans to take on the highest single burden and responsibility of citizenship.

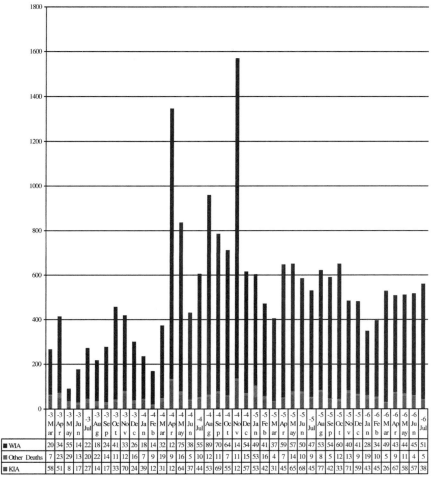

	-3 Mar	-3 Apr	-3 May	-3 Jun	-3 Jul	-3 Aug	-3 Sep	-3 Oct	-3 Nov	-3 Dec	-4 Jan	-4 Feb	-4 Mar	-4 Apr	-4 May	-4 Jun	-4 Jul	-4 Aug	-4 Sep	-4 Oct	-4 Nov	-4 Dec	-5 Jan	-5 Feb	-5 Mar	-5 Apr	-5 May	-5 Jun	-5 Jul	-5 Aug	-5 Sep	-5 Oct	-5 Nov	-5 Dec	-6 Jan	-6 Feb	-6 Mar	-6 Apr	-6 May	-6 Jun	-6 Jul
■ WIA	20	34	55	14	22	18	24	41	33	26	18	14	32	12	75	38	55	89	70	64	14	54	49	41	37	59	57	50	47	53	54	60	40	41	28	34	49	43	44	45	51
■ Other Deaths	7	23	29	13	20	22	14	11	12	16	7	9	19	9	16	5	10	12	11	7	11	15	53	16	4	7	14	10	9	8	5	12	13	9	19	10	5	9	11	4	5
■ KIA	58	51	8	17	27	14	17	33	70	24	39	12	31	12	64	37	44	53	69	55	12	57	53	42	31	45	65	68	45	77	42	33	71	59	43	45	26	67	58	57	38

Source: Defense Manpower Data Center, Statistical Information Analysis Division; http://icasualties.org.

Figure 4.4   Trends in Total U.S. Casualties by Month, March 2003–July 2006

Today, only 0.08 percent of Americans serve in the military—the lowest percentage of the population serving under arms in a century. This compares with just over 4 percent of the population serving in the military during Vietnam.[7] Moreover, the percentage of veterans who bring military experience to American politics, and the other elements of civil society, continues to fall precipitously. Today's soldiers are certainly citizens, but most of today's citizens not only are not soldiers, they have little practical knowledge of just how different military life is and must be. If Vietnam presented the risk that Americans might become involved in the wrong war as a nation,

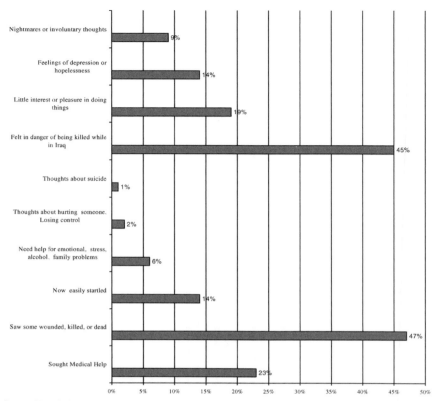

Source: USA Today, October 19, 2005, pp. 1 and 11. Based on Department of Defense Post-Deployment Health Assessment survey of 193,131 personnel.

Figure 4.5   The Impact of the Iraq War on Returning U.S. Forces

Iraq presents the risk that Americans may pay for the sacrifices of other men's sons and daughters with less concern than if they were their own.

Yet, it is far from clear that there is a good alternative. In 2003, Senator Ernest "Fritz" Hollings and Congressman Charles B. Rangel introduced the Universal National Service Act, calling for the reinstitution of the draft. The bill would have reinstituted the procedures for registration, selection, and induction from the prior conscription act—the Military Selective Service Act—with the exception that the new bill called for all "persons" (to include women) to perform a period of military or civilian service to further national defense and homeland security, with the draft age set at between the ages of 18 and 26.

The problem is that no form of the draft seems to be an answer to today's military needs or the problem of sharing the burden of military service. Returning to the draft in an era of nonexistential wars, where there is no apparent threat to the national existence of the United States, would mean flooding a professional military with unwilling, inexperienced, short-service personnel.

Such draftees would have such a short "life cycle" in terms of skill levels and short tours of duty as to make them unsuitable for any demanding military task. They could not be true members of the kind of military team needed in modern warfighting, they would present major problems in morale and motivation, and diverting the truly professional military to train and command them would create a new burden on the professional military that could offset much of their value even in less demanding roles.

Fixing the current system is not an answer to the deeper question of the ethics and morality of paying a small portion of citizens to take the highest burden of citizenship. The fact remains, however, that the United States has long done this in law enforcement and emergency response and simply may not have any practical alternative. A paid, all-volunteer force may not be ethically and morally desirable from a societal viewpoint, but it may well be functionally inevitable.

HUMAN STRAIN ON THE OVERALL U.S. FORCE POSTURE

These human costs show why military manpower is not an accounting issue or one where people can be traded in analytic models against other investments in terms of cost-effectiveness. Strategists and force planners also need to remember that Iraq is only one measure of how adequate the U.S. force posture is to deal with other kinds of stress imposed by actual warfighting. The United States could find itself in a simultaneous conflict in Korea or over the Taiwan Strait, or in a broader war in the Middle East. Nevertheless, the Iraq War has imposed enough strain on U.S. military manpower to provide a clear warning that the United States may need both a different force posture and a larger pool of manpower.

At the same time, many of the data currently available may be misleading and are hard to interpret. The Iraq War has created recruiting and retention problems, but at least on the surface the manpower data issued by the Department of Defense show more of a problem in terms of current and future recruiting and retention costs than in manpower numbers. Such data may, however, be misleading, particularly in the case of retention. The men and women now in the active and reserve forces have a very high sense of mission. While surveys of their attitudes sometimes produce a long list of complaints, they often reenlist out of loyalty to their country, their service, or their unit and immediate companions. As a result, wartime retention data can be misleading. Those serving may be much more willing to leave once "their war" is over, and preliminary estimates of retention for 2007 and beyond indicate that the United States may well be headed for crises in retaining officers at the rank of Captain and below and skilled noncommissioned officers and technicians.

Recruiting data, in contrast, can produce the opposite reaction. Those unfamiliar with military service may decline to enlist during war or may choose to enlist in the military services they see as having lower risks. In this case, however, the problem may end with the conflict. The problems the land forces—the U.S. Army and the U.S. Marine Corps—have in recruiting may end once potential recruits do not face the immediate prospect of repeated combat tours. These manpower issues are compounded by racial issues and the fact that the military has been seen as a more beneficial career path for some minorities in peacetime, but not in wartime.

The existing U.S. force structure is, however, very different from the "hollow force" that existed at the time of Vietnam. Some 98 percent of enlisted men now have high school diplomas versus 75 percent of the nation's 18- to 24-year-olds. More than 70 percent of those actually recruited into the armed services scored in the top half of the Armed Forces Qualification Test versus roughly half of the ordinary population.[8] Nearly 92 percent of the officers now have college degrees, and 35–45 percent of each military service has advanced degrees—a higher percentage than in the total population of graduate students. Racial profiling of today's military forces is difficult because the population is far more mixed than in the past, but over 73 percent of recruits were white in 2004 and 2005, compared with 75.6 percent who identified themselves as white in the 2000 census. While there are slightly more blacks and Hispanics in the recruiting pool than in the general population, there are now less in active combat units. Moreover, if the National Guard and the Reserves are included, there are slightly more whites in the total force mix than in the general population.

The National Guard and Reserves present another kind of problem. The limited pool of active military manpower and a force posture designed to force the services to call up the Reserves in any serious conflict have put extraordinary strains on men and women whose primary career lies outside the military. Repeated, long and extended, or high-risk deployments present special problems in recruiting and retaining such personnel, as well as additional moral and ethical questions as to how much of a burden should be placed on Reserves in anything other than a vital or existential conflict. This not only affects family life, but has a major impact on the self-employed, and on real-world ability to retain jobs in businesses that are not government contractors. It can also have a major impact in civilian areas with high percentages of Reservists like law enforcement, and on small communities with a high percentage of people in the Reserves or the National Guard.[9]

Recruiting and retention data also understate the true strain on military manpower resources because various forms of force retention, major new investments in recruiting and retention activity, and steadily greater bonuses and incentives have a major impact on both retention and recruiting. Such incentives have increased sharply over time.

THE IRAQ WAR'S IMPACT ON RECRUITING

So far, the Iraq War has had more impact on recruiting and retention costs than actual shortfalls, although there have been some changes in the quality of recruits. As has been discussed in the previous chapter, there have been massive increases in the funds used to recruit and retain military personnel, and in the cost per solider.

This includes a 60-precent rise in the personnel and training cost per solider between 2001 and 2006, and a doubling in such spending on Reservists.[10]

The Recruiting Challenge

Most recruiting occurs among young men and women with little military experience and who are heavily influenced by their parents, mentors, and peers. The fact that the war has become steadily more unpopular has had an inevitable impact. In April 2003, a CNN/Gallup poll reported that 73 percent of the American public believed that the war in Iraq was worthwhile and 23 percent did not. Two years later in May 2005 only 41 percent believed it was worthwhile, and 57 percent believed it was not.[11] A year later, in June 2006, a *USA Today*/Gallup poll showed that 57 percent said Congress should pass a resolution outlining a plan for withdrawing U.S. troops, while 39 percent said that decision should be left to the President and his advisers. Precisely half supported withdrawing all U.S. forces immediately or within 12 months, while 41 percent said the United States should keep troops there for as many years as needed.[12]

While the trend in public opinion was not consistent and varied according to the course of the war and the quality of the Administration's case for it, the trends were not favorable to either the war or recruiting:

- A June 2005 Gallup poll reported that the American people had more confidence in the U.S. military than any other institution—this, however, did not appear to translate into support for the war or a willingness of civilians to enlist.[13]

- In a July 2005 Gallup poll, 36 percent of Americans interviewed said that the United States should not have gone to war in Iraq *and* that a timetable should be set for withdrawal. Only 30 percent believed that the United States should have gone to war *and* the troops should remain in Iraq as long as they are needed.[14]

- A *Washington Post*/ABC News poll released in early March 2006 showed that a majority of Americans—80 percent—believed that the Sunni/Shi'ite fighting in Iraq would lead to a civil war. Of those surveyed, 52 percent said they believed the United States should start withdrawing troops immediately. The number of respondents saying they felt the United States was making progress fell to 49 percent, down from 65 percent three months before.[15]

- From January 18 through February 14, 2006, preliminary work began gauging the sentiment of U.S. troops toward the war. Soldiers were questioned for a Le Moyne College/Zogby poll as to their outlook on future U.S. troop levels in Iraq. The poll included 944 military respondents interviewed at several undisclosed locations throughout Iraq. Though the utility of the poll as a barometer for sentiment was uncertain at the time of its release, some of the results were as follows:

  - Fifty-eight percent said their mission was clear; 42 percent said the U.S. role was hazy.

  - Seventy-two percent of troops surveyed said that U.S. troops should exit the country within the following year: 29 percent of members of various services believed the

United States should leave immediately, 22 percent responded that troops should leave in the next six months, and 21 percent said that troops should leave within 6 to 12 months. Twenty-three percent responded that troops should remain "as long as they are needed."

- Only 30 percent said that they thought the DoD had failed to provide adequate troop protection, such as body armor, munitions, and uparmoring for Humvees.[16]

- A CBS poll conducted in March 2006 showed that Americans had become increasingly pessimistic about the current predicament in Iraq, as well as the future of U.S. involvement:

  - More than 7 in 10 Americans said that there was currently a civil war in Iraq, while 13 percent said that a civil war was likely to break out in the future.

  - Just 15 percent said that the United States was likely to succeed in Iraq, down from 21 percent in January 2006. Another 36 percent said that success was somewhat likely, down from 42 percent in January. Forty-seven percent said that it was either not very or not at all likely that the United States would achieve success—up from 35 percent just two months prior.

  - Half of the respondents felt that the government was not giving U.S. troops in Iraq enough resources and military equipment to succeed.[17]

- World Public Opinion conducted a poll of 851 Americans on Iraq from March 1–6, 2006. The following were among the results:[18]

  - Just 31 percent of respondents said it was a "war of necessity, that is, it was necessary for the defense of the United States." Sixty-seven percent held the view that it was a "war of choice, that is, some US interests and values were at stake, but it was not necessary for the defense of the United States."

  - Sixty-eight percent favored beginning to draw down U.S. troops in Iraq. But only 26 percent thought that all troops should be withdrawn within six months. The percentage favoring reductions was up sharply from December 2004, when just 48 percent favored them.

  - Asked to assess the current situation in Iraq, 64 percent said the situation was getting worse, while just 36 percent said it was getting better. Asked to rate how confident they were that "the US intervention in Iraq will succeed" on a 0–10 scale, 58 percent gave a low confidence rating (0–4), while just 28 percent give a high confidence rating (6–10). The mean score was 3.97. These assessments showed a marked downward trend. There was an 11-point increase in those saying that the situation was getting worse as compared to October 2004, when 53 percent saw the situation getting worse and 46 percent saw it getting better.

The broad trends in public opinion do not necessarily affect recruiting, which draws on a much smaller base of the population. It has been clear, however, that the Iraq War is a land war of attrition and one that does not promise a rapid end. It has also been a war where most casualties occur in the Army and the Marine Corps. Potential recruits found joining the Army and Marine Corps increasingly risky.

Analyzing the Trends in Recruiting in Detail

If one looks at recruiting during the Iraq War, some of the data have been ambiguous, but the trends have scarcely been good. Army recruiting and retention had not yet become a problem in terms of sheer numbers, but the recruiting trends were largely negative through 2005.

The Army did get 94 percent of its needed first-term reenlistments in 2004 and 96 percent of its mid-career retentions, but the figures were bad for several months in 2004 and continued to drop off through 2005. The first quarter of FY2006, however, began to show signs of revitalization. New recruiting measures coupled with bonus increases were among the reasons sited for what appeared to be a rebound in recruiting numbers, in particular for the Army National Guard. Figure 4.6 shows recruitment goals and achievements for active Army and Army Reserves from 1990 to 2005.

Trends in 2004

If one looks at the trends in recruiting and military manpower after the first flush of "victory" in 2003, Reservists made up about 40 percent of the 140,000 troops serving in Iraq. By late September 2004, these troops included 5,600 Individual Ready Reserve (IRR) soldiers called up in early July. Meanwhile Reservist deployments were growing longer and longer. As a result, training periods became pinched due to the need to quickly deploy.

Figure 4.6   Army Recruiting Goals/Achievements 1990 to 2005

Year	Active Army		Army Reserve	
	Mission	Accessions	Mission	Accessions
1990	87,000	88,617	56,767	57,357
1991	78,241	78,241	52,500	51,369
1992	75,000	77,583	52,923	52,829
1993	76,900	77,563	42,600	43,088
1994	68,000	68,063	40,000	40,681
1995	63,000	62,967	40,000	40,186
1996	73,400	73,528	43,197	38,440
1997	82,000	82,087	40,000	39,353
1998	72,550	71,749	40,600	37,050
1999	74,500	68,210	45,584	35,035
2000	80,000	80,113	41,961	42,086
2001	75,800	75,855	34,910	35,530
2002	79,500	79,604	28,825	31,319
2003	73,800	74,132	26,400	27,365
2004	77,000	77,587	21,200	21,278
2005	80,000	73,373	28,485	23,859

Source: U.S. Army, http://usmilitary.about.com/od/joiningthemilitary/a/recruitgoals.htm.

At the same time, stop-loss had become a greater issue. While the practice had been employed, to varying degrees, throughout the military services since 2001, leadership in certain reserve forces had begun to complain that the practice had begun to negatively impact on recruiting to the reserve component (RC). Because stop-loss keeps personnel from leaving active duty, these personnel cannot be recruited to the National Guard and the Reserves. Personnel leaving the active component (AC) have been a traditionally strong pool for recruiting to the RC.

A target of 56,000 new recruits for the Army National Guard (ARNG) in FY2004 fell short by 5,000, marking the first missed goal for the Army National Guard since 1994. The 2004 ARNG recruiting goal from the AC was 8,000, with only 3,000 obtained. In late September 2004, ARNG spokesman Scott Woodham stated that there were 5,000 potential recruits lost to stop-loss. While it is not clear that the entire 5,000-man shortfall can be directly linked to stop-loss practices in the AC, evidence did suggest a correlation.

The Army increased the available signing bonuses three times in 2004, from $15,000 to $20,000. There were major new incentives in terms of Army pay. Key veteran Special Operations troops got reenlistment bonuses of up to $150,000 for five-year reenlistments for certain personnel.[19] Military pay, however, was still approximately 5 percent below average private sector pay, according to the Military Officers Association of America, an Alexandria, Virginia, group made up of 370,000 active and retired military officers and surviving spouses.[20]

Trends in 2005

By early 2005, the strain of meeting recruiting requirements had led to increases in the number of recruiting personnel in both the AC and RC Army. The Army National Guard was adding 1,400 new recruiters to its existing 2,700, bringing its force to 4,100—a rise of 38 percent. Other incentives being offered by the Guard included the following:[21]

- $15,000 bonus for new Guard recruits who have served in the military, triple the previous figure.
- $15,000 bonus for Guard soldiers who would reenlist for six years, also three times the previous amount.
- $10,000 bonus for recruits who had never served in the military, up from $6,000 and the largest to-date bonus the Guard had offered to such recruits.

Stop-loss remained an issue as well, in both the AC and RC, with flagging recruiting numbers into FY2005. As of mid-October, 7,845 AC Army soldiers were under stop-loss orders and 13,578 Guard members had been "stop-lossed."

By the summer of 2005, one-third of the U.S. total presence in Iraq was from the Guard—roughly 45,000 troops. There were 8,000 Guardsmen in Afghanistan.[22] As of late June 2005, 7 of the Army's 15 brigades deployed in Iraq or Afghanistan were

National Guard brigades, and 50 percent of the Army's infantry, mechanized, and armored battalions were National Guard units.[23]

The Iraq War was also starting to put serious pressure on U.S. recruiting and end strength. According to General Peter J. Schoomaker, in testimony to the Senate Armed Services Committee on June 30, 2005, the Army was faced with having to recruit 165,000 new troops for active, Guard, and reserve duty each year. This figure accounted for 30 percent of the American males between the ages of 17 and 24. Furthermore, according to Schoomaker, only about 30 percent of males in that age group meet the military's standards for enlistment.[24] Strain to fill the ranks was not helped by the Army's end-strength expansion to 512,400. Similarly, the corresponding increase in the number of total junior officers presented difficulties in an environment where personnel were choosing to leave the service earlier than anticipated. If one looks at the totals in the first figures, they reflect an impressive total manpower pool. If one looks at the active strength of the U.S. Army and Marine Corps, however, the totals are far less impressive. They show both why recruiting and retention are so important in "ground wars" like Iraq and Afghanistan and why the United States was so dependent on reserve forces.

Figure 4.7 shows the recent trends in military end strengths and the active end strengths and mobilization numbers for 2005.

As of July 5, 2005, Iraq and Afghanistan saw 268 Guardsmen fatalities (as opposed to 97 Guardsmen fatalities during the Vietnam War).[25] The Army's National Guard recruiting numbers saw a period of decline in 2005:

- The National Guard met only 70 percent of its May 2005 mission, 86 percent of its June mission (missed its 5,032 target by 695 recruits),[26] and 76 percent of its year-to-date mission.[27] 2004 marked the first year that the Army National Guard missed its mission goal since 1994.[28] Army Lieutenant General H. Steven Blum attributed past recruiting successes to word-of-mouth, adding that when "27% of [the] force [is] deployed overseas, they're not doing much word-of-mouth recruiting."[29]

Figure 4.7   DoD and Services End Strengths for 2005

FY2005	Active	Mobilized*	Guard	Selected Reserve**	Career Civilian	TOTAL
TOTAL	1,415,600	210,252	456,800	404,100	680,466	2,923,966
DoD	–	–	–	–	106,000	106,000
Army	512,400	148,442	350,000	205,000	218,000	1,285,400
Navy	365,900	6,508	–	83,400	193,466	642,766
Marines	178,000	9,717	–	39,600	–	217,600
Air Force	359,300	45,585	106,800	76,100	163,000	705,200

*   FY2004 Supplemental for Guard & Reserve called to active duty, Non-Add.
**   Does not include nondrilling IRR. Source: Adapted from www.globalsecurity.org.
Source: Department of Defense and Stephen Dagget, "Defense: FY 2007 Authorization and Appropriations," Washington, Congressional Research Service, RL33405, October 19, 2006, p. 72.

- The Army Recruiting Command also reported that the Reserves met 82 percent of their May 2005 mission and 80 percent of the year-to-date mission.[30] The Army did, however, lower its accession goal by 1,350 earlier in the spring for the month of May. It did not lower its total goal of 80,000 accessions.

- In June, the Army Reserves exceeded their goal of 5,650 recruits by 507. The Reserves were still approximately 2,350 below their total goal for FY2005.

As of August 25, 2006, however, the number of National Guard and Reserve deaths for the year totaled 54—less than one-third of the 189 recorded at the same point last year. In the comparable period in 2004, the death toll was 92, according to Defense Department casualty records.[31]

These recruiting percentages, however, were also only part of the story. If one looks at the recruiting base and the marginal cost of recruiting, the United States had to make major changes to achieve these numbers. The Army, for example, had cut the average number of days by 50 percent between the time that recruits sign up to the time that they enter boot camp. The sped-up process allowed for a higher short-term intake, but failed to address the longer-term recruiting realities.

The Chief of the Army Reserve and the Chief of the National Guard Bureau both identified potential long-term consequences. The Chief of the Army Reserve wrote the Army Chief of Staff, saying, the Army Reserve was additionally in grave danger of being unable to meet its other operational requirements, including those in named op plans and continental United States (CONUS) emergencies. The Chief of the National Guard Bureau, Brigadier General Bill Libby, expressed concerns that the National Guard would not be ready for the next time it is needed, whether at home or abroad. Meanwhile, governors of various states were also voicing concern about the National Guard's ability to perform in the event of a natural disaster or attack on the homeland.

This was forcing major changes in the use of the Guard and the Reserves. According to Secretary of the Army Francis Harvey, the Army would rely on the Reserve and the Guard much less between 2005 and 2007. He and General Schoomaker both said they anticipated that the current number of seven brigades in Iraq would be reduced to two during the next rotation (in the next two years). Harvey also predicted that the number of Guard units would be reduced to 11 percent of the force in Iraq, as opposed to 41 percent in 2005.[32] The Army said it would be able to do this as a result of restructuring the Army into modular units and the addition of at least ten new active-duty brigades, bringing the total to at least 43.

Though the U.S. Marine Corps (USMC) also plays a major role in Iraq and Afghanistan, it had not struggled with recruiting to the extent that the Army had as of early 2005:

- In January 2005, the USMC met 97 percent of its recruitment goal, but slipped to 93.5 percent in February. In early May, the USMC reached 99 percent of its year-to-date target.

- The USMC saw a positive improvement at the end of May when it shipped 2,674 recruits, 73 above its target.
- The USMC shipping goal for the 2005 fiscal year was 39,150, which included 6,100 Reserves. As of June, the Corps shipped a total of 20,735 recruits, 395 more recruits than required for the year to date, or 102 percent of its accessions target for FY2005.[33]

Nevertheless, the Marine Corps faced challenges. Even though its recruitment numbers did not drop as much as those of the Army, the Marine Corps had to invest more time and money in the recruitment process. According to General Michael W. Hagee, "a [Marine Corps] recruiter today spends about 12 hours for each individual recruited. Before 9/11, they were spending about four hours for each individual recruited."[34]

The Air Force and the Navy faced less severe challenges, but the pressure on recruiting did affect these services. Although its end strength was not at risk, the Air Force went from meeting 111 percent of its recruiting goal in 2004 to meeting only 82 percent of its goal in the first two months of 2005. The Air Guard and the Reserves had become filled with aircrews that planned to leave, posing a serious threat to airlift and the service's "force enablers."

In order to deal with recruiting challenges, all of the services—and the Army in particular—had to take major new steps to provide further incentives:

- General Schoomaker testified in a hearing before the Senate Armed Services Committee on June 30, 2005, that the armed forces had been exploring the possibility of providing home mortgage incentives up to $50,000. (*USA Today* reported that the Army had asked for cash bonuses of $40,000.)[35]
- Under Secretary of Defense for Personnel and Readiness David S.C. Chu proposed a bonus for critical skills retention for the Reserves, as well as a bonus for active-duty soldiers willing to join the Reserves when they complete active duty. He also suggested an increase in hardship-duty pay.
- Along with these bonuses, soldiers were offered an opportunity to participate in either the Loan Repayment Program, which would pay back up to $65,000 worth of federal student loans for soldiers who enlisted for three or more years, or the Army College Fund, which provided soldiers with up to $70,000 for college if they had been selected to work in a "high-priority specialty."

The new incentives had a positive impact on the retention scenario. Task Force Baghdad, for example, was exceeding fiscal year reenlistment goals. By early September, Task Force Baghdad saw 3,100 reenlistments versus a goal of 2,925, which encompassed the combination of all initial term, mid-career, and career soldier reenlistments. The soldiers earned a total payout of more than $23 million in tax-free bonuses for their continued service.[36]

Still, the prospect of serving in Iraq was widely considered to be a factor that contributed to a 7,000-person recruiting shortfall in 2005, despite the additional recruiters and added incentives. According to a study by a Democratic advisory group, chaired by former Defense Secretary William Perry, as of January 2006, the active-duty component of the Army had a deficit of about 18,000 junior enlisted personnel. Overall, the study found that Army manpower had dropped during 2005, with a strength of 492,000 personnel versus a goal of 502,000.[37]

By 2005, the Army and other services also had to change their recruiting strategy. They had to make massive increases in the number of recruiters as well as providing the aforementioned incentives. In early 2005, the Army was adding more than 800 active-duty recruiters to the current 5,201—a rise of 15 percent in a single year.[38] The Army had increased its total number of recruiters in the field by 3,000, raising the total number of recruiters to 12,000, and hired civilian recruiters as well.[39]

The Army assigned Iraq War veterans to work with recruiters to talk about their experiences in Iraq and Afghanistan. Some parts of the Army National Guard had to increase recruiter strength by 30 percent. According to Charles S. Abell, Principal Deputy Under Secretary of Defense for Personnel and Readiness, many recruiters worked 16 or more hours a day, seven days a week.[40] Perhaps partly as a result of Iraq War pressures, 37 Army recruiters had folded under the pressure and gone AWOL by late spring of 2005.[41] Army Secretary Harvey also suggested that the Army would target the approximately 1.1 million home-schooled Americans, increasing its advertising budget as a means of getting the word out more effectively.

By the end of 2005, the services faced significant recruiting problems, although most were able to meet or exceed their numerical goals through new incentives, and others benefited from being seen as lower-risk alternatives. The Army came up 8 percent short of its annual goal, its largest recruiting shortfall since 1979.[42] Secretary of the Army Francis Harvey faced the most difficult recruiting environment of all the military branches and has said that he believed the decreasing popularity of the war to be directly linked to the Army's recruiting troubles.[43]

It was also clear that potential recruits no longer saw joining the National Guard as a safe way of earning extra money with only a limited risk of military service. The Army National Guard fell below the level of any other service component, meeting only 80 percent of its recruiting goal. The Air National Guard, which also had a high deployment level, missed its recruiting goal by 14 percent. By the end of 2005, overall recruiting results were mixed:[44]

- Army Active Component: missed goal of 80,000 by 6,627 recruits, first full-year deficit since 1999.
- Army Reserves: met 84 percent of goal with 23,859 recruits.
- Army National Guard: met 80 percent of goal with 50,219 recruits.
- Marine Corps Active Component: met 100 percent of goal of 32,917 recruits.
- Marine Corps Reserves: met 102 percent of goal.
- Navy Active Component: met 100 percent of goal of 37,635 recruits.
- Navy Reserves: met 88 percent of goal.
- Air Force Active Component: met 102 percent of goal of 18,900 recruits.

- Air Force Reserves: met 113 percent of recruiting goal.
- Air National Guard: met 86 percent of goal.

Trends in 2006

Fiscal Year 2006 saw positive developments in initial recruiting figures, particularly for the Army National Guard, which had experienced perhaps the worst recruiting scenario of the armed services. Coming off of a three-year slump, the ARNG began to bring in soldiers in greater numbers in 2006. On March 10, 2006, the Army Guard announced that it had signed up more than 26,000 soldiers in the first five months of FY2006, exceeding its target by 7 percent in its best performance in 13 years. The performance meant that the Guard was enlisting nearly as many troops as the AC, even though the Guard is a smaller force.

Once again, however, this required major new incentives. The leadership of the Army had threatened to cut funding for the ARNG after the service met only 80 percent of its recruiting goals in 2005. In early January, the ARNG doubled its maximum bonus to $20,000 for recruits who had never served in the military.

The Guard also instituted new recruiting programs. Expanded to 22 states in December 2005, these programs designated 31,000 Guard members as "recruiting assistants," who were awarded $2,000 for every new person they recruited to the ranks. The program was meant to target people on a more personalized basis, as members sought to recruit friends and family into the service. Army leadership expected the Guard to meet its increased Congressionally mandated end strength of 350,000, with a goal of expanding the new recruiting program to 65,000 assistants. Meeting this goal would mean, in essence, that about one-fifth of the force would be recruiters.[45]

Meanwhile, by early 2006, the Navy was offering personnel bonuses of up to $125,000 for a commitment of five more years of service. The bonuses were in compliance with Congressional law setting a $25,000 per year cap on such bonuses. Although the Navy did not have to enact stop-loss policies like other services, high operational tempo—especially in aviation units—created similar strains.

The Army alone spent some $300 million more on recruiting in 2006 than in 2005, and money talked.[46] By October 2006, all of the active services—Army, Navy, Air Force, and Marines—had reported meeting or exceeding 2006 recruiting goals, as did the Marine Corps and Air Force Reserves. The Army Guard achieved 99 percent of its goal for the year, while the Air National Guard achieved 97 percent of its goal. The Navy Reserve saw the greatest shortfall, meeting just 87 percent of its goal, which the Navy attributed largely to a drop in the number of sailors leaving active duty, a normally reliable source of new reserve enlistments.[47]

By the end of the fiscal year, the active-duty Army had exceeded its goal of 80,000 recruits, according to Army officials, after falling short by 7,000 recruits in 2005. Meanwhile, recruiting at the Army National Guard had largely recovered from 2005 figures, when the Guard fell 20 percent short of its recruiting goals. The Guard still fell short of its recruiting goal for the year ending September 30, 2006, but officials reported that the service had exceeded goals for reenlistments during that period.[48]

Recruiting Standards

By the late fall of 2006, however, criticism began to grow regarding the quality of the men and women being recruited. Disputes arose of the Army's claims that successful ad campaigns, increased bonuses for enlistment, and other incentives were the primary forces behind the recovery in numbers. A particular practice that had drawn scrutiny was the increased use of "moral waivers" to accept into the service potential recruits who would have otherwise been disqualified, including drug abusers, persons with other criminal backgrounds, and gang members and former gang members. Nationally, the Army's acceptance of moral waivers increased from 7,640 in 2001 to 11,018 in 2006.[49]

On December 12, 2006, the Pentagon released similarly favorable recruiting data, which showed that the Navy and the Air Force had met their recruiting goals for the previous month, while the Army and the Marines reported exceeding goals for the month. The Army fared the best, signing up 6,484 recruits in November 2006 versus a target of 6,150—meaning 105 percent of its goal.[50]

The problem with such numbers was the steadily rising cost of meeting such goals, coupled with a slow drop in standards for those recruited. The maximum recruiting age also had to be increased to 42, and significant increases had taken place in relaxed educational standards, and waivers for misdemeanors and medical issues. The United States showed that it could still continue to recruit a relatively small percentage of its population to meet relatively limited goals. The trade-off, however, was a rise in cost per soldier at virtually every level from recruiting onward that would almost certainly endure once the Iraq War was over and make it harder to pay for any needed increase in total end strength.

Some accused the services of lowering their standards, sacrificing quality for quantity under the great pressure of the war. On the one hand, the Army could still report in 2005 that it had been able to maintain the quality of its soldiers: 90 percent had high school diplomas, 73 percent scored between category I and IIIA on the Armed Services Vocational Aptitude Battery, [51] and 2 percent received a score in category IV; but these soldiers were the top 10 percent of this group.[52]

The Army reported that it had begun to ease restrictions on recruiting high school dropouts. To face the problem of non-degree-holder would-be recruits, the Army instituted a GED course, allowing dropouts to enroll in the Army-sponsored program to assist them in getting their equivalency degree. The number of high school dropouts recruited doubled to 9 percent, and the percentage of recruits with Category IV test results rose from 0.6 percent in 2004 to 1.8 percent during the first five months of FY2005. Only 60 percent had to be in the top aptitude category, as compared to the 73 percent the Army had in 2005. (Secretary of the Army Francis Harvey said in an interview with *USA Today* that 71 percent of the recruits scored above 50 percent on the aptitude test.)

The issue of waivers also became a growing issue by the end of 2005. Generally approved at the Pentagon, waivers allowed recruiters to sign up men and women who otherwise would have been ineligible for service due to legal convictions, medical problems, or other reasons preventing them from meeting minimum standards. According to statistics provided to Salon.com by the office of the Assistant Secretary of Defense for Public Affairs, the Army said that 17 percent—or 21,880 new soldiers—were admitted under waivers in 2005. In fact, there was further evidence that the 17-percent figure was actually low, as the Army had included data from the Army Reserve and the Army National Guard in determining it.

Furthermore, according to Salon.com, 37 percent of the Army's waivers (or about 8,000 soldiers) in 2005 were based on "moral grounds," essentially meaning criminal activity, ranging from minor infractions like traffic tickets to more serious infractions such as incidents of domestic abuse or narcotics. This represented a 32-percent increase of moral waivers issued compared to 2000, with concerns growing that units were becoming more and more likely to be manned by individuals with criminal backgrounds and increased penchants for undesirable behavior.[53] In FY2005, 15 percent of recruits in all required a waiver to be accepted for active-duty services, or about 11,000 people out of about 73,000 recruited.[54]

Issues of age and physical fitness also came to the fore as the services continued to face recruiting challenges. The Army, for example, raised its maximum recruitment age from 25 to 39, at a time when much attention was being given to the dangers of an aging force, especially in the National Guard and the Reserves.[55] According to a Pentagon spokesperson in March 2006, of the 157,000 troops serving in Iraq and Afghanistan, more than 1,700 were age 55 or older. In all, 1,603 of these older troops came from the National Guard and the Reserve.[56] In January 2006, the Army again raised its maximum age, this time to 40, followed by another hike just six months later to 42, putting the service at the maximum allowable recruitment age set by Congress in the 2006 defense budget authorization.[57]

Likewise, the Army had also begun to loosen physical fitness standards for recruits by early 2006. With much of the "recruitable" young population increasingly over-weight—the U.S. teen obesity rate jumped from 5 percent to 16 percent since 1976—the Army began offering physical fitness tests to overweight recruits. As of February 20, 2006, more than 800 would-be recruits who surpassed the Army's body-weight standards had passed conditioning tests and gone onto basic training. Relaxed rules allowed for recruits of any given height to weigh more for that height than was previously allowed, with male recruits simply needing to measure below 30 percent body fat.[58]

THE IRAQ WAR'S IMPACT ON RETENTION

Like recruiting, retention did not become a critical problem in terms of personnel numbers through 2006, although it did lead to major increases in retention bonuses and costs. The total cost of retention bonuses rose from $85 million in 2003 to $735 million in 2006—a nearly ninefold rise.[59]

By the summer of 2005, retention among the services was high, with both AC and RC components showing good numbers. For June 2005, each active-duty component met or exceeded its goals for retention. Meanwhile, the National Guard showed the following retention figures for the same month: Army National Guard retention was 105.9 percent of the cumulative goal of 23,647, and Air National Guard retention was 110 percent of its cumulative goal of 8,860. Losses in all Reserve components in May 2005 were lower than projected.[60]

By the fall of 2005, retention numbers for the AC remained good across the services, with results beginning to come in mixed for Reserve forces. All services exceeded retention goals for the month of October. The numbers for National Guard retention were as follows: for October, Army National Guard retention was 98 percent of the cumulative goal of 2,456, and Air National Guard retention was 110 percent of its cumulative goal of 986.[61]

As of March 2006, all of the active services were projected to meet their retention goals for the fiscal year. Retention numbers for the Reserves, however, remained mixed into the new year: for February, Army National Guard retention was 106 percent of the cumulative goal of 13,478, and Air National Guard retention was 95 percent of its cumulative goal of 4,046. The Army Guard was at 336,183 of an approved and funded end strength of 350,000, while the Air Guard was at 105,321 of an authorized 106,800.[62]

Meanwhile, another barometer of satisfaction with the service—the desertion rate—showed an overall positive trend by the end of 2005. Since the Iraq War began, at least 8,000 service personnel had deserted the armed forces. Since the fall of 2003, 4,387 Army soldiers, 3,454 Navy sailors, and 82 Air Force personnel had deserted. The Marine Corps listed 1,455 Marines in desertion status as of September 2005. The by-service desertion numbers, however, showed an improvement since 9/11. The Army, the Navy, and the Air Force reported 7,978 desertions in 2001 versus 3,456 in 2005. The Marines, meanwhile, were at 1,603 desertions in 2001, 148 more than in 2005. Overall, desertions represented 0.24 percent of the U.S. forces.[63]

The Human Dimension behind the Recruiting and Retention Base

The Iraq War has, however, raised issues that go beyond current recruiting and retention numbers. Recruiting and keeping the men and women America needs is more than a "mechanical" problem in terms of paying enough to get enough people. In the process of creating an all-volunteer force structure, the United States has also created an unwritten social contract with the men and women in the all-volunteer force. Patriotism is a very real motive, but those who join also join because of the contract that says the United States will offer reasonable incentives relative to reasonable inconvenience and reasonable risk.

This social contract is reinforced by the fact that some elements of the recruiting base for the all-volunteer force have different motives and reactions from others.

- Minorities often join the military to find upward mobility in ways where our civil society still at least partially discriminates against them.

- Poorer Americans often join for college and career benefits.

- Retention and joining the National Guard and the Reserves is shaped largely by prior military service.

- Some join the Guard because they believe they can supplement a limited income or pursue key interests at acceptable levels of deployment and interference with their main career.

Maintaining the Officer Corps

There was evidence that recruiting and retention difficulties were also having an impact on maintenance of the officer corps. In 2005, applications for U.S. service academies were down overall. Applications to West Point, the Naval Academy, and the Air Force Academy were down 9 percent, 20 percent, and 23 percent, respectively, for the year. The downtrend occurred as other four-year universities were seeing increases in applications. An official at West Point, however, said that the school was actually returning to its 5- to 10-year average, after a spike in applications following September 11.[64]

Another point of concern in early 2006 was evidence of declining standards in officer promotion in the Army. In 2005, the Army promoted 97 percent of all eligible captains to the rank of major, according to Pentagon data. This was up from a historical average of 70 to 80 percent. Traditionally, the Army has used the step to major as a winnowing point, sifting lower-performing soldiers out of the military. That same year, the Army also promoted 86 percent of eligible majors to the rank of colonel, up from the historical average of 65 to 75 percent.[65]

The trend was viewed as a consequence of retention woes, as officers left the military, often after multiple deployments to Iraq. According to Army data, the portion of junior officers (lieutenants and captains) choosing to leave the service rose in 2005 to 8.6 percent, up from 6.3 percent in 2004. Meanwhile, the attrition rate for majors rose to 7 percent in 2005, up from 6.4 percent. The rate for lieutenant colonels was 13.7 percent, its highest rate in more than a decade.[66]

The potential hollowing of the middle manager corps was of particular concern to the Navy. Typically staffed at the 0–4 level, these positions include aviation department heads such as maintenance, safety, administration, or operations jobs. Typically, these jobs are not awarded until after a decade of service. Retention of lower-grade officers, therefore, was crucial to the maintenance of these core middle positions. As of late February 2006, however, there was evidence that the bonuses were having some positive effect: while extensions of initial contracts by Navy aviators had stood at about 40 percent since 1986, that figure had risen to about 50 percent since 9/11.[67]

The upshot has been fears that officer candidates who otherwise would not have made muster are being promoted due to the increased stress on manpower. The Army, however, explained the increased percentage of promotions in part as a consequence of the Army's move to create more combat units without expanding the overall force.

As of late fall 2006, concerns began to gather that the hollowing of the officer corps could be seriously exacerbated by mid-level officers leaving the service under the strain of fighting in Iraq and Afghanistan. Officer attrition had also revealed itself as an issue. In 2003, the Army lost 5.7 percent of its company-grade officers. The following year, in 2004, that attrition rate jumped to 8.1 percent and hit 8.5 percent in 2005.

In an attempt to combat the problem, the Pentagon had adopted new incentives, such as enhanced graduate school opportunities, to help keep lieutenants and captains in uniform. Still, the services still continued to face shortfalls. In the Army, as of November 2006, the number of junior officers stood at 40,300 and needed to be increased by 3,000 officers to meet expansion in the coming years. With strong incentive programs already in place, and officer numbers increasing as the wars in Iraq and Afghanistan wore on, the ability to fill these additional spaces became a serious issue heading into 2007.[68]

RECRUITMENT OF MINORITIES

As has been touched upon earlier, today's all-volunteer force structure is much more representative of American society in economic and racial terms than the combat forces the draft sent to Vietnam. In 1973, when the United States instituted its all-volunteer force, 2.8 percent of military officers were African-American. As of March 2002, 8.8 percent of all military officers were African-American. The representation of other minorities—Hispanics, Asian Americans, and Native Americans —increased at an even faster rate over the same period. Also in 2002, minorities comprised 19 percent of the U.S. officer corps and 38.3 percent of total active-duty enlisted soldiers.

The unpopularity of the war has, however, had a growing effect among groups that see peacetime military service as a method of upward mobility, particularly minority groups. Men and women who might have joined the services for college money or career training may perceive the war to be too risky. A GfK Custom Research Inc. August 2004 study conducted for the Army stated that "in the past, barriers were about inconvenience or preference for another life choice. Now they have switched to something quite different: fear of death or injury."[69]

A July 2004 study of the influence parents have on their children's career decisions revealed that African-American parents had a greater influence than Caucasian parents on their children's decision to join the military service. The study further showed that African-American parents had less trust in the military.[70]

The percentage of African-Americans recruited into the Army's active duty demonstrates the war's impact on the recruitment of this minority group. In September 2001, African-Americans made up 22.7 percent of the Army's recruits, whereas in 2003 the percentage dropped to 16.4 percent, and throughout 2004 and the beginning of 2005 the trend continued. As of February 9, 2005, the percentage slipped to 13.9 percent.[71] This trend may be attributable to what the August 2004 CfK report revealed—more "African Americans identify having to fight for a cause they don't support as a barrier to military service."[72]

By late 2005, enlistments of African-Americans had declined 40 percent since 2000. According to the Army Recruiting Command at Fort Knox, Kentucky, in November 2005, the number of black enlistees had dropped from about one in five in 2000 to one in seven. African-Americans have historically been a very important part of the all-volunteer force. Even with the recent downturn in enlistees, blacks made up 25 percent of all enlisted Army soldiers at the end of FY2005, while making up just 13 percent of the general population.[73] Still, as of early 2006, the percentage of African-Americans in the Army dropped from 22.3 to 14.5 percent over the preceding four years.[74]

One reason sited for the decline in recruitment of blacks is the lessened relative dependency on military service for career opportunities. From 1980 to 2002, the percentage of blacks over the age of 25 with at least four years of college had doubled, from 7.9 to 17.2 percent, according to *Digest of Education Statistics.*[75]

There was also evidence that attitudes toward the war in the black and Hispanic/Latino communities played a role in these recruiting difficulties. Two Pew Research Center surveys conducted in mid and late 2005 revealed disparities of opinion toward the war among the black, Hispanic, and white communities. A December survey showed that only 48 percent of blacks expected the United States to succeed in Iraq versus 59 percent of whites.[76] On issues relating to the likelihood of success and positive outcomes and progress, Hispanics were generally more positive than blacks, and in some cases almost in line with white respondents. Meanwhile, black respondents were the most pessimistic nearly across the board.

In December 2005, S. Douglas Smith, a spokesman for Army Recruiting Command, said that the Army had been focusing on recruiting more Hispanics and Asians as a result of the drop-off in enlistments of blacks. Hispanics accounted for 13.2 percent of active-duty recruits in 2005, up from 10.5 percent in 2001, while accounting for 12.5 percent of the U.S. population. Meanwhile, the percentage of Asian-American recruits increased from 2.6 percent in 2001 to 4.1 percent for 2005, about on par with the percent representation in the U.S. population.[77]

THE IMPACT OF THE FAMILY

There is a saying in the Army that "you enlist the soldier, but you reenlist the family." The realities of life in the military, particularly during a period of high deployment, can have a taxing effect on the loved ones of those in military service, which can then impact on reenlistment rates. Families weighing in on recruits, likewise, can affect the decision of would-be recruits, thus dragging down new accessions as well. Lieutenant General James R. Helmly, Chief of the Army Reserve, spoke to this issue before the House Armed Services Committee in February 2005:[78]

We have in each of our Army Reserve centers across the nation and the world either volunteer groups, staff augmented by full-time—or in the region, full-time support. I make
that one of our top priorities with commanders. Early in this conflict and in 2003 we
sent out 300,000 seven-minute CDs, mailed to the home of every Army Reserve
member, both selected Reserve and IRR, seeking to communicate with families and set
proper expectations as opposed to, frankly, previously false expectations of no mobilization or little mobilization stress.

More generally, the Iraq War has shown the importance of the role parents and
mentors play in influencing the recruiting base. The U.S. military is a military where
parents, wives, husbands, and children are all critical factors. Parents have to believe
that enlistees face acceptable risks and burdens. A June 2005 Gallup poll reported
that only 52 percent of Americans would support their child if he or she decided to
enlist in the military, while 48 percent would go so far as to suggest another occupation. In 1999, 66 percent of Americans surveyed said they would support that decision, and only 29 percent said they would suggest an alternative.[79]

Families shape decisions as well—particularly in a world where so large a portion
of the military is married, and their partners have their own careers. In the case of
Reservists and the Guard, the other career is the real career—the center around
which their lives are built.

In early June 2005, the Army released the following information on the impact the
war was having on families:[80]

- In FY2002, 1.9 percent of married officers and 3.1 percent of enlisted soldiers got
  divorced.
- In 2003, married officers saw an increase in the divorce rate to 3.3 percent; the rate
  dropped to 2.8 percent for married enlisted soldiers.
- In FY2004, the trend continued for officers, bringing the percentage to 6 percent,
  while the rate rose slightly to 3.5 percent for the enlisted soldiers. In the same year,
  1.5 percent of officers in the Air Force, 1.7 percent in the USMC, and 2.5 percent in
  the Navy got divorced.

In 2005, the Navy saw an improvement in the divorce rate, dropping from 3.7 to
2.9 percent. There was also a slight pullback in the Army divorce rate, with
3.3 percent of married soldiers getting divorced in 2005. The causes of divorce are
hard to determine, but it is perhaps telling that the Army's divorce rate for 2000,
before the wars in Afghanistan and Iraq, was only 2.2 percent.[81]

These strains were particularly severe and unexpected in the case of the Reserves.
In July 2004, the Defense Manpower Data Center released its "May 2004 Status of
Forces Survey of Reserve Component Members: Leading Indicators." The survey
questioned component members of various ranks regarding the realities affecting
their stress levels, attitudes toward the service, etc. The leading indicator results from
the May 2004 survey of Reserve Component members was intended to reflect the
impact of military operations on members and their families. Issues addressed

included intentions to stay in the military, satisfaction with the military way of life, personal readiness, and unit readiness. The results of the survey showed that each had significantly declined since a prior survey was taken.

For the same time period of the survey, days spent in a compensated status and nights away from home had increased, and roughly one-fourth of the members indicated that time away had decreased their desire to stay in the military. Also, compared to the prior year, significantly fewer members reported that their spouse/ significant other and family favored their participation in the National Guard/ Reserve. Although members' reports of stress in their personal lives had not increased in the covered year, their reports of stress in their military lives had increased. The summary of the report further concluded that the impact of deployments had affected the Army National Guard and the Army Reserve more than other components.[82]

According to a 2004 survey conducted by the Defense Manpower Data Center, the general trend in spousal and "significant other" favorability of participation in the Reserve component was for spousal favorability to peak at about the same time as major combat operations in Iraq in May 2003, then tailor off significantly by the same time in 2004. Meanwhile, the same study showed that family favorability of participation roughly tracked with spousal favorability numbers, revealing a possible source of recruiting difficulties for the time period following May 2003.[83]

Negative family attitudes toward the service continued into 2005. In November, a Department of Defense survey indicated that only 25 percent of parents would recommend military service to their children. In August 2003, that figure had been 42 percent. While the declining numbers could, as some suggested, be a result of distance from a 9/11 rallying point, others contended that the survey data suggested a more significant trend in recruiting.

Another study, carried out by GfK Custom Research Inc., found that the biggest influences in candidates' decisions to join were their mothers, named by 81 percent of respondents, followed by fathers, at 70 percent. In an effort to address declining parental encouragement to join the service in 2005, the Army and Marines began using grassroots initiatives and multimillion-dollar advertising campaigns to appeal directly to the parents of possible recruits.[84]

THE IMPACT ON CIVILIAN EMPLOYMENT

Another key concern growing out of the frequent and extended National Guard and Reserve deployments was the adverse effects on civilian employment scenarios for RC personnel. Extended deployments presented a problem that cut both ways: high RC usage left employers short of personnel, with laws precluding the hiring of new personnel while RC members were on active duty. Meanwhile, RC personnel who found themselves replaced while on active duty—in breach of these laws—often found the complexities and hassle of legal recourse overwhelming.

These conditions created a situation that was unfavorable to both employers and employees. Employers were confronted with the reality that hiring members of the

RC involved inherent risks—and real consequences in the event of wartime mobilization. Superordinary mobilizations and deployments in turn added obvious stress to reserve force personnel in terms of their civilian lives and livelihoods.

In December 2006, the U.S. Labor Department reported that the number of National Guard and Reserve personnel who said they had been reassigned, lost benefits, or been fired from civilian jobs after returning from duty had increased by 30 percent since 2002. The Labor Department said that it had handled 1,548 complaints from returning service members in FY2006 (ended September 30), up from 1,195 in FY2002, of which only about a third of the cases are resolved in favor of the employee, accorded to the department.

Those numbers, however, do not reflect the totality of service members experiencing these issues. The Pentagon reportedly received more than 8,000 such complaints in 2006—nearly double the number of complaints of 2005—but most were resolved without further government action, according to the Pentagon office responsible for trying to resolve such job disputes.[85]

Another growing problem was the high level of military personnel in Iraq who held civilian law enforcement jobs at home, and the positions that were left empty with their deployments. Analysis by the Department of Justice in December 2006 showed that the deployment of thousands of police officers to Iraq, Afghanistan, and other reserve posts was costing local law enforcement agencies up to $1.2 billion per year. The problem was particularly acute with smaller police agencies, as these often experience greater difficulties in filling gaps left by deployed personnel. The analysis further showed that about 2.2 percent of the estimated 683,600 full-time police officers, sheriff's deputies, and state troopers across the nation were in the military reserve at the time of the study.[86]

OVERDEPLOYED FORCES AND THE UNWRITTEN SOCIAL CONTRACT

The Iraq War did more, however, than create recruiting and retention problems. It showed that the current pool of mission-capable active and reserve forces the United States could draw upon when the war began forced the military services to overdeploy large elements of both its active and reserve forces. This may partly be a matter of an outdated force structure still oriented toward the needs of the Cold War, but there are good reasons to suspect it is also a matter of inadequate end strength— particularly in the active forces. This is particularly likely given the fact that the Iraq War is a medium-sized regional contingency, and a major regional conflict like Korea could require far more personnel.

The U.S. government may be able to violate its unwritten social contract under conditions where the military believes the war is so existential and threatening to the nation that personnel will make any sacrifice. Iraq, however, is clearly an optional conflict, one in which military personnel are paying for major problems in our force structure.

According to the Department of Defense, approximately one-third of all military personnel who had served since September 2001 had been on more than one tour as of spring 2005:[87]

- Thirty-seven percent of the active Army manpower sent to Iraq and Afghanistan had been on more than one tour since September 2001. This was also true for 30 percent of the Army National Guard and 34 percent of the Army Reserves.
- Twenty-eight percent of active Marines and 12 percent of USMC Reserves had been on more than one tour since September 2001. As of June 2005, three infantry battalions and three rotary-wing squadrons from the Marine Corps were in the middle of their third tour in Iraq.[88]
- Thirty-three percent of active Air Force, 47 percent of Air National Guard, and 49 percent of Air Force Reserves had also seen more than one tour of duty (largely due to airlift and refueling necessities).
- Over 80 percent of the Army Guard and 60 percent of the Army Reserve units had been mobilized for most of the period authorized by then-current emergency mobilization orders.

By early 2006, usage had reached greater levels. A January 2006 report by the National Security Advisory Group, chaired by William J. Perry, revealed the following data:[89]

- Nearly all of the available combat units in the U.S. Army, the Army National Guard, and the Marine Corps have been used in current operations.
- Every available combat brigade from the active-duty Army has already been to Afghanistan or Iraq at least once for a 12-month tour. Many are now in their second or third tours of duty.
- Approximately 95 percent of the Army National Guard's combat battalions and Special Operations units have been mobilized since 9/11. Short of full mobilization or a new Presidential declaration of a national emergency, there is little available combat capacity remaining in the Army National Guard.
- The average length of tour for Reservists has more than doubled, from 156 days in Desert Shield/Desert Storm to 342 days in Operation Enduring Freedom (OEF) in Afghanistan and Operation Iraqi Freedom (OIF).
- Sixty percent of the Army Reserve, comprised primarily of support units, has been mobilized since 9/11. Only 16 percent of the Army Reserve remains eligible for mobilization to support operations in Iraq and Afghanistan under current authorities, but many of the remaining specialties are not in demand.
- Fielding the necessary combat support/combat service support units has proven particularly challenging for the Army. In the current rotation in Iraq, 20 percent of these units are being manned with soldiers that were removed from their original occupational specialties and rapidly retrained to fill empty billets in cobbled-together units.

- The Marine Corps is also under tremendous strain. All active-duty Marine Corps units are being used on a "tight" rotation schedule of seven months deployed, less than a year home to reset, and then another seven months deployed—meaning that active-duty Marine Expeditionary Units are experiencing two operational deployments per cycle rather than the usual one per cycle. All of the Marine Corps Reserves' combat units have been mobilized.

In the case of the regular military, the initial service contract for active-duty service members varied somewhat, but volunteers still made an eight-year commitment to military service. A service member with a four-year contract, for example, was automatically to be recategorized into the Reserves for that component for another four years once off active duty. Members moved either to the more combat-ready selected reserve or to the individual ready reserve, with a lower level of readiness and with separate legal mobilization procedures.

During the Cold War and for most of the decade that followed, the Reserves, and in particular the IRR, was a low-tempo force, with both active and reserve U.S. personnel largely on stand-by, waiting for the outbreak of World War III. Some have suggested that this bred a false impression that the Reserves were, by design, an unused force. In any case, the Iraq War has forced a reevaluation of what it really means to be a member of the U.S. military reserve forces. The July 29, 2004, call-up of 5,600 IRR personnel to return to active duty made it clear that the Pentagon intended to make use of this pool of manpower.

Operations in Afghanistan and Iraq also had a massive impact on deployments of the National Guard. Under peacetime conditions, the National Guard serves its respective state and governor in Title 32 status. Duties include guarding critical assets, search and rescue, fire control, riot and emergency response, etc. During the decades following the Vietnam War, the National Guard had come to be considered by some as a peacetime/CONUS force. This perception among the rank and file, according to some, proved problematic with the outbreak of the wars in Iraq and Afghanistan.

The Army and other services also emphasized conventional warfighting skills and built the active force around such contingency capabilities. As a result, they had put many of the personnel and units in the skill sets needed for Iraq—such as military police and various intelligence capabilities—in the reserve component. This ensured that the RC became a high-operations tempo (OPTEMPO) force.

The National Guard had to make sustained deployments of many of its combat brigades, which housed many of the warfighting assets and personnel. The National Guard had 34 combat brigades, and these accounted for roughly 40 percent of the total Army's combat brigades, with this number reflected in the breakdown of personnel in Iraq. The heavy use of these brigades—including extended deployments and frequent redeployments—not only affected recruiting into the National Guard, but showed that the Army could not fight counterinsurgency wars, or deal with large-scale nation building and stability operations, without repeatedly deploying them.

- Figure 4.8 provides data on the percentage of the force, by service, that had been subject to multiple deployments as of January 2005. The relative rate of redeployments by service provides information on one key element of "strain" and is useful when comparing relative recruiting/retention success or failures.
- Figure 4.9 illustrates the spikes in RC man-days for operations between 1986 and 2003. The figure contrasts strain in terms of man-days during peacetime versus periods of high OPTEMPO. The contrast has a bearing on force planning constructs, especially in a future based on predictions of more constantly high-operational tempo.

Increases in active and reserve deployments have been well within the letter of the law and regulation, but have no modern historical precedents, raising serious questions about the degree to which the men and women now being deployed had any reason to expect such deployments as the result of a limited and "optional" war.

At the same time, stop-loss policies and multiple deployments cut across the active, Reserves, and National Guard components in ways that raised further questions about a broken social contract. Half of the services faced multiple rotations of at least 30 percent of personnel between September 2001 and January 2005.

Forced retention had to be mixed with multiple rotations. Stop-loss, which was originally envisaged to keep well-trained soldiers during this period of war, is now largely perceived as a means to keep troop levels high enough while recruitment numbers are down. Using stop-loss to keep military personnel on for longer than

Figure 4.8 Percent of Total on Multiple Deployments by Service*

Service	Percentage of Total Deployed More than Once, September 2001–January 2005
Army, Active	37%
Army, National Guard	30%
Army, Reserve	34%
Air Force, Active	33%
Air Force, National Guard	47%
Air Force, Reserve	49%
USMC, Active	28%
USMC, Reserve	12%
Navy, Active	26%
Navy, Reserve	21%
Coast Guard, Active	12%
Coast Guard, Reserve	1%

* Taken from *Washington Post,* "Two Years Later, Iraq War Drains Military" by Ann Scott Tyson, March 19, 2005.

Source: Department of Defense.

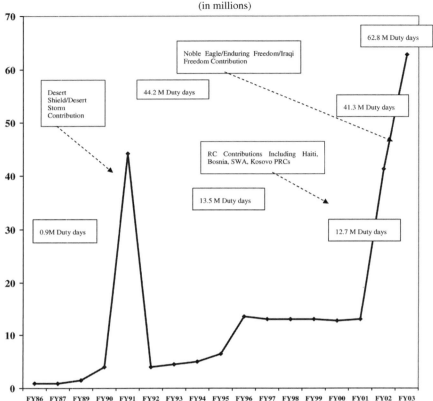

Source: Adapted from a 2004 briefing to CSIS by the Office of the Assistant Secretary of Defense.

Figure 4.9   RC Man-Days, FY1986–FY2003

their eight-year commitment is a serious breach of faith in the promise made to a professional force.

The authority to issue stop-loss orders was granted by Congress during Vietnam, but was not used until the buildup to the Persian Gulf War in 1990 when Dick Cheney, then the Secretary of Defense, allowed the military services to bar most retirements and prolong enlistments indefinitely. A flurry of stop-loss orders was issued after the terrorist attacks of September 11, 2001, intensifying as the nation prepared for war in Iraq. Some of the orders applied to soldiers, sailors, and airmen in specific skill categories—military police, for example, and ordnance control specialists, were in particular demand in Iraq.[90]

The use of stop-loss orders was intended to serve a number of purposes:

- Keep manpower numbers at or above the Congressionally mandated limit,
- Retain certain skill sets that are deemed vital to a mission,

- Retain personnel with combat experience deemed necessary to the continued execution of a successful mission, and

- Retain unit cohesion by keeping the same personnel together for extended periods of time rather than rotating individuals in and out of units on an ongoing basis (standard rotation patterns as of the beginning of the second Iraq War).

As of January 2006, the Army had forced about 50,000 soldiers to continue serving after their voluntary stints ended using stop-loss orders. Under the stop-loss policy, soldiers who would normally leave when their commitments expired had to remain in the Army, starting 90 days before their unit was scheduled to depart, through the end of their deployment and up to another 90 days after returning to their home base. This was meant to "capture" at least six months of additional service from both active and reserve military personnel who were set to exit the service. The affect of the policy, however, was resentment over a broken compact of service. There was also evidence that the policy served as a recruiting liability for the services.

REBALANCING ACTIVES AND RESERVES

The course of the fighting in Iraq, Afghanistan, and the broader war on terrorism is far too uncertain to make a detailed prediction about their cumulative impact on recruiting and retention, how to reshape the force to reduce deployment rates to an acceptable level, and how to reshape the force to find the right balance between active forces and the Reserves. It is clear, however, that all of these aspects of U.S. military manpower must change and that the United States either needs to find a far more effective way of balancing active and reserve forces, or it must increase end strength.

At the outset of the wars in Iraq and Afghanistan, the all-volunteer force had long been structured under a Total Force Policy that ensured the United States could not engage in operations without mobilizing its military reserve component (RC). The primary "social" document underpinning Total Force Policy—itself an outcome of the Vietnam War, and a reaction to the draft—is known as the "Abrams Doctrine," named for General Creighton Abrams. In theory, it was designed to ensure that the United States would go to war only with a full national commitment and would then have to draw on enough Reserves to ensure there would be a suitable political debate over going to war, which would presumably preclude the tensions and political dissent that had occurred in Vietnam.

In practice, the result of the Total Force Policy was very different. Limited military engagements after Vietnam did not force the services to call up the Reserves. The call-up for the Gulf War involved substantial reserve duty for a war that was the subject of intense Congressional debate before the fighting, but which was very popular once it began, involved only short periods of duty, and resulted in very low casualties.

If the Gulf War revealed anything about the Total Force Policy, it was that the insistence on integrating the active and reserve components had made the Army and other services overdependent on the reserve components for power projection and seriously delayed the ability to move combat-ready forces into the theater. It also created a political situation where the Congress responded to the demands of local Guard and Reserve constituencies by constantly increasing their funding and giving them political priority. As a result, the Army largely gave up on its post–Gulf War attempts to reduce dependence on the reserve component; it realized it simply could not win the political struggle.

The end result was that the United States began the Iraq War with a force posture better tuned to the Cold War, conventional combat, and the political heritage of Vietnam than the kind of new requirements that had emerged in the Iraq War and which were set forth in QDR 2006. The U.S. force structure had the wrong balance of active and reserve components to sustain combat in long wars, counterinsurgency operations, stability operations, and nation building. It had also assigned missions to the Reserves that were critical for the counterinsurgency, stability operations, and nation-building missions it faced in Afghanistan and Iraq.

The Iraq War and the Total Force Policy

Ironically, insisting on high RC involvement in the total force needed to go to war did nothing to force the kind of national dialog before the United States went to war that some of its supporters had hoped would take place in supporting a force mix that depended on early deployment of reserve and National Guard forces. The problems in the AC-RC mix began to have a major political impact only after operations in Afghanistan and Iraq were well under way. It did nothing to forge a prewar consensus.

The combination of the Total Force Concept and a force structure that emphasized battles against conventional military forces did ensure that U.S. deployment problems were much worse and that U.S. forces were poorly structured to deal with different types of conflict. Critical units like intelligence, military police, combat, combat support, and combat service support forces were placed in the RC to be drawn upon as a "surge force." Moreover, the Air Force had made much of its airlift dependent on the Reserves and the National Guard—a dependency that worked in short wars but not in long ones. These, however, were precisely the counterinsurgency and nation-building capabilities the United States needed in Afghanistan, Iraq, and elsewhere.

These elements of the Reserves were now needed on a sustained rather than a "surge" basis. Speaking at a hearing of the Personnel Subcommittee of the House Armed Services Committee in February 2005, General Richard Cody, Vice Chief of Staff, Department of the Army, addressed the balance of assets as follows:[91]

> we went from six month rotations in Afghanistan to nine months and then 12 months, so we could balance this force and at the same time do the transformation...what's happened is for the sourcing of OIF II we've had some spot shortages in some of our high demand low density combat support, combat service support in either the National Guard or in the Reserves or in the Active force Some that come to light are the engineers, transportation, quartermaster, as well as MPs. And what we did was we started, one,

going to cross leveling. We went back to the joint staff and we got some joint solutions, like capabilities inside either our other services, and we also went and looked at extending the 12 months boots on the ground to include six months of post-mobilization training so that we could bring units on and get them fully trained up, because some of these units in the Guard and Reserve were at a lower level of manning or equipping.

RESHAPING THE AC-RC MIX TO DEAL WITH THE IRAQ WAR

The high deployment levels of every component of the "Total Force" during operations in Iraq and Afghanistan are forcing military planners to reevaluate the roles that the various components had come to play and what would be their best use for the future.

The Total Force Policy drew both the Guard and Reserves into the fight at high rates of deployment, but it soon became apparent that such a system could not be sustained over the longer term. Rank-and-file personnel expressed their dissatisfaction with the model through attrition while recruiting numbers began to show muted enthusiasm for participation in both the active and reserve components.

The increased use of the RC in Iraq raised concerns about the balance maintained between the AC and the RC. Until 2005, the "180-day rule" ensured that all Reservists who were mobilized for more than 179 days had to be counted against active-duty statistics. In an environment of high mobilization and redeployments of the RC, however, this began to rub up against the concurrent need to adhere to Congressionally mandated end strengths.

It was reported that the Army was using methods to circumvent this restriction: issuing the same person multiple back-to-back active-duty tours of less than 180 each; using more than one Reservist to complete a single task, one who starts the task and another to pick up at the 180-day point; couching a single requirement as several different requirements; and using the same individual to complete each phase of the task, under a different set of orders for each.

Figures 4.10 and 4.11 show the relative increases in deployments among the various services' active and reserve components from September 2001 through August 2004:

- Figure 4.10 shows Army deployments from September 2001 through August 2004. The chart is broken down by AC and RC service. The solid line across the top of the bars indicates deployments of total Army (AC/RC).
- Figure 4.11 shows Marine Corps deployments from September 2001 through August 2004. The chart is broken down by AC and RC service. The solid line across the top of the bars indicates deployments of total Marine Corps (AC/RC).

The Debate over the Future AC-RC Mix

The growing need to reduce the operational distinction between RC and AC personnel in Iraq led to new legislation in the 2005 Defense Authorization Act, which

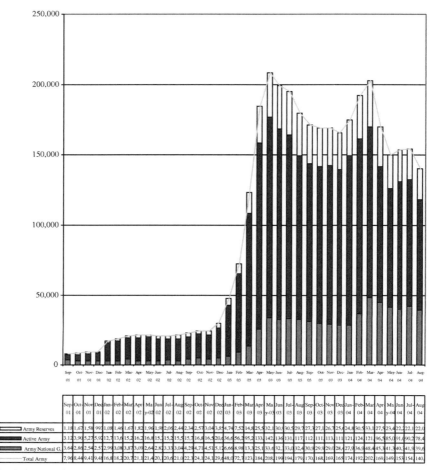

*A deployment of a member occurring at any time during a month is counted in that month's total. Source: Defense Manpower Data Center.

Figure 4.10   Army AC and RC Deployments, September 2001 through August 2004

eliminated the 180-day rule. The act also sought to bring the RC in line with the AC in other ways, particularly bringing RC benefits more in line with those of the AC. The act generally doubled or tripled RC bonuses and increased RC monthly rates under the Montgomery GI bill. Yet some argued that bringing compensation closer to par with the AC would only help to codify the overuse of the RC.

Indeed, the legislation did little more than legalize the problem. The strain on the Reserves triggered a much broader debate over whether a new force planning concept should be developed that would return the RC to its traditional role as a reserve force that is called up only in a major conflict or whether the United States should create a Total Force Concept or "operational RC." At the same time, it raised the issue of

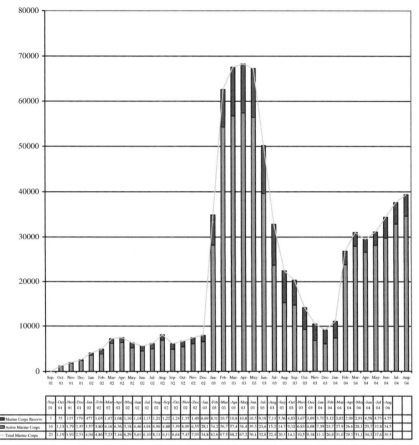

*A deployment of a member occurring at any time during a month is counted in that month's total. Source: Defense Manpower Data Center.

Figure 4.11 Marine Corps AC and RC Deployments, September 2001 through August 2004

whether the problem was finding the right mix of AC and RC components or whether the total pool of men and women in both components was simply too small to carry out the wars and other missions the United States might have to fight in the future.

The decision, so far, has been to try to rebalance the AC-RC mix largely within the limits of the present total pool of personnel in both components and even to seek manpower cuts in the process to allow funds to be shifted to procurement. The U.S. Army and QDR 2006 proposed to deal with this aspect of America's force transformation problems by increasing the number of active military personnel in warfighting roles without increasing end strength and by restructuring and "rebalancing" the active and reserve components of the military.

Politics present another kind of problem. The merits of the case are one thing. The political clout of the National Guard Bureau and various state and local Reserve groups is another. While shifting these assets might reduce future strain on the RC, many in the higher echelons of the National Guard and the Reserves did not want to see their forces stripped of high-demand/low-asset capabilities. One concern is that a loss of critical warfighting assets in the RC would mean a corresponding decrease in funding and equipment deliveries. Because the RC has historically been underequipped relative to the AC, and equipped with older equipment passed on from the active force, senior officers in the National Guard and the Reserves lobbied hard to maintain the RC's relevance in warfighting. In this sense, rebalancing inevitably became a turf battle as well as a debate over what America's future force posture should be.

THE PERSONNEL IMPACT OF FORCE RESTRUCTURING AND MODULARITY

The Iraq War is also forcing the United States to restructure the assignments and skills of the manpower pool in both the active and reserve components and to seek to create a more flexible force structure that emphasizes "modularity" and tailoring the deployed force to the mission, rather than to conventional warfighting.

The Department of Defense has had to make an urgent effort to restructure its force posture to make its forces more deployable, shift men and women into specialties needed for the wars the United States now has had to fight, and seek more lasting solutions to reducing the strain on both the active and reserve components likely to be called up in long wars. It forced the Department of Defense to make a force-wide effort to correct the outdated personnel force structure that had evolved during the Cold War.

Personnel have had to be moved out of low-demand specialties and unit types and redirected to increase personnel in more high-demand units. At the same time, the United States sought to emphasize the kind of forces and skills that could provide a more agile force capable of fighting nonlinear combatants on multiple fronts, dealing with sustained counterinsurgency campaigns, providing for stability and nation-building operations, and dealing with the problems of homeland defense.

As has been discussed earlier, this shift inevitably further complicated the problem of rebalancing the active and reserve components. As Figure 4.12 shows, the Iraq War forced massive increases in the level of deployment by key specialties relative to the Gulf War. The level of combat deployment in the combat, intelligence, engineering, and electronics elements of the Reserves more than doubled. Major further increases took place in the deployment of logistics, maintenance, and technical personnel.

The Broad Outline of Modularity

The DoD's solutions to providing these capabilities are still evolving. As of early January 2006, however, the DoD sought to undertake policy, organizational, and

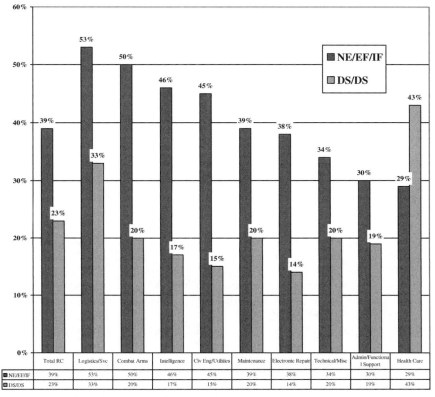

	Total RC	Logistics/Svc	Combat Arms	Intelligence	Civ Eng/Utilities	Maintenance	Electronic Repair	Technical/Misc	Admin/Functional Support	Health Care
NE/EF/IF	39%	53%	50%	46%	45%	39%	38%	34%	30%	29%
DS/DS	23%	33%	20%	17%	15%	20%	14%	20%	19%	43%

Note: NE = Operation Noble Eagle, EF = Operation Enduring Freedom, IF = Operation Iraqi Freedom; NE/EF/IF Total RC percentage reflects: [Total # of mobilized RC members (343,020)]/[SelRes strength (869,003) as of Mar 04]; DS/DS Total RC percentage reflects: [Total # of mobilized RC members (267,330)]/[SelRes strength (1,166,427) as pf Sep 91]; Occupational Categories exclude trainees/students/undesignated specialties. Source: Adapted from DOD briefing to CSIS, "The Reserve Components: Use of -- and Stress on -- the Force (as of March 31, 2004)," June 7, 2004.

Figure 4.12   RC Inventory Use by Skill, as Percent of Total: First and Second Iraq Wars

personnel changes between 2004 and 2009 that would create new "high-demand" units and stabilize the force, providing more predictability for service members and their families. In accordance with the effort to create a more agile force, better suited to address what planners believed to be the new paradigm of warfare, the basic goals of the overall effort were as follows:[92]

- Enhance early responsiveness:

Structure forces to reduce the need for *involuntary* mobilization during early stages of a rapid response operation.

- Resolve stressed career fields:

Structure forces to limit involuntary mobilization to reasonable and sustainable rates.

- Employ innovative personnel management practices:
  - Enhance volunteerism.
  - Provide a range of participation opportunities.
  - Capitalize locally on Reservists' civilian skills (e.g., "reachback").
  - Improve the mobilization process.
  - Provide predictable periods of service.

The end goal is to provide a force not only more capable of tackling asymmetric enemies and carrying out multiple operations and peacekeeping/Stabilization and Reconstruction (S&R) missions, but also a force more friendly to the citizen soldier, with an eye to reducing stress on personnel. In rebalancing the forces, the primary initiatives meant to help reduce stress on the force included the following:

- Continuum of Service: This is meant to provide individual service members greater flexibility in the service. Between the extremes of "downtime" and OPTEMPO is a pool of individuals who may participate at varying levels of service throughout a career. The initiative was meant to reduce the sharp divide between active (365 days per year) and reserve (39 days per year), with greater flexibility of participation for each. As of mid-2006, this model was not yet an operational reality.

- Reachback: Employ advanced technologies to allow more operations to take place from CONUS, rather than deploying to theater.

- Increased use of civilians: Tap timely critical skill sets already available in the civilian population rather than keeping these skill sets [such as specialized information technology (IT)] employed in the force at all times. This sought to save money on certain skill sets as well as free up personnel for other roles, such as combat, combat support (CS), and combat service support (CSS). As of early 2006, procedures and directives to hire greater percentages of civilians were largely ineffective.

- Improvements in mobilization processes: Mobilization remained largely dependent upon unit readiness, which varied greatly from unit to unit. DoD lacked proper readiness tracking. Issues with continuity of health care for Reservists and their families, as well as service inequities in implementing pay and compensation policies, were also cited as issues in the mobilization process.[93]

It is important to note that none of these concepts involved increasing active and reserve end strength. They relied on reorganization, rebalancing, and the deployment of new military technologies. They also placed heavy emphasis on the idea that Iraq and Afghanistan would be the model for determining the need for military personnel in future wars.

The FY2007 budget request and QDR 2006 established a DoD goal to stabilize the Army's end strength at 482,400 Active and 533,000 Reservists, and the Marine Corps' end strength at 175,000 Active and 39,000 Reservists by FY2011. This represented a reduction across the board of personnel for these services from their 2006 levels:

- Active Army: 522,400,
- Active Marines: 178,000,
- Army RC: 555,000 (205,000 Army Reservist and 350,000 Army National Guard), and
- Marine Corps Reserves: 39,600.

The Restructuring of the U.S. Army Personnel Structure and Its "Modular Force"

So far, the Army is the only service where it is clear how these concepts are intended to be put into practice. The Army virtually had to lead in the effort to implement such concepts. The Army Reserve and the National Guard contained more than two-thirds of the Army's psychological operations units, chemical units, and hospital and medical groups. The Army Reserve and the National Guard also contained more than 95 percent of the Army's civil affairs units, internment brigades, Judge Advocate General Corps, training and exercise divisions, and railway units.[94]

As a result, the Army developed force transformation plans that called for moving much of its high-demand, low-density personnel and assets needed for counterinsurgency and long wars into the active component to reduce the strain on the Reserves, give the United States more rapid deployment capability without calling up the Reserves, and provide more personnel in key specialties. The Army rushed changes in the specialties of more than 100,000 soldiers by early 2005. Its goal was to produce a 50-percent increase in infantry capabilities and increases in critical specialties such as Special Operations Forces (SOFs), military police (MP), military intelligence (MI), civil affairs, etc. As of early 2005, the Army claimed to have already converted more than 34,000 spaces.[95] The scale of this shift is illustrated by the Army unit restructuring plan for 2004–2009 shown in Figure 4.13, which shows the increases or decreases in each force element.

Figure 4.13   Army Restructuring of Units: FY2004–FY2009 (Number of Units Increased or Decreased during Period)

Decrease	Increase
36 – Field Artillery Units	149 – Military Police Units
10 – Air Defense Units	16 – Transportation Units
11 – Engineer Units	9 – Petroleum/Water Distribution Units
19 – Armor Units	8 – Civil Affairs Units
65 – Logistics Units	4 – Psychological Operations Units
	11 – Biological Detection Units

Source: Department of the Army briefing to the media on "Building Army Capabilities," February 17, 2004. Adapted from a graph in Andrew Feickert's *U.S. Army's Modular Redesign: Issues for Congress,* Congressional Research Service, updated May 20, 2005, p. 18.

These shifts in military personnel were tied to a modular force plan designed around the Army belief that modular units would be better equipped to conduct "full-spectrum" operations on multiple fronts, as seen in Iraq and Afghanistan. Its ten-division active force was to be transformed into a brigade-level unit of action (UA) force by 2007.

Modularity was also seen as a way of facilitating "jointness," as the new modular units were to be more flexible and adaptive by design. Communications, liaisons, and logistics capacities were to be built into each smaller modular brigade, with the aim being greater autonomy, thereby supporting an enhanced ability to conduct joint multinational missions. An entire echelon of command was likewise being phased out above the brigade headquarters, moving from three levels to two. Several layers of logistics headquarters were also to be removed to increase responsiveness and improve joint logistics integration.[96]

The Army's 2005 Posture Statement claimed that modularity would furthermore increase the number of *total* brigades from 48 to 77, with 10 active brigades (three and one-third divisions, in previous terms), by the end of 2006.[97] The initial estimates of the needed number of such units of action typically ranged between 40 and 48.

The 2006 QDR stated that the DoD would create modular brigades in all three Army components: 117 in the regular Army [42 Brigade Combat Teams (BCTs) and 75 support brigades), 106 in the Army National Guard (28 BCTs and 78 support brigades), and 58 support brigades in the U.S. Army Reserve. According to the report, this would equate to "a 46% increase in readily available combat power and a better balance between combat and support forces."[98]

The 2007 Defense Budget made provisions for the conversion of the Army force from 48 regular combat brigades to 70 modular Brigade Combat Teams at an estimated cost of $40 billion during FY2007–FY2011. Plans called for the number of active Army BCTs to increase from 33 to 42 and for National Guard BCTs to increase from 15 to 28 by FY2011. These numbers had a higher figure for National Guard BCTs than the Army originally planned, reflecting pressure on the Army and the DoD from Congress and lobbyists for the Guard.

The Army's goal was that each new modular BCT, which would include about 3,000–4,000 personnel, would have at least the same combat capability as a brigade under the previous division-base force, which ranged between 3,000 and 5,000 personnel. Although smaller in size, the new modular brigades were planned to be as capable as their predecessors due to different equipment, such as advanced communications and surveillance equipment, and a different mix of personnel and support assets.[99]

At a press briefing on January 25, 2006, Donald Rumsfeld said that as a result of the reforms, "some 75% of the Army's brigade structure should always be ready, in the event of a crisis, and more capacity in modules that are more flexible and more applicable to the new century."[100] The aims of this "modularization" of the force included the following:[101]

- At least a 30-percent increase in the combat power of the active component of the force,

- An increase in the rotational pool of ready units by at least 50 percent,

- Creation of a deployable joint-capable headquarters,

- Force design upon which the future network centric developments (Future Combat System) can be readily applied, and

- Reduced stress on the force through a more predictable deployment cycle:

  - One year deployed and two years at home station for the active component,

  - One year deployed and four years at home station for the Reserve Force,

  - One year deployed and five years at home station for the National Guard Force, and

  - Reduced mobilization times for the Reserve component as a whole.

Progress in 2004

In terms of actual progress, the Army reacted quickly under the pressure of wartime need. Two divisions were fully converted by year-end 2004, and the Congressional Research Service summarized overall progress in 2004 as follows:[102]

In FY2004, the Army began converting three of its ten active duty divisions into modular forces. Two of these divisions—the 3rd Infantry Division from Ft. Stewart, Georgia and the 101st Airborne Division (Air Assault) from Ft. Campbell, Kentucky—were totally converted in FY2004 and their respective division headquarters were converted into units of employment (UEs)—headquarters units which are designed to command up to six units of action (UAs) as well as supporting units of action (SAUs). The 10th Mountain Division (Light Infantry) from Ft. Drum, New York also began its modular conversion in FY2004 by adding a third UA brigade combat team as well as converting its division headquarters to a UE x structure. A fourth UA is scheduled to be added to the 10th Mountain Division in FY2005 and will be stationed at Ft. Polk, Louisiana at the Joint Readiness Training Center. Also in 2004, the Army's third Stryker Brigade Combat Team (SBCT) will be stood up as part of the Hawaii-based 25th Infantry Division (Light).

In March 2005, the converted 3rd Infantry Division was sent back to Iraq for a year-long deployment. The 3rd Infantry Division led the U.S. assault on Baghdad in March of 2003 under the Army's traditional three brigade, division design and experts suggest that the current deployment of the reconfigured 3rd Infantry Division will yield a significant amount of valuable information which could help with ongoing and future modular conversions. The 101st Airborne Division, which also converted in FY2004, is slated to return to Iraq for the second time in late summer or early fall of 2005.

Progress in 2005

Gains were more modest in 2005, although the following conversions were planned:[103]

In addition to the creation of the 10th Mountain Division's fourth UA in 2005, a number of other conversions are planned to occur this year. The 4th Infantry Division at Ft.

Hood, Texas is scheduled to begin its modularization, with the division headquarters converting to a UE x. The 1st Corps headquarters, stationed at Ft. Lewis, Washington is planned to be downgraded and converted to a UE x in 2005 and it has been reported that the Army is attempting to station the former 1st Corps headquarters at Camp Zama, Japan.

In FY2005, the 25th Infantry Division plans to stand up its fourth UA, with an airborne capability for forced entry operations, at Ft. Richardson, Alaska, and the 4th Infantry Division plans to add a fourth UA at Ft. Hood. Also in 2005, the 172nd Separate Infantry Brigade stationed at Ft. Richardson, Alaska is scheduled to convert to the Army's third SBCT.

The 3rd Infantry Division had somewhat mixed success. The division immediately had to be augmented with battalions borrowed from other units, fueling debate about the practice of stripping one "maneuver" battalion from each brigade as part of conversion to modularity.[104] Some argued that Iraq could not be considered the standard test case for modular forces, as future operations were likely to take place in higher security environments. Still others argued that the warfare represented in Iraq was precisely the environment around which modularity was structured, and thus the need to augment the 3rd Infantry Division marked early evidence of weakness in the model.

Growing concerns also emerged over the ability to equip the modular force. The issues involved are discussed in far more detail in Chapters 5 and 6, but a March 2005 Government Accountability Office (GAO) report cast serious doubt on the progress made:[105]

> ...modular brigade combat teams require significant increases in the levels of equipment, particularly command, control, and communications equipment; wheeled vehicles; and artillery and mortars. Examples of command, control, and communications equipment that are key enablers for the modular brigade combat teams include advanced radios, Joint Network Node systems, ground sensors such as the Long-Range Advanced Scout Surveillance System, and Blue Force Tracker, among others. This critical equipment makes possible the joint network communications, information superiority, and logistical operations over a large, dispersed battlespace in which modular forces are being designed to effectively operate. Although the Army has some of this equipment on hand, the levels being fielded to brigade combat teams are well below the levels tested by the Training and Doctrine Command.
>
> ...it is not clear yet how the Army plans to bring brigades that have already undergone modular conversion up to Training and Doctrine Command tested levels of personnel and equipment following their deployments. For example, the design requires a division with four modular brigade combat teams to have approximately 28 tactical unmanned aerial vehicle systems. These systems provide surveillance and reconnaissance for soldiers on the battlefield and enable them to more safely carry out their missions. However, because of current shortages, the 3rd Infantry Division and the 101st Airborne Division are only authorized to have 4 systems, and at the time of our visits, the 3rd Infantry Division had 1 and the 101st Airborne had none on hand. The Army requested funding for only 13 of these systems in the fiscal year 2005 supplemental appropriation

request to the Congress; thus, it remains unclear as to when the 3rd Infantry Division or the 101st Airborne Divisions will receive their full complement of tactical unmanned aerial vehicle systems. Also, the Army may continue to provide other divisions undergoing conversion with limited quantities that fall short of the design requirement.

Progress in 2006

Plans for 2006 and beyond provide considerable detail on the desired completion of the modularization process for active forces and the goal for the Army's restructuring of its ten active divisions to be completed for FY2007:[106]

In FY2006, the Army plans to convert three division headquarters—the Ft. Hood, Texas-based, 1st Cavalry Division, the 25th Infantry Division (Light), and the 82nd Airborne Division from Ft. Bragg, North Carolina—to the UE x structure. These divisions' current brigades are scheduled to convert to UAs during this time period. The 1st Cavalry Division and the 82nd Airborne Division are scheduled to build a fourth UA, respectively and the 25th Infantry Division (Light) will build two additional UAs. The 1st Cavalry Division's fourth UA is planned to be stationed at Ft. Bliss, Texas. The 25th Infantry's third UA will be stationed at Ft. Benning, Georgia and the fourth UA at Ft. Riley, Kansas. In addition, the 173rd Airborne Brigade stationed in Vincenza, Italy is scheduled to add about 2,000 soldiers and become a UA and the Army plans to activate its fourth SBCT at Ft. Lewis, Washington, when the 2nd Cavalry Regiment—the former opposing forces at the Army's Joint Readiness Training Center (JRTC)—converts to a SBCT.

According to the 2005 Army Modernization Plan dated February 2005, the Army will decide in FY2006 whether or not to add five additional UA brigade combat teams (BCTS) to the Active component, eventually resulting in 48 Active component UA BCTs. According to sources, the Army has already decided this year not to add the additional five UA BCTs in FY2007 due to anticipated personnel and funding shortages. In addition, the Government Accountability Office (GAO) reports that the Army is currently considering adding an additional combat battalion to the UAs that could have further personnel and equipment implications for the Army's modularization efforts.

In FY2007, the Army plans to convert the headquarters of the Korea-based 2nd Infantry Division to the UE x structure as well as the headquarters of the Germany-based 1st Armored Division and the 1st Infantry Division. If the Army does decide to add five additional UAs in FY2007, two are scheduled to be stood up in the 2nd Infantry Division, one each in the 1st Armored and 1st Infantry Division, and an additional non-aligned infantry UA would also be created. Also in FY2007, the Army's fifth SBCT is scheduled to be activated under the 25th Infantry Division (Light).

The Army's modernization and campaign plans call for the modularization of the Active Army to be completed by the end of FY2007 but it is not unreasonable to assume that modularization activities will extend beyond 2007. Some suggest that personnel, equipment, and budget demands, as well as modifications to UAs based on experiences in Iraq and Afghanistan could extend the Army's modularization window beyond 2007.

The National Guard and the Reserves

The effort to restructure the National Guard and the Reserves has lagged behind the active Army. Conversion in the reserve component was planned to take place on its own timetable, roughly concurrent with conversion in the AC. Part of the lag in conversion of the RC may, however, have been attributable to the RC's need to realign its support units in accordance with new modular designs for the active force. The Army's 2005 Modernization Plan called for the conversions for the National Guard between 2006 and 2010 as shown in Figure 4.14.

Alternative Views of Modularity

The Army's modularity plans have faced challenges that go beyond affordability and whether it can do the job with existing or less manpower. One such debate is whether the Army's new plans provide the proper mix of warfighting manpower in the field or devote too many men and women to headquarters and other overhead roles. As of early 2006, the Army's plans lowered the number of personnel per brigade, while they increased headquarters and "overhead" personnel in order to facilitate jointness.

A series of eight reports provided to the Pentagon by the Institute for Defense Analysis (IDA) at the end of 2005 found that the Army's plan to reorganize forces into brigade combat teams would reduce net fighting capabilities rather than strengthen them. In order to increase the overall number of brigades without increasing the overall manpower of the service, the IDA studies indicated the Army would have to strip each brigade of one maneuver battalion composed of infantry troops or heavy arms. This would bring the number of such battalions to two per brigade, down from the traditional three, in part because each brigade will also have a reconnaissance battalion for support.

At the same time, each brigade headquarters was planned to grow from less than 100 personnel to 250, a change meant to enhance joint capabilities. The argument for the change was essentially that because each brigade would be redesigned to enable jointness, the brigades would operate effectively as units that could be "plugged into" a larger force structure. Overall, however, the move would mean a net loss of in the neighborhood of 40 maneuver battalions.

Figure 4.14   Army National Guard Modular Conversions, FY2006–FY2010

Fiscal Year	UE x Conversions	UA BCT Conversions
2006	2	6
2007	2	6
2008	2	7*
2009	1	6
2010	0	6
Total	7	31

*   This total includes a National Guard Stryker Brigade Combat Team.
Source: Andrew Feikert, *U.S. Army's Modular Redesign: Issues for Congress,* Congressional Research Service, updated May 20, 2005, p. 5.

The IDA report contended that the essence of land power was resident in the maneuver battalions that occupy terrain, control populations, and fight battles. According to the report, the Army plan would reduce the number of these battalions to 20 percent below the number available in 2003, while increasing BCT head-quarters by 11.5 percent. The report further suggested that the Army's effort was not properly informed by input from global combatant commanders. According to the IDA, the needs of these commanders in the field would be better served by the traditional three maneuver battalions, and perhaps even better served by the addition of a fourth, rather than by a reduction to two.[107]

A second concern was the reliance on new, increased, and enhanced technologies as part of the modularization package. Modularity calls for technology to make up for, in part, what is lost in manpower at the brigade level. Plans called for new tech-nologies and IT personnel operating in the joint structure to streamline combat operations. Concerns arose, however, as to the synchronization of modularizing combat personnel structures with the procurement of new technology and IT per-sonnel, as well as training time frames. Some remained unconvinced that new tech-nologies could be brought online quickly enough to mitigate the structural changes in combat personnel.

SHIFTS IN MANPOWER QUALITY AND NEW TRAINING BURDENS

Looking more broadly at the problem of overstretch, the Army's modularity plans also illustrate the problems every service faces in trying to solve its present manpower problems by making existing personnel more effective and efficient, rather than by addressing the issue of whether the manpower pool is adequate.

The Army's plans call for its modular brigades to be staffed with fewer personnel *per brigade* than the traditional division-base force, although the new brigades do have planned increases in personnel for certain specialties, such as MI, MP, etc. The cost and funding of the increased capabilities in these specialties also remained a key uncertainty. Army plans called for the addition of 2,800 military intelligence specialists by the end of FY2005, with an additional 6,200 needed by FY2010, but the FY2007 budget submission assumed this could be funded within the levels close to the previous force cost.

The Army's personnel plans also depend on the assumption that an increased reli-ance on high technology and "full-spectrum interoperability" would lead to increased effectiveness on the part of the men and women actually in the field. This meant that many of the personnel in the new modular brigades would require differ-ent and increased levels of training over the previous structure. The need for addi-tional training will be further increased by the 2006 QDR call for major new area and language skills and the expansion of Special Forces.

More broadly, the 2006 QDR called for major increases in the level of training and capability. As QDR 2006 recognized, asymmetric warfare, counterinsurgency, stability operations, and nation building also require human skills that cannot be provided by technology. As a result, the FY2007 budget requested $760 million during FY2007–FY2011 to provide U.S. forces with the "language and cultural skills appropriate to the areas and missions in which they will be employed in the 21st Century."[108]

The long wars the United States must fight in the future require the following new human capabilities for a wide range of missions ranging from counterterrorism to dealing with the threat of proliferation and weapons of mass destruction:[109]

- Human intelligence; language and cultural awareness;
- Persistent surveillance over wide areas; fusion of time-sensitive intelligence with operations;
- Capabilities to locate, tag, and track terrorists in all domains and to prompt global strikes to rapidly attack fleeting enemy targets;
- SOFs to conduct direct action, foreign internal defense, counterterrorist operations, and unconventional warfare;
- Multipurpose forces to train, equip, and advise indigenous forces; conduct irregular warfare; and support security, stability, transition, and reconstruction operations;
- Riverine warfare capabilities;
- Authorities to develop the capacity of nations to participate effectively in disrupting and defeating terrorist networks;
- Persistent surveillance over wide areas;
- SOFs to locate, characterize, and secure weapons of mass destruction (WMD);
- Locate, tag, and track WMD; detect fissile materials at stand-off ranges;
- Interdiction capabilities to stop air, maritime, and ground shipments of WMD, their delivery systems, and related materials;
- Joint command and control tailored for the WMD elimination mission;
- Capabilities and specialized teams to render WMD safe and secure; and
- Capability to deploy, sustain, protect, and support SOF in hostile environments.

The 2006 QDR also emphasized expanded joint training as a way of making military manpower more effective. Toward this end, the QDR held that the DoD would do the following:[110]

- Develop a Joint Training Strategy to address new mission areas, gaps, and continuous training transformation;
- Revise its Training Transformation Plan to incorporate irregular warfare, complex stabilization operations, combating WMD, and information operations; and
- Expand the Training Transformation Business Model to consolidate joint training, prioritize new and emerging missions, and exploit virtual and constructive technologies.

Restructuring Manpower to Add New Skills in Stability Operations, Counterterrorism, Counterinsurgency, and Nation Building

The 2006 QDR also called for major increases in specialized manpower skills without increases in end strength. It proposed increases in language and cultural skills, as the report stressed the need for more personnel proficient in languages such as Farsi, Arabic, and Chinese. The Department expressed the need for a level of cultural intelligence about the Middle East and Asia comparable to that developed about the Soviet Union during the Cold War. To this end, the QDR stated that the DoD would do the following:[111]

- Increase funding for the Army's pilot linguist program to recruit and train native and heritage speakers to serve as translators in the active and reserve components.

- Require language training for Service Academy and Reserve Officer Training Corps scholarship students and expand immersion programs, semester-abroad study opportunities, and interacademy foreign exchanges.

- Increase military special pay for foreign language proficiency.

- Increase National Security Education Program grants to American elementary, secondary, and postsecondary education programs to expand non-European language instruction.

- Establish a Civilian Linguist Reserve Corps, composed of approximately 1,000 people, as an on-call cadre of high-proficiency, civilian language professionals to support the Department's evolving operational needs.

- Modify tactical and operational plans to improve language and regional training prior to deployments and develop country and language familiarization packages and operationally focused language instruction modules for deploying forces.

What is far from clear is that the military services can provide such new capabilities without providing more end strength. This kind of planning compounds the overall risk of having an end strength too small to prevent excessive deployments—and strains on recruiting and retention—and adds a serious danger that such concepts will end in calling for "super soldiers," rather than practical and affordable improvements in military manpower. There are only so many skill sets any given mix of men and women can develop and sustain, and an all-volunteer force structure cannot be based on a force in which every man and woman is above average. It certainly is desirable for soldiers to be more than warfighters, to be "joint" in every respect, and to be paragons of the information age. Whether it is practical is a totally different issue.

The QDR calls for capabilities that virtually must involve much longer training cycles to work, and this means that men and women must be deployed in ways that make such training possible. It is not clear how the Army and the Marine Corps can provide both the forces needed for the increased OPTEMPO required for missions in Iraq and Afghanistan and free up enough personnel for training. Redeployments and stop-loss policies kept personnel in theater for extended periods, reducing the available time for training.

The FY2007 budget called for a 33-percent expansion of SOFs and a 33-percent increase in Psychological and Civil Affairs Personnel to support the SOF and the Army's modular force. Finding and retaining linguists and cultural experts, however, was easier to call for than to implement, particularly if there is no immediate mission requirement for such personnel, or new missions emerge in other regions and areas. The FY2007 budget also called for a new Marine Corps Special Operations Component to conduct special reconnaissance and other missions. It further established an SOF Unmanned Aerial Vehicle Squadron and increased the number of SEAL (sea, air, and land) teams.

The total cost of this effort is projected at $28.7 billion for FY2007–FY2011, but these do not seem to be incremental funds, and this means the services must somehow pay for such changes while at the same time meeting existing manpower costs. It also may be harder to make a 33-percent increase in SOFs than the other new manpower specialties. SOFs are extremely difficult to create and set extraordinary standards. The rise in private security forces with far higher pay levels since the beginning of the Iraq War has also made them equally difficult to retain. It simply is not clear that such increases are practical without lowering standards.

MORE CIVILIANS?

It also is not convincing that the problems in military manpower can be solved by more efforts to convert military slots to civilian ones. Chapter 2 has shown that the Department of Defense has become steadily more dependent on civilian manpower since the end of the Cold War, although this is disguised when only career Department of Defense civilian employees are counted. The main increase has occurred in defense-related workers in industry and contractors.

These military-to-civilian conversions have had two fundamental goals:

- Cost savings on the relative expense of contractors/civilians versus uniformed military personnel for certain functions.
- Freeing up money to invest in warfighting capabilities and freeing up uniformed personnel to perform warfighting roles.

In late October 2006, the U.S. Department of Defense indicated it might seek legislation to make it easier to deploy civilians overseas. At an October 18 conference in Falls Church, Virginia, Under Secretary for Personnel and Readiness David Chu said that the Department wanted to review laws that made it difficult to reclassify job descriptions of employees who may be useful abroad. The moves were part of an ongoing effort to identify military jobs that could be filled by Pentagon civilians or contractors. As of the press conference, 20,000 jobs had been converted, with the DoD hoping to double that number by 2008, according to Chu.[112]

Because career civilians have also been cut, however, such conversions have meant growing reliance on contract civilians. At least in some cases, this approach seems to have been based on a political ideology and/or a dubious analysis of cost savings with limited regard to actual performance rather than on real-world life cycle costs and efficiency and the risks that emerge from cutting total military end strength.

Historical Military-to-Civilian Efforts

Since 1954, DoD Directive 1100.4 has required the services to staff positions with civilian personnel unless the services deem a position a military essential for one or more reasons, including combat readiness, legal requirements, training, security, rotation, and discipline. The DoD has, however, given implementing guidance that has provided local commanders with wide latitude in justifying the use of military personnel in their staffing requests.[113]

Several key developments have shaped this military-to-civilian conversion effort:

- Since 1966, Circular Number A-76 has instructed that the Federal Government shall rely on commercially available sources to provide commercial products and services. The idea is that competition enhances quality, economy, and productivity.

- In the 1970s, the services claimed to have replaced nearly 48,000 military personnel in support positions with 40,000 civilian employees. However, the services did not maintain accurate records to substantiate these claims.[114]

- In 1991, the DoD instructed its components to identify essential services provided by contractors (to deployed forces) and to develop plans to ensure the continuation of those services should contractors become unavailable. However, a 2003 GAO report found that DOoD components had not conducted the directed reviews to identify those contracts providing essential services.[115]

  - In 1994, the GAO released a report recommending that the Secretary of Defense study opportunities to convert certain support positions to civilian status. At that time, a DoD Manpower Requirements Report indicated that more than 245,000 military personnel throughout the services and defense agencies were serving in noncombat program areas: service management headquarters, training and personnel, research and development, central logistics, and support activities. The GAO report further suggested that many other job categories generally do not require knowledge or experience gained through military service: finance, administration, data processing, and personnel.[116]

- A 1997 Business Executives for National Security (BENS) report placed blame on Congress for some of the sloth in outsourcing:

  - Current law stipulates that the Secretary of Defense identify core logistics functions which then cannot be outsourced unless Congress is notified. This could theoretically slow conversions of military personnel in the logistics space, although it is not certain how this would have a dramatic impact.

  - The report cites services contracted out already: 9 percent of health services, 12 percent of education and training, 47 percent of data processing, and fully 96 percent of base maintenance is contracted out.[117]

- A 1999 BENS Report estimated that roughly 300,000 DoD civilians perform jobs with direct private sector equivalents. The report predicts that the largest number of transitions would take place in the area of maintenance/repair, base services, and health care.[118]

- In 1998, the 105th Congress passed the FAIR Act (PL 105-270), which required that by June 30 of each year, federal agencies must submit annual lists of jobs that are potential candidates for outsourcing. Jobs must be classified either as (1) inherently governmental, (2) commercial, or (3) commercial exempt.

    - The Act extends, *inter alia,* to military departments named in section 102 of title 5, United States Code (Army, Navy, and Air Force).

    - The Act applies only to activities performed by Federal civilian employees. Military members are not "employees," since they are not appointed to the civil service.[119]

    - Not inherent in the expression "inherently government function," per the terms of the Act, are the following:

        - gathering information for or providing advice, opinions, recommendations, or ideas to federal government officials; or

        - any function that is primarily ministerial and internal in nature (such as building security, mail operations, operation of cafeterias, housekeeping, facilities operations and maintenance, warehouse operations, motor vehicle fleet management operations, or other routine electrical or mechanical services).

    - The Office of Management and Budget (OMB) released its first round of job lists on October 1, 2000. They showed 258,000 employees at 26 agencies, including the DoD, who qualified for conversion consideration. According to the OMB, approximately 75 percent of those jobs could be outsourced.[120]

    - In March 2001, the OMB directed federal agencies to compete 5 percent of all federal jobs considered commercial in nature by October 2002 and 10 percent of all federal jobs considered commercial in nature by October 2003.[121]

Military-to-Civilian Conversions since Afghanistan and Iraq

Iraq and Afghanistan have raised serious questions about the impact of such conversions. As of late 2005, there were an estimated 30,000 civilian contractors working directly with the Pentagon in Iraq, and these figures often understated foreign hires and did not include aid-related workers who often provided some military support functions. Some estimates put the total number of U.S. and foreign hires at over 100,000.

Typical duties included the following:

- Logistics,
- Security,
- Drug eradication,
- Administrative,
- Weapons systems support,

- Linguistics,
- Equipment maintenance,
- Communications,
- Fuel and material transport,
- Medical, and
- Mail.

Many of these personnel played critical roles in supporting the U.S. military, and some provided outstanding performance at considerable personal risk. Many such contract employees were, however, extremely costly. They presented a major "opportunity cost" for the U.S. military because they required extensive force protection and could not be sent into harm's way in the same way as military personnel. Some hires also raised serious questions about corruption, mismanagement, and overspending. The security problem also could not be solved by requiring contractors to provide for their own security. This did more than consume large amounts of the contract. As was documented in the July 2006 report of the Special Inspector General for Iraq Reconstruction, the diversion of time and resources toward increasing security measures continued to detract from many contractors' abilities to focus on and successfully execute their missions in Iraq.

More generally, serious questions arose as to whether the United States had converted so many military positions to civilian contractors that it did not have a large enough pool to provide reasonable deployment levels to be able to convert or reassign personnel in an emergency or to perform support functions in high-risk areas at reasonable cost and with reasonable levels of force protection.

None of these issues, however, have halted the Department of Defense effort to keep converting military positions to civilian ones. In 2002, the Secretary of the Army, Thomas White, announced a new initiative called the "The Third Wave" to outsource approximately 214,000 jobs in the Army (affecting up to 160,000 civilians and up to 60,000 uniformed military personnel). The Third Wave differs from the first and second waves because it includes base operation activities, including logistics, training, information management, and public works.[122]

However, a number of major issues still remained:

- Latitude in services' guidance instruction allows local commanders to choose service members over civilians.
- Local commanders have little guarantee that converted positions will be funded, due to civilian salaries coming from nonguaranteed pools of money that also pay for fuel, etc.
- Some commanders believe that civilian contractors who do not train with the unit are disruptive upon deployment.
- The DoD cannot guarantee that the service provided by contractors would be provided during a hostile situation or a situation of unfavorable OPTEMPO.

- Ongoing military drawdown in the late 1990s is sometimes cited as a reason for not converting more than what was Congressionally mandated until drawdown was complete.

- Using private contractors for CS and CSS runs into the problem of model sustainability. Private sector companies need a constant demand/supply scenario to maintain operability.

In April 2004, the Under Secretary of Defense for Personnel and Readiness introduced a process for managing conversions of military positions to civilian or contractor positions. Specifically, this process was designed to (1) measure the services' progress in achieving military-to-civilian conversion goals, (2) determine which skill sets would receive additional military positions subsequent to conversions, and (3) identify and track the number of civilian or contractor positions added as a result of conversions.

In the FY2005 National Defense Authorization Act (P.L.108-375), Congress directed that the DoD provide new accountability on the reporting of the size and scope of the service contractor workforce. The DoD Inspector General was required to report to Congress by February 1, 2005, on whether the DoD has a sufficient number of employees to conduct public-private competitions.[123] Meanwhile, the FY2005 Defense Budget called for the conversion of 10,700 military jobs to civilian positions. The budget included $572 million to cover the costs of converting or eliminating the positions.

In December 2003 the Office of the Secretary of Defense (OSD) set a goal of converting 20,700 military positions to civilian or contractor positions—10,000 in 2004 and 10,700 in 2005. The GAO reported, however, that only 3,400 positions were converted in 2004, or 34 percent of the original goal. The services had a goal to convert 15,900 positions in 2005, but some service officials said that a lack of funding and the time it takes to properly train and hire replacements were likely to cause the DoD to fail to meet its goal.[124]

The GAO report also noted that the DoD did not have a comprehensive plan to oversee military-to-civilian conversions and that it lacked data-driven metrics to assess whether or not such conversions were fulfilling the goal of providing more active military personnel for combat roles. The GAO report made the following recommendations to the Secretary of Defense regarding military personnel levels and military-to-civilian conversions:[125]

- Establish an OSD-led, systematic approach to assess the levels of active military personnel needed to execute the defense strategy as part of the next quadrennial review and report its analysis and conclusions to the Congress.

- Develop a plan to manage and evaluate the DoD's initiatives to assign a greater portion of active military personnel to warfighting duties.

- In responding to the GAO report, the DoD announced that it generally agreed with the report's recommendations and that the DoD was currently taking steps via the QDR process to address the problems. The DoD response also announced initiatives under way to track and manage military-to-civilian conversions and other programs aimed at reducing the stress on forces.[126]

According to a 2005 GAO Report, senior OSD officials stated that about 300,000 military personnel were performing functions that civilians could perform or that could be contracted out to a commercial source. However, OSD and some service officials acknowledged this estimate was based on a 1997 study that used a methodology that overstated the actual number of military personnel in positions suitable for civilian or contractor performance. Since that time, a comprehensive review of commercial-type positions completed in 2003 identified only about 44,000 military positions as suitable for conversion to civilian or contractor positions.[127]

THE ROLE OF CONTRACTORS

In short, the Iraq War and other recent conflicts have raised serious questions about the possible overdependence on contract employees. Such questions become even more serious when so many such contractors are needed to provide critical combat support functions, and both contractor and career civilians are sometimes unwilling to take on necessary tasks in a war zone.

The Department seems to have almost deliberately avoided providing detailed figures on just how dependent the U.S. military forces in Iraq are on civilian support, the total cost of such support, and the areas where it has not been able to get reliable civilian services because of risk, cost, or lack of specialized expertise. It has also failed to address such issues as the need for reliance on civilian contract security personnel, the impact of large-scale contracting on retention in the U.S. military, and the problems that result from the lack of legal accountability and control over such personnel.

Enough data are available, however, to strongly suggest that a zero-based examination is needed of the growing U.S. reliance on contract personnel. In August 2003, private contracting firm Blackwater USA was awarded a $21-million no-bid contract to guard Coalition Provisional Authority Chief Paul Bremer, and as of July 2006, the company had about 1,000 contractors in Iraq. In June 2006, the U.S. government estimated that there were at least 180 security companies operating in Iraq with more than 48,000 employees—the largest private military deployment in history. Since 2000, in fact, Blackwater alone had won $505 million in publicly identifiable federal contracts, about two-thirds of which were no-bid contracts.

In the first Gulf War, the ratio of private contractors to troops was 1:60; that figure leaped to a ratio of 1:3 in Iraq by the summer of 2006.[128] The presence of military contractors—in particular for security roles—raised a serious debate over the possible resulting negatives implicit in such a large number of personnel who fall outside of the U.S. military command structure and whose status under international law was undefined. Complaints of overly aggressive tactics further raised questions about the effect that these personnel were having in the U.S. effort to "win the hearts and minds" of the Iraqi people, while miscommunication issues between contract employees operating in close proximity with U.S. and Coalition troops also came to the fore.

Contractors can provide some logistics, CS, and CSS functions as well. Contracted support can include traditional goods and services support as well as interpreter, communications, infrastructure, and other non-logistic-related functions. In the initial stages of an operation, the supplies and services provided by local contractors can improve response time and free strategic airlift and sealift for other priorities. Contractor support drawn from in-theater resources can augment existing support capabilities to provide a new source for critically needed supplies and services, thereby reducing dependence on the CONUS-based support system.

When military force caps are imposed on an operation, contractor support can give the commander the flexibility of increasing his combat power by substituting combat units for military support units. This permits the combatant commander to have sufficient support in the theater, while strengthening the joint force's fighting capability. At the conclusion of operations, contractors can also facilitate early redeployment of military personnel.

What is far less clear, however, is that contractors are always more cost-effective in such roles than are men and women in uniform, are as flexible in terms of assignment and training, and should be used extensively in combat theaters. There are good reasons to question the use of contractors on extended battlefields. From a mission-success perspective, placing contractors in security or support positions puts them outside the chain of command, as opposed to military personnel serving in similar roles. The Iraq War has shown that some will not take necessary risks, while contract personnel can be reckless and indifferent to local political considerations and sensitivities.

Army Field Manual 100-10-2 provides the following guidance on contractor command and control:[129]

> Command and control within an area of operations (AO) will be executed by the military Chain-of-Command, which begins with the Theater Commander and extends to the lowest level of command responsible for personnel safety and mission accomplishment. For contractor personnel, command and control is dependent upon the terms and conditions of the contract. The Contracting Officer (KO) or the KO's designated representative(s) is the appointed liaison for monitoring contractor performance requirements and will ensure that contractors move materiel and personnel in accordance with the combatant commander's plan.

Such concerns over reliability are not limited to battlefield scenarios. There are also reasons to fear that contracted personnel cannot be relied upon to deploy to dangerous missions to begin with, barring a legal obligation to deploy. DoD Instruction 3020.41, dated October 3, 2005, was meant to serve as a comprehensive source of DoD policy and procedures concerning DoD contractor personnel authorized to accompany U.S. armed forces. It addressed the issue of contractor deployment reliability as such:[130]

Planning for continuation of essential contractor services during contingency operations includes the following:

- Determining all services provided overseas by defense contractors that must continue during a contingency operation. Contracts shall obligate defense contractors to ensure the continuity of essential contractor services during a contingency operation.

- Developing contractor contingency plans for those tasks identified as essential contractor services to provide reasonable assurance of continuation during crisis conditions.

- Ensuring the secretaries of the military departments and the combatant commanders plan for effective retention or replacement of contingency contractor personnel who are performing essential contractor services in contingency operations. For situations where the cognizant DoD component commander has a reasonable doubt about the continuation of essential services by the incumbent contractor during crisis situations, the commander shall prepare a contingency plan for obtaining the essential services from alternative sources [military, DoD civilian, host nation (HN) personnel, or contractor(s)]. This shall include situations where the commander has concerns the contractor cannot or will no longer fulfill the terms of the contract because the threat level, duration of hostilities, or other factors specified in the contract have changed significantly or because U.S. laws, international or HN support agreements, or status of forces agreements (SOFAs) have changed in a manner that affect contract arrangements, or due to political or cultural reasons.

- Encouraging contingency contractor personnel performing essential contractor services overseas to remain in theater.

This guidance on how to "encourage" contractor personnel to continue performing essential services in a hostile or otherwise unpalatable environment does, however, remain unclear. The task of developing contingency plans to ensure the continuation of essential contracted services and to ensure the proper deployment, visibility, security, accountability, and redeployment was left to the geographic combatant commanders, as per DoD Instruction 3020.41.

Likewise, the undefined status of contractors on the battlefield leaves their U.S. legal status—as well as the U.S. military's ability to impose discipline—unclear, and it has left their status vague under the international conventions defining the terms and rules of war, as well as the treatment and rights of enemy combatants. DoD Instruction 3020.41 addressed the status issue as well:[131]

Contingency contractor personnel remain subject to U.S. laws and regulations. For example, contingency contractor personnel fulfilling contracts with the U.S. Armed Forces may be subject to prosecution under Federal law, including but not limited to the Military Extraterritorial Jurisdiction Act (MEJA), 18 U.S.C. 3261 (reference (k)), which extends U.S. Federal criminal jurisdiction to certain DOD contingency contractor personnel, for certain offenses committed outside U.S. territory. For such cases, the DOD regulations to be followed to comply with MEJA are contained in DOD Instruction 5525.11 (reference (l)). Pursuant to the War Crimes Act, 18 U.S.C. 2441 (reference (m)), Federal criminal jurisdiction also extends to conduct that is determined to constitute a violation of the law of war when committed by a civilian national of the United States. In addition, when there is a formal declaration of war by Congress, DOD contingency contractor personnel may be subject to prosecution under the Uniform Code of Military Justice (UCMJ) (reference (n)). Other laws may allow prosecution of offenses by contingency contractor personnel, such as 18 U.S.C. 7(9) (reference (o)), which may provide for prosecution of U.S. nationals who commit offenses on military facilities in foreign countries. Immediate consultation with the servicing legal office and the contracting officer is required in all cases of suspected criminal conduct by contingency contractor personnel.

This guidance leaves unclear the status of many contractor types in battlefield scenarios, with the status of contractors on the battlefield in the absence of a declared war arising as a particular concern. Army Regulation 715-9, in fact, stipulates that under certain circumstances, contractors may be unable to perform their intended duties due to ill-defined legal status:[132]

> In an area of operations where an international agreement authorizes the presence of US forces (stationing agreement) or regulates their status (SOFA), the status of contractors and their employees, under local law, must also be established by international agreement. Contract provisions or military regulations denoting the contractor as "part of the force" will not suffice to establish such status. When relevant agreements do not address the issue of status for contractors and their employees, the contractor may be unable to perform.

Advocates of increased contractor use, however, cite the use of contractors as a quick way to gain access to certain mission-critical, low-density, high-demand skill sets, particularly in the technology sphere. Use of contractors would furthermore help to ease the strain on the National Guard and the Reserves by providing the CS/CSS that the RC would otherwise provide. Guidance on the DoD relationship with contractors accompanying armed forces on missions abroad stipulates that "hospitalization will be limited to stabilization and short-term medical treatment with an emphasis on return to duty or placement in the patient movement system . . . All costs associated with the treatment and transportation of contingency contractor personnel to the selected civilian facility are reimbursable to the Government and shall be the responsibility of the contingency contractor personnel, their employer, or their health insurance provider." Primary medical and dental care will furthermore not be provided to the contractor unless specifically authorized otherwise in the given contract.[133]

In either case, following the midterm elections of November 2006, there was growing speculation that government contractors operating in Iraq and Afghanistan would begin to see increased scrutiny and oversight from a newly Democratic Congress. A GAO study in 2006 indicated that the government had spent $388 billion on contractors in the previous year and that much of that money was exposed to "potential waste and misuse." Many Democrats in Congress had long been outspoken critics of these contracts and the use of contractors. By late fall, industry leaders were preparing for the possibility of being called to testify before Congress at a moment's notice as a newly invigorated oversight process began to pick up speed.[134]

THE DOLLAR COST OF MAINTAINING THE FORCE

As was discussed at the beginning of this chapter, the FY2007 budget gave priority to procurement and operations and maintenance over military personnel. It also called for cuts in end strength rather than increases. Even so, military personnel were projected to cost $110.8 billion in FY2007, a 4-percent increase over FY2006, and 25.2 percent of the total defense budget less supplementals. This compared with just short of 26 percent in FY2006, and—as a rough rule of thumb—a recent average around 25 percent of total defense spending.[135]

Such figures reflect an important impact of the Iraq War. The United States has been able to keep recruiting and retention as high as it has been only by making major increases in salaries and benefits. The strain on the force in terms of overdeployments, stop-loss, forced retention, the perception of a broken social compact, and uneven political support for the war at home have all had a major impact.

For all of the U.S. military's successes to date, recruiting has become more difficult since the beginning of the Iraq War, with the services struggling to meet their goals or missing them entirely. Retaining those already in the service has become more challenging as well, and such retention has become steadily more important. Even in peacetime, failing to retain military personnel means losing the benefits of a significant investment in training in experience for the services. Military operations in Iraq and Afghanistan have given the force additional in-theater warfighting experience that is lost if the men and women involved are not retained. These troops come home with skills and experience that are crucial to fighting the new forms of warfare, which is how the DoD is now structuring its force.

Paying More for the Same Men and Women

Short-term solutions like stop-loss and forced retention may keep personnel for a while, but have counterproductive long-term consequences. As a result, the DoD has had to pay more to get the recruits it needs and to acquire skilled personnel. This, however, is only part of the cost problem that is rising out of putting so much strain on a fixed end strength.

The U.S. government budget for FY2007, for example, introduced another round of increases in pay and allowances for current service members, in addition to increased funding for the recruitment and pay of certain high-demand personnel. The budget increased military base pay by 2.2 percent over FY2006. This particular annual increase is limited, but pay has increased by an average of 29 percent since 2001. Some service members have received even more.[136]

The FY2007 budget further calls for $263 million in expanded pay increases for certain warrant officers and midgrade and senior enlisted personnel with high-demand skills and experience. An additional $1.9 billion was allotted for retention bonuses and incentives. This increase is only one more step in a long series of major bonuses and incentives since 2001.[137]

The FY2007 budget also called for an increase of 5.9 percent in basic housing allowances for active-duty military members and provided for $1.3 billion to increase the basic housing allowance for off-base family housing. In addition, the budget provided for $1.5 billion for the construction of 48 new barracks projects for enlisted personnel, $68 million for eight new child development centers, and $77 million for four dependent education school projects.

- Figure 4.15 shows the relative percent increases in major DoD funding areas. As the figure shows, spending on military personnel saw the second-largest outlay of

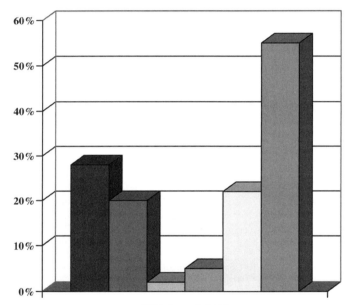

2001 through 2004

■ Military Personnel	28%
▩ Operation and Maintenance	20%
▢ Military Construction	2%
▨ Family Housing	5%
▢ Procurement	22%
▦ R&D	55%

Source: Adapted from the Office of Management and Budget website: http://www.whitehouse.gov/omb/budget/fy2005/defense.html. Margin of error in adaptation +/-2 percentage points.

Figure 4.15   Increases in Major DoD Funding Areas

DoD funds, after research and development costs. Other costs directly related to personnel, such as family housing, were also significant in assessing personnel costs to DoD.

• Figure 4.16 provides a broader view of DoD spending from 2001 through 2005. Of the discretionary budget authority spending listed, military personnel represented the second largest percent increase during this time period—not including "revolving funds and other" expenses—at 28 percent.

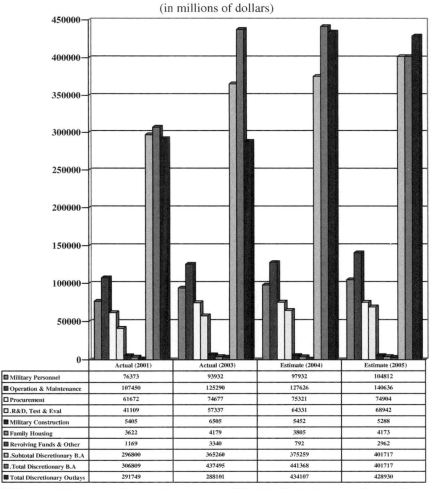

(in millions of dollars)

	Actual (2001)	Actual (2003)	Estimate (2004)	Estimate (2005)
▣ Military Personnel	76373	93932	97932	104812
▣ Operation & Maintenance	107450	125290	127626	140636
▢ Procurement	61672	74677	75321	74904
▢ .R&D, Test & Eval	41109	57337	64331	68942
▣ Military Construction	5405	6505	5452	5288
▣ Family Housing	3622	4179	3805	4173
▣ Revolving Funds & Other	1169	3340	792	2962
▢ .Subtotal Discretionary B.A	296800	365260	375259	401717
▣ .Total Discretionary B.A	306809	437495	441368	401717
▣ Total Discretionary Outlays	291749	288101	434107	428930

* 2003 supplemental funding does not reflect all transfers to other agencies, # 2004 includes CPA administrative costs. ^ For comparability, the 2001 data reflect transfers related to the creation of the Department of Homeland Security. Source: Adapted from Office of Management and Budget, 2005 Website report on DOD trends since 2001, available: http://www.whitehouse.gov/omb/budget/fy2005/defense.html

Figure 4.16   Department of Defense Spending, 2001–2005

The Military Entitlements Cost Squeeze: Health Care

Pay, however, is only one part of the cost story. Increases in pay to retain key personnel within what may well be an inadequate end strength inevitably means future increases in pension payments. There has already been a major increase in the cost of other military entitlements, particularly in the case of health care.

Changes in the nature of combat increase such costs. Higher survival does to some extent mean higher medical costs. Compared to the Vietnam War, when about 12 percent of all wounded soldiers sustained a brain injury, in Iraq, 22 percent of the wounded had serious head wounds, according to data as of late January 2006. However, the wounded in Iraq have a much greater chance of surviving their injuries. In World War II, 30 percent of all injured troops died, compared to 24 percent in Vietnam. In Iraq, just 9 percent of the injured lost their lives. Improvements in body and vehicle armor, as well as advancements in battlefield medicine, were credited with the increased survival rates, among some 16,500 U.S. soldiers and Marines injured in Iraq to date, according to ABC News.[138] Of the 17,000 wounded in Iraq as of March 2006, more than 380 were amputees whose lives were spared by body armor protecting their torsos, but whose long-term medical expenses were expected to be significant given the nature of their injuries.[139]

As a result, more and more personnel have required expensive medical treatment after returning from theater. With the prevalence of blast trauma wounds, long-term care for amputees and brain injury patients became an issue, as well as caring for troops who returned home with Post-Traumatic Stress Disorder (PTSD), a psychological condition often requiring long-term therapeutic care for proper treatment. As of early spring 2006, nearly 150,000 veterans of Iraq and Afghanistan had shown up on the doorsteps of Veterans Affairs (VA) health centers since 2001. About a third of them—46,000—were seen for mental health issues. PTSD was the fastest-growing disability among VA clients at this time, with cases up 80 percent in five years. Of the 46,000 veterans seen for mental health issues, 20,638 had received a possible diagnosis for PTSD that required follow-up monitoring.[140]

By the end of 2006, repeat tours in Iraq had given the issue of PTSD even greater significance. In December 2006, the Army reported that a survey exploring the effect of multiple war-zone rotations on soldiers' mental health showed that soldiers who served repeated Iraq deployments were 50 percent more likely than those with one tour to suffer from acute combat stress, thus raising their risk of PTSD. While earlier Army reports indicated that about 30 percent of soldiers deployed from Iraq suffered from depression, anxiety, and PTSD, these findings suggested a greater risk that some soldiers were returning to the battlefield while still suffering from the psychological scars of earlier deployments.

The report—the Army's third mental health survey conducted since 2003—further suggested that soldiers in Iraq were facing greater exposure to traumatic events than during the periods of previous reports. According to the 2006 report, 76 percent of soldiers said they knew someone who had been seriously injured or killed, and 55 percent had experienced the explosion of a roadside bomb or nearby booby trap.

Other developments included the following:

- The proportion of soldiers who reported that they had suffered a combination of anxiety, depression, and acute stress had risen 17 percent, compared with 13 percent in the previous (2004) report.
- Combat stress was significantly higher among soldiers with at least one previous tour: 18.4 percent compared with 12.5 percent of those on their first deployment.

The Army sought to curb the dangers of personnel with such mental health concerns in the war zone by increasing the number of mental health professionals in Iraq and Afghanistan. The survey also found that 95 percent of respondents said that mental health care was readily available to them. However, 28 percent of soldiers also expressed concern that seeking help for such mental health issues would be a sign of weakness. This stigma was a continuing concern, as Army research showed that only 40 percent of soldiers with mental disorders sought care.[141]

Associated conditions also included alcohol and drug abuse, as well as increased aggressive behaviors, all of which were found to be impacting negatively on soldiers' reacclimation to society and family, and which often required long-term care solutions to properly treat.

Other studies showed that the military health care program has become a key tool in the recruitment and retention arsenal. Providing the DoD's extensive TRICARE benefits [the triple option benefit plan available for military families: TRICARE Prime (HMO option), TRICARE Extra (PPO option), and TRICARE Standard (Fee-for-service option)] for service personnel and their families has proven to greatly increase the attractiveness of the military as an employer with good health benefits, and it provides an incentive to make the military a career.

The services and Congress have come to rely upon health care as a carrot in recruiting personnel to a life in the military. The end result, however, is that the annual health care cost doubled for the military between 2000 and 2005, amounting to $38 billion during that five-year period, or $1 of every $12 the Pentagon spent. Projections called for a price tag of $64 billion by 2015, or 12 percent of the defense budget, up from $19 billion in 2001, or 4.5 percent of the defense budget.

The steady increases in the scale and the cost of such benefits reached the point where they were projected to cost $39 billion in FY2007, or 35 percent of the $110.8 billion allocated to military personnel, and 9 percent of the total $439.3-billion regular budget. They were projected to total $211 billion from FY2007 to FY2011. According to a Department of Defense slide presentation, released alongside the U.S. government budget, this would mean a rise by 31 percent from FY2005 through FY2011. Figure 4.17 depicts historical and projected health care expenditures on military personnel from FY2005 through FY2011.

These costs have not been ones the DoD can predict or control, and the rise in the cost of the medical entitlement benefits for veterans has presented the same problems. By the summer of 2005, FY2005 (ending September 30) estimates for the number of new enrollees seeking health benefits from Veterans Affairs ran at

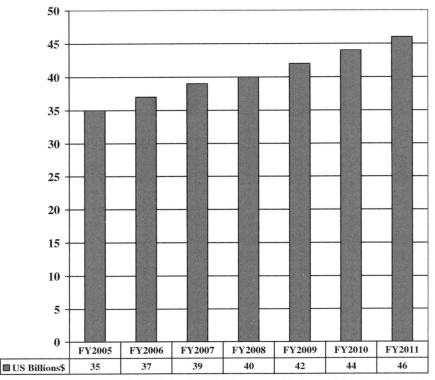

	FY2005	FY2006	FY2007	FY2008	FY2009	FY2010	FY2011
▥ US Billions$	35	37	39	40	42	44	46

Source: Adapted from a chart in DOD Briefing: "FY 2007 Department of Defense Budget," released alongside FY 2007 US Government Budget, February 6, 2006, p. 14.

Figure 4.17 Rising Health Care Expenditures on Military Personnel, FY2005– FY2011

103,000. The number was an upward revision from a previous estimate of 23,553, which Veterans Affairs Secretary R. James Nicholson said was based upon outdated assumptions from 2002. The revision came as the Bush Administration said that it had underestimated the number of personnel returning from Iraq and Afghanistan seeking medical treatment from the Department of Veterans Affairs. The Administration also warned that health care programs would be short at least $2.6 billion in 2006 unless Congress approved additional funds.[142]

On February 6, 2006, Jim Nicholson announced that President George W. Bush would be seeking $80.6 billion for the Department of Veterans Affairs under the FY2007 budget plan. This was to represent an increase of $8.8 billion, or 12.2 percent, above the budget for 2006, including $38.5 billion in discretionary spending, mostly for health care. The budget called for an increase of $3.5 billion for health care alone, more than 11 percent over FY2006. The additional funding was meant to provide for an estimated 5.3 million patients, including over

100,000 veterans of the wars in Iraq and Afghanistan. Specific requests included the following:[143]

- Requests a total investment of almost $3.2 billion in mental health services, which is $339 million above the FY2006 level.
- Requests $1.4 billion for prosthetics and sensory aids, a $160-million increase over FY2006.
- Requests funding for noninstitutional long-term care would increase by nearly 10 percent over FY2006, with a total investment of $535 million in the President's proposed budget.

At the time the budget was introduced, veterans who were deployed to combat zones were entitled to two years of eligibility for VA health care services following their separation from active-duty service, even if they were not immediately otherwise eligible to enroll in VA. This, however, begged the issue of long-term care, which had become an increasing concern due to the nature of injuries being sustained, particularly in Iraq.

As of early 2006, about 9 million current or former military personnel were eligible for TRICARE coverage. Of those, advocacy groups claimed that about a third were retirees under age 65 and their families. TRICARE premiums had not been readjusted since 1995, and some officials saw a readjustment in order as part of the effort to reduce overall costs to the system. The Bush Administration sought to curb some of the rising expenses associated with military health care by proposing increases to the annual cost of coverage under TRICARE Prime, the military's most generous health plan. Annual costs would rise from $230 to $700 for single retired officers younger than 65, and from $460 to $1,400 for married retirees younger than 65. There were to be no increases in TRICARE premiums paid by active-duty families or retirees over 65. The full increases, under this plan, were to be in effect by 2008.[144]

Part of the logic in the new plan was to discourage retired military personnel with second careers from remaining on TRICARE rather than joining the health insurance plans offered by their current employers. Often, TRICARE represented a cheaper or more comprehensive option to the employee, while the option of TRICARE was attractive to employers seeking to avoid the obligation of insuring employees who had alternative means of acquiring health care services. Critics of the plan, however, argued that the Pentagon was overestimating the number of retirees who would opt out of TRICARE once the fee increases took effect.[145]

According to William Winkenwerder, Jr., Assistant Secretary of Defense for Health Benefits, health costs had doubled in the five years leading up to March 2006 and were projected to grow to 12 percent of the estimated defense budget for 2015 at the current rate. According to a CBO analysis, the net cost of the expanded program would rise from $9.3 billion a year in FY2007 to $19.9 billion in FY2024, even without the increases in military end strength that Secretary of Defense Gates called for in January 2007.[146]

Some believed that readjusting the annual cost to beneficiaries was a necessary step to help curb these future costs, similar to rate increases faced by civil service retirees covered by the Federal Employees Health Benefits Program. As of spring 2006, however, legislative efforts were under way to strip the Pentagon of its authority to raise health care enrollment fees without Congressional approval.[147]

INCREASING END STRENGTH: THE NEED FOR AN INDEPENDENT EXAMINATION OF MILITARY MANPOWER REQUIREMENTS IN AN ERA OF STRATEGIC UNCERTAINTY

These data and trends raise serious questions about the size of U.S. military end strength and the need for a zero-based reexamination of the future wartime mix of the military, career civilian, and contracted personnel. They do not, however, make conclusive arguments for a given set of changes in response to this challenge.

Arguments for increasing the size of the armed forces began quickly after the 1990s drawdown overseen by the Clinton Administration. While the Administration and Pentagon officials saw the reduction in force size as a necessary outcome of the ending of the Cold War, cautionary voices soon began to emerge. As early as 1997, members of the House Armed Services Committee voiced concerns that "[t]he post–Cold War defense drawdown and the expanding demands of manpower-intensive peacekeeping and humanitarian operations...are placing at risk the decisive military edge that this nation enjoyed at the end of the Cold War..."[148]

The issue acquired a higher profile after the release of the 2001 QDR, which came in the immediate wake of 9/11 and amid planning for what would quickly become the "global war on terror." The QDR's statement that U.S. forces must be able to fight two major theater battles as well as smaller-scale regional contingencies raised serious questions as to what forces were really needed for a "major theater battle" in an era of asymmetric warfare and to what extent such conflicts would now be differentiated from "smaller-scale contingencies" in terms of manpower needed and the necessary mix of capabilities.

The question of force sizing cannot be divorced from initiatives meant to reallocate human resources from noncombat roles to combat roles or to otherwise free up personnel for deployable warfighting roles, such as conversion of non-war-fighting roles to civilian personnel. The essential goals of all of these initiatives are to free up the proper level of manpower needed to man a more nimble and capable fighting force built around the new enhanced combat brigade structure. Such efforts, however, do not eliminate the need for a debate over manpower levels, and current planning does not give meaningful guidance on what the true numbers of warfighting personnel should be at the undefined time in the future when rebalancing and conversion efforts are "completed."

Temporary versus Permanent Increases in End Strength

Another issue that has served as a stumbling block to seriously examining the end strength the United States really requires is the issue of permanent versus temporary increases in the size of U.S. forces. Today, force levels are nowhere near the "permanent" levels at which they stood throughout the Cold War. Once the Iraq War started, this led to a debate that divided the Bush Administration from many Democrats—and some Republicans—in the Congress.

In November 2003, a bipartisan group of 128 members of the House of Representatives, including 54 of the 61 members of the House Armed Services Committee, asked the Bush Administration to propose funding the FY2005 budget request for two additional divisions, which would amount to 30,000 or more additional soldiers.[149]

In January 2004, the Department of Defense temporarily authorized adding 30,000 troops to the authorized active-duty end strength of the Army. Congress, meanwhile, addressed the issue by raising statutory end strengths in the FY2005 authorization bill, and again for FY2006. However, the Administration remained adamant that the increase remain temporary, as a measure specific to the Iraq War.

A report by the Congressional Research Service explained some of the broader trends taking place in the debate over end strength as follows:

> The Administration proposal to increase the Army's size would only be in effect for four years. This is based on the premises that, in the interim, manpower requirements might decrease, initiatives to find greater efficiencies within the current force might bear fruit, or both. If so, the Army will have avoided some near term and longer term cost differentials between permanent and temporary solutions. A permanent increase would require additional resources for recruiting, retention, and training activities. Also, any change upwards in permanent force structure could possibly negate some anticipated savings from base closures mandated by the 2005 BRAC [Base Realignment and Closure] process.
>
> Critics assert that DOD premises may be faulty; a sudden reduction in military requirements bucks the tide of recent history, and, finding more manpower through internal efficiencies has probably been a goal not well-realized by this and preceding Administrations. Whether or not one accepts DOD premises, the method by which it plans to implement a temporary increase is subject to criticism. Rather than recruiting all new personnel, current personnel are being retained, many through the imposition of "stop loss" orders to extend tours of duty. Some question the fairness of making those currently serving sacrifice further to avoid recruiting additional personnel for the future. Some argue that paying the costs for a permanent increase now would avoid the risk of discovering a few years from now that the forces are inadequate. Congress could revisit and correct end strength in each annual authorization bill. Others, however, believing the situation will ease, would argue that taking such a step is premature.

The Growing End Strength Debate

In January 2004 Secretary Rumsfeld authorized a temporary increase in the Army's end strength by 30,000 through FY2009, and the measure was subsequently approved by lawmakers. The authority to make this decision flowed from the President's Executive Order of September 2001, ordering the Ready Reserve to active duty. The order delegated certain responsibilities to the Secretary of Defense, and, *inter alia,* stipulated the following:[150]

> To allow for the orderly administration of personnel within the armed forces, the following authorities vested in the President are hereby invoked to the full extent provided by the terms thereof: section 527 of title 10, United States Code, to suspend the operation of sections 523, 525, and 526 of that title, regarding officer and warrant officer strength and distribution; and sections123, 123a, and 12006 of title 10, United States Code, to suspend certain laws relating to promotion, involuntary retirement, and separation of commissioned officers; end strength limitations; and Reserve component officer strength limitations.

The issue of increased end strength, however, soon took on a different context. While the order created the temporary circumstance for flexibility in terms of manpower, some began to call for a permanent increase in active component end strengths. Before the House Armed Services Committee on January 28, 2004, the Chief of Staff of the Army, General Peter J. Schoomaker, testified that a permanent, legislated increase would be unwise and unnecessary. He asserted that a permanent increase would create a burden on planned defense budgets in the out-years, citing $1.2 billion annually for each increase of 10,000 troops.

Yet, many in the defense community continued to call for a permanent increase in end strength, particularly in ground forces, to meet the current challenges in Iraq and Afghanistan, as well as to be prepared for future threats. In late 2005, Senators John Reed, Charles Hagel, John McCain, John Kerry, and others proposed a measure (S. 530) that would add 30,000 troops to the Army and 5,000 to the Marine Corps in FY2006, in addition to the troops added in FY2005.

In the House, Representatives Ellen O. Tauscher, Ike Skelton, and others proposed a measure (H.R. 1666) to add 30,000 to the Army, 12,000 to the Marine Corps, 2,000 to the Navy, and 1,000 to the Air Force in FY2006, in addition to the FY2005 increases. Some outside groups proposed adding as many as 25,000 troops per year to the force for the next several years.[151] A group called the Association of the U.S. Army, meanwhile, testified before Congress that Army end strength should grow by 40,000–50,000.

Nevertheless, the Department of Defense continued to stick with the status quo. In late 2005, Deputy Defense Secretary Gordon England told the services to pare a total of $32 billion over the following five years. The Army's share of those cuts totaled to about $11.7 billion. Because the Army said that it would not cut money from its Future Combat System modernization program, the service was left with little other option but to shrink personnel.[152]

The Congress felt differently. For FY2006, the House Armed Services Committee's personnel subcommittee added 10,000 troops to Army end strength and 1,000 to the Marine Corps in markup of the defense authorization bill. The full committee and the full House subsequently approved that measure. In its markup, the Senate Armed Services Committee added 20,000 to Army end strength in

FY2006. Compared to the enacted FY2004 end-strength authorization as a baseline, the Senate provision would add 40,000 troops to the Army and 3,000 to the Marine Corps—13,000 more than the 30,000 additional troops the Administration had decided to maintain for Iraq and Army modularization.[153]

The Department still opposed any such permanent increase in end strength. During a January 25, 2006, press briefing at the Pentagon, Secretary Rumsfeld said that Army leaders were not seeking a permanent increase of 30,000 troops in the deployable active force. Rather, the Army had announced the week prior that it was planning to increase its active-duty combat brigades from its current 33 to 42. This was down from an initial plan to increase to 43. The decision was based upon a strategy review at the Pentagon, which took into account a cut in the National Guard combat brigades from 34 to 28, which would give the Army a total of 70 combat brigades, instead of the originally planned 77.[154]

The *Defense Manpower Requirements Report* for FY2005, prepared by the Office of the Under Secretary of Defense for Personnel and Readiness, forecast that from FY2004 to FY2009 the active number of military personnel would be roughly stable. The report estimated that total active personnel would actually decrease slightly during this period, from 1.39 million to about 1.375 million. Despite this overall decline, the report forecast the active Army and Marine Corps to remain at the same size during this period, at 482,400 officers, enlisted personnel, and cadets for the Army and 175,000 officers and enlisted personnel for the Marines. Meanwhile, they also expected the active Navy to decrease from 373,800 to 357,400, while the Air Force would grow slightly, from 359,300 to 360,000.[155]

Meanwhile, the 2006 QDR called for the following long-term goals:[156]

- Stabilize the Army's end strength at 482,400 active and 533,000 reserve component personnel by FY2011.
- Stabilize the Marine Corps' end strength at 175,000 active and 39,000 reserve component personnel by FY2011.

Defense experts like Senator John McCain responded by stating that the Army and Marine Corps needed another 100,000 people in order to meet their current mission requirements and to allow a proper frequency of deployment for the active, National Guard, and reserve troops, who have been heavily deployed and worn during the operations in Iraq and Afghanistan. Gordon R. Sullivan, former Army Chief of Staff and President of the Association of the United States Army, warned in September 2006 that the Army was too small for the responsibilities it faced and should be expanded from some 500,000 in the active force to 560,000, as well as rebalanced to make better use of the Reserves and National Guard.[157]

The course of the fighting largely supported those who have called for increased end strength. In November 2006, the Army National Guard and the Reserves faced the potential need for more, and even accelerated, call-ups to Iraq. Two Army National Guard brigades with about 7,000 troops were identified for possible rotation to Iraq, it was reported, with the possibility of an additional brigade being diverted from another assignment to Iraq in 2008. As of late fall 2006, projections for 2007 were for the number of Army Guard soldiers in Iraq to surge to 6,000 in about 50 companies, compared to about 20 companies two years prior.[158]

On September 25, 2006, the Pentagon delayed for six weeks the return home of about 4,000 U.S. soldiers from the Army's 1st Armored Division operating in Iraq's volatile Anbar Province—the second extension of U.S. forces in two months. Meanwhile, another brigade, from the Army's 1st Cavalry Division based in Ft. Hood, was ordered to depart for Iraq a month early, in late October, for a year of combat duty in Iraq. According to a Pentagon announcement, the moves came as part of a "shift" aimed at maintaining the current force structure of about 140,000 troops in Iraq at least until spring 2007.[159]

In late October 2006, the Army announced that it planned to maintain its current force level in Iraq through 2010 and that it would be realigning its forces to prevent the wear-out of a small slice of the force that was shouldering the bulk of the combat burden. The new plan entailed moving soldiers from specialties, such as artillery and air defense, to high-demand roles such as infantry, engineering, military police (MP), military intelligence (MI), Special Forces, civil affairs, and psychological operations.[160] The need to shift personnel to account for mounting strains on certain occupations is indicative of wider problems faced by the U.S. military in determining proper force size and mix for the demands of modern warfare. By this time, however, Pentagon records showed that about a fifth of the Army's active-duty forces had already served multiple tours of war duty, while more than 40 percent of the force had not been deployed to Iraq or Afghanistan. Figure 4.18 shows the breakdown of war duty in the Army as of late October.

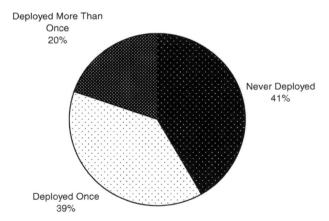

Source: US Department of Defense. Adapted from graphic in article: Tom Vanden Brook, "Army Shifts to Ease Combat Burden," USA Today, October 27, 2006, p. 1.

Figure 4.18   Deployment of Active-Duty U.S. Soldiers to Iraq and Afghanistan as of October 2006

The situation scarcely eased with time. By December 2006, the rising intensity of the fighting, and the risk of wide-scale civil war, led to calls for much larger force increases. Although military manpower for the Iraq War now exceed 140,000 men and women, the need for more soldiers led to serious consideration of surging some 17,000 to 35,000 more troops to Iraq.

Increases in Active End Strength

There is no way to predict the outcome of the war in Iraq, or just how much manpower the United States will eventually deploy. Furthermore, no one can predict another war similar to Iraq, but it *is* possible to predict that the United States is very likely to have to fight another significant regional conflict during the next decade. If so, the results in Iraq strongly indicate that the United States has overstretched its military manpower and needs higher end strengths for its military services. In fact, the Army and the Marine Corps have already moved toward this goal.

It is not surprising, therefore, that the pressures of having to fight even one major contingency in Iraq led the Chief of Staff of the Army, General Peter J. Schoomaker, to change his position on the need for a higher end strength. General Schoomaker had testified before the House Armed Services Committee in January 2004 that, while a temporary boost in end strength was needed, a permanent increase would be unnecessary and costly. General Schoomaker stated that each increase of 10,000 troops would cost an additional $1.2 billion annually.[161]

By early 2006, however, General Schoomaker warned that the active force might need to grow to 560,000 and that there was an immediate priority to bring the Army up to meet a temporary authorization that allowed it to have an additional 30,000 troops through 2011.[162] On December 14, 2006, General Schoomaker went further. He warned that the active-duty Army "will break" under the strain of its current rate of war-zone rotations. He called for expanding the force by 7,000 or more soldiers a year and lifting Pentagon restrictions on involuntary call-ups of Army National Guard and Army Reserve troops. Although 55 percent of the Army's soldiers serving at the time belonged to the National Guard and the Reserves, Department of Defense policy dictated that Reservists could be mobilized involuntarily only once, and for no more than 24 months. As a result, only about 90,000 out of a total of 522,000 National Guard and Reserve members were still available to be mobilized at the time of Schoomaker's statements.[163]

Similarly, the Commandant of the Marine Corps, General James T. Conway, warned in November 2006 that it would take years to train Iraqi and Afghan forces to substitute for U.S. forces and that the Marine Corps probably needed an increase in end strength. He warned that the Marines were badly overdeployed at their current authorized strength of 180,000 men and that more Marines would probably be needed for an era of long wars. At the same time, he warned that the Marine Corps could train and absorb increases only of 1,000 to 2,000 troops a year because all-volunteer professional forces required far higher levels of training and experience than the kind of forces that existed at the time of the draft.[164]

In early November 2006, the Marine Corps went further and advanced a proposal to increase its size by 3,000 to 5,000 Marines. The plan came in response to Donald Rumsfeld's call for the Marines to consider means by which to make more personnel available for Iraq. The plan called for the creation of a new regimental combat team, which would in essence amount to the reconstitution of certain key units that were abolished during the post–Cold War drawdown.

The 2006 Quadrennial Defense Review had called for a Marine Corps of 175,000 Marines, which was funded for in the 2007 budget. Congress had accepted this level and granted temporary authority to increase the size of the Marines by 4,000. The new Marine Corps proposal meant raising the permanent force level to 180,000. Pentagon officials stated in late 2007 that these proposals were being considered in the Pentagon's process of constructing a FY2008 budget proposal.[165] Interviews at the end of 2006 indicated that the Corps would like to increase its end strength to at least 202,000, although its present training base allowed for increases of only around 2,000 men and women per year.

While the Air Force did not seek to raise its end strength, a number of experts warned that plans to cut its active end strength by 40,000 to help to pay for new equipment could leave it without adequate personnel, and similar issues existed for the Navy. The Air Force also faced serious potential problems with the overdeployment of its reserve and National Guard elements, particularly the Reservists staffing critical force enablers like airlift.

This may help explain why Secretary of Defense Robert Gates announced that he had reversed Secretary Rumsfeld's policies regarding cuts in permanent military end strength shortly after Gates came to office; he announced plans to expand the active end strength of the Army from 507,000 to 547,000 total soldiers, reaching 512,000 by the end of 2007. The Marines were to grow from 180,000 to 202,000 by adding 22,000 new Marines and making permanent the 5,000 increase of the past three years.[166]

It was also clear, however, that any such rise in active Army end strength would take time to accomplish. Not only did it mean more recruiting problems, but the Army had a training base that could only easily accommodate increases in end strength of roughly 7,000 a year. Furthermore, added bonuses, recruitment, and other costs had raised the incremental cost of each 10,000-man increase in end strength from around $700 million in 2001 to $1.2 billion in 2006.[167] This may explain why the Army needed time to complete the ongoing 30,000-man increase that had been taking place over the past three years, and why adding an additional 35,000 soldiers would have to take place over the next five years (an average rate of 7,000 troops a year). Similarly, Marines needed years to grow from 180,000 to 202,000 by adding 22,000 new Marines and making permanent the 5,000 increase that had taken place over the previous three years (an average rate of 5,000 a year).[168]

Increases in Reserve End Strength

As General Schoomaker made clear, there was a similar need to address the sizing and use of the manpower in the reserve components. Many experts felt that they were too small and have been overdeployed to the point where they face serious recruiting and retention problems in the future. The Army alone had deployed 186,000 soldiers in the Army Guard and 164,000 in the Army Reserve from the start of the fighting in Afghanistan in 2001 through November 2006.[169]

Once again, the Department of Defense gave reducing force cost priority over the need for more active and reserve forces. The Army National Guard, for example, had a Congressionally mandated end strength of 350,000 for FY2006, yet the Defense Department's FY2007 budget included money for only 330,000 Guardsmen. The Department made this choice to meet its manpower budget ceilings and because of the cost of addressing its growing readiness problems. By the spring of 2006, the Army National Guard had left more than 64,000 pieces of equipment in Iraq, valued at more than $1.2 billion.[170]

Several general officers in the Reserves expressed deep concern in late 2006, however, that major elements of the Reserves were deployed at least twice and sometimes three times the desirable rate. They also noted growing problems with employers and that many Reservists were losing their jobs if they were deployed for more than one year or more than once every four years. Legislation to protect such Reservists was largely ineffective unless the employers had a federal contract, and Reservists with private businesses were increasingly losing them.

At the same time, the fact that the existing Reserves could be involuntarily mobilized only once for no more than 12 months put a heavy burden on the remaining Reserves. By late 2006, the Army had a pool of only around 90,000 men and women in the National Guard out of a total pool of 522,000 that it could still call up on this basis. It also could no longer preserve unit integrity. The Army Reserve was no better off. It had to take 62 percent of its soldiers from other units in deploying forces to Iraq in comparison with 6 percent in 2002 and 39 percent in 2003. In the case of one transportation company, it could deploy only 7 out of 170 soldiers from the unit. It had to pull 163 other soldiers from a total of 65 other units in 49 different locations.[171]

These problems were compounded by the retention of Army Reserves and calling up men and women on the edge of leaving the service. Furthermore, it was clear that cost was given more consideration than military need in decisions to fund the Guard at below authorized end strength. Another concern was the ability to equip such high numbers of Guardsmen. As previously stated, as of early 2006, the Army National Guard had left more than 64,000 pieces of equipment in Iraq, valued at more than $1.2 billion, and had only 40–60 percent of the equipment in the United States needed for many homeland defense missions[172].

The new Iraqi strategy that President Bush announced on January 10, 2007, provided some relief for the immediate problems in the Guard and the Reserves, but left the issue open even in the near term. The Department of Defense also took critical new steps to ease the strain on the Reserves and the National Guard, and the potential American domestic political backlash from implementing the new strategy. The Chairman of the Joint Chiefs, General Pace, announced the following steps at a press conference on September 11,

> General Pace: There will be remobilization of forces, and that remobilization has been contemplated before the announcement of these additional forces, because we have a rotation base of active forces that we try to maintain one year overseas, two years home. And that rotation has gone to one year overseas, one year home.
>
> On the Guard and Reserve side, we try to get one year mobilized and five years demobilized. It's really been more like a year-and-a-half to almost two years mobilized, and then—so the secretary's comments not only allow us to remobilize forces that we need to assist in the total force effort that we've got going on in Iraq, but also significantly ensure that when we do remobilize—or, for those who have not yet been mobilized, when we mobilize them—that their time will be one year. From the time we've called them to active duty, they train up; they deploy, do their mission, come home, and demobilize—all inside of one year, which is a significant planning factor for the folks who have been enormously effective and critical to the success of our overall mission. The Guard and Reserve have been wonderful in the way that they've performed their assignments.
>
> . . . Inside the policy of one year mobilized and five years demobilized, that one year would have been part of the cumulative process. When you have your—what we call "dwell time" at home, you're not mobilized. When you start again, you're starting again. We're not adding that to the previous.
>
> . . . But for any one mobilization, we are constrained not to keep anybody more than 24 months. For subsequent mobilization, we're constrained not to keep anybody more than 24 months. What we're committing to is that we will not keep anybody more than one year on a subsequent mobilization.
>
> Q: So, if you've already been mobilized for 18 months, and you've gone to Iraq for a tour and your unit gets mobilized, and you still have—and you went to Iraq—I'm sorry, this gets very complicated—and you went to Iraq fewer than four years ago, you could be mobilized and have to go. Is that correct?
>
> General Pace: That's correct. But your time, as the secretary has indicated, will be no more than 12 months when you go the second time. Or, if you happen to be a new recruit and you go the first time, it will still be for 12 months.

These steps scarcely deal with the longer-term issues of roles and missions or needed end strength. They at best were a temporary fix.

Finding the Right Numbers

The previous chapter has already noted the need for a zero-based examination of the overall mix of military, career civilian, and contract manpower. It seems very likely that this will end in a call for an increase in military end strength for the active forces at least equal to that proposed by Secretary Gates and quite possibly similar increases in the Reserves.

Success, however, depends on both finding the right end strength and the right mix of at least five major sets of actions:

- First, transform U.S. active and reserve forces to minimize the burden of rotations and service on part of the force, and create a pool of more deployable units tailored to today's missions rather than to the Cold War.

- Second, reexamine contingency plans to make deployment cycles acceptable to the active and reserve military—if necessary paying the cost of rises in end strength—and to explicitly make the need to maintain acceptable deployment rates and cycles part of all war planning.

- Third, restructure the National Guard and the Reserves to eliminate the total force concept of integrating active and reserve forces, break out reserve duty into a clearly defined mix where most of the Reserves are not needed for more than short deployments in limited wars, and men and women must volunteer for units that may have longer and more frequent service and pay them accordingly.

- Fourth, have clear pay and incentive plans for longer and more frequent deployments that make a formal commitment to the U.S. military personnel that they will receive suitable pay and privileges if the U.S. government must violate the unwritten social contract that is a key part of the all-volunteer force structure.

- Fifth, reorganize both the U.S. military personnel system and the U.S. force structure to create a new mix of skills better suited to asymmetric warfare, stability operations, counterterrorism and counterinsurgency, nation building, homeland defense, and the other post–Cold War needs of the twenty-first century.

If one looks at the results of the Department of Defense's efforts in these areas to date, they raise so many serious issues that a zero-based reassessment of both end strength and the social contract between the United States and its all-volunteer military is clearly needed. The issues to be examined include the cost of recruiting and retaining military personnel in an era of long wars. They include finding the right way to restructure military skills and forces to reduce the strain of repeated or forced deployments. At the same time, they include dealing with the risk of shaping the training and the organization of military personnel around the present conflict— "planning for the last war." The types of units currently in high demand for stability and counterinsurgency operations in Iraq, and to some extent in Afghanistan, may not be as much of a paradigm for the future as QDR 2006 and most current military service plans estimate. The United States needs to carefully examine whether the future threat environment warrants shifting the U.S. force structure in this way.

There is a clear need to reorganize the nature and balance of the active and reserve forces, but this is a requirement that the Department of Defense has recognized without yet offering clear solutions. There is no present basis for determining how the DoD will ultimately adjust the AC-RC mix, although it is clear that major adjustments are needed. No service as yet seems to have comprehensively defined how its reserve forces should be structured, manned, and equipped.[173] It is clear, however, that finding a new balance for the AC and RC components must be linked to more realistic budgetary planning and allocation, and clear perceptions of future threats.

Whatever is done to reform and restructure the military manpower pool must provide *both the necessary quality and the necessary quantity*. The United States must size and fund the key elements of its manpower pool accordingly. It must carry out force transformation in ways that make the burden of service acceptable in "nonexistential wars." The AC and RC components must be large enough so that contingency planning and actual warfighting can realistically deploy forces in ways that honor the unwritten social contract that makes an all-volunteer force possible.

The Iraq War is a warning that the United States needs enough military manpower to fight all of the kinds of wars it may face and to meet all of its strategic commitments. Planning on technology, the ability to predict the nature of future conflicts, and improvements in individual manpower quality is meaningful only if every element is fully implemented. If any element falls short, the only answer is more men and women in uniform, and the following chapters strongly suggest that at least one element—U.S. procurement plans—cannot be implemented in anything like the way that current plans dictate.

As a result, the greatest single uncertainty in current military manpower plans seems to be the idea that the United States can solve its manpower problems with the same or a smaller number of men and women in uniform. Increasing active and reserve end strength is not cheap. However, current plans may well rely too heavily on force restructuring to solve these problems without providing a realistic analysis of whether the total military manpower pool is adequate, and of the cost-benefits of increasing the manpower pool in the various AC and RC components. The policy seems to be designed around the thesis that force restructuring and rebalancing will work because they need to work if the United States is to keep defense spending within anything approaching its current limits—and pay for the technology that is being given higher priority than manpower quantity and quality.

Expensive as it may be, raising end strength does seem to be an important alternative, one that may well have a higher priority than emphasizing investment in "transformational" weapons and technology. It is not an alternative to the needed other reforms and qualitative improvements in military manpower described throughout this chapter, but it may well be a necessary supplement. It certainly is an option that needs far more explicit trade-off analysis, with far less ideological emphasis on technology, outsourcing, and supersoldiers.

────────────────────────────────────

Challenge Four: The Challenge of Measuring the Extent to Which We Have the Wrong Forces versus Too Few Forces

The United States may well need more national security resources, but it must also be careful not to rely on simply increasing military spending and manpower. It is all too easy to see the solution to every strategy and military problem as providing more forces. In practice, however, the challenge is to provide the *right* forces and to make the best real-world trade-offs between force quantity and force quality at costs that are politically and economically sustainable over time.

Anyone can (and the American military repeatedly has) advance force goals that are unaffordable and unachievable just as anyone can (and defense "reformers" repeatedly have) advance impractical theoretical concepts that cannot be implemented. Once again, however, two realities intervene:

- First, strategy, doctrines, and force plans are worthless, however, unless they are tightly integrated with long-term programs and budgets that can actually be implemented.
- Second, the answer to "how much is enough?" must be a large enough force posture to do the job, and one that is adequate assuming real-world levels of readiness and effectiveness. Efforts to create "supersoldiers" are no substitute for adequate numbers of real men and women in uniform. Technological "force multipliers" inevitably turn out to be "force improvers" at best.

As the fighting in Afghanistan and Iraq has revealed, revolutions in military affairs become painful evolutions that are only partially successful; force transformations scheduled over a few years take a decade or more. The search for optimal efficiency invariably answers the question of "how much is enough?" by calling for force levels too low to do the job. Budgets and force plans become driven by the illusion that efficiency can do more and more with less and less until it can do everything with nothing.

DECOUPLING STRATEGY AND FORCE TRANSFORMATION FROM REALITY

The United States has made important changes to its forces in recent decades. Major improvements have taken place in areas like joint warfare capability or "jointness"; battle management, combined arms, intelligence and strategic reconnaissance, precision-strike capabilities, targeting, strategic and tactical mobility, and long-range strike capability have been exploited to at least begin what many experts call a "revolution in military affairs." The result has been three striking victories against foreign forces at distances nearly halfway around the world: Iraq in 1991, Afghanistan in 2001, and Iraq in 2003.

The United States has not ignored the need to shift toward forces capable of asymmetric warfare in reshaping its recent strategy and doctrine. This has been a key theme in the Quadrennial Defense Reviews of 2001 and 2006. It has made major progress actually translating such concepts and plans into tangible changes in U.S. forces in some areas.

At the same time, it has become brutally clear that the so-called revolution in military affairs force transformations based on high-technology approaches to defeating conventional enemies does not meet the nation's needs. The Iraq War has helped to expose the deep and long-standing flaws in the U.S. approach to strategic planning.

These problems have been compounded by a system that does not directly integrate the development of strategy, force plans, programs, and budgets. For decades, the Department of Defense's decoupling of strategy and doctrine from a solid foundation in fiscal reality has meant that the U.S. military labors for months (and sometimes years) to produce strategy, doctrine, and plans with little or no real impact on U.S. military capabilities. It has also meant that military advice often has had only a limited impact on the actual budget and the FYDP.

Even when the U.S. military has attempted detailed force planning, the end result has usually been sufficiently decoupled from the programming and the budget process and from real-world cost projections and budget constraints that civilians in the Office of the Secretary of Defense (OSD) and the Office of Management and Budget have had to steadily downsize the military's "requirements" to meet real-world budget constraints or to make key programs affordable.

The United States still treats the need for force transformation more as an exercise in military philosophy than as an effort to produce specific force plans, program budgets and Future Year Defense Programs (FYDPs), and detailed plans for force transformation. As a result, U.S. exercises in strategy and force planning have been ineffective in transforming U.S. forces to prevent the United States from adapting to the needs imposed by ongoing conflicts and strategic confrontations where it would have benefited from planning and precrisis analysis. It has meant that much of the present U.S. force posture evolved far more from downsizing Cold War forces than because of efforts to introduce new strategies, tactics, and concepts of force transformation.

Civilian planners within the OSD have done little better in tying their real-world plans and budgets to either strategic needs or effective plans for force transformation. They have conducted their own vague studies of future trends and potential mission needs, strategy, and possible force transformation concepts. These studies, plans, and net assessments have remained equally decoupled from a systematic effort to formulate detailed plans to implement them, examinations of their potential cost and impact on the FYDP, and transition into the actual defense budget. Major Department of Defense–wide exercises like the Quadrennial Defense Review have developed interesting concepts (as have some of the Joint Staffs' "Joint Vision" series), but they have had surprisingly little real-world impact on the force posture, the FYDP, and the budget.

These problems have been compounded at both the military and civilian levels by the advocacy of given transformational concepts and technologies, which cannot be implemented at anything approaching their planned cost, planned time, and planned effectiveness. The progressive downsizing of virtually every program to fit real-world cost constraints, the constant downward reevaluation of what levels of performance and capability can actually be achieved, and equally constant delays in program execution have virtually ensured that the Department cannot execute its plans even when it has them. Engagement with reality almost inevitably means that programs evolve in ways where drastic escalations in cost mean major cuts in planned strength and numbers, performance falls at least somewhat short of expectations, and implementation experiences major delays.

FORCE RUN DOWNS VERSUS FORCE TRANSFORMATION

The end result is that the U.S. force posture that has developed since the end of the Cold War has been at least as much the result of steady downsizing, or "run down," as force transformation. It has not evolved in response to the needs of the post–Cold War era, and America's new strategic requirements, as it has devolved over time in response to resource pressures and the need to cap defense spending.

Figure 5.1 shows the trends in U.S. forces since the end of the Cold War and just how much the present levels of U.S. forces owe to sheer historical momentum. While the history of U.S. force planning is not the focus of this study, it is important to know that the basic decisions that shaped the changes shown in Figures 5.1 and 5.2 were made during the first Bush Administration and were largely a decision to make an initial series of force cuts based on the end of the Gulf War.

The vast majority of force planning decisions taken during the Clinton Administration, and the second Bush Administration through fiscal year 2007

Figure 5.1 Evolving U.S. Force Plans

Force Element	Gulf War FY1990	FY1995	FY1997	Clinton Goal for FY2002	FY2002	FY2003	FY2004	FY2005	FY2006
Strategic Forces									
Minuteman missiles	–	535	530	500	(500)	500	500	500	–
Peacekeeper missiles	–	50	50(50)	50	50	50(50)	–	–	–
B-52 bombers	–	74	56	56	(56)	–	–	147	–
B-1 bombers	268	60	60	82	(82)	–	–	81	–
B-2 bombers	–	6	10	16	(16)	–	–	20	–
Poseidon/Trident missiles	–	360	408	432	(432)	–	–	432	–
Army									
Active divisions	18	12	10	10	10	10	10	10	10
Active Separate Brigades	8	3	3	3	3	–	–	–	–
Reserve Divisions	–	8	8	8	8	–	–	–	12
Total Divisional and Separate Reserve brigades*	57	46	46	–	42	–	–	–	48
Active personnel (1,000s)	751	59	492	480	475–495	480	482	502	512.4
Reserve personnel (1,000s)	736	629	603	555	–	555	555	555	–
Marines									
Expeditionary Forces**	3	3	3	–	3	–	–	–	3
Active personnel (1,000s)	197	175	174	172	174	175	175	178	178
Reserve personnel (1,000s)	45	41	42	39.5	–	39.5	39.5	39.6	39.6
Active Divisions	3	3	3	–	3	–	–	–	3
Reserve Divisions	1	1	1	–	1	–	–	–	1
Active Combat Aircraft	368/24	320/23	308/21	280/21	280/21	–	–	–	–
Reserve Combat Aircraft	84/8	60/5	48/4	48/4	48/4	–	–	–	–

Navy

Active personnel (1,000s)	583	435	396	371.3	394	375.7	373.8	365.9	352.7
Reserve personnel (1,000s)	149	101	95	90.0	–	87.8	85.9	83.4	73.1
Navy Aircraft Carriers	15/1	11/1	11/1	11/1	11/1	–	–	–	–
Carrier Air Wings	13/2	10/1	10/1	–	10/1	–	–	–	–
Active Combat Aircraft	662/57	528/44	456/36	456/36	456/36	–	–	–	–
Reserve Combat Aircraft	97/9	38/3	38/3	36/3	36/3	–	–	–	–
Battle Force Ships	546	372	354	316	(315)346	–	–	–	–
Support Forces Ships	66	37	26	25	25	–	–	–	–
Reserve Force Ships	31	19	18	15	15	–	–	–	–
Ballistic Missile Submarines	34	16	17	18	(18)	–	–	–	–
Mine Warfare & Coastal	–	13	19	24	(22)	–	–	–	–
Other	–	13	19	24	(22)	–	–	–	–

* Numbers are not comparable in the out-years. The BUR plan calls for 15 enhanced readiness brigades, a goal that DoD will begin to reach in FY1996. Backing up this force will be an Army National Guard strategic reserve of eight divisions (24 brigades), two separate brigade equivalents, and a scout group. Figures in parenthesis show the FY2001 force plan and not the Quadrennial Defense Review (QDR) goal.

** A MEF includes a Marine division, air wing, and force service support group.

Source: William J. Perry, *Annual Report to the President and the Congress, 1995*, Department of Defense (DoD), Washington, February, 1995, p. 274; William S. Cohen, *Annual Report to the President and the Congress, 2000*, Department of Defense, Washington, February, 2000, and material provided by the military services.

Figure 5.2 Evolving U.S. Force Plans

Force Element	Gulf War FY1990	FY1995	FY1997	FY2001	Clinton Goal for FY2002	FY2002	FY2003	FY2004	FY2005	FY2006
Air Force										
Active personnel (1,000s)	539	400	377	354	(375)	358.8	359	359.3	359.7	357.4
Reserve personnel (1,000s)	201	198	182	235	–	–	182.2	182.8	182.9	108.8
Fighter Forces										
Active Wing Equivalents	24	13	13	13	13	–	–	–	–	–
Active Combat Aircraft	1722/76	936/53	936/52	906/45	(906/45)	–	–	–	–	–
Reserve Wing Equivalents	12	8	7	7	7	–	–	–	–	36
Reserve Combat Aircraft	873/43	576/38	504/40	549/38	(549/38)	–	–	–	–	–
Conventional Bombers	33	0	0	36/16	(36/16)	–	–	–	–	–
Total Civilians (1,000s)	1,102	865	786	685	–	–	–	–	–	–
Strategic Lift										
Intertheater aircraft	400	364	345	304	(299)	–	–	–	–	–
C-5	–	199	163	88	(69)	–	–	–	–	–
C-141	–	199	163	88	(69)	–	–	–	–	–
KC-10	–	54	54	54	(54)	–	–	–	–	–
C-17	–	17	24	58	(72)	–	–	–	–	–
Intratheater aircraft	460	416	428	418	(418)	–	–	–	–	–
Active Sealift										
Ships										
Tankers	28	18	13	10	(10)	–	–	–	–	–
Cargo	40	51	48	57	(60)	–	–	–	–	–
Reserve Ships	96	77	87	86	(73)	–	–	–	–	–

(FY2007), had little or nothing to do with declared strategy. They were the result of a progressive downsizing of the Cold War force structure—often driven by the need to pay for the individual new programs advocated by given services.

Moreover, these decisions have usually been shaped more by an effort to preserve both force numbers and programs that originated while the Cold War was still the driving force in U.S. force planning, and there was a tendency to preserve heavy conventional combat forces without adapting them to the post–Cold War world. For all of the talk of asymmetric warfare, the practice was to emphasize conventional warfare, downplay counterinsurgency and counterterrorism, and avoid committing forces to mission capabilities for stability operations and nation building.

UNREALISTIC BUDGET AND FYDP GOALS

The rate of past and planned change in the way the defense budget is allocated is another indication of the lack of a serious effort to transform U.S. forces to implement well-defined and updated strategic goals. As Figures 5.1 through 5.3 have shown, bureaucratic momentum and service rivalry have acted to block fundamental change in the way money has been allocated by military service and the defense component—aside from a slow creep in the amount of money given to defense-wide agencies and spending.

There was a shift away from funding for the U.S. Army after the end of the Cold War, but one driven far more by efforts to sustain procurement spending for the Air Force and the Navy than force planning. Similarly, the sudden surge in spending on the Army from FY2003 on was driven by the unanticipated costs of the counterinsurgency campaign in Iraq and had nothing to do with plans for force transformation.

Figures 5.4, 5.5, and 5.6 show that the Department of Defense planning, program, and budgeting system has remained locked into almost meaningless program categories in which virtually all of the meaningful changes were taking place in the "General Purposes Forces" category—a category that the principal developers of the U.S. Planning, Programming, and Budgeting System (PPBS) had realized was so general that it stood for "no purpose forces" back in the days of the Vietnam War.

The only real change in the structure of the PPBS in nearly half a century has been the addition of a category for Special Forces in 1987, which did at least reflect some significant increase in expenditure on the kind of forces the United States would need for missions other than conventional war.

THE LEGACY OF THE WRONG FORCE POSTURE

The Iraq War is yet another symptom of such problems in force planning and budgeting and not the cause. War is *supposed* to put temporary stresses on the force posture, and some of the pressures on the U.S. force posture have been the inevitable result of going from a state of peace to dealing with the unpredictable exigencies of combat. Nevertheless, much of today's "overstretch" is the result of past failures to

Figure 5.3 U.S. Military Forces in Selected Fiscal Years, 1989–2005

	1989	1993	1997	1999	2001	2003	2005	Percentage 1989–1999	Change 1989–2005
Strategic Forces[a]									
Land-Based ICBMs[b]	1,000	787	580	550	—	—	—	−45	—
Heavy Bombers[c]	310	194	126	143	—	—	—	−54	—
Submarine-Launched Ballistic Missiles	576	408	408	432	—	—	—	−25	—
Conventional Forces[d]									
Land Forces									
Army divisions[e]									
Active	18	14	10	10	—	—	—	−44	—
Reserve	10	8	8	8	—	—	—	−20	—
Marine Corps expeditionary forces[f]									
Active	3	3	3	3	—	—	—	0	—
Reserve	1	1	1	1	—	—	—	0	—
Naval Forces									
Battle force ships[g]	566	435	354	317	—	—	—	−44	—
Aircraft carriers									
Active	15	13	11	11	—	—	—	−27	—
Reserve	1	0	1	1	—	—	—	0	—
Navy carrier air wings									
Active	13	11	10	10	—	—	—	−23	—
Reserve	2	2	1	1	—	—	—	−50	—

Air Forces

Tactical fighter wings

Active	25	16	13	13	–	–	–	–48	–
Reserve	12	11	8	8	–	–	–	–33	–

Airlift aircraft

Intertheater	401	382	345	331	–	–	–	–17	–
Intratheater	468	380	430	425	–	–	–	–9	–

a. Forces with basically nuclear missions.

b. ICBMs = intercontinental ballistic missiles.

c. Includes some long-range bombers that do not have strategic missions.

d. Forces with largely nonnuclear missions.

e. Excludes separate brigades that are not part of a division.

f. A Marine expeditionary force includes a division, an air wing, and supporting forces for those combat elements.

g. Includes all Navy ships involved in combat—for example, ballistic missile submarines, surface combat ships, aircraft carriers, and amphibious craft—as well as some other vessels.

Source: Congressional Budget Office using data from the Department of Defense and the Office of Management and Budget, as shown in "Budgeting for Defense: Maintain Today's Forces," Washington, CBO, September 2000, cbo.gov.

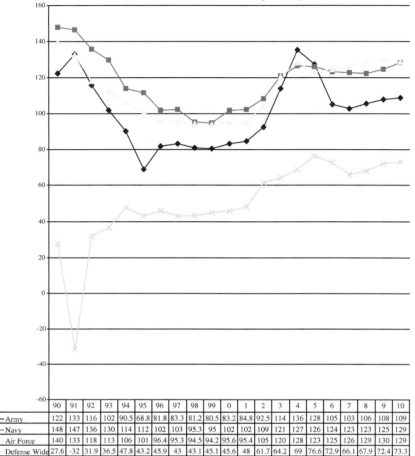

(In Constant FY2006 $US billions in Budget Outlays)

	90	91	92	93	94	95	96	97	98	99	0	1	2	3	4	5	6	7	8	9	10
Army	122	133	116	102	90.5	68.8	81.8	83.3	81.2	80.5	83.2	84.8	92.5	114	136	128	105	103	106	108	109
Navy	148	147	136	130	114	112	102	103	95.3	95	102	102	109	121	127	126	124	123	123	125	129
Air Force	140	133	118	113	106	101	96.4	95.3	94.5	94.2	95.6	95.4	105	120	128	123	125	126	129	130	129
Defense Wide	27.6	-32	31.9	36.5	47.8	43.2	45.9	43	43.1	45.1	45.6	48	61.7	64.2	69	76.6	72.9	66.1	67.9	72.4	73.3

Source: Adapted by Anthony H. Cordesman from data provided by Office of the Under Secretary of Defense (Comptroller), "National Defense Budget Estimates for FY2006", Washington, Department of Defense, April 2005, Table 6-13.

Figure 5.4 Defense Spending by Military Service since the End of the Cold War: FY1990–FY2010

transform Cold War force posture into the forces the United States needs in the twenty-first century, and not the strain imposed by current wars.

It is true that the United States had a much larger pool of forces to draw upon in the past. The United States had an active strength of 2 million for most of the Cold War and wartime peaks of 3.5 million in Korea and Vietnam. Yet, the decline in the U.S. manpower pool since the end of the Cold War scarcely explains any overstretch for a conflict the size of the Iraq War. The United States still had a total of 2.7 million people in uniform in 2005, and it had some 600,000 defense civilians and 100,000

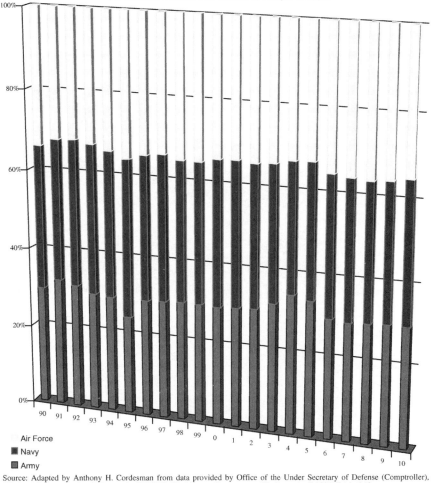

(In Constant FY2006 $US billions in Budget Outlays)

Source: Adapted by Anthony H. Cordesman from data provided by Office of the Under Secretary of Defense (Comptroller), "National Defense Budget Estimates for FY2006", Washington, Department of Defense, April 2005, Table 6.13.

Figure 5.5   Defense Spending by Military Service since the End of the Cold War: FY1990–FY2010

contract civilians. It still had a total force of 1.4 million actives and 1.3 million reserves, while its deployment peaked at only 160,000 men and women in Iraq.

By January 2006, however, a report for a DoD-commissioned study, conducted by Andrew F. Krepinevich, intoned that the Army had become a "thin green line," unable to sustain the pace of deployments necessary for breaking the back of the insurgency in Iraq. Krepinevich, a retired Army officer, suggested that the Pentagon's decision, announced in December 2005, to begin reducing forces in Iraq was driven in part by the realization that the Army was overextended.[1] There was solid evidence

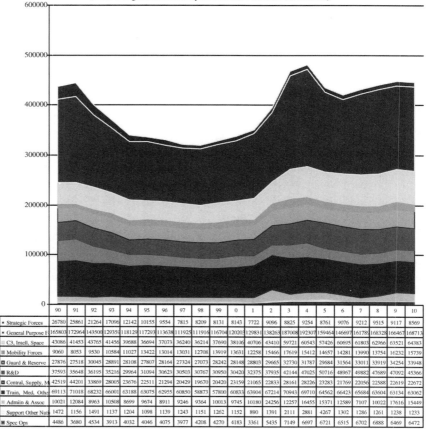

(Total Obligational Authority in Constant FY2006 $US millions)

	90	91	92	93	94	95	96	97	98	99	0	1	2	3	4	5	6	7	8	9	10
• Strategic Forces	26780	25861	21264	17096	12142	10155	9554	7815	8209	8131	8143	7722	9096	8825	9254	8761	9076	9212	9515	9117	8569
• General Purpose F	165803	172964	143500	129359	118129	117293	113638	111925	111916	116704	120203	129831	138263	187008	192307	159464	146697	161789	168328	166467	168713
▨ C3, Intell, Space	43086	41453	43765	41456	39688	36694	37073	36240	36214	37690	38106	40706	43410	59721	60543	57426	60695	61803	62966	63521	64383
▥ Mobility Forces	9060	8053	9530	10584	11027	13422	13014	13031	12708	13919	13631	12258	15466	17619	15412	14657	14281	13990	13754	16232	15739
▣ Guard & Reserve	27876	27518	30045	28891	28108	27807	28164	27324	27073	28242	28148	28803	29665	32730	31787	29684	31564	33011	33919	34254	33948
▪ R&D	37593	35648	36195	35216	29964	31094	30623	30503	30767	30950	30420	32375	37935	42144	47025	50716	48967	49882	47689	47092	45366
▣ Central, Supply, M	42519	44201	33869	28005	23676	22511	21294	20429	19670	20420	23159	21065	22833	28161	28226	23283	21769	22056	22588	22619	22672
▪ Train, Med, Oths	69113	71018	68232	66001	63188	63075	62955	60850	58873	57800	60833	63904	67214	70943	69710	64562	66423	65684	63604	63134	63062
▪ Admin & Assoc	10021	12084	8963	10508	8699	9674	8911	9246	9364	10013	9745	10180	24256	12257	16455	15371	12589	7107	10022	17616	15449
Support Other Nati	1472	1156	1491	1137	1204	1098	1139	1243	1151	1262	1152	890	1391	2111	2881	4267	1302	1286	1261	1238	1233
▪ Spec Ops	4486	3680	4534	3913	4032	4046	4075	3977	4208	4270	4183	3361	5435	7149	6697	6721	6515	6702	6888	6469	6472

Note: GPF=General Purpose Forces

Source: Adapted by Anthony H. Cordesman from data provided by Office of the Under Secretary of Defense (Comptroller), "National Defense Budget Estimates for FY2006", Washington, Department of Defense, April 2005, Table 6-5.

Figure 5.6   Defense Spending by Major Program Category since the End of the Cold War: FY1990–FY2010

for this view. At the time of the report, Secretary of Defense Donald Rumsfeld said that there were 1.4 million Americans on active duty, of whom 138,000 were serving in Iraq at any given time. However, more than 70 percent of the troops to be deployed to Iraq over the following year were to be returning for the third time.[2]

Experts may argue how serious these strains have been and are becoming. But, almost regardless of how the situation is described, the end result provides a clear indication that the United States suffered more from serious problems in the deploy-ability of its existing force structure than overstretch in terms of its total pool of forces and manpower. There are other strong indications that this has been the case:

- U.S. forces are still designed largely for conventional war in an era of asymmetric war and terrorism.

- The United States has an inflated basing and infrastructure from the Cold War era and many support and administrative elements that are overstaffed. This posture is probably around 20 percent too large.

- The National Guard and the Reserves are tailored for a mix of quick-reaction missions, Cold War contingencies, and a total force concept that assumed they would not be deployed in these cases.

- The Army is designed to fight past conventional wars and, as such, far too few elements are suited to counterinsurgency and stability operations or rapid deployment. The Army has to draw on elements of only 17 brigades for Iraq out of total of 33.

- The Marine Corps has been optimized into nonlittoral missions and has gone lighter and lighter for other missions to maintain the size of its active force structure.

- A past focus on air and missile power, "effects-based" precision strikes, has pushed the Air Force and the Navy toward destroying regular military forces and fixed facilities.

- The Guard and the Reserves have been integrated into the "total force" for political reasons without adequate analysis of the resulting expeditionary impact.

- There is no matching deploying component in the civil agencies to support nation building and stability operations. They have civilian elements with little or no operational strength for such missions, and many of their personnel cannot or will not deploy into high-risk areas.

- There are major shortfalls in language and areas skills, police-like forces, and civil-military units in a world where regional and asymmetric conflicts in non-Western areas are likely to be the rule, rather than the exception.

These are problems that present challenges the United States must deal with in reshaping the size and nature of its military forces, regardless of particular problems and strains imposed by the Iraq War.

DETERMINING FORCE SIZE RELATIVE TO FORCE SHAPE AND FORCE FLEXIBILITY

The United States must also deal with a long legacy of various efforts to downsize to meet resource constraints. During the defense drawdown of the 1990s, the size of the U.S. armed forces steadily decreased without any serious opposition. However, since 9/11 and the ongoing operations in Iraq and Afghanistan, there has been much debate over the size of American forces and what the appropriate structure of those forces should be.

As has been discussed in the previous chapter, there are increasing pressures to increase military end strength, and the Congress has already pressed for limited increases in the active and reserve forces that the Administration has not fully accepted or acted upon. This is shown in Figure 5.7. To put these figures in context, U.S. active military end strength is the key measure of actual warfighting capability,

Figure 5.7   Trends in Military End Strength: FY2004–FY2007
(number of personnel at the end of each fiscal year)

	Army	Navy	Marine Corps	Air Force	TOTAL
FY2004 Actual	482,400	373,800	175,000	359,300	1,390,500
FY2005 Authorized	502,400	365,900	178,000	359,700	1,406,000
FY 2005 Actual	492,728	362,941	180,029	353,696	1,389,394
FY 2006 Authorized	512,400	352,700	179,000	357,400	1,401,500
FY2007 Request	482,400	340,700	175,000	334,200	1,332,300
FY2007 House	512,400	340,700	180,000	334,200	1,367,300
FY2007 House vs. Request	*+30,000*	*0*	*+5,000*	*0*	*+35,000*
FY2007 Senate	512,4000	340,700	180,000	334,200	1,367,300
FY2007 Senate vs. Request	*+30,000*	*0*	*+5,000*	*0*	*+35,000*

Source: Department of Defense and Stephen Dagget, "Defense: FY 2007 Authorization and Appropriations," Washington, Congressional Research Service, RL33405, October 19, 2006, p. 72.

and this strength never dropped below 2 million during the Cold War, and it reached
more than 3.5 million during the Korean and Vietnam wars. Since the Cold War, it
has dropped from 2.1 million to 1.4 million, largely as a result of cuts in the active
strength of the U.S. Army from 18 to 10 divisions.[3]

As Chapter 4 has shown, the U.S. force invasion of Iraq in 2003 quickly led to an
occupation that involved elements of every active U.S. Army division, the Marine
Corps, and most elements of the National Guard and the Reserves. It is also important to stress that it has involved only one regional contingency against enemies who
have no regular forces, heavy military equipment, or massive reinforcement and supply from outside Iraq. While Iraq may be anything but typical of future wars, it is
difficult to believe that the United States will not face other kinds of major regional
contingencies during the decades to come.

Increasing Combat Forces

One option to deal with these problems would be to create additional active divisions. Another option would be to move more reserve and National Guard forces
into the active component, especially those for stability and counterinsurgency operations. However, increases in end strength or reducing the dependence upon reserve
forces are even more costly than increases in military manpower and end strength..

Most of the current emphasis on increasing combat force size focuses on the U.S.
Army, and the cost of major force increases would be serious. A Congressional
Budget Office (CBO) report estimated that adding two active divisions to the Army

would increase its active end strength by 57,000 at a cost of $127 billion between 2006 and 2022 (in FY2006 dollars). The same CBO report estimates that adding two active divisions by reducing the support ratio by 15 percent would increase the Army's active end strength by 6,000 at a cost of $54 billion over the years 2006 through 2022. Furthermore, this option might create additional risks by having less artillery and air-defense support units while only modestly increasing end strength.[4]

The CBO report also estimated the costs associated with restructuring the Army to decrease dependence upon reserve units by converting many reserve units into active support units and personnel, thereby eliminating the Total Force Policy currently employed in the reserve structure. The CBO report estimated that adding one additional supported combat brigade under this framework would cost an additional $333 billion between 2006 and 2022. This would also increase the Army's active end strength by 312,000 and decrease the number of Army reserve personnel by 260,000.[5]

Acting on proposals to permanently increase the number of combat forces could easily add more than $6 billion a year to the military budget for a relatively limited increase in force size. It would also mean acting at a time when the cost of the war in Iraq was exceeding $6 billion a month, and estimates of defense spending—including supplementals—were over $500 billion a year.[6]

This makes incremental costs a key factor in any decision as to whether to actually provide more combat power, although it is painfully clear from the escalating cost of the Iraq War that having insufficient combat forces can intensify and lengthen the cost of a war and drive dollar costs far higher. The costs of too few forces can also be far higher in terms of blood and the risk of defeat.

Making Current Forces More Flexible and Combat Capable

Another option is to make further efforts to reorganize the existing force through various transformation initiatives and seek to make them a more nimble and rapidly deployable force—better able to wage irregular warfare. It is also emphasizing continued steady-state conventional deterrence of interstate aggression, with enough surge capacity to wage two nearly simultaneous conventional campaigns (or one conventional campaign if already engaged in a large-scale, long-duration irregular campaign). The practical problem is that—as the previous chapter has discussed—it simply is not clear that such measures can produce an Army and a Marine Corps large enough to meet the nation's needs.

The need for land combat power is also only one of the nation's priorities. The 2006 QDR may have failed to shape detailed force plans, programs, and budgets; but it did look beyond Iraq to other demanding regional contingencies that the United States may have to meet. It recognized that a Korean War or a major conflict in the Taiwan Strait could place far more demanding requirements for naval forces or air forces. In other contingencies, the need may be for amphibious forces and the Marines.

Building on the New Triad priorities developed during the 2001 Nuclear Posture Review, the 2006 QDR called for a force that includes a wider range of nonkinetic and conventional strike capabilities, while maintaining a robust nuclear deterrent, as a continuing keystone of U.S. national power. And while much of the QDR focused notably on the enhancement of Special Operations Forces, and gave greater attention to Stabilization & Reconstruction capabilities, the need for maintaining conventional superiority was also expressed, largely in terms of enhanced joint air and naval capabilities.

The 2006 QDR also called for joint air capabilities to be reoriented to favor, where appropriate, systems with greater range and persistence, larger and more flexible payloads for surveillance or strike, and the ability to penetrate and sustain operations in denied areas. Decisions included the following:[7]

- Develop a new land-based, penetrating, long-range strike capability to be fielded by 2018 while modernizing the current bomber force.

- Reduce the B-52 force to 56 aircraft and use savings to fully modernize B-52s, B-1s, and B-2s to support global strike operations.

- Restructure the Joint Unmanned Combat Air System program and develop an unmanned longer-range carrier-based aircraft capable of being air-refueled to provide greater standoff capability, to expand payload and launch options, and to increase naval reach and persistence.

- Nearly double unmanned aerial vehicle (UAV) coverage capacity by accelerating the acquisition of Predator UAVs and Global Hawks.

- Restructure the F-22A program and extend production through FY2010 with a multiyear acquisition contract to ensure the Department does not have a gap in fifth-generation stealth capabilities.

- Organize the Air Force around 86 combat wings (e.g., fighter, bomber, ISR/Battle Management/Command and Control, mobility, Air Operations Centers, Battlefield Airmen, other missions, and Space/Missile) with an emphasis on leveraging reach-back to minimize forward footprints and expedite force deployments, while reducing Air Force end strength by approximately 40,000 full-time equivalent personnel with balanced cuts across the total force.

Many of the 2006 QDR's decisions regarding maritime capabilities dealt with creating a more nimble force, capable of penetrating smaller potential hot spots, and with the geographical distribution necessary to attend to multiple smaller scenarios. The QDR called on joint maritime forces, including the Coast Guard, to conduct highly distributed operations with a networked fleet more capable of projecting power in the "brown and green waters" of coastal areas. The report called for a future force with greater capacity for riverine operations and other irregular operations. Furthermore, the report called on the future joint force to exploit the operational flexibility of sea basing to counter political antiaccess and irregular warfare challenges.

This proposed change in maritime forces tracked with the concept of "tailored deterrence" outlined in the report. The idea was for the Pentagon to continue its shift from a "one size fits all" notion of deterrence toward more tailorable approaches appropriate for advanced military competitors, regional weapons of mass destruction (WMD) states, as well as nonstate terrorist networks.[8]

At the same time, the QDR concluded that a more traditional large naval deterrence posture remained relevant, with a shift to the Pacific. The Navy would deploy a greater presence in the Pacific Ocean, consistent with the global shift of trade and transport. Accordingly, the Navy planned to adjust its force posture and basing to provide at least six operationally available and sustainable carriers and 60 percent of its submarines in the Pacific to support engagement, presence, and deterrence. Other decisions included the following:[9]

- Build a larger fleet that includes 11 Carrier Strike Groups, balance the need to transform and recapitalize the fleet, improve affordability, and provide stability for the shipbuilding industry.

- Accelerate procurement of Littoral Combat Ships to provide power projection capabilities in littoral waters.

- Procure the first eight ships of the Maritime Pre-Position Force (Future) to improve the Department's ability to operate in restricted access environments.

- Provide a Navy riverine capability for river patrol, interdiction, and tactical troop movement on inland waterways.

- Build partner capacity to improve global maritime security by reinvigorating the Navy Foreign Area Officer program and procuring Disaster Relief Command and Control flyaway communication support capabilities.

- Return to a steady-state production rate of two attack submarines per year no later than 2012 while achieving an average per-hull procurement cost objective of $2.0 billion.

Finally, the QDR called for increased joint operational capabilities. In this case, the FY2007 budget request to seek investment in several related programs:[10]

- Joint air support through the acquisition of the V-22 Osprey tilt-rotor aircraft and the AH-64 Apache, CH-47 Chinook, and UH-60 Black Hawk helicopters;

- Joint air dominance with $10.4 billion for the acquisition of the F-22 and F/A-18 E/F fighter jets, aircraft, and continued development and the first procurement of the F-35 Joint Strike Fighter; and

- Joint maritime capabilities with $11.2 billion for more capable and multimission ships, including two DD(X)—or DDG-1000 Zumwalt-class, multimission surface combatant —destroyers, two Littoral combat ships, one Virginia-class submarine; one landing, helicopter amphibious assault LHA(R) ship, and one Lewis and Clark—called dry cargo/ammunition T-AKE logistics ship.

The key issue is whether any of these proposed measures can either compensate for constant or lower force strength and end strength *or* be made affordable within current budgets and programmed expenditures. This seems doubtful, particularly given the underfunding of the existing force described in Chapter 3 and the chronic failures to contain cost escalation described in the chapters that follow.

At the same time, any such planning efforts raise doubts as to whether the United State can hope to predict the future well enough to continue trying to size its forces around a critical minimum. The previous chapters have shown that the recent history of defense reform and force transformation is a history of efforts based on the wrong assumptions.

Efforts to learn from Afghanistan and Iraq are often no more reassuring. For example, many experts felt the key lesson that should be learned from the initial stages of the campaigns in Afghanistan was that "overmatching power" precision-guided weapons, UAVs, sensors, situational awareness and intelligence, maneuverability, and joint capabilities might mean that the military did not require "overwhelming force" to achieve victory in future campaigns. Some argued that airpower and Special Forces could largely replace traditional ground forces in many areas and that airpower could replace much of the need for armor.

This "lesson," however, quickly proved to be highly contingency dependent. By early 2003, a very different set of lessons seemed to emerge. Even some of those who had just argued that Afghanistan demonstrated the need for airpower now talked about the merits of "legacy" systems like the M-1, the M-2, self-propelled artillery, and the AH-64. Yet, roughly a year later, experts began to argue that the decisive factor in urban warfare and counterinsurgencies might be the sheer number of "boots on the ground."

This lesson changed again by late 2004, along with the tactical situation in both Afghanistan and Iraq. While counterinsurgency operations may have historically been manpower intensive, Vietnam had showed that they also required tailored technology and intelligence systems. In Iraq, calls for boots on the ground were followed by calls for the need to uparmor most support and logistic vehicles, arm support forces involved, and use high-technology approaches to deal with low-technology tactics and devices like improvised explosive devices (IEDs).

Moreover, it became increasingly clear that surviving actual combat in high threat areas still required heavy armor systems to defeat light antiarmor weapons and increase survivability against IEDs and mines. The M-1 and the M-2, the same legacy systems that had helped defeat heavy Iraqi armor in 2003, were now needed as tools to strike at insurgents, to provide intelligence and reconnaissance, and to substitute for ground transportation in high-threat areas.

As the previous chapter has shown, by late 2005, many began to argue that the United States needed both more manpower quality and manpower numbers. The United States did not just need boots on the ground. It needed men and women with special training in area studies, languages, counterinsurgency, civic action, military police functions, etc. Moreover, it also needed a new mix of military and civilians with training in stability operations and nation building. Iraq and Afghanistan reinforced the lessons of similar conflicts that most insurgencies, rebellions, and other forms of resistance movements cannot be addressed with a purely military solution. It became clear that economic, political, and social measures were critical factors in pacifying a region and establishing legitimate authority. The need for skilled forces for stability and support operations was as critical as the need for expertise in counterinsurgency.[11]

These rapid shifts in the lessons drawn from Afghanistan and Iraq provide yet another warning that preparing military forces based on the last war, or planning around a narrow conception of what future wars will look like, will almost inevitably leave serious strategic vulnerabilities in other aspects of military force planning.

Adding in New Missions: Stabilization and Reconstruction

This is particularly true because new missions are being added to U.S. strategy like supporting homeland defense and stabilization and reconstruction (S&R) operations—the Administration's initial posture was one of wariness of U.S. military involvement in "nation building." However, those who asserted that nation building was essentially associated with—or definitionally equivalent to "peacekeeping" or S&R activities—criticized this stance as ignoring a vital aspect of warfighting: consolidation of victory. A Congressional Research Service (CRS) report to Congress, updated January 30, 2006, details a brief history of the problem:[12]

> . . . there has been an evolution in the vocabulary used to refer to activities that are undertaken to maintain, enforce, promote and enhance the possibilities for peace in unstable environments. "Peacekeeping" has been the traditional generic term for the operations undertaken for those purposes by the United Nations and other international organizations, and sometimes *ad hoc* coalitions of nations or individual nations. More recently, in an attempt to capture their ambiguity and complexity, and perhaps also to avoid the stigma of failure attached to peacekeeping, they have become known as "stabilization and reconstruction" operations, or, more simply, "stability" operations. Use of any term with the word "peace" created a semantic dilemma, conveying the misleading impression that an operation is without risk, when in fact, peacekeeping operations can place soldiers in hostile situations resembling war. As knowledge increased about the conditions needed to establish peace, operations increasingly included extensive nation-building (or state-building as some prefer to call it) components to build or reform government structures.
>
> The term "peacekeeping" gained currency in the late 1950s, when U.N. peacekeeping mostly fit a narrow definition: providing an "interpositional" force to supervise the keeping of a cease-fire or peace accord that parties in conflict had signed, but it continued to be used as the range of activities grew. In 1992, the U.N. began to use a broader terminology to describe the different types of activities in securing and keeping peace. It created the term "peace enforcement" to describe operations in unstable situations where peacekeepers are allowed to use force to maintain peace because of a greater possibility of conflict or a threat to their safety. "Peace building" was adopted as a term for activities that are designed to prevent the resumption or spread of conflict, including disarmament and demobilization of warring parties, repatriation of refugees, reform and strengthening of government institutions (including re-creating police or civil defense forces), election-monitoring, and promotion of political participation and human rights.

Organizing and providing security for humanitarian relief efforts can be a part of peace-keeping and peace enforcement operations.

This aspect of the force size and force quality debate seems to be over the combined lessons of "9/11," the Afghan War, and the Iraq War. These campaigns have made it clear that the United States needs new capabilities for stabilization, nation building, and peacekeeping, as well as homeland defense. And, as Figure 5.8 shows, the reality between 1991 and 2005 has been a manifold increase in DoD costs associated with peacekeeping and security contingency operations.

The Afghan War and the Iraq War have shown that S&R operations are of crucial importance to successful conflict termination. These missions have typically been carried out by combat forces at the conclusion of major combat. The effectiveness of this metric was contingent upon large invading forces that were then sufficiently manned to provide effective postconflict peacekeeping capabilities. The wars in Afghanistan and Iraq, however, as well as the ongoing security operations in the Balkans, have helped to push stabilization and reconstruction into the debate over force capabilities and "force packages." Multiple smaller operations, supplanting manpower with technology, have meant a change in planning for S&R operations.

The 2006 QDR addressed the need to "make adjustments to better capture the realities of a long war"[13] in part by focusing on the need for greater S&R assets:[14]

In the post-September 11 world, irregular warfare has emerged as the dominant form of warfare confronting the United States, its allies and its partners; accordingly, guidance must account for distributed, long-duration operations, including unconventional warfare, foreign internal defense, counterterrorism, counterinsurgency, and stabilization and reconstruction operations.

Additionally, the QDR recognized stability, security, transition, and reconstruction (SSTR) as a U.S. government–wide mission of increasing importance and identified military support to SSTR as a core mission.[15] The Report further supported efforts to create a NATO stabilization and reconstruction capability and a European constabulary force.[16] The Report also annunciated some of the current S&R operations employed in the global war on terrorism:[17]

An International Security Assistance Force (ISAF) of 9,000 military personnel, led by NATO since 2003, operates in Kabul and an increasing portion of Afghanistan's territory, with plans to expand into still more Afghan provinces later this year. As part of the ISAF mission, civil-military Provincial Reconstruction Teams operate in the countryside and undertake reconstruction projects, in coordination with local Afghan officials, to help extend the authority of the central government beyond Kabul and build its capacity for the long term.

The force sizing problem in creating effective S&R forces also goes beyond military forces and the authority of the Department of Defense. The 2006 QDR highlights the Department of State's proposal to establish a deployable Civilian Reserve

Figure 5.8 DoD Incremental Costs of Peacekeeping and Security Contingency Operations, FY1991–FY2005
(in millions)

Operation	FY1991–FY2001	FY2002	FY2003	FY2004	FY2005 (Est.)	TOTAL
Areas of Ongoing Operations						
Southwest Asia/Iraq						
Op. Iraq Freedom (OIF)			38,322	52,148	56,200	146,670
Provide Comfort/No. Watch	1405.16					
So. Watch/AEF	6861.80	1372.4	626.2	–	–	11,023.7
Des. Strike/Intrinsic Action/Des. Spring	623.50					
Vigilant Warrior	257.1	–	–	–	–	257.7
Des. Thunder (Force Buildup 11/98)	43.5					43.5
Des. Fox (Air Strikes, 12/98)	92.9					92.9
UNIKOM (UN/Iraq Observer Group)	32.4					32.4
Total SW Asia/Iraq	9451.4	1372.4	38948.2	52148	56200	158120
Afghanistan (Operation Enduring Freedom, OEF)			15,788.1	9,849.2	11,800	37,437
Former Yugoslavia (Kosovo)						
Balkan Calm (Observer Mission, Pre-Air War)	34.6	–	–	–	–	34.6
Eagle Eye (Air Verification, 10/98–03/99)	20.3	–	–	–	–	20.3
Noble Anvil (Air War)	1,891.4	–	–	–	–	1,891.4
Joint Guardian (KFOR)	4,231.5	938.2	590.4	552.9	693.3	7,006.3

Sustain Hope (Refugee Assistance)	141.6	–	–	–	–	141.6
Total Kosovo	**6,319.4**	**938.2**	**590.4**	**552.9**	**693.3**	**9,094.2**
Korea Readiness*	160.6	–	–	–	–	160.6
COMPLETED OPERATIONS						
Former Yugoslavia (Bosnia)						
IFOR/SFOR/Joint Force	16,457.8	932.9	742.2	667.8	150.7	14,405.1
Totals of Haiti, Somalia, Rwanda, Angola, Cambodia,	2603.4	–	3.1	–	–	2,606.5
Western Sahara, East Timor, and Liberia						
GRAND TOTALS	30,446.2	3,243.5	56,072	63,217.9	68,844	221,823.6

* Notes: This chart consists of DoD incremental costs involved in U.S. support for and participation in peacekeeping and in related humanitarian and security operations, including U.S. unilateral operations (including OIF in Iraq and OEF in Afghanistan, which are combat/occupation operations), NATO operations, UN operations, and *ad hoc* coalition operations. UN reimbursements are not deducted. Some totals do not add due to rounding. Other Former Yugoslavia operations include Able Sentry (Macedonia), Deny Flight/Decisive Edge, UNCRO (Zagreb), Sharp Guard (Adriatic), Provide Promise (humanitarian assistance), and Deliberate Forge. Because Korea Readiness has long been considered an ongoing peacetime function of U.S. troops, DoD counts only above-normal levels of activity there as incremental costs.

Source: Defense Finance and Accounting System data through FY2002; Office of the Secretary of Defense FY2005 Budget Estimates: Justification for Component Contingency Operations and the Overseas Contingency Operations Transfer Fund, for FY2003, FY2004, and FY2005 (est) provided by the DoD Comptroller's Office, June 24, 2005. The FY2005 figures are from the FY2005 Supplemental Request of February 2005 and do not reflect approximately $31.6 billion in other support and related costs applicable to OIF and OEF. Taken from CRS Report, *Peacekeeping and Related Stability Operations: Issues of U.S. Military Involvement*, updated January 30, 2006.

Corps and a Conflict Response Fund, as well as the President's National Security Presidential Directive designating the Secretary of State to improve overall U.S. government stabilization and reconstruction efforts.[18] It is clear, however, that outside efforts do not affect the need for increasing U.S. military capability.

The Department of Defense made this clear on November 28, 2005, when it issued DoD Directive 3000.05, providing guidance on military support for SSTR operations. One concern evident in the directive was the question as to whether the DoD had the appropriate and adequate personnel to attend to the complexities of S&R operations. Direction was thus issued to identify these assets and to develop methods to recruit, select, and assign current and former DoD personnel with the relevant skills.

The document made a clear DoD commitment to involvement in these activities in future contingencies and asserted the need for structure and guidance for DoD involvement. The DoD laid out its policy on SSTR as follows:[19]

It is DoD policy that:

- Stability operations are a core U.S. military mission that the Department of Defense shall be prepared to conduct and support. They shall be given priority comparable to combat operations and be explicitly addressed and integrated across all DoD activities including doctrine, organizations, training, education, exercises, materiel, leadership, personnel, facilities, and planning.

- Stability operations are conducted to help establish order that advances U.S. interests and values. The immediate goal often is to provide the local populace with security, restore essential services, and meet humanitarian needs. The long-term goal is to help develop indigenous capacity for securing essential services, a viable market economy, rule of law, democratic institutions, and a robust civil society.

- Many stability operations tasks are best performed by indigenous, foreign, or U.S. civilian professionals. Nonetheless, U.S. military forces shall be prepared to perform all tasks necessary to establish or maintain order when civilians cannot do so. Successfully performing such tasks can help secure a lasting peace and facilitate the timely withdrawal of U.S. and foreign forces. Stability operations tasks include helping:

- Rebuild indigenous institutions including various types of security forces, correctional facilities, and judicial systems necessary to secure and stabilize the environment;

- Revive or build the private sector, including encouraging citizen-driven, bottom-up economic activity and constructing necessary infrastructure; and

- Develop representative governmental institutions.

- Integrated civilian and military efforts are key to successful stability operations. Whether conducting or supporting stability operations, the Department of Defense shall be prepared to work closely with relevant U.S. Departments and Agencies, foreign governments and security forces, global and regional international organizations (hereafter referred to as International Organizations), U.S. and foreign nongovernmental organizations (hereafter referred to as "NGOs"), and private sector individuals and for-profit companies (hereafter referred to as "Private Sector").

- Military-civilian teams are a critical U.S. Government stability operations tool. The Department of Defense shall continue to lead and support the development of military-civilian teams.

- Their functions shall include ensuring security, developing local governance structures, promoting bottom-up economic activity, rebuilding infrastructure, and building indigenous capacity for such tasks.

- Participation in such teams shall be open to representatives from other U.S. Departments and Agencies, foreign governments and security forces, International Organizations, NGOs, and members of the Private Sector with relevant skills and expertise.

- Assistance and advice shall be provided to and sought from the Department of State and other U.S. Departments and Agencies, as appropriate, for developing stability operations capabilities.

- The Department of Defense shall develop greater means to help build other countries' security capacity quickly to ensure security in their own lands or to contribute forces to stability operations elsewhere.

- Military plans shall address stability operations requirements throughout all phases of an operation or plan as appropriate. Stability operations dimensions of military plans shall be:

- Exercised, gamed, and, when appropriate, red-teamed (i.e., tested by use of exercise opposition role playing) with other U.S. Departments and Agencies.

- Integrated with U.S. Government plans for stabilization and reconstruction and developed when lawful and consistent with security requirements and the Secretary of Defense's guidance, in coordination with relevant U.S. Departments and Agencies, foreign governments and security forces, International Organizations, NGOs, and members of the Private Sector.

- The Department of Defense shall support indigenous persons or groups' political, religious, educational, and media's promoting freedom, the rule of law, and an entrepreneurial economy, who oppose extremism and the murder of civilians.

- DoD intelligence efforts shall be designed to provide the optimal mix of capabilities to meet stability operations requirements, taking into account other priorities.

- Stability operations skills, such as foreign language capabilities, regional area expertise, and experience with foreign governments and International Organizations, shall be developed and incorporated into Professional Military Education at all levels.

- Information shall be shared with U.S. Departments and Agencies, foreign governments and forces, International Organizations, NGOs, and the members of the Private Sector supporting stability operations, consistent with legal requirements.

The directive further stipulated that it was the responsibility of the Under Secretary of Defense for Policy, in coordination with the Chairman of the Joint Chiefs of Staff, to develop stability operations policy options for the Secretary of Defense and to coordinate efforts with the Department of State's Office of the Coordinator for Reconstruction and Stabilization (or any successor organization). Further key direction included the following:[20]

- **Stability Operations Curricula:** The directive called on the DoD to ensure that military schools and training centers incorporate stability operations curricula in joint and individual service education and training programs at all levels. It particularly called for developing and incorporating instruction for foreign language capabilities and regional area expertise, including "long-term immersion in foreign societies." It would also broaden the exposure of military personnel to U.S. and international civilians with whom they would work in stability operations by providing them with tours of duty in other U.S. agencies, international organizations, and nongovernmental organizations.

- **Interagency and International Participation in Education and Training:** Responding to calls to enhance the ability of the wide variety of participants in stability operations to work together, the directive provided a number of ways to incorporate military personnel and civilians of many backgrounds in education and training courses, including personnel from U.S. departments and agencies, foreign governments and security forces, international organizations, nongovernmental organizations, and members of the private sector in stability operations planning, training, and exercises. It also proposed that the DoD ensure that instructors and students from elsewhere in the U.S. government be able to receive or provide instruction in stability operations at military schools.

- **Training Other Nations' Security Forces:** The directive also called for the DoD to support the development of other countries' security forces in order to ensure security domestically and to contribute forces to stability operations elsewhere. This was to include helping such forces, including police forces, develop "the training, structure, processes, and doctrine necessary to train, equip, and advise large numbers of foreign forces in a range of security sectors...."

- **Improving Coordination:** The directive called for the creation of "a stability operations center to coordinate operations research, education and training, and lessons learned." The U.S. military had two institutions currently devoted exclusively to such operations, neither of which served a coordinating function: the U.S. Army Peacekeeping and Stability Operations Institute (PKSOI) at Carlisle Barracks, PA, and the Naval Post-Graduate School's Center for Stabilization and Reconstruction Study. PKSOI assisted with the development of Army doctrine at the strategic (i.e., the leadership and planning) and operational levels and helped the Army's senior leadership develop operational concepts. It worked with the UN, U.S. government interagency groups, interservice groups, and foreign militaries.

The directive was hailed by many as a positive shift in the approach to responsibilities and operational posture on S&R. A CRS report to Congress evaluated DoD 3000.05 as follows: "By elevating stability missions to the same priority level as combat missions, DoD acknowledged that future operations will regularly include missions to stabilize areas during transitions from war to peace and to assist with reconstruction during those transitions."[21]

This acknowledgment was reinforced by the new field manual that the Army and the Marine Corps issued on Counterinsurgency in December 2006. It incorporated stability operations into force planning. While the previous manual emphasized that stability operations typically follow combat, the new manual instructed commanders that they cannot wait until the end of combat operations to provide security and services for the population: "Army forces must defeat enemies and simultaneously shape the civil situation through stability or civil support operations."[22]

The Interagency Force Requirement

Similar efforts were made to expand civilian capabilities. On December 7, 2005, President George W. Bush issued a new directive to empower the Secretary of State to improve coordination, planning, and implementation for reconstruction and stabilization assistance for foreign states and regions at risk of, in, or in transition from conflict or civil strife. The Presidential Directive established that the Secretary of State shall coordinate and lead integrated U.S. government efforts, involving all U.S. departments and agencies with relevant capabilities, to prepare, plan for, and conduct stabilization and reconstruction activities. Depending on the situation, these operations could be conducted with or without U.S. military engagement. The directive stipulates that when the U.S. military is involved, the Secretary of State shall coordinate such efforts with the Secretary of Defense to ensure harmonization with any planned or ongoing U.S. military operations across the spectrum of conflict.

The directive further established that the Secretary of State would be supported by a Coordinator for Reconstruction and Stabilization to do the following:[23]

- Develop strategies for reconstruction and stabilization (R&S) activities; provide U.S. decision makers with detailed options for R&S operations; ensure program and policy coordination among U.S. Departments and Agencies; lead coordination of reconstruction and stabilization activities and preventative strategies with bilateral partners, international and regional organizations, and nongovernmental and private sector entities.

- Coordinate interagency processes to identify states at risk of instability, lead interagency planning to prevent or mitigate conflict, develop detailed contingency plans for integrated U.S. reconstruction and stabilization, and provide U.S. decision makers with detailed options for an integrated U.S. response.

- Lead U.S. development of a strong civilian response capability; analyze, formulate and recommend authorities, mechanisms, and resources for civilian responses in coordination with key interagency implementers such as AID; coordinate R&S budgets among Departments and Agencies; identify lessons learned and integrate them into operational planning by responsible agencies.

The Secretaries of State and Defense were directed to integrate stabilization and reconstruction contingency plans with military contingency plans, when relevant and appropriate.[24]

While the Department of Defense was guided by DoD 3000.05, this Presidential Directive, in part, sought to define the Department of State's role in the new process. In a briefing on December 14, 2005, Ambassador Carlos Pascual—coordinator for reconstruction and stabilization under Condoleezza Rice—underlined the joint nature of the new relationship in tackling S&R issues moving forward. Pascual asserted that the rationale for the new relationship came from the National Security Strategy, which stated that the United States was less threatened by conquering states than by failing ones. The joint nature of the relationship, at its broadest point, meant a more structured approach drawing together State and Defense Department assets into a more aligned effort in S&R operations.[25]

One of the first steps in creating jointness in the new S&R relationship was an effort to establish a running database with all U.S. government contracts relating to S&R operations. This project was to be undertaken with the help of the United States Agency for International Development and others in the interagency process, with a goal that it be functional by early 2006.

Problems Implementing S&R Reform

As is discussed in Chapter 10, however, the United States has done even less to provide this kind of "force strength" than it has to ensure its military force levels can meet its commitments. There has been a striking lack of concerted effort among departments—and by Congress—to coordinate a serious S&R apparatus capable of coping with the vast array of challenges faced in operations such as Iraq and Afghanistan. By late 2005, for example, it was noted that the U.S. portfolio of military plans still remained more focused on combat operations than on stability operations. At this point, the United States was at least nominally two-and-a-half years into the Iraqi S&R effort.[26]

A September 2005 report of the Defense Science Board Task Force asserted that in the period between 2004 and 2005, the Executive Branch, ex the DoD, had made very little progress toward the development of operational capabilities applicable to stability operations. Progress made at the Pentagon, meanwhile, was only "modest." Furthermore, the report held that the Congress had not provided departments other than Defense with the appropriate authorities and resources in order to develop those capabilities. Of particular concern was the underresourcing of the Office of the Coordinator for Reconstruction and Stabilization at the Department of State.[27]

Budgetary restraints had become a key issue in the DoD, with the 2007 DoD budget seeking to reduce cost in areas such as manpower, health care, etc. President Bush asked Congress for $92.2 billion in new emergency spending in early 2006. The request included $65.3 billion for the Pentagon and an estimated $2.9 billion for intelligence agencies related to the wider "War on Terrorism." The new funds were to follow on more than $330 billion in prior emergency appropriations for military and intelligence operations since September 2001, of which Iraq accounted for two-thirds. Together with prior funding, the combined cost of Hurricane Katrina and military action in Iraq and Afghanistan was set to approach $500 billion by the end of FY2006.

Furthermore, the rate of annual expenditures on the two wars was going up, not down, with emergency funds in 2006 to total $118.2 billion in FY2006 versus $100.6 billion in FY2005. The push to enhance S&R capabilities in this budgetary environment was further complicated by the already-rising DoD expenditures on peacekeeping operations since 1991, as shown in Figure 5.8. With the line blurred between combat and S&R operations in Iraq, and with combat-type operations continuing to drain DoD resources, the effort to synchronize S&R capabilities—and to properly fund the necessary entities across departments—proved to be challenging.

Special Operations Forces

The one area where the United States has so far called for meaningful increases in force levels is in Special Forces. On April 22, 2005, Army General Bryan D. Brown, commander of U.S. Special Operations Command (SOCOM), told the Senate Armed Services Committee's emerging threats and capabilities subcommittee that since September 11, 2001, the command had become the Defense Department's lead in fighting terrorism.[28] Indeed, the Unified Command Plan, signed by President Bush in 2004, stated that SOCOM now "leads plans, synchronizes, and as directed, executes global operations against terrorist networks" in addition to the more traditional role of training, equipping, and organizing SOCOM forces for missions under regional commanders.[29]

The 2006 QDR sought to define and shape the expanding role of Special Operations Forces (SOF) moving forward. During the QDR process, the Department of Defense concluded that the current size of U.S. forces—both the active and reserve components across the Military Departments—was appropriate to meet current and projected operational demands. At the same time, the report concluded that there remained a need to continue rebalancing the mix of joint capabilities and forces. As part of this process, the DoD sought to recalibrate Special Operations Forces, in particular, vis-à-vis Joint Ground Forces:[30]

> Joint ground forces will continue to take on more of the tasks performed by today's special operations forces. The result will be a new breed of warrior able to move more easily between disparate mission sets while preserving their depth of skill in primary specialties. Future warriors will be as proficient in irregular operations, including counterinsurgency and stabilization operations, as they are today in high-intensity combat. They will be modular in structure at all levels, largely self-sustaining, and capable of operating both in traditional formations as well as disaggregating into smaller, autonomous units.

This reorientation planned to build upon transformational changes already under way, shifting the joint force from dependence on large, permanent overseas garrisons toward expeditionary operations utilizing more austere bases abroad and from focusing primarily on traditional combat operations toward a greater capability to deal with asymmetric challenges. Under this new thinking, the Pentagon sought to create a new Joint Ground Force (JGF) construct with JGF capabilities similar to traditional SOF capabilities, while the future of SOF would be enhanced with more highly trained personnel with an enhanced suite of skill sets:[31]

> As general purpose joint ground forces take on tasks that Special Operations Forces (SOF) currently perform, SOF will increase their capacity to perform more demanding and specialized tasks, especially long-duration, indirect and clandestine operations in politically sensitive environments and denied areas. For direct action, they will possess an expanded organic ability to locate, tag and track dangerous individuals and other high-value targets globally. SOF will also have greater capacity to detect, locate and render safe WMD. For unconventional warfare and training foreign forces, future SOF will have the capacity to operate in dozens of countries simultaneously. SOF will have increased ability to train and work with partners, employ surrogates, operate clandestinely and sustain a larger posture with lower visibility.

The QDR also noted that the Army Special Forces School had increased its training throughput from 282 new active duty enlisted Special Forces personnel in 2001 to 617 new personnel in 2005—the equivalent of an additional SF battalion each year, with a further goal of increasing to 750 students per year. The report cited DoD plans to increase and enhance Special Operations Forces going forward:[32]

- Increase further SOF capability and capacity to conduct low-visibility, persistent presence missions and a global unconventional warfare campaign.
- Increase (starting in FY2007) active-duty Special Forces Battalions by one-third.
- Expand Psychological Operations and Civil Affairs units by 3,500 personnel (33-percent increase) to provide increased support for SOF and the Army's modular forces.
- Establish a Marine Corps Special Operations Command (MARSOC) composed of 2,600 Marines and Navy personnel to train foreign military units and conduct direct action and special reconnaissance.
- Increase SEAL (sea, air, and land) Team force levels to conduct direct action missions. Establish a SOF Unmanned Aerial Vehicle Squadron to provide organic capabilities to locate and target enemy capabilities in denied or contested areas.
- Enhance capabilities to support SOF insertion and extraction into denied areas from strategic distances.

The increased scope of the command's engagement was met with corresponding calls for increased funding in the 2007 Defense Budget. The FY2007 U.S. government budget included $181 million in FY2007 and $760 million in FY2007–2011 to increase language training, pay and recruitment of specialized personnel, and to expand language training for special operations and intelligence units. The budget also called for the expansion of Navy SEAL Commando Teams, as well as for the initiation of a new SOF Unmanned Aerial Vehicle Squadron.

Meanwhile, a DoD briefing released alongside the FY2007 budget on February 6, 2006, set the following goals with regard to SOF increases:

- Grow Special Operations Forces by over 14,000,
- Expand combat battalions by 33 percent (from 15 to 19),
- Complete establishment of Marine Corps Special Operations Command,
- Initiate new SOF Unmanned Aerial Vehicle Squadron, and
- Expand Navy SEAL Commando Teams.

The DoD also sought to expand the role of SOF in intelligence. In 2005, the military began placing SOF personnel in a growing number of American embassies to gather intelligence on terrorists—and to disrupt, capture, or kill them—and to prepare for potential missions. The move had arisen as a point of some friction between the Central Intelligence Agency (CIA) and the DoD, as it was perceived by some as a DoD encroachment into the CIA's traditional turf. SOCOM reported to the Defense Secretary and not to the Director of National Intelligence.[33] The desirability of SOCOM's involvement in intelligence collection—rather than simply the execution of operations based upon intelligence collected—remained a point of debate in early 2006.

MOVING TOWARD THE PROPER REAL-WORLD FORCE POSTURE

This review of current problems and planning mistakes does not show what force size is necessary, but it does show that a major effort of a very different kind is needed to determine what the United States really needs.

Earlier chapters have shown that the United States can resolve these issues only by taking a fundamentally different approach to defense planning, programming, and budgeting. It needs the equivalent of an interagency QDR in which the exercise is clearly tied to formulating a detailed force and procurement plan with a clearly defined program budget. The present decoupling of strategy, planning, programming, and budgeting is a recipe for failure that cannot answer the question of "how much is enough?" for the simple reason that it fails to attempt to, and it does not force strategists, planners, or programmers to work together in an integrated effort.

The following chapters further illustrate how dangerous such failures can be. They show the history of U.S. failures in force transformation, the impact of a growing crisis in defense procurement and cost containment, and a failure to deal realistically with either interagency needs or the need to strengthen U.S. alliances.

These issues cannot be dealt with by simply advocating a new set of strategic principles or slogans, or advancing some new pattern of suggested cost savings, efficiency measures, or force transformations. The fact is that American defense is simply too complex for such efforts to be more than a hollow intellectual exercise. Only a massive, integrated effort within the Department of Defense and the interagency environment can succeed in both addressing all of the issues involved and in translating them into force plans, programs, and budgets.

It also should be clear, however, that it will take repeated efforts to create such a process and make it work; it will take real leadership capable of making hard choices and sticking to them, and major reforms in the Department of Defense PPBS. It also is not meaningful to attempt such an exercise as a quadrennial effort. Reality changes too quickly and any effort that becomes divorced from the annual changes in force plans and budgets loses impact and effectiveness.

What is needed is an annual planning effort of this kind that forces both the Department of Defense and other elements of the national security community to make this their primary focus. It is also a process as open and transparent as possible. There are no real secrets in exercises of this kind, merely data classified for bureaucratic self-protection. The Congress, the American people, and outside critics and experts should be able to see what is being done and have full access to the end result. If it is competent, it will handily survive such examination. If it is not competent, it deserves to fail.

Challenge Five: Determining What Kind of Force Transformation Is Affordable and Needed, and the Extent to Which It Can or Cannot Deal with the Other Aspects of Overstretch

All of the previous chapters help illustrate the fact that the United States pursued the wrong forms of force transformation until the Afghan and Iraq conflicts made it brutally clear that such approaches could not succeed. Put differently, the United States can succeed in dealing with its strategic and resource challenges only if it finds the right way to meet the challenge of force transformation.

This does not mean that U.S. thinking to date has been rigid, conservative, or inflexible. The United States has consistently tried to adapt its tactics, training, and technology to meet constantly changing strategic conditions. U.S. defense policy and strategy has never been static. It has been in a constant state of evolution, and the United States has tried to deal with the problems exposed in Afghanistan and Iraq.

As the previous chapter has shown, the Quadrennial Defense Review (QDR), issued in February 2006, did call for change in many key areas. Similarly, each of the U.S. military services has been restructuring its training, command, control, communications, computers, and intelligence (C^4I) systems, and equipment, to improve its capability for counterinsurgency, stability operations, and asymmetric war for several years. The role of Special Forces is being expanded at every level. The Defense Intelligence Community is restructuring its tactical support capabilities, and the U.S. Army is being restructured to create more, larger, independent, and rapidly deployable brigades. So far, however, performance is at best "mixed," and there is only limited evidence that the United States can meet the challenge of "force transformation" with the programs and resources it now has available.

The level of progress the United States has made, or has not made, becomes clearer, however, when one looks in more depth at the efforts the Office of the Secretary of Defense (OSD), the Joint Chiefs, and the individual services have made to shape the process of transformation. While these efforts cannot be separated entirely from the Pentagon's funding and manpower issues, from its massive program and cost escalation problems, or from its difficulties in cultivating an effective interagency process linking civilian partners to the military, the transformation efforts of the major defense policy makers do, however, provide a tangible picture of how well and how badly the United States is doing in coming to grips with both current "overstretch" and the needs of the future.

THE QUADRENNIAL DEFENSE REVIEW

The strengths and weaknesses in U.S. efforts to meet this challenge are illustrated not only by the current QDR, but by the entire history of the QDR process. The United States initially reacted to the end of the Cold War by conducting a "build down" that left most of its forces postured for a world that was ceasing to exist, but it did conduct a series of major studies, including the 1991 Base Force Study and the 1993 Bottom-Up Review (BUR), designed to reevaluate U.S. military strategy and force structure in the wake of the fall of the Soviet Union. General Colin Powell, former Chairman of the Joint Chiefs of Staff, coined the term "Base Force" to designate a structure representing the minimum military forces necessary for the United States to meet the national security objectives defined by policy makers, notably the capability to conduct two major theater wars (MTW) simultaneously.

The BUR proposed dealing with the changes in the global security environment and preventing conflict by promoting democracy and peaceful conflict resolution while connecting the U.S. military with foreign militaries, especially those of the former Soviet Union. The BUR emphasized peacekeeping and peace enforcement operations and used the two major theater-wars scenario as the primary force-shaping construct.[1]

The BUR produced the plans for substantial U.S. force cuts during the 1990s, but it was widely criticized on various fronts. Critics perceived it as a purely budget-driven review that failed to adequately address the challenges of the new international security environment. Congress was particularly dissatisfied with the BUR and specified three areas of criticism:[2]

- The assumptions underlying the strategy of planning to fight and win two nearly simultaneous major regional conflicts,
- The force levels recommended to carry out that strategy, and
- The funding proposed for such recommended force levels.

These criticisms prompted Congress to pass legislation in the 1994 National Defense Authorization Act that established a Commission on Roles and Missions

(CORM). The CORM recommended instituting a defense strategy review every four years. In turn, Congress responded by passing the National Defense Authorization Act for Fiscal Year 1997 (passed in 1996) mandating the first QDR charged with preparing a "comprehensive examination of the defense strategy, force posture, force modernization plans, infrastructure, budget plans, and other elements of the defense program and policies with a view toward determining and expressing the defense strategy of the United States and establishing a revised defense program through the year 2005."[3]

Because of its doubts about the quality of the traditional defense review process, Congress also authorized the creation of the National Defense Panel (NDP), composed of national security experts from the private sector, to perform its own independent critique of the Department of Defense (DoD)-run QDR. The NDP report would include "an independent assessment of a variety of possible force structures of the armed Forces through the year 2010 and beyond."[4]

The 1997 Quadrennial Defense Review

The QDR process formalized the role of the OSD as the leading voice in the force transformation process. While it sometimes speaks with many tongues, the OSD's QDR exercises do now represent something approaching a single official position.

The first QDR, however, did not significantly alter the status quo. It called for budget cuts across all services in light of forecast fiscal constraints, but most of these cuts had already been programmed into the existing Future Year Defense Program (FYDP) and budget. It did not cut any major weapon systems. It described a broad military strategy that called for the United States to shape the security environment through deterrence and engagement while remaining prepared for a full spectrum of conflicts, ranging from small-scale contingencies to major theater wars. The report endorsed the National Security Strategy's "shape, respond, prepare" doctrine, Joint Vision 2010's "full spectrum dominance," and the BUR's force-sizing requirements to conduct two simultaneous MTWs.[5] In practice, this was more a recipe for status quo than for change and more a series of ambiguous slogans than a tangible strategic plan.

Congress was unimpressed. It viewed the 1997 QDR as a run-of-the-mill DoD budget exercise that reflected what military force structure would look like if funded at present budget levels. As such, it failed to challenge the status quo by making difficult choices and setting priorities. The Congressionally mandated and independent NDP criticized the QDR for rubber-stamping a Cold War defense structure that did not adequately address asymmetric threats and homeland defense.

The NDP, in contrast, recommended a comprehensive look at scaling back or canceling legacy systems, such as the M1A1 Abrams Tank upgrades, the Crusader artillery vehicle, the Comanche helicopter, and the defense-wide tactical aircraft programs [e.g., the F/A-18E/F, the F-22, and the Joint Strike Fighter (JSF)]. Most significantly, the NDP's report challenged the two major theater-wars force posture and suggested that while it was a means to justify a Cold War–based force structure, it had become a roadblock to implementing transformation strategies that would prepare the military for future threats.[6]

The 2001 Quadrennial Defense Review

Despite—or perhaps because of—the weak and ambiguous results of the first QDR, the 106th Congress created a permanent requirement for a Quadrennial Defense Review by inserting Section 118 into Chapter 2 of title 10 of the U.S. Code. This states—in language similar to that of the original 1997 QDR legislation—that every four years, the Secretary of Defense will[7]

> conduct a comprehensive examination of the national defense strategy, force structure, force modernization plans, infrastructure, budget plan, and other elements of the defense program and policies of the United States with a view towards determining and expressing the defense strategy of the United States and establishing a defense program for the next 20 years.

This legislative requirement again attempted to make the QDR a key element of national security planning that would shape the defense program and budget rather than set vague goals for strategy and force changes. The 1947 National Security Act [50 U.S.C. § 404a(a)] already required the President to submit to Congress a national security strategy along with budgets for each fiscal year that (1) identified U.S. interests, goals, and objectives vital to U.S. national security and (2) explained how the United States uses its political, economic, military, and other elements of its power to protect and promote U.S. interests and objectives. The QDR, in turn, was to outline a defense strategy that supported and complemented the National Security Strategy.

The National Defense Authorization Act for Fiscal Year 2000 stated that the purpose of the 2001 QDR would be to (1) delineate a military strategy consistent with the most recent National Security Strategy, (2) define the defense programs to successfully execute the full range of missions assigned the military by that strategy, and (3) identify the budget plan necessary to successfully execute those missions at a low-to-moderate level of risk.

To assist the DoD in formulating a comprehensive military strategy, Congress specifically requested that the following information be provided in the 2001 and future QDRs:

- The results of the review, including a comprehensive discussion of the national defense strategy of the United States and the force structure best suited to implement that strategy at a low-to-moderate level of risk.

- The assumed or defined national security interests of the United States that inform the national defense strategy defined in the review.

- The threats to the assumed or defined national security interests of the United States that were examined for the purposes of the review and the scenarios developed in the examination of those threats.

- The assumptions used in the review, including assumptions relating to (a) readiness; (b) the cooperation of allies, mission-sharing and benefits and burdens resulting from coalition operations; (c) warning times; (d) levels of engagement in operations other than war and smaller-scale contingencies; and (e) the intensity, duration, and military and political end-states of conflicts and smaller-scale contingencies.

- The effect on the force structure and on readiness for high-intensity combat of preparations for and participation in operations other than war and smaller-scale contingencies.

- The manpower and sustainment policies required under the national defense strategy to support engagement in conflicts lasting longer than 120 days.

- The anticipated roles and missions of the reserve components in the national defense strategy and the strength, capabilities, and equipment necessary to assure that the reserve components can capably discharge those roles and missions.

- The appropriate ratio of combat forces to support forces (commonly referred to as the "tooth-to-tail" ratio) under the national defense strategy, including, in particular, the appropriate number and size of headquarters units and Defense Agencies for that purpose.

- The strategic and tactical airlift, sealift, and ground transportation capabilities required to support the national defense strategy.

- The forward presence, prepositioning, and other anticipatory deployments necessary under the national defense strategy for conflict deterrence and adequate military response to anticipated conflicts.

- The extent to which resources must be shifted among two or more theaters under the national defense strategy in the event of conflict in such theaters.

- The advisability of revisions to the Unified Command Plan as a result of the national defense strategy.

- The effect on force structure of the use by the armed forces of technologies anticipated to be available for the ensuing 20 years.

- Any other matter the Secretary considers appropriate.

What the Congress did not do was insist that the next QDR exercise be tied to a force plan and procurement plan, to an overall program and FYDP, and to a budget that would implement what the QDR recommended. The Congressional language was too vague to correct the most obvious and continuing failure in U.S. defense planning: the failure to force the integration of strategy, planning, and budgeting. While its efforts to reform the QDR process were well intentioned, Congress did not force the Secretary of Defense to address the chronic mismatch between strategy, force plans, programs and budgets, and the OSD failed to make any substantive progress in these areas on its own.

The DoD released the 2001 QDR as scheduled on September 30, 2001, less than a month after the September 11 terrorist attacks. The QDR did make conceptual progress in a number of areas and outlined a new defense strategy that encompassed four goals: to assure allies and friends that the United States is capable of fulfilling its commitments, to dissuade adversaries from undertaking activities that could threaten U.S. or allied interests, to deter aggression and coercion, and to decisively defeat any adversary if deterrence fails.

The Review also sought to shift the basis for defense planning from the long-standing "threat-based" model, which focused on specific adversaries and geographic regions, to Secretary of Defense Donald Rumsfeld's vision for a "capabilities-based" construct that emphasized the need to prepare for a broad spectrum of potential military operations against unknown enemies. The "strategy" of winning two nearly simultaneous major theater wars was largely retained, albeit with some clarification. It did not, however, define what this strategy meant in terms of meaningful changes to the force structure, defense program, and budget.

Secretary Rumsfeld stated that the new QDR was not intended to be a strategy *per se,* but a series of goals and priorities for shaping the force structure and sizing the budget. Apart from defending the United States and deterring aggression, the new force-sizing construct called for forces that could do the following:[8]

- Swiftly defeat aggression in overlapping major conflicts while preserving for the President the option to call for a decisive victory in one of those conflicts, including the possibility of regime change or occupation, and
- Conduct a limited number of small-scale contingency operations.

The 2001 QDR identified several steps that the DoD needed to take to achieve the objectives of its new defense strategy, but in vague terms, not as force plans, procurement plans, or resource requirements. These steps ranged from exploiting new approaches and operational concepts to fundamentally changing the way wars are fought. The QDR concluded that the desired transformation objectives could be achieved by exploiting new approaches, technologies, and new organization. The report also described six critical goals to provide focus to the DoD's transformation efforts. These were as follows:[9]

- Protect bases of operation at home and abroad and defeat the threat of chemical, biological, radiological, nuclear, and explosive weapons.
- Assure information systems in the face of attack and conduct effective information operations.
- Project and sustain U.S. forces in distant antiaccess and area-denial environments.
- Deny enemies sanctuary by providing persistent surveillance, tracking, and rapid engagement.
- Enhance the capability and survivability of space systems.

- Leverage information technology and innovative concepts to develop Joint C^{4}ISR (Command, Control, Communications, Computers, Intelligence, Surveillance, and Reconnaissance).

To support these initiatives, the DoD established a transformation office that reported directly to the Secretary of Defense to develop transformation road maps for the services and defense agencies. Moreover, the QDR directed the DoD to develop a prototype for a Standing Joint Task Force Headquarters to improve the services' ability to operate together in situations that required a rapid response. And as an added touch, the Review included the Secretary of Defense's plans for improving DoD business practices—reforming its financial systems, reducing the size of headquarters' staffs, and consolidating the DoD's facilities and supply chain—to increase efficiency and free up resources in support of transformation efforts.[10]

In contrast to the 1997 QDR, the 2001 Review was shaped by the sustained involvement of the Secretary of Defense and senior DoD officials who provided the direction and oversight that the 2001 QDR process required to initiate the development of a new defense strategy. This unified leadership provided for a central, coherent vision of a U.S. defense strategy.

However, several weaknesses in the DoD's review process, analysis, and reporting limited the report's overall utility as a means for reassessing U.S. defense plans and programs. While Pentagon officials did consider postponing the release of the QDR to review how September 11 should affect future military planning, they opted to complete the report on schedule since they felt that it already addressed issues such as homeland defense, asymmetric threats, and potential terrorist surprises.

The 2001 QDR raised a host of new issues about the strategy and force structure the United States should pursue in the future that it failed to resolve in anything other than the vaguest terms. Nevertheless, many experts felt it was a major improvement over the 1997 Review and attributed many of the shortcomings of the 2001 QDR to the compressed timeline in which it was prepared. The Secretary of Defense had delayed starting the review until late spring 2001, after the DoD completed a series of strategic reviews led by outside defense experts. This internal delay compounded the challenge that a new Secretary of Defense and a new administration faced in submitting a national security strategy by June and a QDR by September 30 of the first year in office.

On the whole, the 2001 QDR's focus on the defense policy goals discussed earlier —assuring allies and friends; deterring threats and coercion against U.S. interests; if deterrence fails, decisively defeating any adversary—was clearly aimed at dealing with wars between traditional nation-states or coalitions. The Review did not explore how any of the stated defense policy goals might apply to global terrorism and many aspects of asymmetric warfare, counterinsurgency, peacemaking, and nation building.

As explained in a November 2002 report by the General Accounting Office,[11]

Because the study's principal guidance document was designed to emphasize the Secretary's priorities, there was not always a clear link between the specific reporting requirements in the legislation and the issues assigned to study teams for analysis. Moreover, the thoroughness of the department's analysis and reporting on issues mandated by legislation varied considerably, and some significant issues such as the role of the reserves, were deferred to follow-on studies. Finally, the department's assessment of force structure requirements had some significant limitations—such as its lack of focus on longer-term threats and requirements for critical support capabilities—and the department's report provided little information on some required issues, such as the specific assumptions used in the analysis.

While the 2001 QDR did describe the importance of transformation efforts for dealing with asymmetric and terrorist threats, it offered scant direction on how the services might prevent or respond to so-called fourth-generation warfare attacks like those of September 11, 2001. It did little to describe major changes in U.S. force structures and procurement plans and had only a limited impact on the budget and the FYDP.

For example, the Review stated that the terrorist threat required a faster transformation in forces and operational concepts to address new threats, but offered no changes to the size, composition, or training of military forces. The Review did not offer a timeline for making the transformational changes, nor did it describe them in detail. The QDR's section on research and development also discussed needs regarding homeland defense, but focused almost exclusively on defense against ballistic and cruise missiles and on managing the aftermath of terrorist attacks on U.S. soil.[12]

The Potential of the 2006 QDR

The failures of previous QDRs to shape U.S. force plans and defense spending plans, and to create a match between these goals and actual resources, was not corrected in the 2006 Quadrennial Defense Review. The 2006 QDR exercise was supposed to find ways to carry out a longer-term and far more comprehensive restructuring of U.S. strategy, force posture, and force development plans. Accordingly, the 2006 QDR could have had more impact than previous Reviews for several reasons: (1) it was the first wartime QDR, (2) it was the first QDR completed by a Secretary of Defense who had completed a QDR before, (3) this QDR was the first to be completed as budgets were consistently growing, and (4) this was the first post-9/11 QDR.[13] Moreover, Secretary Rumsfeld had four years to pick senior military officials who subscribed to his philosophy of defense transformation and fighting with smaller, more agile forces.[14]

The terms of reference for the fiscal year 2006 (FY2006) QDR were promising. They looked beyond conventional warfare. They called for the development of a new force posture that relied on a four-way threat matrix that reflected the decline in the likelihood of conventional warfare and Secretary Rumsfeld's intention to counter the concurrent rise in unconventional warfare by shifting from a threats-based force to a capabilities-based force. The matrix, as defined by the March 2005 National Defense Strategy, contained the following threat components:

- Traditional threats: state-based conventional forces.
- Irregular threats: terrorism, insurgency, and civil conflict.
- Disruptive threats: disruption of U.S. operations, electronic warfare, and weapons of mass destruction (WMD) attacks.
- Catastrophic threats: proliferation and attacks on symbols and centers of U.S. power.

The Secretary of Defense also identified four core problems, closely related to the threat matrix, that the QDR must address:[15]

- Partnerships with failing states to combat terrorist threats: The United States has an interest in maintaining a well-managed international system. This interest may push the United States to engage in elective military interventions.
- Defense of the homeland, including offensive strikes against terrorist groups: The United States must be prepared to engage terrorists around the world to prevent domestic attacks.
- Influencing the strategic choices of major countries: Trying to determine the number and type of military forces for this task is difficult.
- Preventing the proliferation of WMD: This is the one likely warfighting issue that could require regime-change operations.

At the same time, three other critical aspects of transformation were supposed to receive attention. These included a long overdue reexamination of the role of the National Guard and the Reserves, an examination of basing and infrastructure, and a look at the role that civilians should play in stability and nation-building operations to reduce the reliance on the military for what are essentially civilian functions.

The 2006 QDR failed to deal with any of these issues. Its transformation efforts were conducted in the face of major budget and cost constraints, serious problems in the existing transformation plans of the individual services, and critical problems in virtually every major procurement program.

The United States faced the problems of dealing with the ongoing Iraq War and with the reality that large-scale transformation could only pay off fully in the 2010 time frame at the earliest. Barring a half decade of almost perfect peace—the lead time needed to execute actual force transformation—transformation could be effective only if it addressed the fact that the United States could not correct its current overstretch problems in the near to medium term with anything like the resources being projected for U.S. defense spending. This was particularly true given the way that the DoD had failed to manage and execute its major procurement programs.

Moreover, the Pentagon chose to repeat its decades-long history of drafting conceptual studies and strategies that were not tied firmly to specific force plans and levels, and which were not then implemented in detail in its budgets, future year defense spending plans, procurement plans, manpower plans, readiness plans, or deployment plans. The DoD ignored the fact that exercises like the QDR have almost inevitably become ineffective intellectual efforts because they have not been tied to concrete, detailed execution. In fact, the entire history of the Department of Defense is a grim warning that theory and policy do not change practices unless they are concretely tied to specific levels of forces, manpower, and dollars.

The Reality of the 2006 QDR

The 2006 QDR was released in February 2006. It did make advances at the conceptual level. It called for a significant shift in DoD policy and planning from an emphasis on fighting conventional, major theater wars against nation-states to fighting a "long war" against terrorism and nontraditional threats and defending the homeland. Where the 2001 QDR largely retained the two major theater-wars construct, the 2006 Review accounted for the possibility that one of those two campaigns would be a large-scale, prolonged, and unconventional conflict. It said that the United States must have the surge capability to "wage two nearly simultaneous conventional campaigns (or one conventional campaign if already engaged in a large-scale, long-duration irregular campaign), while selectively reinforcing deterrence against opportunistic acts of aggression."[16]

The QDR highlighted the risk that the United States might have to fight major conventional conflicts and deal with proliferation. The 2006 Review also focused on the risks posed by rogue, and possibly nuclear, states (like Iran and North Korea), monitoring the rise of a heavily armed rival (like China), and the DoD's domestic role in responding to natural disasters like Hurricane Katrina. The strategy document also called for new investments aimed at countering the proliferation of biological and nuclear weapons, such as teams able to defuse a nuclear bomb.

To accommodate the DoD's newfound role in stability, security, and transition operations—and in response to tough lessons learned in Iraq and Afghanistan—the QDR highlighted and reinforced a November 28, 2005, DoD Directive that gave stability and peacekeeping operations the same priority as major combat operations within the Department.[17] Moreover, the 2006 Review recognized the need for improved interagency relations and more effective cooperation with foreign allies to continue the long war against terrorism.

The 2006 QDR also set several broad priorities for realigning the DoD's resources to support its new strategic initiatives, although some of these were more clearly reflected in the FY2007 budget submission and FYDP.

- Increase Special Operations Forces (SOF) by 15 percent, including a third more Army Special Forces battalions, a 2,600-person Marine component in Special Operations Command (SOCOM), more Navy SEAL (sea, air, and land) capacity, and a new SOCOM Unmanned Aerial Vehicle (UAV) Squadron.

- Improve language skills and cultural awareness.
- Train foreign military units.
- Expand psychological warfare and civil affairs units by 3,500 personnel (an increase of one-third) and enhance the capability of the Army and the Marines to perform SOF missions.
- Field by 2018, rather than by 2037, "a new land-based, penetrating long-range strike capability."
- Accelerate procurement of Predator and Global Hawk UAVs to provide almost double the current UAV coverage.
- Accelerate procurement of Littoral Combat Ships and develop a Navy riverine capability.
- Field within two years a conventional ballistic missile on Trident submarines for conventional prompt global strike.
- Mount a $1.5-billion initiative to develop broad-spectrum medical countermeasures against the threat of genetically engineered bioterror agents.

This marked at least a limited shift away from the DoD's previous focus on vague transformation plans that bore little connection to DoD budgets. The 2006 QDR was, however, anything but an adequate response to the new direction the Department had received from Congress. The Bob Stump Defense Authorization Act for Fiscal Year 2003 amended the QDR mandate in the U.S. Code [10 U.S.C. § 118 (d)] to allow the completion date of the Review to coincide with the President's budget submission. The Congress intended this legislative change to make the Review's delivery and implementation more efficient and to bridge the usual gulf between strategic defense planning and budgeting.

In the spirit of the amended QDR legislation, the DoD did "front-load" a limited number of initiatives into the $439.3-billion defense budget submission for FY2007.

- Increasing SOF by 15 percent corresponded to a $1-billion budget increase in commando forces—Green Berets, Navy SEALs, and Delta Forces—across the board to $5.1 billion.
- Improving foreign language and cultural training programs translated into a $181-billion budget allocation.
- Accelerating the procurement of UAVs connected to $1.7 billion slated for 322 more UAVs.[18]
- Strengthening U.S. homeland defense was linked to $1.7 billion to develop new vaccines against biological weapons and to increase the military's ability to locate and neutralize potential nuclear threats.[19]

Nonetheless, many experts had expected the QDR, and Secretary Rumsfeld, to be far more decisive and explicit in making hard choices about cutting big-ticket defense programs. For example, the Army's Future Combat System (FCS), designed to seamlessly link soldiers and weapon systems in the battlefield, alone cost $150 billion. The

Navy's DD(X) destroyer, an impressive land-attack vessel with limited utility in irregular warfare, cost around $2.5 billion per hull. And the Air Force's F-22 fighter, designed originally as an air superiority platform for waging conventional wars, cost $61.3 billion. Moreover, the proposed acceleration, by nearly two decades, of acquiring a new (manned or unmanned) deep-strike aircraft comprised a significant new liability.

Both the new QDR and the FY2007 budget submission that accompanied it made little more than token progress in creating credible force and procurement plans, and in ending the gap between strategy and reality and between plans and resources. The few cuts the 2006 Review did recommend were relatively small. Programs slated to be scaled back or terminated included the Joint Unmanned Combat Air Systems (J-UCAS) effort, the E-10 surveillance aircraft, and the B-52H standoff jammer. The QDR also recommended cutting 40,000 Air Force personnel, retiring 50 Minuteman intercontinental ballistic missiles, and accelerating the retirement of the F-117 fighter and the U-2 reconnaissance aircraft.

But the 2006 QDR's limited discussion of proposed reductions in force structure and personnel did not substantially alleviate the DoD's mismatch between defense strategy and the budget, nor did the QDR and the budget submission propose cuts that offset the burden associated with new programs proposed in the Review. As Steven M. Kosiak, Director of Budget Studies at the Center for Strategic and Budgetary Assessments, wrote, "some of the proposed shifts in priorities—such as the accelerated fielding of a new long-range strike aircraft—are likely to be dependent, for their implementation, on the willingness and ability of a future administration to make offsetting cuts in other DoD priorities. The [2006] QDR, for the most part, deferred these difficult choices."[20]

The 2006 QDR also failed to make substantive recommendations regarding several key areas. The Review did not propose a forward-looking approach to homeland security operations in the wake of Hurricane Katrina. Nor did it address the new role of the National Guard and the Reserves in transforming the DoD. The QDR's recommendations on acquisition reform fell well short of Congressional expectations, and the Review provided no guidance on the role civilians should play versus soldiers in stability and nation-building operations.

The most glaring flaw of the 2006 QDR was that it called for the DoD to have its cake and eat it, too. Presumably, U.S. force structure had to be realigned to counter the irregular and asymmetric threats posed by international terrorist networks, failed states, and the proliferation of weapons of mass destruction. But this realignment could take place only through a far more dramatic shift in resources away from expensive Cold War–era weapon systems designed for conventional deterrence and major theater wars. Instead, the 2006 QDR and the FY2007 budget request preserved every major weapons system and simply added projects to deal with the new challenges without calling for an increase in the number of troops.

Stephen Biddle of the Council on Foreign Relations summarized the result as follows:[21]

Back when the QDR process started for this round, people tended to frame the thing up as a fundamental choice about what sort of military we wanted to have in the future. Was the Secretary of Defense going to retain the high-tech, capital intensive, speed-oriented transformation concept intended primarily for waging major combat operations or for dealing with potentially emerging peer competitors, or was he going to go to a lower-tech, labor-intensive, lower capital military with an emphasis on persistence oriented towards low intensity conflict, counterinsurgencies of the kind we're waging in Iraq and Afghanistan, counterterrorism, and other lower intensity challenges? . . . The great irony of the QDR that we got, of course, is that they decided to do both. Why choose? So none of the trade-offs embodied in that fundamental choice have been drawn. Instead, the document basically tries to do everything involved with both of those futures and build both of those militaries.

In short, the QDR process had some successes in theory, but failed almost completely to deal with practice. It simply failed to lead to anything approaching the tough decisions that had to be made in defense planning, programming, and budgeting. This occurred even in the 2006 QDT in spite of the fact that Secretary Rumsfeld was one of the most powerful defense secretaries in recent memory and devoted significant resources to completing the 2006 Review—it was drafted over 10 months by some 500 Pentagon employees—and the Secretary staunchly advocated the need for smaller, more agile, and more lethal forces.[22] While the 2006 Review made a significant policy departure from previous Reviews by fully embracing transformation strategies to conduct irregular and counterterrorist warfare, it remained decoupled from detailed force plans, from the budget, and from the FYDP. It did not result in any critical decisions to actually implement its new strategies.

JOINT FORCES AND THE IMPACT OF THE JOINT CHIEFS

The problems raised by the QDR are only one illustration of the U.S. failure to properly meet the challenge of creating strategies and force plans that actually transform into affordable realities. The Joint Chiefs and each of the military services have also advanced strategic concepts, and sometimes force plans, that have compounded the problem of bringing strategy and force transformation into balance with resources. In the case of the Joint Chiefs, the problems have been focused on how to integrate the efforts of the different military services and commands into an effective post–Cold War force structure based on jointness.

Jointness and the joint force have meant different things in various documents over the past decade. In general, however, the word "jointness" and the phrase "joint force" refer to the coordination between any of the U.S. service branches or any U.S. departments or agencies to seamlessly support each other in conducting operations. Neither jointness nor joint force refers to operations involving U.S. and multinational forces.

Creating the Joint Force

The constant changes in the post–Cold War security environment have created a world that requires the combined efforts of U.S. forces to deal effectively with terrorist groups, failed states, stability and reconstruction operations, and homeland security in ways that cannot be assigned to individual services or to major unified and specified commands. The need to transform the military into a joint force capable of operating as a coherent whole has come to shape all U.S. military transformation programs. It is clear from the Balkans, the Gulf War, Afghanistan, the Iraq War, and U.S. contingency planning for other conflicts that the United States requires a joint force that can achieve operational unity of effort across the range of service competencies. While Congress and the DoD have actively pursued doctrinal changes that emphasize joint forces, implementing these changes has been more problematic.

Congress and defense officials alike have focused on the concept of jointness in military operations since the passage of the Goldwater-Nichols Act in 1986 streamlined the U.S. military's command structure. A decade later, the independent Commission on Roles and Missions of the Armed Forces (CORM), established by the National Defense Authorization Act for FY1994, released a report titled *Directions for Defense* (1996) that challenged the DoD to move beyond the provisions of Goldwater-Nichols and prepare for the post–Cold War security environment.[23] The report made more than 100 specific recommendations and argued that the terms of the roles and missions debate should focus on the needs of the commanders in chief (CINCs), on the capability of their forces to carry out joint operations, and on many of the DoD's support activities—not on the capabilities of the individual services. The competition between the near-term visions of the unified commands, CINC visions reflecting diverse regional interests, and service visions indicating their specialized mediums led CORM to recommend that the Chairman of the Joint Chiefs of Staff articulate a unified vision for joint operations.

The CORM report's recommendations led the Joint Chiefs to release *Joint Vision 2010* (JV 2010) in 1996. This report marked the Joint Chiefs' first major effort to provide a comprehensive post–Cold War strategy for U.S. force development. As former Chairman of the Joint Chiefs of Staff General John M. Shalikashvili wrote in the report's Introduction, JV 2010 "is the *conceptual template for how we will channel the vitality of our people and leverage technological opportunities to achieve new levels of effectiveness in joint warfighting.*"[24] JV 2010 detailed a proposed transformational blueprint for the DoD, emphasizing "full-spectrum dominance." Its goal was for U.S. forces, operating alone or with allies, to be able to defeat any adversary and control any situation across the range of military operations, from humanitarian and peace operations to full-scale war.

Significantly, JV 2010 and subsequent joint planning documents (including the 2006 QDR) focused on broad calls for force-wide capabilities rather than on individual services. To accommodate this shift, the 2006 QDR recommended that the Pentagon plan, program, and budget according to joint capability areas and outcomes instead of dividing by and emphasizing individual services. Service core competencies would be assessed through what they brought to the joint fight. As such, the success of JV 2010 (and subsequent joint strategy documents) depended on the ability to truly integrate all of the elements of the total force.

Four capabilities lay at the heart of full-spectrum dominance.[25]

- *Dominant Maneuver* seeks to control the entire range of the battle space and the pace of operations through the multidimensional application of information, engagement, and mobility capabilities to achieve a decisive advantage.

- *Precision Engagement* consists of a system of systems that enables forces to locate an objective or target, provide responsive command and control, generate the desired effect, assess the level of success, and retain the flexibility to reengage with precision when required. Precision engagement will build on current U.S. advantages in delivery accuracy and low observable technologies.

- *Full Dimension Protection* aims to control the battle space so that forces are not just protected, but control the environment and the initiative in all operations. This means that forces can maintain freedom of action during deployment, maneuver, and engagement, while providing multilayered defenses for forces and facilities at all levels.

- *Focused Logistics* undergirds all of the preceding capabilities because the latter rely on the ability to project power with the most capable forces, at the decisive time and place. Focused logistics optimize the previous three capabilities by fusing information, logistics, and transportation technologies to provide rapid crisis response, to track and shift assets even while en route, and to deliver tailored logistics packages and sustainment directly at the strategic, operational, and tactical levels.

JV 2010 stated that realizing these capabilities required the application and development of two enabling concepts—"innovation" and "information superiority"—to fully enable the tailored application of joint combat power. The first of these, innovation, meant the "combination of new things with new ways to carry out tasks."[26] Information superiority was defined as "the capability to collect, process, and disseminate an uninterrupted flow of information while exploiting or denying an adversary's ability to do the same."[27]

Advances in technology lay at the core of both of these force enablers. JV 2010 emphasized technology and "information dominance" for command and control systems as keys to future warfighting. Full spectrum dominance required the services to work together in unprecedented ways, and exploiting U.S. strength in information technology was central to coordinating these joint forces. Specifically, JV 2010 foresaw a future where technology allowed battlefield decision making to have far more information at every level and where technology accelerated battlefield operations through information superiority.

What JV 2010 did not provide, however, was a clear force plan, implementing plans and programs, or any vision of how the required resources compared with available budgets. It came close to calling for jointness without trade-offs, and transparent, near real-time situational awareness without examining when and how the required technology could be provided and paid for. Like the various QDRs and the discussions of the "revolution in military affairs," it was more a wish list than a plan. Moreover, given its timing, it emphasized conventional warfighting and reacted more to the lessons of the Gulf War in 1991 than to the emerging need to deal with asymmetric war, terrorism, peacemaking, and homeland defense.

The Joint Chiefs have not improved the realism and relevance of their planning efforts since JV 2010. Former Chairman of the Joint Chiefs of Staff, Army General Henry Shelton, updated and extended the concepts laid out in JV 2010 with the release of *Joint Vision 2020* (JV 2020) on May 30, 2000. JV 2020 reinforced the importance of building the joint force.[28]

> The joint force, because of its flexibility and responsiveness, will remain the key to operational success in the future. The integration of core competencies provided by the individual Services is essential to the joint team, and the employment of the capabilities of the Total Force (active, reserve, guard, and civilian members) increases the options for the commander and complicates the choices of our opponents. To build the most effective force for 2020, we must be fully joint: intellectually, operationally, organizationally, doctrinally, and technically.

The transformation strategy outlined in JV 2020—and reiterated later in the 2005 Capstone Concept for Joint Operations—again called for integrating the operational capabilities of U.S. forces across the services, especially in the realm of communications, and for improving U.S. capacity for command and control in multinational operations.[29] To achieve these goals, both vision documents emphasized technology as the primary driver behind future warfighting.

While these strategy documents did not provide clear force plans and priorities, they did impact transformation efforts across the armed forces and provided the foundation and justification for various modernization programs including Future Combat Systems, Network Centric Warfare, Sea Power 21, and Advanced Close Air Support Systems.

The strategy documents also helped shape the United States Joint Forces Command's (USJFCOM) proposed framework for future campaigns, "Rapid Decisive Operations" (RDO) released in 2001.[30] The RDO attempted to shift the United States away from engaging in the predictable ways of past conflicts that involved phased deployment, staging, taking airfields and ports, moving progressively to key targets, and taking momentary operational pauses to regroup. Instead, rapid decisive operations would be characterized by immediate, simultaneous, unpredictable, and nonlinear attack. The RDO called for a synchronized application of the full range of capabilities across the width and the depth of the battlefield to overwhelm an enemy. This mode of warfare requires a truly joint and integrated force with clear communications, collaborative planning, and integrated attack capabilities.[31]

Progress in Joint Warfighting

Like the QDRs and the Joint Vision documents, the RDO called for major advances in strategy and capability almost all of which had great potential value. Once again, however, problems lay in realizing affordable and effective implementation and in transforming broad goals into effective action. Joint doctrine has provided the impetus for change; joint command centers have been established; joint training exercises have become the norm. But the tenets of jointness have not yet permeated all levels of the services.

The military has made major progress in establishing a joint command structure. Consistent with the United States Atlantic Command's (USACOM) prominent post–Goldwater-Nichols role in leading joint forces transformation, it was assigned the role of integrating the services into joint operations by combining the roles of Joint Force Provider, Joint Force Trainer, and Joint Force Integrator in 1993. USACOM was renamed United States Joint Forces Command (USJFCOM) in October 1999. Since then, as chief advocate for jointness, USJFCOM has facilitated the transformation of the military through joint concept development and experimentation, recommending joint requirements, advancing interoperability, conducting joint training, simulation, and modeling, and preparing battle-ready joint forces.[32]

The Joint Capability Integration and Development System (JCIDS)—which replaced the old Requirements Generation System in June 2003—now supports the Chairman of the Joint Chiefs of Staff and the Joint Requirements Oversight Council in identifying, assessing, and prioritizing joint military capabilities. It has scarcely reshaped U.S. force plans and programs into an affordable plan for force transformation, but the JCIDS provides an overarching evaluation mechanism that links joint concepts, the capabilities required to execute those concepts, and the systems ultimately required to deliver those capabilities.

Moreover, JCIDS has expanded its list of organizations beyond the scope of the traditional service branches of the Joint Staff. JCIDS now includes representatives from the Office of the Secretary of Defense, the combatant commanders, defense agencies, the intelligence and acquisition communities, and interagency personnel where appropriate. In theory, the documents produced by JCIDS provide the formal communication of capabilities required between the warfighter and the acquisition, test and evaluation, and resource management communities.[33]

Vice Chairman of the Joint Chiefs of Staff and former Commander of USJFCOM Admiral Edmund P. Giambastiani, Jr., highlighted in a statement to Congress in June 2005 several key areas where "significant" joint transformation progress had been made.[34]

- Every major DoD war game since May 2003 has been run as a joint game cosponsored by a service and Joint Forces Command, working on a common set of issues within a common joint context.
- Joint Training has focused on preparing the Joint Task Force Commander and his staff to execute real world joint operations, with a special emphasis on mission rehearsal

exercises for commanders preparing for command in Operations Enduring Freedom and Iraqi Freedom.

- More new flag and general officer have been trained in an expanded CAPSTONE Joint Operations Module. The newly created Joint Task Force Headquarters offers training courses for 2- and 3-star officers and senior enlisted leaders.

- Using the Joint Battle Management Command and Control authorities as directed by the Deputy Secretary of Defense, the Services and Combatant Commands have improved all aspects of Joint Command and Control, issued a detailed Roadmap, and executed their first program, the Deployable Joint Command and Control. USJFCOM has also created the Joint Systems Integration Command (JSIC).

Fully implementing jointness may well take another decade. It not only requires major new capabilities and advances in force transformation, but advances in military training and operational practice. The following anecdotes illustrate the gap between rhetoric and performance.

- In 1998, a prospective Navy battle group [including the Hue City (CG 69) and the Vicksburg (CG 66)] was replaced because the assembled ships were not interoperable. The new Aegis cruiser, with the latest state-of-the-art systems, could not communicate reliably with the older systems due to poor configuration management and the failure to backbit. Here, the Navy could not communicate with itself, let alone with other services or allies.[35]

- In 1999, the Task Force Hawk deployment to Kosovo exposed a number of problems, including the substantial logistical issues and delays in operational readiness. Molding the Army's AH-64 Apache attack helicopters into the primarily Air Force–driven air campaign was exceedingly difficult due both to command failures and technical failures. In effect, the Army and the Air Force could not work together in the theater.[36] Admiral William Owens recounted the situation.[37]

  > The Apaches were unable to integrate with support assets such as the E-8 JSTARS aircraft, the EC-130 Compass Call (radar) jamming aircraft and the F-16CJs equipped to defeat Serbian air defenses...Sixteen years after Grenada—during which Army ground troops found themselves unable to communicate with Navy carrier aircraft providing critical close-air support on the battlefield—the Army and Air Force assets rushed to Kosovo still could not communicate with one another...No one has ever seriously envisioned including Army aviation into a theater strategic air campaign. Everybody trains, organizes, and equips to their service doctrine...When the services come to a war, they come with their service doctrines, not a joint doctrine.

- In March 2002, Operation Anaconda in Afghanistan's Shahikot Valley suffered from major command and control and logistical issues. As Army Major Mark Davis discussed at length in a master's thesis completed at the School of Advanced Air and Space Studies at Maxwell Air Force Base, a "sloppy" chain of command made combat failures almost inevitable from the start. Former U.S. Central Command (CENTCOM) Chief Army General Tommy Franks, who served as the unified commander of all operations in Afghanistan, created an overly complex command structure that established numerous joint task forces and functional commands whose responsibilities could easily overlap.

- Two Special Operations task forces—code-named Dagger and K-Bar—were put in a position where they could be potentially tasked simultaneously by three different commanders: General Franks at CENTCOM, the Combined Forces Special Operations Component Commander, and the Combined Forces Land Component Commander.[38]

- As the Combined Forces Land Component Commander, Army Lieutenant General Paul Mikolashek became the lead general in Afghanistan, and, theoretically, his tactical control extended to all SOF—except for those in Task Force Sword, an elite unit from Fort Bragg, North Carolina, that undertook missions so classified that other task forces were often unaware of them. This made for competing commands between Lieutenant General Mikolashek and the Commander of all of CENTCOM's acknowledged SOF, Navy SEAL Rear Admiral Albert Calland. Because Mikolashek could not direct SOF outside the limits of his original tasking unless General Franks or Rear Admiral Calland approved, Mikolashek was often unaware of mission orders Calland issued. This placed enormous pressure and responsibility on commanders directly responsible for individual Special Operations units like Colonel John Mulholland, commander of Task Force Dagger.[39]

- As a result partially of the serpentine decision-making apparatus and of time con- straints, Operation Anaconda did not have a clear-cut, streamlined joint fire-control network for close air support. CENTCOM had dedicated most frequency band- width for satellite communications to SOF, given their lead role in the opening months of the campaign. As a result, air controllers had only a single frequency on which to coordinate target bombing close to friendly forces. Needless to say, by the second day of the operation, this single frequency was totally inadequate to control the amount of close air support needed for the operation.[40]

  At the heart of the controversy behind Operation Anaconda, however, lay a seri- ous breakdown in direct communication between the commanding officers and a lack of coordination and cooperation between the services.

- At several points during Operation Iraqi Freedom, from March through May 2003, top combat commanders experienced significant difficulties in sharing information across defense installations and coordinating joint fires operations. For example, on March 27, an unmanned aerial vehicle identified two "time-sensitive targets" and the close air sup- port pilot could not engage due to weather. Then, without informing Coalition Force Land Component Command (CFLCC) to deconflict the airspace, the V Corp artillery commander fired three Army Tactical Missile Systems (ATACMS) and only sub- sequently informed CFLCC. A second incident occurred on April 2, when V Corps devised and then cancelled a mission to suppress Iraqi air defenses using the 1st Battal- ion of the 27th Field Artillery Brigade. But V Corp never coordinated the cancellation with CFLCC headquarters. Consequently, the field artillery unit mistakenly launched five ATACMS, having already set a "time on target" for the missiles.[41] A June 2003 study by the National Defense Industrial Association has since emphasized the need to establish joint fires deconfliction guidelines across the services.[42]

While these incidents help illustrate the disjunction between high-level planning and operations in the field, the lag in realizing true jointness has also been delayed by an overly bureaucratic and procedurally focused process. In a December 2005 e-mail memo to the Joint Staff—subsequently published in *Inside the Navy*—Lieutenant General (Ret.) Paul Van Riper contrasted the development of military doctrine by Admiral Stansfield Turner and Generals Donn Starry and Al Gray during the 1970s and 1980s with the development of joint doctrine today.[43]

> Admiral Turner, and Generals Starry and Gray focused on specific problems. This is not surprising for a truly useful military operating concept only results when there is a need to solve a significant problem or through recognition that an opportunity exists to perform some military function better or in a new way.... For this reason alone, recent claims of a "revolution in military affairs" or a "military transformation" ring hollow since there is little to suggest these movements were undertaken to solve clearly identified military problems. Merely to be "transformational" does not qualify as a specific military problem. Mostly, the names of the movements now serve as a mantra for those advocating advanced technologies . . .

Van Riper argued that the new operating concepts expressed in the 1982 and 1986 editions of Field Manual 100-5, *Operations,* and in a 1989 edition of Fleet Marine Force Field Manual 1, *Warfighting,* fundamentally changed the respective services' approaches to war, but that they did not rely on staffs or task forces. They were the products of a few innovative authors supervised by senior leaders.

> After each service promulgated a manual describing its operating concept, no one perceived a need to produce a vast hierarchy of supporting concepts offering increasing specificity. One document "drove" changes in doctrine, organization, material, and training and education throughout each service. Senior leaders expected combat developers, informed by their understanding of war, to exercise considerable judgment in their duties. They could not anticipate additional and more detailed concepts to justify directly their every programmatic decision.
>
> In contrast, today, we see the creation of an overabundance of joint concepts—a Capstone Concept for Joint Operations, four operating concepts, eight functional concepts, and nine integrating concepts with more reportedly under development. Further, some plans I have seen call for the revision of these documents on a regular two-year cycle . . . Rather than a method to drive change, the joint concepts seem to serve more as a means to slow innovation. Services, agencies, and even individuals claim they need ever-increasing detail before they can proceed with force development.[44]

Technology Centric versus Human Centric

From a programmatic and resource perspective, the new joint forces doctrine also suffered from an overemphasis on technology over personnel. The "downside" of the stunning success of advanced weaponry during the 1991 Gulf War was that it helped lead to an emphasis on the role of technology as the primary driver for achieving joint forces transformation. JV 2010 and JV 2020 focused on the application of command and control technologies as they relate to supporting the four operational concepts. But neither JV 2010 nor JV 2020 created concrete force structures, programs, and resource plans to give U.S. forces the level of information dominance that was the foundation of the "joint vision." Colonel Thomas X. Hammes, USMC, wrote the following about JV 2010:[45]

> A cynic might say that the failure to address the issue of information dominance is a bit like the failure to critique the emperor's new clothes. Everyone knows there is not much there but is reluctant to address the issue. A genuine discussion of "information dominance" requires trying to understand and predict the complicated, increasingly fragmented, all-too-human real world.
>
> Because JV 2010 clearly prefers technology to people, it is a bit awkward to address the fact that information collection against today's threats requires investment in human skills rather than technology. In fact, a serious discussion of achieving information dominance might reveal its implausibility, as evidenced by our lack of understanding of the situation in Iraq and Afghanistan and our inability to come to grips with the worldwide al-Qa'ida network. An honest evaluation of our demonstrated inability to achieve information dominance would invalidate the entire concept of full-spectrum dominance that lies at the heart of JV 2010.

The recommendations in the 2006 QDR to increase language and cultural awareness training and to expand Special Forces did focus on developing the human element behind the technology. But the payoff in the field from investments in these education programs may not materialize for a decade or more, and the FY2007 budget submission still placed much more emphasis on technology than on human factors.

Like other strategic goals, jointness has meaning only in practice. The challenge lies in creating an adaptive, flexible, integrated, and multidimensional fighting force out of an organization built on hierarchy, control, stability, career predictability, and command and service separatism.[46] In practice, implementing joint doctrine remains difficult because the individual services are reluctant to give up their power. The *Defense Science Board 2005 Summer Study on Transformation: A Progress Assessment. Volume I,* released February 2006, discussed these problems in a broad context that provided a critical warning about the need for jointness at every level of force transformation as follows:

- The current approach to concepts development is too cumbersome, takes too long, and requires too much consensus building to be useful in driving the needed change;
- JCIDS, rather than strengthening the influence of joint needs, submerges them in a sea of force provider interests. Capability based planning is not widely understood and is sometimes used to justify the progress in programs that are not meeting even known needs;
- JCD&E [Joint Concept Development and Experimentation] is not informing force development;

- Capability based planning is not widely understood; and
- Resource allocation continues to be dominated by the Force Providers and the Joint Staff.

The Defense Science Board also described the JCIDS, the organization designed to monitor the progress of joint transformation as "so unwieldy as to make it ineffective in its intended purpose of focusing on key challenges faced by the warfighters in integrating and employing joint forces."[47]

THE ARMY'S FORCE TRANSFORMATION

Perhaps because the QDR and Joint Vision documents were so general, much of the detailed planning of U.S. strategy and force plans has taken place at the service level. The U.S. Army has shaped many aspects of its own force transformation to deal with problems of overstretch. Although the Air Force and the Marine Corps have experienced serious stress and Navy carrier and aviator forces have come under pressure, the downsizing of the military after the end of the Cold War left the Army more unprepared for the level of strain placed upon it by the simultaneous wars in Iraq and Afghanistan than the other services. It is the only service that has been so badly underfunded that its Secretary has had to openly fight the budget goals set for it in the program objective memorandum (POM) given it by the Secretary of Defense and Office of Management and Budget (OMB). In 2006, the Secretary of the Army, Dr. Francis J. Harvey, refused to submit a budget based on such goals and forced a rise in the Army FY2007 budget goals.

The Army's Chief of Staff, Lieutenant General Peter J. Schoomaker, reacted to these strains on the Army by ordering force structure changes in August 2003. He created four new brigades that would allow the force to be more capable of enduring extended deployments during multiple combat operations, while also improving deployment speed.

The Army is now seeking to create more brigades and implement major force changes through 2006–2007, completing them by 2009 at the latest. These transformation plans depend heavily on the development of two related concepts of operations: Future Combat Systems and Force Modularity.

- The Future Combat Systems program encompasses a joint transformation and modernization effort across all American military services that focuses on networking weapons and systems to create lighter, more agile, and capable forces. The backbone of FCS consists of 18 manned and unmanned ground vehicles, air vehicles, sensors, and munitions connected by a communications network linked to the soldier. In effect, the goal of FCS is to plug the soldier into a vast information network via various sensors and platforms to provide him access to data and give him a more accurate picture of his surroundings.

- On December 23, 2004, the DoD's Program Budget Decision 753 directed "the Army to submit to the Deputy Secretary of Defense by April 1, 2005, an executable plan that rationalizes and integrates its Future Combat System (FCS) and modularity programs." Thus, in April 2005, the Army formally linked the FCS program with the Army Modular Force Initiative to create a Future Combat Force Strategy that established a framework for the continuous progression of the current modular force into the future one.[48] The Modular Force Initiative program was designed to increase the number and deployability of the Army's combat brigades. The Future Combat Force Strategy simply combines efforts to modernize the force (FCS) with efforts to make the force more flexible (modularity).[49]

General Schoomaker's transformation plan called for the following:[50]

- Reorganizing the forces into modular combat and support brigades, thereby creating more flexible divisions. The divisions would take on a new structure because the modular combat and support brigades will plug into the division in differing ratios and numbers depending on the mission—called plug and play combat power, which is similar to the Marine Corps' expeditionary units. Modularity is costly and will compete with FCS, equipment recapitalization, and increases in end strength in the Army budget.[51]

- Converting 33 medium-sized brigades designed for division-centric, conventional warfare into between 43 and 48 lighter, smaller, independent brigade teams with much more modular structures and less dependence on support infrastructure. The goal is to create 10 more brigades with roughly the same manpower and budget resources that can be deployed for 6 months with 18-month rotation vs. brigades/divisions for 12–15 months with 12-month rotation.

- Standardizing Units of Action or combat brigades according to their weight classification: lightweight, medium, or heavy.

- Increasing the Army is increasing its end strength by 30,000 in order to facilitate the force transformation. This is a temporary buildup, and by 2011 the Army should have eliminated 30,000 other positions.

- Reorganizing the role of 100,000 personnel in active and reserve forces and transferring support unit duties from the Reserves to the active Army.

Key aspects of these plans involved a major reorganization of all Army, Army National Guard, and U.S. Army Reserve forces into modular brigade combat teams. The units were intended to be smaller, more agile and deployable, more lethal, and more self-sustaining—in most instances equipped with artillery and reconnaissance assets previously administered at the division level.

The Army's plan called for manning each modular brigade with one-third fewer subordinate combat units than traditional brigades, while adding additional support units to make the brigades more independently deployable. Because of stresses on the force, Secretary of Defense Donald Rumsfeld temporarily authorized an increase in end strength of 30,000 to meet the transformational requirements of the new modular brigades.

In practice, however, the Army's plans quickly collided with reality and provide a case study in the dangers of gaps among strategy, force plans, programs, and budgets.

As of March 2005, the expected costs of the "modularization" program for FY2005–FY2011 increased by 71 percent to $48 billion from the Army's 2004 estimate of $28 billion. The DoD's request for fiscal year 2005 supplemental funds included $5 billion for modularity.

The Army planned for another $5 billion to be funded from fiscal year 2006 supplemental funds and the remaining $38 billion from DoD's annual appropriation from fiscal years 2006 through 2011. A March 2005 Government Accountability Office (GAO) report cautioned, however, that the costs of modularization might be further revised upward and that the Army's proposed modularization costs did not include all potential costs associated with fully equipping the planned brigades. Nor did the Army's plan account for costs associated with the possibility of increasing the number or changing the design of modular brigades.[52]

Many associated costs remained uncertain. The Army could not fully estimate the facility costs of modularization until the DoD determined its base closures and base repositioning overseas, among other decisions. When the Army tried to update its cost estimates for the program, the GAO reported that it could not fully evaluate the new estimates because the Army did not have detailed supporting information.[53]

A Congressional Budget Office analysis in May 2005 argued that "it appears that the 48-brigade plan would increase the *Army's* combat forces by about 5 percent, whereas the 43-brigade plan would produce almost no change in the amount of combat forces available to the Army. In both the 43- and 48-brigade forces, however, more of the Army's combat power would be concentrated in the active component than is the case today, with the active Army's combat forces increasing by either 19 percent or 32 percent and the National Guard's combat forces decreasing by 19 percent."[54]

Congress did generally support the Army's reorganization plans, but raised questions about both the affordability and the effectiveness of the force plan and about the practicality and affordability of the FCS. One key unanswered question was whether the Army would be able to fill out the deployable brigade structure without a permanent increase in end strength. Another key issue was whether, in the long run, the new Army force design would meet strategic requirements. Among others, retired Army Colonel Douglas A. Macgregor, one of the original champions of a brigade-centered force, argued that the new brigades were not sufficiently well equipped to have the necessary flexibility and that the Army was still preserving too many layers of command.[55]

The previous analysis of the possible need for increases in the Army's end strength shows that the current restructuring of U.S. Army forces may only be the beginning of efforts to transform the Army. Like the other services, the Army is attempting to solve the problem of meeting its future mission needs through the use of advanced technology and new methods of warfighting. It is seeking to transform what some have called the "revolution in military affairs."

The initiatives the Army already has under way to accomplish these goals include the following:

- Seeking to reinvent net-centric warfare to focus on improving its intelligence, surveillance, and reconnaissance capabilities, retaining a heavier legacy force, and creating more human intelligence, military police, and civil-military teams with a higher level of regional and language expertise.

- Development of Future Combat Systems. The focus on "going light" and deploying some 18 major new systems as part of a mix of Future Combat Systems, however, has been deferred for roughly a decade, and funds have been freed up for earlier force transformation in less ambitious areas.

- In May 2005, the Army's 3rd Armored Cavalry Regiment completed months of "innovated training, including a requirement that all officers and soldiers receive basic Arabic language and culture training."[56]

The Army's plans are far more tangible than the vague conceptual goals and priorities of the QDR and Joint Vision documents. At the same time, they raise far more tangible issues about jointness, effectiveness, practicality, and affordability. The moment a plan becomes tangible, it illustrates just how critical it is to ensure that plans really can be implemented, are affordable, and represent the best overall mix of trade-offs to meet all the priorities of national security. It also shows just how dangerous it is to rely on procurement programs and future technology that the United States cannot actually deploy or afford.

THE NAVY AND FORCE TRANSFORMATION

The experiences of the other services in transforming their current forces into the forces the United States needs and can afford have been equally uncertain. The Navy and the Air Force have concentrated on cutting their active combat strength to fund future procurement. However, their track record for estimating their ability to trade current strength for future capability has been one of consistent failure. Both the Navy and the Air Force have repeatedly overestimated the potential benefits of cutting current forces, and neither service has demonstrated a consistent capacity to estimate the level of future capabilities it can afford through cutting current forces.

The Navy has done a dismal job of translating its strategy and force plans into actual practice and has been forced to steadily downsize its forces beyond their planned level ever since 1992. It initially sought to rationalize this process with the publication *From the Sea* (1992), which stated the Navy's intent to shift away from mid-ocean combat to littoral waters combat.[57] The end result helped cut the Navy's fleet strength to 288 hulls—approximately half the number it had during the Cold War. However, the Navy correctly said that some of these cuts have been offset by the increased capabilities of its ships, resulting from wireless networks, digital sensors, and precision munitions.[58]

The Navy issued another version of its transformational goals in October 2002 titled *Sea Power 21*. This document outlined the Navy's transformational goals and the possible means of achieving them through a framework that includes Sea Strike,

Sea Shield, and Sea Basing. The Navy assessed that challenges in the twenty-first century may include the following:

- Improved antiaccess or area-denial capabilities of other forces, preventing the United States from penetrating ports, bases, airfields, and littoral areas;
- Terrorism; and
- Weapons of mass destruction.

The framework set forth in *Sea Power 21* was designed to counter these threats by moving toward net-centric warfare, using unmanned vehicles (UVs), creating more flexible and smaller naval formations, and being capable of operating in littoral areas. *Sea Power 21* consisted of four components:

- Sea Strike offensive operations were designed to be "direct, decisive and sustained." In order to accomplish this goal, the Navy emphasized the use of intelligence, surveillance, reconnaissance, total force networking, time-sensitive strikes, ship-to-object maneuverability, extended range gunfire, unmanned vehicles, and stealthy submarines.[59]
- Sea Shield was intended to move the Navy from its traditional defense duties to aid in homeland defense, including detection of and prevention of the use of weapons of mass destruction (WMD), as well as littoral waters domination, which will facilitate its projection of inland defensive power.
- Sea Basing was intended to help the Navy implement Sea Strike and Sea Shield without relying on allies to provide use of their land bases. Although Sea Basing originally was a concept intended for Navy and Marine Corps operations, the Navy would like to use the bases to support joint operations.
- ForceNet was to be a computer program to integrate a network of soldiers, sensors, command and control, and weapons and platforms in the *Sea Power 21* framework.

The Navy has continued to find new rationales for force transformation. According to the "Global Concept of Operations," issued in 2003, the Navy sought to reorganize its fleet "to support the strategy of forward deterrence and flexibility."[60] Its fleet would be organized into 36 entities or force packages, 12 of which would consist of the Carrier Strike Group (aircraft carrier and supporting ships) and 12 of the Expeditionary Strike Group (amphibious assault vessels with helicopters and Marine combat units, and possibly V-22s and F-35s in the future). The final 12 will consist of surface combatants and converted Trident submarines. Like the Army, these units would be self-contained and modular.[61]

Other "transformational" initiatives include a long series of efforts whose net effect was to try to trade force quantity for force quality by freeing money by reducing existing U.S. forces. These initiatives have led to a steady process of downsizing while still meeting the Navy's steadily declining force goals.

- Sea Swap embodies a rotational crewing concept that will allow ships to be continuously deployed while the ship's crew will rotate out every six months, thereby decreasing operational costs and facilitating the Navy's plan to decrease its end strength.

- A new Fleet Response Plan has been implemented with a new readiness posture designed to improve the Navy's surge capabilities while also lowering costs. According to Gordon R. England, U.S. Deputy Secretary of Defense, the Fleet Response Plan "already [has] altered the employment and make-up of naval forces. Today's 290 ships Navy is much more capable than the more than double the size Navy of the late 1980s. Numbers still matter, but only when carefully balanced with capabilities."[62]

- Chief of Naval Operations Admiral Vern Clark said that the Navy no longer needed 375 ships because "Sea Swap and the Fleet Response Plan have changed our Navy. We have literally bought much more operational availability with these concepts, so we can provide the same kind of combat capability for less than 375 ships."[63]

- According to the Navy's 2005 Future Years Defense Plan, the Navy was to reduce its end strength from 373,197 in FY2004 to 345,3000 in FY2007. Military-to-civilian conversions for non-war-fighting positions are already under way. At the end of FY2005, the Navy had converted 2,000 positions and the Marine Corps had converted 1,700 positions. The conversions will help the Navy to decrease its overall end strength and the Marine Corps to add two more infantry battalions.[64] In addition to transferring civilians into previously held uniformed positions, the procurement of newer ships such as the Littoral Combat Ship (LCS), the DD(X), and the CVN-21, which are designed to have smaller crews than their predecessors, will make the decrease in end strength feasible, according to Gordon England.

- While Secretary of the Navy Gordon England stated, "Our vision is to create one fully integrated Navy Team and the Navy's active reserve integration is the cornerstone of that effort. We are aligning organizations, training together, consolidating resources and assets, and financially planning as one so we can better operate as one team and 'train like we fight.'. . . While the numbers of mobilized reserves can fluctuate as GWOT [global war on terrorism] requirements dictate, our objective is. . .to keep the number of mobilized personnel at a minimum."[65] England also believes that the National Security Personnel System will help the Navy to move civilians into non-war-fighting military positions. As more older ships retire and newer, more efficient and capable ones are introduced, the Navy's military personnel needs will decline.

- A 2002 Tactical Air Integration plan will integrate Marine Corps and Navy tactical aircraft while decreasing the size of the tactical fleet to be purchased by 1,296 but increasing capability.[66]

In taking these steps to move away from its Cold War posture, the Navy focused on acquiring new air and maritime systems that would both allow it to perform new concepts of maritime missions and be a critical component of joint operations. The Navy sought to procure several warships that would transform its capabilities and force structure, including the CVN-21 aircraft carrier, the SSN-774, or Virginia-class, attack submarine, the DD(X) destroyer, and the LCS. While these programs have major ongoing cost escalation and program management problems, the platforms have the following goals:

- The CVN-21 is slated to replace the Nimitz-class carrier. The CVN-21 requires 1,000 fewer soldiers to operate than Nimitz-class carriers, and it is estimated to be four times more effective than carriers used during the First Gulf War in 1991. The CVN-21 will also bring naval aviation into a networked environment.[67]

- The SSN-774 Virginia-class attack submarine is designed to maintain sea control, support expeditionary warfare missions, and collect intelligence. The submarines, along with Sea Basing, will aid the United States in maintaining a global presence despite the possibility of decreased access to foreign bases in the future.

- The Littoral Combat Ship was designed to provide access to littoral (near-shore) areas. The LCS will have modular, "plug-and-fight" mission payload packages that can be adapted to its one hull design to meet the needs of various missions.

According to the Navy, these more technologically advanced ships have the long-run potential to save money because they will theoretically drive down the Navy's personnel requirements that contribute to the high cost of maintaining a large personnel force, *if* the procurement costs can be properly managed, *if* each system has the hoped-for effectiveness, *if* the programs can be deployed on time, and *if* future needs conform to current predictions. These prospects are not good and are not getting better. In mid-January 2007, the cost of the third LCS had escalated to $316 million versus $260 million for the second ship, and the Navy was forced to issue a stop work order.[68]

The Navy has also sought to acquire several aircraft designed to be important components of its transformation. These include the F-35 Joint Strike Fighter, the F/A-18 Super Hornet, and the V-22 Osprey. Unfortunately, the one thing all these programs have in common is that they are in deep trouble. The Navy's plans depend on impractical major weapons programs, procurement rates that cannot be achieved, and force improvements that are undercosted to the point of unaffordability. Like the other services, the Navy has been "stretched" far more by its own planning failures than by the burden of ongoing military operations like the Iraq War.

THE MARINE CORPS AND FORCE TRANSFORMATION

The U.S. Marine Corps' (USMC) plans for force transformation have sought both to meet the Corps' future needs and to complement the Navy's vision in *Sea Power 21* (2002) and the joint forces' vision in *Joint Vision 2020* (2000) to ensure that the United States has sufficient expeditionary forces to carry out the full spectrum of roles, missions, and tasks in the new century.

The practical result, however, has been to try to preserve the Marine Corps active and reserve strength while modernizing its equipment. In general, the Corps has also tried to keep its ties to seapower at a time events have steadily pushed it into land operations in Iraq, and joint operations that are scarcely "from the sea." It also has chosen to sacrifice modernization and equipment upgrades for maintaining force strength almost regardless of the content of its strategic plans.

Marine Corps Strategy 21 (2000) set forth how the Marines intended to respond to the challenges of the global century. This document and *Expeditionary Maneuver Warfare* (EMW) lay at the heart of the Marine Corps' force transformation plans.[69] EMW (2001) provided the foundation for twenty-first-century peacetime forward deployments, responses to crises worldwide, and warfighting to protect U.S. citizens, allies, and interests wherever and whenever they may be at risk.

It incorporated two previously published operational concepts, including 1996's *Operational Maneuver from the Sea* (OMFTS) and 1997's *Ship to Objective Maneuver* (STOM). The concepts in EMW focused on the following:[70]

- *Joint enabling,* or the ability to use Marine forces to serve as a lead element of a joint task force, act as joint enablers, or serve as a maneuver element to exploit success.

- *Strategic agility,* or the ability to transition rapidly from precrisis readiness to full combat capability while deployed in a distant theater.

- *Operational reach,* or the ability to project and sustain relevant and effective power across the depth of a battle space.

- *Tactical flexibility,* or the capability to conduct a range of dissimilar missions concurrently, in support of a joint team across the entire spectrum of conflict.

EMW made the Marine Expeditionary Unit (MEU), composed of 2,000 troops, the basic force component. The USMC resurrected Marine Expeditionary Brigades (MEB) in 1999—they had been disbanded in budget cuts after the Gulf War—to improve the ability of Marine forces to deploy quickly with increased firepower. MEBs, which range in size from 4,000 to 20,000 troops, are to be medium-weight fighting forces that include infantry, armored vehicles, and aircraft. They are smaller than MEUs, which have 50,000 or more personnel.[71]

The most dramatic development in Marine Corps strategy, however, came with *Operational Maneuver from the Sea* (1996) and the Navy's sea-basing platform. OMFTS applies maneuver warfare to expeditionary power projection and relies extensively on the tightly integrated capabilities of the Navy-Marine Corps team. In effect, OMFTS described the integration of the Navy's visionary sea-basing facilities with a Marine air-ground task force (MAGTF).

The sea-basing concept sought to eliminate the need for the slow buildup and protection of a traditional beachhead. Rather, sea basing would allow the MAGTF to exploit the sea as a maneuver space while applying combat power ashore, even well inland, without the need to secure enemy territory or get permission from a neighboring country to build a base of operations. OMFTS affords increased operational flexibility, greater force protection, and enhanced capabilities via sea-based logistics and command and control. The success of OMFTS relied on the deliberate design and integration of Navy and Marine capabilities.[72]

The combined future of what the Corps called Expeditionary Maneuver Warfare, Operational Maneuver from the Sea, and Ship to Objective Maneuver came to depend on the development and integration of the following various concepts and platforms:

- Network Centric Warfare (NCW)—also called FORCEnet—is a central element in the integration of Navy and Marine Corps capabilities that will fundamentally transform joint warfighting. NCW aims to overwhelm an adversary by rapidly disseminating critical information to U.S. combatants, allowing them to make accurate decisions before the enemy. The concept relies on connecting future platforms—such as the DD(X) destroyer, the F-35, the V-22, littoral combat ships, Virginia-class submarines, and amphibious assault ships—via a wide array of electronic networks, sensors, decision aids, and supporting systems designed to help warfighters achieve battle-space dominance.[73]

- An important component of STOM, Distributed Operations (DO) encompasses a new training and operations concept that gives small, distant Marine units more autonomy to operate deep inland. It is designed to create more independent and flexible units that can better fight as smaller, squad-sized units. To this end, DO decentralizes the battalion command structure by pushing decision making down to platoon and squad commanders. This new command structure allows platoons to fight and operate farther away from the battalion and company hub, though still linked to those commands via radio and long-range communications systems. Employing DO will require new investments in (1) communications and intelligence-gathering equipment, (2) logistics systems to support units far from headquarters, (3) lightweight body armor and adaptive camouflage, and (4) vehicles to transport units over a large battlefield.[74]

- The Marine Corps also intends to adopt the Navy's sea swap concept. Marines (or sailors) would no longer deploy and return home with the same ship. Instead, Marine expeditionary forces (MEFs) would rotate on and off forward-deployed ships every six months. In between deployments, MEFs would train in the United States.

As is the case with the other services, however, implementing these concepts and platforms depended heavily on high-cost transformational advances in technology. Several platforms were developed to support these transformation concepts, all of which have come to present major problems in terms of cost, effectiveness, and time of availability:

- The Heavy Lift Replacement (HLR) Program became a critical element of EMW and sea basing. The Corps concluded that neither joint operating concept could fully enable according to transformation plans without the heavy-lift capabilities of the HLR. The HLR development effort will replace the aging fleet of the current Marine Corps heavy-lift aviation platform, the CH-53E "Super Stallion" first fielded in 1981. The CH-53E is not suitable for future operational concepts such as sea basing and STOM. The Marine Corps must develop a more capable, survivable, and affordable platform to keep Fleet Maritime Forces effective through the 2025 time frame.[75] An independent *USMC Vertical Heavy-Lift Mission Analysis of Alternatives* determined that a new-build, CH-53 derivative helicopter—with improved survivability and force protection, expanded range and payload performance, improved cargo handling and turn-around capabilities, and lower Operations and Support costs—would be the best HLR solution.[76]

- The MV-22 Osprey—a tiltrotor, vertical takeoff and landing aircraft—was intended to provide the requisite medium lift expeditionary needs of the Marine Corps to engage in EMW operations. Designed to replace the aging CH-46E Sea Knight and CH-53D platforms, the MV-22 addresses the force planning concepts of OMFTS and STOM by allowing Marines to strike from greater distances and to penetrate deeper into enemy territory. The MV-22 adds new capabilities in speed, range, and endurance to the Marine Corps assault support fleet. The most significant advantage offered by the MV-22 is the ability to rapidly self-deploy worldwide and arrive with Marines who are ready to fight.[77]

- The Expeditionary Fighting Vehicle (EFV), also known as the Advanced Amphibious Assault Vehicle, became another central component of EMW—OMFTS and STOM—warfighting concepts. The USMC's only acquisition category I acquisition program is a self-deploying, high-water-speed (23–29 mph), armored amphibious vehicle capable of seamlessly transporting Marines from Naval ships located beyond the visual horizon (25 miles or more offshore) to inland objectives. This increased range would reduce the risk to Navy ships from missiles, aircraft, boats, and mines. Once ashore, the EFV will maneuver with an agility and mobility equivalent, at least, to an M1 Abrams tank. The EFV will replace the current Assault Amphibian Vehicle, which was originally fielded in 1972 and will be more than 35 years old when the EFV begins production in 2008. The Marine Corps plans to procure 1,013 EFVs.[78]

- The new LPD-17 San Antonio class of amphibious landing transport docks was planned to replace four classes of amphibious ships—the LPD 4, the LSD 36, the LKA 113, and the LST 1179—and incorporates both a flight deck and a well deck to support the debarkation of landing craft. The LPD-17 class of ships was designed to transport the Marine Corps' "mobility triad" of EFVs, air-cushioned landing craft, and MV-22s to trouble spots around the world.

- The Joint Strike Fighter (JSF) was planned to enter service with the Marine Corps in 2010. An essential feature of the Marine Corps combined arms operations, the JSF provides the reach, flexibility, and reliability called for in EMW. It will replace both the F/A-18C/D and the AV-8B and will affirm the Marine Corps' goal of limiting its force of attack aircraft to a single model to reduce support requirements and costs. For the Marines, this short takeoff and vertical landing aircraft is particularly appealing for its ability to operate from the decks of amphibious ships, austere sites, and forward operating bases. The JSF's primary mission will be close air support, interdiction, and antiair warfare.[79]

At the same time, events have pushed the USMC into a wide range of missions that involve joint operations on land and which make it a broad power projection asset whose role extends far beyond its ties to the Navy and seapower. The Marine Corps has played a major role in every aspect of the land fighting in Iraq, in part because the U.S. Army is simply too small for the United States not to draw on all of its land force capabilities.

It has also been involved in many additional and more detailed efforts to transform its forces. For example, Marines have begun taking over the training of foreign militaries to help reduce the demands placed on the Army's Special Forces. Part of the 4th Marine Expeditionary Brigade (antiterrorism), the Foreign Military Training

Unit (FMTU), provided tailored basic-military-combat-skills training and advisor support for identified foreign military forces in order to enhance the tactical capability of coalition forces in support of SOCOM. The goal in improving the training of friendly foreign troops would pay dividends by reducing the need for U.S. military involvement.

As Colonel Peter Petronzio, commanding officer of the FMTU, said, "The FMTU is critical because we want to operate in 'phase zero,' Global War on Terrorism–relevant countries. We want to be ahead of the power curve on the GWOT. If you can send a small group of Marines into a country to help stabilize its ungoverned areas to train them to do for themselves early and often, then you preclude the need five or 10 years down the road to have an expeditionary force go and straighten the situation out."[80]

THE AIR FORCE AND FORCE TRANSFORMATION

The U.S. Air Force has actively transformed many aspects of its forces as it has downsized. It has converted its force to highly sophisticated concepts of net-centric warfare and precision-strike operations. In the process it has developed a number of formal concepts for force transformation, but its practice has often been driven largely by budget problems and its decision to fund the procurement of high-cost, high-technology platforms at the cost of total force strength, end strength, and numbers of aircraft and major weapons platforms. Like the Navy, strategy and force plans have consistently been subordinated to fiscal considerations and future procurement programs.

In its Transformation Flight Plan (AFTFP), first published in 2003 and updated in 2004, the Air Force defined transformation as "[a] process by which the military achieves and maintains asymmetric advantage through changes in operational concepts, organizational structure, and/or technologies that significantly improve war-fighting capabilities or ability to meet the demands of a changing security environment."[81] The document described the Air Force's transformation process as an effort to create an effects-based, capabilities-focused expeditionary air and space force.

Rather than employing a Cold War–style, bottom-up, threat-based approach to force planning that focuses on who an adversary may be or where a war may occur, the Air Force sought to achieve the desired military effects against a range of enemies on a variety of battlefields. In a statement "Regarding Air Force Transformation" before the House Committee on Armed Services Subcommittee on Terrorism, Unconventional Threats and Capabilities, Lieutenant General Duncan J. McNabb, the Deputy Chief of Staff for Air Force Plans and Programs, said,[82]

In the past, we improved our capabilities program by program and platform by platform, focusing development efforts on making each individual system go higher, faster, farther, etc. with little consideration of how it would integrate with other capabilities in the Air Force, in other Services, or in allied militaries. We had to turn this around. Now we look at our National Strategy and determine the effects the Air Force must create. We next determine what capabilities we need. Only then do we talk about what platforms, or combination of platforms/systems, we need to provide these capabilities.

As part of the 2003 AFTFP, the Air Force developed Air Force Concepts of Operations (CONOPS) to put effects-based force planning into practice. The CONOPS focused on the effects the military planners would like to produce and on the capabilities the planners need to maintain or develop before they consider what expeditionary platforms are required. The Air Force sought to develop the following six initial CONOPS task forces:

- The Global Strike Task Force developed the Air Force's offensive capabilities—i.e., stealth technology, standoff weaponry, precision, space, and information systems—to defeat enemy defenses and to guarantee that following forces are free to attack and free from enemy attack.

- The Global Mobility Task Force called for the Air Force to provide global mobility, bare basing, and base defense support for combatant commanders in a wide variety of roles ranging from humanitarian aid to evacuation operations.

- The Homeland Security Task Force developed and integrated Air Force capabilities into joint and interagency efforts to prevent, protect against, and respond to a variety of threats against America, including enemy aircraft, ballistic missiles, asymmetric terrorist operations, and cyberterrorism.

- The Global Response Task Force was specifically designed to counter and defeat terrorist targets at immediate risk of attacks. It links intelligence information with alert strike platforms in selected locations so that the platforms can launch and receive updates en route, facilitating rapid, informed responses to fleeting or opportunistic targets.

- The Nuclear Response Task Force comprised the Air Force's contribution to deterring all types of weapons of mass destruction against U.S. or allied forces and works to integrate conventional and nuclear capabilities to provide commanders a full spectrum of responses to counter aggression. Furthermore, the CONOPS made a goal of reducing the number of operationally deployed strategic nuclear weapons to the 1,700–2,200 range.

- The Space and C^{4}ISR (command, control, communications, computers, intelligence, surveillance, and reconnaissance) Task Force integrated manned, unmanned, and space systems to provide commanders with accurate, near real-time intelligence information.[83]

The Transformation Flight Plan also described the expansion of America's space-based military systems as integral to the success of near- and long-term force transformation programs. The Air and Space Expeditionary Force (AEF)—using systems ranging from satellites to advanced weapons systems—sought to transform the Air Force into a capabilities-based force based primarily in the United States that would remain sufficiently flexible to conduct a wide range of operations throughout the world while accommodating the rapid deployment requirements of today's contingency environment.

Moreover, the AEF's capabilities were to support combat soldiers on the ground and to protect the United States from chemical, biological, radiological, nuclear, and high-explosive attacks. All military space programs were to combine the following three capabilities: protect space assets, deny adversaries access to space, and quickly launch vehicles and operate payloads into space to quickly replace space assets that fail or are damaged/destroyed.

In the process, the roster of Air Force space programs—as described originally in the 2003 AFTFP, but not mentioned specifically or ruled out in the 2004 AFTFP —became increasingly futuristic and ambitious.[84]

- The Air-Launched Anti-Satellite Missile, a small, air-launched missile capable of intercepting satellites in low Earth orbit and slated as a development beyond 2015;

- The Counter Satellite Communications System to provide the capability by 2010 to deny and disrupt an adversary's space-based communications and early warning system;

- The Counter Surveillance and Reconnaissance System, a near-term program designed to deny, disrupt, and degrade an adversary's space-based surveillance and reconnaissance systems.

- The Evolutionary Air and Space Global Laser Engagement Airship Relay Mirrors, designed to significantly extend the range of both the Airborne Laser and the Ground-Based Laser by using airborne, ground-based, or space-based lasers in conjunction with space-based relay mirrors to project different laser powers and frequencies to achieve a broad range of effects from illumination to destruction.

- Ground-Based Laser technology to propagate a laser beam through the atmosphere to low orbit satellites to provide robust, post-2015 defensive and offensive space control capability.

- Hypervelocity Rod Bundles to provide the capability to strike ground targets anywhere in the world from space.

- The Orbital Deep Space Imager, a midterm (2010–2015) predictive, near real-time common operating picture of space to enable space control operations.

- The Orbital Transfer Vehicle to add post-2015 flexibility and protection of U.S. space hardware and enables on-orbit servicing of those assets.

- The Rapid Attack Identification Detection and Reporting System encompassed a family of systems that provide near-term capability to determine when a space system is under attack.

- The Space-Based Radio-Frequency Energy Weapon, a post-2015 constellation of satellites containing high-power radio-frequency transmitters that possess the capability to disrupt/destroy/disable a wide variety of electronics and national level command and control systems. That is, it would be used as a nonkinetic, antisatellite weapon.

- The Space-Based Space Surveillance System, a near-term constellation of optical sensing satellites to track and identify space forces in deep space to enable offensive and defensive counterspace operations.

The 2004 AFTFP did not mention these space systems specifically. However, the spirit of the 2004 document was the same as that of the 2003 document. In fact, the 2004 AFTFP stated that it "does not represent new policy guidance or propose what the Air Force should do, but is instead intended to reflect decisions, information, and initiatives already made and/or approved by the Air Force capability-based planning, programming and budgeting process."[85]

The Air Force also pursued new technologies to provide a tactical and operational advantage to dominate air, space, and cyberspace. These programs have all developed serious cost and effectiveness issues. Like the other services and their pet programs, the Air Force considers these new technologies to be central to its ongoing transformation efforts.[86] They include the following:

- The development of high performance stealth aircraft, such as the F/A-22 and the Joint Strike Fighter, to define the Air Force's vision for the future of the world's most affordable, lethal, supportable, and survivable assault aircraft.

- The J-UCAS program—a joint DARPA-Air Force-Navy consortium formed in 2003—to develop unmanned combat aerial vehicles (UCAVs). This joint demonstration program was designed to demonstrate the technical feasibility, operational utility, and operation value of a networked system of high-performance UCAVs to effectively and affordably prosecute twenty-first-century combat missions. The key capabilities of UCAVs currently in development will include Suppression of Enemy Air Defenses, electronic attack, precision strike, surveillance/reconnaissance, and persistent global attack within the emerging global command and control architecture. The system focuses on combat situations and environments that involve deep, denied enemy territory and the requirement for a survivable, persisting combat presence.[87] As of June 2005, the Air Force had 750 UAVs.[88]

- The Advanced Close Air Support System (ACASS) to comprise the Air Force's and the Army's primary joint, network-centric platform for facilitating communication between air and ground forces. Technological advances now allow for the quick generation of accurate geospatial targeting coordinates on the ground and their transfer to strike aircraft waiting above.[89] UAVs also employ ACASS technology to provide streaming video to terrestrial maneuver commanders.

- Directed-energy weapons, nonprojectile weapons that employ directed energy—usually in the form of electromagnetic radiation or particle beams—to damage, interfere with, or otherwise disable enemy equipment, facilities, or personnel. The Air Force's airborne laser program is a plan to mount a chemical oxygen iodine laser on a modified Boeing 747-400F and use it to shoot down ballistic missiles during their boost phase.

The following chapters show just how much such Air Force strategies and plans for force transformation have been blocked by massive problems in cost escalation, delays in planned force modernization, and fiscally driven cuts in force goals. The Air Force has, however, proposed many less ambitious programs to achieve transformational effects.

The Air Combat Command approved the acquisition strategy for smaller, more accurate munitions on January 6, 1998. The Small Diameter Bomb (SDB) program (formerly known as the Miniaturized Munitions Capability Program) addressed two major problems with current munitions. First, stealth aircraft like the F-117, the B-2, the F-22, and the JSF have relatively limited space for weapons if they are flown in a stealthy configuration with their weapons carried internally. The size of current munitions forced pilots to fly more missions to achieve the same battlefield effect. Second, current munitions were often not suitable for destroying specific targets in populated areas with minimal collateral damage—e.g., U.S. attacks on Belgrade during the 1999 NATO-Yugoslavia conflict.

The SDB offered a solution to both problems. At 250 pounds, the SDB was half the weight of the smallest bomb the Air Force uses today (the 500-pound Mark 82), but the SDB has the same penetration capabilities as the 2,000-pound BLU-109. Coupled with either inertial navigation system (INS)/global positioning system (GPS) guidance technology or terminal seeking and automatic target recognition capabilities, the SDB was suitable for either stationary, fixed, or mobile, relocatable targets. The Air Force successfully deployed the SDB in 2006 and made extensive use of the system in both Afghanistan and Iraq.[90]

Another example of the less ambitious and costly transformational programs was advanced C^4I processing, technologies to provide a communicable understanding —a single integrated air picture—of what is going on in a broad geographical area. Commanders use C^4I technologies to convert an understanding of a battle space into missions and assignments designed to affect that battle space.

THE NEED TO TRANSFORM TRANSFORMATION

This examination of U.S. failures in meeting the challenges of force transformation does not reveal fatal defects or some imminent crisis. Chapter 1 showed that the United States has been more successful in adopting new tactics and technologies for conventional warfighting than any other power in the world. For all of their critical defects, the Quadrennial Defense Reviews have made progress in dealing with many of the issues raised by the end of the Cold War, the Iraq War, the War on Terrorism, peacemaking, and homeland defense.

The Joint Staff has failed to provide effective strategic plans and to couple them to force plans, programs, and budgets, but the Joint Vision documents have at least made some progress toward truly integrating the capabilities of the U.S. services. The strategic and force planning documents of the individual services have also made progress in transforming the total force, even if they have failed to achieve true jointness, and helped to create critical problems in realistic force planning, and in matching plans with resources in the process.

It is all too clear, however, that the United States can salvage its overall national security posture only if it can transform the process of transformation. This is partly the need to focus force transformation far more on the grand strategic, counterinsurgency, asymmetric warfare, stability operations, national building, and conflict termination issues described in previous chapters. It is partly a result of the need to tie

Department of Defense efforts to joint interagency operations, and the better use of diplomacy and alliances that is described in the chapters that follow.

Above all, however, the preceding problems in the history of post–Cold War force transformation efforts makes it clear that the United States must transform one critical aspect of its approach to force transformation as quickly as possible. It is brutally clear that strategy and planning documents that are not integrated with force planning and long-term budgets become hollow wish lists or—at a minimum—more of a problem than part of the solution.

It is sometimes argued that planning to meet resource constraints inhibits strategic innovation and the effort to determine what resources are really needed. The reality is that anyone can express broad strategic concepts and ask for more than they can get. The Department of Defense currently wastes tens of thousands of man hours on a process that at best can be described as a "triumph of hope over experience."

As the following chapter makes even clearer, however, meaningful strategy and planning requires explicit decisions about the size and character of forces and programs. It requires explicit identification of major problems and hard, explicit decisions about the necessary trade-offs to make programs realistic and affordable. By this standard, far too many recent U.S. efforts at formulating strategy and force transformation have become symbols of a process of continuing failure—planning by hope and a wish list and an abdication of the fundamental responsibilities of leadership and management.

Challenge Six: Dealing with the Legacy of Cold War Transformation Programs and Past Efforts at Force Transformation That Are Fundamentally Unaffordable

If ideology and the arrogance of power are no substitutes for strategy, neither are massive cost escalation and miserable program management substitutes for planning and management. No single challenge to U.S. security is more urgent than the inability of the Department of Defense (DoD) to create affordable procurement programs, to plan and manage these programs efficiently, and to implement them in ways that support effective force transformation. The failure to meet this challenge is the most serious form of "overstretch" within the Department's control. The DoD's procurement plans and goals have been well intentioned, but the reality has often been an awkward mix of delays, massive cost escalation, failing to foresee real-world future requirements, and unfulfilled promises of effectiveness.

These problems will almost certainly grow worse in the near future. The DoD is deferring and ignoring many of the costs of the Iraq War and faces serious, unfunded out-year costs in terms of massive backlogs in repairs and maintenance, paying for the replacement of worn-out equipment on an accelerated schedule, and dealing with the impact of deferred training. The same is true of the cost of deferred facilities, including military housing and social services.

In short, the problems raised by Iraq have so far been far less serious than the need to deal with cost containment in terms of both the sharply rising personnel costs of its all-professional military and the Department of Defense's failure to effectively manage virtually all of its key procurement problems—including virtually every program in every service that is necessary for effective force transformation.

FORCE DEATH BY MAJOR PROGRAM

The U.S. focus on new weapons and technology as key aspects of force transformation has so far created as many problems as solutions. The very real advantages of technology and modernization threaten to be lost by trying to implement procurement programs that have become a cost escalation nightmare. They are programs so costly that they have led to an ongoing series of cuts both in the U.S. active force and in the numbers of new systems to be procured. They can be financed—even on paper —only by cutting the funds for technology in the out-years as well as limiting other key expenditures like operations and maintenance costs and manpower.

The scale of the budget pressures involved is highlighted in Figure 7.1. The DoD has made cut after cut in the scale of its major procurement efforts or pushed actual

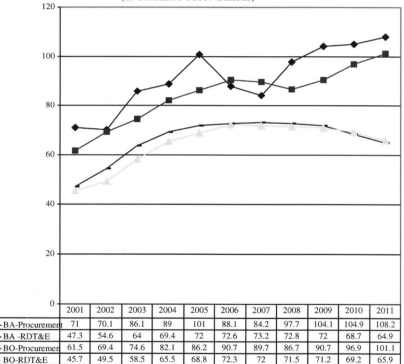

(In Constant FY2007 Billions)

	2001	2002	2003	2004	2005	2006	2007	2008	2009	2010	2011
BA-Procurement	71	70.1	86.1	89	101	88.1	84.2	97.7	104.1	104.9	108.2
BA -RDT&E	47.3	54.6	64	69.4	72	72.6	73.2	72.8	72	68.7	64.9
BO-Procurement	61.5	69.4	74.6	82.1	86.2	90.7	89.7	86.7	90.7	96.9	101.1
BO-RDT&E	45.7	49.5	58.5	65.5	68.8	72.3	72	71.5	71.2	69.2	65.9

Source: FY2007 Green Book: 115 and 133. For a CBO estimate of the cost needs in individual area of defense procurement activity, see "The Long-Term Implications of Current Defense Plans and Alternatives: Summary Update for Fiscal Year 2007." Congressional Budget Office, October 2006.

Figure 7.1 Dancing to the Right: Projected Defense Procurement and RDT&E Expenditures, FY2001–FY2011

procurements into the out-years by "dancing to the right," deferring spending to future years and to future governments.

- Procurement spending increased by 22 percent in Budget Authority from FY2007 to FY2011, appearing to fund major programs, but only by 12 percent in Budget Outlays. Instead of taking hard decisions, the Quadrennial Defense Review (QDR) and Future Year Defense Program (FYDP) stretch out and maintain unaffordable programs, minimize their impact on measures of the balanced budget, and stick President George W. Bush's successor with the burden of either taking hard decisions or a funding nightmare.

- The technology base is underfunded, and not because it is really hard to predict the cost of future programs. The FYDP increases research, development, test, and evaluation (RDT&E) funding by 28 percent between fiscal year 2005 (FY2005) and FY2009, from $144 billion to $185 billion. It then mysteriously drops by 10 percent between FY2009 and FY2011—evidently to allow a shift of funds into procurement.

There is nothing new about the DoD's failure to execute proper program management and to enforce the development of programs the Department can actually produce, make properly effective, and afford. The DoD has been a growing management disaster for decades. Program after program has died in the process. "Success" has meant paying for massive cost escalation, slipping plans years beyond their planned dates, making major cuts in the numbers procured, keeping existing equipment for years to decades beyond the planned retirement decade, and taking additional years and billions of dollars to modify and fix new systems once they enter service.

The problem is that throwing time and money at management failures is no longer affordable, particularly when technology has become the putative solution to force transformation. A March 2005 study by the Government Accountability Office (GAO) was particularly critical of such trends in DoD acquisition programs. The report stated,[1]

> Although U.S. weapons are the best in the world, the programs to acquire them often take significantly longer and cost significantly more money than promised and often deliver fewer quantities and other capabilities than planned. It is not unusual for estimates of time and money to be off by 20 to 50 percent.

The GAO's March 2006 report titled "Assessments of Selected Major Weapons Programs" showed that just five years ago, the top five weapon systems were projected to cost about $291 billion combined. As of March 2006, in the same base year dollars, the top five weapon systems were projected to cost about $550 billion.

The GAO report also found that the DoD had doubled its planned investments in new weapon systems from about $700 billion in 2001 to nearly $1.4 trillion in 2006. Figures 7.2 and 7.3 show just how serious and unaffordable this escalation has become for most of the Department's key programs.

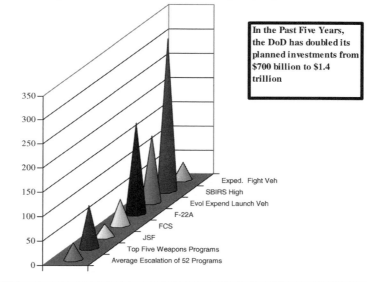

(Measured as Percent Rise in Unit Cost by Program)

In the Past Five Years, the DoD has doubled its planned investments from $700 billion to $1.4 trillion

▣ Average Escalation of 52 Programs	35
■ Top Five Weapons Programs	
▢ JSF	
▢ FCS	
■ F-22A	
▣ Evol Expend Launch Veh	
■ SBIRS High	
▢ Exped. Fight Veh	

Source: Government Accountability Office, "Defense Acquisitions: Assessments of Selected Weapons Systems," GAO-06-391, March 2006.

Figure 7.2   Procuring Defense to Death: The Wonderful World of "Transformational" Cost Escalation, 2001–2005

If one looks in more detail at the problems that have created the cost escalation shown in Figures 7.2 and 7.3, the GAO has projected that RDT&E costs will rise from $147 billion in FY2006 to $178 billion in FY2011, an increase of 21 percent. According to the GAO, maximizing the returns from this investment has proved challenging for the following three reasons:[2]

• The DoD's investment in weapon systems comprises one of the largest discretionary items in the federal budget, so the DoD's budget faces mounting pressure from increases in mandatory federal spending, such as social security, Medicare, and Medicaid. The GAO anticipated that (1) federal deficits will average $250 billion through 2009, (2) budgetary demands stemming from demographic trends will extend beyond that timeline, and (3) discretionary spending will decrease to 33 percent from

(Percent in Constant FY2006 Dollars)

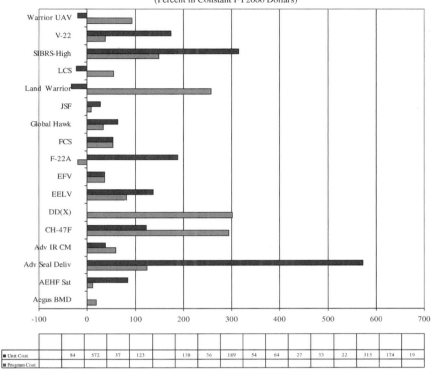

■ Unit Cost		84	572	37	123		138	36	189	54	64	27	33	22	315	174	19
■ Program Cost															

Source: Authors' compilation based on the President's FY2007 budget request, CBO analysis of budget and economic outlook for FY2007-FY2016, and primarily on the range of extrapolations in Congressional Budget Office, and The Long Term Budget Outlook, December 2005. For additional analysis, see US Government Accountability Office, "21st Century Challenges: Reexamining the Base of the Federal Government," GAO-05-325SP, February 2005.

Figure 7.3   Short-Term (2001 or Later) Cost Escalation as of July 2005

39 percent of the federal budget by 2009. As such, the DoD will find it increasingly difficult to increase its budget share to cover cost increases in weapon programs.

- The DoD faces competing demands within its own budget from, among other things, operations in Afghanistan and Iraq. The DoD has required $158 billion in supplemental appropriations to support the global war on terrorism since September 2001. Moreover, ongoing military operations cause faster wear on existing weapons, which will need refurbishment and replacement sooner than planned. All of these budget implications increase the demand on the defense dollar and, therefore, on investment in new weapons programs.

- DoD programs typically take longer to develop and cost more to buy than planned, placing additional demands on available funding. Weapons programs must compete for resources and are often forced to make trade-offs in quantities, resulting in a reduction in buying power. Consequently, funds are not available for competing needs, and programs yield fewer quantities for the same, if not higher cost.

Figure 7.4   Examples of Key Program Management Failures

Program	Initial Investment	Initial Quantity	Latest Investment	Latest Quantity	Percent Unit Cost Increase	Percent Quantity Decrease
Joint Strike Fighter	$189.8 billion	2,866 aircraft	$206.3 billion	2,458 aircraft	26.7	14.2
Future Combat Systems	$82.6 billion	15 systems	$127.5 billion	15 systems	54.4	0
F-22A Raptor	$81.1 billion	648 aircraft	$65.4 billion	181 aircraft	188.7	72.1
Evolved Expendable Launch Vehicle	$15.4 billion	181 vehicles	$28.0 billion	138 vehicles	137.8	23.8
Space Based Infrared System High	$4.1 billion	5 satellites	$10.2 billion	3 satellites	315.4	40
Expeditionary Fighting Vehicle	$8.1 billion	1,025 vehicles	$11.1 billion	1,025 vehicles	35.9	0

Source: Adapted from "Defense Acquisitions: Assessments of Selected Major Weapons Programs," Government Accountability Office Report to Congressional Committees, March 31, 2006, p. 8. Note that the "Latest Investment" and the "Latest Quantity" do not necessarily reflect the latest projections of the total program costs or the total program's procurement quantities.

Figure 7.4, adapted from the 2006 GAO report, illustrates how six critical procurement programs have led to major cuts in planned numbers and inevitably to future U.S. force strength. The GAO's recent assessments have also shown that the majority of weapons programs cost far more and take far longer to develop than initially forecast. Total RDT&E costs for 26 common set weapons programs increased by nearly $44.6 billion, a 37-percent increase over their initial estimates.

The same programs also experienced an increase in the time needed to develop capabilities; the weighted average schedule increase for these programs was nearly 17 percent.[3] The GAO found that critical cost, performance, and delivery schedule problems have mortgaged the force transformation plans of every service and threaten the ability of force transformation to deal with its problems of overstretch.

THE ARMY'S COST-ESCALATION AND PROGRAM MANAGEMENT CHALLENGES

Each of the services faces major problems in transforming its procurement efforts into actual force transformation. In the wake of the wars in Iraq and Afghanistan, the Army has been stretched especially thin. This has led the Army to push for significant increases in investment, to claim it has borne more than its fair share of costs for these conflicts compared with the other services, and to complain that its share of the defense budget has not changed substantially since the invasion of Iraq in 2003.

Without citing specific figures, Army Chief of Staff General Peter J. Schoomaker lobbied hard during 2006 for substantial increases in the Army's budget over the next several years to help finance ongoing operations and to pay for reset costs. However, a large portion of the money the Army sought was not tied to the wars in Iraq and Afghanistan, or the kinds of force transformation that seemed to be emerging from these wars.[4] Instead, the Army sought the money for new weapons, particularly the Future Combat System (FCS) that has become a symbol of the DoD's chronic inability to control procurement costs while still meeting transformation goals.

The Army has had to slow down its near-term funding requests for the FCS because of the need to fund wartime needs, but largely because of major problems in developing concrete procurement plans and finding credible technological solutions to creating a family of light combat vehicles that can meet the Army's steadily evolving requirements for improved protection and firepower.

The end result, however, is to slip the Army's procurement problems into future years, not solving them. A CBO study in late 2006 noted that some of the funding for the FCS program had been slipped two years into the future in the FY2007 budget request, but that the Army planned to buy 1.5 brigades worth of FCS equipment a year beginning in 2015, at a cost of $8 billion to $10 billion—consuming about 90 percent of the funds for ground combat vehicles.

It also found that the Department of Defense's overall investment program for the Army lacked credible programming and budgeting. The Department projected that Army annual average investment spending would decline during FY2007–FY2011 from $30 billion to $29 billion, and total procurement spending would drop from $107 billion in FY2006 to an average of $100 billion a year. This funding level was literally incredible because it made a grossly inadequate allowance for the cost of compensating for wartime losses in Iraq and Afghanistan and for "reset."

The CBO also found that the Department's plans to fund Army investment after 2011, when the major burden of FCS costs would become critical, costed investment at an average of $36 billion a year in FY2007 dollars, but that a reasonable estimate of cost risk based on past spending and cost escalation put the figure at $43 billion a year through 2024—some 20 percent higher.[5]

Future Combat Systems Program Costs

The U.S. Army's Future Combat System is both the Army's key platform for force transformation and its most expensive acquisition project. The program is an ambitious effort to develop a suite of new manned and unmanned ground and air vehicles, sensors, and munitions linked by a new information network that will revolutionize warfighting. The Army has called the FCS "the greatest technology and integration challenge the Army has ever undertaken" and considers the platform key to creating a lighter, more agile, and more capable combat force.

The FCS dominates future investment accounts and faces serious funding problems. Between April 2003 and September 2004 total program costs for FCS escalated 35.2 percent, and research and development costs increased by

50.8 percent. In addition, during the same period, the FCS acquisition cycle time increased 52.7 percent to 139 months. The Army has deferred actual procurement of FCS for roughly a decade to pay for core elements of net-centric intelligence, surveillance, and reconnaissance (IS&R) systems and upgrades/retention of its legacy systems.[6]

The Department of the Army's FCS program office initially estimated total research and development costs in FY2005 dollars of $28 billion and procurement costs for 15 units of action of around $79.9 illion. This meant that the first phase of FCS would equip about one-third of the total force and cost at least $108 billion. The Army then updated its research and development cost estimate to $30.3 billion in 2005 dollars.

By 2004, the FCS program faced major resource constraints. According to a December 2004 report in *Defense News,* the Office of the Secretary of Defense (OSD) considered cutting $1.4 billion from the program each year from then until 2011.[7] The Army's FCS request in the FY2006 budget was $3.045 billion, which was $200 million more than the previous year. The increase in price was partly due to the Army's plan to start incorporating FCS capabilities in two-year increments.[8] The GAO predicted that fully equipping the entire force would cost between $3 billion and $9 billion each year.[9]

In 2005, the cost of the FCS program was so high that the GAO reported that "FCS is at significant risk for not delivering required capability within budgeted resources...Nearly 2 years after program launch and with $4.6 billion invested, requirements are not firm and only 1 of over 50 technologies is mature."[10] The Army estimated the total cost could easily reach $145 billion, or some $53 billion more than originally estimated. In July 2004, the FCS program underwent a restructuring. As a result, the Army expected an additional four-year delay in fielding the first complete FCS brigade—until 2014.

On September 21, 2005, Army Secretary Francis J. Harvey estimated that the program would now cost $125 billion over 20 years.[11] According to the FY2006 Department of Defense Budget, the Army's FCS FY2005 research and development costs were $2.8 billion, a 75-percent increase from FY2004. The Army requested $3.4 billion for the program in FY2006, a 21-percent increase from the previous year. As such, FCS comprised 65 percent of the Army's proposed spending on system development and demonstration programs and 35 percent of the Army's proposed spending on all RDT&E.[12]

The FCS has suffered from more than cost escalation. The program calls for 18 networked new weapons and robotic systems for 18 brigades. The goal of FCS is to create a system of lighter, smaller vehicles without compromising lethality. It is also designed to collect and disseminate intelligence and communications information. It is a complex, interdependent system facing financial, managerial, and technological challenges. The requirements of the program, network, and software are all still in their developmental stages. The program has been given about 9.5 years to complete the development phase and begin production.

There already, however, have been significant cutbacks and delays. The first major deployment of FCS-related equipment is scheduled to take place in FY2008. In 2005, the GAO reported that each of the programs for developing the FCS's communications network was at risk of not delivering its intended capabilities by this deadline:[13]

- The Joint Tactical Radio System (JTRS) Cluster 1 program—tasked with developing radio for ground vehicles and helicopters and slated to be the backbone of the FCS network—has been fraught with immature technologies, schedule delays, and a lack of clearly defined and stable requirements. As such, the program has struggled to mature and integrate key technologies and has been forced to make major design changes without a corresponding boost in intended capabilities. These factors contributed to significant cost and schedule problems that led the Army in December 2004 to propose restructuring the program by adding $458 million and two years to the development effort.

- In January 2005, the prime contractor estimated that the total costs for the Cluster 1 development would be $531 million more than what was originally budgeted, reaching about $898 million. Subsequently, the GAO reported, "A recent review of the [Cluster 1] program concluded that the current program structure is not executable, and in April 2005, DOD directed the Army to stop work and notify the contractor that it was considering terminating the contract."[14]

- JTRS Cluster 5 program—tasked with developing small radios, including those that soldiers carry—has also faced technical challenges and program changes that have impeded progress. For example, the smallest of the Cluster 5 radios will not be able to provide the power and cooling needed for the Wideband Networking Waveform that will serve as the main conduit of information to and from Army tactical units. In light of unresolved issues with the Cluster 1 program, in 2005, the DoD initiated an assessment to restructure the Cluster 5 program that could further delay implementation.

- The GAO estimated in 2005 that none of the critical technologies for the Warfighter Information Network-Tactical program would be fully mature at the time production began in March 2006.

- The System of Systems Common Operating Environment (SOSCOE)—being developed as the operating software that integrates the communications network— faces the dual challenge of a software development that is high risk and has evolving requirements. Army program officials have said that SOSCOE software may not reach the necessary technical maturity level required to meet program milestones.

Congress did exercise some budgetary discretion for the FCS program in the 2007 Defense Authorization Act, and its companion 2007 Defense Appropriations Act. While the 2006 QDR and the accompanying budget submission for FY2007 attempted to keep FCS intact and continue the program's spending binge, lawmakers trimmed back the DoD's requested $3.7 billion by $320 million, citing development and contracting delays.[15] How these cuts will play out for the program remains uncertain, but significant portions of FCS will likely be stretched out over several years.

More generally, recent combat has also raised serious questions about the entire concept behind the FCS. The Army has found heavy armored "legacy" systems like the M-1 main battle tank and the M-2 Bradley to be vital in Iraq. It has had to uparmor many of its lighter systems like the Humvee, and it has had to carry out virtually all of its force movement and sustainment effort by sea. It is far from clear that a new family of lighter, air transportable weapons can really meet the Army's needs, particularly with anything approaching the near-term state of the art in armor and self-protection. The Army might well find it better to invest in upgraded legacy systems, concentrate on improvements in net-centric warfare capabilities, and use its funds to increase end strength.

Force Modularity Program Costs

Similar problems have arisen in other near-term Army transformation efforts. In March 2005, the Army estimated that its modularity program would cost $48 billion from FY2005 through FY2011 to complete, a 71-percent increase from its 2004 estimate of $28 billion.[16] The GAO believed that these cost estimates were unrealistic and would be revised upward, as the Army had yet to fully identify its requirements and costs associated with modularizing the Army. Moreover, some military analysts contended that the Modularity Program would face growing affordability issues because it was being undertaken at the same time that the Army was supporting the Global War on Terrorism, engaged in ongoing operations in Afghanistan and Iraq, and developing new technologies and capabilities (including FCS) that demanded high levels of resources.

While Congress supported the Army's modularity program, it viewed the DoD's FY2005 Supplemental Request for an additional $5 billion for Army modularization with considerable reservation. The House Appropriations Committee directed the Secretary of Defense to submit to the Congressional defense committees a report detailing the DoD's long-range plan for executing and funding Army modularization, specifically identifying the personnel and equipment requirements, unit restructuring timelines, and the associated costs.[17]

Moreover, the Senate cautioned the DoD and the Army in Senate Report 109-52 on the FY2005 Emergency Supplemental. "The Department has now had ample time to incorporate requirements to support Modularity into its annual budget requests. The Committee is unlikely to regard supplemental appropriations as an appropriate vehicle for future efforts supporting modularity."[18] Congress made it clear that it was not pleased with the DoD's and the Army's inability to plan and budget costs and would not look favorably on further DoD and Army efforts to fund modularity through supplemental appropriations.[19]

U.S. AIR FORCE AND NAVAL AVIATION PROGRAM MANAGEMENT CHALLENGES

As in the Army's case, cost-escalation and major problems in development and procurement problems have locked the Air Force into an investment program it simply cannot execute with anything like its currently programmed funds.[20]

A CBO study of Air Force investment costs from FY2007–FY2024 found that the Department of Defense's overall investment program for the Air Force was as lacking in credibility as its program for the Army. The Department projected that Air Force annual average investment spending would rise during FY2007–FY2011 from $57 billion to $62 billion. The CBO did not assess cost risk in detail for this period, but found that the true cost could easily average from $2 billion to $8 billion a year higher.[21]

The main problems with cost-escalation came after 2011, where the CBO estimated that annual investment costs would have to rise to a minimum average of $70 billion a year—16 percent higher than during FY2007–FY2011. It also found that a prudent estimate of actual investment costs based on past escalation would require $77 billion a year—allowing for cost risk. As is the case with the Army, these estimates do not allow for additional procurements to respond to the lessons of the Afghan and Iraq wars.

While cost and development problems with space, C^4I, and weapons programs also drive the Air Force's investment problems, its main problems lie in procuring new aircraft. Air Force and Naval/Marine Corps aviation are mortgaged to a range of major new programs and systems, including the F-22A, the Joint Strike Fighter (JSF), tankers, lift replacements, and special assets. Two of the Air Force's largest programs are the F-22A Raptor and the JSF. Both are examples of how the failure to manage cost escalation can help create a form of overstretch. In fact, they illustrate the risk that "force multipliers" pose when they are so expensive that they create force-planning problems and become "force cripplers."

These programs have also been in existence long enough to be time urgent. If they continue to slip or be cut back, existing systems must be rebuilt or supplemented with unfunded additional production. The average age of the B-52 (41 years) often gets attention. But the average F-15 is 18 years old, and the average KC-135 Stratotanker is 46 years old. Other systems are simply worn.

The F-22A Raptor

The F-22A Raptor has become a cost-escalation nightmare. The OSD restructured the $72-billion program's acquisition schedule twice between 2004 and 2006. In December 2004, the OSD issued Program Budget Decision (PBD) 753, which reduced F-22A funding by $10.5 billion and cut the procurement quantity from 277 to 179 aircraft. (Subsequently, the Air Force transferred one production aircraft to testing, reducing the procurement quantity to 178.) PBD 753 also planned to terminate F-22A procurement in 2008.

The DoD changed the Raptor program again in December 2005. This time the DoD added $1 billion to the program to extend its production for two years through 2010. The move was designed to ensure that a next-generation fighter aircraft production line remained in operation in case the Joint Strike Fighter experienced delays or problems. The change also froze the Raptor's design at its present configuration allowing for the procurement of four additional aircraft for a total planned procurement of 183 F-22As.[22]

But even 183 aircraft is 198 aircraft below the Air Force's current stated need for 381 Raptors to satisfy original air-to-air missions and recently added requirements for more robust air-to-ground attack and intelligence-gathering capabilities. Put simply, because of past cost overruns and current budget constraints, the DoD can afford only 183 aircraft. And as the procurement goal has fallen significantly over the life of the program, the cost per aircraft has escalated dramatically, from $149 million in 1991 to $345 million in 2005. Figure 7.5 illustrates the program's unit cost increase by year.

The history of the F-22 program partially explains its massive cost escalation. Begun in 1986, the original F-22 program was intended to replace the F-15 with a state-of-the-art, air-to-air superiority fighter that would counter large numbers of advanced Soviet fighter aircraft. At the time, the DoD planned to develop the F-22

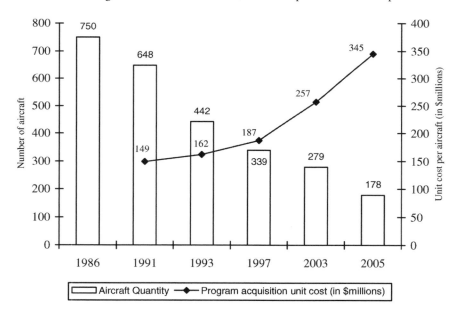

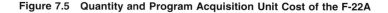

Source: Adapted from "Tactical Aircraft: Air Force Still Needs Business Case to Support F/A-22 Quantities and Increased Capabilities." Government Accountability Office Report to Congressional Committees. 15 March 2005.

Figure 7.5   Quantity and Program Acquisition Unit Cost of the F-22A

over nine years and achieve operational capability by March 1996. However, over the nearly two decades of the Raptor's development, the threat of advanced Soviet fighter aircraft never materialized, and adversarial threats against U.S. aircraft changed.

Consequently, in 2002 the Air Force decided to give the F-22 more robust air-to-ground strike capabilities to increase the utility of the aircraft and to justify continued funding for the program. Redesignated the F/A-22, with the "A" representing the aircraft's expanded ground attack capabilities—the F/A-22 was renamed the F-22A in December 2005—the program embarked on a time-phased modernization program that the OSD's Cost Analysis Improvement Group estimated in 2003 would cost an additional $11.7 billion through 2018. This estimate included costs for development, procurement, and retrofit of modernized aircraft.[23] As of March 2006, the Air Force estimated that modernization costs from 2007 through 2016 would be about $4.3 billion. Additional modernization costs are anticipated, but the content and costs have not been determined or included in the budget.[24]

The modernization and acquisition timeline for the Raptor has become steadily more uncertain as a result of these developments. According to the 2005 timeline, modernization would extend from 2007 to 2015, as summarized in Figure 7.6.[25]

However, the Air Force has not prepared a new business plan for the F-22A to justify the resources needed to implement the proposed modernizations. According to the GAO, the uncertainty surrounding the ongoing modernization program coupled with the 198-aircraft gap between the Air Force's stated need and what the acquisition process is able to deliver have made the F-22As business case untenable. "The business case for the program has changed radically—threats have changed, requirements have been added, costs have increased, funds have been added, planned quantities have been reduced, and deliveries of the aircraft to the warfighter have been delayed."[26]

Moreover, the GAO has argued that "the modernized F/A-22 would differ so significantly from the original aircraft in capabilities and missions that it should have been developed in an entirely separate acquisition program."[27] If the F-22A is

Figure 7.6   Planned Modernization Enhancements for the F-22A Program

	Examples of Capabilities to Be Added
2007	**Air-to-air plus limited air-to-ground capabilities:** Improved capability to launch Joint Direct Attack Munition at fast speeds; upgrade air-to-air capabilities.
2011	**Air-to-ground capability:** Add improved radar to seek and destroy advanced surface-to-air missile systems; integrate additional air-to-ground weapons.
2013	**Additional air-to-ground capability:** Increase capability to suppress or destroy full range of air defenses and improve speed and accuracy of targeting.
2015	**Enhanced intelligence data gathering:** Add integrated intelligence, surveillance, and reconnaissance capabilities.

Source: Adapted from "Tactical Aircraft: Air Force Still Needs Business Case to Support F/A-22 Quantities and Increased Capabilities," Government Accountability Office Report to Congressional Committees, March 15, 2005.

essentially a new program—retired U.S. Air Force (USAF) Colonel Everest E. Riccioni wrote that "only the engines, the canopy, and the fuselage reference line will be common and interchangeable" with the original F-22—then one can expect that implementation of the modernization plan has a good likelihood of causing new delays and problems that are similar to those that a new aircraft program may encounter.[28]

These feared delays and problems became all too real in the spring of 2006 when the Air Force discovered structural flaws affecting nearly 100 Raptor aircraft. Raptor program officials found weaknesses in structures that attach the wing and tail to the plane's fuselage and corrosion in the aircraft's panels. Officials estimated that testing for and fixing these problems could cost around $1 billion.[29]

The GAO has repeatedly asked the DoD to write a new business case for the Raptor program that addresses the need for the aircraft, the quantities required, and the affordability. The DoD did not comply with a March 2004 GAO recommendation to this effect, writing, "The Department evaluates the F/A-22 business case, program progress, need for the aircraft, and quantities required, as part of our routine acquisition and budget processes."[30] Of course, the GAO did not agree that the DoD's routine processes provided sufficient analysis to justify future investments in the new capabilities added by the modernization program, especially considering the prevailing uncertainties surrounding the program issues.[31]

In March 2005, the GAO again recommended that the Air Force develop a new business case that justified additional investments in modernizing the aircraft to include greater ground attack and intelligence-gathering capabilities before moving forward. The Pentagon responded by writing that the forthcoming QDR (released February 2006) would analyze requirements for the F-22A and make program decisions. The 2006 QDR was not forthcoming in addressing these points, as described in March 2006 in testimony before the Subcommittee on Tactical Air and Land Forces of the House Armed Services Committee.[32]

> It is not clear from the [2006] QDR report...what analyses were conducted to determine the gaps in capability, the alternatives considered, the quantities needed, or the costs and benefits of the F-22A program. Therefore, questions about the F-22A program remain:
>
> • What capability gaps exist today and will exist in the future (air superiority, ground attack, electronic attack, intelligence gathering)?
> • What alternatives besides the F-22A can meet these needs?
> • What are the costs and benefits of each alternative?
> • How many F-22As are needed?
> • What capabilities should be included?
>
> Until these questions are answered and differences are reconciled, further investments in the program—for either the procurement of new aircraft or modernization—cannot be justified.

These problems alone threaten the future of the entire U.S. Air Force, but the F-22A program has been criticized on other equally serious grounds.

- The Raptor is more expensive than the JSF; it is less versatile; and presently, it is only an air-to-air combat aircraft, in spite of modernization plans to give the aircraft Global Strike Full and Enhanced Intelligence, Surveillance, and Reconnaissance capabilities.

- Even if the modernization plan is implemented, the utility of the Raptor as a ground-attack aircraft is questionable, considering that the JSF, the A-10, and the F-18E were designed to have or already have this capability.

- An air-to-air fighter is obsolete in this new age of irregular warfare, considering that the program began in 1986 with the intention of it being capable of fighting Soviet fighters. If the aircraft is, in fact, obsolete, then the program's remaining budget dollars could be better invested in enhancing current air assets and in acquiring new and more transformational capabilities that will allow the DoD to meet the evolving threats from asymmetric warfare. As the GAO described the situation, "when DoD's weapon systems, such as the [F-22A], require more time and money than originally anticipated, the extra investment needed to solve problems takes funding away from other priorities, slows DoD's overall modernization effort, delays capabilities, for the warfighter, and forces unplanned—and possibly unnecessary—trade-offs among DoD's many priorities."[33]

- The 2006 QDR shifted the Pentagon's traditional two major theater war strategy to one that accounts for the possibility of waging a conventional campaign and a large-scale, long-duration irregular campaign. The new strategy placed a greater emphasis on homeland defense and counterterrorism. Theoretically, such a shift in strategy should decrease the importance of warplanes like the Raptor.[34]

Unlike the Air Force's failure to manage the F-22A program, such criticisms are debatable. Proponents of the F-22A program argue that the United States requires fifth-generation tactical aircraft like the Raptor to ensure air superiority in the event of a conflict with China, North Korea, or Iran. This argument, however, requires the USAF to be able to fund a suitably large force, and the F-22A so far promises to be more of a force shrinker than a force multiplier.

Colonel Everest E. Riccioni, USAF Ret., argued in his paper, "Description of Our Failing Defense Acquisition System as Exemplified by the History, Nature, and Analysis of the USAF F-22 Raptor Program," that this might not be practical. "Operationally, acquiring only 150–180 aircraft means the USAF will use some 70–80 aircraft for training and home defense, 40–50 for the European theater, and 40–50 for the Pacific theater. These numbers combined with the usual low maintenance readiness for flight of complex stealthy aircraft reduces the operational availability of the fleet to insignificance."[35]

To make matters worse, Congress has not exercised nearly enough budgetary discretion over the F-22. For example, the 2007 Defense Authorization Act and its companion Defense Appropriations Act did nothing to check the F-22A's cost escalation and management challenges. This legislation approved an unusual deal that locked the Air Force into buying 60 F-22As over three years and left open the option for buying more than the planned 183 F-22As. Moreover, lawmakers increased spending on the Raptor by $1.4 billion over the DoD's budget request of $1.5 billion. Lawrence Korb, a former Pentagon official and now a defense analyst, characterized this development as rewarding F-22A maker Lockheed Martin despite 20 years of substandard program performance.[36]

The Joint Strike Fighter

The F-35 Joint Strike Fighter is another high-cost acquisition program led by the United States and co-financed by eight allied countries. The program evolved in the late 1990s in response to the high cost of tactical aviation, the need to deploy fewer types of aircraft to reduce acquisition and operating costs, and the projections of future threat scenarios and enemy capabilities. To these ends, the JSF program is a joint-service project to develop a next-generation multirole aircraft that can be produced in affordable variants to meet the different operational requirements of the Air Force, the Navy, and the Marine Corps. The three primary variants in the JSF family of aircraft—a conventional takeoff and landing aircraft, a carrier-capable (CV) aircraft, and a short takeoff vertical landing aircraft—employ a modular mix of components, systems, and technologies with commonality projected at 70 to 90 percent in terms of production cost. Many high-cost components, such as engines, avionics, and major structural components of the airframe, are common among the three variants.[37] As former Secretary of Defense William Cohen stated, the JSF's joint approach to procurement "avoids the three parallel development programs for service-unique aircraft that would have otherwise been necessary, saving at least $15 billion."[38]

Despite the best cost-saving intentions of the program, however, the history of problems with the JSF is all too similar to that of the F-22A Raptor program. As the GAO wrote in a March 2006 report, "the JSF appears to be on the same path as the F-22A program. After being in development for 9 years, the JSF program has not produced the first test aircraft, has experienced substantial cost growth, has reduced the number of planned aircraft, and has delayed delivery of the aircraft to the warfighter."[39]

- The JSF is the largest defense acquisitions program in history. When its 10-year System Development and Demonstration Phase began in 2001, the program's estimated cost was $183.6 billion for 2,866 aircraft, or about $64.1 million per aircraft.[40] According to a DoD selected acquisition report released March 7, 2006, the cost of the program increased to $276.5 billion for 2,458 aircraft, or about $112.5 million per aircraft. The total program cost has escalated 51 percent, while the cost per aircraft has escalated nearly 76 percent.

- The JSF program is heavily dependent on a business case that invests heavily in production before testing has demonstrated acceptable performance of the aircraft. The program expects to begin low-rate initial procurement in 2007, with less than 1 percent of the flight test program completed and no production representative prototypes built for the three JSF variants. Moreover, technologies and features critical to the JSF's operational success, such as a low observable and highly common airframe, advanced mission systems, and maintenance prognostics systems, will not have been demonstrated in a flight test environment when production begins.[41]

- By 2010, the DoD expects to have procured 126 JSF aircraft with only 35 percent of the flight test program completed. The program expects the first fully integrated and capable development JSF to fly in 2011. By that time, the DoD will have already committed to buy 190 aircraft at an estimated cost of $26 billion. The DoD's low-rate initial production quantities are expected to increase from 5 aircraft a year in 2007 to 133 a year in 2013, when development and initial operational testing are complete. By then, the DoD will have already procured 424 aircraft at an estimated cost of $49 billion. At the same time, spending for monthly production activities is expected to be about $1 billion, an increase from $100 million a month when production is scheduled to begin in 2007. As the GAO described the situation, "concurrently testing and procuring the aircraft adds to the program's costs and schedule risks, further weakening DoD's buying power and jeopardizing its ability to recapitalize its aging tactical air force in a timely and efficient manner."[42]

The DoD made a controversial move to curb the JSF's mounting cost escalation in February 2006 by abandoning investments to develop an alternative engine for the JSF. The DoD had already invested $1.2 billion to develop the alternative F-136 engine, to the current F-135 engine, through FY2006, and by canceling the program, the DoD expected to save $1.8 billion through FY2011. In the past, fighter aircraft programs like the F-15 and the F-16 adopted the practice of developing alternative engines. The practice may help maintain the industrial base for fighter engine acquisition and spare parts, result in price competition in the future for engine acquisition and spare parts, instill incentives to develop a more reliable engine, and ensure an operational alternative should the current engine develop a problem that would ground the entire fleet of aircraft.[43]

Defense analysts criticized the Pentagon's decision to go with a sole source without the support of a strong business case analysis.[44] Christopher Bolkcom of the Congressional Research Service (CRS) explained the DoD's decision: "The argument is that a single engine manufacturer making more engines will climb the learning curve faster and save more money than two manufacturers making fewer engines each...What must also be considered, however, is the innovation and savings that can be derived from competition between two manufacturers, which is lost in a sole source environment." Loren B. Thompson, a defense analyst and CEO of the Lexington Institute, was less sympathetic to the Pentagon's reasoning: "The only learning curve here will be that a contractor will learn how much it can charge for an engine."[45]

The JSF program has also encountered difficulties in accommodating its international partners due to DoD reluctance to share critical technologies. In March 2006, Britain, the United States' principal foreign partner in the program, indicated that it could not buy the aircraft without the requisite technology transfer. Five other partner countries—Norway, Italy, Turkey, Denmark, and the

Netherlands—in the program echoed Britain's reservations about remaining in the program at all.[46]

In addition to the JSF's cost escalation and program management challenges, the JSF, like the F-22A, has faced criticism regarding the need for next-generation tactical aircraft. Some experts have asked whether future threat scenarios require the combat capabilities of the JSF. The implication is that the continued production of modified versions of the Air Force F-16, the Marine Corps AV-8B, and the Navy F/A-18E/F along with the Air Force's B-2 stealth bombers and F-22A fighters and in conjunction with sea-launched missiles and the precision-guided munitions would probably cover most combat scenarios.[47] Moreover, U.S. air dominance during the Gulf War and subsequently in Bosnia, Kosovo, Afghanistan, and Iraq suggests that next-generation aircraft may not be required for U.S. forces to achieve their military objectives in future conflicts.

Proponents of the JSF retort that acquiring next-generation aircraft would be more cost-effective than upgrading current aircraft to perform effectively beyond 2010. Existing planes would require major modifications at considerable cost and would be less effective in combat than a new JSF family of tactical aircraft. This perspective anticipates that the proliferation of Russian and other advanced surface-to-air and air-to-air missiles to hostile countries is likely to continue, posing a more serious threat to U.S. and allied aircraft than they faced during the 1991 Gulf War.

Others have argued that many of the existing operational aircraft will be 20 or more years old and will need to be replaced by the time the JSF is estimated to reach full production in the 2010s. Advocates of the JSF program have also suggested reducing procurement of F-22As and F/A-18E/Fs in order to fund the JSF program.[48] However, this argument is problematic considering that the Air Force often cites the complementary roles of the F-22A and the JSF as analogous to the complementary roles of the F-15 and the F-16. In a March 16, 2006, statement before the House Armed Services Committee, Lieutenant General Carrol H. "Howie" Chandler, Deputy Chief of Staff for Air Force Air, Space, and Information Operations, Plans, and Programs, said, "The [JSF and the F-22A] are very complementary to each other because of the optimization of the F-22A for air-to-air (combat), and its ability to suppress or defeat enemy air defenses. The Joint Strike Fighter is optimized for air-to-surface and its ability to strike hard."[49]

The difficulties in accurately predicting the future threat environment, how combat-effective JSF aircraft would be, and what it would cost to develop, procure, and operate F-35 aircraft leave any assessments of military requirements, combat effectiveness, and budgetary costs open to a range of conjecture and debate.[50] But, it is far from clear that the Air Force and other services have any probable threat or urgent mission need to rush forward into large-scale procurement. It is even more unclear that they can afford both the F-22A and the F-35

It is also precisely these uncertainties regarding the future that the GAO recommended the DoD address with a new analytically based business plan for its tactical aircraft programs. As with the F-22A, the Pentagon's reliance on the 2006 QDR to provide the requisite analytic detail did not live up to expectations. As the GAO pointed out, the 2006 QDR "did not present a detailed investment strategy for tactical aircraft systems that addressed needs, capability gaps, alternatives, and affordability. Lacking a strategy that identifies capability gaps and affordable alternatives, the DoD cannot reasonably ensure that new tactical air capabilities will be delivered to the warfighter within cost and schedule targets."[51]

The Air Force Tanker Problem

Modern military air operations require refueling aircraft, or tankers like the KC-135, that extend the range of fighters, bombers, and other aircraft, increase the deployment times of combat and surveillance aircraft, and boost combat aircraft lethality. The Air Force has estimated that it will need around 600 KC-135-like aircraft. But the need for aerial refueling is likely to increase in the future for two reasons. Over the past several years, the United States has reduced by two-thirds the number of forward bases from which it can operate, and major overseas en route air bases have declined by 69 percent. In order to maintain the same level of engagement capabilities, U.S. forces will be forced to deploy more frequently over greater distances.[52]

Currently, the Air Force's tanker fleet is large and effective, but it is old and requires modernization. The Air Force owns 531 Boeing KC-135 Stratotankers, including 114 E and 417 R models. At an average age of over 46 years, the "Eisenhower Era" KC-135 fleet is the oldest combat weapon system in the Air Force, and the Stratotanker platform is expected to fly until 2040. The Air Force also owns 59 Boeing KC-10A Extenders, with nearly twice the fuel capacity of the KC-135. The average KC-10 has an age of 20.5 years, and the Air Force also plans for the KC-10 to remain active through 2040.[53]

Modernizing or replacing the tanker fleet has been a point of contention for more than a decade, and the DoD faces difficult choices regarding desired capabilities, force structure, and budget options. In 1996, a report by the GAO argued that the long-term viability of the KC-135 fleet was questionable because as the fleet ages, it will take progressively more time and money to maintain and operate. In response to the GAO's recommendation to study replacement options, the DoD countered that KC-135 airframe hours were low and that the fleet was sustainable for another 35 years.[54] The Air Force reiterated this position in its 2001 Economic Service Life Study (ESLS). The ESLS found that the KC-135 would incur "significant cost increases" between 2001 and 2040, but "no economic crisis is on the horizon... there appears to be no run-away cost-growth," and "the fleet is structurally viable to 2040."[55]

The Air Force then reversed this position. Subsequent Air Force studies determined that the ESLS was conceptually flawed because it failed to predict fatigue and corrosion problems in the tanker fleet. The Aging Aircraft Study, released in November 2002, found that corrosion, rather than the number of flight hours flown or the mission assigned to the KC-135, had the most significant impact on the expected life span of each airframe. The May 2003 KC-135 Business Case Analysis reinforced these findings and determined that corrosion, increased operating costs, and other operating uncertainties justified a decision to retire 44 KC-135s in FY2004. Moreover, in a letter dated September 22, 2003, to Senators John Warner and Carl Levin, Deputy Secretary of Defense Paul Wolfowitz noted that between 1991 and the date of his letter, KC-135E corrosion-related depot maintenance increased more than three times and that 30 percent of the tanker's heavy maintenance man-hours were now devoted to the mitigation of corrosion damage.[56]

While most experts finally agreed that the KC-135E fleet suffers from severe corrosion, the Air Force's efforts to solve this problem have been wrought with scandal and political infighting.[57]

- The FY2002 Defense Authorization Act (P.L. 107-117) authorized the Air Force to lease 100 Boeing KC-767 aircraft to replace the oldest KC-135Es. This proved controversial because it appeared to subvert the traditional acquisition process and weaken Congressional oversight. It then turned out that leasing the aircraft would cost more than procuring the aircraft outright. The controversy over the lease proposal was fueled further by four Congressional debates and, ultimately, by alleged and admitted ethical violations by government and industry representatives involved in the proposal.

- The FY2004 Defense Authorization Act (P.L. 108-136, Sec. 135) attempted to reconcile the differences between opponents and proponents of the KC-767 by allowing the Air Force to lease 20 tanker aircraft and purchase no more than 80 aircraft. The legislation also mandated that the Air Force conduct an aerial refueling Analysis of Alternatives (AoA) and that an independent assessment be conducted on the condition of the KC-135E fleet.

- The DoD did not authorize any funds for FY2005 either to lease 20 or procure 80 aircraft even though it had the statutory authority to proceed. Pentagon leaders deferred executing either action until the completion of the independent assessment, tasked to the Defense Science Board (DSB), and an internal investigation by the DoD Inspector General (IG) on potential improprieties by Boeing Company executives negatively affecting the tanker lease program.

- In April 2004, Darleen A. Druyan, the former lead Air Force negotiator on the tanker lease program, pleaded guilty to one count of criminal conspiracy for secretly negotiating an executive job with the Boeing company while still overseeing the $23-billion deal between the Air Force and Boeing.

- Air Force Secretary James Roche submitted his resignation in November 2004 amid allegations of wrongdoing in the tanker lease deal. In February 2005, the *Washington Post* reported that the DoD IG found that Air Force Secretary James Roche misused his office when he lobbied the Office of Management and Budget (OMB) to support the lease proposal.[58]

- The IG's final report found that four other senior DoD officials were guilty of evading OMB and DoD acquisition regulations. The IG determined that senior DoD officials knowingly misrepresented the state of the KC-135 fleet and aerial refueling requirements.[59] In a June 7, 2005, hearing before the Senate Armed Services Committee, DoD IG Joseph Schmitz testified that the U.S. Attorney's Office may file criminal charges.[60]

Despite the fallout from the biggest Pentagon procurement scandal in more than two decades, the Air Force's tanker problem still requires resolution. Given that the FY2005 Defense Authorization Act (P.L. 108-375) terminated the leasing authority granted in the FY2004 Defense Authorization Act, the DoD and Congress again must consider alternatives to modernizing or replacing the Air Force aerial refueling fleet.

The DSB released its independent analysis of the KC-135E fleet in May 2004. In addition to rebutting Air Force claims that the tanker fleet urgently needed to be replaced, the study recommended that "serious consideration be given" to purchasing and converting used aircraft for aerial refueling (especially the DC-10), re-engining some KC-135s, and increasing the use of commercial aerial refueling services. The DSB also pointed out that a tanker fleet composed of two different types of aircraft —large, long-range tankers and smaller, tactical tankers—would likely be most prudent and effective.[61]

Like the DSB study, the RAND Corporation's long-awaited AoA on the Air Force fleet of tankers, completed in January 2006, also argued that the need to replace the tanker fleet was less pressing than the Air Force claimed and that replacement may not need to begin for six to eight years. Rather, the 1,500-page report, classified as secret, advocated that the Air Force weigh budget constraints and other considerations before purchasing new aircraft. Nonetheless, the AoA focused mainly on the question of buying new commercial planes to replace the existing KC-135s. The AoA found that it would cost between $109 billion and $200 billion to buy new planes to replace the existing fleet. It recommended that the Air Force buy new medium or large commercial aircraft—such as Boeing's 767, 777, 787, and 747 or Airbus's A330 and A340—to replace its KC-135 tankers and dismissed recommendations by the DSB and by the CRS to consider leasing tankers, re-engining existing tankers, and converting planes like DC-10s for the job.[62]

Loren Thompson of the Lexington Institute argued strongly against the AoA's recommendations.[63]

> The absurdity of saying you don't need new tankers until some date in the future lies in an inability to predict when the current fleet will begin incurring structural problems... Nobody has ever operated jets for this long, so we can't know when these will become dangerous. They are saying there is plenty of fatigue life in the aircraft, but that's not the problem. Corrosion is, and you can't precisely model that. Each time they open one of these aircraft, they find how inaccurate their models were. This is the oldest fleet of jets operating.

In testimony before the Projection Forces Subcommittee of the House Armed Services Committee on February 28, 2006, Air Force Lieutenant General Christopher A. Kelly, Vice Commander, Air Mobility Command, reinforced these points with concrete dollar figures.

> The KC-135 fleet is over 46 years old, and it has exhibited major technical difficulties with increased costs of operation and decreased aircraft availability, which in turn

increases operation risk. The Fleet Viability Report identifies a window for replacing the KC-135 fleet by the 2023–2030 timeframe. [Air Force Mobility Command] depot forecasts show that an additional $46.8 billion will be needed to sustain the current KC-135 fleet through the year 2040 without addressing the identified gaps and shortfalls that exist today...Affordability is an area of concern. Today our total obligation authority will allow us to buy 12–15 new aircraft per year at costs ranging between $150 million–$200 million per aircraft. At 12 aircraft per year, it would take over 38 years to replace the KC-135 fleet capability to meet the minimum Mobility Capabilities Study requirement, with an annual procurement outlay of $1.9 billion–$3.2 billion. This annual funding outlay increases with every year we delay the replacement program decision.

General Kelly also noted that retiring 114 of the oldest tanker models by 2010 would save the Air Force $6.1 billion, about the cost of 50 new tanker aircraft that would have significantly higher capability than the current KC-135E tankers.

While the FY2007 budget submission included plans to spend $204 million to launch a competition to replace the aging tanker fleet, the 2007 Defense Appropriations Act did not allocate any funding for the Air Force's KC-135 Tanker Replacement Program.[64] In its Report on the 2007 Defense Appropriations Bill, the House Appropriations Committee wrote the following:

> The Committee recommends no funding for advance procurement of KC-X aircraft, a reduction of $36,130,000 below the request for fiscal year 2007.
>
> The Committee continues to strongly support development and acquisition of a replacement for the Air Force's aging KC-135 tanker fleet. To this end, the Committee has fully funded the request in Research, Development, Test and Evaluation, Air Force for the KC-135 Tanker Replacement Program. However, the Air Force has communicated to the Committee that advance procurement funds are early to need as the development program for the KC-135 tanker replacement only recently received authority to resume the acquisition process and issue a Request for Information. The Committee notes that should there be a requirement for procurement funds in fiscal year 2007, significant amounts remain available in the Tanker Replacement Transfer Fund.

Nonetheless, in late September 2006, the Air Force launched a competition for proposals for new refueling tankers from Northrop Grumman/EADS North America and Boeing. At stake is an estimated $20-billion to $30-billion contract to build 179 so-called "KC-X" airframes as the first of three tranches of KC-135 replacements. In order to cover all of the aspects of the commercial aircraft landscape—weighing in the fallout from the tanker-leasing scandal—the Air Force took the unusual step of including in its draft request for information on the tanker deal how an adverse World Trade Organization (WTO) ruling would impact the pricing of the competitors' proposals.[65] The WTO dispute deals with a pending case between the United States and the European Union dealing with allegations on both sides that commercial aircraft subsidies unfairly skew the price of products made by Boeing and EADS subsidiary Airbus. The case will not be resolved by the time the

Air Force wants tanker production to start, as early as 2010, and the Air Force is concerned that a WTO ruling could be applied retroactively to the contract and likely decrement a bid.[66] Thus, the long road to replacing the aging fleet of tanker aircraft continues.

Joint Lift Platforms

For the same reasons that effective U.S. force projection requires a capable tanker fleet, the U.S. military needs a comparable airlift capability. Global tensions have shifted from places like Europe, where the United States had large combat units permanently stationed, to places where the U.S. military presence is much smaller and less welcome. The areas to which the United States must project its forces are increasingly far from the ocean, in locations that are simply not accessible by sea-based forces—sealift alone cannot accommodate forces in Afghanistan. Moreover, as outlined in various strategy documents, the military as a whole is shifting away from forward-deployed forces to U.S.-based expeditionary warfare units that require the capability to surge overseas quickly when threats arise.[67]

Achieving optimal lift for the U.S. military requires procuring, modernizing, and maintaining the right mix of C-5 Galaxy, C-17 Globemaster, and C-130 Hercules aircraft. However, major procurement and cost problems exist in the development of these lift platforms and "joint force enablers."

The C-5 entered service in 1970 and is the biggest airlifter in the U.S. inventory. The C-5 can carry 50 more tons of cargo than the C-17, but the Galaxy requires much longer runways than the C-17 to take off and land and is far less maneuverable on the ground.[68] The C-5 has always been a challenge to maintain—a typical Galaxy has a mission capable rate around 55 percent.[69] The Air Force plans to modernize 125 older C-5 transport aircraft at a cost of around $90 million each to achieve a mission capable rate of at least 75 percent.[70] However, defense planners will not know the viability of the modernization program until 2008, so it is far from certain that upgrading the C-5 fleet with new engines and other reliability improvements will achieve the desired airlifter availability.[71] Moreover, Thomas P. Christie, the Pentagon's Director of Operational Test and Evaluation, said that the C-5 avionics upgrade program suffered from "unrealistic schedules" and "unstable" or "immature" software systems. Christie recommended that the Air Force devise a new acquisition strategy to ensure the program's success.[72]

The C-17 Globemaster has been touted as the best intertheater airlifter that the Air Force has ever bought. Designed to carry heavy or outsized payloads to remote airfields and maneuver in tight spaces on the ground, the C-17 is incredibly reliable with a mission capable rate of 92 percent. Each C-17 costs approximately $200 million that translates to $2.4 billion for each year of production. The C-17 was phased gradually into the airlifter fleet, ultimately taking on most of the responsibilities of the aging C-141 Starlifter.

As of September 2004, all 270 C-141s built in the 1960s were retired from active duty, but the DoD planned to buy only 180 C-17s to replace them.[73] Despite the undeniable success of the Globemaster, the Pentagon's Mobility Capability Study (MCS), the unclassified version of which was released in the fall of 2005, concluded that the military was better served, both strategically and fiscally, by ending procurement at 180 C-17s, 42 aircraft short of the 222 planes that lawmakers had planned. This meant that the DoD would stop purchases of the C-17 after the 180th aircraft is produced in 2008, a move prime contractor Boeing has warned would force the company to close its C-17 production line.

In a last-minute move of election year politicking, lawmakers added $2.1 billion to a $70-billion bridge fund included in the 2007 Defense Authorization Act, and its companion 2007 Defense Appropriations Act, to buy the Air Force 10 unrequested C-17s, keeping Boeing's production line open an additional year through 2009 and providing the Air Force with 190 total Globemaster aircraft.[74] Needless to say, with developments like this, the DoD's MCS and the corresponding decision to close the C-17 production line have been highly controversial in the defense community and on the Hill.

- Loren Thompson, CEO of the Lexington Institute and consultant to the Pentagon and defense contractors, sharply criticized the MCS. He said that "The Mobility Capability Study (MCS) was the latest in a series of deeply flawed [DoD] analyses reflecting both inadequate methodology and poorly constructed guidance." As such, he continued, the MCS "came to conclusions that violate common sense concerning future airlift requirements...It is senseless to terminate the C-17 production line and disband a unique workforce on the basis of airlift requirements early in the next decade when said requirements could double or triple in subsequent years due to [changing] circumstances."[75]

- Senator Jim Talent (R-MO), Chairman of the Senate Armed Services Seapower Sub-committee, expressed his reservations about the MCS during an April 4, 2006, hearing: "I note with concern the variance between the underlying assumptions of the mobility capability study and the more demanding conditions experienced by our lift forces as they adapt to uniquely stressing mission profiles and unplanned loading scenarios." Following the hearing, Talent concluded that as Pentagon officials conducted the MCS, "there were assumptions made [about intratheater needs] that were incorrect or inadequate."[76]

- A September 2005 study by the DSB recommended that the Pentagon maintain the option to acquire additional C-17 airlifters beyond the 180 programmed. The report stated, "The [DSB] task force's concern is that production of the C-17 ends in 2008, and a decision to terminate production at the force level of 180 means that the department will live with the fleet of 100 aging C-5s and 180 C-17s...for many years to come in an environment of great uncertainty."[77]

- In December 2005, U.S. Transportation Command Chief General Norton A. Schwartz said that he would prefer to keep the C-17 production line "warm" after the 180th Globemaster is built, to give the Air Force "insurance" in the event that the Air Force's C-5 modernization program is not as successful as engineers anticipate.[78]

- In March 2006, General Schwartz recommended buying an additional 20 C-17s to account for the extensive use of C-17s to support ongoing inter- and intratheater operations worldwide. But he acknowledged that the DoD simply did not have the funding for these additional aircraft without impacting other strategic airlift programs. General Schwartz emphasized the trade-off between buying additional C-17s versus building a more versatile, multirole tanker aircraft. He said, "From a requirement point of view, from the combatant command point of view, if I had to make a judgment, the first KC-X [the Air Force's next-generation tanker], I think, gives this nation greater payback than does the 181st C-17, the 201st or certainly the 221st."[79]

- A winter 2006 study by the Commerce Department's bureau of industry and security found that C-17 termination contradicts the 2006 QDR's underlying cost savings assumptions. The study estimated the cost of terminating the C-17 production line at $1.26 billion; the estimated cost of reopening the line was $3.2 billion. Thus, the total cost of closing the production line and subsequently reopening it would cost $4.46 billion. However, the Air Force could procure all 42 of the additional C-17s it requires for around $2.5 billion more than it currently plans to spend.[80]

The C-130 Hercules is the most frequently used airlifter in the U.S. fleet. Unlike the C-5 and the C-17, the Hercules is propeller driven and can fly in places jets cannot. This puts the C-130 in high demand by the Air Force, the Marines, and the Special Operations community for everything from aerial refueling to counter-insurgency firepower to electronic warfare.[81] To meet these demands, the Air Force is both acquiring new C-130Js to replace older aircraft and modernizing older C-130s via the C-130 Avionics Modernization Program and center-wing box replacement programs. The newest C-130Js can fly roughly as far as a C-5 or a C-17, but with less cargo. They also can deliver more cargo in a shorter time than older C-130s and have improved combat capability, as well as lower operation and sustainment costs.[82]

Nonetheless, the C-130 program has been riddled with cost overruns and technical problems.

- In 1964, C-130 aircraft cost around $1.5 million each. Adjusted for inflation, that cost is about $11.8 million today.[83] When the Air Force first ordered the latest C-130Js in 1995, they were expected to cost $34 million each. By 2004, the cost per aircraft had escalated to $66.5 million.[84] As of February 2006, the DoD's budget request for FY2007 slated $826.3 million to procure nine C-130Js—that is, $91.8 million per aircraft.

- In 2004, the DoD Inspector General's office said 50 C-130Js delivered to the Air Force did not meet requirements. The IG reported that "the C-130J aircraft does not meet contract specifications and therefore cannot perform its operational mission." Among the plane's problems, the IG reported, were "inadequate range and payload, immature software, lack of an automated mission planning system, and difficulties in cold weather operations."[85]

- A report by the DoD's Operational Test and Evaluation Office, sent to Congress in January 2005, stated that the C-130J aircraft still had "hardware deficiencies, software and technical order deficiencies, manufacturing quality, subsystem reliability" and other problems."[86]

- In December 2004, DoD Program Budget Decision No. 753 planned to end further procurement of C-130J aircraft in FY2006.[87] The decision was supposed to save the Pentagon $4.2 billion through FY2011. After strong opposition from lawmakers on Capitol Hill and estimated costs of between $500 million and more than $2 billion to get out of the deal with Lockheed Martin, the C-130J program was ultimately restored in the FY2006 Defense Appropriations Act.[88]

- The Air Force listed among its list of unfunded priorities submitted to Congress in February 2006 a request for $37.7 million to buy items to fix C-130s currently grounded due to cracks in their center-wing boxes.[89]

- In a rare positive development, in October 2006, C-130 contractor Lockheed Martin Corporation yielded to Congressional pressure on defense contractors over rising weapons costs and agreed to lower prices on the C-130J. The Pentagon began standardizing the C-130J contract in 2005 to give the Air Force greater access to financial-and-pricing data Lockheed had previously been exempted from disclosing. Under the new contract, Lockheed would cut the program cost by 8 percent for the remaining 26 Air Force C-130Js and by nearly 12 percent for 13 Marine planes, saving the Pentagon $244 million.[90]

On the whole, the entire airlift program suffers from a disconnect between proposed strategies and force plans and programmed resources. DoD strategy documents, including the 2006 QDR, suggest that U.S. military roles in fighting increasingly asymmetric and irregular wars, conducting international and domestic humanitarian missions, maintaining a surge capability to rapidly deploy forces worldwide, and waging conventional wars will require more airlift in the future. However, the FY2007 budget request simply does not support these airlift demands. As Loren Thompson of the Lexington Institute said, "There is a mismatch between what the QDR says about troop mobility and what's in the budget. The QDR says air transport is really important, and the budget kills it off."[91]

THE U.S. NAVY FLEET PROGRAM

Like the other services, cost-escalation and development problems have literally made the Navy and Marine Corps investment program incredible.[92] A CBO study of Navy and Marine Corps investment costs from FY2007–FY2024 found that the Department of Defense projected that Navy and Marine Corps annual average investment spending would rise in constant FY2007 dollars during FY2007–FY2011 from $49 billion to $66 billion in 2013, and then decline to $35 billion a year—creating an average annual cost of $49 billion a year. The CBO estimate of cost risk indicated, however, that the program was so badly loaded in terms of annual spending in given years that it could peak at $75 billion in 2013 and then fall back to $39 billion by 2024. It found a prudent estimate of annual investment cost to average $55 billion a year—12 percent higher than the Department's estimate.[93]

In terms of actual practice, the U.S. Navy's procurement programs have helped sink the Navy's force plans far below the "600-ship Navy" of the Reagan years. Some of these cuts are necessary and inevitable. The Navy would like to change the composition of its fleet by increasing the number of ships capable of navigating littoral areas and decreasing the number of deepwater patrolling ships. However, procurement scheduling delays and escalating costs have made it clear that the Navy will not be able to acquire the fleet that it needs. In April 2005, Admiral Vernon E. Clark told Congress that shipbuilding costs "have spiraled out of control," rising so high that "we can't build the Navy that we believe that we need in the 21st century."[94]

The Navy has lost the ability to plan its fleet because of persistent schedule delays and cost escalation. While it did not explicitly mention a total number of ships, the September 2001 report on the 2001 QDR, officially approved and published by the Office of the Secretary of Defense, was generally understood as a plan for a fleet of 310 ships. From around February 2002 until February 2004, Navy leaders mentioned and referred to an alternative proposal for a 375-ship Navy. But during a February 5, 2003, House Armed Services Committee hearing, Secretary of Defense Donald Rumsfeld explicitly declined to endorse a 375-ship fleet as an official DoD goal. In 2005, Admiral Vernon Clark testified that the Navy in future years may require between 260 and 325 ships, or possibly between 243 and 302 ships, depending on how much of the Navy employs new technologies.[95] In December 2005, when the total size of the U.S. fleet comprised 281 ships, Admiral Michael G. Mullen, Chief of Naval Operations, and other senior service officials briefed members of Congress and key Pentagon officials on a new assessment that indicated that the Navy needs 313 ships.[96]

Numerous defense analysts have described the 313-ship goal as unrealistic, given recent trends in naval procurement. In its February 2006 report to Congress, the Navy indicated that its new fleet plan would require spending an average of about $14.4 billion annually (in FY2007 dollars) for ship construction alone and an additional $1 billion annually to refuel nuclear-powered vessels, totaling about $15.5 billion per year.

In May 2006, the Congressional Budget Office (CBO) estimated that the Navy's plan would require an average annual shipbuilding budget of about $19.5 billion. Adding to this figure costs for nuclear refueling, mission modules for littoral combat ships, and modernization of cruisers and destroyers, the CBO estimated that the Navy's new fleet plan would cost an average of $21.6 billion per year through 2035.[97]

The CBO's estimate is around 70 percent higher than what the DoD spent annually on new ship construction and nuclear refueling between 2000 and 2005. Accordingly Ronald O'Rourke, of the CRS, said the Navy's 313-ship plan "appears to depend in large part on the Navy's ability to substantially increase annual funding for construction of new ships and to constrain ship procurement costs."[98]

Moreover, Eric Labs, principal Navy analyst for the CBO pointed out that if the Navy is unable to fund shipbuilding beyond its five-year average, the size of the fleet would shrink to about 200 ships. The Navy would require around $14.7 billion annually (in FY2005 dollars) just to sustain its current fleet of 281 ships.[99] Given these CBO and CRS projections, Senator John McCain said, "There's not a snowball's chance in Gila Bend, Arizona that we're going to be able to maintain this 313-ship Navy [under the current plan]...It's not going to happen."[100]

The 2006 QDR did not endorse the Navy's plan and only increased the uncertainty surrounding the future size and structure of the Navy. At the Pentagon, the comptroller's office may not believe that the Navy's plan is affordable, or defense policy officials may disagree with the Navy's fleet size.[101] In either case and regardless of the ultimate size of the Navy's fleet, the Navy's program management and cost-escalation problems require considerable attention.

The CVN-21

The Navy's problems become even clearer when they are considered on a programmatic basis. The CVN-21 is the next-generation carrier slated to replace the USS Enterprise (CVN-65) when it retires in 2012–2014. In August 2004, the DoD began characterizing the CVN-21 program as a three-ship program encompassing the CVN-21, also known as the CVN-78, and two similar follow-on ships (CVN-79 and CVN-80) to be procured in later years. At the same time, the DoD reported that the estimated development cost for the three-ship program had increased by $728 million, to $4.33 billion. The estimated total acquisition cost for the three-ship program was $36.1 billion ($4.33 billion for development and $31.75 billion for procurement), or an average of about $12 billion per ship.[102]

Congress has been providing advance procurement funding for the CVN-21 since FY2001, and the Navy's proposed FY2007 budget requested $784 million in advance procurement funding and $309 million in RDT&E funding for CVN-78, the lead ship in the CVN-21 program. In June 2005, Ronald O'Rourke of CRS estimated that the total acquisition cost of the CVN-21 would reach about $13.7 billion, or about $2 billion more than the Navy's 2004 estimate.[103]

About $400 million of this cost increase resulted from shifting procurement of the first CVN-21 by one year to FY2008, with follow-on ships beginning construction in 2012 and 2016. However, this move actually posed more significant fleet management problems beyond mere cost escalation. Shifting procurement to FY2008 means that the lead ship will not enter service until 2015. Given that the 2006 QDR called for reducing the number of carriers from 12 to 11 and that the Navy preempted this proposal by deciding to retire the USS Kennedy earlier than projected, delaying procurement until FY2008 creates a minimum one-year gap between the retirement of the USS Enterprise in 2012–2014 and its replacement by CVN-21 in 2015.[104] This will temporarily reduce the size of the carrier force by one ship to 10 carriers, as another carrier is slated for retirement around 2013.[105]

Despite the fact that retiring the USS Kennedy might save the Pentagon an estimated $2 billion through FY2011, the House Armed Services Committee opposed the impending drop in the size of the carrier fleet. The report that accompanied the House version of the FY2007 defense authorization bill, approved by the House May 11, 2006, described its position:[106]

According to the Navy's long range shipbuilding plan, if the Navy retires the Kennedy, then the aircraft carrier force will drop to 11 between now and 2012, and then drop to 10 in 2013 and 2014. With the commissioning of CVN-78 in 2015, the aircraft carrier force increases to 11 and back to 12 in 2019 and beyond...It is apparent to the committee that the decision to allow the force structure to fall to 10 in the near future is fiscally rather than operationally driven...The committee believes that the Navy should continue to maintain no less than 12 operational aircraft carriers in order to meet potential global commitments. The committee believes that a reduction below 12 aircraft carriers puts the nation in a position of unacceptable risk.

The Navy's counterargument is that the CVN-21 and follow-on ships will feature several warfighting benefits over Nimitz-class carriers. These include the following:

- Increased sortie generation rate,
- Improved ship self-defense capability,
- Increased launch and recovery capability/flexibility,
- Increased operational availability, and
- Increased flexibility to support future upgrades.

All of these features are to be supported by a new nuclear propulsion plant that will enable the CVN-21 to operate for 23 years before refueling. The Energy Department's National Nuclear Security Administration, which is responsible for funding efforts to give the Navy safe and reliable nuclear propulsion plants for surface ships and submarines, described the new plant in its FY2007 budget request for the Energy Department's National Nuclear Security Administration. "The new high-energy reactor design for CVN-21 represents a critical leap in capability. The CVN-21 reactor will have increased core energy, nearly three times the electric plant generating capability, and will require half of the reactor department sailors when compared to today's operations aircraft carriers. The extra energy will support high operational tempos and longer reactor life."[107]

Moreover, according to Captain Michael A. Schwartz, the CVN-21 program manager, the new carrier will require 1,000 to 1,200 fewer personnel compared to Nimitz-class carriers currently in the fleet, and the CVN-21's operating costs may be $5 billion less over the ship's lifetime than those of Nimitz-class carriers.[108] There is also little current debate over the value of the carrier in modern warfare. As Ronald O'Rourke of the CRS has written, "Supporters could argue that in spite of their cost, carriers are flexible platforms that in recent years have proven themselves highly valuable in various US military operations, particularly where US access to overseas bases has been absent or constrained...Supporters could also argue that Congress is already heavily committed to procuring CVN-21, having approved more than $3.8 billion of the ship's total acquisition cost from FY 2001 through FY 2005."[109]

Nonetheless, there is good reason to question whether the carriers in the CVN-21 program will be affordable and cost-effective. Promises about enhanced performance and reducing manpower burdens and life cycle costs are notoriously easy to make and are virtually never kept. The need for new carriers is far from urgent when costs escalate to the point that keeping older ships becomes a wiser investment, and some have argued that there may be cost-effective alternatives to CVN-21. Possibilities include the following:

- Smaller carriers, closer in size to the LHA-6 amphibious assault ship that may cost around $3 billion to procure;
- Carriers designed to embark air wings comprised mainly of unmanned aerial vehicles (UAVs) and unmanned air combat vehicles; and
- Small carriers, such as high-speed ships large enough to embark a small number of manned tactical aircraft each.

As for the argument that more than $3.8 billion has already been appropriated for CVN-21, opponents have argued that not all of these funds have been spent and that if large carriers are not cost-effective based on comparisons with alternative platforms, Congress should not "throw good money after bad" by continuing to fund the program.[110]

Other Surface Combatants: The Littoral Combat Ship

As the costs of the Navy's next-generation surface combatant ships continue to rise, the DoD and Congress will have to approve the current programs, sacrifice capabilities for cost, or end the programs altogether. The Littoral Combat Ship (LCS) and the DD(X) are the two most expensive surface combatant platforms and make up a considerable portion of the Navy budget and shipbuilding program.

The Navy identified a capability gap in littoral areas, including penetrating surf zones occupied by enemy mines, shallow water submarines, and fast attack craft. The LCS was tasked to fill this gap for operations in enemy waters and for conducting homeland security missions. Proponents of the program say that the LCS will meet these requirements in keeping with other transformation programs, such as modularity, net-centric warfare, and the use of unmanned vehicles (UVs).

The LCS is a key element of the Sea Shield component of *Sea Power 21*. The LCS was designed to be small, agile, and stealthy, enabling it to operate in the littoral waters that older, larger ships could not navigate effectively or at all. The seaframe is made up of the hull, command and control systems, launch and recovery systems, radar, and other core systems. Moreover, the LCS is a modular weapons platform that can take one of three different "mission packages" to adapt to the specific threats it faces. The specific threats the LCS packages are designed to meet include mine warfare, shallow water submarine warfare, and "swarm boat" or small boat attacks. The LCS will also have intelligence, surveillance and reconnaissance capabilities, and will provide support for Special Operations missions. The LCS's mission packages will use either helicopters and UVs, including UAVs, unmanned combat air vehicles, and unmanned underwater vehicles, in order to counter mines, small boat attacks, and submarines. This will allow the ship to keep its distance from the actual targets of attack.

Supporters of the LCS program cite its relative affordability and versatility due to its various mission packages. The program received $646.2 million between FY2003 and FY2005, and the Navy's Future Years Defense Plan for FY2006 to FY2011 called for $8,801 billion for the entire program. The Navy also placed a $150-million to $220-million cost limit on the seaframe (not including mission packages). In order to meet this range, the Navy is prepared to trade off certain capabilities for less expensive systems without abandoning performance requirements.

A March 2005 Navy report to Congress on potential future Navy force levels showed a potential of a 260- to 325-ship fleet by FY2035 that would include between 63 and 82 LCSs, with a predicted total acquisition cost between $25.3 billion and $32.7 billion.[111] However, the FY2007 budget submission revised these figures upward. According to a U.S. Navy Budget Item Justification Sheet that accompanied the 2007 defense budget request in February 2006, the Navy plans to procure two LCSs each in FY2006 and FY2007, three in FY2008, and then six each year from FY2009 through FY2011. This updated procurement plan showed the average cost per hull breaching the $220-million ceiling after FY2006 and rising by 49 percent to $328.2 million in 2008. Figure 7.7 shows the projected cost escalation by year.[112] In practice, however, the Navy's ability to manage cost escalation was even worse than usual. In mid-January 2007, the Navy had to issue a stop-work order on the third ship because its base cost (a different cost definition from that used in Figure 7.7) had escalated from $260 million for the second ship to $316 million for the third.[113]

Yet, even though projections made in mid-2006 called for an average cost of $317.6 million for each of the 54 planned ships in the class, the LCS was still the least expensive major shipbuilding program in the Navy's long-term shipbuilding plan.[114] Moreover, the cost escalation problems that led to a stop-work order in early 2007 meant the program's total procurement costs remained unclear, the total number of LCSs to be acquired had not yet been determined, and no final decision had been made on the ratio of each of the mission packages to the number of seaframes.

These problems with the LCS program bear a striking resemblance to the acquisition programs in the Army and the Air Force. Critics of the LCS point to both the program acquisition process and to the strategic value of the ship. They feel that the Navy has been aggressive, perhaps prematurely, in its acquisition process:

Figure 7.7   Projected LCS Cost Escalation by Year

	2006	2007	2008	2009	2010	2011
Number of ships	2	2	3	6	6	6
Total cost (in $millions)	440.0	533.4	984.5	1,834.7	1,869.2	1,947.7
Cost per ship (in $millions)	220.0	266.7	328.1	305.8	311.5	324.6

Source: Adapted from "US Navy LCS Costs To Soar, 49%," *Defense News,* March 6, 2006.

- The Navy announced the LCS program in November 2001 and set up a LCS program office in 2002. Before the announcement of the program, the Navy had not analyzed the cost-effectiveness of the LCS in comparison to other alternatives, including manned aircraft, submarines carrying UVs, larger surface ships carrying UVs, or noncombat littoral support craft carrying UVs.[115] Between April 2002 and January 2004, the Navy conducted further analysis. According to a March 2005 GAO report on the LCS, in early 2004 "the Office of the Secretary of Defense and the Joint Staff were concerned that the Navy's focus on a single solution did not adequately consider other ways to address littoral capability gaps."[116]

- As a result, later in 2004, the Navy conducted a formal analysis of alternatives to the LCS, but only "after concluding that the LCS concept was the best option to address challenges of operating US forces in the littorals."[117] Critics referred to the process as "analysis by assertion."

- Even though the Navy emphasized the importance of the LCS's capabilities against small combat boats, the Navy's analysis of surface threats facing U.S. forces in littoral waters "did not include consideration of the potential impact of all threats the LCS is likely to face...the LCS could face threats larger than small boats in littoral waters, including missile-armed warships."[118] These threats may increase the risk to LCS operations when no other U.S. forces are available to help. "Navy officials agreed that the surface threat was focused exclusively on swarms of small boats," even though the LCS is designed to operate independently as well as with larger surface warships.[119]

- The Navy largely agreed with a March 2005 GAO report that found that the LCS program has various manning, logistics, communications, command and control, computer and intelligence gathering issues that have the potential of putting the program at risk if they are not dealt with before Flight 0. In addition, the GAO identified immature technology in the LCS's mission packages that could lead to development cost increases and schedule delays.[120]

- When Gordon R. England testified in front of the Senate Committee on Appropriations' Subcommittee on Defense, he noted that one of the key benefits to the new ships including the LCS and DD(X) is that they require smaller crews—in the case of the LCS, between 15 and 50 core crew members not involved with operating the mission packages. However, the GAO noted that "reduced manning...may not be achievable because maintaining and operating the ship's mission packages, such as the MH-60 helicopter, may require more sailors than the current design allows."[121] If it is determined that this is the case when testing the Flight 0 ships, then the design may have to undergo changes before the Flight 1 ships are built, thereby causing further complications, delays, and cost increases.

- The GAO also recommended that "the Navy revise its acquisition strategy to ensure that it has sufficiently experimented with Flight 0 ships and mission packages before selecting the design for Flight 1."[122]

- Ronald O'Rourke of CRS wrote in an April 2005 report that due to the uncertainty surrounding the Navy's force structure goals, "Critics could argue that...the Navy has no approved force-structure basis for proposing a program to build any significant number of LCSs."[123]

The Navy has established a risk management board to address these problems that put the LCS program at risk, and the GAO determined that the challenges are not "insurmountable, given enough time and other resources to address them."[124] But questions persist about even the mission capabilities of the LCS. From a strategic standpoint, mission packages consisting of helicopters and UVs give the LCS its distinctive antisubmarine, antimine, and anti–small-surface boat attack capabilities.

These packages also allow the seaframe to keep a safe distance from its targets. However, critics argue that larger ships in deeper waters could launch the UVs and helicopters from a safer distance. Taking previous conflicts into consideration, such as Kosovo, Afghanistan, and Iraq, these critics argue that littoral area domination is not an immediate priority. Moreover, the Navy's proposal to use the LCS in homeland security operations is questionable because the Coast Guard is already in the process of procuring the deepwater cutter whose operational costs, the Coast Guard claims, will be lower than those of the LCS.[125]

The DD(X) or DDG1000 Zumwalt-Class Multimission Combat Ship

The DD(X) destroyer is the Navy's next-generation, multimission surface combatant with an emphasis on naval surface fire support. If the ship can be brought in on time and at cost, the mix of new and old technologies being incorporated into the ship's design would provide the following capabilities:

- Carry up to 80 Tomahawk cruise missiles.
- Two 155-millimeter Advanced Gun Systems (AGSs) would have precision-strike capabilities from distances of up to 96 miles, a greater range and accuracy than anything that naval gunfire has previously been able to achieve.
- Stealth technology that makes it look 50 times smaller than the DDG-51, about the size of a small fishing boat.[126]
- Mine avoidance.
- Antisubmarine warfare capabilities (ASW), similar to those of the Arleigh Burke DDG-51.
- Air defense.
- Support Marine Corps land attacks and Special Operation Forces.
- Highly automated functions that reduce manning to 125–175 persons versus 300 on current destroyers and cruisers. Admiral Vernon Clark, Chief of Naval Operations, said that the crew size would be between 95 and 120. He also said that if it were not highly automated, the DD(X) would require between 400 and 500 more soldiers.[127] In testimony before the House Armed Services Committee on July 19, 2005, Kenneth J. Krieg, the Under Secretary of Defense for Acquisition, Technology, and Logistics, said that the DD(X) would require a crew of about 110 where the DDG-51 requires a crew of between 200 and 300.
- Like the LCS, the DD(X) carries unmanned vehicles and helicopters.

- The DD(X) will be about 50 percent larger than the cruisers and destroyers the Navy is operating today. It will also be larger than all Navy destroyers and cruisers since the Long Beach cruiser, which was procured in 1957.[128]

Figure 7.8 summarizes the key technologies that are being incorporated into the ship's design. Like many of the previous figures, such innovations are often intended to produce cost savings, but their real-world effect is likely to be major cost escalation, program slippage, cutbacks in the numbers procured, and further rises in unit cost.

In order to minimize risk in the DD(X) program, the Navy has created ten separate engineering development models for the ship's most critical subsystems. Within each of these models, the subsystems are being designed, developed, and tested simultaneously. Testing has shown that while some of these technologies are mature, others have technical problems that could put a strain on the ship's tight procurement schedule. The models being tested are also not exact replicas of those that will be incorporated into the actual ship and therefore may have to be altered in size.[130]

Figure 7.8   Description of Engineering Development Models

Engineering Development Models	Description
Advanced gun system	Will provide long-range fire support for forces ashore through the use of unmanned operations and the long-range land attack projectile.
Integrated deckhouse and apertures	A composite structure that integrates apertures of radar and communications systems.
Dual-band radar	Horizon and volume search improved for performance in adverse environments.
Integrated power system	Power system that integrates power generation, propulsion, and power distribution and management.
Total ship computing environment	Provides single computing environment for all ship systems to speed command while reducing manning.
Peripheral vertical launch system	Multipurpose missile launch system located on the periphery of the ship.
Integrated undersea warfare system	System for mine avoidance and submarine warfare with automated software to reduce workload.
Infrared mockup	Seeks to reduce ship's heat signature in multiple areas.
Hull form	Designed to significantly reduce radar cross section.
Autonomic fire suppression system	Intended to reduce crew size by providing a fully automated response to fires.

Source: Adapted from testimony by Paul L. Francis, Director Acquisition and Sourcing Management, GAO, before the Subcommittee on Projection Forces, House Committee on Armed Services, July 19, 2005[129]

In a June 2005 report, the GAO found that many of these technologies are still immature. "While progress has been made, the level of technology maturity demonstrated remains below what is recommended by best practices."[131] As described a month later in testimony by Paul L. Francis, Director of Acquisition and Sourcing Management at the GAO, if these core technologies do not become fully mature on schedule, the challenges associated with demonstrating capabilities, developing software, and integrating subsystems must be pushed into the later stages of DD (X) design and construction when the cost of work and delays is much higher and the schedule less forgiving.[132]

Escalating costs in the later stages of development are especially problematic given that the Navy must compete for funding with other programs and support existing platforms and deployments at a time when the discretionary budget is stretched thin. In light of the risks associated with pursuing the DD(X) program, the GAO recommended that decision makers consider trade-offs in reduced mission performance, increased costs, delayed shipyard work, and/or additional manning before constructing the first ship.[133]

Cost control has been the critical issue. The cost of the first DD(X), as reported by the Navy, has increased by approximately 18 percent, from $2.8 billion in 2004 to $3.291 billion, as of May 2005.[134] In July 2005, CBO analyst Michael Gilmore told members of the House Armed Services Projections Subcommittee that the cost of the first DD(X) could be as high as $4.7 billion, above the Pentagon's upper limit for the first DD(X) of between $4 billion and $4.5 billion.[135] Other military and defense experts say that the price of the first ship could be as high as $7 billion.[136]

The cost of the second and subsequent ships has also escalated. The Navy estimated in 2004 that the second DD(X) would cost $2.053 billion. As of May 2005, this estimate increased 49 percent to $3.061 billion, and the FY2007 budget request, submitted in February 2006, included $3.4 billion for each of the first two DD(X) destroyers. Funding for the ships will be split between FY2007 and FY2008.[137] The estimated cost of subsequent DD(X)s also increased roughly 45 percent, from between $1.5 billion and $1.8 billion each in 2004 to between $2.2 billion and $2.6 billion each as of May 2005.[138]

The Cost Analysis Improvement Group (CAIG) within the Office of the Secretary of Defense reportedly estimated that the cost of DD(X) procurement may be 20 to 33 percent higher than the Navy's estimates. The CAIG's estimate for the cost of the lead DD(X) might be $4.1 billion, while its estimate for the fifth DD(X) might be $3.0 billion.[139] If the CAIG projections are accurate, the DD(X) program will certainly breach the $2.3-billion cost cap on the fifth and subsequent DD(X) ships that Congress imposed in December 2005.[140]

Due in part to these increasing costs—and likely also due to changes in operational requirements—the Navy scaled down the number of DD(X) destroyers that it intends to procure from between 16 and 24 ships to between 8 and 12 ships. The Navy's procurement schedule to meet this requirement has also changed significantly. While the 2005 FYDP indicated that the Navy would procure the first DD (X) in FY2005, none in FY2006, and two per year beginning in FY2007, under the 2006 FYDP, the Navy would purchase the DD(X) at a rate of only one per year through 2011.[141]

This schedule changed again in November 2005 when the Defense Acquisition Board approved the Navy's so-called dual-lead ship acquisition plan to procure two DD(X)s in FY2007. The move, proposed in May 2005 in an effort to reduce costs, involves a dual-shipyard construction strategy whereby Northrop Grumman and General Dynamics would build the first two destroyers at the same time. The Navy would then evaluate the shipbuilders and could choose to have all subsequent ships built in one shipyard. The Navy hopes this strategy will increase competition between the shipbuilders and bring down or maintain construction costs.[142]

Some defense experts argue that pursing the DD(X) program is worthwhile despite the program's ever-increasing costs and its shifting procurement schedule:

- Paul L. Francis, Director of Acquisition and Sourcing Management at the GAO, testified before the Projection Forces Subcommittee of the House Armed Services Committee that "the total ship computing environment, which accounts for a large portion of the software [for the DD(X)], will provide a common architecture for major ship systems to facilitate integration and to speed command and control while reducing manning."[143]

- The technologies used in the DD(X) will be spiraled into future ships, including the CG(X) and the CVN-21. As Secretary of the Navy, Gordon England told the Senate Appropriations Committee in March 2005 that the "investment [in the DD(X)] will pay dividends to other surface ship procurements," including the CVN-21, the LHA (R), and the CG(X) cruiser.[144]

- The replacement of manned functions with automated/computerized functions, such as the AGS and fire suppression, allow for a decreased crew size that would help decrease the Navy's end-strength requirements and the DD(X)'s operating costs. The current goal is to decrease the crew size to less than half that of the Arleigh Burke destroyer.

- With smaller crews and improved shore support, ten DD(X)s' operating costs over the course of 25 years would be $4.2 billion lower than the costs of a similar number of DDGs.

- According to Vice Admiral Joseph Sestak, deputy chief of naval operations for warfare requirements and programs, the Navy's analysis indicated that losses due to enemy attacks could be reduced by 31 percent if a DD(X), rather than several DDGs, is present.

- The extended range of the AGS could reduce the need for Marine artillery by 65 percent.

- With better signal processing and radar optimized for a littoral environment, the DD (X) can engage more targets in a coastal region.

- The DD(X) would be more capable in littoral areas. It is about 15 percent more effective than existing surface combatants against attacks from swarming surface craft and is well suited for combating Iranian Boghammers.[145]

Critics of the DD(X) program claim, however, that the Mission Need Statement (MNS) of the DD(X) is outdated and that the program has so many problems with procurement and operational costs and tactical relevance that it should be canceled and existing ships should be kept in service.

- The DD(X) MNS was written in 1994 for the DD(X)'s predecessor, the DD-21 destroyer. However, the combination of ongoing military transformation and the Global War on Terror may make the 1994 MNS obsolete. For example, the DD(X) will carry two AGSs. The AGS will be an important feature of the DD(X) because (1) ship-mounted guns are more cost-effective than ship-launched missiles, (2) AGS ammunition is more economical than missiles, (3) ship-mounted guns can replace air support strikes when aircraft are not ready, and (4) AGS is more reliable in inclement weather. However, taking the wars in Kosovo, Afghanistan, and Iraq as examples of potential future combat situations, there may not be a great need for high-volume fire support when using small ground force units, and the use of missiles may be more effective, as most of the ground operations in Iraq and Afghanistan were beyond the AGS's firing range (approximately 96 miles). Additionally, in keeping with transformational trends, UAVs equipped with precision-guided munitions may be capable of delivering ground support instead.
- *Defense News* reported in July 2005 that military and financial analysts questioned the necessity of the DD(X)'s firepower and stealth capabilities, proposing instead that the Navy pursue a more scaled-down next-generation destroyer.[146] Robert Work, a senior analyst at the Center for Strategic and Budgetary Assessments, argued in the same *Defense News* article that the DD(X) ship-based missile attacks were unnecessary because the Navy already has the necessary capabilities.[147]
- The LCS also has antisubmarine warfare and antisubmarine capabilities, raising the question as to what the DD(X) contributes that other ships do not, other than gunfire support. "If gunfire support is the DD(X)'s primary mission, and if the DD(X) is no longer to be the sole platform for replacing the capabilities resident in the DD-963s and FFG-7s, should requirements for the non-gunfire mission capabilities of the DD (X) design be reduced further? How much further might the cost of the DD(X) design be reduced if its non-gunfire capabilities are reduced and the ship's design is modified to make the ship more of a pure naval gunfire support platform?"[148]
- Michael Gilmore, the Assistant Director of the National Security Division at the CBO, testified before the House Armed Services Projections Subcommittee on July 20, 2005, that the DD(X) may, in fact, not be less expensive to operate in the long run.
- If the Navy keeps its plan to produce one DD(X) a year, according to Ronald O'Rourke of CRS, the procurement rate "might not be enough to introduce the planned new DD(X) technologies in sufficient numbers."[149]

The end result is that a growing number of critics question whether the Navy needs to have the DD(X) and its package of new technology at all, given overall U.S. maritime superiority and the high capabilities of existing ships. If the Navy's discretionary budget is already constrained, how can the DD(X)'s costs continue to grow against the backdrop of two wars, efforts to recapitalize the Navy with

Virginia-class submarines, CVN-21 carriers, Littoral Combat Ships, LHR amphibious ships, the JSF, as well as the remaining Arleigh Burke destroyers. Ultimately, the DD(X) may prove to take up too large a portion of the Navy's shipbuilding budget, especially considering the debate surrounding the true necessity of the ship's capabilities.

U.S. MARINE CORPS' COST-ESCALATION AND PROGRAM MANAGEMENT CHALLENGES

The U.S. Marine Corps faces procurement challenges that are just as serious as those faced by the other services.

The Osprey

The Osprey program now seems to be more an example of a program that will be funded in spite of delays, cost-escalation, and performance failures than a program whose future remains uncertain. Its real-world transformational effect, however, remains questionable. The program was conceived to meet the provisions of the 1995 Joint Multi-Mission Vertical Aircraft (JMVX) Operational Requirements Document (ORD) for an advanced vertical lift aircraft. The JMVX ORD called for an aircraft that would provide the Marine Corps (MV-22) and Air Force (CV-22) with the ability to conduct amphibious assault support and long-range, high-speed missions requiring vertical takeoff and landing capabilities.

The V-22 Osprey was developed as a vertical-lift, tilt-rotor aircraft designed for the amphibious transport of troops, equipment, and supplies from assault ships and land bases. The rotors point upward to fly like a helicopter and forward to fly like a plane. The MV-22 was designed to ultimately replace the CH-46E and CH-53D helicopters. The Osprey has been primarily a Marine Corps program funded by the Navy.

The Marine Corps has faced massive cost, performance, and delay problems with the Osprey during its 16-year development. It has had to reduce many aspects of its original specifications and mission capabilities, including reductions in its potential firepower, survivability, and range payload.

Since its first flight in March 1989, the Osprey has experienced four significant failures during testing—a crash in 1991, a second in 1992 that killed 7, a third in April 2000 that killed 19, and a fourth in December 2000 that killed 4. The Marine Corps grounded the Osprey in 2000 following the December crash, but reinstated the program in 2002.

The Osprey has also had a major cost impact. The Corps may well be able to buy the Osprey only if it does not fund its other lift, and amphibious programs, and must plan to borrow firepower and other assets from the Army in a major contingency. This has occurred at the same time that the Marine Corps has become more dependent on a high-risk vertical take-off and landing version of the Joint Strike Fighter.

- The V-22 Osprey's program costs have soared. The original estimated cost of the program was $48.025 billion. If one holds constant the FY2006 procurement objective of 458 aircraft (360 MV-22 for the Marine Corps, 50 CV-22 for U.S. Special Operations Command (USSOCOM), and 48 HV-22 for the Navy) and the FY2006 average cost per aircraft, the total cost of the program is now approximately $74.1 billion.[150]

- The FY2006 defense budget priced each MV-22 at $126.8 million, a 10-percent increase from FY2005 and a 34-percent increase from FY2004. Including RDT&E costs, the FY2006 per unit cost rises to $149.8 million, an increase of only 1.4 percent from FY2005, but an increase of 11.5 percent from FY2004.[151]

- The CV-22's per unit costs have risen even higher, partly due to the fact that USSOCOM does not require as many aircraft. Between FY2004 and FY2006, the cost per aircraft increased by 25 percent from $145.25 million to $181.1 million. Including RDT&E, between FY2005 and FY2006, the cost per aircraft increased also by 25 percent from $172.13 million to $215.75 million.[152]

Marine generals have consistently defended the merits of the program in spite of these problems. They continue to express sufficient confidence in the future of the Osprey program to discuss the possibility of a four-engine tilt-rotor aircraft with four wings and four tilting rotors called the Quad Tiltrotor whose cost is as yet unknown. Where the standard V-22 Osprey has two wingtip rotors that swivel and is designed to carry 24 troops or 10 tons of cargo, plans for the Quad Tiltrotor envision a plane with four swiveling wingtip rotors that can carry 20 tons of cargo or 132 people up to 1,000 miles at 350 miles per hour.[153]

Critics, however, have stressed the following mission risks:

- Combat helicopters—and, therefore, V-22 Ospreys—remain vulnerable to low-tech, small-arms ground fire.[154]
- The V-22 has an inherently unreliable maneuvering capability.
- The V-22 is larger and weighs four times as much as U.S. helicopters with comparable capabilities.
- The V-22 costs more than four times more than other U.S. combat helicopters.[155]

Nonetheless, the Osprey is being pushed forward toward full-scale deployment. This is despite the growing concerns of some defense analysts who have argued that, in the wake of combat operations in Iraq, the Marine Corps faces an impending helicopter shortage in its fleet of Sikorsky CH-53E Super Stallion heavy-lift helicopters and a potential shortage in its fleet of medium-lift CH-46E Sea Knight helicopters. As such, the Marine Corps' plans to procure 360 MV-22s to replace its fleet of 239 CH-46s offer a particularly costly and risky option.[156]

Some feel that the Navy's MH-60S Knighthawk presents a viable alternative amphibious assault aircraft to the V-22. It is nearly identical to the already well-known and combat-tested UH-60L Black Hawk currently in production for the Army. The MH-60S weighs about one-third as much as the V-22, but can carry nearly the same payload. It has room for only 13 soldiers compared to 18 for the V-22. But unlike the V-22, the MH-60S can also carry machine guns, rockets, and Hellfire missiles.[157] The FY2006 budget requests 26 MH-60S aircraft at a cost of only $22.7 million per aircraft and only $24.2 million per aircraft including RDT&E. That is, the DoD could purchase five MH-60S helicopters for each MV-22 that it buys.[158]

Amphibious Ships

The Marine Corps relies heavily on the Navy's amphibious warfare ships to carry Marines and their equipment and on new prepositioning ships to provide logistical support to Marine expeditionary forces. Amphibious, or L-class, ships currently make up 12 percent of the Navy's fleet, or 35 out of 293 ships. These 35 ships currently provide the lift (transport capacity) to carry roughly 1.9 Marine expeditionary brigades (MEBs), or about 27,000 troops and their equipment. This is about 75 percent of the Navy's stated goal of 2.5 MEBs worth of lift.

The Navy and Marine Corps plan to make fundamental changes to this fleet by implementing the concept the Navy calls Sea Basing. The Navy plans to replace its fleet of amphibious ships over the next 30 years and also buy a new class of logistics ships called Maritime Prepositioning Forces (Future), or MPF(F).

Ultimately, the Navy would like to build a 375-ship fleet that includes 36 amphibious ships and 16 sea-basing ships. Its plan for these forces includes purchasing (1) 10 amphibious assault ships of a new class designated LHA(R) that would carry and support more aircraft than the existing LHD-class ships, (2) 12 LPD-17 San Antonio–class amphibious transport docks, (3) 12 dock landing ships of a new class designated LSD(X), and (4) up to 21 MPF(F) ships.

These plans raise serious cost concerns:[159]

- According to the CBO, the Navy's FY2005 plan for amphibious and maritime prepositioning forces cost an average of $2.4 billion a year (in 2005 dollars), or more than twice as much per year, on average, as the Navy spent on amphibious and maritime prepositioning ships since 1980.

- Including the costs of operating and supporting those ships, the average annual cost of the Navy's plan from 2005 to 2035 may increase to $5.4 billion (in 2005 dollars).

- The CBO estimates that building the proposed 375-ship fleet alone would cost an average of $19 billion annually through 2035, a more than 58-percent increase from the $12-billion average annual funding since 1980. Under the proposed 375-ship plan, amphibious and maritime prepositioning forces comprise about 12 percent of the total shipbuilding costs, up from an average of 9 percent between 1980 and 2004.

- As of March 2006, the cost of building the first and second San Antonio–class amphibious transport docks (LPD-17 and LPD-18) had surged from a Congressionally approved $1.7 billion to an estimated $2.7 billion.[160]

The CBO has proposed four alternative plans for the future of amphibious and maritime prepositioning forces that would decrease the burden the Navy faces with its shipbuilding budget as a whole and with those forces in particular. All four plans would result in a smaller amphibious fleet than exists today, and some would result in a smaller prepositioning force as well. Each option takes a different approach to modernizing the amphibious fleet and the maritime prepositioning force given existing budget constraints. Each illustrates the problems the Marine Corps faces in sustaining and improving its amphibious capabilities. Figure 7.9 summarizes the options proposed by the CBO.[161]

- The first option is to buy fewer, more capable ships whose costs lie within the historical spending level for construction of those vessels (an average of about $1.1 billion per year in 2005 dollars). This approach would gradually reduce the number of expeditionary strike groups by half and reduce the number of prepositioning squadrons from three to two. The Navy's acquisition plans would change as follows: purchase 4 LHA(R) amphibious assault ships through 2035, instead of 10; purchase 7 LPD-17 amphibious transport docks, rather than 12; purchase 5 new LSD(X) dock landing ships, rather than 12; purchase one squadron of 8 MPF(F) ships, instead of 16; and purchase one squadron of 5 conventional cargo ships.

- The second option is to buy more, less capable, ships also within historical spending levels. In this option, the number of expeditionary strike groups would be cut from 12 to 9; the number of maritime prepositioning ships would be cut to just over half a squadron rather than by a whole squadron. Amphibious assault ships would be replaced by ships of similar size and capabilities to existing classes, and maritime prepositioning forces would be replaced by modern cargo ships without sea-basing capabilities. The Navy's acquisition plans would change as follows: purchase 6 LHA(R)s that would replicate the current fleet of amphibious assault ships rather than offer enhanced aviation capabilities as the Navy plans; purchase 9 LPD-17 ships, rather than 12; and purchase 9 LSD(X)s, rather than 12, that are similar in size and capabilities to existing dock landing ships. By 2035, the Navy would have a fleet of 39 amphibious and maritime prepositioning vessels, and the amphibious force would number 27 ships.

- A third option is to create a more survivable sea-basing force that is better able to withstand attack than the force envisioned by the Navy, at a cost below that of the Navy's current plan but above the historical spending level. Currently, MPF(F)s would have little or no ability to defend themselves from attack and would have difficulty operating if they were damaged, even though they would be the largest (except for aircraft carriers), the most detectable, and the most targetable ships in the Navy's theater of operations. To deal with this problem, under this third approach, the Navy would purchase MPF (F)s that were closer in survivability to L-class amphibious ships. Because more survivable MPF(F)s are more expensive, the Navy would purchase only one squadron of 8 ships. Accordingly, the LHA(R) program would acquire 6 ships through 2035 and would not begin until 2022, rather than in 2007. The Navy would purchase 8 LPD-

Figure 7.9   The Amphibious and Maritime Prepositioning Forces in 2035 under Alternative Force Structures

Force Structure	Average Annual Procurement Cost (in $billions)	Lift Capacity (number of MEBs)*		Number of Ships		Number of Deployed ESGs		Number of Marine Infantry Battalions Ashore After		
		All Ships	Amphibious Ships Only	All Ships	Amphibious Ships Only	Using Current Crewing	Using Crew Rotation	4 weeks	6 weeks	10 weeks
Navy's Plan	2.4	5.5	2.3	57	36	2.7	3.6	8	12	15
Option 1	1.1	3.3	1.3	31	18	1.8	2.4	4	6	9
Option 2	1.1	4.3	1.8	39	27	2.2	3.0	2	5	12
Option 3	1.5	2.7	1.7	32	24	2.1	2.8	5	7	7
Option 4	1.5	5.0	2.0	45	30	2.4	3.2	2	5	14
Current Force	n.a.	4.9	1.9	51	35	2.7	3.6	2	6	15

Notes: MEB = Marine expeditionary brigade; ESG = expeditionary strike group.

* Space for vehicles and troops is in relatively short supply on amphibious ships. The Navy has excess capacity in other categories of amphibious lift, such as space for cargo, landing craft, and helicopters. The Navy does not employ crew rotation on expeditionary strike groups, although it is planning to experiment with it. This number is shown only for comparability.

Source: Adapted from Congressional Budget Office, "The Future of the Navy's Amphibious and Maritime Prepositioning Forces," November 2004.

17s instead of 12. And the LSD(X) program would acquire only 8 ships rather than 12. The amphibious warfare force would decline fairly rapidly through 2024, and the fleet of amphibious and maritime prepositioning ships would ultimately total 32. In all, the Navy would spend an average of $1.5 billion a year on ship construction between 2005 and 2035, compared with $2.4 billion a year under the Navy's current plan.

- The fourth option deemphasizes sea basing in favor of forward presence, also at a cost below that of the Navy's current plan but above the historical spending level. In effect, this alternative forgoes the sea-basing concept altogether, but it provides for a greater overseas presence than any of the previous alternatives. It would delay the start of the LHA(R) program from 2007 until 2013 and purchase 8 ships through 2035 rather than 10. The LPD-17 program would stop at 10 ships instead of 12. The LSD(X) program would be delayed from 2020 until 2022 and purchase only 10 ships rather than 12. The MPF(F) program would consist of three full squadrons of 8 ships, but none would have sea-basing capabilities. The amphibious warfare force would remain at around 35 ships through 2012 and then quickly level off at 30 ships. By 2035, the total fleet of amphibious and maritime prepositioning ships would total 45. Given these changes, the Navy would spend $1.5 billion a year between 2005 and 2035 building amphibious and maritime prepositioning ships.[162]

The mounting cost of amphibious capability is another reason the Navy, defense officials, and lawmakers may have to reassess their priorities for transforming the Navy's fleet. If sea basing is essential to future operations, the Navy could procure it without increasing its historical funding level by decreasing the number of amphibious warfare ships (Option 1). Increasing the average funding by only 36 percent could achieve some of the sea-basing capability and make the ships that possess that capability less vulnerable to attack (Option 3). Alternatively, if decision makers determine that the size of the force and its forward presence should take precedence over sea basing, the Navy could have an amphibious warfare force of about 27 ships by 2035 without an increase in funding (Option 2). Or, with the same funding increase as in Option 3, the Navy could retain a force of at least 20 L-class ships through 2035.[163]

DEFENSE AGENCY, SATELLITE, AND SPACE COST-ESCALATION AND PROGRAM MANAGEMENT CHALLENGES

Many key aspects of military transformation rely on the promise of linking new technologies to appropriate revisions in doctrine and organization to achieve revolutionary progress in warfighting performance. This is particularly true in the space sector as key officials at the DoD tout the capacity for orbital systems to offer unique advantages in providing military forces with real-time intelligence, precise targeting, and robust communications.

As might be expected, the Department of Defense has been no more realistic in planning, programming, and budgeting these aspects of investment than it has for the services. A CBO study of defense investment costs from FY2007–FY2024 found that the Department of Defense projected that annual average investment spending for the defense agencies would average $16 billion a year during FY2007–FY2011, and $14 billon a year during FY2007–FY2011. These costs were heavily driven by spending for missile defense and the CBO estimated that annual costs for such programs would peak in 2016. The Department's programs projected a cost of about $15 billion. The CBO estimated that a prudent estimate of cost risk would make the real cost at least $3 billion a year higher—a rise of at least 20 percent a year even in the peak spending year.[164]

The CBO did not examine the implications of other programs, although many defense agencies had historically had cost-escalation problems worse than those of the military services. It also ignored key intelligence and black programs, which are often placed in the service budgets and/or kept secret. The cost of space programs is particularly critical.

The Rising Costs of Space Programs

Although ambitious plans for the future of national security space programs have gained support among policy makers, the space sector has become another cost-performance crisis. Virtually every next-generation constellation being developed has encountered unanticipated cost growth, schedule slippage, and technical difficulties.[165]

These problems are summarized in the following excerpt from the section titled "Problems in DoD Space Programs" in the June 10, 2005, Report of the House Appropriations Committee on the Department of Defense Appropriations Bill, 2006.[166]

> In 2002, DoD leadership saw unsettling trends in the management of these [space] programs and commissioned a Defense Science Board (DSB) task force to conduct an independent review. In 2003, the task force reported numerous systemic problems, including a strong bias towards unrealistic cost estimates, an undisciplined process for requirements definition, and a serious erosion in government management and engineering expertise. Since publication of the DSB report, the programs have collectively gotten worse, with virtually every major space acquisition program under the cloud of a Nunn-McCurdy cost breach. One notable example, the Space Based Infrared High (SBIRS HIGH) satellite, has experienced three Nunn-McCurdy breaches in just four years. SBIRS High costs have grown from $4 billion to over $10 billion.

To further compound matters, the SBIRS HIGH program experienced a fourth Nunn-McCurdy breach for the final quarter of FY2005 when its overall costs swelled by 10.7 percent, from $9.6 billion to $10.6 billion.[167]

The Nunn-McCurdy oversight law represents a key Congressional attempt to force the DoD to learn how to manage and contain its costs. It requires that the Pentagon notify Congress when a major acquisition program's costs grow by 15 percent. If cost growth reaches 25 percent, Nunn-McCurdy requires the Pentagon to justify continuing the program based on three criteria: its importance to national security, the lack of a viable alternative, and evidence that the problems that led to the cost growth are under control.

The Nunn-McCurdy breaches in the Air Force's space portfolio have become so endemic that the House version of the 2006 Defense Authorization Act passed on May 25, 2005, would amend Nunn-McCurdy so as to require the Pentagon to submit to Congress an analysis of alternatives to a given program if its costs grew by 15 percent. The analysis would have to include the costs associated with completing the program with no changes; completing it with some design, requirements, or manufacturing changes; and building alternative systems.[168]

By the spring of 2005, the cost escalation in the DoD's space acquisition portfolio led the Congressional committees reviewing defense budget requests for the next fiscal year to threaten to terminate or drastically cut back several of the Pentagon's most important space initiatives.[169] These included the nation's next generation of missile warning systems, its next generation of photoreconnaissance satellites, its next generation of secure communications satellites, and its first ever constellation of space-based radars.[170]

- The Department of Defense's total budget request for both classified and unclassified space programs was $22.12 billion for 2005 (in 2006 dollars) and $22.66 billion for 2006. While this is an increase of only about 2.5 percent, the investment portion for unclassified programs is 43 percent higher, and investment spending for unclassified programs grew from 22 percent of the DoD's total space budget in 2005 to 31 percent in 2006. Total DoD spending on space programs is expected to rise to at least $25 billion by FY2009, an increase of about $11 billion in 2000.

- According to the FYDP for 2006 through 2011, funding for development and procurement of major unclassified space systems grew by more than 40 percent in 2006 (to $6.9 billion from $4.9 billion in 2005) and will double by 2011.[171]

- Historically, according to the CBO, RDT&E costs for DoD space systems have grown by an average of 69 percent from their original development estimates, and procurement costs have risen by an average of 19 percent. If costs grow at these rates in the future, investment needs would peak at $14.4 billion in 2010, rather than at $10.0 billion under the current FYDP.[172]

- The unclassified data on the five satellites in the SBIRS program have escalated from $3.9 billion eight years ago to $9.9 billion, or by $1.2 billion a satellite. As of July 2005, updating the language in the June 10, 2005, House Appropriations Report quoted above, the SBIRS-HIGH program actually breached Nunn-McCurdy cost growth limits *four* times in as many years.[173] Although the DoD received the full $756 million it requested for FY2006 for the SBIRS-High program, the House Appropriations report called the program "extremely troubled."[174]

- Unclassified space-control programs have also encountered cost overruns. Focused on developing ground- and space-based sensors to enhance situational awareness in space and on developing technology to disrupt, deny, degrade, or destroy enemy space systems, these programs include Spacetrack, the Space-Based Surveillance System, the Rapid Attack Identification, Detection, and Reporting System, and the Counter Communications System. Under the 2006 FYDP, according to the CBO, RDT&E funding for space-control systems would increase from $195 million in 2006 to $768 million in 2011.[175]

- A 2003 report titled "The Full Costs of Ballistic Missile Defense" by Economists for Peace and Security estimated the life-cycle costs for the missile defense program to total $1.2 trillion. The study estimated that the completion date for three of the four major systems planned—that is, the land-based, sea-based, and air-based systems—is 2015.[176] Adhering to this schedule requires a steep spending path. Annual spending for missile defense would have to be about $25 billion in 2005 and $50 billion in 2007. That is, the amount being spent on missile defense is far below what would need to be spent to achieve the DoD's objectives for missile defense.[177]

The High Cost of U.S. National Space Policy

The Bush Administration released a new National Space Policy on October 6, 2006, to govern the conduct of U.S. space activities. The first revision of overall space policy since 1996, the new space policy asserted that space capabilities were vital to U.S. national interests and that the United States will

Preserve its rights, capabilities, and freedom of action in space; dissuade or deter others from either impeding those rights or developing capabilities intended to do so; take those actions necessary to protect its space capabilities; respond to interference; and deny, if necessary, adversaries the use of space capabilities hostile to US national interests.

The policy revision also emphasized the increasing importance of space security, in relation to U.S. economic, national, and homeland security and committed the United States to "encouraging and facilitating" private enterprise in space. Moreover, the document essentially characterized U.S. space diplomacy in terms of persuading other nations to support U.S. policy.

Although administration officials denied it, the new policy seemed to hint at the possibility that the United States would seek to weaponize space by developing, testing, and deploying space weapons. The United States has long rebuffed even the idea of engaging in international talks to ban space weapons, going so far as to submit the only "no" vote against 160 "yes" votes when negotiations on banning space weapons were proposed at the United Nations in October 2005.[178] In keeping with this position, the new space policy opposed the imposition of any international legal regime or other restrictions that would impinge on U.S. access to or use of space.

This approach seems to reflect the fact that many key existing weapons systems, and many transformational systems under development, rely on information and communications from orbiting satellites, and U.S. military officials are bent on protecting these capabilities. Defending the satellites that are both absolutely essential and extraordinarily vulnerable would seem like an obvious course of action. And some advocates of the new policy have argued somewhat naively that no new arms-control agreements are required for a space arms race that does not exist.

The problem with the new space policy is that it could lead to asymmetric space warfare. As Michael Katz-Hyman and Michael Krepon of the Washington, D.C.–based Henry L. Stimson Center point out, "Recent developments highlight the central dilemma of U.S. space policy: the essential and vulnerable nature of satellites used for national and economic security. The more we seek to protect our satellites by the use of force in space, the more vulnerable our satellites will become if our own practices are emulated by others."[179]

If the United States does not pursue "space diplomacy," it forgoes the option of negotiating to produce rules for space that work in conjunction with other U.S. initiatives to help satellites work as intended. Just as the various military services follow codes of conduct that govern military operations on land, sea, and in the air, similar guidelines for responsible space-faring nations could serve the U.S. national interest. For example, basic common sense guidelines could allow for prenotification of unavoidable dangerous maneuvers in space as well as help to manage space traffic and debris mitigation.[180]

Moreover, supporting the new space policy and future space programs could add major new costs to the FYDP. As Theresa Hitchens of the Center for Defense Information stated regarding current trends in the procurement of space platforms,[181]

> Space is an exceedingly expensive place. To fully implement the capabilities necessary to fight "in, from and through" space, hundreds of billions would have to be dedicated to developing new weapons, launching thousands of new on-orbit assets, and maintaining those systems once they are deployed. With launch costs remaining at $22,000 per kilogram, and current satellites in Leo weighing up to 4,000 kilograms, the price tag rapidly becomes exorbitant—hundreds and hundreds of billions of dollars. For one thing, Congress is already expressing concerns about the costs of today's Air Force space programs that have nothing to do with controversial ASAT or space-strike systems. Programs such as the Transformational Satellite system designed to replace current military communications satellites, and the space Radar to replace aging U.S. early warning satellites, are years behind schedule and tens of millions of dollars over budget. Congressional reaction to Air Force budget requests for new space weapons programs based on unproven and yet undeveloped technologies may well not be all that favorable.

Given the ever-increasing cost of space weapons outlined in the previous section and the sheer magnitude of the task that would be controlling space and protecting fragile U.S. space assets from any and all enemies, policy makers may want to rethink their opposition to negotiating international rules, norms, and guidelines to regulate space.

THE BROADER PROBLEM: TURNING FORCE TRANSFORMATION INTO A "LIAR'S CONTEST"

All of these case studies show that the United States faces immediate and critical problems in bringing its strategy and force plans into balance with resources. This summary history of transformational programs is a warning that cost escalation is being dealt with by repeated efforts to downsize the force to pay for new systems—which are then still expected to be both force multipliers and force compensators—somehow enhancing existing capability and compensating for force cuts at the same time.

Taken together, the consistent pattern of problems in such programs is more than a basic failure in management. It strongly suggests that the Department of Defense has been locked into a "liar's contest" at the level of defense contractors, program managers, every military service, and the Office of the Secretary of Defense.

The services compete to place programs in the budget by promising costs, performance, and schedules they cannot deliver. Program managers, contractor managers, and their superiors have to join this competition to survive. Performance specifications are constantly increased to deal with force cuts, make the program more competitive, and justify cost escalation. Major programs take on a life of their own, gather momentum, and become both unaffordable in the process and impossible to cancel. Service secretaries, chiefs of staff, and defense agency heads become advocates and competitors rather than planners and managers.

The review process within the Department of Defense enforces occasional checks and balances, but major programs become too important and too political to cancel. The result is more cuts in the active forces, more program stretch outs to reduce annual cost at the expense of major rises in the cost of the total program, cutbacks in the numbers to be procured, followed by new efforts to improve performance to justify the program and compensate for smaller numbers.

As the previous case histories show, no one is really held accountable. Program survival and advocacy have become more important than the truth in terms of real-world cost, performance, and schedule.

The United States needs to make hard trade-offs and hard decisions, not make further efforts in procurement reform. There are many ways in which the United States might create better procurement experts, better program managers, and more efficient procedures, but the scale of the previous problems in U.S. defense procurement is so great that any such efforts now can have little more impact than putting lipstick on a pig. The level of failure in today's programs represents a basic failure to make hard choices at the level of the Secretary of Defense, Deputy Secretary, Service Secretaries, Chairman of the Joint Chiefs, and Service Chiefs of Staff.

None of these problems could arise without a broad abdication of leadership responsibility throughout the Department. Forcing hard choices on the system is the reason senior positions exist. Tolerating systematic failure is simply cowardice. All of these issues are also a further caution that the United States cannot afford the luxury of planning for what it cannot get. In fact, they show that the most critical single challenge the Department of Defense faces in force transformation is to learn how to plan, manage, and execute force transformation on a program-by-program basis.

Like the Department's response to most of the challenges in this book, they also reflect an even more disturbing failure in leadership and accountability. Over the years, a whole series of efforts have been made at procurement reform. Some have helped at the margins. Most have simply created more bureaucracy, paperwork, and need for contract support. In balance, they have done at least as much harm as good and many have bordered on the absurd.

The United States does not need new management techniques or procurement reforms. It needs top-down accountability for making hard strategic decisions that kill programs that get out of control, which do not deliver on schedule and at planned cost, and which force the wrong kind of trade-offs in force size and capability. The current system would work fine if the senior officials and officers in the Department of Defense made the decisions they should when they should. No system can be effective if it fails to act, dithers and delays, and lies to itself and to others.

A Secretary of Defense who cannot end cost escalation and who cannot make the hard decisions necessary to force true cost containment on the Department should be very publicly fired for incompetence. The same is true of the Deputy Secretary, Director of Defense Research and Engineering (DDR&E), Under Secretaries, and other senior officials in the Office of the Secretary of Defense.

The United States also cannot afford Joint Chiefs of Staff who create unaffordable force plans and tolerate major program cost escalation to purse their own interests, or those of their services, in an effort to "win" the procurement game by being the most successful liar. The Chiefs, and the Office of the Joint Chiefs, needs to be given the same responsibility for affordable force plans and procurement plans given to civilians. This may well require formal legislation, or Department of Defense Directives, forcing the Chiefs and the Office of the Joint Chiefs to provide program and budget costs for all strategic documents, force planning exercises, net assessments, and annual inputs to the planning, programming, and budgeting cycle. Decades of unrealistic force and procurement plans, and strategies decoupled from reality, have shown that freeing the military from programming and budgeting does not lead to better plans, but only to unworkable ones.

Similar responsibility for cost containment and realistic and affordable programs and budgets needs to be forced on the Service Secretaries and all of the senior officers and officials in each of the four services. In an era of joint warfare, no one needs service advocates and no one should tolerate any service official or officer who cannot control costs and budget effectively. One possible solution is to expand the long-term planning, programming, and budgeting role of the major unified and specified commanders. The argument that they are too operational and too short term in their thinking and role is a dangerous self-fulfilling prophecy. Service-oriented planning and budgeting is increasingly obsolescent, if not obsolete. Both force and procurement plans should be tailored to joint missions, not service priorities.

The argument that talent is scarce at the top and deserves collegial protection is absurd. The competition for top positions ensures that there will always be a new and potentially competent replacement for any official or officer who fails, and no one is more expendable than Secretary of Defense or service Chief of Staff.

Finally, the cult of the CEO or defense contractor is equally dangerous. Corporate officials and senior program managers should be held personally responsible for program success, and this includes cost control and containment. Contracts should have cost, performance, and schedule penalties, and these too should be enforced without exception. Defense companies and contractors need to know that their personal careers and corporate bottom line will suffer severely if they underbid, overpromise, let program costs escalate, or go along with pressure from officers and officials to change specifications and indulge in program growth that leads to cost escalation.

In short, the only real answer to a potentially crippling failure to develop affordable programs does not lie in new procurement methods or endlessly reporting the failure to manage costs and meet performance and delivery goals. It does not require more studies. The fact is that the steady rise in problems and cost escalation is the result of a system in which failure to make difficult and timely decisions is not only tolerated but encouraged. There is no single area where the Department of Defense and the Congress should be less forgiving in firing senior defense officials including Secretaries, Deputy Secretaries, and DDR&Es. The same is true of service secretaries and the Chiefs; the CEOs, the vice presidents, and the program managers in the defense industry who fail to contain costs and deliver effective programs should be faced with being forced to resign or seeing their companies barred from future defense contracts. There will never be an effective system until failure is punished from the top down. As for replacements, the competent will always emerge if given the chance and the incentive.

Challenge Seven: Creating an Effective Interagency Capability to Perform National Security Missions

Salvaging American defense does, however, require measures that go far beyond the Department of Defense. The Iraq War, the Afghan conflict, and the broader war on terrorism have all shown that the United States cannot define "overstretch" in terms of military resources and capabilities. If it is to develop effective capabilities for modern warfare, it must do so as an entire government. It must create the civilian components and interagency progress necessary to place the burden on a government-wide basis.

To return to points made earlier, a substantial part of the burden that the Iraq War, the Afghan conflict, and the war on terrorism have placed on U.S. military forces in Iraq is the result of failures in interagency planning and coordination in going to war, in fighting the war, and in stability and nation-building operations. It is also the result of the fact that the civilian elements of the U.S. government (USG) did not assume their share of the burden and properly perform their functions.

- A State Department–led interagency process proved able to diagnose many of the problems that were likely to emerge in Iraq, but failed to create an operational capability to deal with them in the field. Under pressure from neoconservative ideologues in the Office of the Secretary of Defense (OSD), the Bush Administration let the interagency process collapse and effectively excluded it from the actual execution of stability and nation-building operations in Iraq. At the same time, both the U.S. military and the OSD chose to focus almost exclusively on defeating Iraq's conventional forces, planning for instant liberation, rather than preparing for meaningful stability and nation-building operations.

- The United States ignored the warnings of the interagency community before the war. It did not provide, or even have, anything like the civilian elements in other agencies it needed, and much of the capability it did have was not willing to take risks in the field.

- The Bush Administration recruited short-term civilian teams, many chosen for ideological and political reasons, without area expertise to make up for the lack of trained and experienced personnel. These teams were then rotated by civilians and the military through the country far too quickly to develop the expertise, interpersonal relationships with Iraqis, and other skills necessary for effective stability operations.

- The United States compounded its problems by improvising a massive aid operation after the fall of Saddam and during the initial occupation that sought to transform Iraq's economy on American terms using outside U.S. and other contractors and relying on private security forces. The result was a hopelessly flawed effort U.S. administrators could not plan or manage, that failed to efficiently substitute dollars for bullets, and which has had to be repeatedly restructured and reprogrammed because of its inherent impracticality.

- Postwar planners tried to improvise a contractor-implemented approach to key elements of stability operations where it was clear that U.S. officials did not have the talent necessary to manage the programs and the contractors available lacked core competence. U.S. officials then tried to force the contractors to hire mercenaries to protect themselves from the developing insurgency.

If the United States is to find the right match between its strategy and resources, it must make major changes in the civilian contribution to war. The existing interagency process failed at least as badly in Iraq as it did during critical periods in Vietnam, and many observers feel it was much worse. If the United States is to have an effective match between its strategy and resources, it needs to do so on a civil-military basis, not simply on a military one. This means that the United States not only needs interagency tools to allocate both civil and military efforts, but central direction and clear lines of authority that do not allow one agency to bypass another or to stonewall or partially comply in working as part of a common effort.

Put bluntly, the interagency process needs clear and unambiguous lines of authority, and almost certainly from the National Security Council down. Iraq has simply exposed long-standing realities. The State Department cannot lead or direct interagency operations in wartime, and its theoretical authority is an exercise in futility when it comes to practice. The Department of Defense (DoD) cannot be allowed to operate in the field or at the central command level without a broader grand strategic direction. Civil agencies cannot be allowed to put domestic priorities first without interagency review and coordination.

Allocating civilian resources is as important as improving the interagency process. The United States needs to rethink "jointness" to force united efforts by both the DoD and the civilian agencies. It not only needs this jointness in Washington, it needs it in the field. There must be a single decision maker clearly in charge of each major effort and capable of compelling interagency cooperation and holding individuals directly responsible.

The military needs adequate staffs of civilian counterparts in the field if the United States is to efficiently conduct asymmetric war, counterinsurgency, counterterrorism, stability operations, nation building, and peacemaking. These kinds of missions and struggles cannot be shaped and won in Washington and rear areas; they must be won on the scene in the countries involved. If this is to happen, civilians in the State Department, intelligence services, and other relevant agencies must be recruited and retained on the basis of their willingness to operate in hostile areas and accept significant risk. Stability and nation-building operations must have an effective civilian component, where "effective" means in the field and not in fortress-like embassies.

The U.S. government has recognized these needs in theory, but so far has failed to go beyond ineffective good intentions. State Department efforts to create new coordinating bodies have created the image of progress and the reality of failure. Its U.S. Agency for International Development (USAID) has failed in Afghanistan and has been an incompetent disaster in Iraq. The DoD's new Quadrennial Defense Review (QDR) and other efforts like DoD directive 3000.05 have called for many of the right actions, but done little to accomplish them. The results are already costly in both Iraq and Afghanistan and could be far more costly in future missions.

IMPROVING INTERAGENCY OPERATIONS

> The primary challenge of interagency operations is to achieve unity of effort despite diverse cultures, competing interests, and differing priorities of participating organizations.
>
> —*Joint Vision 2020* (2000)[1]

Jointness is just as important at the interagency level as at the military level. If the United States is to meet the challenges of stability operations, nation building, peacemaking, asymmetric warfare, and homeland defense, it must forge a civil-military partnership that can provide the full mix of talent and resources needed for each new crisis and task.

As the Iraq War has demonstrated, the need for this partnership goes far beyond simply cooperating in military and stability operations once a conflict or mission has begun. When war must succeed at the ideological, political and economic levels—as well as at the level of military operations—close interagency cooperation is needed to determine what kind of operation is needed and what kind of operation is feasible. The most critical single moment in interagency cooperation is in determining what to do and whether it is possible to create a real-world operational plan that the U.S. government can implement.

The First Steps on the Road to Interagency Failure

In the case of Iraq—and Afghanistan to a lesser degree—the system failed dismally in this regard. The rush to war at the military level led the State Department and intelligence agencies to be largely ignored and the DoD to focus on warfighting and not on stability operations and nation building. No real strategy existed for integrating military and civilian efforts to support military operations with ideological, political, and economic operations. There was no systematic assessment of risks and costs, operational needs, or resource requirements.

The interagency planning that did take place was largely diagnostic, rather than operational, in part because there was no pool of civilian competence with experience in anything approaching an operation on the scale of Iraq, and because area expertise was oriented far more toward intelligence and political reporting than operations. The U.S. government could not provide a convincing answer as to how to deal with Iraq's or Afghanistan's ethnic and sectarian problems. It had no core expertise in dealing with either an economy as large or different as Iraq's command kleptocracy, or Afghanistan's war-ruined and drug-dominated economy. The U.S. interagency process was incapable of dealing with the fact that religion, not democracy, was the dominant ideological issue and local culture was of far more popular concern than Western concepts of human rights.

In fairness, the most senior political leaders did not want to know, or hear, many of the concerns that were raised at the interagency level. A "can do" approach rejected objections and concerns as obstructionist, and the issue of "should do" was not one the White House and Secretaries of State and Defense wished to address. The President chose to reject the interagency approach to the Iraq War that had begun in 2002 and instead chose to give the mission to the DoD in early 2003—setting aside the interagency effort that the State Department had begun.

In retrospect, the most important single aspect of the Iraq operation was the need to determine whether the United States could actually take on the mission of nation building at every level and create a realistic operational plan that could integrate all U.S. government activities and that could actually be manned and funded. A combination of Bush Administration rejection of the need for the mission, a general Administration opposition to nation building, and a strong DoD and military desire to avoid being "bogged down" in stability operations in Iraq meant that the choices between containment and invasion were never realistically assessed, and senior U.S. political and military leaders effectively went to war with one-third of a war plan and no real idea of what to do at the interagency level once Saddam fell.

The key lesson is that no moment in interagency cooperation is more critical than the first one: whether to go, how to go, and whether the necessary resources are there?

Failing Once the Mission Begins

The ideological and political failures in the U.S. approach to Iraq once the mission began have been described in Chapter 2 and again revealed many of the same weaknesses in the interagency process. The economic failures, however, provide a new illustration of just how serious the need for a full-scale civil-military partnership really is. Once Saddam fell, the almost immediate collapse of a grossly undermanned and understaffed Office for Reconstruction and Humanitarian Assistance (ORHA) then led to a Coalition Provisional Authority (CPA) where heavy reliance was placed on recruiting neoconservatives and volunteers from outside government, most of whom had virtually no area or subject experience and were on three- to six-month tours. A massive staff of constantly shifting personnel built up in Baghdad's Green Zone with grossly understaffed civilian efforts in the field. The headquarters tripped over itself, while the military was left with token support from a few dedicated career personnel.

The United States had grossly inadequate capability to use either the Iraqi funds left over from Saddam Hussein's regime or the massive aid funds Congress voted for once the CPA was created. USAID, which had shrunk over the years from some 3,000 to 1,000 personnel, was a project-oriented group with no real experience in reshaping entire economies, limited operational capability in the field, and dependence on outside contractors. Department of the Army and Corps of Engineers personnel brought into the aid process to provide support had no real competence relevant to the task.

The private contractors that were then hired to perform virtually all tasks in the field had no experience either. They at best had operated with the semi-market economies in the Middle East. They had no ability to survey and plan what Iraq needed and no functioning Iraqi government existed to help them. The U.S. military would not provide security as Iraq became a functional war zone, and private security was extremely expensive and limited in coverage. A lack of experience, a lack of functional audits and measures of effectiveness, and a blizzard of pointless paperwork and regulations further crippled U.S. prime contractors that had no real ability to work in an alien country and command an economy. Prime contractors were forced to be dependent on a host of local contractors with little or no motive other than sheer profiteering. The situation also created a climate of uncontrolled expenditure that led to massive corruption and waste.

The end result was one of the worst and most incompetent operations in the history of the U.S. government, covered up in far too many cases by worthless official reporting that claimed progress that did not exist, politicized and spun failure into success, denied the scale of the security problem, and attempted to ignore the fact that American corruption outpaced that of Iraq. As the reports of the Special Inspector General for Iraqi Reconstruction made brutally clear, at least $10 billion were thrown away to minimal effect, sometimes in ways that actively aided the insurgents or encouraged the division of the country.[2]

It was not until well into 2005, and once Ambassador Zalmay M. Khalilzad brought some of the same planning techniques to Iraq that he had used in Afghanistan, that the United States attempted two critical steps. The first was a meaningful strategic plan for overall action. The second was to transfer aid planning and implementation to the Iraqis. The lack of an Iraqi government through June 2006, however, ensured further delays. The United States effectively wasted three years at the civilian level of war that it simply did not have to waste.

The Afghan Case

The situation in Afghanistan has been more favorable, but still has important parallels to that in Iraq. This was not an optional war, but the focus on military action and the assumption that American and Western values could "win" the political and ideological side of the battle was equally flawed. The interagency process worked better in the sense that strategic plans to integrate ideological, political, economic, and military action were developed soon after the Taliban fell—although more through the efforts of outside advisors than because of interagency efforts.

The creation of Provincial Reconstruction Teams (PRTs) made a deliberate effort to put integrated civil-military teams into the field early in the operation—a step that did much to force integrated civil-military efforts where they counted most. This same step was later instituted in Iraq, but years too late and with extraordinarily badly managed initial recruiting efforts and plans for operations and security.

There was, however, the same lack of realism about the time scale needed to succeed, about the level of resources required, and about the need for U.S. civil and military efforts with the kind of language, cultural, and area expertise needed to transform a country. Premature and unrealistic efforts were made to pass critical parts of the mission on to NATO allies. The dependence of a war-torn country on a drug economy was dealt with largely in terms of denial. The depth of ethnic and sectarian division was not fully addressed, and the probable impact of religious and cultural values was downplayed.

The Nature of the Problem

Half a decade into the first major step in the "long war," and more than three years into a major counterinsurgency struggle in Iraq, the United States still has not made a serious effort to create an effective civil-military partnership even in Washington. In spite of cosmetic efforts at improved interagency coordination, there is still a fundamental mismatch between the international threat environment and the current national security structure. In complex contingency operations from Somalia to Iraq, the lack of a joint, integrated interagency process undermined the ability of the United States to develop appropriate policies and implement comprehensive strategies. At a time when national security challenges increasingly required the combined efforts of multiple agencies, the United States continued to cling to an *ad hoc* and improvised interagency process that made policy difficult to develop and even more difficult to implement.

It is easy to create new staffs and committees, talk about interagency coordination, and promise progress. The interagency progress, however, remains one of rivalry, turf battles, and Washington-oriented parochialism. It does not work on a voluntary basis; it works only when some higher authority forces it to do so. This situation is much worse when civilian agencies are involved that do not normally have personnel who take risks or work with the military in the field, and when most of the action must be taken overseas and at the Embassy and command levels. It is further complicated by the natural tendency of intelligence agencies to grossly overclassify, exclude, and seek to compartmentalize their operations. Progress must be forced on both the bureaucracy and the political appointees; in Washington terms, meaningful interagency action is an "unnatural act."

An article by Martin J. Gorman and Alexander Krongard put it this way: "[W]hen the Government confronts conflated or melded problems that are beyond the capacity of any single department or agency to solve, it rarely develops comprehensive policies; instead it poorly coordinates its actions, badly integrates its strategies, and fails to synchronize policy implementation."[3]

These problems were highlighted in the first phase of a Center for Strategic and International Studies' study on defense reform and improving the interagency process titled *Beyond Goldwater-Nichols, Phase I Report* (2004). The chronic disconnect between governmental agencies in conducting operations owes to several factors:[4]

- Unlike the military, the U.S. government as a whole lacks established procedures for developing integrated strategies and plans. Each new administration issues its own policies and plans for devising strategy and often overlooks the best practices and lessons learned by its predecessors.

- Outside of the DoD, there is no long-term "planning culture" that would facilitate institutionalizing an interagency process. Military officers are taught that planning is critical to successful operations and receive training to this end. With the exception of USAID, which plans long-term development projects, the civilian departments and agencies tend not to have dedicated planning staffs or expertise.

- As an unfortunate aftereffect of the Oliver North era, when a National Security Council (NSC) staffer conducted foreign operations from the Old Executive Office Building, the NSC has little capacity dedicated to integrating agency strategies and plans or to monitoring their execution. However, coordinating interagency strategies and plans and monitoring their execution under some central authority is critical to achieving unity of efforts across the U.S. government and success on the ground. The tendency to assign integration functions to a lead agency—as the Bush Administration designated the DoD the lead agency for postconflict operations in Iraq—rarely works because the lead agency has no authority over its counterparts and cannot bring the President's authority to bear.

- Most civilian agencies lack meaningful pools of rapidly deployable U.S. government experts who are trained for field missions and can offer them meaningful pay or career incentives—although it can easily offer massive pay incentives to private contractors. Moreover, the agencies do not have the authorities or resources to quickly establish programs in the field. Consequently, the U.S. military does not have the requisite civilian partners on the ground with whom to share the burden of conducting operations. At the same time, military personnel are forced to execute tasks for which they were not trained, which, in turn, leads to longer deployments.

During the Iraq War and the Afghan conflict, the weaknesses in other federal agencies have placed the main burden of stability operations and nation building on the U.S. military. They have been supported largely by a limited number of carrier civilians in the State Department willing to take risks, work in the field, and put the mission before a promotion system that has favored those who either remain in Washington or keep their visibility through the State Department's reporting back to Washington. In practice, far too many career foreign service officers have proved so risk averse that the State Department has had to rely heavily on short-term contract personnel, many with limited qualifications. Other government departments and agencies have been notably less forthcoming than the State Department, often leaving critical gaps in aid and other civil efforts.

Intelligence personnel have been more willing to volunteer, but career intelligence operatives have suffered from constant reorganizations, cutbacks and shakeups, and the same Washington-centric focus on bureaucratic careerism. This has put an undue strain on a military whose forces are simply not trained or equipped to establish law and order and effective governance, relief, and reconstruction programs.

The problem has been made far worse by an over-reliance on contractors, many of which compete with the military and the government for the same skilled personnel, and who often outbid the government in ways that lead military officers and career civilians to leave government service. In far too many cases, such contractors have not been able to perform effectively, and there has been massive waste, fraud, and abuse in many of the aid programs in Iraq. As was discussed in Chapter 2, this has been a major problem in creating an effective U.S. approach to counterinsurgency and one well-documented by the Special Inspector General for Iraqi Reconstruction.

Other critical difficulties include a system where both government civilians and contractors must provide for security, relying on the equivalent of mercenaries, rather than on the U.S. military. In many cases, they also are given far less priority for the use of military transportation than would be the case in an integrated system where priority was assigned on the basis of overall need or must provide their own transportation. The end result is that government civilians do not operate as part of a common team and contractors often cannot function or choose security over mission effectiveness. It is also the creation of mercenary security forces that often show little concern for local sensitivities and political considerations, and sometimes conduct "cowboy" or rogue operations.

As Senator Richard Lugar said in March 2004 in his Opening Statement to the Hearing on the Stabilization and Reconstruction Civilian Management Act (S 2127, 108th Congress, commonly known as the Lugar-Biden initiative),[5]

> While recognizing the critical challenges that our military has undertaken with skill and courage, we must acknowledge that certain non-security missions would have been better served by a civilian response. Our post-conflict efforts frequently have had a higher than necessary military profile. This is not the result of a Pentagon power grab or institutional fights. Rather, the military has led post-conflict operations primarily because it is the only agency capable of mobilizing sufficient personnel and resources for these tasks. As a consequence, military resources have been stretched and deployments of military personnel have been extended beyond expectations. If we can improve the capabilities of the civilian agencies, they can take over many of the non-security missions that have burdened the military.

Balancing peacekeeping and nation-building responsibilities more evenly across key federal agencies—the Intelligence Community, the State, Treasury, Commerce, and Justice Departments, and USAID—requires enhancing the civilian capacities for complex contingency operations.[6] In the same way that the 1986 Goldwater-Nichols Department of Defense Reorganization Act created a major impetus for the military to operate more efficiently and effectively, many experts have intimated that the interagency process may require a Goldwater-Nichols–like change.[7]

FAILED EFFORTS TO FIX THE INTERAGENCY PROCESS

Past efforts to improve U.S. effectiveness in managing complex contingency operations have yielded mixed results. President Bill Clinton directed an interagency review of peacekeeping policies, programs, and procedures that led to the issuance of a series of three Presidential Decision Directives (PDDs) aimed at improving U.S. capability to respond to inter- and intrastate conflicts. The first of these, PDD 25, addressed reforming multilateral peace operations. It established instructions for conducting peace operations and focused attention on the need for improved dialogue and decision making among governmental agencies.

The Clinton Beginning

In 1997, the Clinton Administration issued PDD 56, *Managing Complex Contingency Operations*.[8] This document built on PDD 25 and incorporated some important lessons learned from such operations in Haiti, Somalia, Northern Iraq, and Bosnia.[9] PDD 56 institutionalized policies and procedures for managing complex crises and established an interagency framework for coordinating the U.S. response to postconflict situations. It was, at least, partly responsible for the better international organization, greater unity of command, quieter interagency squabbles, and overall success of U.S. nation building and stability operations in Kosovo.[10]

While the overall approach of PDD 56 would have been successful in enhancing the effectiveness of interagency coordination and managing complex contingency operations, it suffered from several weaknesses.[11]

- Too few civilian and military leaders embraced the process. Without sufficient support among agency leaders for interagency education and training, the required generational shift from insulated, agency thinking to horizontal, interagency cooperation could not occur.

- The directive underemphasized transitional periods and failed to provide an adequate framework to manage operations between peacekeeping and peace building.

- PDD 56 had no institutional mechanism for integrating regional specialists into an operation even though such regional experts would ultimately be asked to chair the interagency Executive Committee in the latter stages of peace building.

- PDD 56 failed to address the civil-military relationship in clear terms. The directive overemphasized the military role and downplayed the civilian role in the latter stages of peacekeeping and peace building.
- PDD 56 also provided no guidance for crisis recovery operations that typically require a coordinated effort across a range of issues including funding, logistics, political will, commitment of time, and understanding host nation customs, laws, and culture.

The U.S. effort to prepare for complex contingency operations also suffered from a lack of qualified and trained civilian police (CIVPOL) units, particularly ones that had competence involving warfighting at the level of serious counterinsurgency operations or the kind of counterterrorism that must counter the almost unrestricted violence of Islamic extremist terrorist movements. Carrying out the provisions of PDD 56 required not only a more substantial civilian contingent of area experts to conduct peacekeeping and nation-building operations, increasing the efficacy of these operations required the presence of a centralized CIVPOL presence beyond that provided by the State Department.

One key problem was that the Department of State's Bureau for International Narcotics and Law Enforcement Affairs manages the training, oversight, and coordination of the U.S. CIVPOL program on a case-by-case basis for each mission. To this end, the State Department recruits civilian police personnel from local and municipal law enforcement agencies through a commercial contractor. But because there is no specific authority and thus no dedicated budget line for the U.S. CIVPOL program, it is usually funded on an *ad hoc* basis through various State Department regional bureaus and the State Department's Peacekeeping account.[12] Furthermore, the Bureau was deliberately organized for civil police operations in an environment where a rule of law existed and levels of violence were largely civil and matters of crime. As became all too clear in Iraq, it was unprepared to help create paramilitary and police forces for civil war, asymmetric warfare, or large-scale terrorism and insurgency or send advisors into this kind of violent environment.

The third Clinton Administration Directive, PDD 71 (2000)—issued in the wake of United Nations peacekeeping operations in Kosovo and East Timor—aimed at reforming the management of the U.S. CIVPOL program.[13] PDD 71, titled *Strengthening Criminal Justice Systems in Support of Peace Operations and Other Complex Contingencies,* directed the State Department to establish a new program that would train U.S. CIVPOL for international peacekeeping missions around the world. While PDD 71 was left largely unimplemented during the final year of the Clinton Administration—which, some have argued, owed to insufficient political will, including ineffective interagency cooperation and the lack of statutory authority and funding mechanisms—it remains in effect, and the Bush Administration has begun implementing some of its provisions.[14]

Bush Administration Action

The Bush Administration came to office believing that the United States should not become deeply involved in "nation building" or peacemaking missions that would tie down high-cost, high-technology forces in long-term, low-technology missions that were felt to have limited strategic priority.

It initially did not support the directives of the Clinton Administration for the need to create a permanent, institutionalized mechanism for conducting postconflict operations. It was only after the terrorist attacks on 9/11 that policy makers again began to perceive unstable or failed states as significant threats to U.S. national security interests. Even then, it took American involvement in Afghanistan and Iraq to convince the Bush Administration that wars had to be fought, terminated, and brought to a successful peace as a civil-military operation.

Nina M. Serafino and Martin A. Weiss of the Congressional Research Service summarized this requirement as follows:

> The perception that international terrorism can exploit weak, unstable states has convinced many policymakers of the need to strengthen US and international capabilities to foster security, good governance and economic development, especially in post-conflict situations. Most recently, the 9/11 Commission and the Commission on Weak States and US National Security have judged weak states, as well as unsuccessful post-conflict transitions, to pose a threat to US security.[15] Such states often experience economic strife and political instability that make them vulnerable to drug trafficking, human trafficking and other criminal enterprises, and to linkage with non-state terrorist groups (such as the links between the previous Taliban government in Afghanistan and the Al Qa'ida terrorist network)...These commissions argued for assistance to the governments of weak states and of post-conflict transitions regimes to help them control their territories, meet their citizens' basic needs, and create legitimate governments based on effective transparent institutions.[16]

The new threat posed by weak and failed states and by terrorist networks requires the breadth of vision, speed of action, and management of resources that could be accomplished only through synchronizing all the elements of national power to achieve what General Richard B. Myers, then Chairman of the Joint Chiefs of Staff, called *integrated operations* that would impact all phases of conflict, from planning and war to stability and reconstruction.[17]

The United States did take some steps to make such operations possible. General Tommy Franks, Commander of U.S. Central Command, created Joint Interagency Coordination Groups (JIACG) for each Regional Combatant Command in October 2001 and approved a Joint Interagency Task Force–Counterterrorism (JIATF-CT) in November 2001.[18] JIACGs spearheaded the development of operational connections between civilian and military departments linking the DoD with the Central Intelligence Agency (CIA), Federal Bureau of Investigation (FBI), Diplomatic Security Service, Customs Service, National Security Agency, Defense Intelligence

Agency, Defense Human Intelligence Service, New York's Joint Terrorism Task Force, and the Justice, Treasury, and State Departments.

These JIACGs had their first test during operations in Afghanistan and Iraq and, in many ways, provided a "test bed" for the development of an institutionalized interagency process in the field. Their success in organizing and managing such tasks as hunting for senior Al Qa'ida and Ba'ath Party members, facilitating non-DoD law enforcement operations, establishing border security programs, investigating bombings with U.S. civilian casualties, and pooling intelligence demonstrated the importance of fielding an effective and integrated interagency group in conflict operations.

Despite their successes, however, JIACGs were restricted by several factors that reinforced persistent weaknesses in the overall interagency process, and the United States encountered far more serious problems at the interagency and national levels. The most serious limitation stemmed from the fact that JIACGs were never intended to coordinate large-scale stability and nation-building operations that required the creation of host-country security forces, paramilitary forces, and police forces. Nor were JIACGs meant to coordinate major U.S.–host-country operations of this kind. In addition, they had the following problems:

- There was no real support for effective stability and nation-building operations at the national level. The NSC did not lead. State Department efforts at coordination and leadership were bypassed, ignored, or thrust aside, particularly in the case of Iraq. The DoD policy cluster acquired *de facto* authority over planning and operations in Iraq and effectively denied the need for the mission, ignoring the planning and warnings developed earlier by a State Department–led interagency effort.

- The U.S. military and the DoD lacked the personnel with the skills, background, and area expertise for such missions and was organized for conventional warfighting. It lacked the civil-military, counterterrorism and counterinsurgency, military police, human intelligence, and other components needed for such missions.

- The State Department could diagnose many of the requirements for such missions, but had little operational capability. It had a very small pool of personnel with civil-military and nation-building experience. Its aid staffs were small, poorly led, and had little real capability to deal with tasks as large as Afghanistan and Iraq. Moreover, a past focus on security had created a risk adverse, "fortress embassy" culture that meant far too few career personnel were willing to volunteer for the necessary missions in the field and take the necessary risks.

- Other agencies gave such missions only limited priority at the national level. They were slow to respond to urgent needs in the field and slow to provide the necessary personnel and resources. They had only limited staff with field experience and little background in dealing with the risks inherent in civil-military operations in high-risk areas.

- There was no single, national-level organization issuing guidance, managing competing agency policies, and directing agency participation in JIACGs.

- JIACGs lacked the resources to develop a theater- or national-level interagency strategy. Thus, while JIATF-CT proved to be a highly effective operation-specific task force, converting the JIATF-CT to a more comprehensive JIACG better able to wage the long-term war on terrorism was problematic.

- JIACGs were created to execute and implement policy, not to make it. Moreover, JIACGs were designed to establish interagency links, not to replace habitual relations or traditional chains of command.

- There was no single standard directing when individual agencies must begin interagency participation in their crisis- or deliberative-planning processes.

- There was a lack of government-wide standards for information sharing among agencies, exacerbated by the lack of a communications architecture linking those agencies.[19]

- There was no plan or experience for creating effective interagency teams of the kind suddenly needed in Afghanistan and Iraq. The "embassy team" concept did not prepare the United States for the scale and nature of the operations required. This situation was made much worse by the failure to plan for such operations before and during military operations. It took years, and painful experiments in Afghanistan and with ORHA and the CPA in Iraq, to see the need for an integrated interagency plan and strategy, adequate staffing and experiences, tours of duty long enough to be effective, and the creation of joint civil-military teams that would deploy into the field with military leadership in high-risk or combat areas and civil leadership as an area became more stable and secure.

- There was no understanding of the level of aid required to be effective, and no initial willingness on the part of the Administration to provide it. Once aid funding did begin to flow there was little practical or competent experience in planning nationwide efforts, and it took months to realize that immediate aid funds were needed for commanders in the field and to provide money to help bring immediate stability at the local level. The sheer cost of stability and nation-building operations came as a shock, one the United States is still having problems dealing with.

- The tendency to contract out became a nightmare of uncontrolled waste and inefficiency. Contractors with no real experience or competence were given vast responsibility and funds and had to rush to recruit and subcontract without effective fiscal controls and checks on their effectiveness. At least in Iraq, the United States did not "contract out," it abdicated responsibility.

- The entire process failed to anticipate the scale of the security problem, its costs, and the risk of contracting this mission out. The U.S. military was not prepared to provide security, at least in Iraq. Controls over private security were weak to nonexistent, and no overall security plan was developed to deal with aid or reconstruction activities.

- The lack of experienced and competent U.S. personnel did not lead the United States to place suitable reliance on local advice, authority, planning, and execution. This situation was largely corrected in Afghanistan, but was not corrected in Iraq. The United States made vast mistakes and incurred vast waste, often with the rationale that Iraqis could not make their own decisions or would be corrupt or inefficient. In practice, the United States did much more harm with less useful effect than letting the Iraqis do it would have accomplished.

Given the logistical challenges interagency operations faced at the joint task force level, creating a permanent framework to facilitate a true, horizontal interagency process has proven long and arduous.

THE OFFICE OF THE COORDINATOR FOR RECONSTRUCTION AND STABILIZATION AND THE CONGRESS

The one major effort at reorganization the United States has taken would almost certainly have been grossly inadequate under the best of circumstances, and Congress ensured that it never had a chance. The most ambitious effort to boost civilian capacity to deal speedily and efficiently with complex emergencies came with the establishment at the State Department of the Office of the Coordinator for Reconstruction and Stabilization (S/CRS) in August 2004.

The S/CRS was tasked with designing and establishing the new structures within the State Department and elsewhere that would allow civilian agencies to develop effective policies, processes, and personnel to build stable and democratic states. Ambassador Carlos Pascual, then Coordinator for the Office of Reconstruction and Stabilization, identified the following five core functions for the new office:[20]

- **Monitor and Plan:** Identify states and regions of greatest risk and importance, and lead U.S. interagency planning focused on these priorities to avert crises, when possible, and to prepare for them as necessary. Integrate planning and exercises with the military.

- **Prepare Skills and Resources:** Establish and manage an interagency capability to deploy personnel and resources in an immediate surge response through an Active Response Corps to deploy as first responders in Advance Civilian Teams, and a Standing and Technical Corps for immediate deployment, backed by quick-start flexible funding through a proposed Conflict Response Fund.

- **Mobilize and Deploy:** Coordinate the deployment of U.S. resources and implementation of programs in cooperation with international and local partners, to be expedited through interagency Country Reconstruction and Stabilization Groups in Washington and within regional bureaus.

- **Leverage International Resources:** Work with international organizations, international financial institutions, individual states and NGOs to harmonize approaches, coordinate planning, accelerate deployment of assets, and increase the interoperability of personnel and equipment in multilateral operations.

- **Learn from Experience:** Incorporate best practices and lessons learned into functional changes in training, planning, exercises, and operational capabilities that support improved performance.

Despite the pressing need for reform, Congress was slow to respond to the proposed recommendations and did not follow through with the funding for various initiatives. Through the end of 2004 and throughout 2005, Congress made some gradual progress in realizing the goals of the new office.[21]

- Eight positions and $536,000 were reprogrammed for S/CRS in FY2004 with Congressional support.

- S/CRS received $7.7 million (though it requested $17 million) in the enacted FY2005 supplemental budget request that provided for reconstruction and stabilization management support for Sudan, including assistance to Darfur.

- By the end of August 2005, S/CRS had 54 staff members including personnel from USAID, the Office of the Secretary of Defense, the Joint Staff, the Joint Forces Command (JFCOM), the Corps of Engineers, Justice, Treasury, and the intelligence community.

- S/CRS established a Policy Coordinating Committee on stabilization and reconstruction with interagency working groups on transitional security, rule of law, democracy and governance, infrastructure, economic and social well-being, humanitarian issues, management, and monitoring and resources.

Despite these advances and the enthusiastic verbal support of Congressional leaders, especially Senators Lugar and Biden, and the Pentagon, the S/CRS had to struggle to gain even the most minimal funding. The FY2006 Budget requested $100 million for a Conflict Response Fund and $24.1 million for operational costs—i.e., for the staff, training, exercises, developing skills, and capabilities.

The Conflict Response Fund was to pay for a multilayered organization tasked to avert conflict and instability when possible and to respond quickly to reconstruction needs after war. But the House and Senate Foreign Operations Appropriations Conference report, completed November 1, 2005, rejected the Conflict Response Fund entirely for FY2006.[22] And even as of December 14, 2005, Ambassador Pascual said that he did not yet know the actual amount allocated to cover S/CRS operational expenses for FY2006.[23]

Ironically, and as a sign that State and Defense were learning about the need to cooperate from Iraq and Afghanistan, it was the DoD that saved the situation by giving up $200 million for stabilization and reconstruction from its own $420 billion budget for FY2006 to help the State Department fill the civilian deployment gap until S/CRS is able to do so. The DoD's rationale was that an organized effort to prevent conflict and prepare staff for postconflict reconstruction would be a cheaper and better answer than relying on the military to do the work.

In the end, Congress passed a FY2006 Defense Authorization Act that approved a transfer of up to $100 million from the DoD to the State Department or other agencies for the rapid overseas deployment of reconstruction, security, or stabilization assistance.[24] This would allow civilian agencies to deploy more quickly by giving them contingency funds without having to wait for a supplemental appropriation. Secretary of State Condoleezza Rice took the funding setbacks to S/CRS in stride and proposed $75 million, including a Conflict Response Fund, for S/CRS in the FY2007 Budget Request.[25]

The resources involved, however, were far too small for the function involved. The entire structure depended on the assumptions that (1) agencies not only would cooperate but had the necessary core competence, skill sets, and personnel; (2) the State

Department could direct interagency cooperation at the level required; and (3) the center of operations was Washington and not the field. The S/CRS was at best a deeply flawed concept on all of these grounds.

DIRECTIVES SEEKING INTERAGENCY PROGRESS: DOD'S DIRECTIVE 3000.05 AND NSPD 44

More progress has been made in setting the right policies. The DoD and the Bush Administration issued two important directives in November and December 2005 that addressed the importance of conducting stability operations and of managing interagency efforts for these operations.

The DoD's Directive 3000.05 on Military Support for Stability, Security, Transition, and Reconstruction Operations was intended to change the priorities of the military so that leaders plan for what happens after they win, in order to avoid the kind of prolonged problems that have plagued Afghanistan and Iraq.[26] It stated that "stability operations are a core US military mission that the DoD shall be prepared to conduct and support. They shall be given priority comparable to combat operations and be explicitly addressed and integrated across all DoD activities including doctrine, organizations, training, education, exercises, materiel, leadership, personnel, facilities, and planning."

The directive said that postconflict rebuilding efforts should be mainly civilian operations, involving civilians from the host country whenever possible, but that, initially, the work of restoring order and public services and rebuilding damaged facilities will likely fall on the military.

This set an important institutional precedent and was a clear recognition of how wrong the Bush Administration, the DoD, and the military had been in rejecting nation building as key missions, in downplaying the importance of stability operations and conflict termination, and in seeking to bypass the interagency process. It was effectively an admission that fundamentally different policies were needed. However, it was also a Directive that could have meaning only if the rest of the interagency forum took on the required missions and could provide the needed resources.

The White House released a complementary National Security Presidential Directive (NSPD 44) on the Management of Interagency Efforts Concerning Reconstruction and Stabilization on December 7, 2005.[27] Where the DoD's Directive 3000.05 addressed how the military would undertake its security stabilization and transition and reconstruction activities, the Presidential Directive outlined the broader umbrella structure of how the interagency community would operate.

Specifically, NSPD 44 was designed to avoid the disputes that erupted between Foreign Service officials and the Pentagon early in the occupation of Iraq. It designated the Secretary of State to improve coordination, planning, and implementation for reconstruction and stabilization assistance for foreign states and regions at risk of, in, or in transition from conflict or civil strife. Ambassador Pascual said of the Directive, "What is new is that it puts on paper a very clear mandate that says that the Secretary of State has the responsibility to lead and coordinate an integrated US government response and clearly lays out the specific functions that are expected of a secretary of state."[28]

As has been discussed previously, however, the NSPD 44 had all of the critical defects that made the S/CRS at best an extremely dubious tool. It assigned responsibility by the book, but ignored the fact that the book was wrong.

THE PUSH FOR INTERAGENCY REFORM

The massive problems and failures in interagency operations from Haiti and Bosnia to Afghanistan and Iraq have spurred several studies on U.S. postconflict operations that focused on the need for a unified interagency process.[29] While different in breadth and scope, these studies largely pointed to five key areas that dealt with U.S. capacity to respond to and organize postconflict stabilization, reconstruction, and development missions.[30]

- The existing *ad hoc* system must be replaced with a permanent mechanism for developing contingency plans and procedures for joint civil-military operations led by civilians. To make a difference, this would likely translate into creating a new National Security Council office dedicated to integrating interagency planning for complex contingency operations, establishing planning capacity for operations in civilian agencies, and ensuring that a standard approach exists for coordinating civil-military actions.

- Mechanisms to rapidly deploy U.S. civilian government and government-contracted personnel need to be put in place. This covers the creation of crisis management teams composed of regional and functional experts from all of the agencies involved, and it requires civilian training for postconflict stabilization and reconstruction missions.

- Civilian activities in reconstruction and development situations require a flexible funding mechanism to facilitate timely deployment of human and financial resources during crisis situations. This is especially true for civilian operations because, unlike the military, the civilian effort does not have a large budget to reorganize priorities and reprogram funding to meet short-term challenges. Civilian budgets are already stretched and overextended, and they do not have the luxury of being resubmitted to Congress for supplemental appropriations.

- Preventive action must be considered. This requires identifying and mitigating potential sources of conflict in postconflict regions and underlines the need to standardize training, deployment, and funding for civilian police forces.

- The U.S. government must enhance multinational capabilities to carry out postconflict security tasks and to better coordinate international aid.

Building on these broad recommendations, *Beyond Goldwater-Nichols: Phase 2 Report* (2005) made more specific proposals for enhancing interagency capabilities.[31]

- The NSC needs to move beyond its traditional and well-accepted role of preparing decisions for the President and take a more active oversight role to ensure that Presidential intent (as reflected in those decisions) is realized through USG actions.

- Establish planning capacity for complex contingency operations in civilian agencies.
- Establish a standard, NSC-led approach to interagency planning at the strategic level for complex contingency operations.
- Create rapidly deployable Interagency Crisis Planning Teams for interagency campaign planning.
- For any operations involving security, stability, transition, and reconstruction operations, the Combatant Commander (COCOM) and his Commander Joint Task Force (CJTF) should fully integrate these elements into their military plans. The COCOM should designate a subordinate commander to lead the military's participation in the interagency planning process.
- Enhance USG capacities for training and equipping indigenous security forces by amending Titles 10 and 22 to permit direct DoD funding of these activities.
- For each complex contingency operation, establish an Interagency Task Force in the field to integrate the day-to-day efforts of all USG agencies and achieve greater unity of effort on the ground.
- Establish a standing Interagency Task Force Headquarters core element that is ready to deploy to an operation on short notice.
- Provide the DoD with more flexible contracting authorities and vehicles more responsive to the operational environment.
- Congress should rewrite and fully fund the recommendations outlined in the Lugar-Biden Initiative.
- Strengthen existing operations capacities at USAID.
- Create a new Training Center for Interagency and Coalition Operations.
- Increase U.S. funding for programs that support building the operational capabilities of allies and partners.
- Enhance peacetime opportunities for civilian planners and operators to work with their counterparts from various countries.

Many such recommendations are now under study. However, the United States is already at war, and it is vital that effective reforms be implemented as soon as possible both in Washington and in the field. Such recommendations also leave open several critical issues in creating effective interagency operations. One is the need for a clear and direct line of authority from the top that gives the NSC the power (and the staff) to compel Department of State, DoD, other civil agency, and intelligence agency co-operation. Bureaucrats and cabinet members may talk about coordination and co-operation, but this is a fundamentally unworkable approach to war and large-scale national building.

A second issue is the need to focus on the interagency role in advising on the options for carrying out a mission: whether given approaches are feasible, whether a meaningful operational plan can be created, and what kind of resources are necessary. The decision to commit is at least as critical as actual execution.

Third, success at the interagency level in Washington will be meaningless without success in the field. Interagency operations of the kind in Iraq and Afghanistan, and in any asymmetric struggle with high political and ideological constants, are won or lost in the field. It is the quality of the country team, field groups like the PRTs, and local civil-military actions that will be critical. Even the best "Beltway" or Washington-centric approach to interagency action will still fail to deal with any difficult or serious case. Hands-on operations and expertise, and partnership with host-country officials and military, are simply too critical.

Fourth, critical problems exist in the present culture of the State Department. More and more emphasis has been placed in recent years on protecting embassies, creating fortress-like compounds, and avoiding losses of Foreign Service and other State Department personnel. This has been combined with career patterns that favor officers who remain visible in Washington, report back to Washington, or have safe profiles in safe countries. If the State Department is to be an effective partner, it must take risks in terms of its facilities overseas; it must give career and cash benefits to risk takers; and it must select out non–risk takers no matter how good they may to be in routine bureaucratic functions and writing cables. Fortunately, there is a vast supply of graduates from foreign service and international relations schools who are more than willing to replace those foreign service officers who are not risk takers.

Fifth, one key aspect of this change may be the need to abolish USAID and create a new bureaucracy and group of experts who are truly field oriented, can work directly with the U.S. military and staffs of the countries involved, and can meet the mission needs that conflicts like Iraq have shown exist. USAID is a long-standing embarrassment in the U.S. government, and its performance in Iraq has been dismal. Some personnel have been outstanding in the field. There is no similar evidence of such capability in the State Department headquarters.

Sixth, the United States must develop integrated civil-military teams in the field that operate with the same transportation and security systems, and the U.S. military must assume full responsibility for security in the area of operations. If the United States is to develop real country teams and use civilians effectively, they must be given the same priorities for protection and transportation as the military members of the team. More generally, contract security personnel and mercenaries are part of the problem and not the solution. They should be used only as a last resort, subject to full oversight and control, subject to criminal penalties under U.S. law for any misconduct and abuses, and ruthlessly prosecuted for any infraction.

Seventh, the United States must never again rely on private contractors for critical military, stability, and nation-building functions to the extent it has in Iraq. There are many roles where contractors can be a cost-effective substitute for military personnel and career civilians, but there are many where they cannot. This includes support functions where the personnel involved must be capable of self-defense and many functions in major aid projects. In practice, it is clear that U.S. contractors are no more effective or less corrupt than local contractors and officials and that aid and nation-building money is almost always better spent on local nationals than in ways that have no visibility in the area of operations. This, however, means that the United States must develop civil-military teams that can carry out such aid projects and actually monitor their effectiveness in the field. It also means that contractors should be precluded from hiring active military or career civilians or those who have left the service for at least several years and that contractors should be forced to limit salaries and benefits to levels approaching those offered by the government. If this means they cannot attract suitable personnel, then they should not be awarded a contract.

Finally, the United States must have a local partner, must work on a government-to-government basis, and cannot rely on contractor operations. Iraq has shown once and for all that contract operations can have value in some support missions, but must not be given a major security role or responsibility for major economic and aid missions. Only the U.S. military can provide U.S. government civilians with adequate security and ensure that the military and civilians act as a team. U.S. contractors lack expertise, continuity, area and language skills, security capability, and the ability to avoid massive waste and corruption. They cannot save a failed state from itself, and they do not lead host governments to take responsibility, plan, use resources effectively, or create projects and development efforts that suit a given economy and culture and that can be sustained once U.S. aid and contract support ends.

THE IMPACT OF A NEW INTELLIGENCE HIERARCHY

The Intelligence Community is another critical part of an effective interagency effort. The Afghan conflict and the Iraq War have provided a clear warning that the U.S. Intelligence Community needs to move beyond a reliance on technical means and analysis outside the operational area and join with the State Department, the Department of Defense, and the U.S. military to create an integrated civil-military capability to deal with counterinsurgency, nation building, and stability operations.

The new threat matrix laid out in the 2006 QDR was certainly one where technical means can still play a vital role, but it was also one that is people intensive in terms of collection and analysis, where human intelligence plays a critical role, and where much of the activity must occur in the field. Iraq and Afghanistan provided clear field demonstrations of just how simpleminded many proposed aspects of the Revolution in Military Affairs were before the Iraq War. "Effects-based operations" are a case in point. The targeting aspect was never honestly addressed, nor was the ability to provide the quality of battle-damage assessment at the speed required. Transformation must look beyond the narrow role of intelligence and consider how to integrate intelligence and operations in realistic and achievable ways in a world of soft targets, buildings with uncertain functions, and where collateral damage imposes steadily growing political consequences.

Ironically, "intelligence reform" has threatened to make these tasks more difficult. Congress has legislated such reform in a way that ignores most real-world operational needs. The President's approval of the Intelligence Reform and Terrorism Prevention Act of 2004 (P.L. 458 108-458) on December 17, 2004, codified the most significant restructuring of the Intelligence Community since 1947. But the principal provision of the Act—the creation of Director of National Intelligence (DNI), separate from the Director of the CIA (DCIA), to manage the Intelligence Community—lays the groundwork for major new turf fights among the DoD, the National Security Council, and the new DNI. If these do not occur, it will be a triumph of strong personalities over bad legislation.

The Director of National Intelligence

The Intelligence Reform Act assigned two of the three principal responsibilities to the DNI that had formerly been performed by the now defunct Director of Central Intelligence (DCI), including providing intelligence to the President, other senior officials, and Congress and acting as head of the Intelligence Community. The DNI would not oversee the CIA; rather, the DCIA will report directly to the DNI. Moreover, the DNI would have to prepare and deliver the President's Daily Brief (PDB), manage the Intelligence Community, and serve as the principal intelligence advisor to the President. This forced the DNI to walk a fine line. A DNI who saw his role as primarily managerial would risk losing the credibility to manage; a DNI who saw his role as primarily advisory would risk losing the time to manage.[32]

The Act also strengthened the DNI's authorities to carry out responsibilities by providing the DNI additional powers in personnel, tasking, and acquisition. That is, the DNI was given responsibilities in areas that affected every aspect of asymmetric warfare, stability operations, nation building, counterterrorism, counterinsurgency, peacemaking, and humanitarian operations:[33]

- The DNI, with the approval of the Office of Management and Budget (OMB), may transfer or reprogram funds unilaterally, but within certain limits. The DNI can annually reprogram or transfer up to $150 million provided that sum is less than 5 percent of the affected agency or department's budget.

- The DNI, with the approval of the OMB, may transfer Intelligence Community personnel for up to two years. Should the DNI decide to establish a new national intelligence center, the Director also has the authority to transfer up to 100 personnel to man that center.

- The DNI has appointment authority. That is, the department or agency head having jurisdiction over the appointment must seek the approval of the DNI. If the DNI does not approve, the position cannot be filled.

- The DNI will serve as the exclusive authority on major acquisitions. This authority is limited only when acquisitions concern DoD programs. In these cases, the DNI and the Secretary of Defense share acquisition authority with the President acting as final arbiter.

- The DNI shall "manage and direct the tasking of, collection, analysis, production, and dissemination of national intelligence... by approving requirements and resolving conflicts" [P.L. 108-458, §102A(f)].

- The Intelligence Reform Act also created a new National Counterterrorism Center (NCTC). The Center has a dual reporting structure owing to a differentiation the Act stipulates between intelligence joint counterterrorism operations and nonintelligence joint counterterrorism operations. Thus, the DNI has authority over the Center's budget and programs, NCTC's intelligence activities, and intelligence joint counterterrorism operations. Because strategic planning for nonintelligence joint counterterrorism operations is considered an Executive Branch–wide function, the Director of the NCTC reports directly to the President with respect to joint counterterrorism operations other than intelligence.

The Intelligence Reform Act gave the DNI substantial budgeting control over the 15 agencies. It also formally gave the DNI budget authority that the DCI may have had, but was not given explicitly and never chose to exercise:[34]

- The Director of the Office of Management and Budget, at the exclusive direction of the DNI, will apportion, or direct, how Congressionally appropriated funds will flow from the Treasury Department to each of the cabinet level agencies containing Intelligence Community elements. Consequently, the DNI will control the pace of spending and could, for example, withhold funds until recipients comply with DNI spending priorities, an option never available to DCIs.
- The DNI will be able to allot appropriations directly at the subcabinet agency and department levels. The Act further requires that the DNI notify Congress if a departmental comptroller refuses to act in accordance with a DNI spending directive.
- The DNI will "develop and determine" the National Intelligence Program budget [P.L. 108-458, §102A(c)(B)].
- The DNI will "ensure the effective execution of the budget" and monitor the implementation and execution of the National Intelligence Program [P.L. 108-458, §102A(c)(4)].
- The DNI shall provide budget guidance to those elements of the Intelligence Community not falling within the National Intelligence Program.

There were, however, serious *de facto* limits on the DNI's capabilities. Despite his enhanced budgeting powers over the National Intelligence Program, the DNI's authority to affect intelligence support to military operations—i.e., the DoD's Military Intelligence Program which, as of September 2005, encompassed all programs from the former Joint Military Intelligence Program and most programs from the Tactical Intelligence and Related Activities Program—remained limited and was more comparable to that of former DCIs. In theory, the DNI was to develop intelligence programs falling under the purview of the DoD with the Secretary of Defense.

The Need to Reform the "Reformed" System

These limitations highlight a more general problem in the way intelligence is now intended to support the interagency process. The Intelligence Reform Act never seriously addressed the process of intelligence, or how operational capabilities could be improved in areas like counterterrorism, counterinsurgency, nation building, stability operations, etc. In many ways, the Act was an organizational chart-driven effort designed to create new lines of authority reporting to the President.

The end result was that the Act further bloated an already vast intelligence bureaucracy, layering new boxes on top of the existing organizational chart without clearly identifying roles or how the boxes will support actual intelligence functions and users other than the President. For example, while even critics of the Intelligence Community usually cite the creation of the NCTC as a valuable addition, its dual role in uniting terrorism analysis and in conducting strategic operational planning for counterterrorism clearly overlapped the responsibilities of the CIA's Counterterrorist Center, the unit responsible for pursuing Al Qa'ida operatives around the world.[35]

The DNI's authorities also lacked clarity. As discussed in the Commission on the Intelligence Capabilities of the United States Regarding Weapons of Mass Destruction Report to the President (also known as the Robb-Silberman Report), released March 31, 2005, "The DNI's role could have been a purely coordinating position, with a limited staff and authority to match. Or it could have been something close to a 'Secretary of Intelligence,' with full authority over the principal intelligence agencies and clear responsibility for their actions…In the end, the DNI created by the intelligence reform legislation was neither of those things; the office is given broad responsibilities but only ambiguous authorities."[36] Thus, the degree to which the DNI can actually exert control over the allocation of intelligence resources—particularly those whose main function is the support the Department of Defense—remains to be seen.

Other problems lie in the fact that many of the provisions of the Intelligence Reform Act could be interpreted differently by different agencies, and certain provisions of the Act potentially undermined the DNI's authorities. For example, Section 1018 required that the President issue guidelines to ensure that the DNI's authorities are implemented in "a manner that respects and does not abrogate the statutory responsibilities of the heads of the departments of the United States Government." Exactly how the DNI was to implement reforms that conflicted with the standard operating cultures of the various components of the Intelligence Community was not clear.

Iraq has shown that close partnership is needed among intelligence collection, analysis, and operations and every other aspect of the interagency activity in warfighting, at the embassy level, and in the field. As Gregory F. Treverton of the RAND Corporation has pointed out, real reforms depend far more on changing actual operations and an organizational culture than on redesigning an organizational chart. If the Intelligence Community is to be an optimal partner in asymmetric warfighting and nation building, it must address several general areas of reform, some of which are important to create effective interagency capabilities to meet the kind of mission needs that the Iraq War has shown are necessary.[37]

- Implement the change made by the Intelligence Reform Act to create national intelligence centers under the authority of the DNI that organize intelligence around issues, missions, wars or threats, rather than around collection sources or agencies. These centers, with the NCTC as the prototype, would be the intelligence version of the military's unified commands and would both deploy and use the information, technology, and staff resources of the existing agencies. Of course, the Act does not specify the creation of centers other than the NCTC, so the DNI must decide which other centers to create and be prepared to change the culture to accommodate them. The existing agencies surely will resist becoming force providers rather than "force doers," and they will argue that the centers will be consumed only by the hottest current issues.

- Improve intelligence analysis using recommendations from the Weapons of Mass Destruction (WMD) Commission's Report to avoid intelligence failures like those before the Iraq War. "This failure was in large part the result of analytical shortcomings; intelligence analysts were too wedded to their assumptions about Saddam's intentions."[38] The Cold War model where analysts could work alone or in small groups to address clearly defined threat areas no longer applies. To understand terrorism, analysts must integrate themselves into larger virtual networks across specialties and agencies and be more innovative in their approach to analysis. The WMD Commission's Report made several recommendations on how to enable analysts to better analyze intelligence, how to put that intelligence in context, and how to communicate gaps in intelligence to decision makers.[39]

  - Empower "Mission Managers" to coordinate analytic efforts on a given topic. Mission Managers would be members of the DNI's staff responsible for developing strategies for all aspects of intelligence relating to a priority intelligence target. Mission Managers would not be responsible for providing a single, homogenized analytic product. Rather, they would be responsible for encouraging alternative analysis and for ensuring that dissenting views are expressed to intelligence customers.

  - Strengthen long-term and strategic analysis. A common complaint among intelligence analysts has been that the pressing need for current intelligence does not allow them to conduct long-term and strategic analysis. To address this problem, the WMD Commission recommended establishing an organization to perform only long-term and strategic analysis under the National Intelligence Council.

  - Encourage diverse and independent, or "competitive," analysis from many sources including the proposed long-term research and analysis unit and the national Intelligence Council. To further address the need for a nonconsensus, devil's advocate perspective, the WMD Commission also recommended the creation of a nonprofit "sponsored research institute" outside the Intelligence Community.

  - Improve the rigor and "tradecraft" of analysis. To address the apparent lack of analytic rigor within the Intelligence Community and to compensate for weak leadership, insufficient training, and budget cutbacks in analyst ranks, the WMD Commission made several recommendations. Notably, increase analyst training, ensure that managers and budget writers allot time and resources for analytical training; standardize structures and practices to increase competitive analysis, enable joint and rotational assignment opportunities, and implement other changes in human resource policies—such as merit-based pay—to encourage the best analysts to stay in government.

- Communicate better intelligence products to policy makers. To improve the PDB and other senior policy-maker briefs, the WMD Commission recommended eliminating misleading "headline" summaries. The DNI's staff would also ensure that the PDB reflects alternative views from the Community. Moreover, the Commission recommended that the DNI assume responsibility for the President's three primary sources of intelligence—the PDB, the President's Terrorism Threat Report, and the FBI briefing. The DNI should coordinate this intelligence in a manner that eliminates redundancies and ensure that only material necessary for the President is included.

- Demand more from analysts. Policy makers must actively probe and question analysts. Analysts should expect this demanding and aggressive testing without allowing it to subvert their judgment.

- Deal more effectively with a very changed intelligence workforce that poses both challenges and opportunities. The dramatic growth of the intelligence agencies since September 11, 2001, has drawn a large crop of young, fearless, technology savvy recruits who do not stand for the compartmented, slow, and source-driven information environment that the current intelligence framework provides. The Intelligence Community must take advantage of demographics and create teams of veterans with entry-level newcomers. The Community must be more accommodating of lateral entry applicants and be prepared to deal with young professionals who do not intend to stay for their entire careers. Moreover, intelligence officers should not be deterred from training by the imperative to gain experience on the job. Intelligence training should emulate the military in being joint and integral to careers.

- Pursue new, more targeted collection and, in the process, address the problem of information overload, even from secret systems, that threatens to overwhelm analysts, not to mention policy makers. Because U.S. adversaries are familiar with standard, passive U.S. surveillance techniques—like satellite imagery and eavesdropping—the Intelligence Community must move toward more directed collection and shorten the cycle of innovation so as to be less predictable for would-be targets. Intelligence must adapt faster to stay ahead of adversaries. In imagery, this means using more small satellites, drones, and stealth technology. In signals, this means finding new ways to get very close to targets. The DNI must lead the development of an analytic capacity to make trade-offs between certain collection techniques and the existing Collection Concepts Development Center, which assesses collection against particular targets, across the stovepipes, is one place to start.

- The intelligence culture of secrecy and "need to know" is dangerously outdated. Unlike fighting more conventional threats from nation-states, fighting terrorism demands information sharing across intelligence agencies and with state and local authorities. The WMD Commission's Report made specific recommendations on how to facilitate information sharing.[40]

  - Designate a single official under the DNI who will be responsible for both information sharing *and* information security, in order to break down cultural and policy barriers that have impeded the development of a shared information space.

  - Apply advanced technologies to the Information Sharing Environment to permit more expansive sharing with far greater security protections than currently exist in the Intelligence Community.

- Establish clear and consistent Community-wide information sharing and security policies.
- The DNI should also jettison the phrase "information sharing" because it reinforces the (incorrect) notion that information is the property of individual intelligence agencies, rather than of the government as a whole.

The most important step, however, is to ensure that intelligence provides focused and comprehensive support to major missions like Iraq and Afghanistan as part of an integrated team without artificial compartmentation and excessive security and compartmentation. There are certain long-standing tendencies in the Community that intelligence reform has not addressed, but which present constant problems and often make Intelligence Community security officers *de facto* enemies of the United States.

There has been a steady improvement in some aspects of the "fusion" of intelligence, planning, and operations in recent years. Intelligence agencies, however, have to be forced to fully cooperate with each other and share information. Joint experience is still limited, particularly in areas outside the military. The legitimate protection of sources and methods still leads to gross overclassification. Members of the Community still do not have common clearance procedures and often differ sharply in special access. The mystique of operations leads to physical as well as security compartmentation, often isolating intelligence from policy and operations at various levels.

The Intelligence Community sometimes seems to have never learned that the Cold War is over and that no peer threat exists to challenge U.S. intelligence capabilities and security in most asymmetric wars. The fact that what is needed is real-time sharing and fusion of information of all kinds at every level, rather than the protection of information that is inherently of short-term value, is still forgotten. So is the fact that the low-level user in the field often has a far more urgent need for support than an analyst in Washington or the glorified "comic book" that has become the President's daily brief. It is how well the Intelligence Community serves this level of user with operational and planning information that is perhaps the most important single test of its success.

The Issue of Congressional Oversight

Probably no user of intelligence is less important at a functional level than the U.S. Congress, but Intelligence will get adequate funding and legislation only if Congress is properly briefed and can properly exercise its oversight authority. The United States requires a strong, stable, and capable Congressional committee structure to provide the national intelligence agencies oversight, support, and leadership.

The 9/11 Commission made several related recommendations in this area.[41] The Commission called on Congress to model its oversight practices after those of the 1970s and have either a single joint committee to oversee intelligence (like the old Atomic Energy Committee) or single committees in each house. In either case, "the intelligence committees cannot carry out their oversight function unless they are made stronger, and thereby have both clear responsibility and accountability for that oversight."[42]

The Commission also called for more transparency about the intelligence budget as an important step toward more effective oversight. In practice, this recommendation could translate into creating intelligence appropriations subcommittees in both houses of Congress. Critics argue that oversight of the Intelligence Community will remain weak if the overall intelligence budget remains classified and dwells primarily within the Pentagon.

To date, progress in reforming intelligence oversight has been almost nonexistent. Thomas H. Kean and Lee H. Hamilton, the former Chair and Vice Chair of the 9/11 Commission, headed the 9/11 Public Discourse Project to oversee the implementation of the 9/11 Commission's recommendations. Just before the Public Discourse Project ceased operations on December 31, 2005, Kean and Hamilton released a report card that gave the government a grade of D for progress in reforming intelligence oversight and a grade of F for progress in declassifying the intelligence budget.[43]

Congress has been resistant to any institutional changes that would improve legislative oversight. In 2005, Congress rejected the 9/11 Commission's proposal to create a joint, bicameral intelligence panel with power both to authorize and appropriate funding for intelligence activities. Legislators were reluctant to enact any provision that would cede any of their power to allocate money as they saw fit. In 2004, the Senate passed a resolution to create an intelligence subcommittee of the Senate Appropriations Committee, but the House did not follow suit. The House Republican leadership opposed the creation of an intelligence appropriations committee, in part, to avoid the 9/11 Commission's proposal to disclose the Intelligence Community's budget figures. Even though the Senate attached a proposal to declassify the intelligence budget to the Intelligence Reform Act of 2004, GOP-led House leadership and the White House objected to and ultimately killed the provision.[44]

Critics maintain that as long as the overall intelligence budget remains classified and dwells primarily within the Pentagon, legislative oversight of the Intelligence Community will remain weak. As Lee Hamilton, former Vice Chair of the 9/11 Commission said, "The intelligence community goes around the authorizing committees because they don't have control over the money...You need a subcommittee that focuses exclusively on intelligence to have robust oversight."[45] Some have suggested that part of the problem is that the bureaucratic stakes became higher after the passage of the Intelligence Reform Act. Declassifying the intelligence budget would boost the stature of the DNI at the expense of the Defense Secretary. Obviously, the Pentagon would oppose any such move.

THE PROBLEM OF HOMELAND DEFENSE

The best that can be said of homeland defense is that it is a massive bureaucratic mess that is still in transition and which may someday produce improvements that offset the disruption and cost of actions like creating a Department of Homeland Security (DHS). The practical problem is that the end result is to put a further strain on the DoD and the military while creating a level of turmoil in several key civil agencies that makes it even harder to get support for missions outside the United States, new kinds of core competence, and personnel willing to take risks in the field.

The 2006 QDR outlined various initiatives designed to reorient defense capabilities and forces to defend the homeland from transnational terrorist movements, from extremist ideologies and advanced weapons, as well as from disease and natural disasters. The stated end goal was to deter potential aggressors, defeat threats at a distance, and mitigate the consequences of any attack or natural disaster.

The QDR and Homeland Defense

The following points from the 2006 QDR spell out what the DoD has done and intends to do to improve U.S. homeland defense capabilities:

- Created a new combatant command, U.S. Northern Command (US NORTHCOM), in 2002 to consolidate homeland defense missions under a single headquarters.
- Created the new civilian post of Assistant Secretary of Defense for Homeland Defense to coordinate the efforts of NORTHCOM and increase the DoD's emphasis on homeland defense.
- Over the next five years the DoD will fund Project BioShield, a $1.5-billion initiative to develop broad-spectrum countermeasures against bioterrorism. In Project BioWatch, the DoD will collaborate with other federal agencies to improve technologies and procedures to detect and identify a biological attack.
- The DoD will work as part of an interagency effort with the Department of Homeland Security and other federal, state, and local agencies to address threats to the U.S. homeland.
- Improve the homeland defense and consequence management capabilities of its national and international partners. Improve the DoD's capabilities by sharing information, expertise, and technology as appropriate across military and civilian boundaries.
- Develop new or expanded authorities to improve access to National Guard and Reserve forces for use in the event of a man-made or natural disaster.

The FY2007 Defense Budget Submission sought to address many of these points.

- $5 billion was allocated to the DoD for defending against catastrophic threats including activities to research, develop, and deploy technologies, systems, and medical measures to detect and counter threats from chemical, biological, radiological, and nuclear (CBRN) weapons.
- $536 million was allocated to the Domestic Nuclear Detection Office, created in 2006 within the DHS. This was a 70-percent increase over the 2006 allocation.

- $1.9 billion—a $120-million increase from FY2006 and a $1.9-billion increase from FY2005—was invested in the Department of Health and Human Services for developing medical countermeasures to CBRN threats.

- $160 million was allocated to the National Institutes of Health for the advanced development of medical countermeasures against threats of bioterrorism.

Throwing Money at the Problem

The practical problem is that the DHS is still in a state of turmoil, and a vast amount of money is being thrown at the problem of interagency cooperation in homeland defense with little real planning, uncertain cost-effectiveness, and few measures that monitor progress efficiency or provide meaningful measures of effectiveness.

The cost of homeland defense may not be high relative to total defense expenditures, but it is high by any other standard. Overall, the FY2007 budget provided $58.3 billion—a $3.4 billion or 6-percent increase over FY2006—to support the homeland defense activities of 32 government agencies, including the DoD. The monies were directed toward improving nuclear detection and defense, safeguarding critical infrastructure, establishing interoperability standards for first responders, and improving terrorism information sharing among all levels of government. Some other highlights in the FY2007 budget submission for homeland defense included the following:

- Increased funding by $176 million (41 percent) for intelligence and warning,

- Increased funding by over $1.8 billion (10 percent) for homeland security activities focused on border and transportation security,

- Increased funding by over $100 million (3 percent) for domestic counterterrorism,

- Increased funding by nearly $500 million (3 percent) for protecting critical infrastructure and key assets,

- Increased funding by $240 million (3 percent) for defending against catastrophic threats, and

- Increased funding by over $550 million (11 percent) for homeland security–related emergency preparedness.

Of the 32 government agencies that received homeland security funding in FY2007, 5 agencies—the Department of Homeland Security, Department of Defense, Department of Health and Human Services, Department of Justice, and Department of Energy—account for approximately 93 percent of total government-wide homeland security funding. Figure 8.1 shows the baseline funding estimates for FY2005 through FY2011 allocated by agency.

The Department of Defense Role in Homeland Defense

Not surprisingly, the DoD assumes a substantial role in homeland defense. Most of the DoD's funding goes toward two national strategy mission areas for homeland

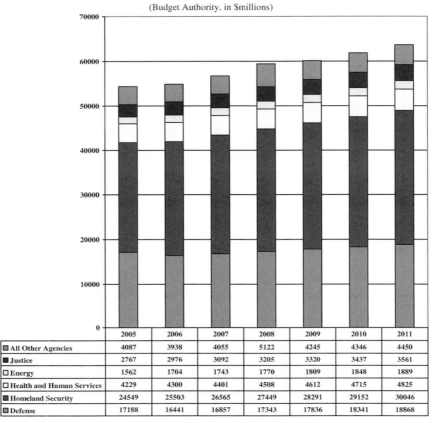

Figure 8.1 contents:

(Budget Authority, in $millions)

	2005	2006	2007	2008	2009	2010	2011
All Other Agencies	4087	3938	4055	5122	4245	4346	4450
Justice	2767	2976	3092	3205	3320	3437	3561
Energy	1562	1704	1743	1770	1809	1848	1889
Health and Human Services	4229	4300	4401	4508	4612	4715	4825
Homeland Security	24549	25503	26565	27449	28291	29152	30046
Defense	17188	16441	16857	17343	17836	18341	18868

Source: Adapted from "Homeland Security Funding Analysis," Fiscal Year 2007 Defense Budget Submission. Estimates for FY 2005 include supplemental appropriations; estimates for FY 2006 - FY 2011 do not.

Figure 8.1   Baseline Estimates of Total Homeland Security Spending by Agency

defense: protecting critical infrastructure and key assets ($11.3 billion requested for FY2007) and defending against catastrophic threats ($4.9 billion requested for FY2007). The remainder of the DoD's homeland defense funding goes to emergency preparedness and response ($407 million requested for FY2007). Figure 8.2, Figure 8.3, and 8.4 illustrate the DoD's contribution to these mission areas.

DoD efforts are not yet part of a meaningful common strategic plan, program, or budget for homeland defense, and the civil agencies have no clear plan, core competence, or responsibility for supporting DoD in missions outside the United States like the war in Iraq. It is possible to trade the allocation of homeland defense money by agency within the federal budget, but not what it actually buys. In far too many cases, when expenditures are traced by capability or function, there is little capability to serve domestic needs relative to the scale of potential tasks, efforts are still

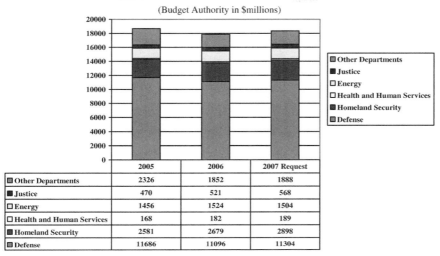

(Budget Authority in $millions)

	2005	2006	2007 Request
Other Departments	2326	1852	1888
Justice	470	521	568
Energy	1456	1524	1504
Health and Human Services	168	182	189
Homeland Security	2581	2679	2898
Defense	11686	11096	11304

Source: Adapted from "Homeland Security Funding Analysis," Fiscal Year 2007 Defense Budget Submission. Figures for FY 2005 include supplemental appropriations; figures for FY 2006 and FY 2007 do not.

Figure 8.2   Protecting Critical Infrastructure and Key Assets Funding by Agency

developmental or shifted to contract study, or there is little evidence of overall federal, state, and local coordination.

One major problem is the present and future role of the National Guard. The Guard serves state interests until a national emergency takes place and is a key potential tool in homeland defense. Major progress has taken place in ensuring that the Guard can play that role in some areas, and in coordination at the state and local level. Exercises have improved coordination as well, although in many cases they have done more to identify problems and new requirements than demonstrate adequate existing capability.

If the DoD is to find the right balance of active and reserve forces, it must define the right role for the Guard in homeland defense. To do this, however, there must be some common plan and definition of roles and missions on an interagency (and state and local) level that ensures the DoD and the Guard are part of a common structure. There is no evidence that this has advanced beyond a "state of becoming" and little evidence that it is "becoming" very fast.

This may not matter in the case of low-level terrorist threats or various natural emergencies. There is time to react, and the level of planning and coordination required is less demanding—although Hurricane Katrina is a warning that "worst cases" do happen. It could be critical in the case of any use of weapons of mass destruction, and particularly in the case of any use of infectious biological agents. The most coordinated and efficient effort might well fail to prevent massive casualties and damage.

Moreover, it is far from clear that efforts like the S/CRS or NSPD 44 have even begun to identify what other civil agencies that now concentrate on homeland

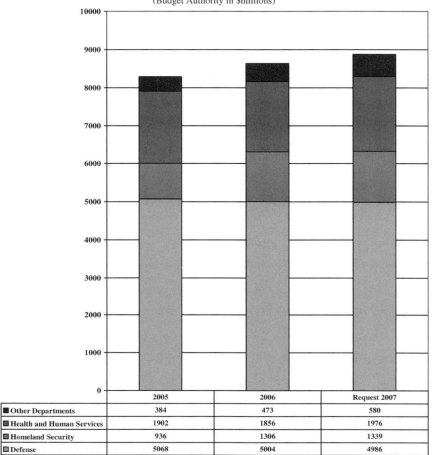

(Budget Authority in $millions)

	2005	2006	Request 2007
■ Other Departments	384	473	580
▩ Health and Human Services	1902	1856	1976
▨ Homeland Security	936	1306	1339
▢ Defense	5068	5004	4986

Source: Adapted from "Homeland Security Funding Analysis," Fiscal Year 2007 Defense Budget Submission. Figures for FY 2005 include supplemental appropriations; figures for FY 2006 and FY 2007 do not.

Figure 8.3　Protecting Critical Infrastructure and Key Assets Funding by Agency

defense can or should contribute by way of civilian support to future asymmetric struggles like Iraq and Afghanistan, and what new levels of core competence and arrangements to send U.S. government civilian personnel need to be established. There is not much "talk" and even less "walk."

CREATING AN EFFECTIVE INTERAGENCY CAPABILITY TO PERFORM NATIONAL SECURITY MISSIONS

It is terribly easy to make anodyne-like calls for more interagency coordination, write new directives, and budget more studies. Changing organization charts is as

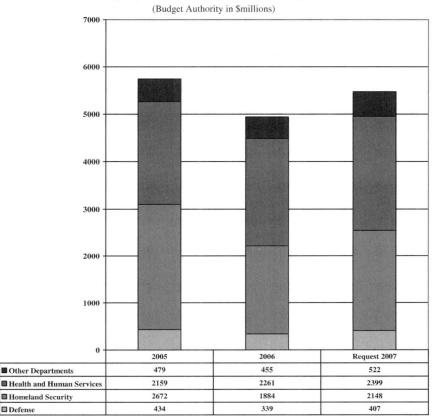

(Budget Authority in $millions)

	2005	2006	Request 2007
■ Other Departments	479	455	522
▨ Health and Human Services	2159	2261	2399
▨ Homeland Security	2672	1884	2148
▨ Defense	434	339	407

Source: Adapted from "Homeland Security Funding Analysis," Fiscal Year 2007 Defense Budget Submission. Figures for FY 2005 and FY 2006 include supplemental appropriations; figures for FY 2006 and FY 2007 do not.

Figure 8.4   Emergency Preparedness and Response Funding by Agency

easy, if not easier, as playing musical chairs. The reality is, however, that the United States has only begun to create an effective interagency structure and move toward the level of civil-military jointness that Iraq and Afghanistan, and many contingencies before them, have shown are necessary.

There are no simple solutions, and in many cases it will take years of pragmatic experience to determine exactly what is needed. The preceding analysis does indicate, however, that the following steps are necessary:

- *If the United States is to have an effective match between its strategy and resources, it must do so on a civil-military basis and not simply a military one:* This means it not only needs interagency tools to allocate both civil and military efforts, but central direction and clear lines of authority that do not allow one agency to bypass another or to stonewall or partially comply in working as part of a common effort.

- *Jointness is just as important at the interagency level as at the military level:* If the United States is to meet the challenges of stability operations, nation building, peacemaking, asymmetric warfare, and homeland defense, it must forge a civil-military partnership that can provide the full mix of talent and resources needed for each new crisis and task.

- *The interagency process must have a clear and unambiguous line of authority from the National Security Council down:* Iraq has simply exposed long-standing realities. The State Department cannot lead or direct interagency operations in wartime, and its theoretical authority is an exercise in futility when it comes to practice. The Department of Defense cannot be allowed to operate in the field or at the central command level without a broader grand strategic direction. Civil agencies cannot be allowed to put domestic priorities first without interagency review and coordination.

- *The most important interagency role is in deciding whether a given mission is necessary, whether a full operational plan is possible, and whether the necessary resources exist:* The United States must never again go to war or into large-scale missions in ways that bypass the interagency process, without a clear plan and without providing the needed interagency resources. The interagency role is critical in advising on the options for carrying out a mission, whether given approaches are feasible, whether a meaningful operational plan can be created, and what kind of resources are necessary. The decision to commit is at least as critical as actual execution.

- *At the same time, the need for this partnership goes far beyond simply cooperating in military and stability operations once a conflict or mission has begun:* When war must succeed at the ideological, political, and economic levels—as well as at the level of military operations—close interagency cooperation is needed to determine what kind of operation is needed and what kind of operation is feasible. The most critical single moment in interagency cooperation is in determining what to do and whether it is possible to create a real-world operational plan that the U.S. government can implement.

- *The key to success will be the civil-military partnership and quality of interagency cooperation at the embassy, regional, and local levels. This requires fully integrated teams of military forces, State Department and other civilian department personnel, and members of the Intelligence Community.*

- *The State Department requires a major change in culture:* There cannot be a successful civil partnership as long as far too many foreign service officers are risk averse, career advancement is not directly linked to taking risks, and force protection and fortress embassies have priority over the ability to act throughout a country and in direct contact with the people. A fundamental change is needed in accepting risk and making this an essential aspect of State Department operations.

- *The military must provide security for U.S. civilians:* The United States must never again rely on contract civilians to provide security instead of U.S. soldiers. A civil-military partnership is a two-way street. U.S. commanders and officers at every level must understand this and also understand that their careers are dependent on their success in joint assignments that work with civilians and ensure that those civilians are properly protected by U.S. forces.

- *There must be an efficient way to allocate civilian resources:* The United States not only needs this jointness in Washington, it needs it in the field. There must be a single decision maker clearly in charge of each major effort and capable of compelling interagency cooperation and holding individuals directly responsible.

- *The necessary pool of trained personnel must exist and must accept the possibility of being assigned to high-risk tasks overseas:* The military needs adequate staffs of civilian counterparts in the field if the United States is to efficiently conduct asymmetric war, counterinsurgency, counterterrorism, stability operations, nation building, and peacemaking. These kinds of missions and struggles cannot be shaped and won in Washington and rear areas; they must be won on the scene and in the country involved. If this is to happen, civilians in the State Department, intelligence services, and other relevant agencies must be recruited and retained on the basis of their willingness to operate in hostile areas and accept significant risk. Stability and nation-building operations must have an effective civilian component, and "effective" means in the field, not in fortress-like embassies.

- *Intelligence operations must serve both military and civilian users in the field:* The Intelligence Community does not exist to write briefs for the President, Congress, or officials in the Beltway. Wars and crises are won and lost in the field and generally in real time. The recent reorganization of intelligence has focused on virtually every user but the operator. This needs fundamental review and a clear new focus.

- *The Intelligence Community must be a true partner collocated and integrated into civil military operations and not compartmented in terms of security or location:* The Cold War is over. The priority today is for efficient joint operations, not layers of classification or compartmentation.

- *The role of the Department of Defense needs to be fully integrated into an overall strategy, plan, program, and budget for homeland defense on an interagency basis:* Homeland defense is still a broken mess, and this is particularly true of the Department of Homeland Security. It will be impossible to create an effective system unless there is a fully integrated plan, program, and budget that cut across all organizational lines.

- *The National Guard needs a clear long-term plan and program for a role in homeland defense as part of the rebalancing of the active and reserve forces:* The Guard is the natural core of the DoD and the military role in homeland defense. It needs a clear plan for assigning resources to this role and one that takes into account the overall mission needs of U.S. military forces and the future role of the Reserves relative to the active force.

- *The civilian components in homeland defense, and particularly in the Department of Homeland Security, need to have a clear allocation of personnel for assignment as partners to the military in operation in asymmetric war, stability operations, nation building, etc.:* The United States must not wait for volunteers who never come, rely on contractors that cannot perform, and/or look for skill sets and core competencies that do not exist. Special pay and other incentives may be needed to build the competence and volunteer pool needed, but this aspect of career development is critical to providing real-world capability.

- *The United States must have a local partner, must work on a government-to-government basis, and avoid any serious reliance on contractor operations:* Iraq has shown once and for all that contract operations can have value in some support missions, but must not be given a major security role or responsibility for major economic and aid missions. Only the U.S military can provide U.S. government civilians with adequate security and ensure that the military and civilians act as a team. U.S. contractors lack expertise, continuity, area and language skills, security capability, and the ability to avoid massive waste and corruption. They cannot save a failed state from itself, and they do not lead host governments to take responsibility, plan, use resources effectively, or create projects and development efforts that suit a given economy and culture and that can be sustained once U.S. aid and contract support ends.

We make one final point. Iraq has already shown that it is terribly easy to call for interagency solutions, but very difficult to create, fund, and sustain them. Iraq is more than a demonstration that new forms of interagency coordination are needed. It is also a warning that there are some things that the United States may never have the resources or strategic priorities to do. Iraq may have been too complex a task from the start. The combination of ideological, political, economic, and military challenges of "fixing" or "constructing" a state of 27 million people in a country the size of California may simply have been too difficult, and a more objective interagency risk assessment, planning effort, and examination of the probable costs might have shown this.

The ability to predict what kinds of expertise and core competence, languages, and area expertise that will be needed for the "next war" will always be limited. Dealing with "failed states" with failed political elites and/or major ethnic, religious, racial, and tribal problems will always be difficult at best and often require far more resources than aiding neighboring states, reinforcing success in other parts of a region, and relying on deterrence and containment.

Much also depends on the capability of the nation or people that the United States is seeking to aid and must adopt as a partner. The United States must act when it is faced with true strategic necessity. The level of unavoidable problems and limits to interagency action are, however, a warning that optional or limited wars, nation-building efforts, and similar missions will often need to be avoided or have to be terminated when their real-world cost exceeds their value. There also will always be a necessity to make other kinds of choices. It will often be the case that it is the nation that can easily be fixed or strengthened, not the nation that has failed, where American resources can be most effective and have the greatest real-world impact in helping those involved.

Challenge Eight: Creating Effective Local Governance and Forces

The problem of creating effective Afghan and Iraqi governance, and military and security forces, is only one example of the challenges the United States faces in restructuring its alliances to reduce the strains on its forces and to make American military action more effective. At the same time, the U.S. experience in both Iraq and Afghanistan has shown that building local allied forces and capabilities is almost certain to be a major mission requirement in other wars and U.S. military interventions.

Placing greater reliance on local forces provides a mechanism for reducing the demands placed on U.S. forces. It helps the United States compensate for the religious, ideological, and cultural differences that the United States faces in fighting the war on terrorism. And it can help compensate for the lack of U.S. civilian counterparts to the U.S. military that can take up many of the potential burdens in stability operations and nation building.

Far more is involved, however, than making the maximum possible use of allied forces and reducing the burden on the United States and the risk of "overstretch." There are many things the United States can do to improve the counterinsurgency capabilities of its forces, their area and language skills, and expertise in civil-military and nation-building operations. There is much the United States can do to improve its interagency capabilities to provide civilian support to military operations, and there is much it can do to improve its overall structure of alliances and its ability to obtain allied support. This is a key point touched upon in part in the Department of Defense Directive on stability operations, DoD Directive 3000.05, that was issued on November 28, 2005, and that is highlighted in the new U.S. Army Field Manual (FM 3-24) on Counterinsurgency issued in December 2006.[1]

The United States needs to go much further if it is to deal with a world filled with nonstate actors who fight on asymmetric terms and use new methods of terrorism and insurgency. Many future wars will involve nations that at least partially qualify as "failed states" as well as states that have very different cultures and values from those of the United States. This is particularly true of the areas where the United States faces its most severe challenges in the "long war." As long as the United States struggles against Islamist extremists, it will have to deal with different religious and ideological values and the perception that the United States is a "neoimperialist," a "crusader," or an "occupier."

Moreover, major stability and nation-building operations will always present serious problems in terms of U.S. force quantity and force quality. Unless the United States can rely on local forces, it will face the potential need to make long-term deployments of large numbers of U.S. troops and civilians. It will simultaneously need large numbers of personnel with highly specialized areas, language, cultural, and administrative skills. In most cases, the United States simply will not be able to have the numbers and kinds of personnel it needs, whether military or civilian, unless it can develop strong local forces and civil capabilities to supplement its resources.

Political and ideological dimensions will likely dominate many future asymmetric wars. Only using or creating local forces and local governance can minimize the inevitable frictions between U.S. efforts and the local populace, and the ability of terrorists, insurgents, and other hostile forces to exploit the alien status of a U.S. presence. In most cases, this will mean that the United States must expend significant resources to create the local capabilities it needs to win. Almost by definition, the kind of local forces and governance required will be missing. If they were there in the first place, there would be no need for U.S. intervention short of a major invasion or series of operations from a neighboring state.

In most such cases, the United States will still have to send in combat forces, but the ultimate focus of its operations will not be the direct defeat of an enemy by U.S. forces, but rather the creation of local capabilities that can defeat the enemy and the establishment of political and economic stability, even in sustained asymmetric struggles and wars of attrition.

Furthermore, even when local allies already have substantial capabilities, extensive U.S. training and financial and equipment aid will still be needed. So will the ability to rapidly deploy and sustain a balanced U.S. assistance effort that mixes the development of military and police forces with political and economic aid, and efforts to create an effective criminal justice system and rule of law.

BALANCED "CONSTRUCTION," NOT "RECONSTRUCTION"

History provides consistent warnings about the need for the United States to build up local forces and capabilities. It also warns, however, that each case must be treated differently. This is not the place for case-study comparisons, but even a casual acquaintance with history makes it clear that Vietnam was not Lebanon, which was not Haiti, which was not Somalia, which was not Afghanistan, which was not Iraq.

If one looks at UN and other peacemaking operations, the case-specific nature of efforts to create local forces and capabilities is even clearer.

At the same time, in most cases, the use of the word "reconstruction" was a fundamental misnomer. Existing local capabilities provided some foundation, but the primary task was actually to improve or construct new local capabilities and not to reconstruct old ones. In each case, it was also clear that the end goal had to be developing a balanced mix of local capabilities, and not simply creating local military forces. Action was also required at the ideological, political, security, and economic levels or local forces could not win and often became part of the problem.

Establishing security also always required a broad effort at the regional and local levels to create a mix of military forces to deal with the main threat. It also, however, required the development of police or paramilitary forces to deal with local or lesser threats. It required some kind of local government presence and services to give governance and the political process credibility. Finally, it required the development of courts and legal institutions to establish a rule of law that kept corruption, arbitrary official violence, and the abuse of minorities and human rights within workable limits.

This is why the new field manual on Counterinsurgency and new Department of Defense Directive 3000.05 on stability operations are only initial guidance in dealing with far more serious problems in working with local forces.[2] The United States does not simply need to transform its military forces to fight terrorists or insurgents. It needs to transform its national security structure to be able to fight civil-military warfare in ways that rely far more heavily on the development of local forces and capabilities. One of the most serious U.S. strategic failures in Iraq was the lack of effective planning to ensure the continuity of government, police, and legal operations. Another was the failure to see the transformation of the Iraqi military and the various militias into an effective force as the key both to providing local stability with a local face and to keeping such elements from becoming part of the security threat.

The United States was slow to see the need to create new military forces, restructure and reform the police, match military and police efforts with the deployment of a local Iraqi government presence, and provide courts and a functional rule of law. It was not until 2005 that the development of Iraqi military forces gathered full momentum. And it was not until late in 2005 that officials recognized the potential importance of the Ministry of Interior and its security forces as a source of Shi'ite sectarian violence.

Preserving or creating effective police forces was treated as a tertiary or passing priority until it became brutally clear that local civil, sectarian, and ethnic violence was becoming as much of a threat as the insurgency and that many of the police and other security forces were part of this problem. This led to 2006 being called the "year of the police," but it was not until mid-2006 that the United States and its allies recognized just how important such efforts really were, and how dangerous private militias and security forces were. Even then, there was limited recognition of the need for a matching government presence at the local level, and functional courts and legal institutions. The same was true of the need to fight crime and soft ethnic cleansing, not just the insurgents and militias, and the importance of providing the kind of economic aid that could actually deal with the worst problems of unemployment.

It is worth noting that in Afghanistan's case, the problems were different. Heavy reliance was placed on local capabilities and forces from the start, but few resources were provided to create them. A single-minded military concentration on defeating the Taliban and a political concentration on creating a national democracy and government were combined with minimal local security efforts, an attempt to create Afghani military forces that were a small fraction of what was needed, no serious effort to create effective police or rule of law, grossly insufficient economic aid, and denial of Afghanistan's real-world dependence upon a drug economy. The importance of Afghanistan's ethnic and sectarian problems, and particularly its religious and cultural conservatism and traditions, was sharply underestimated. This was particularly true of the Pashtun problem and its overlap into Pakistan, which helped create the Taliban in the first place.

The United States has generally done a better job of helping countries develop local capabilities to fight the war on terrorism. In most cases, this was the only real option since occupation or a major U.S. presence was not practical. The task was also easier because the United States was not dealing with failed states. In general, developing local capabilities in these other countries required limited training, technology, and other assistance and expertise in counterterrorism and could build on existing ideological, political, security, and economic structures.

Egypt, Jordan, and Saudi Arabia are all cases in point where the United States effectively gained "force multipliers" in terms of local counterterrorism capabilities that it could aid and encourage and which acted not only as substitutes for U.S. action and forces, but as more capable forces than the United States could generate because they were native, were perceived as legitimate, and had the necessary religious, cultural, and linguistic identities.

THE U.S. STRATEGY FOR IRAQ AND ITS PROGNOSIS

At this point, there is no way to be sure whether the United States can succeed in building such balanced local capabilities in Iraq. The historical record in other countries has not been good, almost regardless of the effort involved. The internal divisions and forces that cause failed states are extremely difficult to change, and UN Secretary General Kofi A. Annan has noted that over 50 percent of all the countries where the UN sends in peacekeeping missions revert to violence within five years.

The United States has, however, gradually come to focus on such a balanced approach in both Afghanistan and Iraq, although this may well have come too late to be effective—at least in Iraq. President George W. Bush formally announced such an approach for Iraq on November 30, 2005,[3] While this announcement came more than two years after Saddam's fall, the United States government clearly laid out the need to simultaneously address the political, security, and economic dimensions of its activity in Iraq:[4]

Our Strategy for Victory Is Clear

- We will help the Iraqi people build a new Iraq with a constitutional, representative government that respects civil rights and has security forces sufficient to maintain domestic order and keep Iraq from becoming a safe haven for terrorists. *To achieve this end, we are pursuing an integrated strategy along three broad tracks,* which together incorporate the efforts of the Iraqi government, the Coalition, cooperative countries in the region, the international community, and the United Nations.

- *The Political Track* involves working to forge a broadly supported national compact for democratic governance by helping the Iraqi government:
  - *Isolate* enemy elements from those who can be won over to the political process by countering false propaganda and demonstrating to all Iraqis that they have a stake in a democratic Iraq;
  - *Engage* those outside the political process and invite in those willing to turn away from violence through ever-expanding avenues of participation; and
  - *Build* stable, pluralistic, and effective national institutions that can protect the interests of all Iraqis, and facilitate Iraq's full integration into the international community.

- *The Security Track* involves carrying out a campaign to defeat the terrorists and neutralize the insurgency, developing Iraqi security forces, and helping the Iraqi government:
  - *Clear* areas of enemy control by remaining on the offensive, killing and capturing enemy fighters and denying them safe-haven;
  - *Hold* areas freed from enemy influence by ensuring that they remain under the control of the Iraqi government with an adequate Iraqi security force presence; and
  - *Build* Iraqi Security Forces and the capacity of local institutions to deliver services, advance the rule of law, and nurture civil society.

- *The Economic Track* involves setting the foundation for a sound and self-sustaining economy by helping the Iraqi government:
  - *Restore* Iraq's infrastructure to meet increasing demand and the needs of a growing economy;
  - *Reform* Iraq's economy, which in the past has been shaped by war, dictatorship, and sanctions, so that it can be self-sustaining in the future; and
  - *Build* the capacity of Iraqi institutions to maintain infrastructure, rejoin the international economic community, and improve the general welfare of all Iraqis.

This Strategy Is Integrated and Its Elements Are Mutually Reinforcing

- Progress in each of the political, security, and economic tracks reinforces progress in the other tracks.
- For instance, as *the political process* has moved forward, terrorists have become more isolated, leading to more intelligence on security threats from Iraqi citizens, which has led to *better security* in previously violent areas, a more stable infrastructure, the prospect of *economic progress,* and expanding *political participation.*

Victory Will Take Time

- **Our strategy is working:** Much has been accomplished in Iraq, including the removal of Saddam's tyranny, negotiation of an interim constitution, restoration of full sovereignty, holding of free national elections, formation of an elected government, drafting of a permanent constitution, ratification of that constitution, introduction of a sound currency, gradual restoration of neglected infrastructure, the ongoing training and equipping of Iraqi security forces, and the increasing capability of those forces to take on the terrorists and secure their nation.

- **Yet many challenges remain:** Iraq is overcoming decades of a vicious tyranny, where governmental authority stemmed solely from fear, terror, and brutality.

  - It is not realistic to expect a fully functioning democracy, able to defeat its enemies and peacefully reconcile generational grievances, to be in place less than three years after Saddam was finally removed from power.

- Our comprehensive strategy will help Iraqis overcome remaining challenges, but defeating the multi-headed enemy in Iraq—and ensuring that it cannot threaten Iraq's democratic gains once we leave—requires persistent effort across many fronts.

Our Victory Strategy Is (and Must Be) Conditions Based

- With resolve, victory will be achieved, although not by a date certain.

  - No war has ever been won on a timetable and neither will this one.

- But lack of a timetable does not mean our posture in Iraq (both military and civilian) will remain static over time. As conditions change, our posture will change.

  - We expect, but cannot guarantee, that our force posture will change over the next year, as the political process advances and Iraqi security forces grow and gain experience.

  - While our military presence may become less visible, it will remain lethal and decisive, able to confront the enemy wherever it may organize.

  - Our mission in Iraq is to win the war. Our troops will return home when that mission is complete.

There is no way to be certain how much better the situation would be if the United States had begun with such a strategy, if it had not committed the strategic mistakes described in Chapter 2, or if it had begun its invasion with the plans and resources to preserve as many existing Iraqi capabilities as possible and encourage Iraqis to take the lead in the areas where new capabilities were needed. It seems likely, however, that much of the tragedy that followed the fall of Saddam Hussein could have been avoided, although no one can ever be sure. The sheer scale of the task of reshaping a nation of some 27 million people in a divided state after decades of dictatorship, war, and economic mismanagement may well have been beyond U.S. capability even if it had chosen such a strategy to begin with, committed the necessary resources, and chosen to work closely with every faction in Iraq. Unfortunately, U.S. efforts to implement such strategy came so late that Iraq may plunge into civil war, divide, or simply fail to emerge as a strong and viable state that meets its peoples' needs.

It is equally clear that time and experience have forced the United States to look beyond its own warfighting and security capabilities and to focus on the development of local forces and capabilities in both Iraq and Afghanistan and that this is a serious warning about how the United States should shape its strategy and military interventions in the future. The United States found in practice that the only strategy that could allow it to remove most or all of its forces from Iraq and Afghanistan within a few years, produce some kind of victory, and solve America's immediate problem of "overstretch" on a timely basis was to create a mix of Iraqi forces and Iraqi governance that could relieve the burden on the United States and then support this effort with added economic aid.

Both Iran and Afghanistan have shown that wars must be won at the local political and economic levels as well as the military and security levels. They have also shown that the way governments are chosen—whether democratic or not—is far less important to both victory and achieving a stable long-term outcome than their ability to govern and actually meet the needs of their peoples. Ordinary citizens do not live in the dawn of tomorrow, they live in the noon of today. Security, jobs, education, medical services, and utilities are far more serious measures of legitimacy than the ability to vote.

The United States has found that it cannot hope for any kind of victory in conflicts like Iraq and Afghanistan until it is clear that the government has created a relatively stable political structure and effective government services. It cannot hope for victory without forging a suitable mix of military, police, and legal forces in the field. It cannot hope for victory without maintaining major military advisory and aid efforts, providing continuing support from U.S. heavy and Special Forces, and eventually reshaping Iraqi military capabilities to deter and defend against Iraq's neighbors. The United States has also found that winning long wars requires patience and time. Many of the wars the United States must now fight do not involve "tipping points" in Iraq; they involve "tipping years" that may well play out for more than a decade.

THE MORE DETAILED LESSONS OF U.S. INTERVENTION IN IRAQ AND AFGHANISTAN

It is too early to draw a full set of conclusions about the more detailed lessons the United States should draw from its intervention in Iraq and Afghanistan, and it must be stressed that the lessons from one contingency may not apply to the next. At the same time, the United States cannot afford to prepare for an era of asymmetric warfare, and a long war against Islamist extremism and terrorism, without acting on such lessons as quickly as possible. It is also clear that some lessons are certain to apply to many future contingencies.

Risk Assessment and Operational Planning

One critical grand strategic lesson that does clearly emerge from the Iraq War is that the decision to intervene is the moment at which the United States can do the most to limit the strain on its forces. The United States must learn from Iraq what it did not learn from Vietnam. It cannot unilaterally reshape the world or even other nations. Moreover, limited wars are always optional; they are not crusades, they do not merit open-ended commitments, and diplomatic and military alternatives must always be fully considered.

Risk assessment must always look beyond the narrow issue of the immediate rationale for military action, and the prospects for short-term success, and consider the cost-benefits in terms of stability operations, nation building, and long-term efforts. Such assessments must also be regional and global. The United States can never take serious military action without affecting its overall strategic and diplomatic position, affecting regional and global perceptions, and impacting on other nations.

Risk assessment must also be realistic and consider failure as well as success. One of the few iron laws of contingency planning is that planning for success is often a good way to plan for failure. It is far better to be cautious and pessimistic in deciding whether to act, and—if that decision is taken—to plan for much higher force levels, costs, and periods of commitment than may ultimately be necessary. A nation with America's resources can afford waste—which may often be its best secret weapon. It cannot afford too little and too late.

If there are any clear parallels between Iraq and Vietnam, it is that risk assessments cannot be based on responding to the desires of policy makers or their political ideology. The Neoliberals who took the United States to war in Vietnam were strikingly similar to the Neoconservatives who took the United States to war in Iraq. They both learned the hard way that in a confrontation between reality and political hope and belief, it is reality that tends to win.

It is equally clear that these decisions should explicitly consider how much the United States can and must rely on local capabilities. No matter how many other members may be in a given coalition of the willing, with or without a UN mandate, the center of gravity in such wars will always be local forces and governance. Grand strategic success does not depend on who deploys or invades; it depends on the local government and forces that remain once U.S. and allied forces leave.

Accordingly, the United States has several lessons to learn from its experience in Iraq, almost all of which have been reinforced by its experience in Afghanistan:

- *Fully assess the risks in going to war as objectively as possible, and do so in the light of both explicit analysis of all the alternatives and the risks through successful conflict termination and nation building if necessary:* A "can do" approach is both stupid and self-destructive. So is bypassing the interagency process or seeking to serve the policy maker, rather than the nation.

- *Look carefully at containment, diplomacy, and alternative uses of resources:* Containment was not an ideal solution to Saddam Hussein, but it is clear in retrospect that it had succeeded in both crippling Iraq's conventional military capabilities and denying Iraq the ability to reconstitute its weapons of mass destruction. If one uses Congressional Budget Office estimates—which are lower than those estimated by the Congressional

Research Service—the Iraq War alone cost $290 billion between March 2003 and the end of FY2006 and was likely to cost at least $166 billion more to terminate successfully (with a high-end estimate of $368 billion).[5] Even if one ignores the human, political, and diplomatic costs of the fighting to the United States, these are immense opportunity costs in terms of alternative spending on U.S. military forces, U.S. allies and influence, and aid programs. Furthermore, many experts put the predicted total cost at $800 billion to $1 trillion.

- *Do not commit U.S. forces without a detailed operational plan for integrated interagency action:* One of the major problems in the U.S. approach to the Iraq War was that the interagency analysis before the war was far more diagnostic than operational. This was partly due to a lack of core competence. The United States simply did not have a large pool of personnel, or outside experts to draw upon, with detailed knowledge of Iraq's internal politics, methods of governance, security forces, or economy. It lacked meaningful generic experience in counterinsurgency prevention, ensuring continuity of government, and stability operations in general. The United States had virtually no experience with command economies, particularly one as distorted and corrupt as Iraq's, and lacked the most basic data and expertise to do sectoral analysis and planning.

  If the United States is to conduct stability operations and nation building, it must go to war with clear plans for the entire conflict to the final conflict termination stage, with estimated costs, or at least go to war with a clear and honest understanding of the area where it lacks core expertise and the ability to plan. This is also an essential aspect of risk and cost-benefit analysis. If the United States cannot create workable operational plans, this is a major additional risk that must be weighed as such. If the United States lacks suitable assets in terms of core competence to plan, it will be far worse off when it comes to executing the plan. If the United States cannot estimate the full range of costs over time before engaging, decision makers need an explicit analysis of what the United States can and cannot cost.

  If the United States faces a long war, and many such operations do involve military and advisory presences that last years and often a decade, a clear decision must be made to make such a commitment. The American political and policy-making culture looks for quick and simple solutions. In many, if not most, cases involving failed states, or countries with serious internal problems, the search for speed and simplicity is an exercise in self-delusion. Shaping history is complex and it takes time. American strategic planning and military operations must accept this.

  Such plans cannot eliminate risk or produce any certainty. They will inevitably be wrong in many areas and require constant change and adaptation. All of the tired military homilies about the war plan being the first casualty of combat apply even more strongly to comprehensive operational plans. If the United States does not start with a plan, however, its efforts to improvise one will be far worse than if there were no plan at all, and its risk assessments will have little meaning.

- *Do not commit U.S. forces without committing U.S. resources:* The United States went to war in Iraq with no commitment to providing an enduring military presence, with no meaningful plan or resources for civilian support, and with no meaningful costing of the possible contingencies that could emerge and no funds for foreign aid. In 2006, the Bush Administration still could not provide Congress with even the crudest plan for future expenditures and relied on supplemental budget requests that were decoupled from its ability to execute the strategy it had developed. Once again, there are no certainties in such planning.

The failure to even begin realistic efforts to plan was, however, inexcusable and helped make meaningful risk and cost-benefit analysis impossible. It should also be clear that the level of planning required to ensure success will at least take months and often years. Iraq strongly indicates that the United States needs integrated plans to be developed now for possible contingencies on the scale of Iran, North Korea, and the Taiwan Strait.

- *Make the role of local governments and forces an essential part of risk assessment and planning:* In retrospect, U.S. action in Iraq is the model of what not to do in the future. The United States relied far too much on the hopes of exiles and a "coalition of the willing." The United States failed to assess what aspects of the Iraqi system of governance, legal system, military, and police services it should seek to preserve or work with. It sought to impose a new constitution rather than alter the old one and ended in doing the same for the legal code. It saw the Ba'ath Party as a whole as a potential problem or threat, rather than the political cover that most secular Iraqis have been forced to adopt. It did not plan for, or provide, forces to secure government offices and operations as it advanced.

  U.S. planning should, from the start, focus on how to use and develop local capabilities as a key force multiplier. Even the best and most willing outside allies cannot be an enduring presence, and they too have every reason to encourage local governments and forces. More important, no end game is possible except through the success of local forces and governments. Indefinite occupation is simply not an option.

- *Anticipate the fact that conflict or crisis almost inevitably exacerbates sectarian/confessional and ethnic/tribal divisions and other local fault lines:* The idea that "liberation," peacemaking interventions, outside assistance, and the urgency of humanitarian crises somehow unite a people is false far more often than it is true. In most cases, the opposite is true. Both risk assessment and plans cannot be based on political and ideological assumptions based on hope and good intentions. They must reflect the fact that any kind of national turmoil tends to uncap previous local fault lines and divisions and that operations can succeed only if they anticipate this and are willing to commit the necessary effort and resources to deal with the result.

- *Look beyond military force development and plan accordingly:* One key lesson that Iraq provides that has emerged out of one insurgency, stability operation, and nation-building exercise after another is that developing stability and security means a tight focus on developing local military, security, and police forces and not simply military forces. Equally important, security forces without courts and the rule of law inevitably become corrupt, abusive, or factional.

  Moreover, any serious stability operation requires police and security forces, and courts and prisons, strong enough to withstand serious paramilitary and insurgent attacks. U.S.–style police cannot survive or function under the conditions required, and the resulting local power vacuum will cause far more human rights abuses than creating effective forces. On the one hand, this means the precedent that the Multi-National Forces–Iraq and the Multi-National Security Transition Command–Iraq set in October 2005 of combining advice through the U.S. military to the Ministry of Interior, Ministry of Defense, army, security forces, and police is one that should be followed in all similar cases. On the other hand, it makes it equally important to provide immediate and parallel civilian support to creating effective courts and prisons and ensuring a civil government presence in the field.

- *Do not seek to narrowly impose U.S. goals and values on a foreign country and culture:* The United States cannot, however, make effective use of local capabilities unless it is willing to defer to many local values and sensitivities. There is nothing new about the United States treating war as a moral crusade and seeking to impose its values on a foreign country and defeated enemy. Hans Morgenthau and James Reston talked about these American tendencies, and the strengths and weaknesses, more than half a century ago. In Iraq's case, however, this was carried to unique and dangerous extremes.

  Neoconservatives, and many others including leading liberals in Congress, assumed that U.S. values were global, the values Iraq should choose, and the values Iraqis either already had or would quickly acquire once Saddam Hussein and his elite were removed from power. Even today, the United States often tacitly rejects the right of Iraqis to put religion before secular values, and their own culture before U.S. concepts of human rights. It is one thing to influence and persuade and quite another to impose and assume. It is particularly naive to assume the United States can achieve massive, sudden change when a society has a different religion that is key to its political life, such different cultural values, a history of colonial occupation and tensions going back to the crusades, and so many unresolved internal ethnic and sectarian differences.

  Moreover, the United States is still saddled in part with the problems it created for itself by placing excessive reliance on exiles. There has never been a historical reason to place great trust in exiles as a source of objective information or as proxies for local citizens and governments. A few succeed, most fail, and all serve their own—not U.S.—interests. Choosing the few with capability, credibility, and common interests is an art form at best, and it is particularly important to recognize that the fact exiles have acquired, or claim to have, U.S. values and goals does not mean they speak for their country or are politically viable. The United States should also not forget the historical irony that ever since ancient Greece, and the Napoleonic wars in Europe, exiles have done a surprisingly better job of using the governments that tried to use them.

  As a corollary, it is dangerous and absurd to assume that U.S. action will not only transform the country where operations take place, but also create a transformational example. Nations are too different, peoples are too sensitive to outside action, and change (when it occurs) is too long and too time-consuming.

- *The United States needs to have a clear plan from the start that it can communicate to the population of the country where it will go to war or conduct military operations:* It is not enough to say the United States has good intentions and noble goals. The United States must be able to communicate its intentions in terms of clear plans and actions that the local populace and leaders can see and judge. It must anticipate local concerns (and hostility and conspiracy theories) and do its best from the start to defuse them. Broad, unsupported slogans and rhetoric are not tools in political and psychological warfare; they are paths to defeat.

These lessons do not mean that there will not be many low-level contingencies where limited U.S. military action cannot achieve decisive results without such coordinated approaches to risk assessment and planning. However, almost all of the above lessons apply in some form to Afghanistan, and most apply to the U.S.

experience in Vietnam and Somalia. If the contingency and the risks are serious, they must be considered.

Wartime Execution and Adapting to Circumstances

Another critical lesson the United States must learn from Iraq, Afghanistan, and many other modern wars is the need to look beyond struggles between conventional forces. It is becoming harder and harder to define "war" as struggles between the armed forces of state actors. The conventional phases of recent conflicts have often been episodic or brief, while the low-level periods have lasted years. Asymmetric conflicts are generally wars of attrition, and this means the so-called conflict termination, stability operation, and nation-building phases of a conflict can involve years of armed struggle after the main phase of conventional fighting is over. Vietnam, Lebanon, and the Balkans are just a few additional examples.

Iraq and Afghanistan show that stability operations and nation-building activities not only should begin before hostilities or any other form of military intervention, they should be an integral part of even the most intense conventional warfare. Political and psychological operations are a critical aspect of seeking to influence local and enemy behavior. Targeting and the location and intensity of tactical operations must consider both the political dimension and the needs of the postconflict environment. This is not simply a matter of reducing collateral damage; it is a matter of shaping operations.

One key issue is how to integrate ideological and political warfare, and the need to combine conventional warfighting at the command level with effective stability operations. In the Balkans, Afghanistan, and Iraq, the United States benefited from allied military personnel and sometimes allied political interference. In many cases, allies vetoed or "red carded" operations and air strikes whose political cost outweighed their military value. There was not, however, a political planning cell to provide coherent advice on the political dimension of operations or support activities for stability operations and nation building. Such a cell may well be needed as the definition of "joint operations" is broadened to look beyond interservice coordination.

Actual operations, however, are equally important. Iraq provides a clear warning that rapid maneuver does not mean that the United States does not need to either secure or occupy rear areas and preserve security as its forces advance. Tactical operations need to explicitly consider continuity of government. The fall of Baghdad provides an example of extraordinary tactical success against the enemy, but under conditions where the U.S. forces involved were small, exposed elements in a potentially hostile city, and could not secure it against looting. Having civil-military teams to work immediately with local police and local governments, and military units to work with Iraqi military units to keep them in place and preserve potential cadres for future Iraqi forces, would have been critical. Local aid teams might have done much to defuse hostility, particularly if they had worked through local authorities, mosques, and institutions.

Creating Force Quality as Well as Force Quantity

Iraq also provides a clear message that calls to deploy far higher U.S. troop levels to solve these problems will not solve the problems involved and may actually increase them. The United States almost certainly did have too few troops on the ground to deal with rear areas and urban security missions. At the same time, it provides little evidence that sheer numbers of troops would have solved the problems that emerged after the fall of Saddam Hussein. "Boots on the ground" alone simply highlight the alien nature of the occupying force unless the "brains above them" have the right training and skills.

The United States went to war in Iraq with virtually no overall area and cultural training for its troops, and far too few translators. Most of its forces had no real training and experience in modern counterinsurgency or counterterrorist warfare. The United States had only token numbers of civil-military personnel and military police, most with few if any area or language skills. Much is made of the military's lack of close liaisons with the Office of Reconstruction and Humanitarian Assistance and of the feuding between Ambassador L. Paul Bremer and General Ricardo Sanchez.

What was equally serious was that neither the U.S. military nor the U.S. State Department had recent experience of working closely together in the field or in rear areas, and the military had no pool of competent civilians to draw upon to substitute for its own lack of experience and specialization. This was certainly made worse once the Coalition Provisional Authority (CPA) was established by the Administration's screening of politically correct civilian volunteers, almost all of whom had no experience in working under local conditions or meaningful experience of any kind, little real area expertise, no training for working in the field under threat conditions, and who were recruited for tours as short as three months.

There simply was no pool of qualified U.S. civilian or military personnel to provide the level of skills required. Sending in another 100,000 men and women in uniform who did not know what to do and did not have the required training would have helped in terms of "boots," but would not have provided "brains." Things could have been better, but they could not possibly have been adequate.

This experience does provide the lesson that the United States must do more to create the necessary mix of military and civilian skills and a pool of personnel it can send into operations as soon as combat begins, not simply once the intense phases of combat are over. However, the United States needs to be far more honest with itself about the acute limitations that are inherent in any such efforts. Whatever the United States does, its numbers will still be limited; it will often lack the right mix of skills and experience, and it will not be able to substitute for local personnel.

"Warehousing" semicompetent "specialists" and "experts" in full-time jobs to wait for missions they may never perform is an expensive recipe for failure. The competent will not wait, and only the failed or mediocre will remain. Creating reserve volunteers will waste far less personnel, but still have acute limitations. The competent will already be doing similar jobs somewhere else. The U.S. military and the State

Department cannot possibly maintain a large pool of operationally ready personnel with the full range of area and language skills that may be needed and certainly cannot maintain a pool of personnel with practical experience if such personnel do not exist.

Dealing with the Transition to Stability Operations and Nation Building

Many of the same lessons apply during the transition to stability operations and nation building as during any phase of intense conventional military operations. Iraq and Afghanistan both demonstrate, however, that there may be a narrow window of opportunity in which to create local government and security capabilities out of existing elements of local forces, reduce the image of U.S. forces as "invaders" or "occupiers," and avoid local tensions and ethnic and sectarian rivalries from exploding into terrorism or insurgency.

The United States will probably always face the problem of impossible local expectations, coupled with hostility and conspiracy theories. Iraq does warn, however, that the United States will make things far worse if it cannot provide an immediate civil-military presence, if it does not turn immediately to local leaders, and/or if it attempts another procounselor operation like the Coalition Provisional Authority (CPA). Going from the illusion that Iraq was essentially self-healing to trying to remake the entire country by a massive occupying presence—particularly one sited in Saddam's former palace—was exactly the wrong approach.

The United States needs to stop congratulating itself on mythical versions of its success following World War II. The first few years of occupation in Germany and Japan involved massive suffering and poverty. Germany recovered largely because of its own leaders and because of the aid that came out of the Marshall Plan and the Cold War. Japan recovered from the flood of money that also came as a result of the Cold War, but most of all from spending in Japan during the Korean conflict.

Few wars today will be fought against conventional secular enemies like Germany and Japan or lead to the same level of acceptance by the occupied. Even those oppressed by the former regime often will not welcome a foreign presence unless it clearly is working with local authorities. Even the best trained U.S. troops will not be police or be suited for low-level law enforcement work or providing security that requires an exact knowledge of, or intelligence on, local factions and tensions. Too low a profile may be seen as a power vacuum, but too high a profile—coupled with the declared goal of transforming a country—will often be seen as intolerable.

In most divided countries and failed states, military action will cause a significant part of the population to see U.S. forces as a threat or an enemy from the start, and large portions of the populace will blame every failure or problem that follows on U.S. forces. This will interact with the kind of internal turmoil that encourages core settling, violence, and political divisions between sects and ethnic groups. U.S. actions to act as a broker or to enforce stability will make the United States seem to oppose factions on any side that do not directly benefit from such U.S. involvement.

The United States must make every conceivable effort to avoid fighting limited wars where it must actually occupy a nation, where it would be seen by that nation's people as an occupier rather than as a liberator committed to the earliest possible transfer of the largest possible amount of power, and actually executing that commitment.

The alternative to "occupation" is U.S. civil-military action to bring as many existing local leaders into the government as soon as possible. It means reviving existing ministries and provincial and local governments. It means using local police and at least consulting with and paying the military and security elements that may otherwise become unnecessarily hostile. It means putting more emphasis on effective governance and security than instant efforts to introduce democracy or sort out exactly who might have been guilty of abuses in the past. It is one thing to remove the clearly dangerous and hostile, and another to attempt to remove broad categories of people from power and any form of employment, particularly when no aid or economic opportunity is created to tie the country together.

Such U.S. efforts will require broad action at the local and provincial levels, not just attempts at building central governments. Power may be concentrated in the capital, but security and development are national. Massive fortress embassies cannot reach out to a nation, try to defuse local flash points, or find ways to use local nationals to substitute for inadequate governance and security. Getting as many civil-military teams into the field as soon as possible, having all commanders begin civil-military operations immediately, and seeking as much local national participation as possible from the start are key steps. Having personnel ready from the start in the field, giving them aid funds and equipment, and providing military—not contract—security are also key steps.

This does not mean early action can always ensure popularity or stop decades of contained sectarian and ethnic tension from exploding. Afghanistan, Iraq, and Somalia have all shown that it will generally be critical to avoid taking a transformational approach to creating rapid democracy, Western standards of human rights, and secular approaches to change in deeply religious societies. One key step will be to determine how fast a given society can and wants to change. It is one thing to encourage what is already there; it is another to seek changes that create alienation and enemies.

Operations from the Start of Stability to the "Advisory" or Active Conflict Termination Phase

Iraq and Afghanistan also teach that the United States must be prepared for long-term efforts that are costly, require an enduring U.S. presence, and call for progress at levels local governments and forces can actually provide. Both countries have confirmed the lessons of Vietnamization, the Balkans, Lebanon, and Somalia.

Deeply troubled nations can sometimes be abandoned when it is strategically expedient, but they cannot be "fixed" quickly. Iraq, for example, can be placed only in an even worse position by premature U.S. disengagement. Iraq cannot hope to reshape its political process and establish effective governance throughout the country for years, and this effort could easily have cycles of success and failure that take a decade. The same is true of Afghanistan.

Iraq is also a good example of a case where withdrawal is not strategically expedient, although circumstances could make this necessary. The United States cannot exit from a strategic situation involving more than 60 percent of the world's proven oil reserves and some 40 percent of its gas, and where the United States and the global economy are dependent on steadily increasing the flow of some 17 million barrels of oil a day through the Strait of Hormuz without paying a heavy price tag.

The United States may well be able to reduce its troop presence in Iraq, and it may even be forced to leave and seek to influence Iraq from the outside. One way or another, however, it must try to make Iraq succeed for years, if not a decade, to come. It also cannot abandon Iraq without appearing to be defeated by Islamic extremism and asymmetric methods of war, and without being seen as abandoning some 27 million people it pledged to rescue from tyranny. The U.S. bull is seen throughout the world as having broken the Iraqi china shop it claimed to rescue. It must now live with the political and strategic consequences.

The lessons that the United States should have learned from Iraq, Afghanistan, and similar contingencies to date fall into four major categories: ideological, political, security, and economic.

IDEOLOGICAL LESSONS

Much will depend on whether the United States is seeking to carry out missions in nations with fundamentally different values and cultural norms, where deep divisions have produced ethnic and sectarian conflict or are likely to do so and, above all, where deep distrust exists of the United States on religious grounds and/or because of fears it seeks to occupy a country or shape it as some form of neocolonial proxy.

This may not be the case in many contingencies. The Balkans is one such example. It may well, however, be the norm in the Middle East and Islamic nations in Asia and Africa. It can easily be the norm in much of Latin America. One key lesson from Iraq and Afghanistan, and Lebanon and Somalia before them, is that the United States must not go to war assuming that its actions and values are popular or transcend local values. It must recognize that rhetoric about the universal support for democracy, secular views of law and human rights, and/or capitalism is simply not realistic and that a thin veneer of exiles and Western-educated citizens who may claim to share such views does not provide a picture of what the people of a country want or can accept.

There are several lessons to learn from this experience.

- *The United States must make it clear from the start that it has no intention to remain in a given country, that its goal is to create effective local governance and forces, and that it will leave as soon as this task is accomplished or a sovereign government asks it to; it must constantly reiterate this at the Presidential and Secretary of State level:* One of America's most serious problems in conducting effective stability and nation-building exercises is that it attempts to enforce its own values and goals, rather than adapt and reinforce local goals. The United States cannot achieve political or psychological victory, or conduct successful public diplomacy, by remaining silent as to its objectives or by stating it will impose its own values and political system. It can exert powerful influence for change and reform, but only if it works through local leaders and reinforces natural forces for change. Values are local and relative, not Western and universal. Crusades are the road to failure; persuasion is the road to success.

- *Operations must be conducted with the knowledge that many of the people may be hostile to, or angry at, the United States and that the United States will not be greeted as a friend or liberator:* The United States needs to understand that it will normally face large elements in any given country where it introduces military forces that are hostile or angry, oppose such American action, deeply distrust America, or at best tolerate U.S. action or support it conditionally. America's ability to fall in love with itself is not contagious. This situation will also tend to deteriorate, not get better, over time. Exaggerated hopes and expectations will not be met. It is easier to blame outsiders. Factions will perceive the United States as taking sides, and military and security actions will breed a legacy of anger and revenge. Conspiracy theories and hostile political groups will grow more sophisticated. It will take constant political and ideological efforts to minimize or reverse these trends.

- *Operations must anticipate the risk of ethnic, sectarian, and factional divisions and warfare or be based on the fact it is already a reality. Every effort must be made to preserve the political center and process of governance that can unite the government and to avoid encouraging such divisions or letting them accelerate:* Ever since Woodrow Wilson's massive miscalculations following World War I, it has been clear that "self-determination" can cause at least as many problems as it solves, and the postwar period since World War II has reinforced the constant risk of nations dissolving into warring factions. The very conditions that lead to U.S. military involvement will often have made this risk even worse or have either created civil war or brought the nation to the edge. This has already proven true even in supposed ethnically cohesive nations like Somalia. For the vast majority of citizens, security, stability, and national cohesion will offer more than attempts to intervene in readjusting the balance of power between national factions and have priority over efforts to introduce democracy or redefine power in terms of demographic equity.

- *Ideological, political, and psychological efforts must be focused on local conditions and factions, not on regional or national:* "Winning hearts and minds" will often succeed with only part of the population, consist of tolerance and not admiration or support, and depend heavily on factional and local support for the local government and forces the United States backs. National and regional efforts to persuade a nation or people will be important, but success will generally require an ongoing, focused effort to win such support on a faction-by-faction basis and at the local level. This means that radio and TV campaigns are not substitutes for in-country efforts and that a focus only on what happens at the national level or in capitols is no substitute for dialog and action in the field.

- *The United States must seek out local attitudes and views, not anticipate them or guess at them:* The United States should not make assumptions about local attitudes wherever tools like polls, local dialog, media analysis, Internet surveys, etc., are available. One of the problems with U.S. efforts to support political and psychological warfare and political operations in general is that the United States often either does not actively measure local attitudes or looks for reinforcement of its current approach. It is particularly important to monitor opinion at a level of detail where the United States has both a picture of national and regional trends and in key local areas of operations.

- *Extreme care must be taken to avoid alienation and "negative political and ideological warfare":* Iran has shown just how easily incidents like Abu Ghraib and the killings and rapes of Iraqi civilians can happen. Both Iraq and Afghanistan have reinforced the lessons of the Kosovo campaign that collateral damage must be kept limited and explained. Tactical operations like house-to-house searches or urban sweeps can be as important. All operations are now political operations and most are reported or misreported locally in near real time. It is particularly important that the handling of detainees and prisoners conform with the standards set by the Geneva Convention and that actual crimes against civilians be rigorously investigated and punished. America's image, and seeing justice done, will often have more of an impact than any amount of political and psychological warfare.

- *Wherever possible, local authorities and forces should speak for themselves:* The United States made a serious mistake early in the Iraq War in having U.S. spokespersons dominate communications and efforts at dealing with the political, ideological, and religious dimensions. As is the case with most operations at the local level, every effort should be made to have local authorities and forces take over every possible aspect of such operations. They should be clearly sovereign and independent, speak in terms of their own values, and be free to criticize the United States. (In many cases, the United States will also be better off relying on allied spokesmen, minimizing the image of U.S. control and dominance.)

- *The United States needs to persuade Congress and the American people as well as those outside the United States:* The struggle for hearts and minds is as much a domestic one as a foreign one. This requires honest reporting, not spin, and reporting with depth and content, not meaningless metrics and reassurances.

This latter point is difficult for those inside government to raise, but the Bush Administration did serious damage to its own cause by trying to spin the course of war in Iraq into images of turning points and success and in failing to address the real risks and issues. Credibility is the key to success in persuading both foreign and domestic opinion. Short-term propaganda efforts are sometimes necessary, but political and information campaigns must focus on honest admissions of risk and cost, and realistic time scales rather than easy ways out.

The U.S. military and senior U.S. officials must avoid "cheerleading." They must present the real facts and options and provide metrics that give an honest picture of what is happening, good and bad. Americans need to see that there are practical plans, they need to be able to trust what senior military and civilian officials say, and they need to see a case for patience that builds credibility and trust. There is a reason polls show a growing lack of confidence and support. The U.S. government simply has failed to earn it.

POLITICAL AND GOVERNANCE LESSONS

Some of the key lessons about the political side of operations that emerge from the U.S. experience in Iraq are to rely as much as possible on local government and expand its role and capability as soon as possible, to work within the limits imposed by local conditions, and to set a clear strategy for encouraging the kind of compromises and consensus that allows the political process to function and governance to operate.

There are several other key lessons for sustained operations and a successful transition to handing over power:

- *Politics are no substitute for governance:* The United States often seemed far more concerned in Iraq with how governments were chosen than with whether they could govern effectively. Democracy is a possible path to effective governance and the day-to-day services and security that define true legitimacy in the state. It is meaningless, however, unless such governance is its end result. The Western obsession with elections and legal forms at best addresses the lesser half of successful political operations. It is what governments do that determines their success, not how they are chosen. This is particularly true in an environment where stable national political parties do not yet exist and where elections produce service politics, ideological or religious parties, or divide the people along factional lines.

- *It is far more important to find ways to reduce local ethnic, sectarian, tribal, and other tensions and fracture lines than to attempt rapid democratization and political, legal, and human rights reform by U.S. or Western standards:* This does not mean abandoning ultimate goals, but it is a clear matter of priorities. The image or illusion of political progress is no substitute for civil order and creating the conditions that make democracy and the rule of law function on a national, not special interest, basis. Similarly, the United States must avoid participating in excluding key factions from power and appearing to take sides.

- *Build on existing institutions, constitutions, and legal codes wherever possible:* To mix a metaphor, reinventing the wheel will often open up Pandora's box. It does not make sense to force nations to confront the task of totally reinventing their political structures, constitutions, legal codes, procedures, and other aspects of governance in the midst of war, insurgency, or crisis where this can be avoided. Such efforts almost force the resurfacing of every major issue that divides a country. Seeking reform of the most important features of existing structures is far less provocative. Where possible, it will be particularly important to avoid efforts to draft new constitutions or other sweeping legislation that can force national factions to struggle over the issues that divide them most in a formal and legalistic context.

  The same is true of the practice of law. It is one thing to reform or prevent key abuses. It is another to try to reinvent the legal system or courts, create whole new police forces, and leave gaps and uncertainty in the day-to-day functioning of courts and law enforcement.

- *Do not conduct major purges or dismissals:* It may be necessary to remove all top leaders, but all others should be removed on a case-by-case basis, and only for cause. It is far better to supplement than purge, particularly when any other course of action exacerbates sectarian and ethnic divisions.

- *Do not set artificial or impossible deadlines:* Iraq is yet another demonstration that trying to do too much too soon does not act as a forcing function. Too many quickly repeated elections, constitutional drafts and redrafts, and referendums create political instability. It is better to let local authorities advance and compromise at their own pace, setting broad goals and timelines for progress.

- *Effective aid and liaison with ministries and civil government offices are critical:* For all of the previous reasons, ministries and regional and local government offices and services must be made to work and be improved as soon as possible. People must see their government operate and benefit from its services to be encouraged to support it. This puts a high premium on rushing in competent U.S. advisors in the numbers required and giving them the aid funds and authority to have influence and provide the local support.

- *National politics are only part of political operations, and national governance does not have meaning without local governance:* Important as capitols may be, most people do not live in them, and even those who do, interface on a day-to-day level with local governments. U.S. advisory, aid, and civil-military efforts need in any case to be concentrated on improving governance in high-threat and high-risk areas. The operational center of gravity at the political level will sometimes be at the national level, but far more often it will be regional and local. It also will often be much easier to build workable, functioning elected governments at the local level—where ethnic and sectarian tensions are less intense—than at the national level.

- *Give local authorities both power and responsibility as soon as possible:* Governments do not become effective by waiting for training and advice. Iraq and Afghanistan have shown in different ways that governments develop by acting and taking responsibility.

- *Strengthen planning, budgeting, and fiscal control functions:* The United States may not have the expertise to govern or do many jobs by itself. It can usually provide expert support in planning and improve budget planning and control. Helping to create inspector generals, audit boards, and other tools that prevent overspending and limit corruption can have great value. It should be noted, however, that wartime or crisis is not the moment to try to introduce ideal Western standards of accounting and anticorruption measures. Local standards of performance should be the goal.

- *Use U.S. influence, but keep a low profile:* The United States should be proactive, but not deliberately visible or seen as taking the lead. The United States must still actively "interfere" in Iraqi politics. Iraq and Afghanistan have shown that if top-level U.S. officials do not to engage local political leaders, and if the U.S. ambassador does not act as a forceful "agent provocateur," efforts to create a workable political process and efforts at governance are likely to bog down, and the risk of failure and division increases. Such U.S. action will inevitably lead to protests by whatever Iraqi faction feels the United States is opposing or failing to support it. It will provoke some Iraqi nationalists and outside critics on principle.

In cases that approach anything like the status of a failed state, the local government and political leaders will need active outside pressure, criticism, and effort to force it to actually make decisions and move. It also needs constant reminders that Iraqis are now responsible and that there are limits to U.S. and other outside support. Iraqis need to know that the United States will provide support where it is productive, but there are no open-ended commitments.

- *Create strong civil-military teams to lead integrated action in the field:* Build on the Provincial Reconstruction Teams (PRTs) example used in Afghanistan rather than the Provincial Support Teams and Regional Embassy Office used initially in Iraq. The PRTs should have been in place years ago. According to the latest State Department reporting, however, they have been established only in Ninawa, Babil, Kirkuk, and Anbar Provinces, and they seem to have serious recruiting problems and difficulties in getting experienced and qualified personnel.

- *Avoid the central headquarters, fortress embassy, and overstaffed central facility problem that developed in Iraq as the advisory and support mission developed:* The United States does not need grossly overstaffed "white elephants" like the Green Zone in Baghdad. It does need local efforts at every level to provide a full civilian component to support the U.S. military in the field.

- *Make participation in in-country and field efforts a key to military, foreign service, and other U.S. government career development and promotion, and enforce this:* Such efforts will require a major reorientation in the U.S. presence in Iraq, a "go or be fired" approach to ensuring full staffing by the most qualified people in the foreign service, and direct Presidential pressure on Cabinet officers to provide the rest of the needed staff. It needs the kind of Congressional funding, and flexibility in using U.S. aid funds at the local level, necessary to give such a presence.

- *Ensure that the U.S. military, not contractors, provide the necessary security for civil aid and advisory teams:* While some contractor security teams have provided outstanding service, far too many have been careless and have alienated local populations. The reliance on contractors has also meant inadequate military support for civilian operations in the field, including transportation. The U.S. military must be ordered to provide security for such missions. They will have the highest possible priority, and U.S. officials simply should never have been made dependent on contract and civilian security in a war zone.

- *Develop plans and assessments to aid local political development and governance that can shape a structured effort:* Exercising U.S. political influence requires effective long-term plans backed by aid to Iraq's emerging political structure. Moreover, effective U.S. influence demands governance that recognizes the need for at least a five-year strategy funded to have a major impact in aid at the regional and local levels. Iraq's politics are as much urban and local as they are national, and U.S. strategy must recognize this.

- *Give priority to direct action in the field, and give the personnel in the field the freedom of action to be effective:* Research and study efforts will generally be far too slow and distant from real-world issues to pay off, and there is no way to wait for half-informed attempts to manage and control funds from Washington. Advisory teams need to be able to act. It should also be noted that contractor and nongovernmental organization (NGO) efforts in such areas often waste considerable amounts of money with little local impact and focus. At a minimum, they need to be ruthlessly audited for efficiency and patterns of expenditure.

None of these lessons can be acted upon without sufficient U.S. personnel and aid, and without giving field personnel the proper funds and authority. The United States needs to accept the fact that such operations require relatively large staffs of responsible military or career personnel and that such advisors will need aid funds they can allocate without constant reference to Washington or other authorities. As is the case with all aid and liaison efforts, it is also critical to ensure relatively long deployments with suitable overlap when personnel are rotated and to ensure enough personnel to allow leaves to be taken without creating gaps. There are no potential countries where personnel relationships, continuity, and direct hands-on contact will not be critical.

SECURITY LESSONS

The most important security lesson is the need for immediate and sustained action to create an effective mix of military and police and security forces and to support them with aid and support to courts and the criminal justice system. The need for a matching presence in terms of government services has been addressed above and is equally important.

Another lesson is that it is far more cost-effective to act decisively from the start to create or strengthen local forces, giving such aid and force development missions at least the same priority as combat assignments and overfunding and overstaffing them to help ensure success, than to delay, let terrorism and insurgency fester, and leave the mission to militias and other security forces not controlled by governments. The same is true of providing immediate transfers of funds and equipment, and using existing facilities, even when inadequate. Time is a critical resource, and every step forward in creating local capabilities minimizes the risk of serious low-level or asymmetric conflict, will be far cheaper than maintaining and committing U.S. forces, and will save American lives.

In practice, the United States has also learned (or relearned) a long list of practical lessons about how best to accomplish these tasks. The most important are the following:

- *Treat the local force as a partner that must take the lead as soon as possible:* It can take years before some forces will be able to act as full partners or truly take the lead in all aspects of operations. Local forces must, however, be treated as true partners from the start, be respected as sovereign and not proxies, and be shown that the United States gives them responsibility and the lead as quickly as possible. They must not be treated as tools or proxies, and it must be clear to all concerned that the U.S. goal is to enable them to serve their national interest in ways that serve all concerned, not to create forces that simply serve the interests of the United States.

- *Act immediately to build up local security capabilities to defeat terrorist and insurgents, but act simultaneously to create balanced forces:* Priority does need to be given to providing immediate security capabilities, but local forces need adequate intelligence, headquarters, combat and service support, and logistic capabilities. The transfer of responsibility, keeping U.S. forces and activities to a minimum, and expediting U.S. and allied withdrawal requires the creation of balanced forces.

- *Give equal priority to controlling, disarming, disbanding, or integrating factional militias and other nongovernmental forces wherever possible, but ensure they have a secure and properly funded transition away to civil life:* Iraq and Afghanistan are simply more lessons in how dangerous it is not to act immediately to control any factional forces that can challenge the stabilization and nation-building effort or can provide armed support to civil violence or civil war. The dedicated teams that tried to deal with this issue at the time of the CPA were never given more than limited support, and a potentially successful effort was allowed to collapse during the transfer of power in June 2004. Lebanon, Somalia, and Haiti are just a few other examples of how militias, factional forces, and rogue elements in national forces must be brought under control as quickly as possible and of how serious a threat they present to the success of U.S. efforts.

- *Tailor the use of local and U.S. forces to reduce the presence and the visibility of U.S. forces to the local population as soon as possible:* The United States will never have enough trained forces with suitable area expertise to deal with most medium- to large-scale stability, nation-building, and counterinsurgency capabilities and will always be seen as a hostile or alien presence by a large part of the population. U.S. forces also should be concentrated on direct operations against the most dangerous insurgent, factional, or terrorist elements. Putting a local face on local wars is a key priority.

- *Set realistic force goals and create effective short-, medium-, and long-term plans; do not attempt minimal manning or minimal standards:* There is no way to suddenly create large numbers of effective forces that do not already exist. At the same time, rushing to meet short-term, expedient levels with forces too small to do the job is an inevitable road to failure. There must be clear plans to train, equip, and facilitize the number of forces actually required, and calls for half measures or inadequate force levels and force quality must be strongly resisted. Rushing forward without clear plans also ensures inadequate levels of effort, ones that may either alienate large elements of local forces or produce unsustainable and unaffordable programs.

- *Do not rush the job: it takes time to create new training centers and methods and train effective forces:* Rushing inadequate local forces into the field, however, not only has a vast opportunity cost in terms of force disintegration and failure, it creates serious political problems both between the United States and local forces and between local forces and various local factions.

- *Pay the cost for proper facilities and equipment:* It took years in Iraq to begin to plan and pay for the facilities and equipment needed, and Iraqi forces still lack protected vehicles, adequate firepower, and adequate facilities. Local forces do not need to be built up to U.S. standards, and must be equipped with weapons and other systems they can maintain and support, but they must be capable of self-defense, given adequate facilities by local standards, and be properly equipped to take on offensive missions.

- *Advise and listen; do not attempt to create a mirror image:* Local forces must work to local norms and under local conditions. They cannot be mirror images of U.S. or Western forces, and their leaders and officers must take responsibility for force planning, doctrine, and shaping training efforts as soon as possible. There are many U.S. and Western techniques and methods that can be rapidly and effectively adapted to strengthen the capabilities of forces in developing countries and fill in the gaps in forces in failed "states." Ultimately, however, each case requires careful attention and adaptation to how local leaders and forces want their forces to be developed, and enduring success requires them to believe the forces that have been created meet their expectations and needs.

- *Build national forces with careful attention to sectarian and ethnic divisions and rivalries; create balanced and mixed forces rather than units that serve some factional interest:* No effort to build local forces can have perfect representation, but every effort must be made to convince both those in the forces and the people in the nation involved that the forces being developed will not serve factional interests or divide along such lines if they come under pressure.

- *Develop military, security, and police forces in tandem, not in sequence:* There is a natural and dangerous tendency for military advisors to give priority to military forces. Areas cannot be secured, however, unless specialized internal security forces operate at a different level from conventional military forces and police provide day-to-day security at the local level. The failure to act on this principle means either that military victories do not last or that military forces must stay in every liberated area, often alienating the local populace and not providing the kind of security required.

- *Seek better ways to shape local capabilities to provide guard forces and the ability to protect key government and economic facilities and religious and cultural facilities:* Like developing police forces, the United States cannot simply focus on combat development. It must help local governments and forces develop effective low-cost guard and protection forces.

- *Pay close attention to developing local human intelligence (HUMINT), translation, and liaison:* There will always be security problems with local forces, but there will always be even more severe problems for U.S. forces in establishing human intelligence, getting the necessary pool of language skills, and having local forces or personnel that can guide U.S. forces in operations from the raid to the strategic level. Once again, the United States needs to adopt a "partner" ethnic.

- *Ensure that all of the ministries involved have adequate advisors and aid. Force development cannot really work or be sustained unless the key ministries involved can function effectively:* These will, at a minimum, involve the Ministry of Defense, the ministry handling local security, relevant elements of the Ministry of Finance, and some element directly under the nation's prime minister or president. Ministries are key elements in determining whether forces and security efforts are national or factional, have sound financing, have controls to keep corruption to reasonable levels, and develop plans and the ability to implement them. A focus on forces in the field or on the Ministry of Defense, without a matching concern for the ministries handling internal security, police, justice, and finance, is a recipe for failure.

- *Constantly assess local vulnerabilities and casualties, and develop plans for local force protection:* The United States has often been slow to see that developing local forces and capabilities will often require at least some U.S. military role in protecting them, and it will take major efforts to train, organize, and equip local forces to protect and defend themselves. This is a key aspect of the mission.

- *Do not isolate or ignore existing members of the military, security forces, and police:* Punishing the truly guilty is necessary, but numbers must be kept to an absolute minimum. Broad amnesty and inclusion in the government and local forces should be introduced immediately where possible, and as quickly as possible in other cases.

Former military, security, and police should not be left without jobs or funds to make a transition to new careers when they cannot be included in the new security structure. This is particularly true when the former members of the security forces are largely composed of a single or disenfranchised faction.

- *Vet individuals, not groups, and continue performance-based review:*. Iraq once again validates the need to introduce vetting systems immediately to review recruits and those already in service in terms of individual capability and performance, rather than former position, or political, sectarian, and ethnic background. It also stresses the need to keep up performance review to exclude those who cannot perform or take sides on behalf of a given faction. When those with prior service must be dismissed, some kind of financial support and transition aid will normally be needed.

- *Learn from the U.S. experience in embedding training teams and creating partner units in Iraq:* It is not enough to train and equip local forces. They will often need cadres of U.S. advisors and partner units as they actually move into the field. This is essential to holding them together, giving them support in initial periods of combat, and going from theory to practice. It is also clear that the need for embedded training teams can be just as important in security and police units as in combat units.

- *Develop case histories and studies of the lessons learned in terms of training, tactics, support, intelligence, etc., for use by future U.S. force development efforts and local forces:* Formal field manuals and efforts to create standard rules can be useful starting points, but can never predict or adapt to local circumstances. The United States needs to develop case material for use by local forces, and case material for use by U.S. trainers and liaison teams, and an inventory of practical methods and tactics that users can both draw upon and adapt to a particular contingency.

- *Treat other allies as full partners in the local force development effort from the start:* The U.S. military was often slow to listen to and learn from its allies, and sometimes it turned a coalition of the willing into a coalition of the unheard or ignored. Other nations have a great deal to teach, and multilateralizing the local force development effort reduces the image of the United States as dominating the country and local forces involved, as well as reducing the burden on U.S. forces.

- *Ensure that the U.S. aspects of security and force development efforts remain under U.S. military control until suitable levels of local stability and security are actually achieved:* The United States must never repeat the experience of dividing its advisory and force development efforts, and it must ensure that security, paramilitary, and police forces can deal with terrorists, insurgents, and organized crime and not simply act as police forces in a normal U.S. sense. This requires the Department of Defense and the military to be in charge of a unified effort with a single line of command and a comprehensive plan and effort. The State Department may be able to recruit and deploy training teams for regular police development, but cannot handle the mission of dealing with ministerial level aid or police development in counterinsurgency or serious antiterrorist environments.

- *Make it clear to the military command that creating effective local forces may have the same or higher priority as using U.S. and outside allied forces:* The U.S. military in Iraq was slow to see the need for developing local forces and took years to respond to the need to support this mission effectively in Washington and at the headquarters level. Issuing DoD Directive 3000.05 and improving some aspects of U.S. training will not change this situation. Making effective use of local forces, like adding the political and economic dimensions to military operations, requires a change in military culture as well.

- *Develop effective accounting, planning, and budgeting tools that can rapidly be transferred and require minimum training and support:* Iraq shows that it is dangerous to deny local commanders the freedom to use aid funds and equally dangerous at every level of command not to provide near real-time accountability. The result is corruption and waste and a loss of Congressional confidence. But creating a massive paper chase is not the answer. Off the shelf automated aids that allow rapid, functional accounting and simple follow-up reporting of execution and effectiveness need to be available, and the goal should be operational effectiveness, not meeting the needs of bean counters and rear-area bureaucrats.

- *Create reporting tools and software to control, manage, and account for actual manning, how salaries are paid, and how weapons and equipment are allocated and inventoried:* The same issues apply to reporting on other aspects of local force development.

- *Develop meaningful measures of effectiveness and tools to determine progress and report them honestly, without exaggeration or spin:* Far too much of the reporting on progress in Iraqi force development and performance has had the same misleading reporting of success that the U.S. military provided in Vietnam and Lebanon. The United States took far too long to develop useful measures of performance in the training and equipment effort. It still uses meaningless measures of combat performance like taking the lead and control of battle space. Much more demanding measures are needed, and much better unclassified reporting is needed to build Congressional, public, and media confidence.

One of the most consistent challenges to effective U.S. security action will be the need to resist false economies, cost-effectiveness analysis, and bureaucratic downsizing of the required effort. Iraq and Afghanistan are warnings that advice and requests from the field to assign adequate personnel and resources to the development and support of local forces can easily become the stepchildren of efforts to support U.S. forces and meet immediate bureaucratic resistance from personnel in Washington with no competence to make judgments as to what is required.

Iraq and Afghanistan should fundamentally change the command ethic and policy makers' priorities in this regard, but it is far from clear that they will. The same should have been true of "Vietnamization" or the failure of U.S. force development efforts in Lebanon after 1982. This is an area where far too many people are generally in the loop, with no real understanding of practical needs and priorities in the field, and where the U.S. military tends to "forget from experience" rather than learn from it.

ECONOMIC AID AND DEVELOPMENT LESSONS

Iraq is scarcely a unique example of the problems in using foreign aid to help a developing country. The whole course of aid efforts since World War II has shown that aid can be of great value in helping a country get organized and become capable of helping itself. It has also shown that outside efforts to use aid to reshape the econo-mies of failed states rarely produce meaningful results and that the United States has little competence in planning such efforts even under peacetime conditions.

The United States should learn three important lessons from its experiences in Iraq and Afghanistan, as well as from other conflicts and aid efforts:

- *The first is that the U.S. government simply does not know how to do jobs of this kind on this scale and lacks the core competence to do it:* The illusion that the United States can remake a national economy, as distinguished from aiding a nation to do so, is simply dangerous. So is the idea that the United States has, or ever will have, the cadre of experts necessary to carry out such tasks at the career civilian, contract, and military levels.

  There were critical problems in policy and planning that made things far worse than they had to be, but the CPA, United States Agency for International Development (USAID), and Corps of Engineers simply showed again and again that the United States could not provide workable plans and program management for an aid effort of the scale involved and that reliance on U.S. prime contractors and their subcontractors did nothing to reduce waste and corruption and did a vast amount to increase security costs and divert large amounts of money away from the intended objective and outside Iraq.

- *The second is that in stability and wartime operations, the first priority is to use aid and money as a tool to bring order and stability, one that responds to operational needs:* There simply is no time to wait for structural change in the economy, for mid- to long-term projects to pay off, for interesting economic experiments to work, by acting as if war, insurgency, crime, and social violence can be ignored.

  Iraq and Afghanistan have also shown that U.S. military officers and their U.S. government civilian counterparts must have great discretion in using aid at the local level and essentially substitute dollars for bullets. Buying stability is cheaper by far than shooting for stability and much less provocative and destructive. It also provides quick benefits in terms of results the local populace wants and sees, disperses aid into the most troubled areas, and builds political trust.

  At the same time, it is clear that NGOs and international institutions are often unsuitable for such activities. They cannot protect themselves and often will not allow the U.S. military to do so. They bring their own institutional agendas and priorities into the field and will not act in concert to achieve the kinds of operational results needed for security operations or to buy political support and consensus. There are often times where this independence frees the United States of political pressure, but stability operations and nation building need to use short-term aid for just the opposite purpose.

- *The third is that, whether it is an efficient method or not, the United States must rely on local governments, businessmen, entrepreneurs, and contractors for longer-term planning and implementation of aid projects—and not on U.S. control of the aid and economic construc-tion effort or the use of U.S. personnel and contractors:* The United States does need more experts capable of dealing with the economic aspects of stability operations and nation building. Iraq, however, is scarcely the first country where the United States has shown that it may not be able to restructure an entire economy, but can provide direct help to large numbers of people and use economy aid to help bring stability. A reliance on local governments, businessmen, entrepreneurs, and contractors at least keeps aid money in the country it is intended to benefit, shows the local populace that the United States is directly aiding them, and responds to local needs and priorities.

It may take time to build local capabilities, but short-term direct U.S. assistance can buy such time. It is also far too easy to fall into the trap of attempting too much, changing whole sectors of a local economy, restructuring the nation's infrastructure, etc. Such projects inevitably are too complex to plan and manage, and they leave half-implemented legacies built to U.S. standards using U.S. chosen equipment and methods that the country cannot finish or sustain.

These, however, are only the most serious lessons that the United States should learn in terms of what it must do once conflict termination, stability, and nation-building operations begin. Following is a list of the more technical lessons that have emerged out of Iraq that can be of considerable importance in future contingencies.

- *Treat aid and economic development as short-term operational necessities until sufficient security and stability exist to give workable priority to longer-term efforts:* Stability operations, counterterrorism, counterinsurgency, and true humanitarian emergencies in high-risk areas must firmly put security and stability first. Trying to build on longer-term and more ambitious goals without a functioning short-term foundation will simply lead to waste or failure.

- *Give top priority to local jobs, local services, and efforts with immediate visibility and targeted impact on the local populace:* Aid and development must actually benefit ordinary people directly, make the local government seem useful and credible, and show people that the United States is actually helping. In stability operations and any form of conflict, perception will be as important as performance.

- *Focus on sustaining and expanding key sources of government revenue:* Iraq and Afghanistan are scarcely new demonstrations of the fact that planning local forces and stability efforts that cannot be financially sustained by the host country rapidly develop serious problems in distorting the local economy and operations of the government. They also show in very different ways the need to rapidly help local governments develop or protect their sources of revenue.

- *Do not count on donor conferences and third-party pledges of aid:* Efforts to seek allied and international aid can be useful, but produce far more pledges and aid with strings attached than actual results, and they inevitably fall short of the requirement. The United States must plan to pay for the aid efforts necessary to succeed.

- *Do not attempt ambitious efforts to restructure infrastructure unless these can be managed and implemented at the local level:* The task will be to meet local expectations as much as possible on local terms and to avoid creating unrealistic demands and expectations. Small- or medium-sized efforts to fix and improve existing capabilities will go a long way toward building positive expectations and confidence in the local population.

- *Do not attempt to remake the national economy in mid-crisis or wartime, and attempt major structural or sectoral change only if the local government and people want it and can clearly sustain it:* The United States lacks the core competence to do this. It places an impossible burden on U.S. forces and on the entire U.S. mission and creates major new problems for local leaders.

- *Let local governments take the lead and make their own mistakes; focus on reviewing and vetting requests for aid and ensuring they have suitable monitoring and fiscal controls:* Iraq is only one of many case studies that show that the United States is no better than local authorities at trying to undertake such large-scale efforts and that the moment the United States takes responsibility, it not only acquires the blame but finds it progressively harder to transfer responsibility back. By contrast, advising, vetting, demanding suitable accounting, and demanding measures of progress and effectiveness can be highly effective.

- *Do not rely on or use U.S. contractors or other outside contractors unless absolutely necessary and by exception:* The purpose of operations at both the political and economic levels will be to win local support and strengthen local capabilities. It will also be to get maximum operational benefits from the funds involved, and these will be heavily dependent on local employment and on the perception and the reality that aid efforts and projects meet local needs.

- *Provide U.S., allied, or local military security or do not attempt the effort; do not use mercenaries or private personal security details (PSDs) again:* If the United States is to commit major resources to stability operations, nation building, and counterinsurgency, it must commit military forces to protect them, provide transportation, and provide support in high-risk areas.

    Contractors and PSDs cannot do this, and separating the military from such responsibility inevitably decouples it from the broader mission of supporting aid efforts at the project, local, and regional levels. Mercenaries in any form also will always have profit and expediency as their primary objectives, will create popular hostility, and will be a source of abuses and corruption.

- *Accept the fact that some level of waste and corruption is inevitable and that meeting urgent needs on local terms has the higher priority:* Bringing waste and corruption under reasonable control is necessary. Setting U.S. standards and giving anticorruption and similar measures the same priority as success is absurd. Quite aside from the pressures and uncertainties of war and crisis, local standards of honesty and efficiency have to be accepted.

- *Develop effective accounting, planning, and budgeting tools that can rapidly be transferred and that require minimum training and support:* Regardless of who plans, manages, and spends aid projects, off-the-shelf tools like computer programs should be ready that allow the immediate capability to properly control funds and measure progress and compliance with contracts.

- *Ensure that a fully independent inspector general like the Special Inspector General for Iraqi Reconstruction covers all aid activity, and maintain an ongoing grand jury for rapid prosecution of U.S. contractors and officials:* Nothing about the history of U.S. aid activity in Iraq indicates that trust can be placed in U.S. officials and contractors or that agencies like USAID or the Corps of Engineers can be trusted to set realistic standards or report anything like success.

- *Create contractual tools that require detailed accounting and measures of effectiveness, and adopt a "zero tolerance," "public declaration" policy in dealing with U.S. officials, local officials, and contractors who do not fully comply:* The United States tied up much of its aid activity in precisely the wrong kind of regulation, law, and red tape. It failed to require regular reporting of progress, set effectiveness measures, or ensure suitable accounting; and abuse after abuse was tolerated on the grounds of necessity. Effective aid does need to give great flexibility to the embassy or command in the field, but it cannot mean tolerance of poor or nonperformance, failure to establish accounting and progress reports, or activities with no measures of effectiveness. Excusing problems and poor performance on the grounds of time pressure or exigency simply leads to failures and far more problems than it solves.

- *More broadly, legislation and regulation are needed to do the following:*
  - Establish civil and criminal penalties for U.S. government personnel, military personnel, and contractors who do not meet proper standards for accountability or try to waive them. Iraq is to some extent a history of American incompetence and corruption. The answer is a zero tolerance approach.
  - Make the U.S. military responsible for protecting aid activity. Contractor security is too expensive and wasteful, and far too often the end result is that the aid goes where things are more secure rather than where it is needed.
  - Require U.S. government agencies to provide long-term planning and mandated measures of effectiveness reporting in submitting aid requests, and mandate that all contracts to U.S. companies require evidence of performance and accountability with far more severe criminal and civil penalties.
  - Require all civil U.S. and non-Iraqi security contractors accepting money for U.S. aid to accept criminal and civil liability for their actions. Leave no gaps.
  - Require clear transition plans, reporting, and measures of effectiveness to show that completed programs and projects have a lasting impact and become sustainable, rather than are completed and dumped.
  - Offer major "whistle blowing" rewards.

A very different approach to economic aid and development should generally be adopted once true stability and security are provided and a government is capable of acting at the local, regional, and national levels. International organizations and NGOs can play a major, if not lead, role; multilateralizing aid efforts will be far more important, and so will a focus on mid- and long-term development based on national priorities.

The same measures under these conditions are recipes for failure in the face of major security threats of any kind, particularly when U.S. and local forces are involved in major counterterrorist or counterinsurgency campaigns. The focus must be on operational success and security first.

LESSONS FOR THE BROADER WAR AGAINST TERRORISM

The need for local forces and governments may be different in the case of the broader war on terrorism, but it is no less important. The United States does not face the risk of overstretch in the broader war on terrorism in terms of having enough total forces and resources to fight a long war against Al Qa'ida and other nonstate actors. These groups will not even be serious military threats as long as they do not control governments or acquire large-scale sanctuaries.

The United States will often, however, face a different kind of overstretch. It will lack expertise in the form of linguists and area experts. It will never have the local popularity, or even tolerance, necessary to directly defeat terrorists and extremists in countries where they have broad popular support and can exploit ideology and religion as weapons. As a result, the United States may be even more dependent on local allies for success, and there already are many individual lessons from the war on terrorism that have close parallels to the lessons the United States should learn from Iraq and Afghanistan.

Once again, the key lesson is that the United States needs local allies and forces that are able and willing to act. Yet again, the problem is the lack of effective allies and local counterterrorism capabilities and forces. One key lesson from the war on terrorism over the last half decade is that a mix of Western action and Islamic inaction cannot win.

The United States may be "politically correct" when it calls the current struggle a long war or "global war on terrorism," but the reality is very different. Most terrorism is a minor and largely local or national threat. The real threat is Islamic extremism, and specifically neo-Salafi Sunni Islamist extremism. The violent transnational movements that support these beliefs, symbolized by Al Qa'ida, are the only serious global threat that uses terrorism. Isolated terrorist movements do need to be defeated, but Irish, Spanish, Palestinian secular, Sri Lankan, Japanese, and other such groups are peripheral threats at most.

The U.S. ability to recognize this fact, and focus on it, is critical to winning the "war on terrorism." This struggle is religious and ideological, not military or driven by secular values. It is a struggle for the future of Islam, not generic, global, or focused on political or economic systems. It is, however, regional, covers a wide range of nations, includes hundreds of millions of people, and is enduring. U.S. counterterrorism doctrine has not been updated to deal with the challenges involved as counterinsurgency doctrine has. While the State Department reports on terrorism do focus on international cooperation, it is purely in terms of direct cooperation in activity against terrorism organizations. The new *National Strategic Plan for the War on Terrorism* issued by the Joint Chiefs in 2006 virtually ignores the issue. So does the new *National Security Strategy of the United States* issued by the White House in March 2006, which focuses on transforming the Middle East and "cooperative action with the other main centers of global power."[6]

It may be possible to defeat Islamist extremist movements at the local and national levels using the kind of strategies the United States has chosen for Iraq and Afghanistan, but it is already clear that the United States would have been far better off if it had focused on local sensitivities and creating local capabilities. The last half decade has also made it clear that there will always be places where such movements can regroup and resume operations. Just as counterinsurgency must be defeated at the political level by local forces and governments, the real war on terrorism is a religious war of ideals that can be won only within Islam and at the religious and ideological levels.

This does not mean that U.S. efforts are not needed to improve every aspect of counterterrorism at the national, regional, and global levels. It does mean that no amount of outside action by the United States, Europe, or non-Islamic states will be enough to contain and end such violence. It is only the religious, political, and intellectual leaders of Islamic countries and communities, particularly in the Arab world, who can successfully engage and defeat Islamic extremism at the religious, intellectual, political, and cultural levels.

The Limits on U.S. and Western Military Intervention and on Building Local Capabilities

The United States and the West cannot simply defend themselves on their own territory. They must seek to deny movements like Al Qa'ida sanctuaries in places like Afghanistan, Iraq, and Somalia. Whether or not anyone likes the word "war," Islamist extremist violence is so dangerous that it must be met with force. The current efforts to transform U.S. and other Western forces to give them better area and language skills, and true expertise in counterinsurgency and counterterrorism, are also vital.

The United States needs to firmly understand, however, that none of these measures will ever enable it or the West to "win" at the critical ideological and political levels. They at best enable Western forces to score limited tactical victories, help local forces contain major terrorist movements, defend home territory, and buy time. If the West seeks to use major long-term deployments of U.S., British, or other non-Islamic forces to fight sustained struggles in Islamic countries, the end result will be to breed new extremists and terrorists. As Afghanistan and Iraq have shown, military and counterterrorist battles need to be won by local and Islamic forces, not by occupiers, "crusaders," and "neoimperialists."

There are too many memories of colonialism and too much anger against U.S. ties to Israel for Western forces to succeed unless they act in alliance with local forces and local governments are clearly sovereign. Moreover, even the United States will never be able to deploy the number of troops needed or have enough forces with language skills and area expertise. It will always have to rotate too much of its force too quickly to build up the personal relationships critical to success.

Islamist extremists have already shown how well they can exploit any long-term presence from "outside" forces, but Western efforts to train and equip effective local forces can have a very different effect. They can create enough local forces to do the job, and such forces will start with all the necessary area and language skills and personal relationships. They will be able to stay on the scene and create the lasting interpersonal relations that are a key to victory. Moreover, Western military, counterterrorism, counterinsurgency, and intelligence training and advisory efforts can introduce methods and tactics that have a lasting impact on improving respect for human rights and the rule of law in those cases where such reform is necessary.

The Need to Change the Image of the United States in the Muslim World

This requires far more, however, than simply changing the focus of U.S. operations. The United States needs to understand that it can use its influence, counterterrorism capabilities, and military capabilities effectively only if it can change its image in the Islamic world. The importance of changing the image of the United States does, however, go far beyond public diplomacy. In fact, it is important to all Western efforts to push for reforms in the Middle East and is essential to "winning" the global campaign against counterterrorism. While U.S. public diplomacy has been a failure, it is the policies that are being communicated that create the problem, not the way they are being "sold."

The American image in the Islamic and Arab worlds is a key factor in building popular support and tolerance for extremist and terrorism movements.[7] The anger against the United States is not directed at its values or "democracy," but rather at tangible issues like the U.S. role in the Arab-Israeli conflict, the Iraq War, and the other U.S. policies in the Middle East. It is shaped by the perception that the U.S. reaction to "9/11" has gone beyond counterterrorism to a broad hostility toward Islam and Arabs.

Such anger does not mean that the United States should change its core policies in any of these areas, but leaders in the Administration and Congress, and the American people, must understand the impact of such U.S. actions in the Islamic and Arab worlds. One key to winning the real war on terrorism is to do everything possible to execute U.S. policies in ways that minimize their negative impact in the region.

One key is the Arab-Israeli peace process. Most Arabs have reluctantly come to accept the reality that the United States is, and will remain, an ally of Israel. What they will not accept is what appears to be a passive or one-sided U.S. approach to the Arab-Israeli peace process. The perception in the Muslim world is that the United States cannot be evenhanded in seeking peace because administration after administration has taken the Israeli point of view.

It is fair to say that the Arab and the Islamic approach to an Arab-Israeli peace has been at least as biased and has often drifted toward rejection of Israel's right to exist. The fault is scarcely American alone. From a practical point of view, what matters to both Israel and the Arabs is a just and lasting peace. While that may or may not be possible at a time when Israel and the Palestinians are fighting a war of attrition that has now lasted half a decade, it is clear that "a good faith" and a high-profile U.S. effort to constantly push both sides toward peace will go a long way in winning many people in the Muslim world who are on the margin. This is key to easing Islamic and Arab anger toward both the United States and other Western states.

Islamic and Arab perceptions of the war in Iraq are an equally serious cause of anger and of tolerance or support for Islamic extremism and terrorism. Once again, both U.S. intentions and actions create the problem. The United States may think in terms of democracy, but many in the Islamic world see a crusader and neoimperialist attack from outside the Islamic and Arab worlds. This has been compounded by the fact that weapons of mass destructions were not found, the insurgency has been increasingly dominated by those who claim to speak for all of Islam, and the Iraqi people have suffered greatly since the overthrow of Saddam Hussein.

These attitudes usually ignore the fact that the war has happened and cannot be undone and that a U.S. presence in Iraq is now essential to keeping Iraq together and ensuring regional stability. The United States again, however, needs to be far more visible in seeking to aid the Iraqi people, creating a fully sovereign Iraqi government, and committing itself to leave without seeking bases and any control of Iraqi oil.

The U.S. focus on the role Iraq now plays in the larger war on terror is valid, but far too many outside the United States see this nearly monolithic focus on terrorism and military victory, and on imposing an American political system, as proof the invasion of Iraq was motivated by Israel's security, Iraq's oil, and the search for military bases in the region. Once again, the United States does not need to change its core policies, but it needs to give the highest possible visibility to aiding the Iraqi people, deferring to a sovereign Iraqi government, showing that Iraqi oil is for the Iraqis, and that it has no intention of maintaining any military presence that the Iraqi government does not need or want.

What is far more important than any such policy pronouncements, however, is that the United States avoid alienating the Arab and Muslim worlds and inadvertently waging "negative political and ideological warfare," for the same reasons that apply in fighting terrorism also apply in fighting counterinsurgency. There must be no more Abu Ghraibs or Hadithas.

Mistakes in war will happen, and history is full of such mistakes. The implications, however, of mistakes like Haditha go beyond their tactical importance in the field and strike at the heart of the U.S. posture in the region—the way Iraqis, Arabs, and Muslims see the United States—and such mistakes are used repeatedly by Al Qa'ida and other extremist groups as recruiting cries. Both the war in Iraq and the war on terrorism are religious, political, and ideological battles. Every true American abuse of the values the United States truly stands for does far more harm in this battle than any direct act of treason.

Local versus Outside Political Reform: The Need for Evolutionary Change

More generally, the United States and its Western allies need to understand that the wrong kind of efforts to "reform" the Middle East can lose the war on terrorism at precisely the ideological, political, cultural, and religious levels at which it must be won. Outside efforts to transform the region, rather than influence it, will be no more successful than U.S. efforts to transform Iraq. Like it or not, the short- and midterm battles against Islamist extremism, and day-to-day action in counterterrorism, are going to have to be won or lost by existing regimes. Creating open-ended political instability, and broad popular hostility in the process, cannot win a religious and ideological struggle fought by those with a different culture and faith.

U.S. efforts to push instant political change and "democracy" are dangerously self-defeating. As Algeria, Iraq, Kuwait, the Palestinians, and Saudi Arabia have shown, elections do not mean progress unless there are national political movements that advocate practical courses of action. Electing Islamists, and/or provoking civil war, does not bring political stability and cannot defeat a religious and ideological movement. Democracy can make things better only if it is built on sound political and legal checks and balances that protect minorities and prevent demagogues and extremists from coming to power. Elections do more harm than good if they divide a nation to vote in ways that encourage violence and civil conflict.

As Iraq has shown all too clearly, the long history of sectarian violence and tribal wars has not been erased from the minds of much of the Middle East. Western efforts to achieve instant democracy can easily provoke a crisis in traditional societies. Where parties do not now exist, rushing to create new parties will make most of these sectarian, ethnic, or tribal in character. Where parties do exist, the better-organized and disciplined parties will come to power. In most cases, such parties have an Islamist nature, such as Hamas, Egyptian Islamic Jihad, and the Islamist parties in Kuwait.

Efforts by occupiers, crusaders, and neoimperialists to impose change from the outside, rather than encourage it from within, cannot succeed. In fact, neo-Salafi Islamist extremists often do a fine job of using such efforts to discredit internal reform efforts and reformers. Furthermore, the West needs to accept the fact that an evolutionary approach to change means working with many local leaders who are not democratic, fall short of Western ideals, or are traditional in character. Calls for "regime change" and other efforts that introduce political instability, and produce more resistance to reform, will do far more harm than good.

Political reform must be built on a foundation of moderate political parties, a real rule of law, and a respect for human rights that protects all but the most extreme voices in a society. However, creating a true culture of political participation will take a decade or more to develop, and most of the impetus for political reform must come from within and be led by local political leaders and reformers.

Local versus Outside Economic, Social, and Cultural Reforms: The Limits to "Draining the Swamp"

It is equally impractical to call for rapid economic, social, and demographic reforms to remove the causes of terrorism. In practice, such calls to "drain the swamp" and eliminate popular support for extremism are at best, a well-meant fantasy. Iraq and Afghanistan may be two extraordinarily difficult cases, but the demographics of virtually all Arab and Islamic states have already created a youth explosion of new students and entrants to the labor force that will be a major problem for the next two decades.

Economies, societies, and birth rates do not change quickly. When they do change, they can change in ways that bring internal stability only if change in response to internal political and social dynamics move at a measured pace. As is the case with political reform, the West can do a great deal over time by working with moderate political leaders and local reformers, by focusing on the internal dynamics and windows of opportunity in individual nations, and by supporting what is really practical to accomplish. The United States cannot, however, win by calling for instant change through efforts to impose change from the outside without giving the enemy new ammunition.

As in the case of counterinsurgency, the United States cannot win through broad efforts at public diplomacy, regional meetings and initiatives, or part-time efforts. At least in the case of the United States, it is going to take strong embassy teams that work hard on a country-by-country level and tailor their actions to what can be achieved and what is productive on a case-by-case basis. Clear national strategies will be needed for military and counterterrorism cooperation and advisory efforts, for supporting balanced political reform at the pace a given nation can accept, and for balancing political reform with economic, social, and demographic reforms.

Here, both governments and analysts in the West need to understand that people in the Islamic world do not make politics or Western approaches to human rights their main priority. They look for personal security, for jobs, for education for their children, for health services, and for other government services. The key to defeating Islamic extremism, and the broad popular base that sympathizes with such extremism, comes first from providing popular security without oppression and then from providing economic opportunity for both today's workers and their children. Survey after survey has shown this. It does not make those in the region who call for political change and more sweeping human rights reforms unimportant—they are voices that will help shape the longer-term future of the Islamic world—but first things first.

Regional polices, meetings, and slogans will not deal with real-world needs or provide the kind of dialogue with local officials and reformers, tailored pressure and aid, and country plans and policies that are needed. Strong country teams both in Washington and in U.S. embassies are the keys to success. Quiet, steady advocacy—and well-staffed and funded efforts tailored to a given country—should replace noisy, episodic, region-wide pressures and demands.

Above all, successful efforts at counterterrorism, reform, and public diplomacy must have a national focus. The Arab and Islamic worlds are not monolithic. In fact, country-to-country differences are generally far greater than in the West. Each country requires different kinds of help in counterterrorism and different kinds of help in moving toward reform.

Some countries need help in reforming their political process and enhancing citizen participation; others need help dealing with economic development difficulties; still others need special attention paid to their demographic dynamics and population control. The West, therefore, must avoid any generalized strategy of dealing with the Arab-Islamic world as one entity and avoid making policy pronouncements that are as vague as they are unhelpful to local reformers who have been working on reforming their societies for decades.

The Burden Is on the Islamic Nations and Communities, Not the West

At the same time, this critique of the U.S. and Western approach to winning the long war in no way means that the political, religious, and intellectual leaders in Islamic nations do not have to make even more striking changes in their behavior. Once again, local forces and efforts are the ultimate keys to success.

The real war on terrorism can be won only if the religious, political, and intellectual leaders of Islamic countries and communities actively confront and fight neo-Salafi Sunni Islamist extremism at the religious and ideological levels. The long war will be lost if such leaders stand aside, take half measures, or compromise with enemies that seek to destroy them and what they believe in. It will be lost if they deny that the real issue is the future of Islam, if they tolerate Islamist violence and terrorism when it strikes at unpopular targets like Israel, or if they continue to try to export the blame for their own failures to other nations, religions, and cultures.

One message the United States needs to firmly communicate to the religious, political, and intellectual leaders of Islamic countries and communities is that they cannot be passive or hope to have this struggle won from the outside. No strategy can succeed that is not based on their broad acceptance of the fact that this is a war within a religion, not a clash between civilizations, and that they must take an active role. The war to defeat Islamic extremism can be won only at a religious and an ideological level if every religious, political, and intellectual leader accepts the fact that the only choice is to actively engage Islamic extremism or engage in cowardice and self-defeat.

Islamic regimes can win their part of the war only if they accept the fact that repression, counterterrorism, and stifling local reform efforts ultimately aid the very Islamist extremists they are trying to defeat. Algeria, Egypt, and Syria have already shown that long wars fought on this basis may bring the threat under partial control, but cannot defeat it.

If the United States has pushed too hard, too quickly, and sometimes for the wrong thing, the Islamic or Arab leader that tries to defeat Islamic extremism by blocking or delaying reform, or making concessions to Islamic extremism, is guilty of committing self-inflicted wounds to his own faith and country—a failure far worse than any failure by Western states.

The Muslim world is starting to deal with these failures, although several decades after the fact. In December 2005, the Organization of the Islamic Conference met in Mecca and issued a clear statement advocating moderation. The Mecca declaration read in part, "we reaffirm our unwavering rejection of terrorism, and all forms of extremism and violence."[8] In addition, the declaration endorsed the creation of an International Counterterrorism Center to improve global cooperation against the fight against terrorism.

The Islamic World Must Take Responsibility at Every Level

The Islamic world must do far more to confront its own failures and must stop blaming the West for its self-inflicted wounds. It must react immediately and decisively every time neo-Salafist terrorists, Islamists, Shi'ites, and other extremist organizations use the Islamic faith as their recruiting platform. While various Muslim leaders have condemned violence against civilians, they have done little to defeat these groups at the ideological level.

Winning any kind of victory requires a massive additional effort by Islamic politicians, religious leaders, educators, and media to beat these extremists at their own game by using religious text and historical facts to counter them. Educational and religious reforms, use of the media, statements by leaders, sermons, articles, dialog, and intellectual debate are weapons that cannot be ignored. They ultimately will be more important than internal security forces and counterterrorism campaigns.

Time is also an issue. The United States has dubbed the fight against transnational terrorism as a "long war," but this may be a dangerous misnomer. Islamic leaders do not have time in which to react. They confront a world in which Islamic media and the Internet make inaction and attempts at censorship a certain path to losing popular support and seeing extremists gain by default. There is no time for tolerance of inaction, or political and religious cowardice, within the Islamic world. The religious and ideological struggle needs to be made as short as it possibly can be.

Steady progress toward meeting popular needs and goals is equally important. Such progress may often be slow, and change will normally have to be evolutionary. But it must be a constant and publicly credible pursuit that leaders are seen to push forward. Extremists have capitalized on the dissatisfaction on the Arab street and in the majority of the Muslim world with their economic, political, and economic situations—the steady decay of public services, corruption, and the narrow distribution of income. Governments must be more proactive in ensuring personal security, job creation, improving education, improving health services, providing the environment for the private sector to flourish, and ensuring the rule of law to protect property and the right of the public.

Islamic regimes also have to at least move toward some form of centrist, moderate political pluralism. Leaders for life, hereditary presidents, one-party systems, and monarchies with captive political parties or none at all help breed extremism by denying the rise of moderate Islamic and secular movements that would give local political leaders practical experience and provide a basis for useful compromise. The tolerance of moderate dissent is another key weapon in the real-world war on terrorism.

The need for action is scarcely limited to regimes. Far too many Islamic intellectuals have learned to ignore the candle, live in the dark, and curse the West or outsiders for their plight. They wallow in the problems of the past and ignore the need to shape the future. They turn history into a self-inflicted wound and tolerate extremist violence when they perceive it as being directed at their enemies.

Elites in the Muslim world must act on the reality that they cannot survive without contributing to the building of viable civil societies that are sustainable in the long run. Many elites in the Arab and Muslim worlds argue—rightly so—that the West's push for democracy is backfiring. They also, however, do far too little themselves to provide viable alternatives and put far too much blame for the current level of stagnation on their own governments. An intellectual or businessman who fails to actively help build viable private sectors, erect educational institutions, and provide employment opportunities for the youth in his own society is little more than a whining parasite.

Both leaders and elites must be far more willing to try to end regional conflicts in ways that actually benefit the peoples involved. Pretending that the conflicts in Iraq, Afghanistan, Chechnya, Darfur, and Palestine are the problems of others or are going to solve themselves is not a solution. Blaming the West and waiting for the United States to solve them is no better. Holding endless summits and issuing countless declarations have not solved anything for the last 50 years. These conflicts not only impact their Muslim brethren, but have the potential to impact their own stability. For example, a civil war in Iraq, an Iraq that disintegrates into three countries, or an Iraq that suffers chronically from the threat of insurgency not only impacts the livelihood of Iraqis, but also of every neighboring state and every country in the Middle East.

The Need for Common Western and Islamic Action

Terrorism can never be totally eliminated as a tactic, but the ideology that drives organizations like Al Qa'ida can be discredited and isolated. Support for extremism is still extremely marginal in Islamic nations. Osama bin Laden and Abu Musab al-Zarqawi have killed innocent civilians, including Arabs and Muslims, have tarred the image of Islam in the world through suicide bombings and beheadings, and have destroyed the livelihood of Muslim nations like Iraq and Afghanistan. Poll after poll has shown that people in the Muslim and Arab worlds want moderate alternatives to the status quo, *if* their political, religious, and intellectual leaders will actually provide them.

The Muslim world has wasted far too much time complaining about history and spent far too little time building for the future. Governments in the Islamic world must understand that in order to salvage the image of Islam, and ensure stability in their countries, they must actively destroy support for Islamist extremism at every level.

The United States and its allies must join in this struggle, but their roles should be to help Islamic nations develop the military and security capabilities they really need and intervene only as allies when it is absolutely necessary. The West should support long-term sustainable and evolutionary efforts at reforms geared toward helping Islamic nations improve their own economic, political, and social systems.

The West must reinforce local reform efforts and avoid being seen as meddling in countries' internal affairs by supporting secular over religious Islamists, driving reform from the outside, or trying to change the Islamic character of Islamic countries. The West must not be seen as picking sides in the "sectarian game" between Sunnis and Shi'ites, Arabs or Persians, and Afghanis or Pakistanis. To the extent possible, the United States and other Western nations must be seen as an even-handed broker in the Arab-Israeli conflict.

Both sides, however, need to get their true priorities straight. The key to victory is ultimately in Islamic, not Western, hands. Implementing a "winning" strategy in this struggle does require mutual cooperation, but the key lies in the ability of those who are part of the Islamic world to exploit the real-world limitations and capabilities of the enemy and defeat them at the heart of their ideological arguments in the mosques, in the classrooms, on the television screens, and at all levels of civil society. This is not the job of Western nations or intellectuals, but of Muslim religious, government, business, and intellectual leaders.

THE COMBINED PRIORITIES OF COUNTERINSURGENCY AND COUNTERTERRORISM

The United States is almost certain to face many of the same demands for enhanced counterterrorism and counterinsurgency capabilities over the coming decades that it does today in Iraq, Afghanistan, and many other countries. It will also face a complex mix of steadily more sophisticated state and nonstate actors. These will normally operate with a high degree of independence, but they have collectively and individually already found a form of low-technology "swarm" tactics that can defeat high-technology U.S. forces unless the United States can depend on local allies.

Time literally is on the side of such enemies. They can afford to fight wars of attrition, outwait the United States, and pause their activities to regroup. They can swarm slowly around targets of opportunity. They can operate in cycles, and episodically, and concentrate on vulnerable local, regional, and transnational targets at the time of their choosing.

They do not need high-technology communications, "bandwidth," or coordination. Media coverage, word of mouth, and penetration into U.S. and local governments and forces will usually give them good intelligence and a good picture of what tactics work in military, political, and media terms.

These tactics reinforce a point raised by General Sir Rupert Smith.[9] Such threats will seek to operate *below* the level of U.S. and allied conventional superiority. They will use proxies and avoid battles when they can. They will prefer low-level wars of attrition and avoid present conventional targets. They will attack U.S., allied, and local civil targets using suicide bombings, kidnappings, assassinations, and other tactics in ways that are hard to anticipate or fully defend against.

At the same time, terrorists can exploit religion, ideology, culture, and ethnic and sectarian identity to attack and isolate the United States and outside allies. This means such threats will also seek to fight *above* the level of U.S. conventional superiority. They will try to shape the ideological, political, and psychological battlefields in ways that make the United States an invader, occupier, or crusader. They will use the support they gain to disperse and hide among the population and seek to force the United States to use tactics and detainments that alienate the people in the areas where they operate.

Unless the United States can rely on local forces and local allies, this mix of attack tactics will often deprive the United States of much of its ability to exploit superior weapons, intelligence, surveillance, and reconnaissance assets, and conventional war-fighting expertise. It will succeed in using a far lower cost "countervailing strategy" to exploit U.S. weaknesses, and no amount of talk about "fourth-generation" war, changes in tactics or field manuals, or creation of new specialized forces will change this.

This leaves the United States with some hard choices. It needs to realize that no matter what it does to improve its counterterrorism capabilities, counterinsurgency capabilities, and area expertise, it will fight an uphill battle if it fights alone or without substantial support. Winning local and regional support, however, means accepting allies that often will have different values. The United States cannot simultaneously seek to impose its own vision of democracy or reform and cannot count on quick and rapid progress. It cannot assume that its Western values will always be right or triumphant, and it will have to be far more realistic about the possible pace of reform in much of the world, the need to work with individual countries and groups at their own pace, and defer to local leaders and reformers.

Challenge Nine: Dealing with Alliances, International Cooperation, and Interoperability at the Regional and Global Levels

The development of local forces is only one of the sets of lessons the United States needs to learn about the value and management of alliances. The United States needs to learn that allies are partners, and independent ones at that. It should learn from the strains that Iraq and other recent contingencies have put on its forces and defense resources. One key lesson is that allies are not wrong simply because they disagree with U.S. policy and will not change their views because the United States acts. The United States entered the war without several of the key allies it initially counted on for support. One was Turkey, which failed to permit the United States to operate from its soil. Others included France and Germany. In retrospect, it is hard to argue that their strategic reasoning was more flawed than that of the United States.

Another key lesson is that creating "coalitions of the willing" can be a very dangerous action in terms of future support if they are really largely coalitions of the pressured, and they do not subsequently become coalitions of the consulted and the victorious. A similar lesson may be emerging from Afghanistan. By late 2005, many allies were concerned that the United States led them into a combat situation where the mission involved serious combat against a resurgent Taliban. They were also concerned that the United States was reducing its combat forces in Afghanistan, leaving allies with an added burden and set of risks.

It is too soon to say that the United States has done any lasting damage to its alliances. Several nations that would not join the U.S. invasion of Iraq continued to support the United States in Afghanistan, and some have supported the United States in other security initiatives since the invasion. The same is true of many of the nations that have withdrawn forces from Iraq, and many of America's past allies still seem likely to support the United States in any contingency where both countries have clear common interests.

It is more than possible, however, that the United States has reduced the willingness of its allies to support it in local conflicts that do not clearly and directly serve their interests, and it has broadly damaged its credibility in forming coalitions and sustaining them. Public opinion polls have shown the damage already extends to critical allies like Australia, Britain, and Japan. The leaders of these countries were able to act in spite of a broad lack of popular support, but such action tends to mortgage future success to success in the present. Even if the United States does achieve a favorable outcome in both Iraq and Afghanistan, the legacy will still be one of a major loss of popular confidence and political support in many allied nations.

If the United States does not achieve a favorable outcome in both Iraq and Afghanistan, the results may be far worse. Vietnam, Lebanon, and Somalia still evoke strong memories and concerns about U.S. ability to conduct coalition operations. These concerns were overshadowed by U.S. success in the Gulf War and by initial U.S. successes in Afghanistan and Iraq. Even limited victory is going to leave both allies and potential allies with lasting concerns about how well the United States formulates its plans for military engagement, the role it seeks from its allies, and the way it interfaces with its allies.

More broadly, the United States needs to learn how to listen and follow, not always insist on taking the lead. The United States has created problems in the Balkans, Iraq, and Afghanistan by not treating the allies who serve with U.S. forces as full partners. Many allied military officers and advisors who served with the United States during the time of the Coalition Provisional Authority feel that the United States did not consult, did not listen, and gave allies positions in joint allied commands with more symbolic rank than real meaning. No one who talks to a range of such allied officers and officials can ignore the extent to which they feel they were bypassed by U.S. officials and commanders who were caught up in their own internal divisions and goals and failed to take their allies seriously.

THE UNITED STATES AS LEADER VERSUS ALLIES AS PARTNERS

Allies are vital and fragile military and strategic assets that the United States cannot do without. The Cold War is over. There is no single threat that forces current and potential allies to unite behind the United States or follow its lead even in Europe. NATO's capability to operate outside Europe is particularly sensitive to consensus and success. The European Union (EU) may talk about contingency forces, but looks inward. Europe is and will remain primarily concerned with Europe and the nations on its immediate periphery.

There is no alliance between Russia and China or Russian ability to interfere in Asia that pushes Asian nations to support the United States. South Korea and Taiwan have shown, in very different ways, that they will pursue strong independent policies, and Japan is increasingly emerging as an ally that will take both a stronger and more independent stand in Asia.

The United States has never had the same degree of allied support in other regions. The Middle East will be a particular problem for all of the reasons outlined in the previous chapter. Latin America, sub-Saharan Africa, Central Asia, South Asia, and the Caspian have always been areas where the United States has had to compete for allies on a contingency-by-contingency basis—a problem that may be far more important in an era of nonstate actors, and loose coalitions of nonstate actors and radical states, than today.

U.S. strategy needs to deal with these challenges by constantly strengthening local alliances and emphasizing partnership, cooperation, and mutual interest. Instead, it has emphasized unilateral U.S. efforts to reshape the world around democracy on U.S. terms.

The National Strategy the United States issued in March 2006 paid suitable rhetorical deference to the value of alliances, but its first four sections focused almost solely on advancing "democracy" with little regard to working with allies as partners in any form.[1] When it does turn to diplomacy and alliances, it focuses on "transformational diplomacy" before turning to a region-by-region analysis of alliances in which the litmus test in each case is not how to reinforce mutual interests and security, but rather how to achieve the ideological and strategic goals of the United States.[2]

The Quadrennial Defense Review (QDR) issued in February 2006 placed more emphasis on partnership and allied interests, but placed its primary emphasis on the "transformational defense agenda directed by the President" and raised many of the same themes as the National Strategy.[3] The QDR's primary focus was on the war on terrorism, homeland defense, emerging powers like China, and the threat of proliferation.[4] Transformation is seen largely in terms of unilateral U.S. action.[5] The section on "developing a 21st Century force" does not mention allies at all and assumes that the United States can successfully restructure its own forces to substitute for local forces and support.[6]

When the QDR finally did touch upon the need for allies, it provided little meaningful detail except to call for allied capabilities that supplement the United States in missions that it has found to be difficult and wants assistance on its own terms:[7]

> The nation's alliances provide a foundation for working to address common security challenges. NATO remains the cornerstone of transatlantic security and makes manifest the strategic solidarity of democratic states in Europe and North America. NATO is evolving through the addition of seven new allies, the Partnership for Peace Program, the creation of the NATO Response Force, the establishment of the new Allied Command Transformation, the Alliance's leadership of the International Security Assistance Force in Afghanistan and the NATO Training Mission in Iraq. In many European allied states, however, aging and shrinking populations are curbing defense spending on capabilities they need for conducting operations effectively alongside U.S. forces. In the Pacific, alliances with Japan, Australia, Korea and others promote bilateral and multi-

lateral engagement in the region and cooperative actions to address common security threats. India is also emerging as a great power and a key strategic partner. Close co-operation with these partners in the long war on terrorism, as well as in efforts to counter WMD [weapons of mass destruction] proliferation and other nontraditional threats, ensures the continuing need for these alliances and for improving their capabilities. The Department will continue to strengthen traditional allied operations, with increased emphasis on collective capabilities to plan and conduct stabilization, security, transition and reconstruction operations. In particular, the Department supports efforts to create a NATO stabilization and reconstruction capability and a European constabulary force. The United States will work to strengthen allied capabilities for the long war and countering WMD. The United States, in concert with allies, will promote the aim of tailoring national military contributions to best employ the unique capabilities and characteristics of each ally, achieving a unified effort greater than the sum of its parts.

Consistent with the President's emphasis on the need to prevent, rather than be forced to respond to, attacks, the Department recommends that the United States continue to work with its allies to develop approaches, consistent with their domestic laws and applicable international law, to disrupt and defeat transnational threats before they mature. Concepts and constructs enabling unity of effort with more than 70 supporting nations under the Proliferation Security Initiative should be extended to domains other than WMD proliferation, including cyberspace, as a priority.

ALLIES AS AN ESSENTIAL PART OF U.S. SECURITY

Neither the national strategy document nor the QDR presented a workable strategy for creating effective ties or partnerships with allied forces or for reducing the strain on U.S. forces or strategic commitments. The U.S. need for allies as an essential supplement to, and substitute for, its own forces has not diminished since the Cold War, and Iraq and Afghanistan are only one type of case where allied support is necessary. It is one thing to set unilateral strategic goals and another to create a global structure of alliances that can actually provide partners in real-world contingencies.

The United States may be the leading military power in the world, but as Chapters 1 and 2 have made clear, this gives it little leverage in making nations follow its lead. Iraq and Afghanistan have also shown just how much the United States needs allies to reduce the burden on its forces and on the skills and capabilities it lacks or has in short supply. This is particularly true in four critical cases:

- NATO and Europe have scarcely become unnecessary because of the collapse of the Soviet Union and the Warsaw Pact; they have simply become successful. Their very success has sharply reduced the need for U.S. forces and strategic commitments to Europe and the risk that large numbers of U.S. forces will be needed for warfighting contingencies.

- Iraq is not the only threat in the Middle East and is not the primary one in any case. Transnational terrorism and neo-Salafi extremism pose a more enduring and broader threat. So does the risk of a nuclear Iran and coalitions among Iran, Syria, and Shi'ite radicals.

- The primary large-scale warfighting contingencies the United States now faces are in the Korean Peninsula and the Taiwan Strait. In the case of Korea, South Korea has evolved to the point where it, not the United States, is the leading military partner.

- In the case of Taiwan, the United States has an ally that should assume far more responsibility for its own security and act with far more responsibility. The result is a government that is far more of a strategic liability than a strategic asset.

IMPLEMENTING MULTILATERALISM

The Department of Defense may be learning some of these lessons from experience. The Office of the Secretary of Defense (OSD) did make moves to restructure its policy shop to reflect the growing importance of America's allies during the fall of 2006. In keeping with the multilateral coalition goals laid out in the QDR, the OSD initiated, and Congressional defense authorizers approved, a push to reorganize the Office of the Under Secretary of Defense for Policy.[8] The goal was to better integrate key Department of Defense offices given the growing emphasis on managing international military coalitions, equipping partner nations to fight terrorists, and managing the U.S. military response to transnational threats.

This initiative involved several potentially important steps:[9]

- Expand the number of Assistant Secretaries of Defense from four to five, adding a new Assistant Secretary for Global Security Affairs that would oversee the Pentagon's new focus on "building partnership capacity," the ability of foreign militaries to fight terrorists within and near their own borders. The new office would also deal with transnational threats.

- Establish several new Deputy Assistant Secretary of Defense posts under the Assistant Secretary for Global Security Affairs, including the following:
  - Deputy Assistant Secretary for Security and Cooperation,
  - Deputy Assistant Secretary for Coalition Management, and
  - Deputy Assistant Secretary for Support to Public Diplomacy to spearhead strategic communications efforts.

- The Deputy Assistant Secretary for Counternarcotics would become the Deputy Assistant Secretary for Counternarcotics and Global Threats to emphasize its expanded focus on transnational challenges from drug trafficking to avian flu. The new counternarcotics office would report to the new Assistant Secretary for Global Security Affairs.

- Establish a new Global War on Terrorism Task Force that would report directly to the Policy Under Secretary. This Task Force would work closely with the National Counterterrorism Center and would bring a more comprehensive picture of ongoing activities ranging from Special Operations capabilities to strategic communications.

- Remove and rename Deputy Assistant Secretaries for Negotiations Policy and Forces Policy. These portfolios will be folded into new organizations.

- The Assistant Secretary of Defense for Special Operations and Low-Intensity Conflict (SO/LIC) would become the Assistant Secretary for SO/LIC and Interdependent

Capabilities. The office is intended to present a more unified and coordinated policy position on the future combat capabilities of the U.S. military.

- Establish under the Assistant Secretary for SO/LIC and Interdependent Capabilities a Deputy Assistant Secretary for Strategic Capabilities and a Deputy Assistant Secretary for Forces Transformation and Resources. The new Forces Transformation and Resources Office would use the expertise of the former Deputy Assistant Secretary of Defense for Resources and Plans and would likely absorb the Office of Force Transformation.

- Relieve and reassign the responsibilities of the offices of International Security Affairs and of International Security Policy. As part of a regional reorganization, the Assistant Secretary for International Security Affairs, supported by three deputies, would focus on Europe, the Middle East, and Africa. The other Assistant Secretary, also supported by three deputies, would focus on Asian and Pacific security affairs.

It is still far from clear what this means in practice, however, or just how sensitive the U.S. national security community is to need to take a new approach to rebuilding and strengthening America's alliance. In late 2006, the details of implementing these new proposals had not yet been decided upon. Congress had voiced several concerns with the OSD's reorganization, especially with regard to the military's counternarcotics mission.

Moreover, bureaucratic changes are not substance or actions; no matter how well intentioned, it will not necessarily change how the OSD conducts business. In 1993, Les Aspin, President Clinton's first Secretary of Defense, attempted a drastic OSD overhaul that did not last a full year. OSD can neither shape the actions of the interagency community nor reshape the U.S. military to emphasize partnership, interoperability, reliance on the use of allied forces, and the development of allied military and police forces in nations where insurgency and terrorism are key issues.

It is clear that the United States must respond to an ever-widening array of transnational threats that require managing international coalitions and equipping partner nations to fight terrorists. It is clear that the United States must try to compensate for the problems of the last few years and be more sensitive to the fact that other nations can not only disagree with the United States, but be right in doing so. Ultimately, however, this is a matter of Presidential leadership and one that no amount of reorganization, whether in part of the Department of Defense or the entire interagency community, can accomplish without sustained Presidential leadership and action.

THE CHANGE IN THE U.S. FOCUS IN NATO

The United States has not turned away from NATO, but it has taken advantage of NATO's success and the collapse of the Warsaw Pact to shift the U.S. force posture to focus on missions in less secure areas. The United States no longer requires large heavy maneuver forces to maintain its defense posture in Europe. In keeping with transformation programs described in Chapter 5, the United States is transforming its European forces to provide lighter, more deployable ground capabilities. The United States has also shifted its European forces south and east to allow for easier deployment to volatile regions in the Caucasus and in the Middle East. The United States has increased the capabilities of its Italy-based 173rd Airborne Brigade, strengthened ground and air rotations in southern and southeastern Europe, and increased access to facilities and training sites in the Romanian and Bulgarian areas as part of establishing the Eastern European Task Force.[10]

Europe and the "Peace Dividend"

These U.S. moves come, however, at a time when most European countries have also taken advantage of the collapse of the Warsaw Pact to cut the size of their forces and the cost of force modernization. Europe has far fewer reasons to transform and modernize its forces than the United States, and it has altered its defense policies and force plans accordingly.

Since the end of the Cold War, NATO has steadily shifted from collective defense against a threat from the East to a collective security organization, charged with organizing peacekeeping missions and facilitating democratization in Eastern Europe. As of July 2006, NATO had peacekeeping, security, and/or stabilization missions with various mandates in the Balkans, in Sudan, in Iraq, and in Afghanistan. *Military Technology* magazine described NATO's newfound role in the twenty-first century: "Since 1990, NATO has rapidly established itself as the world's most experienced peacemaking and peacekeeping force, and is becoming a major enabler for the United Nations...As a result, the world is demanding more of NATO, not only to assist with failing states, but also to counter the growing threats of terrorism, drugs, and the proliferation of weapons of mass destruction (WMD), well outside of its traditional areas of responsibility."[11]

At the same time, European powers have fallen behind in modernization and warfighting capability. The trends in European defense spending have clearly reflected these shifts. Excluding the United States, NATO member states have steadily cut military manpower and defense funds since 2001. A comparison of force structures compiled by the International Institute for Strategic Studies showed that between 2001 and 2005 Britain, Canada, France, Italy, Poland, Spain, and Germany cut their active-duty forces. Meanwhile, during the same period, the United States increased its ranks from 1.37 million to 1.42 million.

More tellingly, while NATO has urged its members to maintain defense spending levels of at least 2 percent of gross domestic product (GDP), the burden carried by the NATO nations collectively, excluding the United States, dropped from 2.02 percent of their GDP in 2001 to 1.8 percent in 2006.[12] And even this number is inflated by high levels of defense spending in Turkey and Greece, where the armed forces are preparing not for NATO missions but for fighting one another.[13]

By contrast, during the same five-year period, U.S. core defense spending—less some wartime supplemental expenditures—increased from 3 percent of GDP in 2001 to 3.7 percent in 2005. In response to these trends, in May 2006 Secretary of

Defense Donald Rumsfeld commented, "A growing concern is that this declining spending is likely to drop even further given the demographic trends of much of Europe, coupled with their prevailing threat assessments."[14]

NATO operations in Kosovo and the NATO-led International Security Assistance Force (ISAF) operation in Afghanistan showed that the European members of NATO lag far behind the United States, both in high-tech weapons and in their ability to get useable troops speedily to where they are needed. Moreover, NATO has not developed a cohesive set of tactics and rules of engagement for such missions. In some cases, like Afghanistan, these have to be laboriously negotiated among the deployed forces of 26 nations; there will invariably be a wide variance in the propensity of individual combatant commanders to engage.

For example, Afghanistan has shown that British and Canadian commanders may take a broad and flexible view of their mandate, while other commanders are forced to be relatively inflexible. This is why Afghan government officials were leery of U.S. troops turning over their areas to NATO replacement forces in July 2006. At the same time, the ISAF in Kabul, run by NATO since 2003, was not authorized to fight drug production and trafficking in Afghanistan—whose insurgency is intimately linked to drug barons. This is just another restriction limiting the utility of NATO forces in furthering U.S. objectives.[15]

These differences need to be taken account of when the United States decides what roles and capabilities it should seek from its NATO and European allies, and how it can best seek the kind of partnership that will aid both sides while reducing the need for unilateral deployments of U.S. forces. Ever since the First Gulf War, the United States has sought to transform NATO's military forces into high-technology conventional forces with as many interoperable elements as possible. At the same time, NATO has sought to develop added out-of-area and power projection capabilities —many again modeled on U.S. capabilities. The NATO Response Force is the symbol of such an intention.

What the United States, Europe, and NATO may really need, however, are forces that can deal with the broader problems of asymmetric warfare, counterinsurgency, stability operations, and nation building. If so, such forces must by fully integrated under a single NATO commander, operate according to the same rules of engagement, and be prepared for both actual combat and the full range of civil-military operations. Afghanistan has shown all too clearly that separate national approaches to such missions are a recipe for failure and that when given contingents are not allowed to fight and become stand-aside forces, they become part of the problem and not the solution.

NATO has made some progress along these lines, but much of it is more cosmetic than real. Institution building is not force transformation. Ministers may agree to force modernization priorities and to create power projection capabilities, but most country defense plans and budgets reflect slow progress, a continuing lack of interoperability, and the inability to move and sustain more than a small fraction of national forces much beyond national boundaries. NATO Europe is spending well over $220 billion on military forces and has some 2.2 million active military and

2.6 million Reservists. Virtually all defense analysts agree, however, that most of its procurement efforts are scarcely properly coordinated and interoperable and are not coming close to providing U.S. levels of technology and warfighting capability. More generally, only a small fraction of NATO's total manpower is deployable outside NATO, and most European forces are really usable and sustainable in warfighting only if Europe goes to war with itself.

This situation has not been aided by the fact that a *de facto* competition has emerged between NATO and the European Union over who should plan and control Europe's defense capabilities, particularly its rapid-reaction and power-projection capabilities. Various arrangements have papered over these differences, but the tensions in the NATO Alliance created by the Iraq War have made the situation worse. French and U.S. tensions run deep, in spite of President George W. Bush's recent fence-mending visit to Europe, and figures as senior as former German Chancellor Gerhard Schröder have said that the NATO alliance is "no longer the primary venue where transatlantic partners discuss and coordinate strategies." The reality seems to be that NATO is now an alliance where member statements will form *ad hoc* coalitions in reaction to given crises and contingencies far more often than they act in unison.

NATO and Europe Have Already Freed Major U.S. Forces for Other Missions

Yet, before one starts mourning the death of NATO, or seeing its force transformation efforts as a failure, it is necessary to consider several factors that highlight the importance of NATO and Europe in spite of such issues. First, it is not a bad thing—or an abdication of Europe's security needs—if European integration and stability are the primary focus of Europe. Century after century of past conflict is a lesson in just how important it is that Europe completes this process of change. Two world wars have shown that it is also as vital to the strategic interests of the United States and Canada as to Europe. NATO does not need a new unifying mission outside Europe to replace the Cold War; it needs to remember that the purpose of a transatlantic alliance is transatlantic security, and this is an area where the West is having outstanding success.

Second, a European focus on Europe has already allowed the United States to make major shifts in its force posture and allocate far more forces to missions outside Europe. In 1990, the United States still had some 317,000 men and women stationed in Europe, and virtually all of its reserve and active force posture in the United States had the reinforcement of Europe as its primary mission. The U.S. Army still had some 204,700 personnel in West Germany alone, with some 5,000 main battle tanks. The U.S. Air Force (USAF) had 41,000 additional personnel and some 264 aircraft. The United States had large land, air, and naval forces in many other European countries, including 27,500 USAF personnel and 279 combat aircraft in Britain.[16] In 2006, the United States had some 50,377 U.S. Army personnel in Germany and 568 main battle tanks; the USAF had 15,460 personnel and one fighter wing with a normal combat strength of less than 60 aircraft. USAF strength in Britain was under 10,000 and combat strength was one fighter wing with 48 combat aircraft plus a Special Forces group with 10 combat aircraft.[17]

U.S. and European Specialization

Third, specialization is often a more effective form of partnership than active coalitions, and there is nothing all that new about the fact that the United States focuses on security missions outside of Europe or the fact that transatlantic cooperation is based on *a la carte* force mixes and coalitions of the willing, rather than reliance on formal arrangements with NATO. NATO has shown its relevance in the Balkans and Afghanistan, but virtually all of the out-of-area operations that have involved both U.S. and European forces over the last half century have been *ad hoc* mixes of forces from the United States and a few European states. Moreover, a study done after the Gulf War by the Center for Naval Analysis found that the United States had used power projection forces outside the NATO area more than 240 times between the founding of NATO and the end of the Cold War, and the list of contingencies involved was one where more than three-quarters of the U.S. actions did not involve any European role.

NATO Europe, and European forces as a whole, are not a failure because they are not designed for power projection or modernized to the same level of force transformation as those of the United States. A situation in which Europe focuses on Europe and the United States focuses on the rest of the world with contingency-driven support from individual European states may, in fact, be the only way in which the West can act in most out-of-area contingencies. The NATO Alliance does not create common interests and perceptions. In many cases, alliance-wide consensus is a recipe for paralysis, and alliance-wide force transformation of any kind will never happen at more than token levels because many—if not most—European states have no clear motive to become involved and pay the cost.

NATO as an institution may be most useful as a common security forum that ensures suitable dialogue and cooperation where cooperation is seen as both necessary and affordable and is still successful by any rational standard. The "specialization" of Europe and the United States also reflects the reality that two of the most important security priorities for the United States are outside of Europe: the security of Korea and stability in the Taiwan Strait. Both are military arenas where Europe can at most play a token role. Even in the Gulf and Central Asia, Britain is now the only European power with any real-world prospect of deploying and sustaining serious out-of-area deployments.

Setting New Goals for Partnership in Force Transformation

Fourth, the preceding chapters show that the priorities for force transformation must change to set more realistic goals for investment and cost containment. They also show that even the "rich" have budget problems, and cost containment is proving to be as serious an issue for the United States as for Europe, in spite of the massive U.S. advantage in total military spending.

The United States has found that it cannot afford many of the programs it once thought it could include in its "revolution in military affairs." The USAF has an unaffordable mix of combat aircraft procurements. The U.S. Marine Corps is mortgaged to the Osprey and faces serious cost constraints in many other areas of force modernization. The U.S. Army has had to slip procurement of its new family of future combat system vehicles by at least a decade, and the U.S. Navy has what virtually every expert inside and outside the Navy accepts as a massive gap between its shipbuilding requirements and what it can actually afford. The United States faces the same reality as every other member of NATO. Budgets cannot be shaped to meet the priorities of force transformation; force transformation must be shaped to fit budgets. In the absence of some peer conventional threat, the primary criterion for force transformation is now affordability.

Focusing on Different Mission Requirements

Fifth, it is all too clear that mission requirements are changing as well. The capability to fight asymmetric wars and to carry out stability and peacemaking missions is at least as important as the ability to fight high-technology conventional wars. There are still important conventional threats in Asia and the Middle East, but the United States has recognized, in terms of reference, from its most recent QDR that such "traditional threats" are only part of the problem. It is moving away from a focus on high-technology conventional forces to a "four-way matrix" in which irregular, disruptive, and catastrophic threats have equal priority. The lessons of 9/11, Afghanistan, and Iraq—and the prospect of proliferation by Iran and terrorist groups—have forced the United States to give equal priority to asymmetric warfare, counterinsurgency, counterterrorism, and homeland defense. They have also forced the United States to rethink the need for interagency cooperation, creating civil components that can perform national security tasks, and assigning the military roles in nation building, peacemaking, and stability operations.

Dealing with irregular, disruptive, and catastrophic threats are all mission areas where technology can play a critical role, but where new high-cost weapons platforms, extremely expensive space-based programs, and very high performance munitions have far less priority. The Iraq War has demonstrated, for example, that the quality of intelligence, surveillance, and reconnaissance was more important than having the most advanced aircraft. It showed that precision warfare could be fought largely with affordable laser and global positioning system–guided bombs. It has also demonstrated that existing major weapons platforms not only retain their value, but also can be adapted to new missions.

Existing "legacy" systems purchased during the Cold War are also proving to be valuable in new types of wars. Systems like the M1A1 heavy tank and the Bradley armored fighting vehicle not only helped smash Saddam's conventional forces, they have since been critical in urban warfare and in dealing with the insurgency. Attack helicopters and unmanned aerial vehicles have proven easy to adapt to a wide range of counterterrorism and counterinsurgency missions. Existing combat aircraft can deal with the air threat in developing countries, and relatively simple precision-strike weapons not only enable them to "stand off" from land-based air defenses, but strike at urban terrorist and insurgent targets. Older systems like the A-10 War-thog have proved so useful that they may well get a major upgrading.

More importantly, the Iraq War and the Afghan conflict have shown the importance of human skills, area expertise, civil-military units, and a host of "human-centric" capabilities that depend on men and women in uniform, not things. Counterterrorism, counterinsurgency, peacemaking, and nation building are all people and skill intensive. They are also areas where existing European forces can play a critical role in those contingencies where states perceive a common need. Special Forces, military police, linguists, civil-military action teams, human intelligence experts, combat engineers, service support units, and transport helicopters are just a few examples of the type of "transformational" capabilities that are needed that are not high-technology systems.

Defense and response to terrorist attacks on national soil involve new mixes of regular military, paramilitary, law enforcement, and emergency response forces where civilian capabilities can be at least as important as military ones, and where the priority for increased resources requires "transformation" in a far broader sense of the term. Counterterrorist experts, information technology security experts, critical infrastructure protection, specialized medical facilities, and emergency responders like firefighters are as important to national security as regular military forces.

These are areas where Europe often has the same or more capability than the United States and where there may well be a much more common set of transatlantic priorities and needs than in out-of-area operations and power projection. If terrorism leads to the combination of irregular and catastrophic threats, as many experts fear, the need for transatlantic cooperation may become even greater. This could mean transforming and increasing many of NATO's nascent efforts in areas like counterterrorism and giving it a much larger role in some aspects of homeland defense.

Resetting NATO's Force Transformation Goals

In short, much of the U.S. criticism of NATO's force transformation efforts may be based on the wrong strategic assumptions and the wrong priorities. Transatlantic differences will remain. Europe and the United States are not going to agree on some common set of NATO out-of-area missions in many—if not most—cases. European forces are not going to be transformed to have the level of conventional technology or power-projection capability as the United States or that their Foreign Ministers have officially agreed to.

Such differences, however, are scarcely anything new, and the unifying and cohesive impact of the Cold War is largely a matter of bad history and false nostalgia. NATO had a "transatlantic crisis" over the phase out of U.S. Point Four military aid, U.S. refusal to support colonial out-of-area operations, efforts to convert to theater nuclear options and then to restore conventional options, Charles de Gaulle's partial withdrawal from the Alliance, the U.S. role in Vietnam, the deployment of Pershing II missiles and the ground-launched cruise missile, and planning for mutual and balanced force reductions and Conventional Forces in Europe. NATO has never lived up to a single major force plan in any unified way, even one as vital in its day as a cohesive deployment of land-based air defenses for the Central Region.

If one judges the NATO Alliance by real-world standards, it is scarcely a perfect success, but it is anything but a failure. Moreover, it has far more affordable opportunities for the kind of force transformation that member states really need than many military analysts that focus solely on traditional threats seem to realize. NATO should rethink many of its present force transformation priorities from the ground up, but it remains a considerable success. As for the future, what NATO really needs is a little less hubris from the United States, a little less bickering from Europe, and a lot more strategic realism about what NATO can and should do.

THE BROADER MIDDLE EAST

The previous chapter has already touched upon the changes needed in the way the United States builds its alliances in the Middle East. It should be clear, however, that more is involved than counterterrorism and counterinsurgency. The United States must work with North African and European allies to avoid any risk of more conventional conflict in that region. It must continue to try to find ways to reduce the constant buildup of conventional military capabilities in the Levant, but ensure that key allies like Egypt, Israel, and Jordan can deter and defend in the interim.

Iran presents a conventional threat as well as an asymmetric one and is a potential nuclear power. There will be a continuing need to strengthen regional alliances to deter conventional war in the Gulf, and there may well be a need to contain and deter Iranian long-range missile forces and possibly its nuclear weapons. If the United States is successful in Iraq, there will be a broader need to find some new security structure to deal with Iraq that allows it to deter and defend against foreign enemies as well as internal ones without creating problems for nations like Turkey, Jordan, and Saudi Arabia. If the United States fails, civil conflict in Iraq must be contained, and alliances will need to be built up to avoid the division of the region into Sunni and Shi'ite powers with a host of new security problems.

NEW FOCUS ON ALLIANCES IN ASIA

The greatest challenge the United States faces in shaping its alliances seems likely, however, to be in Asia, and it will be a very different kind of challenge from the one the United States has faced in Iraq, Afghanistan, and the war on terrorism. The United States has already begun to realign its force posture to focus on Asia. This, in part, is a response to the emergence of Japan as a more active power on a regional basis. It is a response to the steady growth of South Korea and the decline of North Korea. Finally, it is a response to the emergence of China and the risk that tensions between China and Taiwan could involve the United States in a major clash or conflict over the Taiwan Strait.

The Korean Case and Japan

The United States faces different risks in each case, and potential partners have very different capabilities. South Korea is a major military power, and its primary needs have evolved from having the United States reinforce it in every aspect of military power to a need for high-technology U.S. strike support and U.S. deterrence of North Korea's nuclear threat. Japan's needs are for defense against North Korea and China, although Japan is both expanding its regional role and steadily modernizing its forces.

No one can ignore the fact that North Korea is developing nuclear weapons and long-range missiles, has long kept its forces on a near wartime footing near the demilitarized zone with South Korea, and presents a serious risk in any conventional war. The balance of forces in Northeast Asia is shown in Figures 10.1 through 10.7.

North Korea clearly maintains one of the world's largest military forces. On the other hand, so does South Korea, and the United States can deploy an extraordinary mix of long-range precision-strike assets, provide its own nuclear umbrella over South Korea, as well as deploy missile defenses and provide advanced intelligence collection, analysis, and targeting tools.

These developments explain why the composition of U.S. alliances and partnerships has shifted, and policy makers would like to convert existing relations with Japan, Australia, and South Korea into a robust, integrated anti-Chinese alliance system. Bringing other nations, especially India, into this system can also further U.S. interests.

Ryan Henry, Principal Deputy Under Secretary of Defense for Policy, summarized the realignment of U.S. forces in Asia as follows in testimony before the House Armed Services Committee on June 20, 2006:

> In the Asia-Pacific region, we are improving our ability to meet our alliance commitments by strengthening our forces' deterrent effect and our capability for rapid response with forward deployment of additional expeditionary maritime capabilities and long-range strike assets in Alaska, Hawaii, and Guam.
>
> We also seek to help allies in the region strengthen their own military capabilities and to solidify relationships with newer partners who can help in the prosecution of the global war on terrorism.
>
> On the Korean peninsula, our planned enhancements include the reallocation and consolidation of stationed forces from the Seoul area to two hubs in the central and southern sections of the country. We are strengthening our overall military effectiveness for the combined defense of the Republic of Korea.
>
> And through the defense policy initiative, we have consulted closely with Japan on several important force realignment initiatives that will have far-reaching beneficial impact for the US–Japanese alliance.

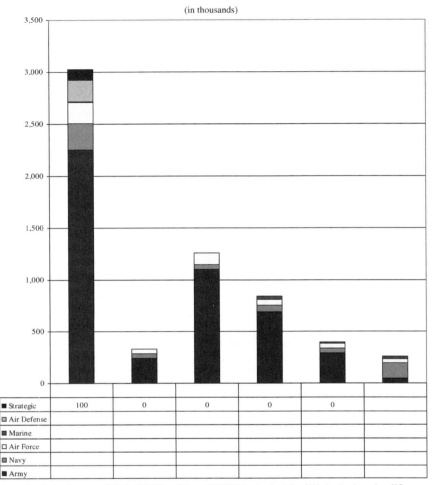

(in thousands)

	Strategic	Air Defense	Marine	Air Force	Navy	Army
■ Strategic	100	0	0	0	0	

Source: Based primarily on material in the *IISS Military Balance, 2005-2006*, London, Routledge, 2005 plus data drawn from U.S. Pacific Command (USPACOM) sources and US experts. Some data estimated or corrected by the author.

Figure 10.1   Northeast Asian Military Manpower in Key Powers: 2006

Among these initiatives is a significant realignment and reorganization of the Marine Corps posture in Okinawa to include relocating approximately 8,000 marines and 9,000 dependents from Okinawa to Guam.

The United States has taken several steps to pursue this agenda. In February 2005, Secretaries Condoleezza Rice and Donald Rumsfeld hosted a meeting with top Japanese officials. The parties signed a "Joint Statement of the U.S.–Japan Security Consultative Committee," which called for greater collaboration between American and Japanese forces in the conduct of military operations in an area stretching from

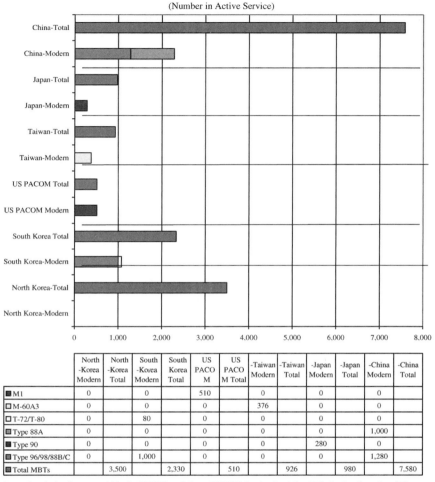

(Number in Active Service)

	North -Korea Modern	North -Korea Total	South -Korea Modern	South Korea Total	US PACO M	US PACO M Total	-Taiwan Modern	-Taiwan Total	-Japan Modern	-Japan Total	-China Modern	-China Total
■ M1	0		0		510		0		0		0	
□ M-60A3	0		0		0		376		0		0	
□ T-72/T-80	0	80	0		0		0		0		0	
■ Type 88A	0		0		0		0		0		1,000	
■ Type 90	0		0		0		0		280		0	
■ Type 96/98/88B/C	0		1,000		0		0		0		1,280	
■ Total MBTs		3,500		2,330		510		926		980		7,580

Source: Based primarily on material in the *IISS Military Balance, 2005-2006*, London, Routledge, 2005 plus data drawn from U.S. Pacific Command (USPACOM) sources and US experts. Some data estimated or corrected by the author.

Figure 10.2 Northeast Asian Modern Main Battle Tanks (MBTs) versus Total Holdings: 2006

northeast Asia to the South China Sea. In October 2005, Washington and Tokyo released the Alliance Transformation and Realignment Report to guide the further integration of U.S. and Japanese forces in the Pacific and the simultaneous restructuring of the basing system in Japan.[18]

The United States has also reached out to South Korea and Australia to bring them closer into the U.S. alliance system. While South Korea has been reluctant to work closely with Japan because of Japan's brutal occupation of the Korean Peninsula from 1910 to 1945, the Bush Administration has continued to promote what it calls

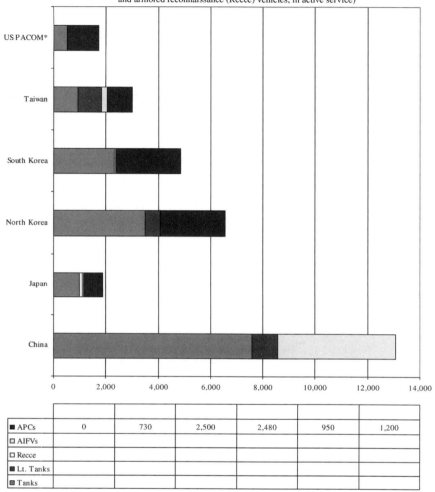

(Number of Tanks, other armored fighting vehicles (OAFVs), armored personal carriers (APCs), and armored reconnaissance (Recce) vehicles, in active service)

■ APCs	0	730	2,500	2,480	950	1,200
☐ AIFVs						
☐ Recce						
■ Lt. Tanks						
▣ Tanks						

Source: Based primarily on material in the *IISS Military Balance, 2005-2006*, London, Routledge, 2005 plus data drawn from USPACOM sources and US experts. Some data estimated or corrected by the author. *APCs number includes APCs, AIFVs, and Recce.

Figure 10.3   Northeast Asian Armored Fighting Vehicles: 2006

"trilateral military cooperation" among Seoul, Tokyo, and Washington. The United States has encouraged South Korea to adapt to the changing security environment and take a more regional view of security and stability that is not focused solely on North Korea.[19]

Australia has been a staunch ally of the United States, and Secretary of State Rice has made it a priority to bring Australia into the merging anti-Chinese network. In March 2006, Australia hosted tripartite talks with the United States and Japan. As

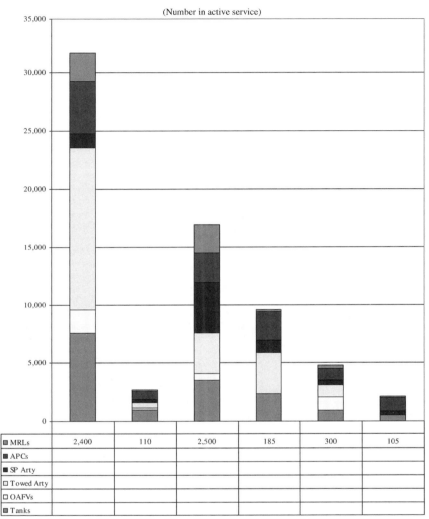

Source: Based primarily on material in the *IISS Military Balance, 2005-2006*, Routledge, 2005 plus data drawn from U.S. Pacific Command (USPACOM) sources and US experts. Some data estimated or corrected by the author. *SP artillery number includes both towed and artillery.

Figure 10.4   Northeast Asian Artillery Weapons in Key Powers: 2006

Steven R. Weisman reported in the *New York Times*, Secretary Rice convened the trilateral meeting "to deepen a three-way regional alliance aimed in part at balancing the spreading presence of China."[20]

The Taiwan Case and China

What the United States has not been able to do is to rebalance its relations with Taiwan. Relations with Taiwan and China have always been a major domestic

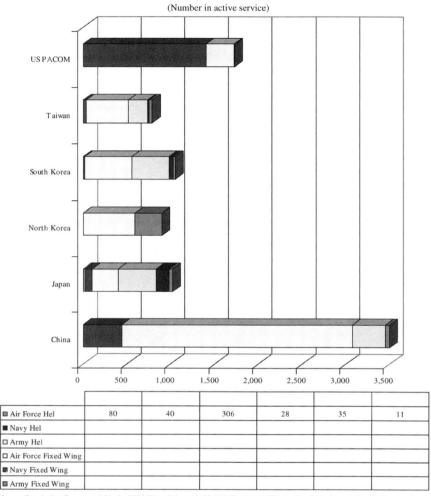

(Number in active service)

▣ Air Force Hel	80	40	306	28	35	11
■ Navy Hel						
☐ Army Hel						
☐ Air Force Fixed Wing						
■ Navy Fixed Wing						
▣ Army Fixed Wing						

Source: Based primarily on material in the *IISS Military Balance, 2005-2006*, Routledge, 2005 plus data drawn from U.S. Pacific Command (USPACOM) sources and US experts. Some data estimated or corrected by the author. *Figures for navy contain fixed and rotary wing aircraft.

Figure 10.5   Northeast Asian Fixed- and Rotary-Wing Combat Aircraft: 2006

political problem for the United States. A Republican Administration and a highly partisan Congress are naturally reluctant to put the kind of pressure on Taiwan that could force it to act more responsibly and build up its military capabilities.

As a result, Taiwan is the wild card in terms of stability, deterrence, and defense. It faces vastly superior Chinese forces, as is shown in Figures 10.1 through 10.7. Taiwan is also the "problem child" of America's structure of global alliances. Taiwan's political leadership has taken risks in provoking China that could involve the United States in a pointless conflict. Taiwan has also let its forces deteriorate and has failed to

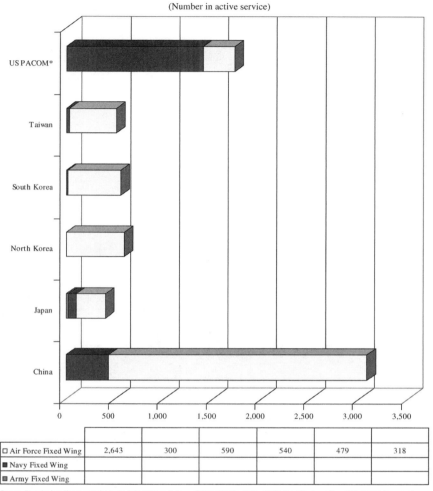

(Number in active service)

☐ Air Force Fixed Wing	2,643	300	590	540	479	318	
■ Navy Fixed Wing							
■ Army Fixed Wing							

Source: Based primarily on material in the *IISS Military Balance, 2005-2006*, Routledge, 2005 plus data drawn from U.S. Pacific Command (USPACOM) sources and US experts. Some data estimated or corrected by the author. *Figures for navy contain fixed and rotary wing aircraft.

Figure 10.6   Northeast Asian Fixed-Wing Combat Aircraft: 2006

modernize them. No other ally now presents so many risks and problems while doing so little to ensure its own security.

At the same time, China is emerging as the one power that may eventually present a major warfighting challenge to the United States. China has devoted substantial resources to its military over the past decade. China has some 2.5 million soldiers and the largest armed force in the world. The uncertainty surrounding China's ultimate military ambitions along with continuing tensions in the Taiwan Strait and on the Korean Peninsula demand a reassessment and a possible realignment of U.S. forces in response.

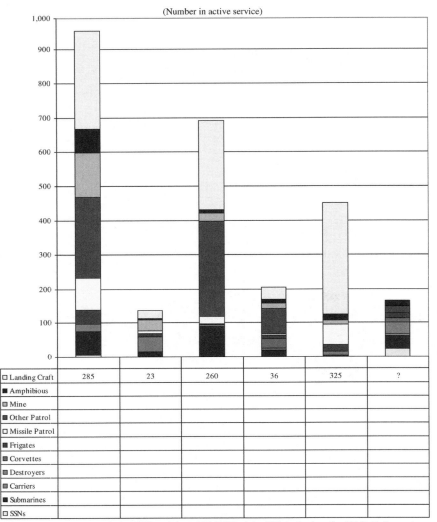

(Number in active service)

□ Landing Craft	285	23	260	36	325	?
■ Amphibious						
□ Mine						
■ Other Patrol						
□ Missile Patrol						
■ Frigates						
▤ Corvettes						
▤ Destroyers						
▤ Carriers						
■ Submarines						
□ SSNs						

Source: Based primarily on material in the *IISS Military Balance, 2005-2006*, Routledge, 2005 plus data drawn from U.S. Pacific Command (USPACOM) sources and US experts. Some data estimated or corrected by the author. *Missile Patrol numbers includes all patrol craft.

Figure 10.7   Northeast Asian Naval Combat Ships: 2006

As articulated by Condoleezza Rice in a much-cited *Foreign Affairs* article published during the 2000 presidential campaign, "China's success in controlling the balance of power [in Asia] depends in large part on America's reaction to the challenge. The United States must deepen its cooperation with Japan and South Korea and maintain its commitment to a robust military presence in the region."[21]

A Department of Defense report issued in June 2006, titled "Military Power of the People's Republic of China," summarized U.S. concerns as follows:[22]

Several aspects of China's military development have surprised US analysts, including the pace and scope of its strategic forces modernization. China's military expansion is already such as to alter regional military balances. Long-term trends in China's strategic nuclear forces modernization, land- and sea-based access denial capabilities, and emerging precision-strike weapons have the potential to pose credible threats to modern militaries operating in the region.

The 2006 QDR echoed these concerns about the rise of China and illustrates the fact that the United States cannot size or shape its forces around its experience in Iraq or the "long war."[23]

Of the major and emerging powers, China has the greatest potential to compete militarily with the United States and field disruptive military technologies that could over time off set traditional U.S. military advantages absent U.S. counter strategies. U.S. policy remains focused on encouraging China to play a constructive, peaceful role in the Asia-Pacific region and to serve as a partner in addressing common security challenges, including terrorism, proliferation, narcotics and piracy. U.S. policy seeks to encourage China to choose a path of peaceful economic growth and political liberalization, rather than military threat and intimidation.

The United States' goal is for China to continue as an economic partner and emerge as a responsible stakeholder and force for good in the world. China continues to invest heavily in its military, particularly in its strategic arsenal and capabilities designed to improve its ability to project power beyond its borders. Since 1996, China has increased its defense spending by more than 10% in real terms in every year except 2003. Secrecy, moreover, envelops most aspects of Chinese security affairs. The outside world has little knowledge of Chinese motivations and decision-making or of key capabilities supporting its military modernization.

The United States encourages China to take actions to make its intentions clear and clarify its military plans. Chinese military modernization has accelerated since the mid-to-late 1990s in response to central leadership demands to develop military options against Taiwan scenarios. The pace and scope of China's military build-up already puts regional military balances at risk. China is likely to continue making large investments in high-end, asymmetric military capabilities, emphasizing electronic and cyber-warfare; counter-space operations; ballistic and cruise missiles; advanced integrated air defense systems; next generation torpedoes; advanced submarines; strategic nuclear strike from modern, sophisticated land and sea-based systems; and theater unmanned aerial vehicles for employment by the Chinese military and for global export. These capabilities, the vast distances of the Asian theater, China's continental depth, and the challenge of en route and in-theater U.S. basing place a premium on forces capable of sustained operations at great distances into denied areas.

The United States will work to ensure that all major and emerging powers are integrated as constructive actors and stakeholders into the international system. It will also seek to ensure that no foreign power can dictate the terms of regional or global security. It will attempt to dissuade any military competitor from developing disruptive or other capabilities that could enable regional hegemony or hostile action against the United States or other friendly countries, and it will seek to deter aggression or coercion. Should deterrence fail, the United States would deny a hostile power its strategic and operational objectives.

Shaping the choices of major and emerging powers requires a balanced approach, one that seeks cooperation but also creates prudent hedges against the possibility that cooperative approaches by themselves may fail to preclude future conflict. A successful hedging strategy requires improving the capacity of partner states and reducing their vulnerabilities. In this regard, the United States will work to achieve greater integration of defensive systems among its international partners in ways that would complicate any adversary's efforts to decouple them. The United States will work with allies and partners to integrate intelligence sensors, communication networks, information systems, missile defenses, undersea warfare and counter-mine warfare capabilities. It will seek to strengthen partner nations' capabilities to defend themselves and withstand attack, including against ambiguous coercive threats.

To dissuade major and emerging powers from developing capabilities that could threaten regional stability, to deter conflict, and to defeat aggression should deterrence fail, the United States is further diversifying its basing posture.

Based on the Department's Global Defense Posture Review, the United States will continue to adapt its global posture to promote constructive bilateral relations, mitigate anti-access threats and off set potential political coercion designed to limit U.S. access to any region. The United States will develop capabilities that would present any adversary with complex and multidimensional challenges and complicate its offensive planning efforts. These include the pursuit of investments that capitalize on enduring U.S. advantages in key strategic and operational areas, such as persistent surveillance and long-range strike, stealth, operational maneuver and sustainment of air, sea and ground forces at strategic distances, air dominance and undersea warfare.

These capabilities should preserve U.S. freedom of action and provide future Presidents with an expanded set of options to address all of the QDR focus areas and a wide range of potential future contingencies. The aim is to possess sufficient capability to convince any potential adversary that it cannot prevail in a conflict and that engaging in conflict entails substantial strategic risks beyond military defeat.

Consistent with this approach, shaping the choices of countries at strategic crossroads highlights the need for the following types of capabilities:

- Security cooperation and engagement activities including joint training exercises, senior staff talks, and officer and foreign internal defense training to increase understanding, strengthen allies and partners, and accurately communicate U.S. objectives and intent. This will require both new authorities and 21st century mechanisms for the interagency process.

- Considerably improved language and cultural awareness to develop a greater understanding of emerging powers and how they may approach strategic choices.

- Persistent surveillance, including systems that can penetrate and loiter in denied or contested areas.

- The capability to deploy rapidly, assemble, command, project, reconstitute, and re-employ joint combat power from all domains to facilitate assured access.

- Prompt and high-volume global strike to deter aggression or coercion, and if deterrence fails, to provide a broader range of conventional response options to the President.

This view of China, and the suggested U.S. response, is to some extent a prudent response to the unknown. There also, however, are serious risks in treating China as a potential threat when it may be possible to treat it as a partner, in failing to recognize that all of Chinese history combines to make it seek full status as a major military power, and in refusing to pay the domestic political cost of keeping U.S. commitments to Taiwan in strict proportion to its strategic value. The end result may ultimately do far more to encourage U.S. overstretch than the Iraq War and have far more dangerous results.

PARTNERSHIP IN OTHER AREAS

The nature of the partnerships the United States should build in other areas is more uncertain. U.S. ties to its allies are less formal and less well structured; future contingencies are more uncertain. At the same time, these are areas where the 2006 QDR pays far more attention to the need to work with other countries and indicates that the United States had learned several of the lessons outlined in the previous chapter.

Interoperability Initiatives

The QDR states that "US operational and force planning will consider a somewhat higher level of contributions from international allies and partners, as well as other Federal agencies, in surge operations ranging from homeland defense to irregular warfare and conventional campaigns. This assumption is consistent with the increased level of security cooperation and other activities to enable partners as required by the refined Force Planning Construct."[24]

The QDR also emphasizes the need to foster better working relationships with newer nontraditional allies:[25]

...the Department must be prepared to develop a new team of leaders and operators who are comfortable working in remote regions of the world, dealing with local and tribal communities, working with local networks to further U.S. and partner interests through personal engagement, persuasion and quiet influence—rather than through military force alone. To support this effort, new authorities are needed. During the Cold War the legal authorities for military action, intelligence, foreign military assistance and cooperation with foreign police and security services were separately defined and segregated from each other. Today, there is a need for U.S. forces to transition rapidly between these types of authorities in an agile and flexible manner, to meet the challenges of the 21st century.

Based on operational experiences of the last four years, the QDR recommends that Congress provide considerably greater flexibility in the U.S. Government's ability to partner directly with nations in fighting terrorists. For some nations, this begins with training, equipping and advising their security forces to generate stability and security within their own borders. For others, it may entail providing some assistance with logistics support, equipment, training and transport to allow them to participate as members of coalitions with the United States or its allies in stability, security, transition and reconstruction operations around the globe.

The Department will seek to:

- Establish a Defense Coalition Support Account to fund and, as appropriate, stockpile routine defense articles such as helmets, body armor and night vision devices for use by coalition partners.
- Expand Department authority to provide logistics support, supplies and services to allies and coalition partners, without reimbursement as necessary, to enable coalition operations with U.S. forces.
- Expand Department authority to lease or lend equipment to allies and coalition partners for use in military operations in which they are participating with U.S. forces.
- Expand the authorities of the Departments of State and Defense to train and equip foreign security forces best suited to internal counterterrorism and counter-insurgency operations. These may be non-military law enforcement or other security forces of the government in some nations.

The United States cannot count on success in these areas, however, unless it pays attention to the political and ideological lessons discussed in the previous chapter. It also needs to develop far more specific plans to create new forms of alliance and partnerships to deal with individual security tasks; there are many areas like creating a more stable security structure in the Gulf that require far more detailed planning to create better partners and alliances.

The United States also should not define interoperability in terms of the high-technology forces needed for the Cold War. It should seek interoperability in other missions, including asymmetric war, counterterrorism, counterinsurgency, peace-making, and humanitarian action. These are far cheaper areas for most allies to prepare for, and also areas where heavy U.S. forces are not suitable. It simply does not make sense to push allies to mirror image the United States when the end result may actually make them less useful at higher cost.

PLANNING AND PROGRESS IN COMPLEX CONTINGENCY OPERATIONS

As with the interagency process, the lack of standardized mechanisms for coordinating the planning and conduct of complex operations with coalition partners has prevented the United States from effectively and efficiently working with its allies. Given the nature of the post–Cold War security environment and the demand for the United States and its international partners to conduct operations that require political, military, economic, and humanitarian integration, consultation and coordination mechanisms should not be reinvented *ad hoc* for every new operation. While the purpose and rationale will certainly vary between operations—from preventing the use of WMD to fighting terrorism, rebuilding failed states, and preventing genocide—these operations require a level of organization beyond what the defense community is currently capable of providing.

The 2004 Center for Strategic and International Studies report, *Beyond Goldwater-Nichols* (BGN), made several recommendations for improving multinational interoperability. In addition to providing opportunities for civilian planners and operators to work alongside their foreign counterparts, the report recommended that Congress fund two international training and exercise programs to develop and institutionalize standard operating procedures for the planning and conduct of operations involving U.S. civilian and military personnel and their foreign counterparts.[26]

- The first program should target civilian and military planners at the headquarters level and should aim to establish civil-military mechanisms for coordinating planning among allies or coalition partners for a particular operation.
- The second program should involve field-level operators and should aim to refine civil-military coordination mechanisms for the coalition on the ground, based on best practices from past operations.

These programs could be hosted by the proposed Interagency Training Center and should be ongoing activities to ensure that the United States has a standard forum for establishing and refining standard operating procedures for multinational interoperability.

BGN also recommended that Congress increase U.S. funding for programs that support building the operational capabilities of allies and partners in priority task areas in complex operations. This is largely because multinational operations are likely to become more common in the future and because the United States has interests in helping its allies and potential coalition partners to enhance their capabilities, especially in areas where the United States does not have a comparative advantage and cannot afford to fill the need by itself. Funding could be targeted toward training and equipping international civilian police, as well as international constabulary and peacekeeping forces. The United States could also support the development of deployable civilian teams expert in areas ranging from justice reform and the rule of law to civil administration.[27]

Past Progress with Coalition Partners

In other cases, the United States should build on its past success in creating multinational interoperable forces and not rely on its own power-projection capabilities. America's most dependable allies in the current global war on terror have been committed to a program for more than 50 years to facilitate multinational operations. Known as ABCA (for the armies of America, Britain, Canada, and Australia, with New Zealand as an associate member), these armies have fought together in operations from Kosovo and Somalia to Afghanistan and Iraq.

The ABCA standardization program is undergoing its own transformation agenda as comprehensive requirements for combat interoperability emerge. In response to a 2002 top-to-bottom review to assess how to make the ABCA framework more relevant and responsive, ABCA nations proposed a radical restructuring of their program to respond to a post–Cold War world that is characterized by transnational, asymmetrical, and nonstate actors possibly engaging on more urbanized battlefields and possibly using weapons of mass destruction.[28]

ABCA's new approach aims to meet the next-generation concept of interoperability: the ability to fight together in a coalition, anywhere in the world, at any force level or structure. That is, ABCA will focus increasingly on integrating ABCA armies' capabilities in a joint environment that will optimize interoperability through collaboration and standardization. The new doctrine prioritizes clustering resources around identified interoperability gaps, particularly regarding battlefield operating systems. To these ends, with transformation goals analogous to those in the U.S. joint forces doctrine, the new ABCA program will focus on the full spectrum of coalition land operations in a joint and interagency environment.[29]

During operations in Afghanistan and Iraq, ABCA allies fought together almost seamlessly in several arenas. Special Operations Forces fighting alongside conventional units from the United States, Australia, and Great Britain engaged regular and paramilitary enemy forces in northern and western Iraq. U.S. regular and Special Operations Forces were interoperable with British forces in the Basra region, capturing the city and the al Faw Peninsula with the oil fields and the petroleum piers. Canada and New Zealand provided both Special Operations and regular forces to Operation Enduring Freedom in Afghanistan.[30]

The progress that ABCA has made in streamlining and transforming coalition doctrine to facilitate complex contingency operations provides a starting point for standardizing future military operations with other allies. Such standardization procedures will become increasingly important force enablers in the future. As written in the Chairman of the Joint Chiefs of Staff Instruction 3165.01, released January 24, 2006, in support of the activities of the Multinational Interoperability Council (MIC), it states the following:

> Interoperability with multinational partners is in the best interests of the United States Armed Forces. This policy is enunciated in various international agreements and policy documents. The level of interoperability to be achieved cannot be ascertained within a general statement of policy.

- CJCS policy encourages the joint Staff, combatant commands, Services, Defense agencies, and other DoD activities to participate in multinational organizations, with the objective of enhancing national security as expressed in the National Security Strategy and the supporting National Military Strategy.

- The degree of Military interoperability achieved is subject to resource, technical and policy considerations.

- Enhancing the planning and execution of multinational military operations is a key objective.

- Coalition interoperability is a continuing challenge, which could be enhanced via multinational for like the MIC.

The former British Army Chief, General Sir Roger Wheeler, emphasized the importance of interoperability in future warfighting. "There is simply no point, in my view, in developing battle-winning capabilities at the national level if it's muted through lack of interoperability in coalition."[31]

BROADER GRAND STRATEGIC LESSONS

In conclusion, there are broader grand strategic lessons that need to be learned about America's structure of alliances. As discussed in detail in Chapter 2, Iraq sends a warning about the dangers of American arrogance and that allies must not be treated as tools or proxies. The United States cannot focus on its ideological goals and ignore its allies' goals and needs. It needs to constantly reinforce individual partnerships rather than seek to transform the world.

Trust and commitment must be earned, and allies must be courted and won for each new contingency. With such preparations, other nations can be immensely valuable in reducing "overstretch," but only where they are true partners. The UN, other international organizations, and nongovernmental organizations can also have great value in some cases, but they are sources of help, not force multipliers or force substitutes.

At the same time, the United States must not wander off in search of enemies and new commitments. Iraq also teaches the dangers of committing U.S. forces to areas where conflicts are optional, not forced on the United States, and where there is no clear strategic interest proportionate to the risk. The United States does not need to engage everywhere in the world and should not let hope and ideology overrule realism and common sense. There are many areas, like much of the Caspian Sea region and Central Asia, where there is no reason to provoke Russia or China, and little to gain. Strategic neglect is often as valid a choice as strategic engagement, and some games are best won by refusing to play them.

Challenge Ten: The Challenge of Responsibility

The analysis of the previous challenges has been a practical exercise in complexity theory. Salvaging American defense requires new approaches to an extraordinarily wide range of issues, and integrating a wide range of activities both within the Department of Defense and the overall U.S. national security community.

It is easy to talk about defense transformation or reform in simplistic terms and ideological slogans or simply to go with the historical flow and avoid making truly difficult programming and management decisions. The fact remains that there is no royal road to making U.S. defense more effective, more efficient, or cheaper. Each of the preceding chapters has made it clear that progress is needed in many areas to address the current failures in the ways in which the United States chooses its strategy, the ways it plans and programs its military forces, and the ways it manages its manpower and defense budgets.

Iraq is only one of the problems the United States must deal with and is not the most serious problem the United States faces in force transformation and shaping an effective mix of strategy, force plans, programs, and budgets. U.S. policy makers cannot deal with issues like "overstretch" or force transformation in simple terms or by focusing on a few key aspects of the problem. All of the issues analyzed in this book are closely interlinked, and no matter how complex the range of challenges covered in this analysis may seem, U.S. policy makers must confront all of them simultaneously. Any effort to deal with them in terms of ideology or oversimplification has already produced a dangerous decline in America's national security position. It is not enough for America to be able to "walk and chew gum," it must also be able to play three-dimensional chess.

At the same time, the United States does not need massive new institutions, complex new procedures, new technologies, special cadres of trained personnel, or new studies to deal with its most serious security problems. The United States does need leaders with vision; but above all, it needs leaders who take responsibility for actually implementing fundamental reforms in the way it plans and uses its national security resources. It cannot go on taking half measures, denying the scale of existing problems, or deferring key issues. The United States must soon address major additional challenges like proliferation, reshaping "net-centric" and "human-centric" warfare into a "system-centric concept," developing all the capabilities needed for stability operations and nation building, the need to meet new developments in terrorism and asymmetric war, and a host of other issues.

SETTING KEY PRIORITIES FOR CHANGE

The success that the United States enjoyed after the end of the Cold War, and even at the beginning of the Iraq War, is rapidly eroding as is America's reputation and prestige. This is not the product of any one administration. Some of the driving failures discussed in previous chapters go back to mistakes made as early as the Kennedy Administration—if not before. The fact remains, however, that the United States has already wasted time and capital it cannot afford to waste and is on an unworkable path toward the future. This means that the United States must make the following major changes in its approach to national security:

- *The United States needs to integrate its efforts to shape its strategy, force plans, programs, and budgets:* Creating separate strategy documents almost ensures that they will fail to be fully and properly implemented and are never tested in terms of the ability to create practical and affordable force plans to implement them. Documents like the Quadrennial Defense Review (QDR), Joint Vision series, and various service strategy documents are exercises in futility. The same is true of force planning and force requirements documents that are not tightly constrained by the need for force plans and budgets. At the same time, budget-driven exercises hurt or cripple effective force development and planning.

- *The United States must revise its approach to war planning at many levels:* It needs far more realistic efforts to assess the cost-benefits of taking military action and to assess risks on an interagency basis. It needs to place more reliance on winning allied support and consensus. The wrong strategy and the wrong perception of the rationale and support for a war will almost inevitably create a strain on U.S. forces regardless of transformation. At the same time, it must plan from the start for both conventional and asymmetric conflict, and for the aftermath of defeating the enemy. Conflict termination, stability operations, and nation building are critical aspects of war and the key to obtaining successful grand strategic outcomes. This must include creating outcomes that maintain coalitions and alliances and not simply those that serve U.S. interests in a narrow sense.

- *While the United States must carry out a major transformation of its forces for a wide range of missions, that transformation must be both top to bottom and affordable:* As part of this transformation, it is clear that oversimplistic concepts like the "revolution in military affairs" and technology-oriented force transformation are not relevant, practical, or affordable. The United States must not simply talk about new threats and missions, it must have comprehensive force plans that are fully affordable to deal with them. Force transformation must be real and every aspect of actual plans and spending must reflect the effort to make it real. The QDR may lead to a workable plan, but it is not clear that it will produce a realistic future year defense plan.

- *The United States needs to reform its budget process and create an effective program budget that is mission oriented, projects costs at least five years into the future, and can be rapidly updated in a matter of days:* The internal divisions and rigidities in the U.S. programming and budgeting process are a bureaucratic nightmare inflicted on the Department of Defense by its own internal divisions and rigidities. The ruthless enforcement of single, integrated, computerized accounting and programming systems has been needed for years. The present program categories in the program budget make no sense in terms of most current needs and budgets, and the line item or "input" budgets required by Congress are dysfunctional except as a method of adding special appropriations and "pork" to the defense budget. Both military and civilian planners and system analysts need to work on a common integrated program and budget.

- *The United States needs to complete the transition to forces capable of both conventional and asymmetric warfare and to forces with rapid expeditionary capability without reliance on Reserves or excessive deployment times:* The United States cannot predict or choose the nature of future war. Iraq, Afghanistan, and the "war on terrorism" illustrate that asymmetric warfare is an ongoing reality. The Taiwan Strait, the Koreas, and Iran show, however, that the risk of conventional war is all too real. The United States also faces the risk of high-intensity asymmetric warfare in the form of major conflicts using weapons of mass destruction, and attacks on the global economy ranging from energy attacks to information warfare. The United States cannot base its future transformation efforts on any past war, including Iraq. It must deal with proliferation, asymmetric war, irregular war/terrorism, and disruption. The United States must constantly adapt to future possibilities; it cannot afford to remain in the past at any level.

- *Cost containment and performance metrics need to be ruthlessly enforced at every level:* There can be no separation between force requirements, procurement plans, and any other defense activity and the ongoing, near real-time enforcement of cost ceilings, performance milestones, and measures of effectiveness. The military must be held accountable from the Chairman of the Joint Chiefs down for ensuring that force costs and procurement costs are not allowed to escalate. Force plans must be practical and affordable. Service secretaries, Directors of Defense Research and Engineering (DDR&Es), and other senior policy makers must be held personally responsible for success. The same is true of the chief executive officers (CEOs) and top corporate personnel in the companies that contract with the Department of Defense. There must be direct and immediate personal penalties for failure.

- *Technology must become the tool of force planning and not its master:* The United States has obtained many benefits from advances in technology, but half a century of unrealistic searches for force multipliers, force transformation, and other technological achievements that are grossly undercosted, with sharply exaggerated warfighting benefits, and unrealistic development and production schedules have greatly increased the cost of U.S. forces, done much to disrupt effective force development, and turned much of the Department of Defense's procurement efforts into the equivalent of a liars' contest.

- *The United States needs to reexamine its approach to defense manpower to provide a zero-based examination of the role of active and reserve military personnel, career civilians, and contractors:* The Iraq War has not shown what the new balance of manpower resources should be, but it has clearly shown that the present balance is wrong. The total force concept that tied all major deployments to the use of both active and reserve forces did not make going to war harder; it just made it far slower and less efficient. The United States is also making trade-offs between military, career civilian, and contract personnel that seem to be far more matters of ideology than the result of a comprehensive cost-benefit analysis of given levels of military end strength, the value of career civilians, and the actual cost-performance of contractor personnel. The United States now seems reliant on a bloated, inefficient, and over-costly mix of contractor personnel for both peace and war.

- *The United States must develop an effective interagency process for national security planning and management and make it work:* The National Security Council needs clear lines of interagency authority to enforce cooperation at every level and ensure that the Department of Defense cannot bypass the policy-planning process, while civilian agencies must be organized to provide counterpart skills and personnel who are deployable and prepared to take the necessary risks. The civilian parts of the federal national security structure must become risk oriented and be prepared to carry out their functions even when they must go in harm's way. They must be ready to play a critical role in stability operations, nation building, and humanitarian operations in high-threat environments. It is particularly important that the State Department develop risk-oriented expertise and career patterns for such missions, along with several critical elements of the Department of Homeland Security (DHS).

- *Homeland defense needs to be planned, programmed, and budgeted on an integrated civil-military level:* Just as the military must be able to count on the support of civilian counterparts in key missions in war, the military must be part of a fully integrated approach to homeland defense and supporting DHS in domestic defense against terrorism and a wide range of recovery, humanitarian, and emergency missions. This requires more than an efficient assignment of roles and missions. It requires a major reexamination of the future role and organization of the National Guard and an integrated effort within DHS to create a single integrated plan, program, and budget for all dedicated interagency homeland defense activity.

- *Intelligence must serve warfighting, not be oriented toward the President or policy makers:* The recent reorganization of U.S. intelligence has given far too much weight to fixing problems by changing organization charts and creating clear lines of responsibility to the President. The bulk of intelligence users are in the field and need effective interagency efforts to "fuse" intelligence with plans and operations at the mission or combat level.

- *The United States needs to rethink its approach to NATO:* The best single way to minimize the burden of U.S. defense commitments is to limit the scale of U.S. action to what is truly necessary. The second best method is to rely as much on allied political, diplomatic, military, and economic support. The United States does need to make major changes in its traditional alliance structure. In the case of NATO, it needs to reestablish allied confidence in the United States and to stress the kind of interoperability that takes advantage of real-world allied capabilities and strengths, rather than seeks to make NATO forces mirror images of the United States. The United States needs to plan, however, for the fact that its primary areas of operation will probably be in the Middle East and Asia and that Britain will be the only European state capable and willing of sustained and consistent out-of-area operations.

- *The United States will probably see its alliances in Asia become steadily more important in security terms than NATO and its alliances with Europe:* Europe has not diminished in strategic importance since the end of the Cold War, but the risks to Europe and the need for U.S. involvement have sharply diminished, while those in Asia and the Middle East have not. The United States faces a future in which South Korea and Japan may well be its key allies in conventional warfighting and where Taiwan's failure to modernize its military forces and make them effective presents major and unnecessary risks. This shift to Asia reflects the continuing threat posed by North Korea and the uncertain nature of China's emergence as a major world power.

- *More broadly, the United States needs to rethink its approach to all of its formal and informal alliances and to interoperability and see them as integral parts of its efforts to deal with resource issues and overstretch:* In most cases involving asymmetric wars—as is the case in Afghanistan, Iraq, and many countries involved in the war on terrorism—the United States will need to rely on local forces and capabilities, many of which it will have to create or greatly improve on the scene. In many cases, this means allies with different religions, cultural values, and languages who do not wish to be transformed to have values similar to the United States. The United States must prepare for such warfare, particularly in the Middle East and in working with Islamic allies. It must also accept the fact that often such forces must take the lead as soon as possible and that the U.S. military will always be seen as an outside and alien force.

UNCERTAINTY AND COST

More broadly, this analysis provides two consistent warnings about how the United States must deal with its future strategic needs and cope with the risks of overstretch.

The first such warning is that the United States must plan for continuing uncertainty about the nature of future threats and war. Success in past conventional wars, and the Cold War, is already a failed recipe for the future. Moreover, the roles and missions of the Department of Defense will be in a constant state of flux for at least the next decade. The United States faces a volatile mix of threats that means no year will go by in which the United States will be able to avoid altering some aspects of its current plans and perceptions.

The second warning is one that both defense planners and defense reformers tend to forget. No matter what improvements the United States makes, the resulting plans and programs will still be costly, involve serious risk, and be experimental. Success will require making many future mistakes, and often involve considerable waste—even if the Department of Defense does learn how to manage. Any transformation plan or model for defense reform that depends on high levels of efficiency, cost-effectiveness, and "right-sizing" of U.S. forces is a dream that will collapse under its own weight. The United States can never get it exactly right; all it can do is to avoid getting it very wrong.

This need to hedge against uncertainty means the United States can never afford to size its forces in terms of some calculation about exactly how much is enough or what is needed. It cannot afford to simply have the critical minimum or what it knows is cost-effective. This goes against the grain of an ethic that constantly seeks to make new cuts to military spending and force size. The fact is, however, that the United States cannot succeed by focusing on finding ways of doing more and more with less and less—particularly if this unconsciously ends in trying to do absolutely everything with absolutely nothing.

The good news is that the United States has already emerged as the world's dominant power in ways that are eminently affordable in terms of the strains they impose on American labor, the gross domestic product (GDP), and the federal budget. The United States can easily afford to do more if it makes intelligence trade-offs that cap entitlements and a distorted health-care sector, and it will almost certainly have to do so. The bad news is that it must spend more as well as spend more wisely.

THE CHALLENGE OF RESPONSIBILITY

Increased spending, however, is scarcely the answer to the most serious problems in America's defense culture. America has had too many failures at the cabinet level and with an increasingly politicized top level of military command. As has been discussed in earlier chapters, the United States can deal with its strategic challenges, and the problems of force transformation and overstretch, only if it finds far more exacting ways of actually holding senior civilian and military policy makers responsible for achieving success, for realism and transparency in their action, and for solving key long-standing problems in areas like procurement and cost containment.

The U.S. government has made massive strategic mistakes at every stage of its actions in Iraq and at least some of the same mistakes in Afghanistan. Its strategic position has eroded in Korea, in dealing with the Taiwan Strait, and on a global level. Its overall management of manpower and procurement is at least as bad as any failed corporation or business scandal of the last decade.

In fact, it is hard to think of any American CEO in recent history that has done as bad a job of managing critical programs as what has become the norm for managing major defense procurement programs. Similar problems are emerging in managing the all-volunteer force structure and at least some aspects of military readiness. They clearly exist at the interagency level as well as in the Department of Defense.

U.S. national security management cannot be perfect, but it must at least be mediocre. No U.S. military service or major element of the Office of the Secretary of Defense can currently meet this test, nor can the present levels of efficiency and effectiveness in the interagency process. America is so wealthy that it can afford this, but wealth is not an excuse or rationale for what has happened.

In retrospect, the causes do not seem to lie in management systems, organization, or processes. They rather lie in a cumulative failure to hold senior decision makers accountable for problems and failure, and a tendency to blame either lower level personnel or current methods of organization and the "system." U.S. national security is good at rewarding success, and there have been many, but it seems to be equally good in rewarding failure—particularly at the level of the Assistant Secretary and two-star officers and above.

Changes to organization charts and processes cannot be the answer. Senior defense decision makers need to be held to a far higher standard of performance, as do the senior executives of the nation's defense industries and other players in the interagency process. The cult of the CEO is bad enough in industry, but it is inexcusable in defense. Failure must be followed by dismissal, and no part of the national security structure should be free of personal and public accountability at the top that is both demanding and ruthless.

Notes

CHAPTER 1

1. International Institute of Strategic Studies (IISS), *Military Balance 2004–2005,* Oxford, IISS, 2004, Table 38.

2. Department of Defense, Quadrennial Defense Review Report, Washington, Department of Defense, February 6, 2006, http://www.defenselink.mil/qdr/, p. 31.

3. See Col. Ernie Howard, "The Strategic Logic of Suicide Terror," Air University Warfare Studies Institute, April 2004.

4. Department of Defense, Quadrennial Defense Review Report, Washington, Department of Defense, February 6, 2006, http://www.defenselink.mil/qdr/, p. 24.

5. For the full text, see www.dtic.mil/whs/directives/corres/html/300005.htm.

6. U.S. Army Field Manual FM 3-24 and U.S. Marine Corps manual MCWP 3-33.5, *Counterinsurgency,* Washington, Department of Defense, December 2006.

CHAPTER 2

1. For many of the problems involved, see Robert M. Perito, "The Coalition Provisional Authority's Experience with Public Security in Iraq," Washington, U.S. Institute of Peace, Special Report, 137. April 2005.

2. Nina Serafino, Curt Tarnoff, and Dick K. Nanto, "U.S. Occupation Assistance: Iraq, Germany and Japan Compared," CRS Report for Congress, RL33331, March 23, 2006.

3. See the various reports listed on the Web page of the *Special Inspector General for Iraqi Reconstruction,* http://www.sigir.mil/.

4. Department of Defense, Global War on Terrorism, Casualties by Military Component —Active, Guard, and Reserve, October 7, 2001 through November 18, 2006, Defense Manpower Data Center, Statistical Information Analysis Division, November 24, 2006, http://siadapp.dior.whs.mil/personnel/CASUALTY/castop.htm.

5. Iraq Coalition Casualty Count, http://icasualties.org.oif/, December 28, 2006.

6. Edward Wong and Kirk Semple, "Civilians in Iraq Flee Mixed Areas as Killings Rise," *The New York Times,* April 2, 2006.

7. Jonathan Finer, "U.S. Troops Fatalities Hit A Low; Iraqi Deaths Soar," *Washington Post,* April 1, 2006.

8. Iraq Body Count, http://www.iraqbodycount.org/, August 4, 2006.

9. UN Assistance Mission for Iraq, *Human Rights Report,* September 1, 2006–October 31, 2006.

10. Iraqi Body Count, December 28, 2006.

11. For a detailed estimate of the problems in estimating casualties without actual surveys, and the probable lack of credibility in the higher estimated totals, see the work done by Royal Holloway at the University of London by Professor Michael Spagat, Sean Gourley, and Professor Neil Johnson, http://www.rhul.ac.uk/Economics/Research/conflict-analysis/iraq-mortality/index.html.

12. ABC News, December 20, 2006; Ann Scott Tyler, "Repeat Iraq Tours Raise Risk of PTSD, Army Finds," *Washington Post,* December 20, 2006, p. A19; Greg Zoroya, "Suicide Rate Spikes Among Troops Sent to Iraq War," *USA Today,* December 20, 2006, p. 8.

13. General Accounting Office, "Global War on Terrorism: DoD Needs to Improve the Reliability of Cost Data and Provide Additional Guidance to Control Costs," Washington, GAO-05-882, September 2005, p. 34; Amy Belasco, "The Cost of Iraq, Afghanistan, and Other Global War on Terror Operations Since 9/11," Washington, Congressional Research Service, RL33110, April 24, 2006, p. 10.

14. General Accounting Office, "Global War on Terrorism: DoD Needs to Improve the Reliability of Cost Data and Provide Additional Guidance to Control Costs," Washington, GAO-05-882, September 2005, p. 34.

15. Amy Belasco, "The Cost of Iraq, Afghanistan, and Other Global War on Terror Operations Since 9/11," Congressional Research Service, RL3311014, June 2006: 2–3.

16. Peter Cohn, "CRS: Wars Will Top $500B by Next Year," National Journal's Congress Daily AM, June 27, 2006; Rick Maze, "Extra Funds Push U.S. War Costs Beyond $500B Mark," *Defense News,* October 2, 2006.

17. Amy Belasco, "The Cost of Iraq, Afghanistan, and Other Global War on Terror Operations Since 9/11," Congressional Research Service, RL33110, September 22, 2006: 2–3.

18. Amy Belasco, "The Cost of Iraq, Afghanistan, and Other Global War on Terror Operations Since 9/11," Congressional Research Service, June 14, 2006: 6.

19. Amy Belasco, "The Cost of Iraq, Afghanistan, and Other Global War on Terror Operations Since 9/11," Congressional Research Service, June 14, 2006: 2–3.

20. Amy Belasco. "The Cost of Iraq, Afghanistan, and Enhanced Base Security Since 9/11," Congressional Research Service, October 7, 2005.

21. Amy Belasco, "The Cost of Iraq, Afghanistan, and Other Global War on Terror Operations Since 9/11," Congressional Research Service, June 14, 2006.

22. Amy Belasco, "The Cost of Iraq, Afghanistan, and Other Global War on Terror Operations Since 9/11," Congressional Research Service, June 14, 2006.

23. Amy Belasco, "The Cost of Iraq, Afghanistan, and Other Global War on Terror Operations Since 9/11," Congressional Research Service, June 14, 2006; Jonathan Weisman, "Unforeseen Spending on Materiel Pumps Up Iraq War Bill," *Washington Post,* April 20, 2006.

24. Amy Belasco, "The Cost of Iraq, Afghanistan, and Other Global War on Terror Operations Since 9/11," Congressional Research Service, June 14, 2006: 10 & 14.

25. For an overview of then current estimates, see Alan B. Krueger, "The Cost of Invading Iraq: Imponderables Meet Uncertainties," *New York Times,* March 30, 2006.

26. Jonathan Weisman, Unforeseen Spending on Materiel Pumps Up War Bill," *Washington Post,* April 20, 2006, p. 1; and "Projected Iraq War Costs Soar," *Washington Post,* April 27, 2006, p. 16.

27. For background on these issues, see Jonathan Weissman, "Unforeseen Spending on Material Pumps Up Iraq War Bill," *Washington Post,* April 20, 2006, p. A1.

28. For an overview of then current estimates, see Alan B. Krueger, "The Cost of Invading Iraq: Imponderables Meet Uncertainties," *New York Times,* March 30, 2006.

29. Amy Belasco, "The Cost of Iraq, Afghanistan, and Other Global War on Terror Operations Since 9/11," Congressional Research Service, RL33110, September 22, 2006: p. 3

30. Congressional Budget Office, "Additional Information About the Alternative Spending Path for Military Operations in Iraq and Afghanistan and for the War on Terrorism," CBO working Note, September 22, 2006; Luis E. Martinez, "The Rising $ Cost of Iraq and Afghanistan, $70 Billion More to be Requested," ABC News, February 2, 2006, 4:16 P.M.; Gail Russel Chaddock, "War Costs Irk Congress," *Christian Science Monitor,* February 21, 2006, p. 1; Dave Ahearn, "House Panel Advances Budget with $2.5 Trillion for Defense," *Defense Today,* March 30, 2006, p. 1; Tony Capaccio, "War Funds Request Setting Yearly Record, *Bloomberg News,* December 15, 2006.

31. See Congressional Budget Office, "Paying for Iraq's Reconstruction: An Update," CBO, December 8, 2006.

32. Matthew Cox, "U.S. Army Gets $17B To Reset Equipment," *Defense News,* October 9, 2006.

33. James Jay Carafano, "That Hollow Feeling," *New York Post,* September 29, 2006.

34. Peter Spiegel, "Army Warns Rumsfeld It's Billions Short," *Los Angeles Times,* September 25, 2006.

35. Nina Serafino, Curt Tarnoff, and Dick K. Nanto, "U.S. Occupation Assistance: Iraq, Germany and Japan Compared," Congressional Research Service, March 23, 2006.

36. Nina Serafino, Curt Tarnoff, and Dick K. Nanto, "U.S. Occupation Assistance: Iraq, Germany and Japan Compared," Congressional Research Service, March 23, 2006.

37. General Accounting Office, "Global War on Terrorism: DoD Needs to Improve the Reliability of Cost Data and Provide Additional Guidance to Control Costs," Washington, GAO-05-882, September 2005, p. 34; Amy Belasco, "The Cost of Iraq, Afghanistan, and Other Global War on Terror Operations Since 9/11," Washington, Congressional Research Service, RL33110, April 24, 2006, p. 10; Office of the Under Secretary of Defense (Comptroller), "National Defense Budget Estimates for FY2006," April 2006, Table 7.7.

38. Bill Gertz, "S. Korea to Get War Control Over US Troops in 3 Years," *Washington Times,* August 4, 2006, p. 5.fsd.

39. Richard Halloran, "US 'Turning Out the Lights' in S. Korea," *Honolulu Advertiser,* July 30, 2006.

40. Department of Defense, Quadrennial Defense Review Report, Washington, Department of Defense, February 6, 2006, http://www.defenselink.mil/qdr/, p. 31.

41. See the work of Richard F. Grimmett of the U.S. Congressional Research Service, including "Conventional Arms Transfers to Developing Nations, 1997–2004," Washington, Congressional Research Service, CRS RL33051, August 29, 2005.

42. Department of Defense, Quadrennial Defense Review Report, Washington, Department of Defense, February 6, 2006, http://www.defenselink.mil/qdr/, p. 24.

43. Energy Information Administration, *International Energy Outlook, 2005,* Washington, D.C., Department of Energy, pp. 7–8.

44. Based on the defense expenditure as a percent of GDP and federal budget data in Table 7-7 in Office of the Under Secretary of Defense (Comptroller), "National Defense Estimates for FY2007," March 2006.

CHAPTER 3

1. For a detailed analysis of such Congressional action, see Stephen Dagget, "Defense: FY2007 Authorization and Appropriations," Washington, Congressional Research Service, RL33405, October 19, 2006. Especially the tables in pages 70–72.

2. Congressional Budget Office, "The Budget and Economic Outlook, Fiscal Years 2007 to 2016," CBO, Washington, January 2006, p. 7.

3. Gopal Ratnam and William Matthews. "DoD Looses Supplemental Rules." *Defense News,* November 11, 2006.

4. Andrew Taylor, "Democrats Expected to OK Bulk of War Funding," *Miami Herald,* December 1, 2006; Richard Wolf, "Military May Ask $127 Billion for Wars," *USA Today,* November 17, 2006, p. 1; "Incoming Senate Leader Wants $75 Billion More for U.S. Military," *Wall Street Journal,* November 15, 2006.

5. William Matthews, "Bush Says He May Ignore New War-Funding Law," *Defense News,* October 23, 2006.

6. Gopal Ratnam and William Matthews, "DoD Looses Supplemental Rules," *Defense News,* November 11, 2006.

7. Ibid.

8. Ibid.

9. Office of the Under Secretary of Defense (Comptroller), National Defense Budget Estimates for FY2007, Washington, Department of Defense, March 2006, Table 6-11.

10. Congressional Budget Office, "Long Term Implications of Current Defense Plans: Summary Update for Fiscal Year 2007," Washington, CBO, October 2006, p. 2.

11. Office of the Under Secretary of Defense (Comptroller), National Defense Budget Estimates for FY2007, Washington, Department of Defense, March 2006, Table 7-7, p. 217.

12. Ibid.

13. For a detailed analysis of such Congressional action, see Stephen Dagget, "Defense: FY2007 Authorization and Appropriations," Washington, Congressional Research Service, RL33405, October 19, 2006.

14. Office of the Under Secretary of Defense (Comptroller), National Defense Budget Estimates for FY2007, Washington, Department of Defense, March 2006, Table 7-7.

15. Office of the Under Secretary of Defense (Comptroller), National Defense Budget Estimates for FY2006, Washington, Department of Defense, April 2005, Table 7-7.

16. Office of the Under Secretary of Defense (Comptroller), National Defense Budget Estimates for FY2007, Washington, Department of Defense, March 2006, Table 7-7.

17. Congressional Budget Office, "Long Term Implications of Current Defense Plans: Summary Update for Fiscal Year 2007," Washington, CBO, October 2006, p. 3.

18. Office of the Under Secretary of Defense (Comptroller), National Defense Budget Estimates for FY2006, Washington, Department of Defense, April 2005, Table 7-7.

19. Office of the Under Secretary of Defense (Comptroller), National Defense Budget Estimates for FY2007, Washington, Department of Defense, March 2006, Table 7-7.

20. Office of the Under Secretary of Defense (Comptroller), National Defense Budget Estimates for FY2007, Washington, Department of Defense, March 2006, Table 7-6.

21. Includes the unemployed.

22. Office of the Under Secretary of Defense (Comptroller), National Defense Budget Estimates for FY2007, Washington, Department of Defense, March 2006, Table I-10.

23. Greg Jaffe, "U.S. Army Still Faces Cash Crunch, Despite Its $168 Billion Budget," *Wall Street Journal,* December 13, 2006, p. 14.

24. Ibid.

25. Congressional Budget Office, *Growth in Medical Spending by the Department of Defense,* September 2003, pp. 1–6.

26. Ibid.

27. Congressional Budget Office, "The Budget and Economic Outlook, Fiscal Years 2007 to 2016," CBO, Washington, January 2006, p. 7.

28. Congressional Budget Office, "Long Term Implications of Current Defense Plans: Summary Update for Fiscal Year 2007," Washington, CBO, October 2006, pp. 4–13.

29. Ibid., p. 6.

30. Ibid., pp. 8–10.

31. Luis E. Martinez, "Army and Marines Increase Size," ABC News, 10:40 A.M., January 11, 2007.

32. Office of the Under Secretary of Defense (Comptroller), National Defense Budget Estimates for FY2007, Washington, Department of Defense, March 2006, Table 6-11, pp. 128–129.

33. Greg Jaffe, "U.S. Army Still Faces Cash Crunch, Despite Its $168 Billion Budget," *Wall Street Journal,* December 13, 2006, p. 14.

34. Office of the Under Secretary of Defense (Comptroller), "National Defense Budget Estimates for FY2006", Washington, Department of Defense, April 2005, Tables 6.8 and 6.11.

35. Congressional Budget Office, "Long Term Implications of Current Defense Plans: Summary Update for Fiscal Year 2007," Washington, CBO, October 2006, pp. 13–15.

36. Comptroller, Office of the Under Secretary of Defense, *National Defense Budget Estimates for FY 2006,* March 2006, p. 67.

37. Statement by General Peter J. Schoomaker, "The Army's Reset Strategy and Plans for Funding Reset Requirements," testimony before the House Committee on Army Services, June 27, 2006.

38. Ann Scott Tyson, "U.S. Army Battling to Save Equipment," *Washington Post,* December 5, 2006, p. A1; Greg Jaffe, "U.S. Army Still Faces Cash Crunch, Despite Its $168 Billion Budget," *Wall Street Journal,* December 13, 2006, p. 14.

39. Ann Scott Tyson, "U.S. Army Battling to Save Equipment," *Washington Post,* December 5, 2006, p. A1; Matt Kelley, "Wars Wearing Down Military Gear at Cost of About $2 Billion a Month," *USA Today,* November 29, 2006, p. 1.

40. Greg Jaffe, "U.S. Army Still Faces Cash Crunch, Despite Its $168 Billion Budget," *Wall Street Journal,* December 13, 2006, p. 14.

41. Richard Whittle, "U.S. Air Force Loses Out in Iraq War," Christian Science Monitor, December 19, 2006.

42. Andrew Feickert, "U.S. Army and Marine Corps Equipment Requirements: Background and Issues," Washington, Congressional Research Service, RL33757, December 20, 2006. Also see U.S. Government Accountability Office, "Defense Logistics: Preliminary Observations on Equipment Reset Challenges and Issues for the Army and Marine Corps, Washington, GAO-06-604T, March 30, 2006.

43. Andrew Feickert, "U.S. Army and Marine Corps Equipment Requirements: Background and Issues," Washington, Congressional Research Service, RL33757, December 20, 2006, p. 22; Statement by General Peter J. Schoomaker, "The Army's Reset Strategy and Plans for Funding Reset Requirements," testimony before the House Committee on Army Services, June 27, 2006.

44. U.S. Government Accountability Office, "Reserve Forces: An Integrated Plan is Needed to Address Army Reserve Personnel and Equipment Shortages, Washington, GAO-05-660, July 2005, p. 15.

45. Steven M. Kosiak, "Analysis of the FY2006 Defense Budget Request," Center for Strategic and Budgetary Assessments, 2005, pp. 13–14.

46. Office of the Under Secretary of Defense (Comptroller), "National Defense Budget Estimates for FY2007, March 2006.

47. See Stephen Dagget, "Defense: FY2007 Authorization and Appropriations," Washington, Congressional Research Service, RL33405, October 19, 2006, especially pages 7 and 70.

48. Office of the Under Secretary of Defense (Comptroller), "National Defense Budget Estimates for FY2007, March 2006, p. 207.

49. Ibid.

50. Ibid., p. 216.

51. Ibid.

52. Adapted from Office of the Under Secretary of Defense (Comptroller), "National Defense Budget Estimates for FY2007, March 2006, pp. 4 and 5.

53. Congressional Budget Office, "The Budget and Economic Outlook: Fiscal Years 2007–2016," January 2006; and Donald B. Marron, "The Budget and Economic Outlook: Fiscal Years 2007–2016," testimony before the Committee on the Budget, U.S. Senate, February 2, 2006.

54. Marron, "The Budget and Economic Outlook," p. 5.

55. Ibid.

56. Ibid., p. 4.

57. Ibid.

58. Congressional Budget Office, "The Budget and Economic Outlook: Fiscal Years 2007 to 2016," p. 19.

59. Ibid., p. 2.

60. Donald B. Marron, Acting director, "The ABCs of Long-Term Budget Challenges, Washington, Congressional Budget Office, December 8, 2006; also see Brian W. Cashell; "The Economics of the Federal Budget Deficit," Washington, Congressional Research Service, RL31235. October 6, 2006.

61. Marc Labonte, "Social Security and Medicare: The Economic Implications of Current Policy," Washington, Congressional Research Service, RL32747. January 24, 2006.

62. Concord Coalition baseline estimate, http://www.concordcoalition.org/issues/fedbudget/charts/0601-plausible-baseline.pdf.

63. U.S. Government Accountability Office, "21st Century Challenges: Reexamining the Base of the Federal Government, Washington, GAO-05-3255, corrected edition of March 4, 2005.

64. Ibid., pp. 7–8.

65. Alice M. Riviln and Isabel Sawhill, *Restoring Fiscal Sanity—2005: Meeting the Long-Range Challenge,* Washington, Brookings Institution, 2005.

66. U.S. Government Accountability Office, "21st Century Challenges, pp. 7–8.

67. Congressional Budget Office, "The Budget and Economic Outlook: Fiscal Years 2007 to 2016," p. 23.

68. Ibid., pp. 21–24.

69. Ibid., p. 23.

70. Marron, "The Budget and Economic Outlook," p. 5.

71. Congressional Budget Office, "The Long Term Budget Outlook," December 2005, p. 19.

72. Marron, "The Budget and Economic Outlook," p. 3.

73. Congressional Budget Office, "The Long Term Budget Outlook," December 2005, pp. 29 and 30.

74. Ibid., p. 19.

75. Ibid., p. 31.

76. Congressional Budget Office, "The Budget and Economic Outlook: Fiscal Years 2007–2016," January 2006, p. 9.

CHAPTER 4

1. Luis E. Martinez, "Army and Marines Increase Size," ABC News, 10:40 A.M., January 11, 2007.

2. Ann Scott Tyson and Josh White. "Wars Strains US Military Capability, Pentagon Reports," *Washington Post,* May 3, 2005, A6.

3. Office of the Under Secretary of Defense (Comptroller), "National Defense Budget Estimates for FY2007, March 2006, pp. 115 and 133.

4. David S. Cloud, "Military Eases Its Rules for Mobilizing Reserves," *New York Times,* January 12, 2007.

5. Patrik Jonsson, "Third Round in Iraq to Test US Troops," *Christian Science Monitor,* January 9, 2007, p. 1.

6. Percentages based on the count in Iraq Coalition Casualty Count, September 4, 2006, http://icasualties.org/oif/.

7. Mark Benjamin. "2,000 Dead? Who Cares? Why Is the Country so Oblivious to the Iraq War's Casualties?" *Salon.com,* October 10, 2005.

8. Jack Kelly, "Military Mockery" *Pittsburgh Post-Gazette,* December 3, 2006.

9. For typical reporting on these problems, see Barbara Slavin, "Reserve Troops' Job Woes Increase," *USA Today,* December 8, 2006, p. 1; Kevin Johnson, "Impact of Police Being Sent to Iraq Felt on Street," *USA Today,* December 8, 2006, p. 18. The stress over overdeployment sharply increases job retention problems after more than one deployment every four years, and it has a significant impact on divorce.

10. Greg Jaffe, "U.S. Army Still faces Cash Crunch, Despite Its $168 Billion Budget," *Wall Street Journal,* December 13, 2006, p. 14.

11. Jay Bookman, "Ominously, Army Recruiting Tumbles," *Atlanta Journal-Constitution,* May 9, 2005, p. 11.

12. "Poll: Majority of Americans Want Withdrawal Plan for Iraq," *USA Today,* June 26, 2006, http://www.usatoday.com/news/world/iraq/2006-06-26-iraq-poll_x.htm.

13. Lydia Saad, "Military Again Tops 'Confidence in Institutions' List," *Gallup News Service,* June 1, 2005.

14. David W. Moore, "Public: Pullout From Iraq Would be Harmful to U.S.," *Gallup News Source,* July 1, 2005.

15. Richard Morin, "Majority of Americans Believe Iraq Civil War Is Likely," *Washington Post,* Monday, March 6, 2006.

16. "U.S. Troops in Iraq: 72% Say End War in 2006," *Zogby International,* poll released February 28, 2006, http://www.zogby.com/news/ReadNews.dbm?ID=1075.

17. "Poll: Americans Pessimistic On Iraq," *CBS News,* March 13, 2006, http://www.cbsnews.com/stories/2006/03/13/opinion/polls/main1396372.shtml.

18. Steven Kull, *Americans on Iraq: Three Years On,* report on poll conducted by World Public Opinion, March 15, 2006.

19. Dave Moniz, "Army Plans to Test Another Increase in Recruit Bonuses," *USA Today,* May 5, 2005, p. 5.

20. Bob Deans, "Army Blitz to Fight Dip in Recruits," *Atlanta Journal-Constitution,* June 20, 2005, p. 1.

21. Dave Moniz, "National Guard Triples Bonuses for Some Recruits," *USA Today,* December 16, 2004.

22. Thomas M. Defrank, "Heavy Toll on Guard in Iraq War," *New York Daily News,* July 5, 2005.

23. Ibid.

24. General Peter J. Schoomaker, "Hearing on the Status of the U.S. Army and Marine Corps in Fighting the Global War on Terrorism," Senate Armed Services Committee, June 30, 2005.

25. Defrank, "Heavy Toll on Guard in Iraq War."

26. Michael Kilian, "Army Study: US Facing Hard Choices," *Chicago Tribune,* July 12, 2005.

27. U.S. Army Recruitment and Retention Fact Sheet," June 9, 2005.

28. "Army National Guard Seen Missing Recruit Goals," *Associated Press,* September 24, 2004.

29. Ibid.

30. U.S. Army Recruitment and Retention Fact Sheet."

31. Robert Burns, "Guard, Reserve Iraq Death Toll Declines," CBS News, August 25, 2006, http://www.cbsnews.com/stories/2006/08/25/ap/national/mainD8JNM8100.shtml.

32. Interview with Secretary of the Army, Francis Harvey, "An Expectation of 'Less Reliance' on Guard, Reserve," *The Forum,* May 5, 2005, p. 13; and Bradley Graham and Josh White, "National Guard Troops in Iraq," *Washington Post,* July 1, 2005, p. 17.

33. Unattributed, "Army and Marines Fall Short of Recruiting Goals.," *USA Today,* May 3, 2005, p. 5.

34. General Hagee, "Hearing on the Status of the U.S. Army and Marine Corps in Fighting the Global War on Terrorism," Senate Armed Services Committee, *Gallup News Service,* June 30, 2005.

35. Dave Moniz, "Army Bonuses May Rise to $40K," *USA Today,* June 20, 2005, p. 1.

36. Spc. Maria Mengrone, "Task Force Baghdad Tops Reenlistment Goals," Media Release, HQ-MND Baghdad, September 8, 2005.

37. Ann Scott Tyson, "Rumsfeld: Army Not 'Broken,'" *Washington Post,* January 26, 2006, p. A18.

38. Ann Scott Tyson, "Army Having Difficulty Meeting Goals in Recruiting," *Washington Post,* February 21, 2005, p. A01.

39. Interview with Secretary of the Army, Francis Harvey, "An Expectation of 'Less Reliance' on Guard, Reserve," *The Forum,* May 5, 2005, p. 13.

40. Charles S. Abell, "Hearing on the Status of the US Army and Marine Corps in Fighting the Global War on Terrorism, Senate Armed Services Committee," June 30, 2005.

41. Robert Novak, "Army's Recruitment Crisis Deepens," *Chicago-Sun Times,* May 26, 2005.

42. Mark Benjamin, "Out of Jail, into the Army," *Salon.com,* February 2, 2006.

43. Dave Moniz, "Army Plans to Test Another Increase in Recruit Bonuses," *USA Today,* May 5, 2005.

44. Robert Burns, "For 2005, Only Army Missed Its Recruiting Goal among U.S. Military Services," *Associated Press,* October 11, 2005.

45. Ann Scott Tyson, "Army Guard Refilling Its Ranks," *Washington Post,* March 12, 2006, p. A1.

46. Greg Jaffe, "U.S. Army Still Faces Cash Crunch, Despite Its $168 Billion Budget," *Wall Street Journal,* December 13, 2006, p. 14.

47. David Axe, "Military Meets Most Recruiting Goals," *Military.com,* October 27, 2006, http://www.military.com/features/0,15240,117873,00.html.

48. Associated Press, "Army Guard Recruiting Recovers from 2005, Barely Missing Its Goal," *USA Today,* October 4, 2006, p. 5.

49. Rick Sallinger, "CBS4 Investigates Army Recruits' 'Moral Waivers,'" *CBS News,* November 20, 2006, http://cbs4denver.com/investigates/local_story_325001958.html.

50. "Troops Recruitment at a High," *Long Island Newsday,* December 13, 2006, p. 28.

51. General Peter J. Schoomaker, "Hearing on the Status of the U.S. Army and Marine Corps in Fighting the Global War on Terrorism," Senate Armed Services Committee, June 30, 2005.

52. "U.S. Army Recruitment and Retention Fact Sheet," June 9, 2005.

53. Mark Benjamin, "Out of Jail, into the Army," *Salon.com,* February 2, 2006.

54. Associated Press, "Military Candidates Fall Short," *Washington Times,* March 13, 2006, p. 9.

55. Benjamin, "Out of Jail, into the Army."

56. Tom Vanden Brook, "For Older Warriors, Experience Beats Athleticism," *USA Today,* March 15, 2006.

57. Lisa Burgess, "Army Raises Maximum Enlistment Age," *Stars and Stripes,* June 23, 2006, http://www.military.com/features/0,15240,102539,00.html.

58. Douglas Belkin, "Struggling for Recruits, Army Relaxes Its Rules," *Boston Globe,* February 20, 2006, p. 1.

59. Greg Jaffe, "U.S. Army Still Faces Cash Crunch, Despite Its $168 Billion Budget," *Wall Street Journal,* December 13, 2006, p. 14.

60. U.S. Department of Defense, Office of the Assistant Secretary of Defense (Public Affairs), News Release, "DOD Announces Recruiting and Retention Numbers for June," July 11, 2005, http://www.defenselink.mil/releases/2005/nr20050711-3941.html.

61. U.S. Department of Defense, Office of the Assistant Secretary of Defense (Public Affairs), News Release, "DOD Announces Recruiting and Retention Numbers for October," November 10, 2005, http://www.defenselink.mil/releases/2005/nr20051110-5089.html.

62. U.S. Department of Defense, Office of the Assistant Secretary of Defense (Public Affairs), News Release, "DOD Announces Recruiting and Retention Numbers for February," March 10, 2006, http://www.defenselink.mil/releases/2006/nr20060310-12635.html.

63. Bill Nichols, "Fewer Troops Desert Since 9/11," *USA Today,* March 7, 2006, p. 1.

64. Brian MacQuarrie, "Fewer Applying to US Military Academies, Observers Cite Iraq Conflict, Decline from Post-9/11 Surge," *Boston Globe,* June 13, 2005, p. A1.

65. Mark Mazzetti, "Army's Rising Promotion Rate Called Ominous," *Los Angeles Times,* January 30, 2006, p. 1.

66. Ibid.

67. Kate Wiltrout, "Navy Pilots Debate Taking $125,000 Bonus or Running," *Norfolk Virginian-Pilot,* February 20, 2006.

68. Bob Deans, "Officers Leave Army Hurting," *Austin American-Statesman,* November 5, 2006, p. 13.

69. Robert Burns, "Army: Young Blacks and Females Are Less Willing to Join, Fearing Combat," *The Associated Press,* March 8, 2005.

70. Ibid.

71. Ibid.

72. Burns, "Army: Young Blacks and Females"; and GfK Custom Research, Inc., "U.S. Military Image Study: for U.S. Army," August 4, 2004, http://dccw.hqda.pentagon.mil/downloads/Army/ArmyEquityStudyConDeck1.pdf.

73. Dave Moniz, "Opportunities, Opposition to Iraq War Cut into Recruiting," *USA Today,* November 4, 2005.

74. Lizette Alvarez, "Army Effort to Enlist Hispanics Draws Recruits, and Criticism," *New York Times,* February 9, 2006, http://www.nytimes.com/2006/02/09/national/09recruit.html?ex=1297141200&en=36fc581180571a86&ei=5088&partner=rssnyt&emc=rss.

75. Moniz, "Opportunities, Opposition."

76. "Modest Election Optimism, Positive Views of Iraq Troop Training, Public Unmoved by Washington's Rhetoric on Iraq," *The Pew Research Center,* December 14, 2005, p. 4.

77. Drew Brown, "Fewer African Americans Enlisting; Iraq War a Factor—Army Has Depended on Blacks to Meet its Recruiting Goals," *Knight Ridder Newspapers,* December 22, 2005, p. A6.

78. The Federal News Service, "Hearing of the Personnel Subcommittee of the House Armed Service Committee: The Adequacy of Army Forces," transcript, February 2, 2005.

79. Charlie Savage and Bryan Bender, "As Bush Calls for More to Sign up, Military Recruitment Lags," *Boston Globe,* June 30, 2005; and Jeffery Jones, "Many Americans Reluctant to Support Their Child Joining Military," June 22, 2005.

80. Reuters, "US Army Misses 4th Monthly Recruiting Goal in a Row," *Yahoo News,* June 8, 2005.

81. Carol Ann Alaimo, "Army Helps Couples Stressed by Iraq Duty," *Arizona Daily Star,* February 21, 2006, p. 1.

82. "May 2004 Status of Forces Survey of Reserve Component Members: Leading Indicators," Defense Manpower Data Center, released July 26, 2004.

83. Ibid.

84. Rick Jervis, "Army, Marine Recruiters Shift Focus to Wary Parents," *USA Today*, April 5, 2005, p. 1A.

85. Barbara Slavin, "Reserve Troops' Job Woes Increase," *USA Today*, December 8, 2006, p. 1.

86. Kevin Johnson, "Impact of Police Being Sent to Iraq Felt on Street," *USA Today*, December 8, 2006, p. 18.

87. Ann Scott Tyson, "Two Years Later, Iraq War Drains Military," *Washington Post*, March 19, 2005.

88. Sylvia Moreno, "'I'm Not Going to Come Home': One Marine's Third Iraq Tour," *Washington Post*, July 5, 2005, p. A01.

89. William J. Perry, *The U.S. Military: Under Strain and at Risk*, The National Security Advisory Group, January 2006.

90. Lee Hockstader, "Army Stops Many Soldiers From Quitting," *Washington Post*, December 29, 2003, p. A01.

91. The Federal News Service, "Hearing of the Personnel Subcommittee of the House Armed Service Committee: The Adequacy of Army Forces," transcript, February 2, 2005.

92. Office of the Assistant Secretary of Defense, Reserve Affairs briefing to CSIS, June 2004.

93. Office of the Secretary of Defense Reserve Forces Policy Board, "Mobilization Reform: A Compilation of Significant Issues, Lessons Learned and Studies Developed since September 11, 2001," October 2003, p. 3.

94. Government Accountability Office, *Reserve Forces: An Integrated Plan Is Needed to Address Army Reserve Personnel and Equipment Shortages*, July 2005, p. 1.

95. Francis J. Harvey and Peter J. Schoomaker, *2005 Posture Statement*, U.S. Army, February 6, 2005, p. ii.

96. Ibid., p. 8.

97. Ibid., p. ii.

98. U.S. Department of Defense, *2006 Quadrennial Defense Review Report*, February 6, 2006, p. 43.

99. Janet St. Laurent, *Force Structure: Preliminary Observations on Army Plans to Implement and Fund Modular Forces*, Government Accountability Office, March 16, 2005, p. 5.

100. U.S. Department of State, *Department of Defense Report: Army Not Broken (U.S. Military Capable of Meeting Global Tasks, Rumsfeld Says)*, distributed by the Bureau of International Information Programs, January 25, 2006.

101. *Army Strategic Planning Guidance 2005*, January 15, 2005, p. 9.

102. Andrew Feickert, *U.S. Army's Modular Redesign: Issues for Congress*,, Congressional Research Service, updated May 20, 2005, p. 3.

103. Ibid., pp. 3–4.

104. Elaine M. Grossman, "Study Finds Army Transformation Plan Weakens Combat Capability," *Inside the Pentagon*, January 26, 2005, p. 1.

105. Janet St. Laurent, *Force Structure: Preliminary Observations on Army Plans to Implement and Fund Modular Forces*, Government Accountability Office, March 16, 2005, p. 6.

106. Feickert, *U.S. Army's Modular Redesign*, pp. 4–5.

107. Grossman, "Study Finds Army Transformation Plan," p. 1.

108. Department of Defense, "President Bush's FY2007 Defense Budget," February 6, 2006.

109. Department of Defense, "Quadrennial Defense Review Results," February 3, 2006.

110. U.S. Department of Defense, *2006 Quadrennial Defense Review Report,* February 6, 2006, pp. 77–78.

111. Ibid., pp. 78–79.

112. Daniel Friedman, "Pentagon Eyes Civilian Workers for Overseas Posts," *Defense News,* October 23, 2006.

113. Government Accountability Office, "Converting Some Support Officer Positions to Civilian Status Could Save Money," October 1996.

114. Government Accountability Office, "Greater Reliance on Civilians in Support Roles Could Provide Significant Benefits," October 19, 1994.

115. Government Accountability Office, "Contractors Provide Vital Services to Deployed Forces but Are Not Adequately Addressed in DOD Plans," June 2003.

116. Government Accountability Office, "Greater Reliance on Civilians."

117. Business Executives for National Security, "Outsourcing and Privatizing of Defense Infrastructure," 1997.

118. Business Executives for National Security, "Defense Department Jobs in Transition," 1999.

119. Fairnet, http://web.lmi.org/fairnet/faq.htm#4 (accessed August 1, 2005).

120. Congressional Research Service Report for Congress (2001), "Foreign Affairs: Defense, and Trade Policy: Key Issues in the 107th Congress."

121. Congressional Research Service Report for Congress (2003), "Foreign Affairs: Defense, and Trade: Key Issues for the 108th Congress."

122. Ibid.

123. Ibid.

124. Government Accountability Office, "DOD Needs to Conduct a Data-Driven Analysis of Active Military Personnel Levels to Implement Defense Strategy," February 2005, pp. 17–18.

125. Ibid., p. 4.

126. Ibid., pp. 35–36.

127. Ibid., pp. 3–4.

128. Bill Sizemore and Joanne Kinberlin, "Blackwater: On the Front Lines," *The Virginian-Pilot,* July 25, 2006.

129. U.S. Army, *Army Field Manual 100-10-2: Contracting Support on the Battlefield,* August 4, 1999, Appendix F.

130. U.S. Department of Defense, *DOD Instruction 3020.41: Contractor Personnel Authorized to Accompany the U.S. Armed Forces,* October 3, 2005, pp. 8–9.

131. Ibid., p. 7.

132. U.S. Army, *Army Regulation 715-9: Contractors Accompanying the Force,* October 29, 1999, Section 3-1, g.

133. U.S. Department of Defense, *DOD Instruction 3020.41,* p. 19.

134. Griff Witte and Renae Merle, "Contractors Face More Scrutiny, Pinched Purses," *Washington Post,* November 8, 2006, p. D01.

135. Department of Defense, "President Bush's FY2007 Defense Budget," February 6, 2006.

136. Office of Management and Budget, 2005 Web site report on DOD trends since 2001, http://www.whitehouse.gov/omb/budget/fy2005/defense.html.

137. Ibid.

138. "Body Armor and Medicine Save Lives in Iraq," *ABC News Online,* January 30, 2006, http://abcnews.go.com/GMA/OnCall/story?id=1556540 (accessed February 13, 2006).

139. Craig Gordon, "Ailing Vets Overwhelming System," *Long Island Newsday,* March 20, 2006.

140. Ibid.

141. Ann Scott Tyson, "Repeat Iraq Tours Raise Risk of PTSD, Army Finds," *Washington Post,* December 20, 2006, p. A19.

142. Thomas B. Edsall, "VA Faces $2.6 Billion Shortfall in Medical Care," *Washington Post,* June 29, 2005, p. A19.

143. "Veterans Get Nearly $81 Billion in Historic FY 07 Plan," United States Department of Veterans Affairs Web site, February 6, 2006, http://www1.va.gov/opa/pressrel/PressArtInternet.cfm?id=1075 (accessed February 13, 2006).

144. Dale Eisman, "Increase in Military Retirees' Health Premiums Appears Dead," *Norfolk Virginian-Pilot,* March 15, 2006.

145. "Military Retirees' Health Care May Rise," *New York Times on the Web,* February 21, 2006.

146. Congressional Budget Office, "Long Term Implications of Current Defense Plans: Summary Update for Fiscal Year 2007," Washington, CBO, October 2006, p. 10.

147. Stephen Barr, "Plan to Raise Military Retirees' Health Costs Faces a Tough Fight," *Washington Post,* March 16, 2006, p. D4.

148. House Committee on National Security, "Military Readiness 1997: Rhetoric and Reality," April 9, 1997, p.1.

149. Peter Brownfield, "Debate Over Size, Shape of Army," *FoxNews.com,* August 30, 2004, http://www.foxnews.com/printer_friendly_story/0,3566,130541,00.html.

150. The White House, Office of the Press Secretary, "Executive Order Ordering the Ready Reserve of the Armed Forces to Active Duty and Delegating Certain Authorities to the Secretary of Defense and the Secretary of Transportation," September 14, 2001.

151. Congressional Research Service, "Defense: FY2006 Authorization and Appropriations," updated November 17, 2005, pp. 33–34.

152. Greg Jaffe, "Army Weights Slower Troop Growth to Keep Modernization on Track," *Wall Street Journal,* December 7, 2005, p. 3.

153. Congressional Research Service, "Defense: FY2006 Authorization and Appropriations," pp. 33–34.

154. Ann Scott Tyson, "Rumsfeld: Army Not 'Broken,'" *Washington Post,* January 26, 2006, p. A18.

155. Office of the Under Secretary of Defense for Personnel and Readiness, *Defense Manpower Requirements Report, Fiscal Year 2005,* March 2004, p. 11.

156. U.S. Department of Defense, *2006 Quadrennial Defense Review Report,* February 6, 2006, p. 43.

157. Thom Shanker and Michael R. Gordon, "Strained, Army Looks to Guard for More Relief," *New York Times,* September 22, 2006, p. 1.

158. Ann Scott Tyson, "Possible Iraq Deployments Would Stretch Reserve Force," *Washington Post,* November 5, 2006, p. 1.

159. Ann Scott Tyson, "US Extends Iraq Tour for Another Army Unit," *Washington Post,* September 26, 2006, p. 16.

160. Ton Vanden Brook, "Army Shifts to Ease Combat Burden," *USA Today,* October 27, 2006, p. 1.

161. Remarks by Chief of Staff of the Army, General Peter J. Schoomaker, "Operation Iraqi Freedom Force Rotation Plan," House Armed Services Committee Hearing, January 28, 2004.

162. Matthew Cox and Sean D. Naylor, "Calls for Bigger US Army on the Rise," *Defense News,* October 16, 2006.

163. Ann Scott Tyson, "General Says Army Will Need to Grow," *Washington Post,* December 15, 2006, p. 1.

164. Lolita C. Baldor, "Marine Corps May Need to Grow, General Says," *Washington Post,* November 23, 2006, p. A6.

165. "Marines Want Another Infantry Regiment," *Military.com,* November 7, 2006, http://www.military.com/features/0,15240,118468,00.html.

166. Luis E. Martinez, "Army and Marines Increase Size," ABC News, 10:40 A.M., January 11, 2007.

167. Ann Scott Tyson, "General Says Army Will Need to Grow," *Washington Post,* December 15, 2006, p. A1; Peter Baker, "Bush to Expand Size of Military," *Washington Post,* December 19, 2006.

168. Martinez, "Army and Marines Increase Size."

169. Tyson, "General Says Army Will Need to Grow," p. A1; Baker, "Bush to Expand Size of Military."

170. Dan Balz, "Governors Lobby Bush about Guard," *Washington Post,* February 28, 2006, p. 4.

171. Tyson, "General Says Army Will Need to Grow," p. A1.

172. Balz, "Governors Lobby Bush About Guard," p. 4.

173. Government Accountability Office, *Reserve Forces: An Integrated Plan Is Needed to Address Army Reserve Personnel and Equipment Shortages,* July 2005, pp. 4–5.

CHAPTER 5

1. Robert Burns, "Study: Army Stretched to Breaking Point," *San Francisco Chronicle,* January 24, 2006.

2. Julian Borger, "US Military Stretched to Breaking Point," *The Guardian,* January 26, 2006.

3. See Edward F. Bruner, "Military Forces: What is the Appropriate Size for the United States?" Washington, Congressional Research Service, RS21754, January 4, 2007.

4. Congressional Budget Office, *Options for Restructuring the Army,* May 2005, pp. xv–xvi.

5. Ibid.

6. Remarks by Chief of Staff of the Army, General Peter J. Schoomaker, "Operation Iraqi Freedom Force Rotation Plan," House Armed Services Committee Hearing, January 28, 2004.

7. U.S. Department of Defense, *2006 Quadrennial Defense Review Report,* February 6, 2006, pp. 46–47.

8. Ibid., p. 49.

9. Ibid., pp. 46–47.

10. Donna Miles, "Budget Request Focuses on Irregular Warfare, Transformation," *Defenselink,* February 6, 2006, http://www.defenselink.mil/news/Feb2006/20060206_4125.html.

11. For further discussion of Congressional attitudes and action, see Edward F. Bruner, "Military Forces: What Is the Appropriate Size for the United States?" Washington, Congressional Research Service, RS21754, January 4, 2007.

12. Nina M. Serafino, *Peacekeeping and Related Stability Operations: Issues of U.S. Military Involvement,* CRS Report, updated January 30, 2006, p. 2.

13. U.S. Department of Defense, *2006 Quadrennial Defense Review Report,* February 6, 2006, p. 3.

14. Ibid., p. 36.

15. Ibid., Appendix-4.

16. Ibid., p. 88.

17. Ibid., p. 10.

18. Ibid., p. 86.

19. *DOD Directive 3000: Military Support for Stability, Security, Transition, and Reconstruction (SSTR) Operations,* March 2, 2006, http://www.thomaspmbarnett.com/weblog/archives2/002755.html.

20. Serafino, *Peacekeeping and Related Stability Operations,* pp. 7–8.

21. Ibid., p. 1.

22. Julian E. Barnes, "Army Gives Rumsfeld Doctrine A Rewrite," *Los Angeles Times,* November 20, 2006, p. 1; U.S. Army FM 3-24 and USMC MCWP 3-33.5, "Counterinsurgency," Washington, Department of Defense, December 2006.

23. State Department Fact Sheet, *President Issues Directive to Improve the United States' Capacity to Manage Reconstruction and Stabilization Efforts,* December 14, 2005, http://www.state.gov/r/pa/prs/ps/2005/58067.htm (accessed March 2, 2006).

24. Ibid.

25. State Department Special Briefing, *Signing of a Presidential Directive to Improve management of US Efforts for Reconstruction and Stabilization,* December 14, 2005, http://www.state.gov/r/pa/prs/ps/2005/58085.htm (accessed March 2, 2006).

26. Report of the Defense Science Board Task Force, *Institutionalizing Stability Operations Within DOD,* September 2005, p. 29.

27. Ibid., p. 5.

28. Donna Miles, "Special Operations to Increase in Size," May 1, 2005, http://usmilitary.about.com/od/jointservices/a/specopsincrease.htm.

29. Thom Shanker and Scott Shane, "Elite Troops Get Expanded Role on Intelligence," *New York Times,* March 7, 2006.

30. U.S. Department of Defense, *2006 Quadrennial Defense Review Report,* February 6, 2006, p. 42.

31. Ibid., p. 44.

32. Ibid., pp. 44–45.

33. Shanker and Shane, "Elite Troops Get Expanded Role on Intelligence."

CHAPTER 6

1. "Quadrennial Defense Review: From 1997 to 2001," *Defense Report,* June 2001.

2. Public Law 104-201, The National Defense Authorization Act for Fiscal Year 1997 Subtitle B—Force Structure Review.

3. Ibid.

4. Ibid.

5. Jeffrey D. Brake, "Quadrennial Defense Review (QDR): Background, Process and Issues," Congressional Research Service, June 21, 2001.

6. *Transforming Defense: National Security in the 21st Century,* Report of the National Defense Panel, December 1997.

7. *Congressional Record,* August 5, 1999, p. H7527.

8. Department of Defense, *Quadrennial Defense Review,* September 30, 2001, p. 17.

9. Ibid., pp. 42–47.

10. U.S. General Accounting Office, "Quadrennial Defense Review: Future Reviews Can Benefit from Better Analysis and Changes in Timing and Scope," Report to the Chairman and Ranking Minority Member, Senate Armed Services Committee, November 4, 2002.

11. Ibid., p. 3.

12. Elaine M. Grossman, "Key Review Offers Scant Guidance On Handling '4th Generation' Threats," *Inside the Pentagon,* October 4, 2005.

13. Jack Spencer and Kathy Gudgel, "The 2005 Quadrennial Defense Review: Strategy and Threats," Web memo published by the Heritage Foundation, April 20, 2005.

14. Gopal Ratnam, "QDR May Devolve Into Budget-Cutting Recipe," *Defense News,* November 7, 2005.

15. Spencer and Gudgel, "The 2005 Quadrennial Defense Review."

16. Department of Defense, *Quadrennial Defense Review,* February 6, 2006, p. 38.

17. Department of Defense Directive, "Militay Support for Stability, Security, Transition, and Reconstruction (SSTR)," November 28, 2005.

18. Steve Komarow, "Proposed Boost for Pentagon Among Biggest.," *USA Today,* February 7, 2006.

19. Ann Scott Tyson, "Pentagon Adds Initiatives, Retains Old Ones," *Washington Post,* February 7, 2006.

20. Steven M. Kosiak, "FY 2007: DOD Budget Continues to Grow, Modest Program Cuts," Center for Strategic and Budgetary Assessments, February 6, 2006.

21. Stephen Biddle, comments made at The Council on Foreign Relations Journalist Roundtable: The QDR, February 8, 2006.

22. "The Quadrennial Defense Review—Rummy's Wish List." *The Economist,* February 10, 2006.

23. *Directions for Defense,* Report of the Commission on Roles and Missions of the Armed Forces to Congress, the Secretary of Defense, and Chairman of the Joint Chiefs of Staff, May 24, 1995.

24. General John M. Shalikashvili, *Joint Vision 2010* (Washington, DC: U.S. Government Printing Office, July 1996), p. 1.

25. Shalikashvili, *Joint Vision 2010.*

26. General Henry H. Shelton, *Joint Vision 2020* (Washington, DC: U.S. Government Printing Office, June 2000), p. 13.

27. Ibid., p. 10.

28. Ibid., p. 2.

29. Joint Chiefs of Staff, Department of Defense, "Capstone Concept for Joint Operations, Version 2.0," August 2005, www.dtic.mil/futurejointwarfare.

30. U.S. Joint Forces Command, A J9 Directorate White Paper, "A Concept for Joint Experimentation: Rapid Decisive Operations," February 16, 2001.

31. Ellen Maldonado, "Matching Investment to Strategy: Preparing the Department of Defense for the Future," Winner of the Brigadier General A.A. (Rick) Sardo, USMC Award for Best Paper at the National Defense University, 2001.

32. "Joint Warfighting Center History," United States Joint Forces Command Web site, http://www.jfcom.mil/.

33. Vice Admiral Robert F. Willard, Director Joint Staff, J-8 and Lt. General Robert M. Shea, Director Joint Staff, J-6. Combined Statement Before the Terrorism, Unconventional Threats and Capabilities Subcommittee, March 3, 2005.

34. Admiral Edmund P. Giambastiani, Jr., United States Navy, "Advance Questions for Admiral Edmund P. Giambastiani, Jr., USN, Nominee for the Position of Vice chairman of the Joint Chiefs of Staff," The Senate Armed Services Committee confirmed Admiral Giambastiani's nomination on June 29, 2005.

35. Maldonado, "Matching Investment to Strategy," p. 9.

36. David Atkinson and Hunter Keeter, "Apache Role in Kosovo Illustrates Cracks in Joint Doctrine," *Defense Daily*, May 26, 1999.

37. Admiral William Owens, *Lifting the Fog of War* (New York: Farrar, Straus and Giroux. 2000), p. 199.

38. Elaine M. Grossman, "Army Analyst Blames Afghan Battle Failings on Bad Command Set-Up," *Inside the Pentagon*, July 29, 2004.

39. Ibid.

40. Elaine M. Grossman, "Anaconda: Object Lesson in Poor Planning or Triumph of Improvisation?" *Inside Defense*, August 12, 2004.

41. Elaine M. Grossman, "Lapses in Coordinating Missile Launches in Iraq Pinned on V Corps," *Inside the Pentagon*, June 19, 2003.

42. Emily Hsu, "New Study Highlights Urgency for Joint Fires Deconfliction," *Inside the Army*, June 23, 2003.

43. Lt. General (Ret.) Paul Van Riper, "Van Riper's Email to Pace, Hagee, and Schoomaker Regarding JCIDS," *Inside the Navy*, January 23, 2006.

44. Ibid.

45. Colonel Thomas X. Hammes, USMC, *The Sling and the Stone: On War in the 21st Century* (St. Paul, MN: Zenith Press, 2004), Chap. 1.

46. Maldonado, "Matching Investment to Strategy."

47. Defense Science Board, Department of Defense, "Summer Study on Transformation: A Progress Assessment Volume I," February 2006, p. 19.

48. "Army Announces Business Restructuring of the FCS," *U.S. Army News Release*, April 5, 2005.

49. Andrew Feickert, "U.S. Army's Modular Redesign: Issues for Congress," Congressional Research Service, May 20, 2005, p. 10.

50. Edward F. Bruner, "Military Forces: What Is the Appropriate Size for the United States?" Congressional Research Service, February 10, 2005.

51. Sean D. Naylor, "Overhauling the U.S. Army: New Chief Redesigns Force, Sets Review," *Defense News*, September 29, 2003.

52. Government Accountability Office, "Preliminary Observations on Army Plans to Implement and Fund Modular Forces," March 16, 2005.

53. Ibid., p. 9.

54. Congressional Budget Office, "Options for Restructuring the Army," May 2005, p. 8.

55. Congressional Research Service, "Defense: FY2006 Authorization and Appropriations," November 17, 2005, p. 56.

56. Stephen Hedges, "Critics: Pentagon in Blinders," *Chicago Tribune*, June 6, 2005.

57. Ronald O'Rourke, "Naval Transformation: Background and Issues for Congress," Congressional Research Service, February 10, 2005, p. 3.

58. Loren Thompson, "QDR 2005: Issues Facing the Navy," *Lexington Institute*, May 1, 2005.

59. Admiral Vern Clark, "Sea Power 21 Series—Part I: Projecting Decisive Joint Capabilities," October 2002, http://www.navalinstitute.org/proceedings/Articles02/proCNO10.htm

60. Thompson, "QDR 2005."

61. Ibid.

62. Gordon R. England, "Winning Today while Transforming for Tomorrow," testimony for the House Appropriations Committee on Defense, March 10, 2005.

63. "Chief of Naval Operations Says Future Navy Is Right Navy," *US Fed News*, March 25, 2005.

64. England, "Winning Today while Transforming for Tomorrow."

65. Gordon England, Testimony for the Senate Appropriations Committee—Defense, March 16, 2005.

66. Statement of Gordon England before the Senate Appropriations Committee—Defense, March 16, 2005.

67. Thompson, "QDR 2005."

68. Christopher P. Cavas, "Stop Work Ordered for Third LCS," *Defense News*, January 15, 2007, p. 1.

69. James L. Jones, *Marine Corps Strategy 21*, Department of the Navy, Washington, DC, November 3, 2000.

70. Frank Hoffman, "A Marine Corps for a Global Century: Expeditionary Maneuver Brigades," in *Globalization and Maritime Power*, ed. Sam J. Tangredi (Washington, DC: Institute for National Strategic Studies, National Defense University, 2002), Chap. 22.

71. Harold Kennedy, "Naval Transformation Gets Boost from War on Terror," *National Defense Magazine*, December 2002.

72. Hoffman, "A Marine Corps for a Global Century."

73. Kennedy, "Naval Transformation Gets Boost from War on Terror."

74. Gidget Fuentes, "Distributed Ops, Up Close and Personal," *Defense News*, September 12, 2005, p. 66.

75. Christian Lowe, "Practicing Distributed Ops," *Defense News*, October 3, 2005, p. 82.

76. Statement by Mr. William Balderson, Deputy Assistant Secretary of the Navy, Mr. Thomas Laux, Program Executive Officer for Air ASW, Assault and Special Mission Programs, and Brigadier General Martin Post, Assistant Deputy Commandant for Aviation, before the Tactical Air and Land Forces Subcommittee of the House Armed Services Committee on FY 2006 Marine Corps Major Rotocraft Programs, April 14, 2005.

77. Major John W. Bullard, USMC, "MV-22 Osprey: Future Role and Impact for Medium Lift," 1997, www.globalsecurity.org.

78. "Expeditionary Fighting Vehicle/Advanced Amphibious Assault Vehicle," www.globalsecurity.org.

79. The Naval Strike Forum, The Lexington Institute, "Marine Corps Transformation: Expeditionary Maneuver Warfare," July 2003.

80. Cpl. Sharon E. Fox, "Foreign Military Training Unit Activates," *Marine Corps News*, October 7, 2005.

81. U.S. Air Force, *The USAF Transformation Flight Plan, FY03-07*, HQ USAF/XPXT, p. iv.

82. Statement by Lieutenant General Duncan J. McNabb, Deputy Chief of Staff for Air Force Plans and Programs, before the House Committee on Armed Services Subcommittee on Terrorism, Unconventional Threats and Capabilities, February 26, 2004.

83. Staff Sgt. A.J. Bosker, "Air Force Changing How It Buys Weapons," *Air Force Print News,* May 24, 2002.

84. Leonard David, "U.S. Air Force Plans for Future War in Space," *Space.com,* February 22, 2004.

85. Center for Defense Information, "The U.S. Air Force Transformation Flight Plan 2004: A Kinder, Gentler Space Strategy? Not Really," January 12, 2005, www.cdi.org.

86. Christopher Bolkcom, "Air Force Transformation," Congressional Research Service, January 25, 2005.

87. Joint Unmanned Combat Air Systems Web site, http://www.darpa.mil/j-ucas/index.htm.

88. "Think Differently, U.S. Air Force Chief Says," *Defense News,* June 6, 2005.

89. Michael Sirak and Joshua Kucera, "Back to the Future: US Looks to Bolster Close Air Support Mission, Coupling Past Experiences with New Technologies and Tactics," *Jane's Defense Weekly,* April 21, 2004.

90. Adam J. Hebert, "Smaller Bombs for Stealthy Aircraft," *Air Force Magazine,* July 2001.

CHAPTER 7

1. Government Accountability Office, "Defense Acquisitions: Assessments of Selected Major Weapon Programs," Report to Congressional Committees, March 31, 2005, p. vii.

2. Government Accountability Office, "Defense Acquisitions: Assessments of Selected Major Weapon Programs."

3. Ibid.

4. Peter Spiegel, "Army Warns Rumsfeld It's Billions Short," *Los Angeles Times,* September 25, 2006.

5. Congressional Budget Office, "Long Term Implications of Current Defense Plans: Summary Update for Fiscal Year 2007" (Washington, DC: CBO, October 2006), pp. 13–15.

6. Government Accountability Office, "Defense Acquisitions: Assessments of Selected Major Weapon Programs."

7. Christian Lowe, "Lighter, Faster, More Flexible," *Defense News,* May 23, 2005, p. 11.

8. "Army Budget Plan Advances Modular Force and FCS," *Army Logistician* 37, no. 3, p. 1.

9. Government Accountability Office, "Defense Acquisitions: Future Combat Systems Challenges and Prospects for Success," March 16, 2005.

10. Ibid.

11. Greg Grant, "Full FCS Fielding Slips 5 Years," *Defense News,* October 3, 2005.

12. Government Accountability Office, "Defense Acquisitions: Future Combat Systems Challenges and Prospects for Success."

13. Government Accountability Office, "Defense Acquisitions: Resolving Development Risks in the Army's Networked Communications Capabilities Is Key to Fielding Future Force," June 2005.

14. Ibid., p. i.

15. William Matthews, "2007 U.S. Defense Spending on Track for Post-WWII Record," *Defense News,* October 2, 2006.

16. Government Accountability Office, "Force Structure: Preliminary Observations on Army Plans to Implement and Fund Modular Forces," March 16, 2005, p. 2.

17. House Report 109-16, Making Emergency Supplemental Appropriations for the Fiscal Year Ending September 30, 2005, and For Other Purposes, March 11, 2005.

18. Senate Report 109-52, Emergency Supplemental Appropriations Act for Defense, the Global War on Terror, and Tsunami Relief, 2005, April 6, 2005, pp. 33–34.

19. The Department of the Army, "The Army Campaign Plan (Unclassified)," March 31, 2004, p. 5; Andrew Feickert, "U.S. Army's Modular Redesign: Issues for Congress," Congressional Research Service, May 20, 2005.

20. Congressional Budget Office, "Long Term Implications of Current Defense Plans," pp. 19–21.

21. Based on discussions as well as the analysis in Congressional Budget Office, "Long Term Implications of Current Defense Plans," pp. 19–21.

22. Government Accountability Office, "Tactical Aircraft: Recapitalization Goals Are Not Supported by Knowledge-Based F-22A and JSF Business Cases," testimony before the Subcommittee on Tactical Air and Land Forces, House Committee on Armed Services, March 16, 2006.

23. Government Accountability Office, "Tactical Aircraft: Air Force Still Needs Business Case to Support F/A-22 Quantities and Increased Capabilities," Report to Congressional Committees, March 15, 2005.

24. Government Accountability Office, "Tactical Aircraft: Recapitalization Goals Are Not Supported."

25. Government Accountability Office, "Tactical Aircraft: Air Force Still Needs Business Case."

26. Government Accountability Office, "Tactical Aircraft: Recapitalization Goals Are Not Supported," p. 6.

27. Ibid., p. 7.

28. Col. Everest E. Riccioni, USAF Ret., "Description of Our Failing Defense Acquisition System as Exemplified by the History, Nature and Analysis of the USAF F-22 Raptor Program," Project on Government Oversight, March 8, 2005, p. 14, http://www.pogo.org/m/dp/dp-fa22-Riccioni-03082005.pdf.

29. Laura M. Colarusso, "Fixing the F-22A: USAF Finds Structural Problems that Affect Nearly 100 Raptors," Defense News, May 1, 2006.

30. General Accounting Office, "Tactical Aircraft: Changing Conditions Drive Need for New F/A-22 Business Case," Report to Congressional Committees, March 15, 2004, p. 26.

31. Government Accountability Office, "Tactical Aircraft: Air Force Still Needs Business Case."

32. Government Accountability Office, "Tactical Aircraft: Recapitalization Goals Are Not Supported," pp. 8–9.

33. Government Accountability Office, "Tactical Aircraft: Air Force Still Needs Business Case," p. 1.

34. Thom Shanker and Eric Schmitt, "Pentagon Weighs Strategy Change to Deter Terror," New York Times, July 5, 2005.

35. Riccioni, "Description of Our Failing Defense Acquisition System."

36. Matthews, "2007 U.S. Defense Spending on Track."

37. Christopher Bolkcom, "F-35 Joint Strike Fighter (JSF) Program: Background, Status, and Issues," Congressional Research Service Report for Congress, August 29, 2005.

38. Letter from Secretary of Defense William S. Cohen to Rep. Jerry Lewis, June 22, 2000, transcript made available by *Inside the Air Force,* June 23, 2000.

39. Government Accountability Office, "Tactical Aircraft: Recapitalization Goals Are Not Supported," p. 9.

40. Bolkcom, "F-35 Joint Strike Fighter (JSF) Program"; Government Accountability Office, "Tactical Aircraft: Recapitalization Goals Are Not Supported."

41. Government Accountability Office, "Tactical Aircraft: Recapitalization Goals Are Not Supported."

42. Ibid., p. 2.

43. Christopher Bolkcom, "Air Force Aerial Refueling," Congressional Research Service Report for Congress, September 19, 2005.

44. Carlo Munoz, "Defense Analysts Slam Pentagon's Proposed Axing of Second JSF Engine," *Inside the Air Force,* March 31, 2006.

45. Michael Fabey, "Report: JSF Costs Increase 7.7%, Reach $276 Billion," *Defense News,* April 17, 2006.

46. Leslie Wayne, "U.S. and Allies' Fighter Jet Program Hits Turbulence," *International Herald Tribune,* March 17, 2006.

47. Steven Kosiak, "U.S. Tactical Aircraft Plans: Preparing for the Wrong Future?" Center for Strategic and Budgetary Assessments Backgrounder, October 3, 1996.

48. Lawrence J. Korb, "Should We Pay $21 Billion for This Plane?—Yes, It's a Bargain for the Future," *Christian Science Monitor,* November 25, 1996.

49. Lt. General Carrol H. "Howie" Chandler, as quoted in Staff Sgt. C. Todd Lopez, "Joint Strike Fighter Program Crucial to Future Air Dominance," *Air Force Print News,* March 20, 2006.

50. Bolkcom, "F-35 Joint Strike Fighter (JSF) Program."

51. Government Accountability Office, "Tactical Aircraft: Recapitalization Goals Are Not Supported," p. 3.

52. Bolkcom, "Air Force Aerial Refueling."

53. Ibid.

54. General Accounting Office, "US Combat Airpower: Aging Refueling Aircraft are Costly to Maintain and Operate," August 8, 1996.

55. "KC-135 Economic Service Life Study," Technical Report F34601-96-C-0111, February 9, 2001.

56. Christopher Bolkcom and Daniel Else, "Observations on KC-135 Corrosion and KC-767 Sole-Source Logistics Support," memorandum to Senate Commerce Committee, October 23, 2003.

57. Bolkcom, "Air Force Aerial Refueling."

58. R. Jeffrey Smith, "Roche Cited for 2 Ethics Violations," *Washington Post,* February 10, 2005.

59. Office of the Inspector General of the Department of Defense, *Management Accountability Review of the Boeing KC-767A Tanker Program,* Report No. OIG-2004-171, May 13, 2005.

60. Hearing of the Senate Armed Services Committee, "Management Accountability Review of the Boeing KC-767A Tanker Program," *Federal News Service,* June 8, 2005.

61. Defense Science Board Task Force, Office of the Under Secretary of Defense for Acquisition, Technology, and Logistics, "Report on Aerial Refueling Requirements," May 2004.

62. Michael Fabey and William Matthews, "USAF Tanker Could Cost $200 Billion," *Defense News,* January 30, 2006.

63. Comments by Loren Thompson, quoted in Fabey and Matthews, "USAF Tanker Could Cost $200 Billion."

64. John T. Bennett and Carlo Munoz, "USAF Seeking $204 Million in FY-07 to Replace Aging Tanker Fleet," *Inside the Air Force,* February 10, 2006.

65. Amy Butler and David A. Fulghum, "Risk Avoidance," *Aviation Week & Space Technology,* November 6, 2006.

66. Amy Butler and David A. Fulghum, "Fair Play: The U.S. Air Force Is Seeking a Level Playing Field for Tanker Bid," *Aviation Week & Space Technology,* October 2, 2006.

67. Loren B. Thompson, "Lift," Lexington Institute Issue Brief, April 13, 2006.

68. Ibid.

69. Lt. General Donald Hoffman, Military Deputy, Office of the Assistant Secretary of the Air Force (Acquisition), presentation to the Senate Committee on Armed Services AirLand Subcommittee, March 28, 2006.

70. Bob Cox, "C-17 Flying on Wing and Prayer: Defense Budget Would Halt Work," *Fort Worth Star-Telegram,* February 22, 2006.

71. John A. Tirpak, "Rising Risk in Air Mobility," *Air Force Magazine,* March 2006.

72. Martin Matishak, "Testing Chief Says C-5 Modernization Needs New Acquisition Strategy," *Inside the Air Force,* January 27, 2006.

73. Rep. Jim Saxton, "Air Mobility Lifeline," *Defense News,* April 4, 2005.

74. Matthews, "2007 U.S. Defense Spending on Track."

75. John T. Bennett, "Sweeping DoD Mobility Study's Focus on Intratheater Needs Questioned," *Inside the Air Force,* April 7, 2006.

76. Ibid.

77. Jason Sherman, "Advisory Panel to Rumsfeld Suggests More C-17s Are Required," *Inside the Air Force,* November 11, 2005.

78. John T. Bennett, "Schwartz Sees C-17's Fate Hinging on C-5 Modernization Efforts," *Inside the Air Force,* December 9, 2005.

79. Michael Sirak, "TRANSCOM Chief Says 20 Additional C-17s Would Be Ideal, But Not More," *Defense Daily,* March 3, 2006.

80. Center for Security Policy, "The QDR and Strategic Mobility: Air Bridge or Air Bust?" Decision Brief, March 7, 2006.

81. Thompson, "Lift."

82. Hoffman, presentation to the Senate Committee on Armed Services.

83. John A. Tirpak, "Older Aircraft Problems Need Attention; Unfunded List of $3 Billion; Teets Voices Disappointments," *Air Force Magazine,* May 2005.

84. William Matthews, "US Air Force Officials Praise Threatened C-130J." *Defense News,* January 24, 2005.

85. Ibid.

86. Ibid.

87. John Liang, "Wynne: Changing Transport Needs Triggered C-130J Cancellation," *Inside the Air Force,* February 11, 2005.

88. Cynthia DiPasquale, "Pentagon Reviewing Estimated Cost of Terminating C-130J Hercules," *Inside the Air Force,* April 8, 2005; John T. Bennett, "Appropriations Conferees Restore C-130J Advanced Procurement Funds," *Inside the Air Force,* December 23, 2005.

89. Tirpak, "Older Aircraft Problems Need Attention."

90. Jonathan Karp and Andy Pasztor, "Lockheed Cuts Cargo-Plane Profit Amid U.S. Pressure," *Wall Street Journal,* October 26, 2006.

91. Cox, "C-17 Flying on Wing and Prayer."

92. Congressional Budget Office, "Long Term Implications of Current Defense Plans," pp. 16–19.

93. Ibid.

94. Tim Weiner, "The Navy's Fleet of Tomorrow Mired in Politics of Yesterday," *New York Times,* April 19, 2005, p. 1.

95. Ronald O'Rourke, "Potential Navy Force Structure and Shipbuilding Plans: Background and Issues for Congress," Congressional Research Service Report for Congress, June 23, 2005.

96. Jason Sherman, "Navy Leader Says Service Will 'Stick' with Goal of 313-Ship Fleet," *Inside the Navy,* December 12, 2005.

97. Congressional Budget Office, "Options for the Navy's Future Fleet," May 2006.

98. Quoted in Grace Jean, "Plans to Expand Fleet May Be Unrealistic," *National Defense Magazine,* April 2006.

99. Michael Sirak, "Navy Shipbuilding Plan Doesn't Float, Analysts Warn," *Defense Daily,* January 13, 2006.

100. Quoted in Christopher P. Cavas, "USN Shipbuilding Cost Assailed at Budget Hearing," *Defense News,* March 13, 2006.

101. Jean, "Plans to Expand Fleet May Be Unrealistic."

102. Ronald O'Rourke, "Navy CVN-21 Aircraft Carrier Program: Background and Issues for Congress," Congressional Research Service Report for Congress, June 24, 2005.

103. Ibid.

104. Ibid.

105. Roxana Tiron, "Carrier Industry Mounts Budget Defense," *The Hill,* April 12, 2006.

106. Christopher J. Castelli, "Carrier's Future in Dispute on the Hill," *InsideDefense.com,* News Stand, May 18, 2006.

107. Rati Bishnoi, "CVN-21 Design Nearly Half Complete: 100 'Hull Units' to be Built in 2006," *Inside the Pentagon,* March 2, 2006.

108. Ibid.

109. Ronald O'Rourke, "Navy Littoral Combat Ship: Background and Issues for Congress," Congressional Research Service Report for Congress, June 24, 2005.

110. Ibid.

111. Ibid.

112. Christopher P. Cavas, "U.S. Navy LCS Costs to Soar 49%," *Defense News,* March 6, 2006.

113. Christopher P. Cavas, "Stop-Work Ordered for Third LCS," *Defense News,* January 15, 2007, p. 1.

114. Cavas, "U.S. Navy LCS Costs to Soar 49%."

115. Ronald O'Rourke, "Navy Littoral Combat Ship: Background and Issues for Congress." Congressional Research Service Report for Congress, April 1, 2005, p. 4.

116. Government Accountability Office, "Defense Acquisitions: Plans Need to Allow Enough Time to Demonstrate Capability of First Littoral Combat Ships," Report to Congressional Committees, March 2, 2005, p. 11.

117. Ibid., p. 3.

118. Ibid.

119. Ibid., p. 16.

120. Ibid.

121. Ibid.

122. Ibid., p. 5.

123. O'Rourke, "Navy Littoral Combat Ship: Background and Issues for Congress," April 1, 200, p. 3.

124. Government Accountability Office, Defense Acquisitions: Plans Need to Allow Enough Time, " p. 20.

125. O'Rourke, "Navy Littoral Combat Ship: Background and Issues for Congress, " April 1, 2005, p. 3.

126. Admiral Vernon Clark, testimony before the House Armed Services Committee, Subcommittee on Projection Forces, July 19, 2005.

127. Geoff Fein, "The Navy 'Desperately Needs DD(X),' CNO Says," *Defense Daily,* June 22, 2005.

128. Ronald O'Rourke, "Navy DD(X), CG(X)m and LCS Ship Acquisition Programs: Oversight Issues and Options for Congress," Congressional Research Service Report for Congress, May 9, 2005, p. 15.

129. Paul L. Francis, Direction Acquisition and Sourcing Management, Government Accountability Office, "Defense Acquisitions: Progress and Challenges Facing the DD(X) Surface Combatant Program," testimony before the Subcommittee on Projection Forces, House Committee on Armed Services, July 19, 2005.

130. Ibid.

131. Government Accountability Office, "Progress of the DD(X) Destroyer Program," report to Congressional Committees, June 14, 2005, p. 3.

132. Francis, "Defense Acquisitions: Progress and Challenges Facing the DD(X) Surface Combatant Program."

133. Ibid.

134. Ronald O'Rourke, "Navy DD(X) and CG(X) Programs: Background and Issues for Congress." Congressional Research Service Report for Congress, May 31, 2005.

135. Peter Kaplan, "Analysts Question Cost of New U.S. Navy Destroyer," *Reuters,* July 21, 2005.

136. Christopher Cavas, "New DD(X) Plan: Build 2 Competing Ships in '07," *Defense News,* May 20, 2005, p. 8.

137. Christopher Cavas, "Experts Agree: U.S. Navy Fleet Plan Unaffordable," *Defense News,* April 3, 2006; Chris Johnson. "GAO Notes Low Confidence Level in Meeting DD(X) Projected Costs," *Inside the Navy,* April 3, 2006.

138. O'Rourke, "Navy DD(X) and CG(X) Programs."

139. J. Michael Gilmore, Assistant Director for National Security, Congressional Budget Office, testimony before Projection Forces Subcommittee of the House Armed Services Committee, July 20, 2005.

140. Christopher Castelli, "Congress Backs DD(X), Littoral Ship," *InsideDefense.com,* December 28, 2005.

141. Congressional Budget Office, "The Long-Term Implications of Current Defense Plans and Alternatives: Summary Update for Fiscal Year 2006," October 2005; Congressional Budget Office, "The Long-Term Implications of Current Defense Plans and Alternatives: Summary Update for Fiscal Year 2007," October 2006.

142. Christopher Cavas, "USN's DD(X) Wins Approval," *Defense News*, November 28, 2005.

143. Paul L. Francis, Director Acquisition and Sourcing Management, GAO, "Defense Acquisitions: Progress and Challenges Facing the DD(X) Surface Combatant Program," testimony before the Projection Forces Subcommittee of the House Armed Services Committee, July 19, 2005, p. 14.

144. Gordon England, Secretary of the Navy, statement before the Senate Appropriations Committee, March 16, 2005.

145. Christopher Cavas, "U.S. Navy Rises to Defend DD(X)," *Defense News*, June 27, 2005, p. 20.

146. Peter Kaplan, "Analysts Question Cost of New U.S. Navy Destroyer," *Reuters*, July 21, 2005.

147. Ibid.

148. Ronald O'Rourke, "Navy DD(X), CG(X)m and LCS Ship Acquisition Programs: Oversight Issues and Options for Congress," Congressional Research Service Report for Congress, May 9, 2005, p. 29.

149. Ronald O'Rourke, "Navy DD(X) and GC(X) Programs: Background and Issues for Congress," Congressional Research Service Report for Congress, May 9, 2005, p. 4.

150. "Procurement Acquisition Costs By Weapons System," *Dept. of Defense Budget for Fiscal Year 2006*, February 2005.

151. Ibid.

152. Ibid.

153. Richard Whittle, "One Giant Step For Tilt-Rotors," *Dallas Morning News*, September 20, 2005.

154. Stacy Schultz, "Why Choppers Go Down," *U.S. News & World Report*, April 7, 2003.

155. "V-22 Costs Soar," *G2mil Quarterly Online*, www.g2mil.com.

156. William Matthews, "Experts: USMC Faces Helicopter Shortage," *Defense News*, August 28, 2006.

157. "V-22 Costs Soar."

158. "Procurement Acquisition Costs By Weapons System."

159. Congressional Budget Office, "The Future of the Navy's Amphibious and Maritime Prepositioning Forces," November 2004.

160. Eric Rosenberg, "Admiral Keelhauls Execs Over USS San Antonio," *San Antonio Express-News*, March 15, 2006.

161. Congressional Budget Office, "The Future of the Navy's Amphibious and Maritime Prepositioning Forces."

162. Ibid.; Roxana Tiron, "Ships' Cost Could Sink Plans for Floating Military Bases," *National Defense Magazine*, January 2005.

163. Congressional Budget Office, "The Future of the Navy's Amphibious and Maritime Prepositioning Forces."

164. Congressional Budget Office, "Long Term Implications of Current Defense Plans: Summary Update for Fiscal Year 2007," Washington, CBO, October 2006, pp. 22–24.

165. Loren B. Thompson, "Can the Space Sector Meet Military Goals for Space? The Tension Between Transformation and Federal Management Practices," The Lexington Institute, September 2005.

166. "Problems in DoD Space Programs," Department of Defense Appropriations Bill, 2006, Report of the House Committee on Appropriations (House Report 109-119), June 10, 2005, pp. 205–206.

167. John T. Bennett, "SBIRS HIGH Surpasses Nunn-McCurdy Threshold for the Fourth Time," *Inside the Air Force,* November 18, 2005.

168. Jeremy Singer, "House Bill Would Strengthen Nunn-McCurdy Provision," *Space News,* June 6, 2005.

169. National Defense Authorization Act for Fiscal Year 2006, Report for the House Committee on Armed Services, May 20, 2005, pp. 208–209, 213–217.

170. "Problems in DoD Space Programs," pp. 205–206.

171. Congressional Budget Office, "The Long-Term Implications of Current Plans for Investment in Major Unclassified Military Space Programs," September 12, 2005; Congressional Budget Office, "The Long-Term Implications of Current Defense Plans and Alternatives: Summary Update for Fiscal Year 2007," October 2006.

172. Congressional Budget Office, "The Long-Term Implications of Current Plans for Investment"; Congressional Budget Office, "The Long-Term Implications of Current Defense Plans and Alternatives."

173. Marcia S. Smith, "Military Space Programs: Issues Concerning DOD's SBIRS and STSS Programs," Congressional Research Service, August 8, 2005.

174. "Problems in DoD Space Programs," pp. 205–206.

175. Congressional Budget Office, "The Long-Term Implications of Current Plans for Investment"; Congressional Budget Office, "The Long-Term Implications of Current Defense Plans and Alternatives."

176. "The Full Costs of Ballistic Missile Defense," ed. Richard F. Kaufman, Center for Arms Control and Non-Proliferation, January 2003.

177. Richard F. Kaufman, "The Folly of Space Weapons," *TomPaine.com,* June 15, 2005.

178. Marc Kaufman, "Bush Sets Defense As Space Priority" *Washington Post,* October 18, 2006.

179. Michael Katz-Hyman and Michael Krepon, "Space Responsibility: U.S. Policies Endanger Satellites, Space Access," *Defense News,* October 16, 2006.

180. Ibid.

181. Theresa Hitchens, "U.S. Military Space Policy and Strategy," presentation to the e-Parliament Conference on Space Security, September 14, 2005.

CHAPTER 8

1. General Henry H. Shelton, *Joint Vision 2020* (Washington, DC: U.S. Government Printing Office, June 2000), p. 26.

2. These reports can be found in full at http://www.sigir.mil.

3. Martin J. Gorman and Alexander Krongard, "A Goldwater-Nichols Act for the U.S. Government," *Joint Forces Quarterly,* no. 39, 4th Quarter 2005, p. 52.

4. Clark A. Murdock, Michèle A. Flournoy, Christopher A. Williams, and Kurt M. Campbell, principal authors, *Beyond Goldwater-Nichols: Defense Reform for a New Strategic Era, Phase 1 Report* (Washington, DC: Center for Strategic and International Studies, March 2004).

5. Senator Richard G. Lugar, hearing on the Stabilization and Reconstruction Civilian Management Act Opening Statement, March 3, 2004.

6. Murdock et al., *Beyond Goldwater-Nichols.*

7. Gorman and Krongard, "A Goldwater-Nichols Act for the U.S. Government"; James Dobbins, testimony before the Senate Committee on Foreign Relations, March 3, 2004.

8. The White House/National Security Council, Presidential Decision Directive 56, "Managing Complex Contingency Operations," Washington, DC, May 1997.

9. William P. Hamblet and Jerry G. Kline, "PDD 56 and Complex Contingency Operations," *Joint Forces Quarterly,* Spring 2000.

10. Francis Fukuyama "Nation-Building 101," *The Atlantic Monthly,* January/February 2004.

11. Hamblet and Kline, "PDD 56 and Complex Contingency Operations."

12. Nina M. Serafino, "Policing in Peacekeeping and Related Stability Operations: Problems and Proposed Solutions," Congressional Research Service, March 30, 2004.

13. The White House/National Security Council, Presidential Decision Directive 71, "Strengthening Criminal Justice Systems in Support of Peace Operations," Washington, DC, February 24, 2000.

14. William Lewis, Edward Marks, and Robert Perito, *Enhancing International Civilian Police in Peace Operations,* Special Report, United States Institute of Peace, April 22, 2002; Serafino, "Policing in Peacekeeping and Related Stability Operations."

15. *The 9/11 Commission Report: Final Report of the National Commission on Terrorist Attacks upon the United States* (New York: W. W. Norton & Co., 2004); *On the Brink: A Report of the Commission on Weak States and US National Security,* sponsored by the Center for Global Development, May 2004.

16. Nina M. Serafino and Martin A. Weiss, "Peacekeeping and Conflict Transitions: Background and Congressional Action on Civilian Capabilities," Congressional Research Service, June 28, 2005, p. 5.

17. Matthew F. Bogdanos, "Joint Interagency Cooperation: The First Step," *Joint Forces Quarterly,* no. 27, April 2005.

18. The original idea for JIACG arose at the Joint Forces Command annual exercise in June–July 2001.

19. Bogdanos, "Joint Interagency Cooperation."

20. Drawn from Ambassador Carlos Pascual's testimony to the Senate Foreign Relations Committee, June 16, 2005.

21. Ibid.

22. Pamela Hess, "Congress Rejects Post-War Planning Fund," United Press International, November 2, 2005.

23. Ambassador Carlos Pascual, statement at a State Department news briefing, December 14, 2005.

24. H.R. 1815 National Defense Authorization Act for FY2006 §1207(b).

25. Secretary of State Condoleezza Rice, testimony before the Senate Foreign Relations Committee, February 15, 2006.

26. Department of Defense Directive 3000.05, Military Support for Stability, Security, Transition, and Reconstruction Operations, November 28, 2005.

27. National Security Presidential Directive 44, Management of Interagency Efforts Concerning Reconstruction and Stabilization, December 7, 2005.

28. Quoted in Steven R. Weisman, "Bush Gives State Department Priority in Helping Nations to Rebuild," *New York Times,* December 15, 2005.

29. *Play to Win: the Final Report of the Bi-partisan Commission on Post-Conflict Reconstruction,* Center for Strategic and International Studies (CSIS) and the Association of the U.S. Army, 2003 (a book-length version was published in mid-2004); Robert C. Orr, ed., *Winning the Peace: An American Strategy for Post-Conflict Reconstruction* (Washington, DC: CSIS, 2004); Murdock et al., *Beyond Goldwater-Nichols;* Hans Binnendijk and Stuart Johnson, eds. *Transforming for Stabilization and Reconstruction Operations,* National Defense University Center for Technology and national Security Policy, April 2004; *On the Brink: Weak States and US National Security,* Center for Global Development, May 2004; Office of the Undersecretary of Defense for Acquisition, Technology, and Logistics. *Defense Science Board 2004 Summer Study on Transition to and From Hostilities,* December 2004.

30. William L. Nash and Ciara Knudsen, "Reform and Innovation in Stabilization, Reconstruction and Development," Princeton Project on National Security Working Paper, October 26, 2005.

31. Murdock et al., *Beyond Goldwater-Nichols.*

32. Gregory F. Treverton, "The Next Steps in Intelligence," Occasional Paper by the RAND Corporation, 2005.

33. Richard A. Best, Jr., Alfred Cumming, and Todd Masse, "Director of National Intelligence: Statutory Authorities," Congressional Research Service Report for Congress, April 11, 2005.

34. Ibid.

35. Scott Shane, "Year Into Revamped Spying, Troubles and Some Progress," *New York Times,* February 28, 2006.

36. The Commission on the Intelligence Capabilities of the U.S. Regarding Weapons of Mass Destruction Report to the President of the United States, March 31, 2005, p. 6.

37. Adapted from Treverton, "The Next Steps in Intelligence."

38. The Commission on the Intelligence Capabilities of the U.S., p. 3.

39. The Commission on the Intelligence Capabilities of the U.S.

40. Ibid., p. 29.

41. *The 9/11 Commission Report: Final Report of the National Commission on Terrorist Attacks Upon the United States* (Washington, DC: U.S. Government Printing Office, July 22, 2004).

42. Ibid., p. 25.

43. Final Report on 9/11 Commission Recommendations, 9/11 Public Discourse Project, December 5, 2005.

44. Shane Harris and Greta Wodele, "Miles to Go," *The National Journal,* January 14, 2006.

45. Quoted in Harris and Wodele, "Miles to Go."

CHAPTER 9

1. See Chapter 6, Field Manual, *Counterinsurgency,* FM-3-24/ FMFM 3-24, Headquarters, U.S. Army, Washington, June 16, 2006, especially Chapters 3 and 6, and Appendix C; and Department of Defense Directive, "Military Support for Stability, Security, Transition, and Reconstruction (SSTR) Operations," DoD Directive 3000.05, November 28, 2005.

2. See Chapter 6, Field Manual, *Counterinsurgency,* FM-3-24/ FMFM 3-24, Headquarters, US Army, Washington, June 16, 2006, especially Chapters 3 and 6, and Appendix C; and Department of Defense Directive, "Military Support for Stability, Security, Transition, and Reconstruction (SSTR) Operations."

3. White House, "Executive Summary," *National Strategy for Victory in Iraq,* November 30, 2005, http://www.whitehouse.gov/infocus/iraq/iraq_strategy_nov2005.html.

4. Ibid.

5. Congressional Budget Office, "Estimated Costs of US Operations in Iraq Under Two Specified Scenarios," July 13, 2006, pp. 1–3.

6. See Chairman of the Joint Chiefs of Staff, *National Strategic Plan for the War on Terrorism,* Department of Defense, Washington, February 1, 2006; and *National Security Strategy of the United States,* Chapters VII and VIIII, edition issued by the White House on March 16, 2006.

7. For an excellent survey of the problems in Arab and Muslim public opinion that help shape these problems, see Andre Kohut and Carroll Doughtery, "The Great Divide: How Westerners and Muslims View Each Other," Pew Global Attitudes Project, 22 June 2006, www.pewglobal.org.

8. Makkah Al-Mukarramah Declaration, issued at the completion of the Third Session of the Islamic Summit Conference, December 7–8, 2005.

9. See General Sir Rupert Smith, *The Utility of Force* (London: Allen Lane, Penguin imprint, 2005).

CHAPTER 10

1. White House, "The National Strategy of the United States," March 15, 2006.

2. Ibid., pp. 33–42.

3. Department of Defense, "Quadrennial Defense Review," February 6, 2006, pp. 2, 19–39.

4. Ibid., pp. 19–39.

5. Ibid., pp. 40–62.

6. Ibid., pp. 75–79.

7. Ibid., pp. 88–89.

8. Roxana Tiron, "Pentagon Gets New Office," *The Hill,* October 3, 2006.

9. Jason Sherman, "In Sweeping Overhaul, DOD Reorganizes Policy Office," *Inside Defense,* August 28, 2006.

10. Ryan Henry, Principal Undersecretary of Defense for Policy, testimony before the House Armed Services Committee, June 20, 2006.

11. *Military Technology* 30, no. 3 (March 2006): 38.

12. Rowan Scarborough, "NATO Allies Cut Military Since 9/11," *Washington Times,* February 15, 2006.

13. Max Boot, "Proactive Self-Defense," *The Weekly Standard,* July 3, 2006.

14. Shannon McCaffrey, "Rumsfeld Cites Importance of Building Non-traditional Partnerships with Foreign Militaries," *Associated Press,* May 4, 2006.

15. Boot,l "Proactive Self-Defense."

16. IISS, *Military Balance, 1988–1989,* pp. 27–28.

17. IISS, *Military Balance, 2006,* pp. 40–44.

18. Michael T. Klare, "Taking Aim at the Sleeping Dragon," *Salon.com,* April 19, 2006.

19. Ibid.

20. Steven R. Weisman, "Rice Seeks to Balance China's Power," *New York Times,* March 19, 2006.

21. Condoleezza Rice, "Campaign 2000: Promoting the National Interest," *Foreign Affairs,* January/February 2000.

22. Department of Defense, "Military Power of the People's Republic of China," Annual Report to Congress, June 2006, p. I.

23. 2006 Quadrennial Defense Review, pp. 29–31.

24. Ibid., p. 38.

25. Ibid., pp. 89–90.

26. Murdock et al., *Beyond Goldwater-Nichols.*

27. Ibid.

28. Robert L. Maginnis, "ABCA: A Petri Dish for Multinational Interoperability," *Joint Force Quarterly,* no. 37, 2nd quarter 2005.

29. Ibid.

30. Ibid.

31. Kevin L. Robinson, "Interoperability Key to Future Success British Army Chief Says," *Army News Service,* October 19, 1999.

About the Authors

ANTHONY H. CORDESMAN holds the Arleigh A. Burke Chair in Strategy at the Center for Strategic and International Studies and is an analyst and commentator for ABC News. He has written extensively on energy and Middle Eastern politics, economics, demographics, and security. He has served in a number of senior positions in the U.S. government, including the Department of Energy, and several assignments in the Middle East.

PAUL S. FREDERIKSEN has been a consultant to the Post-Conflict Reconstruction Project (PCR) at the Center for Strategic and International Studies where he worked on a World Bank–funded project devising strategies to assess and develop governance and state capacity for the Government of Iraq. Prior to joining PCR, Frederiksen spent a year as a defense policy analyst with the CSIS Arleigh A. Burke Chair in Strategy, conducting research and writing on a wide range of U.S. defense topics including the Iraq War, defense transformation, stabilization and reconstruction programs, and the interagency process. He received his B.A. magna cum laude in political science and economics from Washington University in St. Louis where his thesis won the Center for the New Institutional Social Sciences Award. He subsequently completed his Master's degree in politics as a MacCracken Fellow at New York University where he focused on humanitarian interventions in civil wars.

WILLIAM D. SULLIVAN is a research associate at the Arleigh A. Burke Chair in Strategy at the Center for Strategic and International Studies. He joined CSIS in 2004 with the Eastern Europe Project to study narcotics and weapons trafficking in the Western Balkans. In 2005, Sullivan joined the CSIS International Security Program to focus on a Department of Defense initiative to reorganize the U.S. military's reserve component. He currently works on Middle East energy and security strategies as well as domestic and overseas U.S. defense issues. Prior to joining CSIS, Sullivan spent three years at a portfolio advisory and publishing group in McLean, Virginia. He is a frequent speaker and radio commentator on his areas of expertise and is published on both financial and geopolitical topics. Sullivan is a graduate of the University of Virginia with a B.A. in politics and English literature.

Recent Titles by Anthony H. Cordesman

2006

Arab-Israeli Military Forces in an Era of Asymmetric Wars
The Changing Dynamics of Energy in the Middle East, with Khalid R. Al-Rodhan
Gulf Military Forces in an Era of Asymmetric Wars, with Khalid R. Al-Rodhan

2005

The Israeli-Palestinian War: Escalating to Nowhere, with Jennifer Moravitz
National Security in Saudi Arabia: Threats, Responses, and Challenges, with Nawaf Obaid
Iraqi Security Forces: A Strategy for Success, with Patrick Baetjer

2004

The Military Balance in the Middle East
Energy and Development in the Middle East

2003

The Iraq War: Strategy, Tactics, and Military Lessons
Saudi Arabia Enters the Twenty-First Century: The Political, Foreign Policy, Economic, and Energy Dimensions
Saudi Arabia Enters the Twenty-First Century: The Military and International Security Dimensions

2001

Peace and War: The Arab-Israeli Military Balance Enters the 21st Century
A Tragedy of Arms: Military and Security Developments in the Maghreb
The Lessons and Non-Lessons of the Air and Missile Campaign in Kosovo
Cyber-threats, Information Warfare, and Critical Infrastructure Protection: Defending the U.S. Homeland, with Justin G. Cordesman
Terrorism, Asymmetric Warfare, and Weapons of Mass Destruction: Defending the U.S. Homeland
Strategic Threats and National Missile Defenses: Defending the U.S. Homeland

2000

Iran's Military Forces in Transition: Conventional Threats and Weapons of Mass Destruction